Understanding Sexual Offending

D1557100

Patrick Lussier • Evan C McCuish • Jesse Cale

Understanding Sexual Offending

An evidence-based response to myths
and misconceptions

 Springer

Patrick Lussier
School of Social Work and Criminology
Universite Laval
Quebec, QC, Canada

Jesse Cale
School of Criminology and Criminal Justice
Griffith University
Gold Coast, QLD, Australia

Evan C McCuish
School of Criminology
Simon Fraser University
Burnaby, BC, Canada

ISBN 978-3-030-53303-8   ISBN 978-3-030-53301-4   (eBook)
https://doi.org/10.1007/978-3-030-53301-4

This Springer imprint is published by the registered company Springer Nature Switzerland AG
The registered company address is: Gewerbestrasse 11, 6330 Cham, Switzerland

Acknowledgements

This book was written over the course of about 2 years. It involved a lot of traveling across the globe for us to meet, discuss, write, plan, organize, and structure many ideas into a single book. The overarching ideas included in the book, however, were formulated, developed, tested, modified, and clarified for over a decade. The three of us have been involved in many formative research projects that helped shape the ideas for this book along the way. In fact, these ideas and conclusions have been initially pretested in the form of conference presentations, research reports, talks and seminars, university lectures, book chapters, and scientific articles.

This book would not have been possible without the numerous debates, exchanges, critiques, comments, and suggestions from hundreds of individuals. At every step of the way, we have been grateful to receive support, assistance, feedback, and helpful ideas from not only research collaborators, colleagues, anonymous reviewers, conference attendees, graduate and undergraduate university students, but also criminal justice professionals, psychologists and psychiatrists, probation and parole officers, police investigators, and many more.

We would like to acknowledge the contribution, collaboration, and support of various research centers, scientific and professional organizations who gave us the opportunity to present many of the ideas presented throughout this book, such as the Association for the Treatment of Sexual Abusers, and the American Society of Criminology to name a few. The opportunity to present innovative and challenging ideas, to raise critical questions, and to challenge preconceived ideas and what many consider established facts was key to the origin and the development of this book.

We have been fortunate enough to receive significant funding over the years from various granting agencies, research centers, organizations, and our affiliated universities. Without their support along the way, this project would not have been possible. We would like to acknowledge, among others, the generous contribution of the Social Sciences and Humanities Research Council of Canada (SSHRC) and the Fonds Québécois de Recherche Société et Culture (FRQSC).

For university professors, an important source of inspiration are university students. Lectures, seminars, and conferences are key opportunities to present these ideas, exchange and debate, and clarify our thoughts on certain issues. Many graduate students have helped shape these ideas through the completion of a master's thesis or a doctoral dissertation. In that context, we would like to acknowledge the terrific work and contribution of three graduate students, Julien Fréchette, Claudele Gagnon, and Jeff Mathesius, who helped collect information and organize some sections of the book.

We cannot speak enough about our appreciation of our publisher, Springer, and its team for their availability, patience, assistance, and support throughout the process, which made a significant difference. A special thank you to Judith Newlin for her trust and belief in this project.

Finally, we would like to thank our respective families for the support, help, ideas but most importantly, coping with us throughout the writing of this book. Of note, the last stretch of this book was written during the COVID-19 pandemic, which affected millions of individuals worldwide and made multiple thousands of victims. Without the support of our close ones, it is unclear whether this book would have come through.

Contents

viii   Contents

Part IV   Conclusion

**10 The Great Policy Gap: Toward More Proactive Sex Offending
Research**   359

Index   395

List of Figures

List of Tables

About the Authors

Patrick Lussier is a Professor of criminology at the School of Social Work and Criminology at Université Laval, Canada. After completing a Ph.D. in criminology at the University of Montreal under the supervision of Drs. Jean Proulx and Marc Le Blanc, he completed postdoctoral studies at the Institute of Criminology at the University of Cambridge under the supervision of Prof. David P. Farrington. He was Professor at the School of Criminology at Simon Fraser University for 8 years. He is currently a regular researcher at the International Centre for Comparative Criminology (ICCC). His field of expertise is at the intersection of criminology and criminal justice and includes, among other things, the etiology of criminal conduct, sexual offending, risk assessment and management, and quantitative research methods. He has published five books and has about 140 publications, including several scientific articles in leading criminology/criminal justice scientific journals, including Criminology, Criminal Justice and Behavior, Justice Quarterly, Journal of Interpersonal Violence, Psychology, Public Policy and Law, and Sexual Abuse: A Journal of Research and Treatment. He is an Associate Editor of the Canadian Journal of Criminology and Criminal Justice and a member of the Editorial Board of the Journal of Criminal Justice. He has also been a member of the American Society of Criminology for more than 15 years. In 2005, he received the Academic Gold Medal from the Governor General of Canada for the excellence of his PhD dissertation. Since 2019, he has been the Editor of the Canadian Journal of Criminology and Criminal Justice.

Evan McCuish received his PhD in Criminology in 2016. He is currently an Assistant Professor at Simon Fraser University and is the Principal Investigator of the Incarcerated Serious and Violent Young Offender Study, the largest and longest-running study on young offenders in Canada. His research interests include criminal careers, desistance, developmental criminology, foster care, gang involvement, psychopathy, sexual offending, and violence. His work is published in Psychological Assessment, Crime and Delinquency, Sexual Abuse, Justice Quarterly, and Journal of Criminal Justice. He is on the Editorial Boards of the Journal of Criminal Justice, Journal of Youth and Adolescence, and Youth Violence and Juvenile Justice. He is an Associate Editor of the Canadian Journal of Criminology and Criminal Justice. He is the recipient of Simon Fraser University Dean's Convocation Medal for Academic Excellence, the American Psychology-Law Society Outstanding Dissertation Award, and the American Society of Criminology Division of Developmental and Life-Course Criminology Early Career Award.

Jesse Cale is an Associate Professor of Criminology in the School of Criminology and Criminal Justice, at Griffith University in Brisbane, Australia. He completed his PhD in 2010 at Simon Fraser University in Canada and was awarded the Governor General of Canada Academic Gold Medal for his doctoral studies. Following his Ph.D., he was awarded a prestigious research fellowship with the Griffith Youth Forensic Service, a clinic that provides treatment for youth who have committed sexual offences, at Griffith University in Brisbane, Australia. His main areas of research involve the causes and consequences of sexual violence, developmental criminology, and criminal justice policy and evaluation. He is a Chief Investigator on several large-scale research grants in Australia funded by the Australian Research Council and different state governments and agencies examining the development of delinquency and criminal offending and the effectiveness of criminal justice policy responses. He has published his research in leading international criminology and criminal justice books, and journals such as Sexual Abuse: A Journal of Research and Treatment, Journal of Criminal Justice, Aggression and Violent Behavior, Journal of Interpersonal Violence, and Youth Violence and Juvenile Justice. He is a member of the American Society of Criminology and the Australian and New Zealand Society of Criminology and serves on the Editorial Board of the Journal of Developmental and Life-Course Criminology. He is also a Visiting Scholar at the Institute of Criminology at the University of Cambridge.

Part I
Introduction

Chapter 1
Sexual Offending: An Elusive Phenomenon in Criminology's Blind Spot

Introduction

"Sexual" and "offending" are two words that, in isolation, suggest a *contradiction*. On the one hand, the term sexual is generally associated with something intimate, physical, and pleasurable; it suggests an instinct, a physical and emotional attraction, excitement, a desire or an urge, love, and even life. Offending, on the other hand, alludes to a transgression, to do wrong, to cause discomfort, pain, anger, even injury, or death. These two words together, however, leave very little in contradiction. Sexual offending affects us all, directly or indirectly. In general, whatever images, thoughts, memories, stories, or ideas that these two words together generate, they have a profound and immediate impact for various reasons. For some, this impact is extremely difficult to put into words, but this difficulty is not a matter of indifference. Nowadays, it sparks strong opinions, potent beliefs, and judgment, often very divisive stances, and certainly powerful emotional reactions. Despite these strong emotional reactions, at the same time, sexual offending is something that most people find difficult to comprehend, and thus many are often left without answers to their questions and their emotional reactions are left unresolved. In effect, sexual offending compels an immediate reaction, a powerful response, and very concrete and affirmative actions despite a general lack of awareness regarding fundamental questions about the origins of such behavior and its likelihood of continuing.

This book offers a different type of approach to researching, preventing, and responding to sexual offending. What may come as a surprise to most is the fact that for more than eighty years, scholars, scientists, researchers, clinical researchers, and graduate students from various academic disciplines and backgrounds have approached the complex issue of sexual offending through the lens of science. Science requires time, patience, and objectivity. It demands information, but also skepticism, measure, debate, and reason. It necessitates a method, testing and re-testing, and more time. Science provides the tools to challenge common sense, faith,

© Springer Nature Switzerland AG 2021
P. Lussier et al., *Understanding Sexual Offending*,
https://doi.org/10.1007/978-3-030-53301-4_1

gut feelings, dogma, and myths (Pinker, 2018). In other words, science calls for a response to sexual offending that is diametrically opposed to the swift, powerful, and emotive responses that define today's status quo. For over eight decades, scientists have investigated questions such as what is sexual offending? Why sexual offending? How often? By whom? In what context? Through a scientific lens, researchers have attempted to define the costs and consequences of sexual offending. How do societies respond to sexual offending, and when a response is given, what is the intended outcome? The long and hazardous road to knowledge is not without pitfalls, issues, challenges, and limitations. In fact, taking the long road of scientific discovery makes it difficult to keep up with societal changes, and in particular, society's relatively swift responses to the problem of sexual offending. By the time researchers begin to understand some key policy aspects about sexual offending, society and the legal system have already changed their perspective on sexual offending and researchers must start anew. It is too often the case that society and the legal system dictate to researchers the agenda for understanding the problem of sex offending. While addressing questions held by the public, policymakers, and practitioners within the legal system is an important part of being useful as an academic, the ability to be useful also hinges on first having an adequate understanding of the phenomenon that society has questions about.

This book, therefore, is based on four important premises that the authors will attempt to shed light on.

First, in North America and other Western countries, social policies and strategies _have been mainly reactive_ rather than proactive in terms of their response to sex offending. These social policies have been implemented following some form of pressure imposed on the government and its institutions "to do something" about sexual offending. Such pressure has been fueled by often brutal sex crimes against children that elicit, understandably, emotionally charged reactions from the public. The kidnapping, disappearance, and sexual homicide of a child leave a strong imprint not only on a family, but also on a community and society as a whole. Such crimes have been described as manifestations of inept and incompetent governments; as manifestations of broken criminal justice systems, failed institutions, and an inadequate correctional service system; they have also been described as symptoms of poor judgment and malpractices of criminal justice professionals and corrections and law enforcement agencies. As a result, governments often react to such pressure in ways that are more symbolic than instrumental, focusing on short-term goals and objectives. These short-term goals may include tempering the public's resentment toward the government agencies that they feel are responsible for the crime occurring in the first place, which has little to do with crime prevention. In that regard, when it comes down to how to best tackle the issue of sexual offending, the term "prevention" is commonly used by government officials and policymakers. While the narrative seems to imply governmental actions designed to keep sex offenses from happening, we suggest that goals and objectives of social policies with respect to sexual offending have little in fact to do with the prevention of sexual offenses.

Secondly, over the years, _scientific research has had very little influence_ on the development and implementation of social policies in response to sexual offenses.

There is more than eight decades of scientific research on sexual offending. During that time span, research from various academic disciplines has examined, described, and measured the phenomenon, its origins and investigated its causes. Research has shed light on the nature of the phenomenon, the complexity of the factors involved, as well as the profiles of the concerned people. For many years now, researchers have also evaluated policies to interpret their impact on the prevention/reduction of sexual offenses. In some cases, researchers have even examined the unintended and sometimes negative consequences of such policies. Nevertheless, the contribution of scientific research to the establishment of policies for the prevention of sexual offending appears to be marginal compared to ideological and popular discourse, media coverage and clinical interpretations and impressions of sexual offending. Let's be clear. To date, scientific research in the field of sexual offending, like many other fields of research in the social sciences, has not always been very rigorous conceptually, theoretically, and methodologically. Research has been at times fragmented and conducted in vacuum. The results of scientific research have appeared inconsistent and somewhat contradictory at times. To some, scientific research on the issue of sexual offending has appeared somewhat disconnected and disjointed from current events of the time. This is reminiscent of Popper (1962, p. 216) who once wrote that "The history of science, like the history of all human ideas, is a history of irresponsible dreams, of obstinacy, and of error. But science is one of the very few human activities—perhaps the only one—in which errors are systematically criticized and fairly often, in time, corrected. This is why we can say that, in science, we often learn from our mistakes, and why we can speak clearly and sensibly about making progress there."

This brings us to the third premise of the book, which is that social science has done a poor job of debunking *myths, misconceptions, and hasty and erroneous conclusions about sexual offending* that remain numerous and widespread among the general population, but also among the policymakers and practitioners that play a key role in the sociolegal response to sexual offenses. Social advocacy groups have, for many years, not only challenged myths and misconceptions about victims of sexual offenses, they have shed light on how such misconceptions had a serious and primarily negative societal, cultural, legal, and individual impact. These myths and misconceptions about victims of sexual offenses (e.g., victim-blaming stereotypes) have played an important role in shaping negative attitudes and distorted beliefs that have significantly impacted: (a) the sociolegal response to sexual offenses and (b) the willingness of victims to come forward. While the general public and policymakers are more aware of these myths and misconceptions about victims of sexual offenses, the same is not true about the myths and misconceptions established regarding perpetrators of such actions. In fact, there is a substantial gap between scientific knowledge and public perceptions of the individuals that perpetrate sexual offenses. These myths and misconceptions are sufficiently widespread that, over the years, they have fueled the populist, ideological, and pseudo-scientific discourse that has left a strong imprint both on the social construction of sexual offending and on the legal and penal responses to it.

Lastly, and perhaps most importantly, an overarching issue with direct implications for the social construction of sexual offending and the resulting social policies that follow is *the absence of a clear conceptualization of the phenomenon*. Some would argue that sexual offending refers to undesirable behaviors that are sexual in nature. Some social scientists would add that sexual offending is to impose, coerce, or force someone into sex. To other social scientists, it refers to specific acts of violence perpetrated against women and children. From that perspective, the sexual component is somewhat irrelevant, and the focus should be on the reprehensible, power imbalances involved in sexual offenses. This includes attention to the victim's experience, perspective, and perceptions as the defining aspects of sexual offending. Some would instead refer to sexual offending as odd, bizarre, irrational, or sexually deviant behaviors. In this regard, sexual offending is represented as a significant departure from behaviors that are considered normal by conventional standards. In fact, labeling particular behaviors as examples of sexual offenses remains, to this date, not only a challenge for social scientists, but for the public, the persons involved, law enforcement, lawyers and judges, lawmakers and policymakers, as well as criminal justice professionals and practitioners.

Sexual Offending: An Elusive Term

What is sexual offending? What constitutes a sexual offense? What actions are socially defined as a sexual offense, and do social definitions differ from legal ones? Sexual offending is a particularly complex phenomenon to circumscribe, define, and describe for any social scientist. Not unlike several other social phenomenon, sexual offending is not a static, fixed, and agreed upon set of behaviors. The ideas that we have of a sex offense may come from our own personal experiences, from family members and family friends, friends, and acquaintances. They may also come from media sources such as news coverage, documentaries, films and novels, and websites. They may also come from public inquiries, trials, and public demonstrations and events. These different sources may portray a range of different contexts in which sexual offending occurs. Some may describe a college student who has been sexually assaulted after a night with friends. Others may describe a co-worker who recollects having been sexually abused by a former sports coach during his teenage years; a cousin who remembers a stranger, naked, masturbating outside his apartment window in the middle of the day; the young daughter of a family friend who reports to a social worker having been molested by the next-door neighbor who was babysitting her; a young woman who was lured into an alley only to be raped and murdered by a male stranger pretending to be someone else. While these examples are diverse, they all tend to be uniformly recognized as sex crimes by the public.

Descriptions of other scenarios may receive less consensus or, at least for most people, do not represent the prototypical scenario involving a sexual offense. A man introduces himself into the apartment of an adult female stranger and steals her underwear. A young female teenager is unknowingly recruited and groomed by a new, older female acquaintance into performing sexual acts with adult strangers in exchange for money and drugs. A young man runs naked in a football stadium during the middle of a game as part of a lost bet. A neighbor discovered that a young man was attempting to lure his young son into performing sexual acts over the internet. A 14-year-old teenager engages in a sexual act with a 13-year-old that he is dating. A man fantasizes about sexual activities with the young boy he met at a camping site. A young female exposes her breast at a public event, with slogans written on her body, in the name of women's rights. Over a three-month period, a co-worker regularly flirts, talks about sex, and is aggressively asking his colleague for a date, despite her expressing discomfort with the situation. An older man hides a camera in the vent of a hotel room to film strangers. Clearly, these examples involve deviant acts, including sexually deviant behavior, but not all are defined as sexual offenses. Nevertheless, they certainly raise issues about sets of actions that constitute a sexual offense.

For several decades, the description, explanation, and sociolegal response to sexual offending have given rise to much debate and controversy within the scientific community. At the heart of many of these debates and controversies is the inability to reach a consensus regarding the concept of sexual offending. The lack of consensus is not limited to academic pedantries about the definition and defining criteria for sexual offenses. Debates also involve the labels used to represent a specific set of actions. For many, sexual offending is synonymous with a male raping a female. For others, sexual offending reflects a broader spectrum of acts of sexual violence and abuse. To confuse the matter further, some assert that specific sexual offenses represent larger political and social issues and engender motivations to label certain actions as genocide, sexual terrorism, or acts of war. In fact, different terms, labels, and amalgams have been proposed over the years for this relatively complex and multidimensional concept. More specifically, there is no universal definition of sexual offending. Some definitions are broad and inclusive while others are much more circumscribed and specific. The concepts of violence and consent are usually at the heart of debates surrounding the definition of sexual assault. Sexual offending, however, is not limited to this phenomenon. From the outset, it is important to emphasize the complexity of the terminology that sometimes makes communication between researchers from different academic disciplines as well as practitioners and professionals from various backgrounds, not only difficult but, also at times potentially hazardous.

Perspectives on Sexual Offending

First, it is important to recognize that different academic disciplines and societal institutions use various terms to label, define, and describe sexual offending. In that regard, it is important from the outset to distinguish terms stemming from three main sources, with their respective knowledge-based tradition in education, research, and real-life applications of such knowledge: (a) criminal law and legal studies; (b) the medical sciences and psychiatry; and (c) the social sciences. With respect to the phenomenon of sexual offending, terms and concerns will be dramatically different. The methods of inquiry will also be very different. From a criminal law standpoint, criminal codes and written statutes are the key reference to name, discuss, and label behaviors as sex crimes (or not) under the law. A situation and a person's behavior will be interpreted according to the criminal code to determine whether a crime has been committed. Statutes can vary according to (a) geography (e.g., from one state to another, from one country to another), (b) time (e.g., the addition of new crimes or the modification criteria defining what constitutes a sexual offense or who can be held responsible for a sexual offense), and (c) group status (e.g., differences in laws for youth versus adults, differences in ability to consent according to age). A sex crime, therefore, does not reflect a theoretical entity, but rather is defined by the rules and regulations stipulated in a code of law of a particular jurisdiction at a particular moment in time for a particular group of people. Sex crimes are, at least in part, a reflection of a society's attitudes toward certain actions, or at least the response of those in power, and the criminal justice system mirrors this attitude through a set of laws. In the process, various professionals from the criminal justice system can be solicited to assist with responding to a sexual offense; from the occurrence of an event to the determination of whether someone has committed a crime as defined by these rules, to the determination of whether the evidence for the impugned behavior is sufficient to present to a judge and/or jury, and to determine whether the perpetrator is likely to repeat their behavior in the future, and so on.

From the medical science and psychiatry perspective, understanding the development of a sexual offense and the likelihood that the actor repeats such behavior is primarily determined by evidence of mental health problems. Therefore, from this perspective, mental health professionals will refer to mental health guides and manuals to determine whether the specific thoughts, motives, and actions of a person are manifestations of mental health problems. Mental health professionals, particularly psychiatrists, will examine someone's actions, their motives, the context in which such actions took place, any history of similar actions, and so on. Mental health professionals, therefore, are concerned with whether a person is sexually deviant. From a medical science standpoint, sexual deviance does not reflect a theoretical entity, but rather a general agreement and consensus among medical science experts that certain actions are atypical of expected societal norms, values, and beliefs and therefore the rarity of the sexual behavior warrants the "deviant" label, especially if these actions have a negative impact on the person's general functionning. Similar to laws, what is considered sexually deviant is not fixed and stable across time. Behaviors regarded as sexually deviant, how they are defined, and associated criteria are subject to change. Until relatively recently, homosexuality was considered a mental illness, a sexual deviation requiring mental health intervention (e.g., Green, 1972). Psychiatrists will determine whether their patient is characterized by specific and pre-determined criteria that justify labeling their mental health problems as a reflection of sexual deviance (e.g., exhibitionism, sexual sadism, pedophilia, frotteurism).

In the presence of sexual deviance, more commonly referred to as a paraphilia, specialized therapies and treatment programs will be offered to the person whether or not the person has been convicted for a sex crime in a court of law. In fact, having perpetrated a sexual offense is not a necessary condition indicative of a paraphilia. A person may experience uncontrollable urges and persistent sexual fantasies associated with a sexual offense and thus can be defined as sexually deviant, yet this same person may not act on these urges or fantasies and thus never have actually perpetrated a sexual offense. From this standpoint, sexual deviance reflects another form of societal response through a government institution, only this time it is the health care system rather than the criminal justice system.

Second, the legal studies and the medical sciences are concerned by a set of phenomena, but use terms, concepts, criteria, tools, and methodologies that are somewhat specific to their fields and reflect relatively distinct concerns and issues about a given behavior, even if these two disciplines agree that a behavior constitutes a sexual offense. Indeed, these terms and the definitions associated with distinct disciplinary fields are not equivalent to the extent that certain actions and attitudes, commonly linked to the description of sexual offenses, are not necessarily in and of themselves criminal behaviors. Similarly, certain criminal behaviors are not necessarily sufficient for labeling someone as sexually deviant (Fig. 1.1). For example, pedophilia is not criminal in the sense of the law, insofar as it remains at the stage of sexual thoughts and fantasies. Similarly, an adult having sexual contact with a seven-year-old girl is considered a criminal offense under section 151 of the Canadian Criminal Code, yet this behavior alone does not meet the criteria used in psychiatry for the diagnosis of pedophilia. The imperfect relationship between these terms and concepts *across* disciplines is further complicated by disagreements and debates *within* disciplines and fields of study. For example, while the phenomenon of rape is not considered a paraphilia or mental health problem according to the *Diagnostic and Statistical Manual of Mental. Disorders* (DSM-V; American Psychiatric Association, 2013), some psychiatrists have long argued that it should be the case (see in particular, Laws & O'Donohue, 2008). This portrait is even more complex because psychiatry and legal perspectives are not completely independent; rather, they often intersect when responding to a person involved in a sexual offense. An act of fetishism may lead an individual to commit a crime within the meaning of the law (for example, breaking into a residence to steal underwear). An adult with pedophilia may commit acts of sexual abuse on a prepubescent child, which constitutes a criminal act within the meaning of the law. Few individuals commit theft in relation to fetishism, and in the same way, only a minority of people who have sexually abused a child are diagnosed with pedophilia within the meaning of the DSM-V (American Psychiatric Association, 2013).

Third, sex crimes as defined by the law and sexual deviance as conceptualized by the medical-psychiatric experts are permeable to changes. Indeed, sex crimes and sexual deviance remain an important issue that continues, even today, to provoke strong emotional reactions that can spark changes. In North America, for example, since the 1970s, the phenomenon of sexual assault has been the subject of much reflection and legal reforms. The latter have their origins in the legal definition of

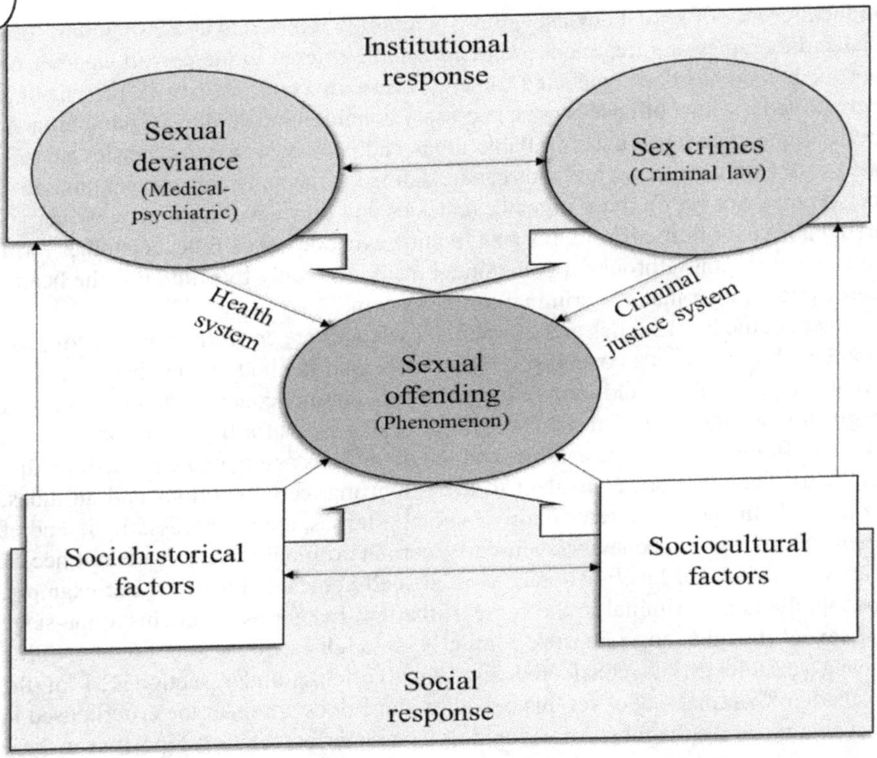

Fig. 1.1 Institutional responses to sexual offending

"rape" and the problems raised by traditional definitions of the concept. Historically, the legal definition of rape refers to the use of physical force to constrain a woman into sexual penetration. Notably, it is not uncommon to find in rape trials that the issue of victim consent is at the heart of the trial and becomes the main focus of the defense (Little, 2005). The legal definition of rape has been vilified by critics, as it leads to situations where the victim and the victim's reputation are on trial, rather than the accused and his behavior (Spohn & Horney, 1992). As part of this focus on the victim, many myths and misconceptions are presented regarding the meaning-fulness of a victim's prior behavior, sometimes behavior engaged in long before the sexual offense in question, that are asserted to be informative of the likelihood that the victim would consent (Burt, 1980). During the 1970s and 1980s, several aspects of the definition of "rape" were questioned, including spousal immunity, the sex of the victim, the notion of consent, physical resistance from the victim as evidence of non-consent, as well as physical strength as an inherent element of the crime (Seidman & Vickers, 2005).

These questions led to important reflections and significant legal changes regarding the victim's experience in court. In particular, significant changes were made to criminal proceedings, most notably the type of evidence about the victim that could be raised by the defendant's lawyer, otherwise known as Rape Shield Laws, such as the victim's personal and sexual history, the victim's reputation, the presence of physical injuries, and the presence of an eyewitness. It also led to significant changes regarding the victim's experience in court (e.g., being able to provide testimony). In Canada, during the 1980s, the concept of rape was abandoned in favor of the term "sexual assault" (Roberts & Gebotys, 1992) to reframe the phenomenon, legally speaking, as a violent crime and to raise public awareness about the seriousness of these acts. These changes, however, have not had the desired effect on public opinion, as emphasized, in particular, by the work of Roberts, Grossman, and Gebotys (1996). Indeed, the term "rape" raises public outrage more than the term "sexual assault." Criticisms of legal definitions of rape and sexual assault, as well as variations in terms and definitions from one jurisdiction to another have reinforced the importance of examining the phenomenon outside the realm of the legal terms and their definitions. However, the lack of consensus within the scientific community has quickly resulted in the emergence of a multitude of confusing terms. Moreover, the scientific community has not been immune to definitions that were politically motivated or ideologically bound, which consequently have further reinforced confusion and negative reactions regarding the definition of sexual offending.

Sexual Offending from a Social Science Perspective

From the social science perspectives, the focus is put on sexual offending as a social phenomenon. Such social phenomenon exists irrespective of whether or not a crime has been committed as defined by the criminal code of a particular jurisdiction. It also exists independently as to whether or not a person meets all criteria of a paraphilia according to a mental health manual, such as the DSM-V. Social scientists' work is guided by theory, concepts, measurement, observation, and generalization. In social sciences, each sub-discipline is concerned with describing, measuring, and understanding: (a) various aspects of the phenomenon (e.g., nature of the actions, actors involved, context in which these actions took place); (b) the social construction of the phenomenon across time and place (e.g., what is considered a sex offense); (c) the social costs and consequences of such phenomenon (e.g., the long-term impact of sexual victimization); and (d) the societal response to such phenomenon (e.g., the context in which societies decide to implement sex offender registries). An anthropology researcher could be interested in the characteristics of tribes and clans where the appropriation of women is more common as well as the social function of these actions within these societies (e.g., Chagnon, 1988). A sociologist could be interested in the role and impact of pornography on men's attitudes and behavior toward women (e.g., Baron & Straus, 1987). An evolutionary psychologist could be interested in the phenomenon of forced copulation in the animal kingdom, in particular among non-human primates, and how it reflects on human evolution (e.g., Smuts & Smuts, 1993). From a social work perspective, for example, research could focus on the psychosocial consequences of experiencing sexual abuse during childhood and how it affects later life adjustments (e.g., Bagley & Ramsey, 1986). From a psychology standpoint, a researcher could use a standardized questionnaire to measure young men's adherence to distorted beliefs supportive of rape and sexual assault (e.g., Rapaport & Burkhart, 1984). A criminology researcher could be interested in describing the sequence of events characterizing a sexual assault (e.g., Beauregard, Proulx, Rossmo, Leclerc, & Allaire, 2007).

Social scientists, therefore, do not limit their study of sexual offending to specific behaviors defined by the law as sexual offenses or defined from a medical-psychiatric perspective as sexually deviant. They do not limit the scope of their inquiry to actions that are defined as criminal by a code of law or individuals who have been convicted for a crime. Various terms, concepts, and sources of information can be found in the scientific literature, which highlights the diversity of theoretical and methodological considerations and perspectives. The scientific community commonly use terms such as sexual assault, rape, sexual violence, sexual coercion, and sexual abuse, to name a few. Their definitions are not mutually exclusive, which can lead to conceptual confusion. For example, in the social sciences, sexual assault typically refers to sexual contact without the consent of the victim. Unlike rape, sexual assault is not limited to situations where the abuser penetrates or tries to penetrate the victim. In addition, unlike sexual violence, sexual assault is not limited to situations where the abuser uses physical violence to coerce the victim. Sexual coercion generally refers to all situations and tactics used to coerce a victim into sexual acts. These "tactics" can range from sustained insistence to intimidation and threats to physical violence. Sexual abuse is a term commonly used by researchers and specialists whose focus is on situations where the victim is a child (notably, Finkelhor, 1984). Some definitions of sexual assault in the social sciences are highly inclusive and describe situations where the abuser makes sexual contact with a victim without the consent of the victim, whether through the use of physical force, threats, verbal or psychological pressure, through a position of authority over the victim, or simply by disregarding the victim's inability to consent to acts, for various reasons (victim's age, intoxication of the victim) (notably, Koss, Gidycz, & Wisniewski, 1987). However, these definitions lack consensus within the academic community. This lack of consensus often relates to debates about the description, explanation, and prevention of sexual offending.

Some of the key issues and problems in social science regarding the study of sexual offending, therefore, include the lack of conceptual clarity and the absence of theoretical integration. Cleary, social scientists will agree that sexual offending encompasses a wide range of manifestations that present some similarities but also some distinctions. Some manifestations are more similar than others. The similarities and distinctions of sexual offending manifestations suggest, therefore, the presence of a conceptual structure. In the absence of clarity regarding the conceptualization of sexual offending, an integrative conceptual model of sexual offending is proposed (Fig. 1.2). This model, first proposed by Lussier and Mathesius (2019), is based on the assumption that the phenomenon of sexual offending is multidimensional and encompasses a set of actions and behaviors that are distinct in form, nature, and context. These behaviors vary in terms of the nature of the actions taken,

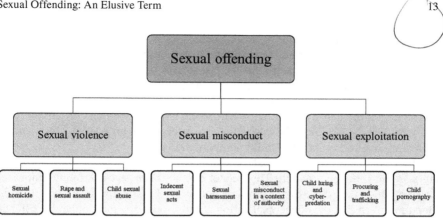

Fig. 1.2 Sexual offending: a multidimensional conceptual model

the context surrounding these acts, the seriousness of the acts, and their underlying motivations. Within this model are three distinct dimensions of sexual offending, all of which have been recognized, to different degrees, in the scientific literature. These dimensions include sexual violence, sexual misconduct, and sexual exploitation.

Sexual violence refers to a set of behaviors that involve sexual contact, with or without sexual penetration, against one or more victims that did not consent, either explicitly or because they were unable to do so. These coercive behaviors are imposed via threats, aggressive behavior, physical violence, or by taking advantage of the victim's inability to give consent (e.g., intoxication, young person, intellectual disability; Koss et al., 1987; Koss et al., 2007). More specifically, sexual violence refers to the sexual abuse of children (also known as child molestation), rape and sexual assault (also refer to as sexual aggression), as well as sexual homicide. These actions, as well as the attempts of sexual violence, may be committed against strangers, acquaintances, friends, intimate partners or a spouse, as well as close or extended family members.

Sexual misconduct refers to a set of actions and behaviors that violate a particular rule or code of conduct in which one or more non-consenting victims are involved. Sexual misconduct includes, from the perspective of the victim, unwanted sexual attention (e.g., Fitzgerald, Magley, Drasgow, & Waldo, 1999; Koss, Wilgus, & Williamsen, 2014). Sexual misconduct includes indecent sexual acts, for example, acts of gross indecency, acts of exhibitionism, and voyeurism. Sexual misconduct also refers to inappropriate sexual behaviors in an authoritative or professional context (e.g., military, psychologist, teacher, sports coach, etc.). These inappropriate behaviors, also referred to as sexual coercion, involve situations where a person takes advantage of their position of authority (e.g., rewards, promotion, threats, demotion, etc.) to obtain sexual gratification. Finally, sexual misconduct also includes behaviors that are considered sexual harassment. This involves persistent psychological pressure to obtain sexual gratification or sexual contact.

Finally, *sexual exploitation* refers to behaviors in which the individual takes advantage of or benefits from the body of a minor or an adult (Clayton, Krugman, & Simon, 2013; Reid & Piquero, 2014). It concerns online luring and cyberpredation (Fortin & Paquette, 2018), prostitution and the exchange of sexual favors for money or other valuable goods (housing, drugs, food), procuring and trafficking, and other commercial sexual activities involving a minor or a non-consenting adult (Clayton et al., 2013). Sexual exploitation also refers to the production, distribution/ exchange, and consumption of child pornography.

This conceptual model of sexual offending is proposed as a platform for developing a framework for research. This model has not been tested through empirical observation. In fact, these dimensions are not yet well-distinguished in the scientific literature given that the conceptualization and operationalization of sexual offending have not been given particular attention by scholars and researchers. Also, the fact that researchers have either studied sociolegal responses to these behaviors (e.g., how sex crimes are dealt with by the courts) or the underlying mental health problems that may lead to such actions (e.g., sexual deviance) has also limited the development, measurement, and testing of a conceptual model of sexual offending. This may seem surprising given that there has been over 80 years of research on the topic, at least in North America. This omission is symptomatic of the difficulties, debates, and controversies surrounding the phenomenon for several decades. Clearly, the central aspect and common theme underlying the proposed three dimensions of sexual offending are the lack of victim consent to actions that vary in nature, frequency, motive, and context.

These conceptual considerations should not be taken lightly since they are used to help guide the measurement of the phenomenon in order to understand the extent to which they occur within a given location. To determine their prevalence and the extent of the "problem," it is necessary to have a clear understanding of what "is" and "is not" considered an example of a particular problem. As the work of Mary Koss and her colleagues illustrates, the definition used greatly influences the prevalence observed in a given population. For example, the results of victimization surveys of young women indicate that the rates of sexual victimization observed (at least one event since the age of 14) ranged from 12% to 46% depending on whether the definition was limited and specific (rape) or broader and more encompassing (sexual assault; Koss et al., 1987). Thus, by virtue of a limited and specific definition, the phenomenon is rarer, whereas a more encompassing definition suggests that the phenomenon affects almost one in two women. It is therefore not surprising that the conceptualization and definition of the phenomenon are so important and continues to raise many debates within the scientific community. It should be noted that these prevalence rates rarely include items that refer to sexual exploitation and sexual misconduct. The absence of a consensus remains an important issue in this field of research. Moreover, it is important to note that the scientific literature, including both theoretical and empirical work as well as reviews of social and penal policies have focused, until this day, mainly on sexual violence. In other words, the majority of the literature has focused on crimes that are not applicable to the majority of those that have experienced sexual victimization.

Myths, False Beliefs, and Erroneous Conclusions

During the 1970s and 1980s, feminist writings brought to light a series of myths and mistaken beliefs about women, sexuality, and victims of rape and sexual assault. These writings have had important repercussions in society, in legal proceedings of rape and sexual assault cases, and attitudes toward victims, which are still felt today. These writings and their implications will be given special attention in Chap. 2. Although their writings have brought to light myths and erroneous beliefs about sexuality, women and victims of sexual assault, many misconceptions and myths about sexual offending are still widespread today. While writings from the feminist literature have been heavily focused on victims and victims' rights, perpetrators of sexual offenses have been largely neglected. As a result, many false beliefs, hasty and erroneous conclusions and myths about perpetrators of sexual offenses are still firmly rooted in ideological and populist beliefs. These false beliefs have played and continue to play an important role in the sociolegal reaction to sexual offending. This context explains this book's almost exclusive focus on perpetrators in order to highlight the important differences between popular image and rigorous scientific observation, and how the gap between the two has influenced societal response and social policies aimed at preventing sexual offenses.

One common theme espoused throughout the book is that ideological thinking has and continues to play a key role in the construction of sexual offending as a social problem. Ideologies involve three key overarching and interrelated components: cognitions, society, and discourse (van Dijk, 1998). First, they involve a set of ideas, thoughts, and beliefs about a phenomenon. Who are sex offenders? What is sexual violence? What should we do with sex offenders? How should society respond to the sex offender problem? What is the scope of the problem? Second, ideologies are also fundamentally social, political, and cultural, often associated with a specific group's interests. In fact, the perpetration of sexual offenses is fundamentally social. It involves victims, sometimes child-age victims. Sometimes, the same perpetrator offended against multiple victims. In that context, it can easily become political as occurrences of sexual offending immediately reflect upon the safety and the protection for a group, even a community. Finally, the discourse is a pivotal social practice by which group members articulate and convey their ideology to other group members, acquire new members, and defend their ideology against outsiders. Not all sex crimes come to the attention of the public. In fact, most do not. But when they do, these cases can attract a lot of media coverage, especially if there is something unique, atypical, and particular about them (e.g., well-known public figure, high number of victims, involved a kidnapping, highly violent, multiple offenders). These atypical cases highlighted by the media are what facilitate the three components of ideologies. Exposure to these cases by the media influences a person's reflection on how they think about the case and what should be done. It also gives viewers ideas about what sexual offending is. These reflections can spawn a call to action; engagement with groups to call for social change. Finally, these views can be shared by individuals or by groups, at work, over coffee, in the classroom, and across social media. Because the media typically highlights only atypical cases that poorly reflect the multidimensional, varied nature of sexual offending, this process favors the emergence and proliferation of myths, misconceptions, and erroneous conclusions about sexual offending and perpetrators of sexual offenses.

The popular image of "sex offenders" as sexual pariahs and monsters, strange and mentally disturbed individuals hunting stranger victims in dark alleys is alive and well. This image generally involves a man who cannot be rehabilitated and who is prone to perpetrate multiple offenses involving hundreds of victims. This popular image of a person with uncontrollable deviant sexual urges is widespread in the general population as shown by a study by Levenson, Brannon, Fortney, and Baker (2007). There are multiple inaccurate beliefs and false assumptions about individuals having perpetrated a sex crime, but also about their motives, risk factors, amenability to therapy and rehabilitation, as well as their dangerousness, all of which, over the years, have been challenged by researchers through scientific methods of inquiry (Caldwell, 2002; Letourneau & Miner, 2005; Lussier, 2005; Lussier & Blokland, 2014; Sample & Bray, 2003; Simon, 1997; Simon, 2000; Zimring, 2004).

Several factors explain the persistence of these false beliefs about individuals who have perpetrated sexual offenses. A common and recurrent explanation for this important gap between rigorous scientific writings and the popular image outlined above is partly the media's emphasis on covering atypical and often extreme cases with a sensationalistic slant that fuels these myths and false beliefs. In recent years, the rapid growth and popularity of social media have also contributed to the wide circulation of myths and erroneous ideas about sexual offending and perpetrators of sexual offenses. One of the most persistent ideas is that sexual offending is something inherently part of the person who perpetrates such actions. In fact, it defines the perpetrator; the person is reduced to the act they commit. We refer to them as a sex offender as if these persons are life-course persistent perpetrators of sex crimes. Among the misconceptions and myths that are widespread, the following are particularly prevalent (see also Lussier, 2017; Lussier & Cale, 2013):

- Perpetrators of sex offenses are generally portrayed according to the adage that "once a sex offender, always a sex offender," yet research shows that sexual offending tends to be circumscribed to a very short period of the life course.
- Adolescents who have committed a sexual offense are considered to be the adult perpetrators of sex offenses of tomorrow, yet empirical research clearly shows that such adolescents rarely continue to sexually offend in adulthood.
- Individuals convicted of a sex crime are often portrayed as sex crime "specialists," which means that their criminal activity is limited to sex crimes, whereas the extant research shows that the criminal history of these individuals mainly consists of a variety of non-sex offenses (e.g., theft, drug trafficking, noncompliance to their legal conditions, car theft, burglary, etc.).
- Individuals who have committed a sexual offense are often portrayed as individuals with "sexual deviance" requiring psychosexological expertise, while clinical and empirical research shows that sexual offending is only rarely motivated by underlying deviant sexual urges and sexual fantasies.

- Perpetrators of sexual offenses are often portrayed as representing a high-risk of sexual recidivism, while longitudinal research shows that the risk of reoffending is relatively low.
- Individuals who have committed a sexual offense are often perceived as predators who attack strangers using different subterfuges to confuse victims and police, while research has shown for years that sexual offending is more commonly committed by people well known to their victim (e.g., father, stepfather, partner, ex-partner, neighbor, co-worker, new acquaintance).
- The risk of sexual recidivism of individuals convicted for a sexual offense is presented as fixed and stable over their life course, while research shows that the risk is dynamic and it fluctuates over time; even those nowadays considered "high-risk sex offenders" are not always high-risk offenders.
- Popular belief suggests that all perpetrators of sexual offenses require specialized sex offender therapy given their mental health problems that fuel their sexual and behavioral problems; this belief, however, is not based on empirical observations or findings, but rather on ideological views about perpetrators of sex crimes.
- Concentrating preventive actions by targeting individuals convicted of a sex crime is seen as a reasonable, valid, and effective preventative approach, while research shows that repeat offenders are responsible for a very small proportion of sex crimes in society.

This is not to say that there are no dangerous, life-course persistent offenders repeatedly involved in sex crimes. This phenomenon does exist, but it is certainly the exception rather than the rule. Criminological research provides a scientific framework to describe and measure the criminal activity of perpetrators of sex offenses and the factors responsible for such actions (Blokland & Lussier, 2015). It provides a framework, key concepts, and methods to study these long-held ideas and views about sexual offending and perpetrators of sexual offenses. These statements will be revisited in future chapters, particularly in Chap. 3, in light of emerging social science research.

The Relative Absence of Criminology

Within the social sciences, criminology refers to the study of deviance, delinquency, and crime. It concerns the description, measurement, and explanation of these phenomena through scientific methods. It also refers to the study of the sociolegal construction, reaction, and response to these phenomena. This includes the processes by which a phenomenon or certain actions become deviant or criminal. This also includes the social forces and institutions responsible for the regulation of these manifestations. Historically, criminology has borrowed theories, concepts, and methods of investigation from various academic disciplines such as anthropology, sociology, psychology, history, political sciences, philosophy, social work, medical sciences, as well as legal studies. Criminology, as a result, is not only fundamentally interdisciplinary but also examines criminological phenomenon from a broader perspective. Nowadays, at least in North America, criminology is no longer seen as a mere field of study, but as a distinct academic discipline, with history, debates, and research paradigms, its own theories and explanations, as well as its own unique research methodologies. The scientific contribution of criminology to the description, measurement, and explanation of crime and delinquency is now undeniable.

Sexual offending, as a social problem, is not absolute and set in stone. In fact, a key aspect to the understanding of sexual offending is being able to take into consideration and situate its social construction and society's response to its manifestations. How certain actions and behaviors become regarded, interpreted, and defined as sex crimes and others as sexual deviance is pivotal to adequately understand the issue as well as the social roots of these issues. In fact, the actions and behaviors that are considered a sex crime or a sexually deviant behavior have substantially changed over the years. The groups, associations, organizations, and the so-called experts that have played a key role in the social construction of the sexual offending problem can change. The social forces that come together to identify the nature of the problem, define the problem, and respond to the problem can also change. In fact, since the postwar period, the problem of sexual offending and how to best respond to it has significantly evolved and changed. A criminological examination of the sociohistorical context suggests that, in North America and other Western countries, the social construction of sexual offending has now entered a fourth cycle, with important implications and ramifications at the societal, social, and individual level. These issues will be explored in Chap. 2.

Theoretically speaking, criminology is concerned with the phenomenon of sexual offending and society's response to this phenomenon. Criminology possesses the concepts and theories to describe and explain its multiple manifestations; it is capable of answering questions regarding why certain groups or certain people are more prone to perpetrate sexual offenses and why sexual offenses are more likely under certain social circumstances. Criminology has the methodologies to measure the nature, prevalence, frequency, and seriousness of these various manifestations in various contexts and under different social circumstances. Criminology also includes the study of sociocultural, sociohistorical, and sociopolitical factors as well as the mechanism by which certain phenomena become criminal and/or deviant. This entails the study of the criminal justice system and its various institutions and agencies and how they respond to sex crimes. Criminology, therefore, is concerned with the role of law enforcement (e.g., investigation, police interrogation), the courts (e.g., prosecution, conviction, sentencing), as well as corrections (e.g., carrying out sentences, supervising and monitoring, risk management). This line of research is also concerned with those who are arrested, charged, and convicted for a crime as well as the victims of such crimes. Criminology deals with questions regarding whether there are some groups more likely to have legal problems or be a victim of a crime; whether some groups are more likely to avoid legal problems or avoid detection; whether some groups are less likely to report crimes to law enforcement, etc. Criminology is also concerned with the role and importance of other institutions in regulating crime and deviance, such as the mental health system and social services; the processes involved in defining sexual deviance; understanding the role and impact of treatment and services offered to individuals considered sexually deviant; and the impact of mental health system services on the lives of individuals considered to be sexually deviant. There are also those whose behavior and actions lie at the intersection of the law and the mental health system; some of these individuals have committed a crime but may not be criminally responsible for their actions due to mental health problems.

Over the years, several important scientific breakthroughs have been made with respect to the description and the explanation of crime and delinquency. Most notably, significant discoveries have been made in the field of environmental criminology (the study of crime variation across geographical spaces), developmental and life course criminology (the study of the origin and development of crime and delinquency from birth through to the end of the life course), and more recently, biosocial criminology (the study of biological, genetic, and hereditary factors influencing crime and delinquency). Several methodological innovations have been developed and tested to measure criminological phenomenon, to estimate the prevalence of hidden behaviors and difficult-to-reach populations, to examine criminological phenomenon from a longitudinal standpoint using various types of data, etc. Important views and thoughts by critical and realist criminologists have helped highlight problems, issues, gaps, and contradictions about the response to crime and delinquency; legal and ethical issues with respect to correctional services and their impact on the lives of individuals convicted of a crime; the factors impacting perceived fear of crime and, in turn, how such fears influence social policies. Researchers have helped distinguish sociolegal responses that help reduce the prevalence of crime and delinquency from strategies that do not help, or even harm, broader attempts to reduce crime and delinquency. However, these theoretical, conceptual, ethical, and empirical research developments have not had a concrete, immediate, and significant impact on social policies related to the prevention of sexual offending. Paradoxically, until recently, criminology researchers have remained somewhat hesitant, even reluctant, to discuss issues specifically related to sexual offending, sex crimes, and sexual deviance (Lussier & Beauregard, 2014).

Historically, the scientific contribution of criminology to the description, explanation, and prevention of sexual offending, sex crimes, and sexual deviance has been relatively marginal, even modest at best. Of course, this does not mean that over the years criminology has not paid attention to the phenomenon. Criminology's contribution to the field of research of sexual offending has remained, for the most part, on the fringe of issues related to sexual offending. There are notable exceptions to this trend, however, but such exceptions have been limited to social policies and sex offender laws. Consider, for example, Sutherland's (1950) description of the evolution of sexual psychopath laws, which are still very relevant today and align with the emergence of sex offender registries and public notification laws in the USA. Consider also the notable and insightful examination of contemporary sociolegal responses to sex offenses committed by adolescents by Zimring (2004). In recent years, criminology's footprint within the research literature aimed at describing and evaluating society's response to sexual offending has become more pervasive and influential (Lussier & Beauregard, 2018). It is hard to avoid the impactful scientific work of criminology and criminal justice scholars such as Richard Tewksbury and his thought-provoking criminological analyses of sex offender laws and Keith Soothill, who was one of the first to bring key criminology concepts into the field of research on sexual offending. Nevertheless, the contribution of criminologists in the field of sexual offending has had only a minor influence on the development of scientific thought, empirical knowledge and investigation methods, as well as on the development of crime prevention strategies.

One area of scientific investigation where criminological scholars have remained silent, if not invisible over the years, is with respect to the description, measurement, and explanation of sexual offending. From the outset, it is important to highlight that, nowadays, criminology researchers tend to have a preference for general explanations of crime and delinquency. This means that all crimes can be explained by the same risk factors, and sexual offending is no exception to this trend (see Chap. 3). Accordingly, from this perspective, unique studies of sexual offending are presumed to be unnecessary. Indeed, for contemporary researchers who have studied the theoretical work of Gottfredson and Hirschi (1990), Agnew and White (1992), Akers and Jennings (2009), and Le Blanc (2005), it is difficult to conceive that sexual offending requires a specific theoretical framework given that existing theories and their concepts can explain various forms of crime and delinquency. That is, major criminological theories imply that all crime-types can be explained by the same underlying set of factors; sexual offending is no exception and thus it is needless to specifically study perpetrators of sexual offenses. For contemporary researchers, general theories of crime and delinquency can explain a myriad of phenomena including sexual offending. That being said, while these assertions are implicit, rarely have criminological theorists directly and explicitly posited that their theory explains sexual offending or some form of sex offense (Cusson, 2005; Gottfredson & Hirschi, 1990; Le Blanc, 2005; Moffitt, 1993). In other words, general explanations for delinquency and criminal behavior are believed to be parsimonious and equally applicable to rape and sexual assault as they are to, for example, drug trafficking, homicide, car theft, and burglary. Of course, if general explanations of crime and delinquency are sufficient to describe and explain sexual offending and its various behavioral manifestations, this should be scientifically measured, tested, and demonstrated. To this point, criminologists have favored making assumptions over observations. In fact, only a handful of empirical studies have examined criminological theory assertions to explain sexual offending (e.g., Boutwell, Barnes, & Beaver, 2013; Cale, Lussier, & Proulx, 2009; Felson & Cundiff, 2014; Harris, Mazerolle, & Knight, 2009; Lussier, LeBlanc, & Proulx, 2005; McCuish, Lussier, & Corrado, 2016).

Another reason for the relative lack of a criminological view of sexual offending is due to a long-held belief by some that sexual offending is a phenomenon that requires a specific expertise in mental health and mental health problems. In fact, for some, criminology has little to offer in order to describe, explain, and prevent sex offenses compared to psychology and psychiatry. To date, research on sexual offending has been disproportionately represented by researchers within psychology and psychiatry. The important role played by these disciplines can be partly explained by the long history of clinical practice with perpetrators of sex crimes in prison settings and individuals with deviant sexual preferences in psychiatric units. In fact, the first direct observations about perpetrators of sex offenses and their motives stemmed from clinical and hospital settings (e.g., Freund, 1967; Krafft-Ebing, 1886/1965; Magnan, 1890; McGuire, Carlisle, & Young, 1964). These clinical researchers were involved in the clinical assessment of individuals involved in unusual, odd, compulsive, bizarre, and extremely violent sexual behaviors that were often motivated by overwhelming sexual thoughts and urges. Those first observations helped to shape the first explanatory models of what is more commonly referred to nowadays as sexual offending and motives for sexual offending. Their pioneering work, however, lacked theory, methodological rigor, longitudinal and prospective data, comparison groups, and controlled-study designs guide their examination and interpretation.

We can safely posit that, ever since these first clinical observations were publicly reported more than one century ago, no other offender type has been under more scientific scrutiny than individuals having perpetrated a sex crime (see Chap. 4). This scrutiny, however, has been heavily focused on perpetrators' motives, conscious or unconscious, cognitions and cognitive processes, as well as emotions and emotional regulation. Psychology researchers have also attempted to determine the causes of sexual offending by analyzing the different aspects of the individual, and the interpersonal and sexual functioning of those who commit it. For example, researchers have studied physiological responses to sexual stimulation, sexual thoughts and fantasies, sexual urges, social skills, (false) beliefs about women, children, and sexual relationships, also known as cognitive distortions, intelligence and cognitive abilities to encode and interpret situations, attachment styles, coping strategies, personality traits and disorders, and psychopathological profiles. Such an examination projects an image of someone incapable of rational decisions or someone whose rationality is bounded by long-term individual deficits (e.g., neuropsychological problems) or more transient factors (e.g., anger, rage, alcohol, stress, anxiety). This image contrasts with several criminological perspectives on general offenders that describe such individuals as rational and reasoning (Cornish & Clarke, 1994; Cusson, 1981).

On the other hand, the fact that there have been very few studies comparing individuals having perpetrated sexual offenses to those not having perpetrated such offenses also contributed to the persistence of the notion of "sex offender specificity." This specificity hypothesis (see Simon, 1997) suggests that individuals having perpetrated a sexual offense are a distinct group characterized by unique and distinct motives, individual deficits, and personal experiences and trauma, all of which set them apart from other offenders. Their unique and very distinct behaviors and actions are in fact reflective of such specificity and the roots of such specificity can be found in these individuals' biological makeup, their upbringing, and early formative years. These assumptions, however, have not been the subject of extensive empirical investigation. Yet, more recently, researchers have observed that differences between perpetrators of sex offenses and perpetrators of non-sex offenses are only marginal and are often limited to a small subgroup of perpetrators of sex offenses. A meta-analysis by Seto and Lalumière (2010), which combined the results of nearly 60 separate empirical studies, compared various background characteristics of adolescents who have committed a sexual offense to those of youth involved in other delinquent acts. More than 40 individual and family characteristics were compared between the two categories of adolescents. None showed large differences between the two groups: 7% showed moderate differences, 33% small differences, and finally, about 60% showed no difference at all. Some will interpret these findings as evidence of the specificity of juvenile sexual offending, however, the empirical evidence, as a whole, points in a different direction. This point will be elaborated in Chap. 5. In recent years, scientific breakthroughs have been witnessed in the field with respect to the identification of risk and protective factors. Departing from previous research seeking confirmation about the specificity of sexual offending, this recent wave of research has espoused a developmental life course perspective recognizing the importance of individual factors, environmental factors, and their interplay at different life stages (Chap. 6). It offers a more complex view of the origins and the development of sexual offending, but one that also recognizes the uncertainties and the discontinuity of its development over time.

This point is pivotal given that the specificity hypothesis dictates the need for a unique, special, distinct societal response to sexual offending. It demands that its institutions, the criminal justice system, and its various agencies and organizations adapt their practices and respond differently to sex crimes and individuals having perpetrated sex crimes. In recent years, American criminal justice systems as well as those from the United Kingdom, Canada, and Australia have adopted, to differing extents, rather exclusionary and managerialist penal policies around ideas of incapacitation and continued surveillance and monitoring, which involves public shaming and populist themes (e.g., McAlinden, 2012). Such a response style to the problem of sexual offending is directly related to the social construction of risk of sexual offending, which emphasizes that prevention must target known perpetrators of sexual violence and abuse given their presumed lifelong risk for repeating such behavior. Chapters 7, 8, and 9 will address various response models to the issue of sexual offending, their nature, their crime prevention impact as well as the unintended consequences of such models. The tendency to respond swiftly with concrete and affirmative actions based on false assumptions comes with a heavy price and negative long-term consequences that policymakers have vastly overlooked. Therefore, not only will contemporary response models be described, examined, and compared, but other reasonable and humanistic, theoretically grounded, empirically based alternatives could be proposed by taking stock of more than 100 years of criminological research in crime prevention (Chap. 10).

Conclusion

This chapter proposes that sexual offending is a complex, multidimensional phenomenon that can take many shapes and forms. It is suggested that sexual offending is best described by three key dimensions, which encompass different behaviors and manifestations: sexual violence and abuse, sexual misconduct and sexual exploitation. Societies, across space and time, react differently to those manifestations. Since the postwar period, the criminal justice system has been the most predominant institution by which a society responds to this phenomenon. It deals with actions that are described as criminal by a code of law. It deals with a subset of sexual offending manifestations, those that are designated as criminal offenses or sex crimes. The mental health system also has been called upon to respond to the phenomenon of sexual offending. It focuses on mental illness and more particularly what is considered to be sexual deviance. The criminal justice system and the mental health system have historically played a key role in measuring, describing, and explaining sex crimes and sexual deviance. In doing so, however, important gaps remain with respect to the measurement, description, and explanation of sexual offending as a whole and its three dimensions. It is argued that the social sciences, criminology in particular, offer an important and additional avenue to address these gaps.

References

Agnew, R., & White, H. R. (1992). An empirical test of general strain theory. *Criminology, 30*(4), 475–500.

Akers, R. L., & Jennings, W. G. (2009). The social learning theory of crime and deviance. In M. Krohn, A. Lizotte, & G. Hall (Eds.), *Handbook on crime and deviance*. New York: Springer.

American Psychiatric Association. (2013). *Diagnostic and statistical manual of mental disorders* (5th ed.). Washington DC: American Psychiatric Association.

Bagley, C., & Ramsay, R. (1986). Sexual abuse in childhood: Psychosocial outcomes and implications for social work practice. *Journal of Social Work & Human Sexuality, 4*(1–2), 33–47.

Baron, L., & Straus, M. A. (1987). Four theories of rape: A macrosociological analysis. *Social Problems, 34*(5), 467–489.

Beauregard, E., Proulx, J., Rossmo, K., Leclerc, B., & Allaire, J.-F. (2007). Script analysis of hunting process in serial sex offenders. *Criminal Justice and Behavior, 34*(8), 1069–1084.

Blokland, A. A. J., & Lussier, P. (2015). *Sex offenders: A criminal career approach*. Oxford: Wiley-Blackwell.

Boutwell, B. B., Barnes, J. C., & Beaver, K. M. (2013). Life-course persistent offenders and the propensity to commit sexual assault. *Sexual Abuse: A Journal of Research and Treatment, 25*, 69–81.

Burt, M. R. (1980). Cultural myths and supports for rape. *Journal of Personality and Social Psychology, 38*(2), 217–230.

Caldwell, M. F. (2002). What we do not know about juvenile sexual offense risk. *Child Maltreatment, 7*(4), 291–302.

Cale, J., Lussier, P., & Proulx, J. (2009). Heterogeneity in antisocial trajectories in youth of adult sexual aggressors of women: An examination of initiation, persistence, escalation, and aggravation. *Sexual Abuse: A Journal of Research and Treatment, 21*, 223–248.

Chagnon, N. A. (1988). Life histories, blood revenge, and warfare in a tribal population. *Science, 239*(4843), 985–992.

Clayton, E. W., Krugman, R. D., & Simon, P. (Eds.). (2013). *Confronting commercial sexual exploitation and sex trafficking of minors in the United States*. Washington, DC: National Academies Press.

Cornish, D. B., & Clarke, R. V. (1994). Modeling offenders' decisions: A framework for research and policy. In D. P. Farrington (Ed.), *Psychological explanations of crime*. Aldershot, UK: Dartmouth Publishing Company.

Cusson, M. (1981). *Délinquants pourquoi?* Montréal: Hurtubise HMH.

Cusson, M. (2005). *La délinquance, une vie choisie: entre plaisir et crime*. Montréal: Hurtubise HMH.

Felson, R. B., & Cundiff, P. R. (2014). Sexual assault as a crime against young people. *Archives of Sexual Behavior, 43*(2), 273–284.

Finkelhor, D. (1984). *Child sexual abuse*. New York: Free Press.

Fitzgerald, L. F., Magley, V. J., Drasgow, F., & Waldo, C. R. (1999). Measuring sexual harassment in the military: The sexual experiences questionnaire (SEQ-DoD). *Military Psychology, 11*(3), 243–263.

Fortin, F., & Paquette, S. (2018). Online sexual exploitation of children: Reactive and proactive policing. In P. Lussier & E. Beauregard (Eds.), *Sexual offending: A criminological perspective*. Abingdon, UK: Routledge.

Freund, K. (1967). Erotic preference in pedophilia. *Behavior Research and Therapy, 5*(4), 85–93.

Gottfredson, M., & Hirschi, T. (1990). *A general theory of crime*. Palo Alto: Stanford University Press.

Green, R. (1972). Homosexuality as a mental illness. *International Journal of Psychiatry, 10*(1), 77–98.

Harris, D. A., Mazerolle, P., & Knight, R. A. (2009). Understanding male sexual offending: A comparison of general and specialist theories. *Criminal Justice and Behavior, 36*(10), 1051–1069.

Koss, M. P., Abbey, A., Campbell, R., Cook, S., Norris, J., Testa, M., et al. (2007). Revising the SES: A collaborative process to improve assessment of sexual aggression and victimization. *Psychology of Women Quarterly, 31*(4), 357–370.

Koss, M. P., Gidycz, C. A., & Wisniewski, N. (1987). The scope of rape: Incidence and prevalence of sexual aggression and victimization in a national sample of higher education students. *Journal of Consulting and Clinical Psychology, 55*(2), 162–170.

Koss, M. P., Wilgus, J. K., & Williamsen, K. M. (2014). Campus sexual misconduct: Restorative justice approaches to enhance compliance with title IX guidance. *Trauma, Violence & Abuse, 15*(3), 242–257.

Krafft-Ebing, R. (1886/1965). *Psychopathia sexualis*. New York: Putnam's Sons.

Laws, D. R., & O'Donohue, W. T. (Eds.). (2008). *Sexual deviance: Theory, assessment, and treatment*. New York: Guilford Press.

Le Blanc, M. (2005). An integrative personal control theory of deviant behavior: Answers to contemporary empirical and theoretical developmental criminology issues. In D. P. Farrington (Ed.), *Integrated developmental and life-course theories of offending: Advances in criminological theory* (pp. 125–163). New Brunswick, NJ: Transaction Publishers.

Letourneau, E. J., & Miner, M. H. (2005). Juvenile sex offenders: A case against the legal and clinical status quo. *Sexual Abuse: A Journal of Research and Treatment, 17*(3), 293–312.

Levenson, J. S., Brannon, Y. N., Fortney, T., & Baker, J. (2007). Public perceptions about sex offenders and community protection policies. *Analyses of Social Issues and Public Policy, 7*(1), 137–161.

Little, N. J. (2005). From no means no to only yes means yes: The rational results of an affirmative consent standard in rape law. *Vanderbilt Law Review, 58*, 1321.

Lussier, P. (2005). The criminal activity of sexual offenders in adulthood: Revisiting the specialization debate. *Sexual Abuse: A Journal of Research and Treatment, 17*(3), 269–292.

Lussier, P. (2017). Juvenile sex offending through a developmental life course criminology perspective: An agenda for policy and research. *Sexual Abuse: A Journal of Research and Treatment, 29*(1), 51–80.

Lussier, P., & Beauregard, E. (2014). Sex offending: A criminological perspective. *Journal of Criminal Justice, 2*(42), 105–110.

Lussier, P., & Beauregard, E. (2018). *Sexual offending: A criminological perspective.* Abingdon, UK: Routledge.

Lussier, P., & Blokland, A. (2014). The adolescence-adulthood transition and Robins's continuity paradox: Criminal career patterns of juvenile and adult sex offenders in a prospective longitudinal birth cohort study. *Journal of Criminal Justice, 42*(2), 153–163.

Lussier, P., & Cale, J. (2013). Beyond sexual recidivism: A review of the sexual criminal career parameters of adult sex offenders. *Aggression and Violent Behavior, 18*(5), 445–457.

Lussier, P., LeBlanc, M., & Proulx, J. (2005). The generality of criminal behavior: A confirmatory factor analysis of the criminal activity of sex offenders in adulthood. *Journal of Criminal Justice, 33*(2), 177–189.

Lussier, P., & Mathesius, J. (2019). Trojan horse policies: Sexual predators, SORN laws and the American experience. *Psychology, Crime & Law, 25*(2), 133–156.

Magnan, V. (1890). Des exhibitionnistes. *Les Archives de l'Anthropologie Criminelle et de Sciences Pénales, 5*, 456–471.

McAlinden, A. M. (2012). The governance of sexual offending across Europe: Penal policies, political economies and the institutionalization of risk. *Punishment & Society, 14*(2), 166–192.

McCuish, E., Lussier, P., & Corrado, R. (2016). Criminal careers of juvenile sex and nonsex offenders: Evidence from a prospective longitudinal study. *Youth Violence and Juvenile Justice, 14*(3), 199–224.

McGuire, R. J., Carlisle, J. M., & Young, B. G. (1964). Sexual deviations as conditioned behavior: A hypothesis. *Behaviour Research and Therapy, 2*(2-4), 185–190.

Moffitt, T. E. (1993). Adolescence-limited and life-course-persistent antisocial behavior: a developmental taxonomy. *Psychological Review, 100*(4), 674–701.

Pinker, S. (2018). *Enlightenment now: The case for reason, science, humanism, and progress.* New York: Penguin.

Popper, K. (1962). Conjectures and refutations: The growth of scientific knowledge. New York: Basic Books.

Rapaport, K., & Burkhart, B. R. (1984). Personality and attitudinal characteristics of sexually coercive college males. *Journal of Abnormal Psychology, 93*(2), 216.

Reid, J. A., & Piquero, A. R. (2014). On the relationships between commercial sexual exploitation/prostitution, substance dependency, and delinquency in youthful offenders. *Child Maltreatment, 19*(3-4), 247–260.

Roberts, J. V., & Gebotys, R. J. (1992). Reforming rape laws: Effects of legislative change in Canada. *Law and Human Behavior, 16*(5), 555.

Roberts, J. V., Grossman, M. G., & Gebotys, R. J. (1996). Rape reform in Canada: Public knowledge and opinion. *Journal of Family Violence, 11*(2), 133–148.

Sample, L. L., & Bray, T. M. (2003). Are sex offenders dangerous? *Criminology & Public Policy, 3*(1), 59–82.

Seidman, I., & Vickers, S. (2005). The second wave: An agenda for the next thirty years of rape law reform. *Suffolk University Law Review, 38*, 467.

Seto, M. C., & Lalumière, M. L. (2010). What is so special about male adolescent sexual offending? A review and test of explanations through meta-analysis. *Psychological Bulletin, 136*(4), 526–575.

Simon, L. M. (1997). Do offenders specialize in crime types? *Applied and Preventive Psychology, 6*(1), 35–53.

Simon, L. M. (2000). An examination of the assumptions of specialization, mental disorder, and dangerousness in sex offenders. *Behavioral Sciences & the Law, 18*(2-3), 275–308.

Smuts, B. B., & Smuts, R. W. (1993). Male aggression and sexual coercion of females in nonhuman primates and other mammals: Evidence and theoretical implications. *Advances in the Study of Behavior, 22*(22), 1–63.

Spohn, C., & Horney, J. (1992). *Rape law reform*. New York: Plenum.

Sutherland, E. (1950). The sexual psychopath laws. *The Journal of Criminal Law and Criminology, 40*(5), 543–554.

Van Dijk, T. A. (1998). *Ideology: A multidisciplinary approach*. London: Sage.

Zimring, F. E. (2004). *An American travesty: Legal responses to adolescent sexual offending*. Chicago: University of Chicago Press.

Part II
Understanding Sexual Offending

Chapter 2
The Construction of Sexual Offending as a Social Problem: A Historical Perspective

Introduction

Social policies are created to address social problems. There are many situations and social manifestations that are perceived as social problems. Some of these receive widespread recognition and command a great deal of societal attention. Others, that are equally important and damaging, are not as easily or as universally recognized as a social problem (e.g., Blumer, 1971). Sexual offenses fall into both scenarios when it comes to their construction as social problems. There exists a broad range of sexual behaviors that are coercive and harmful and are recognized as such. Over the years, however, from a societal perspective, not all sexual offenses have been described as important. Not all forms of sexual harm lead to public outrage and not all forms of sexual harm raise the same level of public concern. Certain behaviors that are sexually harmful are overlooked, endured, or even tolerated. For example, sexual harassment in the workplace was not part of society's collective attention two decades ago. Whereas today, public demonstrations, students' marches, and public inquiries related to the issue of sexual harassment are more and more common. Is it because sexual harassment was non-existent two decades ago? Is it because workplace social cultures have profoundly changed in recent years? Two decades ago, public attention was focused on the issue of sexual predators. How many news stories, documentaries, fiction and non-fiction books, television shows, and movies about sexual predators captured the public attention in the early 2000s? In the present, one may argue the fear of a child being kidnapped, sexually abused, and even murdered by a complete stranger is not at the forefront of the collective public consciousness as it once was. Have sexual predators suddenly disappeared in the past decade? Has the problem of sexual predators become less important in recent years? Clearly, the "importance" of these situations has very little to do with the reason explaining sudden shifts in public attention calling for immediate government action to address them (Hilgartner & Bosk, 1988). As such, there is a clear distinction to be made between sexual offending, as a social

© Springer Nature Switzerland AG 2021
P. Lussier et al., *Understanding Sexual Offending*,
https://doi.org/10.1007/978-3-030-53301-4_2

phenomenon, and what we will refer to as the "sexual offending problem" or in other words, the public perception of a social problem.

It is a mistake to believe that all forms of harmful sexual behaviors have been perceived as social problems over the years. It is also a mistake to think that all forms of sexual harm have led to swift, immediate, and powerful societal responses from governmental agencies. For many years, certain harmful sexual behaviors have gone unnoticed and unattended to by social institutions while others have become a focal point. For the most part, social scientists have played little to no role in pre-emptively identifying harmful sexual behaviors that subsequently become identified as social problems. Instead, social science researchers tend to recognize and identify these situations only after they are recognized as such by the public. This situation is not specific to the issue of sexual offending and this has been reported elsewhere for various social phenomena (e.g., poverty, racism, drug use, driving while impaired). When a social phenomenon is recognized as a social problem, it is rarely depicted as a nuisance or unpleasant behavior. Indeed, when certain behaviors causing sexual harm are recognized as social problems, they are described as being very serious in need of immediate societal attention and powerful governmental response or as a gateway to more serious behaviors and, in that context, similar societal attention and a governmental response are also warranted for prevention purposes.

The emergence of social problems and the process by which certain social phenomena are socially constructed as social problems has garnered much attention from social scientists since the 1970s (e.g., Blumer, 1971; Hilgartner & Bosk, 1988; Schneider, 1985). In criminology, researchers have also used similar processes to describe and explain the sudden emergence of "crime waves" (e.g., Fishman, 1977). This process is generally described as a series of stages by which a social phenomenon becomes a social problem. Sexual offenses, however, are no "ordinary" social problem and criminological phenomenon. Cormier and Simons (1969) argued that the idea that an individual causes harm, including sexual harm, out of pleasure is likely to exacerbate strong, negative public reactions. Such reactions, by themself, are unlikely to lead to the public perception that there is a social problem. A key initial step of this process involves obtaining social recognition and such recognition is facilitated by the interplay of social forces, namely, on one side, interest and ideological groups,[1] and, on the other side, media organizations, news outlets, and more recently, social media. Historically, sexual offending issues have become social problems once they have been contextualized by advocacy claims and culturally resonant news themes that are filtered, shaped, and delivered by the media (see Sacco, 1995). In the process, the portrayal and characterization of the social

---

[1] Ideologies involve three key overarching and interrelated components: cognitions, society, and discourse (van Dijk, 1998). First, they involve a set of ideas, thoughts, and beliefs about a phenomenon. Ideologies are also fundamentally social, political, and cultural, often associated with a specific group interest. Finally, the discourse is a pivotal social practice by which group members articulate and convey their ideology to group members, acquire new members, and defend their ideology against outsiders.

phenomenon too often become biased, one-sided, and over simplified, if not sensa-
tionalized, leaving little room for alternative explanations of the problem (e.g.,
Dowler, Fleming, & Muzzatti, 2006).

This chapter is not focused on the process responsible for the social construction
of sexual harm as a social problem. The motives and factors responsible for a specific form of sexual harm becoming a publicly recognized social problem is well
beyond the scope of this chapter. Rather, the chapter presents a brief historical
account of the evolution of the social construction of sexual offending as a social
problem. It aims to provide some baseline information about the dynamic nature of
sexual offending as a social problem. In doing so, the current chapter provides an
examination of the evolution of the sexual offending problem since the postwar
period with an emphasis on the situation in North America. This is not meant to say
that the situation in North America is representative of all Western countries. In fact,
we illustrate that even in North America, where very similar social constructions
were witnessed between the United States and Canada, very significant differences
were also noticeable (Petrunik, 2003). These similarities and differences highlight
the importance of taking into account sociohistorical, sociocultural, and sociopolitical factors in the description and explanation of social problems such as sexual
offending. This analysis reveals not only that the sexual offending problem has considerably evolved over the years, the collective and popular representation of the
"sex offender," as a result, has been profoundly impacted as well and so has our
societal response to the problem.

The Sex Offender as a Social Problem

Since the 1940s, in North America, the sex offender problem has considerably
changed. These significant changes have been addressed in whole or in part in previous work by several researchers (e.g., La Fond, 2005; Lieb, Quinsey, & Berliner,
1998; Lussier, 2018; Lussier & Cale, 2016; Petrunik, 1994, 2002). This characterization includes the prevalence of the phenomenon in society, the perpetrator's
motives, the factors responsible for their behavior, and the context of their perpetration of a sexual offense. The research conducted so far suggests that the interplay of
social forces has led to the characterization of individuals having perpetrated sexual
offenses in a very specific way. In fact, the central thesis for this chapter is that,
since the postwar period, the characterization of the "sex offender" has changed
profoundly, and multiple times. To be clear, researchers are not suggesting that the
actual phenomenon, the perpetrators, or that the factors responsible for someone
perpetrating a sexual offense have profoundly changed during this same period.
Social scientists do not have valid and reliable information to make such claims. But
perceptions have changed and so too has the collective narrative about perpetrators
of sexual offenses. To that effect, Karpman (1954, p. 4) once wrote that "A sexual
offense is sexual behavior that offends the particular society in which the offender
lives…" More specifically, he suggested that the characterization of the sex offender

problem is what has changed, profoundly. Furthermore, the evolution in the characterization of the sex offender problem was not the result of scientific advancements, but rather the result of a complex interplay of social forces that social scientists have problems fully understanding to this day.

To illustrate this point, Edwin H. Sutherland, a prominent criminology scholar, suggested that the enactment of sex offender laws was flawed and had no merit (Sutherland, 1950). He suggested that enactment of these laws followed a particular process where science had little to no role to play. Sutherland, reflecting on a series of events unfolding during his time, argued that sex offender laws emerged as a result of the following conditions. First, a community is plunged into a state of fear by a series of a few serious sex crimes occurring in rapid succession: A woman being raped by a stranger; a child kidnapped in broad daylight and never seen again; another person being sexually attacked in public. According to Sutherland, these few instances perpetrated in quick succession can be interpreted as a "sex crime wave" if other conditions are met. After all, not all sexual offenses lead to new sex offender laws and policies. Indeed, collective fear can follow if these few events are the subject of heavy and regular media coverage. Sutherland argues that such fear is likely when the behaviors that are the subject of constant media attention, especially those that are particularly brutal and involve children, are incomprehensible to citizens. This incomprehension is necessary for the enactment of sex offender laws as such laws require agitation in the community to mobilize support for the law. This agitation involves scattered and conflicting reactions by individuals and groups demanding that actions be taken to address the problem. In doing so, such collective agitation in the community creates pressure on government officials to act. As a result, a third element of the process is the creation of a committee of experts, in the form of a public inquiry, whose role is to shed light on the problem and to propose solutions. The so-called "experts" are appointed by the government and their role is to accumulate "facts," examine how others respond to similar situations elsewhere and, ultimately, make some recommendations to address the problem. These recommendations are customarily accepted without further investigation or critical examination. They are also typically presented to the public as science even if such recommendations may be fundamentally flawed and biased by ideological thinking, reflecting a predominant social movement of the time.[2]

While almost seven decades have passed since these earlier writings, Sutherland's description, while only hypotheses, still resonate today with the proliferation and evolution of sex offender laws and associated policies that have been documented by social scientists. Three important generations of societal responses have been identified in North America (Lieb et al., 1998; Petrunik, 1994, 2002). These societal responses were not based on scientific evidence about sexual offending and perpetrators of sexual offenses, but rather based on ideological thinking that reflected the

---

[2] Paradoxically, Sutherland's hypotheses were later misrepresented as an ideological attack on medical sciences and psychiatry (see Galliher & Tyree, 1985). In fact, Sutherland's criticism of psychiatry and psychiatric interpretations of crime and delinquency was not central to his ideas about the *emergence* of sexual offender problems.

predominant social movement of the time. The evolution of sex offender laws and associated policies is far more reaching as it also reflects changes in the characterization of the sex offender problem. Since the postwar period, it is hypothesized that offenders have been portrayed as: (a) sexually deviant individuals who need therapy; (b) angry misogynistic men who need to be punished; and, (c) sexual predators who need to be contained. Each of these portrayals captured the collective attention for some period and such characterizations influenced societal responses during a particular time. This is not meant to say that these social constructions of the sexual offending problem perfectly followed one another: quite to the contrary, they overlapped with each other over time. The relative importance of these social construction and social responses, however, changed quite dramatically from one period to another. Moreover, an analysis of more recent events suggests the gradual emergence of a fourth social construction of the sex offender problem, portrayed as the sexual violence of the powerful. The following section provides a brief chronological overview of these periods and the evolution of the sex offender problem up to this day (Table 2.1).

Of importance, over the years and across the aforementioned periods, each of these characterizations has garnered much attention from researchers. Claims about sexual offending and perpetrators of sexual offenses have been examined through the lenses of different disciplines. Researchers from various fields, beginning with psychiatry, and gradually including researchers from the social sciences, such as psychology, anthropology, sociology, legal studies, criminology, and social work have shed new light on these claims over the years. In each of these periods, social scientists raised very different questions, posited distinct hypotheses, and approached sexual offending research from distinct theoretical perspectives, by and large, independent of one another. Each of these periods, as a result, produced specific methodologies to examine ideas, thoughts, claims, and impressions about sexual offending and perpetrators of sexual offenses. Since the 1940s, given the importance of addressing social problems of the time, social scientists have produced research that, when taken together, is relatively fragmented and disjointed, narrow in focus, and overly focused on policy evaluation. Some of these scientific advancements are presented as well as their role and importance in shaping scientific knowledge on sexual offending.

The Sexual Deviant (1940s–1970s)

In the 1940s, many commentators were concerned about the presence of a sex crime wave in the USA (Sutherland, 1950). In 1947, the FBI director of the time, J. Edgar Hoover, commented in the American Magazine that the most rapidly increasing crimes were those perpetrated by "degenerate sex offenders" (see Lave, 2009). Such views were endorsed by others, such as James M. Reinhardt, a sociology professor, who pressed the government to make legal provisions to deal with these dangerous individuals. These specific words and associated perceptions echoed those of the

Table 2.1 The evolution of sex offender laws and policies

Period (years)	Social construction	Sex offender portrayal	Focus	Key themes	Conceptualization of sexual offending	Responses and privileged reactions
1940s–1970s	Clinical and medical model	"Sexually deviant individuals"	Abnormal sexual behaviors	Individuals with a mental health problem, more specifically sexual deviancy	Rare, exceptional, irrational, unpredictable, and inexplicable phenomenon	Specialized therapy, behavioral modification, sexual psychopath laws
1970s–1980s	Feminist and sociolegal model	"Angry misogynistic men"	Rape and sexual assault	Rational and calculating individuals who use sexuality as a means for another end (power, retaliation, control)	Major social problem that is relatively common and widespread, domestic, rational, and explicable	Rape law reforms; women's shelters and crisis centers; modifications to the CJS to ease victims' experience in court
1990s–2010s	Risk and community protection model	"Sexual predators"	Serial offenders and sexual murderers	If given the opportunity, convicted sex offenders will inevitably sexually reoffend	All convicted sex offenders are sexual predators who prey on their victims	Risk management, sex offender registries, public notification, electronic and GPS monitoring
2010s–	Social justice model	"Sex crimes by powerful men"	Sexual harassment and sexual misconduct	Men in positions of power use status to achieve sex regardless of consent	Sexual offending is widespread in the workplace; men using their power, reputation, and prestige to take advantage of others, sexually; sexual harassment and misconduct are constructed as rape and sexual violence	Victims need a voice, rules and regulations on university campuses, at the workplace, in the military, etc.

time; that individuals having caused sexual harm were: "abnormals"; "perverts"; "sex deviates"; "fiends"; "monsters"; or even, "sex maniacs" (e.g., see, East, 1946; Karpman, 1951; Reinhardt & Fisher, 1948; Roth, 1952; Tappan, 1955). Frederick Hacker, a chief psychiatrist in California, critically observed during this period that various sex offender laws had been passed to address the sex offender problem as a result of "insistent demands on the part of medical and legal leaders, as well as some enlightened civic groups" (Hacker & Frym, 1955; p. 766). Hacker's comment suggests that the portrayal of the sex offender problem as a social problem was in reaction to pressures and not the result of scientific advancements. In fact, a predominant theme that would emerge in Hacker's time was the need to address the mental health problems of sex offenders. Importantly, not all scholars and psychiatrists of the time agreed (see also Sutherland, 1950). In fact, sociologists such as Prof. Paul Tappan highlighted the lack of sound empirical research combined with myths and misconceptions as key factors explaining the portrayal of individuals having perpetrated a sexual offense (e.g., Tappan, 1955). That said, it was certainly the predominant and prevailing idea of the time that perpetrators were sexually deviant individuals whose sexual offense was a symptom of mental health problems.

During this first postwar characterization of the sex offender problem, sexual offending was perceived as exceptional, irrational, unpredictable, and inexplicable phenomena (e.g., Abrahamsen, 1950). In 1939, an English translation of a treatise written by a German–Austrian psychiatrist, Richard von Krafft-Ebing, entitled *Psychopathia Sexualis*, would become accessible almost three decades after he passed away (Krafft-Ebing, 1939). The book, originally published in 1886, provided one of the first detailed accounts of more than 200 clinical cases of individuals having perpetrated sexually deviant behaviors (see also, Magnan, 1890). Krafft-Ebing advocated for a greater role of medical experts in the criminal justice system, specifically for sexual offense cases. In fact, he stated that "even at the present time, in the domain of sexual criminality, the most erroneous opinions are expressed and the most unjust sentences pronounced, influencing laws and public opinion" (Krafft-Ebing, 1939, p. iv). He asserted that medical experts were needed to examine scientifically the "psychopathology of sexual life," such as masochism and fetishism. He hypothesized that, for some individuals, these abnormal sexual behaviors were reflective of psychopathic predispositions. There was no general consensus about the definition of the term, indeed it took nearly a century later for the assessment of psychopathy to become more formalized; sexual psychopathy[3] was a common theme of that period and it encompassed any aberrant, deviant sexual activity that was also considered antisocial and criminal. According to Karpman (1951), a chief psychotherapist of the time, sexual psychopaths were not consciously perpetrating their sexual offenses, rather, they were victims of an uncontrollable disease. This idea was prevalent and echoed by others, such as Dr. Nathan Roth, a senior psychiatrist in the State of New York, who concluded that "the sexual offender is not the master of his own home: he is powerless before the onslaught of forces within himself" (Roth, 1952, p. 632). In that sense, it was believed that minor sexual misbehaviors or sexually deviant acts were precursors of more serious forms of sexual

---

[3] The term "sexual psychopathy" used during that period should not be confused with the modern-day clinical conceptualization and operationalization of psychopathy (Hare, 1999).

violence. Although the idea was prevalent, a uniform understanding of the sexual psychopath was not.[4]

From 1940–1970, professional membership in the American Psychiatric Association increased tenfold (Jenkins, 1998). It is, therefore, unsurprising that such professionals, following the war, were available to screen and assess individuals involved in sex crimes and that psychopathology was identified as the most important explanatory variable for this behavior. One of the predominant ideas of the time was that the perpetrators' sexual functioning played an important role in the origin and development of sexual offending. As such, from a psychiatric standpoint, sexual offending was conceptualized as one more indicator of deviant sexual problems, along with other manifestations such as fetishism, abnormal sexual urges, compulsive masturbation, homosexuality, transvestism, masochism, and necrophilia to name a few. A predominant idea of the time was that a perpetrator's behavior originated with abnormal sexual development: experiences of sexual victimization, deviant sexual fantasies, compulsive masturbatory activities, deviant sexual preferences (e.g., Abel & Blanchard, 1974; Groth & Burgess, 1977). Sexual offending was, therefore, perceived as a deviant sexual behavior resulting from abnormal sexual development. In that context, the clinical evaluation of the sex offender's pathology, therapeutic modalities, and the assessment of dangerousness in a psychiatric setting gradually became the cornerstone of early criminal justice responses to the sex offender problem.

Sexual Psychopath Laws

The sexual psychopath laws enacted during the first postwar period highlighted the common perception of the time that perpetrators of sexual offenses were mentally disordered individuals who needed to be removed from society until their pathology had been properly addressed through some form of medical treatment. This idea required the use of indeterminate sentences in order to address, in custody, the causes of the offender's behavior until they were rehabilitated and no longer dangerous (Tappan, 1951). It is in this context that the first sexual psychopath laws emerged, starting in the 1930s (e.g., Hacker & Frym, 1955). The medical viewpoint of the time suggested that traditional criminal justice responses to crime involving custody and punishment were not appropriate for sex offenders. Instead, given the assumptions that sex offenders had mental health problems, the appropriate societal response needed have rehabilitative objectives. As a result, sex offender treatment

---

[4]As outlined by Lieb et al. (1998), among the first adjudications under New Jersey sexual psychopath laws included an individual involved in public masturbation (without exposure), a Black man who followed a white woman (there was no assault or approach towards the victim), and a homosexual man that passed illegitimate cheques. In effect, these crimes did not reflect the types of violent, random, and uncontrollable behaviors initially described by J. Edgar Hoover that were used to justify the passing of sexual psychopath laws.

programs were gradually developed and implemented in psychiatric units using primarily either psychodynamic or behavioral therapeutic approaches (e.g., Cormier & Simons, 1969; Groth & Burgess, 1977; Karpman, 1954; Maletzky & McGovern, 1991; Quinsey & Earls, 1990). The modification of deviant sexual preferences in a laboratory setting using orgasmic reconditioning techniques would gradually become one of the preferred specialized behavioral therapeutic modalities (Marshall & Barbaree, 1978). Although there was no consensus among clinicians and very little empirical research about the origins and cause of sexual offending, there was general consensus about the importance that the best way to address these causes was through specialized sex offender therapy. There were also some wildly experimental treatments that had no empirical basis for implementation. In Canada, Dr. Elliott Barker treated what were perceived to be violent psychopaths by locking them in a room for over a week. The prisoners were stripped naked, given high doses of LSD, forced to take their meals through a straw connected to the room's walls, and had no say in their entry into, or exit from, the "treatment" program (see Barker & Mason, 1968; Barker, Mason, & Wilson, 1969; Weisman, 1995).

The American sexual psychopath laws also had consequences across the border on the Canadian criminal justice system. The sex offender problem became the subject of governmental actions that ultimately led to the implementation of special measures that comprised two complementary mechanisms: (1) the identification of dangerous offenders among offender populations; and, (2) the imposition of indeterminate prison sentences for those identified as dangerous. In Canada, these legal provisions for the imposition of an indeterminate prison sentence are rooted in the Habitual Offenders Act (Bonta, Zinger, Harris, & Carrier, 1998; Wormith & Ruhl, 1986). Although this provision targeted "chronic offenders" (i.e., multi-recidivist offenders, for any types of offenses), the Sex Psychopaths Act, introduced in 1948, was specific to sex offenders and modeled after the Massachusetts law (Greenland, 1972). This provision was proposed and implemented to neutralize people considered incapable of controlling their sexual urges. Shortly thereafter, amendments were made to the Criminal Code of Canada (CCC) and this provision was renamed the Dangerous Sex Offender (DSO) provision. The abandonment of the term "sexual psychopath" reflected the opinion of some experts that sex offenders are responsible for their actions and deserved some form of punishment (for a discussion, see Petrunik, 1994). Following the report of the Canadian Committee on Corrections (Ouimet, 1969), several questions were raised. For example, the relatively vague concept of sexual psychopathy was highlighted. Of note, while initially the Canadian legal dispositions were directed toward dangerous and violent sex offenders, it became clear that, in practice, individuals who had perpetrated nonviolent sexual crimes (e.g., voyeurism) were prime candidates for the sexual psychopath label and associated legal dispositions. As Greenland (1972) reported, Canadian judges were reluctant to use the disposition given the ambiguity of the law and reluctance to impose indeterminate sentences where there were no guarantees for treatment.

Dr. Bruno Cormier, a Canadian psychiatrist reflecting on the general perception of the time, raised the paradox that there were very few dangerous, violent sex offenders yet there was social pressure to implement special programs and even institutions specifically for these individuals (Cormier & Simons, 1969). Others would also challenge the idea that the sex offender problem was best approached through the medical sciences. For example, Sutherland (1950) noted this viewpoint had emerged in response to rare, unique, very publicized cases that involved the sexual murder of a child. Sutherland further suggested that the media coverage of such cases fueled strong negative emotional reactions in the community, such as confusion (difficulty in understanding these acts), fear (of being the next victim), and anger (toward the perpetrator but also the criminal justice system). The confusion, fear, and anger surrounding a child's sexual homicide and the media coverage of the tragedy would serve to foster the emergence of beliefs that the criminal justice system did not provide sufficient protection for the community. In some localities, such reactions culminated with public demonstrations involving civil groups, law enforcement representatives, and government officials (see Lave, 2009). It was suggested that these emotional reactions and the associated media coverage had put pressure on the government to react quickly by setting in motion new measures to address the problem and to reassure the public. The government reacted by setting up an expert committee to propose solutions. At that time, the government turned to the medical science and psychiatrists, considering the predominant view of the time that such behaviors were inexplicable, irrational, and rather unpredictable. Decades later, governments would turn away from the medical sciences and look for other forms of expertise.

Social scientists of the time pointed out that the medical viewpoint on the sex offender problem was based on misconceptions and false assumptions. To put things in perspective, there was very little academic research prior to the 1940s on the problem of sexual offending. The scientific research along these lines gradually increased in the 1940s and social scientists grew increasingly concerned over the validity of the Sexual Psychopath Laws. Researchers could not agree on whether the 1940s had witnessed a sex crime wave or not (e.g., Lave, 2009). Most notably, Prof. Paul Tappan (1951, 1955) observed that the emerging evidence of the time highlighted a great deal of heterogeneity among sex offenders, casting doubts about the use of a single, unilateral approach with all perpetrators of sexual offenses. He also observed that the empirical evidence of the time did not support the view that all perpetrators were sexual recidivists or that a specialized treatment program would help to rehabilitate these individuals. Instead of describing perpetrators as sexual psychopaths, he described perpetrators as immature, sexually inexperienced, and typically involved in minor sexual offenses; only about five percent of perpetrators were involved in sexual offenses that involved coercion or injury. Joining his voice to others (e.g., Cormier & Simons, 1969), he also raised doubts surrounding claims that perpetrators of minor sexual offenses escalated to more serious sexual offenses, including sexual homicide. In that context, Tappan argued that there was little empirical evidence to use indeterminate prison sentences with all sex offenders, especially given the lack of resources and training to provide effective therapeutic services. Tappan's observations challenged some important preconceived ideas that had remained scientifically unchallenged for many years. More fundamentally,

Cohen (1956) questioned the very core aspect of the Sexual Psychopath Law that individuals should be confined until they have fully and permanently recovered, and, whether such conclusions could even be drawn by psychiatrists. The emerging social science research along these lines, although minimal, supported these assertions. The New York Mayor's committee for the study of sexual offenses indicated that, in 1930, 555 individuals perpetrated a sex crime and yet only seven percent (*n* = 40) of such individuals were charged with another sex crime in the next decade. Despite this evidence, the committee nevertheless stipulated, as their very first recommendation in the report, that indeterminate sentences be used for sexual psychopaths. Another recommendation mandated a medical and psychiatric examination of all sex offenders before their sentence. The report concluded "a considerable proportion of sex offenders are abnormal" (The New York City Mayor's Committee Reports on the Study of Sex Offenses, 1944, p. 327).

It was during this period that research on sexual offending and perpetrators of a sexual offense gradually began increasing. Given the sociohistorical context, it is not surprising that the first empirical studies were conducted with individuals admitted to psychiatric hospitals (e.g., Abrahamsen, 1950; Apfelberg, Sugar, & Pfeffer, 1944; Brancale, Ellis, & Doorbar, 1952; Ellis, Doorbar & Johnston, 1954; Karpman, 1952). Thus, the first generation of studies was limited to the examination of persons who have been arrested, charged, convicted, and incarcerated for a sexual crime. These investigations were very limited in scope: they typically were based on a very small number of observations; included only persons having perpetrated a sexual offense; generally did not include any kind of comparison group; and, only included retrospective information, with a focus on sociodemographic (e.g., age, marital status, ethnic origin) and criminometric (e.g., criminal history, type of offense perpetrated, victim's age) information. Not only did the methodological quality vary greatly from one study to another, often it was extremely difficult to assess the methodological properties given the lack of information provided in studies (e.g., sampling, test procedures, etc.). Likewise, ethical concerns were rarely discussed in reports and scientific articles, raising important questions about the context in which a study was conducted. As researchers of the time noted, it was unlikely that their observations were representative of all individuals having perpetrated a sexual offense, especially those who had not been apprehended for their offense. It was even correctly suggested that individual characteristics frequently observed for this group, such as the presence of emotional disturbances, might have contributed to their arrest and conviction, therefore raising doubts about the generalization of the study findings (e.g., Ellis, Doorbar, & Johnston III, 1954).

The first studies investigating perpetrators of sexual offenses were mainly descriptive and aimed to answer fundamental questions such as: who are these individuals? What have they done? Who have they offended against? and, what was their motive for acting in such a way? The group of individuals these early studies described had been involved in a wide variety of behaviors including, but not limited to: homosexual acts; incest; child sexual abuse; indecent exposure; rape, and sexual homicide. Not surprisingly, a common theme often reported by the investigators of the time was the heterogeneity of this population. Of importance, sexual deviance, and the measure of it, was at the heart of the concerns of this first generation of research on sexual offending (e.g., Peek & Storms, 1956; Yamahiro & Griffith, 1960). Researchers from the medical sciences grew increasingly concerned with sexual behavior that deviated from social norms, most notably those that involved: (a) non-human objects (e.g., animals); (b) the suffering or humiliation of oneself or another person (e.g., sadomasochistic behavior); (c) children or non-consenting persons (e.g., necrophilia, offenses against an intellectually disabled person); and, (d) atypical sexual preoccupations (e.g., a sexual attraction to a specific body part). Given the difficulties discussing, and taboos surrounding, sexual behavior in general, and sexually deviant behaviors specifically, a growing concern was that perpetrators did not admit guilt or denied any deviant sexual interests. Clinicians were faced with serious issues and challenges (e.g., Calder, 1955), namely, how to properly establish the presence and extent of these individuals' sexual deviance.

More than thirty years after the enactment of the first Sexual Psychopath Laws and associated legal dispositions that framed the sex offender problem as sexual deviance, scientific research helped design a method, albeit a controversial one, to assess sexual deviance. Phallometry (also called penile plethysmography) is a tool used in a laboratory setting to evaluate sexual preferences in men. Introduced in North America by Kurt Freund (Freund, 1963; Freund, Sedlacek, & Knob, 1965), it gradually became a clinical instrument considered by many to be the most objective for assessing the sexual preferences of individuals having committed a sexual offense (e.g., Proulx, 1989). In short, this tool makes it possible to measure, according to a particular protocol, men's sexual arousal in a laboratory setting. Over the years, various laboratory protocols have been tested and explored. These protocols include the presentation of various stimuli in the form of videotapes, pictures, or audiotaped recordings. The protocol generally involves the person being assessed placing a small rubber-type device around their penis. This device is connected to a plethysmograph. This device allows the recording of any changes in penile circumference (or volume) during the presentation of different stimuli. The content of these stimuli was designed to vary in order to measure different sexual interests, from pedophilia to sexual violence with humiliation, including consenting sex with an adult partner (see Freund & Blanchard, 1989). These stimuli were purposely designed to elicit significant but minimal sexual arousal in order to assess the person's sexual interests. Together, these results are used to make an assessment of a person's sexual interests and sexual preference.

Despite a lack of standards and guidelines to frame this practice, phallometric assessment gradually became the preferred instrument for assessing sexual deviance. Indeed, the encouraging results of validation studies made it possible to establish this practice (Lalumière & Quinsey, 1994; Lalumière, Quinsey, Harris, Rice, & Trautrimas, 2003; Launay, 1999), even if it was questioned on methodological bases (Marshall & Fernandez, 2000). Not only did this method become popular for clinical assessment but also for research purposes. The relative absence of guidelines combined with ethical questions about the proliferation of this intrusive method, especially among minors, raised serious concerns (Robinson, Rouleau, &

Madrigrano, 1997; Seto, Lalumière, & Blanchard, 2000). Moreover, if the phallo-metric assessment of several hundreds of perpetrators of sexual offenses have shown a diversity of sexual interest profiles (notably, see Michaud & Proulx, 2009), this method has provided empirical evidence that only a minority of convicted offenders are in fact characterized by deviant sexual preferences. Given the abovementioned methodological limitations of these laboratory studies, researchers still have not been able to specify the role of sexual deviance in the perpetration of sexual offenses. For example, it remains unclear whether deviant sexual interests are a cause of sexual offending or a consequence of perpetrating sexual offenses. Is it that indi-viduals became overwhelmed by deviant sexual fantasies to the point of acting them out, or, did the sexual pleasure obtained from committing these offenses lead to the development of deviant sexual thoughts? These fundamental questions remain rela-tively unanswered to this day.

This first postwar characterization of the sex offender problem was embedded in a rehabilitation ideal that was very much part of a social movement of the time (e.g., Sutherland, 1950). Furthermore, the idea that perpetrators of sexual offenses could be rehabilitated through some form of therapy or treatment would not suddenly disappear thereafter. In fact, therapeutic programs for sex offenders would remain an avenue by which society would respond to the sex offender problem to this day. At the same time, social scientists would continue to think, examine, and test how to best approach the rehabilitation of sex offenders, but theoretical models would drastically change (e.g., Marshall, 1996). The most sophisticated and rigorous anal-yses of the impact of sex offender treatment would occur three decades later. While scientists turned their attention to the development of a theoretical foundation for the treatment of perpetrators of sexual offenses, social movements would soon change the dominant narrative about what the sex offender problem was and how to best respond to it.

The Angry Misogynistic Man (1970s–1980s)

In the early 1970s in North America, a significant shift in the characterization of the sex offender problem would gradually take place. The psychiatric approach with respect to the description and explanation of sexual offending came under attack on many fronts. The role and importance of mental health problems as a common denominator among perpetrators of sexual offenses became somewhat brushed aside in favor of other novel ideas about the etiology of sexual offending at the time. The common view that offenders lacked control over their deviant sexual urges as the key explanatory factor of sexual offenses became seriously challenged. While sociologists like Sutherland (1950) and Tappan (1951) had challenged some of the key assumptions of the psychiatric perspective decades earlier, their view remained somewhat marginal for their time. This was especially true considering the lack of influence these scholars had on public sentiment. In contrast, pushed by a social progressive movement that was initiated in the 1960s, which included an anti-psychiatry movement (e.g., Szasz, 1960), the second-wave feminist movement (e.g., Friedan, 1963), alongside a counterculture movement that initiated a sexual revolution, all left a profound impact on society that challenged traditional norms of the time.

In the 1960s, the rising women's liberation and civil rights movements were defined by social attitudes that advocated for equal opportunities across employment, equal pay for equal work, and a demand for a radical shift in gender roles (Evans, 1980). The advocacy for civil rights of minorities and women became increasingly sophisticated and organized (e.g., the National Organization for Women). This movement took aim at various institutions, including the labor market, family structures, and the church (Evans, 1980). It is, therefore, not necessarily surprising that this movement also later subsumed victim advocacy and mobilization of women and their allies against patriarchal judicial systems as another institution responsible for the oppression and repeated victimization of women. It is also not surprising that those responsible for identifying the causes of the sexual offending problem were feminist scholars.[5] Two branches typically associated with the women's liberation movement, "radical" and "reform," that focused on the liberation and rights of women, respectively (Freeman, 1973; Hole & Levine, 1971), each played a role in the 1960s in reshaping responses to the sexual offending problem. The radical branch was associated with shedding the status quo of women as subservient housewives (Friedan, 1963). Some argued that the sexual revolution marked a shift in state legitimization of cultural individualism that favored individual pleasure as opposed to family-based procreative sexuality (e.g., Treas, 2002). In that context, North American society became gradually more familiarized with premarital sex among young people, extramarital sex, homosexuality, and pornography, but also divorce, abortion, and sexually transmitted diseases. At the dawn of the 1970s, this social movement would shake the image and the characterization of the sex offender problem in many important ways.

While there were notable but very modest scientific advancements by the 1970s about perpetrators of sexual offenses, their mental state, and therapy, the collective narrative surrounding the sex offender problem moved away from the focus on mental health toward the etiology of sexual offending. Susan Brownmiller's (1975) writing symbolized in many ways the shift that marked this period in which the sex offender problem was conceptualized, not as a problem caused by a selective few mentally ill men, but one historically caused by all men: male perpetrators, male jurors, male police officers, male lawyers, and male judges. The widespread perception of the "sexual deviant" gradually became replaced by one characterizing perpetrators of sexual offenses as "angry, misogynistic men" in a decisively patriarchal society that contributes to aggression against females and children. In other words, the sex offender was no longer characterized by a sexual pathology in the collective imagery, but as an individual who uses force and threat, including sexual violence

---

[5] As evidence of the intertwining of different eras, the lack of a feminist movement prior to the 1960s was in part because of arguments to replace earlier waves of feminism with psychotherapy. Feminism, like sex offending, was treated as pathology (Evans, 1980).

and coercion, as strategies to maintain women in a state of oppression. From this feminist perspective, sexual offending is not motivated by sexual impulses, fantasies, or preferences, but by nonsexual motivations, such as a desire for power and control. In this context, the sex offender is portrayed as a rational, calculating individual who uses sexuality to control and subjugate women and children and to keep them in a state of fear (Brownmiller, 1975; Sanday, 1981). More specifically, perpetrators are frustrated, angry men seeking to reaffirm their power, social status, masculinity, and their superiority through various means, including sexual violence. Sexual violence, and more specifically rape, was considered another means to keep women "in their place" (e.g., Brownmiller, 1975). This idea was certainly not a shared viewpoint outside feminist scholars' circles at the time. For example, Shorter (1978), a history professor, challenged Brownmiller's historical account of rape as being biased, selective, and misconstrued. He also pointed out that, while the incidence of reported rape was recently on the rise in the 1960s, particularly in the USA and Canada, a broader analysis revealed that incidence of rape and other violent offenses had been dropping in Western countries for the past century. As implied by Hartmann and Ross (1978), Brownmiller's writings were not intended to represent a historical account of rape. Rather, her contribution, they argued, was one in which she highlighted this phenomenon as an important social problem that had been historically ignored.

Bryden and Grier (2011) argued that during this period feminist groups replaced psychiatrists as the authority figure with respect to the sex offender problem largely because of their role in defending victims' rights. A victim-centered approach emerged in the 1970s. Some would argue that an Anti-Rape movement that emerged in the 1970s could not be dissociated from the feminist movement of the time as the women having adopted a feminist perspective had formulated the ideology behind the movement (e.g., Rose, 1977). With the sexual revolution of the 1970s in place, sex outside marriage became more common and carried important legal and social implications. In fact, sex crimes perpetrated, not so much by strangers, but rather by acquaintances, friends, ex-partners, and partners became the focus of much concern (Amir, 1971). While sex crimes perpetrated by such individuals were more common compared to those perpetrated by strangers, they were also more difficult to prove in court. Legal and feminist commentators argued that rape laws of the time were largely based on traditional attitudes about social roles and sexual customs; faithful wives and "virgins" deserved the law's protection while the others were deemed unworthy of it (LeGrand, 1973). As a result, these laws were unfit to address societal changes of the time and the rampant idea that, consciously or not, victims precipitated their own rape as a result of their perceived behavior and attitude (Amir, 1971). In the absence of scientific theories of rape, popular ideas filled the gap and influenced the behavior of criminal justice practitioners (Schwendinger & Schwendinger, 1974). These ideas were responsible, as activists argued, for the sympathy that men accused of rape received from the public while the victim was too often vilified and portrayed as malicious and a liar afflicted by sexual and emotional problems (e.g., promiscuity, deceitfulness; see Wood, 1973).

Feminist groups and victims' rights advocates condemned the myths and prejudicial stereotypes of the time about women and rape victims (Brownmiller, 1975; Clark & Lewis, 1977; Wood, 1973). It was suggested that these myths and stereotypes were not only found in the general population, but also in professionals working in the criminal justice system. Accordingly, victims' experiences with the criminal justice system were negative. As Burt (1980) and others (e.g., Schwendinger & Schwendinger, 1974) recollect, ideas that victims "asked for it," "deserved it," "that only bad girls get raped" or that "any healthy woman can resist rape" created a hostile environment for rape victims. Robin (1977) spoke of the institutionalized sexism toward rape victims as a result of the combination of a male-dominated criminal justice system influenced by victim-precipitation theory (e.g., the offender was "lead on"). Robin and other feminists scholars and legal commentators of the time spoke of the increasing number of cases involving women who had been raped where the accused was acquitted on the grounds that: the victim's testimony was unreliable; that she had not physically resisted her assailant; that she was a "sexual libertine"; that the victim had previous sexual relations with the accused (e.g., Wood, 1973). It was argued by these commentators that cases resulting in the perpetrator's acquittal received more and more media coverage, reinforcing rape myths and the stigmatizing effects of the criminal justice process on victims. A turning point, however, might have been the media coverage and the ensuing public outrage over a few cases involving women who had fought back and subsequently were later charged for a homicide after killing their assailant in self-defense (e.g., Rose, 1977). These cases became a rallying point and fueled the Anti-Rape movement of the time. By the mid-to-late 1970s it became clearer that changes had to be made to the criminal justice system, especially the law itself and associated criminal justice system procedures, to obtain more equitable treatment for rape victims (Wood, 1973).

Rape Law Reforms

In addition to the radical branch of the women's liberation movement, the reform branch emphasized that laws were not representative of women's interests (Freeman, 1973). This emphasis was witnessed in the 1970s with the emergence of a second wave of sex offender related policies that led to significant changes to traditional rape laws. Feminists and legal scholars emphasized that previous sex offender policies had been focused on mentally disordered offenders and that it was time to propose social policies that focused on "normal rapists" (LeGrand, 1973). The Anti-Rape movement challenged the general perception that rape perpetrated by an intimate partner was not a "real rape" and that such perceptions and stereotypes impacted how the criminal justice system processed these cases. It was argued at the time that in such rape cases, it was the victim, not the offender, who was unjustly on trial. Rape laws of the time were framed around the traditional Anglo-Saxon role of the wife as the husband's property through the contract of marriage and expectations about how she should act when forced to perform sexual acts. It became more and more clear that perceptions, beliefs, and norms, therefore, could all influence the criminal justice processing of a case. The Anti-Rape movement stressed that reform was necessary and that the focus should not be on perpetrators and their rehabilitation, but the acts themselves, society's perceptions of these acts, and the associated legal response to the act and the victim. In other words, symbolic (e.g., perceptions) and instrumental (e.g., legal and procedural) changes were demanded by women's groups.

In effect, the women's liberation movement as it applied to responding to the sexual offending problem was a complementary, two-pronged approach. This first prong addressed women's liberation issues (i.e., the radical branch) by changing how society, and the law that reflected society's belief, viewed victims of sexual offenses. Victims were not someone whose loose morals placed them in a dangerous situation but rather were the victim of everyday attitudes towards women that made rape acceptable. It was believed that changes in these perceptions would also result in an increase in victims' reporting rates. This changing perception would help bring about the aims of the second prong of the liberation approach, which concerned reforming statutes and associated criminal justice system practices in order to make police investigators, prosecutors, and jurors more sensitive to the issue, which should in turn increase the arrest and conviction rates of male perpetrators of rape. In that context, legal procedures and the issues and challenges associated with providing a fair trial and establishing the evidence in rape cases came under much more scrutiny (e.g., Hibey, 1973).

In the USA, Rape Laws were re-examined starting with their definition, which also led legislators to fundamentally question: (a) the spousal exemption; (b) the notions of force, consent, and resistance; (c) the admissibility of evidence of the complainant's prior sexual behavior; and, (d) corroborative evidence that the event actually took place (e.g., Backhouse & Schpenroth, 1983; Robin, 1977). Across the USA, various legal amendments were made to one or more of these dimensions of the law. For example, by the mid-1970s, several American states amended the traditional rule that non-consensual sexual intercourse by a husband with his wife could not be prosecuted as rape. In some states, these legal changes were met with much resistance (Geis, 1977). In Canada, important legislative changes as part of the Sexual Assault Act were made in 1982, and, as a result, the term rape was removed altogether from the Criminal Code in favor "sexual assault" which was considered a violent crime, not a sexual crime. The Anti-Rape movement would also raise awareness surrounding the importance of addressing other issues beyond the legal dimension of rape cases (e.g., Rose, 1977). Victims reported the frustrating and futile experience they had with the criminal justice system, whether the police or the courts (e.g., Wood, 1973). The inadequate training of police officers and investigators dealing with victims of a sex crime and the traumatic experience of victims in court was also noted. It the midst of these changes and espousing the ideological social movement of the time, sexual assault centers providing services to victims proliferated in North America (e.g., Valentich & Gripton, 1984).

It was only in the 1980s that social scientists finally caught up with the themes that had emerged for the past decade. This period marked a burgeoning in social science research on rape and sexual assault, a period in which the focus of research was not so much on perpetrators, but rather the scope of the problem in society. Groundbreaking research was observed in many areas, especially the measurement of the prevalence of rape and sexual assault (e.g., Koss, Gidycz, & Wisniewski, 1987; Malamuth, 1981, 1989). In line with expectations of feminist scholars and in contrast to the earlier psychiatric-based study of sex offenders, self-report studies of sexual offending indicated that this behavior, even with respect to violent sexual offenses like rape, was often unrelated to psychopathology (Koss, Leonard, Beezley, & Oros, 1985). In a context during which the entire criminal justice system was on trial for its handling of rape cases, starting with official data on rape, it became obvious that alternative data were necessary to measure to scope of rape in society. Police data underestimated the number of rapes, the so-called dark figure of rape, but the extent to which this number was underestimated was unclear.

The best way to measure the actual scope of the rape problem was to bypass the biases that characterize data from the criminal justice system and its handling of rape cases and ask women directly. Not only was this approach considered more reliable for identifying the prevalence of sexual offending, it was also in line with the renewed emphasis of victims' rights advocates that emerged from the second-wave feminist movement and called for increased attention to the experiences of victims instead of remaining solely focused on the characteristics of offenders. If the preceding period was defined by the emergence of phallometric assessment and the study of sexual arousal and sexual preferences, this period was defined by the emergence of victimization surveys to shed light on the problem. Among others, Mary Koss and colleagues proposed the Sexual Experience Survey (SES; Koss et al., 1987), which was designed to estimate the scope of rape and sexual aggression. Koss and her colleagues' research showed not only that the scope of rape and sexual aggression could be assessed but also that its prevalence was largely dependent on the definition and the type of behavior being estimated. While it was predominantly used at first with young adults attending colleges/universities, the SES was later used in various contexts to estimate the prevalence of rape and sexual assault among different segments of the population. It is in this context that studies of this generation determined that about 5% of the victims of rape and sexual assault reported their victimization to police (e.g., Fisher, Cullen, & Turner, 2000). Victims surveys revealed a number of additional factors that explained the decision not to report these acts; among other things, victims often tend to blame themselves or deny their sexual victimization; they tend to believe that there is not enough legal evidence and that they will not be taken seriously; they are afraid or ashamed that their social circle would learn what happened to them; they may be victimized again by their perpetrator in the event of the disclosure of the original act(s); and/or, the perpetrator is a family member who financially supports the victim, just to name a few.

An important part of social science is debate and disagreement about how to do research, how to collect data, and how to interpret research findings. Some argued that these emerging studies were somewhat limited to the description of what is commonly referred to as date rape, and, as a result, was not representative of all forms of sex crimes against women and for that matter, of sexual offenses more broadly. While this criticism is certainly warranted, it is important to reiterate that most sexual offenses generally occur in a context where the perpetrator and the victim know each other relatively well (e.g., Fisher et al., 2000). Others questioned the validity of this line of research on grounds that it did not properly reflect sex crimes as recognized in a court of law (e.g., Bryden & Lengnick, 1997). This point is important because it is commonly a point of contention that leads to important debates among scholars. Among others, Gylys and McNamara (1996) presented the SES to 156 US state prosecutors for legal evaluation. While respondents seemed to agree on the concordance between the legal and SES wording surrounding "rape" and "attempted rape" behaviors, other items were more ambiguous. More specifically, when the questionnaire items referred to sexual behaviors that occurred while the respondent felt under the influence of alcohol or drugs, or sexual behaviors in a context of "verbal pressure, the state prosecutor's perception became more varied. In fact, more than 75% of the prosecutors consulted raised doubt that the behaviors measured by the SES about sexual contact or sexual intercourse under verbal pressure (what social scientists tend to refer to as sexual coercion) corresponded to the legal definitions of sexual assault. This was important because, first, these behaviors were most frequently reported in sexual victimization surveys and therefore were largely responsible for estimates of the prevalence of sexual offending victimization. Second, these behaviors were least commonly reported to the police (Koss et al., 1987). Methodological limitations aside, women surveyed reported negative sexual experiences that went far beyond the contexts and situations recognized by the criminal justice system as criminal offenses. In other words, social scientists were measuring a social phenomenon instead of capturing only those behaviors that resulted in a legal response.

As time passed and legal reforms were put in place, social scientists found themselves in a position to examine the potential impact of Rape Law reforms. More specifically, rather than relying on broad and general perceptions, data regarding the instrumental consequences of the reforms could be examined using a scientific approach. Relatively scarce research was conducted to examine the possible impact of the Rape Law reform on the reporting of sexual offenses to law enforcement, the criminal justice processing of these cases, the number of arrests and convictions subsequently observed, and so on. Despite these reforms, it remained equivocal whether these changes had any significant impact on sexual offending and the criminal justice response to it (e.g., Polk, 1985). What made the task difficult for social scientists was that the type and nature of the reforms varied across states. Single state studies, therefore, could not speak to the impact of the movement as a whole. Using a multi-state study approach, social scientists reported either inconsistent findings or findings that showed, at best, a limited impact on the number of reports to the police or the probabilities of a conviction for rape. The most in-depth analyses would come in the early 1990s (e.g., Spohn & Horney, 1992; Bachman & Paternoster, 1993) and cast further doubt about the instrumental impact of the Rape Law reform of the 1970s. In Canada, very pessimistic conclusions were also drawn by other social scientists about the associated Canadian Law Reforms of the 1980s (e.g.,

Roberts & Gebotys, 1992). Early reports suggested the Canadian Rape Law reform had contributed to the increase in reporting of sexual assault cases; but commentators of the time failed to mention that the general crime rate was on the rise and sexual assault cases simply followed that same trend (Lussier, 2018).

Most importantly, by conceptualizing rape and sexual assault as a social rather than a mental health problem, this second characterization of the sex offender problem contributed to: (a) several key legislative changes by expanding the extent of the scope of laws and behaviors recognized as criminal (e.g., Lieb et al. 1998; Petrunik, 2002); and, (b) increased awareness about victims' experiences with the criminal justice system, thus highlighting the shortcomings of the criminal justice system response to such victimization experiences (e.g., Campbell & Raja, 1999; Kilpatrick, Best, Saunders, & Veronen, 1988). As social scientists then began to examine what some of the key risk factors were for sexual offending, a first in the study of this field, the sex offender problem was about to take on a different image and a new collective narrative that would rapidly gain prominence, particularly in the criminal justice context.

The Sexual Predator (1990s–2010s)

In the 1980s, the Reagan government in the United States, the Thatcher government in England, and the Mulroney government in Canada reflected a rise in conservative attitudes that included a heightened demand for personal responsibility over social welfare services. After the Cold War, attention turned to defunding federal social programs (Somers & Block, 2005) and rehabilitative services within criminal justice systems did not escape this new policy (Krisberg, 1991).[6] At the core of this political philosophy were notions about the "necessity of private sector management and planning" (Amott & Krieger, 1982, p. 14).

In North America, while the feminist and Anti-Rape movements were concerned with the "normal rapist" and the courts, a significant shift occurred around the early 1990s. The characterization of the sexual offending problem as misogynistic males forcing or coercing women into sex was gradually replaced by one portrayed by the "sexual predator." The image of the sexual predator is clearly a departure from the irrational mentally ill individual depicted in the 1950s, or, men seeking to establish power and dominance over all women depicted in the 1970s. Rather, the sexual predator image suggests a cold, callous, ruthless, and calculating individual who can go to great length to hunt down and capture prey. Predators hide, are deceptive and secretive about their identity or true nature (e.g., a wolf in sheep's clothing). The predator personification also suggests someone who is patient, meticulous, and who has a sophisticated *modus operandi*. A predator is willing to refine their

---

[6] It should also be noted that these conservative policies emerged shortly after Martinson's (1974) "almost nothing works" claims about rehabilitative services (Gendreau & Ross, 1987).

offending strategy based on past hunting experiences. Perhaps most importantly, the predator, unless stopped, will commit sexual offenses again and again. Therefore, "get tough on crime" strategies that characterized many criminal justice system philosophies of the 1980s become a central guiding approach for criminal justice responses to perceived sexual predators in society. The image of a stranger who preys on his victim, especially young children, dominated the collective narrative of the sex offender problem between the 1990s and 2010s. This image became over-whelmingly present in biographies, documentaries, movies, and television shows. As a result, terms like serial offenders and sexual murderers became more common in the collective narrative; some convicted sex offenders who perpetrated multiple brutal sex crimes often achieved substantial public notoriety.

Around the early 1990s, the characterization of the sex offender problem was refocused along these lines on the small number of individuals who were "known" sex offenders. These known sex offenders were those individuals who had previous convictions for a sex crime. The public became acutely aware of the fact that con-victed offenders do not typically spend the rest of their lives in a mental institution or prison following their convictions, but rather, after completing their sentence, or upon receiving parole, they more often than not return to their communities unan-nounced. This increased awareness that known sexual predators were anonymously living among law-abiding residents in the community became the source of much preoccupation and fear, especially surrounding the real or perceived threat that these individuals represent to the community, particularly women and children. The pub-lic discourse that questioned the police work, the courts, jurors, and the handling of the rape cases throughout the 1970s was largely replaced by one focusing on correc-tions and the risk management of dangerous individuals. Investigative journalists began hunting down convicted sex offenders in the community and publicly inform-ing communities about their whereabouts. Citizens also mimicked these vigilante behaviors and, in the process, would routinely publicly identify sexual predators using posters, and eventually websites and Facebook pages, among other means. In fact, for feminists and Anti-Rape movements, while the notion of injustice was a key theme throughout the 1970s and 1980s for victims, their family members and victims' rights advocates, the notion of risk largely took its place and subsequently characterized the sex offender problem of the 1990s up to the 2010s.

The emergence of this third characterization of the sex offender problem can be explained, at least in part, by the convergence of three key factors.

First, there was substantial media coverage across North America in the 1990s of a series of rare cases involving kidnappings, disappearances, and homicides of chil-dren that marked the collective mindset of this period. In fact, during this period, the names of several young victims became well known in North America; from Canada, "Alexandre" (Quebec) and "Christopher" (Ontario). These victims' names became symbols of a new wave of Canadian legal dispositions and changes in cor-rectional practices. Similarly, in the USA, "Megan" and "Jacob," and in the United Kingdom, "Sarah," were all names of child victims that symbolized corresponding waves of sex offender policies. Although each of these cases is unique, they share some similarities that were central to the characterization of the sex offender problem. These children were all homicide victims whose perpetrators, generally, were previously known to police and corrections in that they had a criminal record and had served time in prison for previous offenses. Some of the perpetrators were even under some form of community supervision (e.g., parole) at the time they committed their crime. For some citizens, it is a shock to learn that these perpetrators, known to the criminal justice system, lived in their very neighborhoods and had easy and regular access to places such as public parks and pools, bus stations, malls, and even schools.

Second, there was important and significant progress made in terms of archiving increasingly large amounts of individual information about perpetrators of sexual offenses. Correctional records of individuals convicted for a crime, including sex offenders, became more standardized and detailed. The proliferation of computers in workplaces significantly contributed to the standardization of data collection practices among criminal justice professionals (e.g., parole/probation officers, psychologists, social workers) and allowed for the development of large databases of individual information about offenders that included, but was not limited to: sociodemographic information; educational background and professional experiences; criminal record and past prison experiences; family history and general impressions about each of these individuals' personality characteristics; and, detailed information about their past sex crimes. Gradually, the government increasingly collected systematic and standardized information about multiple thousands of individuals convicted for sex crimes. All these factors facilitated, within corrections and correctional services, the development of new practices focusing on the statistical analysis of aggregated information, particularly about this offender population.

Finally, a third factor was the emergence of a significant shift in correctional practices, particularly in North America, but other jurisdictions as well, which Feeley and Simon (1992) designated as the "new penology." These two scholars were among the first to describe a series of fundamental changes in American correctional practices that occurred in this period. They observed that rehabilitation, or the transformation of the offender through some form of treatment, was no longer a central objective of correctional practices. Instead, risk management and community protection slowly became the key objective and one that would dictate correctional practices for quite some time. As a result, the identification of 'dangerousness' through risk assessment, risk classification, and the risk management of a subgroup of dangerous individuals among convicted offenders came to the forefront of correctional practices. The management of offenders throughout their sentence was mainly characterized by correctional services' assessment of these individuals' level of risk in terms of the likelihood of being rearrested and reconvicted again for another crime once released. One subgroup most affected by this significant shift in correctional practices was individuals convicted for a sex crime (e.g., Simon, 1998). The risk of criminal recidivism, especially sexual recidivism, would have a significant impact on these particular individuals' trajectory through the criminal justice system like never before.

The focus on sexual recidivists at risk of perpetrating a sexual homicide, the identification and archiving of information regarding these individuals, and increasing concerns surrounding the risk management of dangerous individuals over and above the rehabilitation of offenders not only significantly influenced the characterization of the sex offender problem from the 1990s forward, but also the social and criminal justice response to it. Together, these three contextual factors converged to mark the characterization of a new series of sex offender laws and social policies that gradually emerged in the 1990s (e.g., La Fond, 2005; Lussier, 2018; McAlinden, 2012; Petrunik, 2003). The momentum of the anti-rape movement and associated law reforms were largely replaced by a social movement composed of victims and victims' rights advocates who were demanding increased community protection against the threat posed by convicted sex offenders. These concerns were addressed, in part, by the criminal justice system through the creation of computerized databases including the names and personal information of individuals convicted for any sex-related crimes. Furthermore, unlike the past (e.g., Doshay, 1943), adolescent offenders also became targeted as potentially dangerous individuals and potentially subjected to adult-like sentences by the criminal justice system as they also represented a risk.

Sex Offender Registries

In the 1990s, in North America, various legal dispositions set the stage for the creation of sex offender registries. Sex offender registries (SOR) require by law that once released, those convicted of a sexual offense regularly provide valid personal information to police. Although the actual content of sex offender registries varies from state to state in the USA, they typically include information such as: the offender's name and any aliases, gender and ethnic origin, photos of the person's face that are updated; the person's physical characteristics (e.g., height, weight, tattoos, scars); home address; and information about prior sex crime convictions including if the victim was a minor (e.g., see Brewster, DeLong, & Moloney, 2012). Information that is less commonly found in SOR includes: the offender's education level; employment status and the location of their workplace; the license plate of his/her vehicle; the date and the location of past sex crimes; detailed information about past sex crimes; and the relationship between the offender and the victim. Convicted offenders on SOR must regularly contact authorities to verify their personal information, anywhere, at least once a year, for a minimum of 10 years (this may be imposed for life). In the USA, SOR laws were promulgated in 1994 as a result of the Jacob Wetterling Crimes against Children and Sexually Violent Registration Program. This law was adopted following the disappearance of Jacob Wetterling, an 11-year-old boy who was abducted by a stranger while he was playing outside with his friends in October 1989. Looking for the kidnapped boy, many local residents were surprised to learn about the presence of a halfway house in their neighborhood. This discovery then prompted them to request governmental actions to increase community protection in the neighborhood. Only decades later we would learn that the alleged person responsible for the disappearance and homicide of this boy was not one of the halfway house residents nor was his residence in the neighborhood where the abduction took place (e.g., Steve Visser, CNN, September 7th, 2016).

American laws on public notification make these government records and the information they contain about convicted offenders accessible to the public through various means, including the Internet. These practices became federal law with the enactment of Megan's Law. Proposed by the State of New Jersey following the death of young Megan Kanka, Megan's Law became a Federal law in 1996. Megan was 7 years old when she was the victim of a sexual homicide perpetrated by a neighbor, who was previously convicted of sexual assaults. The offender lured the victim into his house to play with his puppy before sexually assaulting her multiple times (State of New Jersey v. Jesse Timmendequas). It was believed that the passage of Megan's Law could prevent similar crimes from happening in the future. Together, the laws surrounding SOR and public notification, commonly called "SORN Laws" (i.e., "Sex Offender Registration and Notification Laws"), came into force in all US States. Some of the rationale for SORN laws include: (a) increasing awareness so that local residents can be informed of the presence of sex offenders in the neighborhood and can take appropriate actions to prevent a sexual offense; (b) increasing public safety by facilitating law enforcement work, police investigations of sex crime cases, and police surveillance of convicted sex offenders; and, (c) creating an additional deterrent effect against sex crime perpetration by increasing the negative consequences that result from these laws (Lussier & Mathesius, 2019). To be sure, these laws were not based on any scientific evidence about the prevention of criminal behavior, but rather, as Logan (2003, p. 342) suggested, an "untested article of faith." Other countries would eventually pass similar laws in the decades following the enactment of the Jacob Wetterling Act and Megan's Law (e.g., Whitting, Day, & Powell, 2014). In Canada, the province of Ontario established a provincial sex offender registry before the Canadian government put in place the National Sex Offender Registry in 2004 (e.g., Murphy, Fedoroff, & Martineau, 2009). This registry, however, is not accessible to the public and is strictly used by the law enforcement (e.g., Royal Canadian Mounted Police) for police investigation purposes.

Up to this point in history, past decades demonstrated that researchers were relatively slow to catch up with social movements and the enactment of new sex offender laws and policies, but this period s somewhat different, sort of. Almost immediately observable in the 1990s was a growth of scientific research in line with the social movement and policies of the time described above. Furthermore, the research that emerged along these lines was increasingly focused on the empirical examination of risk for sexual recidivism among individuals convicted for a sexual offense. Research programs in Canada and the USA were being developed to follow cohorts of individuals convicted of sexual offenses over time after their prison release. The growth of computers in research offices, the archival of personal information that could be accessed and used by researchers, including risk assessments completed by practitioners, as well as the growth of criminology, correctional psychology, and criminal justice university programs, were all useful for promoting this burgeoning of research. In the process, a growing number of longitudinal studies, in academia and government policy contexts, investigated the long-term risk of sexual recidivism of the so-called sexual predators. After all, the sex offender policies associated with the enactment of SORN laws and related regulations were based on the idea that convicted offenders remain at risk of sexual recidivism for long periods, in spite of having gone through prison and even possibly having completed sex offender treatment programming. During this era, scientific advancements in the field of risk assessment and risk prediction were made along three key lines of investigation.

More specifically, this generation of research was distinct from previous ones in that the key foci involved examining: (a) the proportion of individuals who have been rearrested or reconvicted for a sex crime after their prison release (e.g., Hanson, Morton, & Harris, 2003); (b) the individual characteristics of persons rearrested for a sex crime after their prison release compared to those who were not arrested for such offenses (e.g., Hanson & Bussière, 1998); and, (c) using various sophisticated statistical modeling techniques—individual risk factors were used to predict the risk of sexual recidivism (e.g., Quinsey, Rice, & Harris, 1995). These empirical studies highlighted, first and foremost, that the risk of sexual recidivism across these perpetrators of sexual offenses varied substantially. Contrary to the popular idea that all convicted sex offenders are long-term persistent sex offenders, this line of research demonstrated that only a minority of these individuals were rearrested and reconvicted again for a sexual offense. In other words, even the early scientific research in this context suggested that advocates of sex offender registries might have grossly overestimated the risk of sexual recidivism.

Nonetheless, these research findings also contributed to the development of actuarial risk assessment tools to identify high-risk sex offenders (see Chap. 7). The key aim was that actuarial risk assessment instruments could be used by criminal justice practitioners (e.g., psychologists, parole/probation officers) to determine, statistically speaking, the likelihood that a convicted sex offender in custody will be reconvicted for a sexual offense. These actuarial tools consist of a series of items (i.e., risk factors) that have an empirically demonstrated statistical association with sexual recidivism based on longitudinal studies. Other research at the time provided evidence that these tools were also more accurate than psychologists and psychiatrists using their clinical intuition and judgment to predict who is likely to sexually reoffend and when. Several actuarial tools were proposed and developed during this period (Hanson & Thornton, 2000; Quinsey, Harris, Rice, & Cormier, 1998), establishing a solid foundation for this field of research and expertise. While recognizing the heterogeneity of risk within the sex offender population, actuarial risk assessment instruments gained notoriety to the point where they became commonly used, or even required by law, throughout an offender's trajectory within the criminal justice system (e.g., at pre-sentencing and sentencing decisions, offender prison admission for assignment to minimum versus maximum security institutions, admission into sex offender treatment programs, parole board committees, etc.).

In the process, the use and reliance of these instruments created a shift toward what some have called "actuarial justice" (e.g., Logan, 2000). However, many questions remained unanswered as to the efficacy and accuracy of these instruments, largely because of the lack of a clear theoretical framework and the focus almost exclusively targeting sexual "recidivists." Because of the static nature of the risk factors typically included in risk assessment instruments, the risk of sexual recidivism is portrayed as constant and fixed over time. This portrayal is not representative of the dynamic aspect of sexual offending over time (Lussier, Tzoumakis, Cale, & Amirault, 2010). The risk of recidivism changes over time, but this change is still not well accounted for by risk assessors and risk instruments. In fact, empirical studies that lead to the creation of risk assessment instruments were not properly designed to examine offenders' level of offending over long periods. Not only were these studies based on relatively short follow-up periods (4–5 years), they also combined individuals at different stages of their criminal career (first offense, second offense, etc.) and at different stages of the life course (e.g., adolescence, emerging adulthood, adulthood; Lussier & Cale, 2013). In other words, this generation of sexual recidivism studies was not well suited to examine long-term risk of sexual offending in a context where the burden of being a registered sex offender potentially carried lifelong consequences. Although sufficient data were available, the sophistication of social science research methods and analytic strategies were insufficient for addressing important questions about the applicability of actuarial risk assessment tools to individuals of different ages, ethnicities, and whether such tools were appropriate to use on the same individual at different stages of their trajectory through the criminal justice system.

More importantly, this period marked a significant shift in sex offender policy where important criminal justice resources were diverted toward the risk management of the dangerous few. This shift was supported by the well-intentioned idea, albeit based on untested and unproven assumptions, that the allocation of important criminal justice resources could help prevent the occurrence of serious sexual offenses. This idea, however, would later be seriously challenged by the media portrayal of high-profile cases showing that in spite of these extensive criminal justice measures, some individuals were able to cause sexual harm to dozens if not hundreds of victims over long periods. These individuals would sexually offend and reoffend without being noticed, without having to face the criminal justice system and without being punished. Such injustice was a prelude to the rise of another type of social problem and the portrayal of another of type of sexual predator, one that would be in sharp contrast with the convicted sex offender of the community protection era, was someone with no known criminal record, a fairly well-educated, well-respected, influential professional who may in some case be an authority figure or in a position of power.

Sexual Violence by the Powerful (2010s-)

A fourth conceptualization of the sex offender problem gradually emerged toward the end of the 2010s. The imagery and label of the sex offender was recently revisited, jostled, and, once again, challenged. New social movements have gradually reframed sex crimes in a broader perspective, increasingly sensitive to issues of sexual misconduct, which were previously absent from debates and discussions that up to this point tended to focus on perpetrators of sexual violence including sexual homicide. The media, and particularly social media, began identifying a multiplicity of behaviors in different contexts that were increasingly and repeatedly becoming subsumed under the broad term of sexual violence. While the term sexual misconduct was relatively absent from this social movement's early narrative, the behaviors that are the target of this movement suggest the need to broaden the scope of what is considered sexual violence. In other words, the term sexual violence is used for rape and sexual assault, but also for sexual harassment, sexual misconduct in the military, sexual harassment at the workplace, etc. In social media, spoken words, specific gestures and attitudes toward women, and questionable intimate relationships involving, among other things, power discrepancies, became framed as new forms of sexual violence alongside rape, sexual assault, and sexual abuse. Social movements advocated that these new forms of sexual violence were the result of a rape culture that allows, facilitates, and breeds these behaviors. As a result, these social forces began aiming to challenge public perceptions about not only who sex offenders are, but also what constitutes a sexual offense.

The social context that gave rise to this social construction is one where increasing disparities in wealth between the lower, middle, and upper class resulted in a backlash towards the elite "one-percent" culminating in marches on, and against, major symbols of those in power (e.g., Occupy Wall Street). Those in power came under scrutiny not only because of their disparate wealth but also because of the belief that this power facilitated the control of employment opportunities. This line of reasoning was, in turn, extrapolated to understand how these dynamics also facilitated the perpetration of sexual offenses. In effect, what began as a movement specifically targeting disparities in wealth/power pivoted to focus on how such disparities influenced the perpetration of sexual offenses. Central to the Occupy Wall Street and other movements was the use of social media, including the use of specific hashtags, to engage with, mobilize, and further the cause (Gleason, 2013; Theocharis, Lowe, Van Deth, & García-Albacete, 2015). Similarly, responses to the alleged sex crimes perpetrated by powerful men have also received far more attention in public over social media than within any criminal court (e.g., the #metoo movement).

During this period, the emerging image of the sex offender contrasts quite starkly with those of all previous periods discussed. The images of the seemingly irrational and mentally ill "sexual psychopath," the angry misogynist, and the convicted sexual predator were replaced by one involving well-respected, suit-wearing, males, who may be: very influential business executives, wealthy entrepreneurs, famous actors, prominent medical doctors, well-known radio hosts, television icons, or well-respected priests. Although the notion of the sexual predator still has a place in the collective societal mindset, at this time, the emerging image of the offender is not one of an irrational person or an angry misogynist male, but one in a position of privilege and/or power. In effect, this rendition of the "sexual predator" is one that depicts a male who is able to hide in plain sight because of their status, which in turn was central in providing them with opportunities to perpetrate sex crimes. The portrayal of a few high-profile individuals suggested that these men use their power, in the form of social networks and influence, money and prestige, authority and image, to take advantage of their victims, not only sexually, but also in terms of employment opportunities, and career advancement. While second-wave feminists of the 1970s challenged public perceptions about victim-precipitated rape and sexual assault, third-wave feminists of the 2010s targeted power imbalances in society that not only favor these behaviors, but also create a context that facilitates victim silence and the avoidance of detection and sanctions for wealthy and privileged men.

Importantly, this fourth emerging characterization of the sex offender problem is increasingly being framed around social justice principles. In this context, perceptions of social justice are fueled by victims' accounts of their previous and often undisclosed sexual victimization experiences. These individuals would increasingly speak in public, on television shows or through some form of social media (e.g., Facebook, Twitter) about their own sexual victimization experiences, identifying their perpetrator(s), and the context in which alleged offenses took place as well as their perception of the social responses to these acts. Perceptions of injustice, being treated unfairly, and feeling powerless were at the core of this emerging movement that slowly shaped the new characterization of the sex offender problem. Importantly, social justice issues often concern how decisions are made, what those decisions are, and the inequities that result. As such, in this context, the criminal justice system's handling of sexual violence cases once again comes under scrutiny, but with a slightly different focus away from management of offenders in corrections toward law enforcement decisions to investigate allegations of sex crimes or not, prosecutors' decision to lay charges or not, and, jury decisions to find defendants guilty or not. Along these lines, power imbalances are often portrayed as the underlying explanation for seemingly unfair and unjust decisions made at these different stages of the criminal justice process. Furthermore, these power imbalances are exacerbated by the victimization context that involved a perpetrator who was wealthy, or in a position of trust, power, or even authority. Importantly, although social media served as a tool for raising awareness along these lines, and continues to do so, one of the negative consequences of its scope is that it also has been used as a way to inundate victims with criticisms aimed toward their credibility and "why they did not speak out sooner." In addition to this, some have argued it interferes with the process of natural justice, the right to the presumption of innocence on the part of the accused, and thus a fair and objective trial.

Paradoxically, while this influential mainstream social justice movement is concerned with the issue of social justice for victims of sexual violence, another, less known social movement that emerged alongside it was centered on the issue of social justice for convicted sex offenders (e.g., Madden, 2008). This social justice movement, again focusing on how decisions are made, what those decisions are, and the inequities that result, was focused on the stigmatization and labeling effect of public policies (particularly SORN laws) directed toward *certain* perpetrators of sexual offenses (i.e., convicted sex offenders). More specifically, considering sensitivities about the negative impact and heavy burden that the sex offender label carries, offenders' advocates, family members, and legal scholars have become increasingly critical of sex offender policies, and view sex offender registration and public notification as significant barriers to rehabilitation and community reintegra-tion and possibly even increased the risk of reoffending and therefore further endan-gered the public. For example, these advocates highlighted instances where convicted offenders as young as 14 years old were ultimately under lifelong sen-tences in the form of sex offender registration and public notification. Furthermore, reports of the sometimes-dramatic real-life social consequences of being a regis-tered sex offender increasingly emerged in media outlets (e.g., victimization experi-ences at the hands of vigilante groups). In effect, a paradox emerged insofar as the consequences of social justice advocacy for some, but not others, ultimately results in social injustice.

Conclusion

Since the postwar period, the characterization of the sex offender problem has changed and evolved as suggested by the various types of sex offender laws and reforms proposed over the years. These laws and reforms reflected the key societal concerns of the time but also the lack of scientific knowledge on sexual offending issues, particularly the etiology of sexual offending. The analysis in this chapter suggests the presence of three clear social constructions of the sex offender prob-lem, with a fourth one currently emerging since the 2010s and into the 2020s. This evolution underlines the importance of taking into account the sociohistorical con-text to explain the social construction of the sexual offending problem. Each period is marked by a relative focus on a particular sexual offending phenomenon socially constructed as a critical social problem. These periods are constructed around a particular portrayal of the sex offender and characterized by means to address this social problem. These reactions to the social construction of the sexual offending problem did not emerge as tailored, empirically-driven solutions designed with the express purpose of responding to the phenomenon. In effect, across these different eras, the response to the sexual offending problem was neither tailored nor special-ized. Instead, it represented a broader social movement and social issues of a par-ticular period in which public opinion played a large part. In sum, four different eras in which there are distinct social responses to the sexual offending problem were identified and these responses reflected the broader tools/approaches of societies, organizations, and individuals that happened to be available at the time. Social reac-tions to sexual offending helped shape what was defined as the "sexual offending problem," whether a mental health problem, a patriarchal conspiracy, a risk of sex-ual recidivism, and more recently a social injustice.

Although there does seem to be a pattern, this pattern seems much easier to define retrospectively than prospectively. These major social movements that give rise to responses to sexual offending are difficult to clearly identify prior to, or at, the time they begin. Recognizing not only that a movement is emerging but that it is also influencing the response to the sexual offending problem is likely difficult to do in real time. Thus, our point is not to try to use social movements of the time to predict how responses to sexual offending will occur. Rather, the purpose is to simply understand that responses are often simply what was convenient and understood at the time. Responses are atypically exclusive of all other social movements of the time (e.g., each of the four periods was defined by a social response that was not unique to sexual offending but rather reflected broader social, cultural, and political attitudes of the time). Finally, responses to sexual offending problems were not driven by experts in the field according to the data available. Instead, especially because those brought before the criminal justice system for their involvement in sex offending reflected the individuals that society of the time were most interested in seeing punished, researchers relying on official criminal justice system data were effectively relegated to studying particularly narrow samples of perpetrators of sexual offenses.

The social forces and the actual process by which these generational social constructions of the sex offender problem emerge and evolve over time remain somewhat elusive to this day. The observed pattern suggests, however, that the social construction of the sex offending problem has swung like a pendulum from the rare, atypical, and individual-specific phenomena to a more widespread, common, and social one. In the 1940s, the clinical-medical approach focused on sexual deviant individuals and their need for psychotherapy. In the 1970s, the pendulum moved and the social construction of the sexual offending problem, rape, and sexual assault, became portrayed as widely underestimated but widespread and requiring societal and legal changes. In the 1990s, the pendulum moved back to the portrayal of the sexual offending problem as an individual-focused issue with the identification and the risk management of the sexual predator. Since the 2010s, the pendulum has gradually shifted again, with the sexual offending problem being constructed as a more widespread issue requiring societal, legal, and procedural changes to detect and bring to justice powerful men. Contrary to Sutherland's hypothesis that a few atypical even brutal sexual offenses committed in quick succession initiate a sequence that helps define the sexual offending problem of the time, history seems to suggest that other social forces play a much larger role in initiating this process. These social forces, in the form of social movements, appear to play a more significant role in the conceptualization of the sexual offending problem and how to best respond to it: from a clinical-medical, a feminist-legal, a community protection, and more recently, a social justice approach. Social scientists have neglected the examination of these fundamental questions in favor of the examination of the impact of sex offender laws and reforms that are too often based on ideological thinking, misconceptions, and erroneous conclusions. In the meantime, the gap between the understanding of sexual offending and the social construction of the sexual offending problem remains wide and large.

References

Abel, G. G., & Blanchard, E. B. (1974). The role of fantasy in the treatment of sexual deviation. *Archives of General Psychiatry, 30*, 467–475.

Abrahamsen, D. (1950). Study of 102 sex offenders at Sing Sing. *Federal Probation, 14*, 26.

Amir, M. (1971). *Patterns in forcible rape*. Chicago, IL: University of Chicago Press.

Amott, T., & Krieger, J. (1982). Thatcher and Reagan: State theory and the "hyper-capitalist" regime. *New Political Science, 2*(4), 9–37.

Apfelberg, B., Sugar, C., & Pfeffer, A. Z. (1944). A psychiatric study of 250 sex offenders. *American Journal of Psychiatry, 100*(7), 762–770.

Bachman, R., & Paternoster, R. (1993). A contemporary look at the effects of rape law reform: How far have we really come. *The Journal of Criminal Law and Criminology, 84*, 554.

Backhouse, C., & Schpenroth, L. (1983). A comparative survey of Canadian and American rape law. *Canada-United States Law Journal, 6*, 48.

Barker, E. T., & Mason, M. H. (1968). Buber behind bars. *Canadian Psychiatric Association Journal, 13*(1), 61–72.

Barker, E. T., Mason, M. H., & Wilson, J. (1969). Defence-disrupting therapy. *Canadian Psychiatric Association Journal, 14*, 355–359.

Blumer, H. (1971). Social problems as collective behavior. *Social Problems, 18*(3), 298–306.

Bonta, J., Zinger, I., Harris, A., & Carrier, D. (1998). The dangerous offender provisions: Are they targeting the right offenders. *Canadian Journal of Criminology, 40*, 377.

Brancale, R., Ellis, A., & Doorbar, R. R. (1952). Psychiatric and psychological investigations of convicted sex offenders: A summary report. *American Journal of Psychiatry, 109*(1), 17–21.

Brewster, M. P., DeLong, P. A., & Moloney, J. T. (2012). Sex offender registries: A content analysis. *Criminal Justice Policy Review, 24*(6), 695–715.

Brownmiller, S. (1975). *Against our will: Men, women, rape*. New York: Simon and Schuster.

Bryden, D. P., & Grier, M. M. (2011). The search for rapists' real motives. *The Journal of Criminal Law and Criminology, 101*(1), 171–278.

Bryden, D. P., & Lengnick, S. (1997). Rape in the criminal justice system. *The Journal of Criminal Law and Criminology, 87*(4), 1194–1384.

Burt, M. R. (1980). Cultural myths and supports for rape. *Journal of Personality and Social Psychology, 38*, 217–230.

Calder, W. (1955). Sexual offender: A prison medical officer's viewpoint. *British Journal of Delinquency, 6*, 26.

Campbell, R., & Raja, S. (1999). Secondary victimization of rape victims: Insights from mental health professionals who treat survivors of violence. *Violence and Victims, 14*(3), 261–275.

Clark, L. M., & Lewis, D. J. (1977). *Rape: The price of coercive sexuality*. Toronto: Women's Press.

Cohen, E. S. (1956). Administration of the criminal sexual psychopath statute in Indiana. *Indiana Law Journal, 32*, 450.

Cormier, B. M., & Simons, S. P. (1969). The problem of the dangerous sexual offender. *Canadian Psychiatric Association Journal, 14*(4), 329–335.

Doshay, L. J. (1943). *The boy sex offender and his later career*. Oxford: Grune & Stratton.

Dowler, K., Fleming, T., & Muzzatti, S. L. (2006). Constructing crime: Media, crime, and popular culture. *Canadian Journal of Criminology and Criminal Justice, 48*(6), 837–850.

East, W. N. (1946). Sexual offenders. A British view. *The Yale Law Journal, 55*(3), 527–557.

Ellis, A., Doorbar, R. R., & Johnston III, R. (1954). Characteristics of convicted sex offenders. *The Journal of Social Psychology, 40*(1), 3–15.

Evans, S. M. (1980). *Personal politics: The roots of women's liberation in the civil rights movement and the new left* (Vol. 228). New York: Vintage.

Feeley, M. M., & Simon, J. (1992). The new penology: Notes on the emerging strategy of corrections and its implications. *Criminology, 30*(4), 449–474.

Fisher, B. S., Cullen, F. T., & Turner, M. G. (2000). *The sexual victimization of college women: A research report (NIJ research report: NCJ 182369)*. Washington, DC: U.S. Department of Justice.

Fishman, M. (1977). Crime waves as ideology. *Social Problems, 1*, 531–543.

Freeman, J. (1973). The origins of the women's liberation movement. *American Journal of Sociology, 78*(4), 792–811.

Freund, K. (1963). A laboratory method for diagnosing predominance of homo-or heteroerotic interest in the male. *Behaviour Research and Therapy, 1*(1), 85–93.

Freund, K., & Blanchard, R. (1989). Phallometric diagnosis of pedophilia. *Journal of Consulting and Clinical Psychology, 57*(1), 100–105.

Freund, K., Sedlacek, F., & Knob, K. (1965). A simple transducer for mechanical plethysmography of the male genital. *Journal of the Experimental Analysis of Behavior, 8*(3), 169.

Friedan, B. (1963). *The problem that has no name.* New York: Norton.

Galliher, J. F., & Tyree, C. (1985). Edwin Sutherland's research on the origins of sexual psychopath laws: An early case study of the medicalization of deviance. *Social Problems, 33*(2), 100–113.

Gendreau, P., & Ross, R. R. (1987). Revivification of rehabilitation: Evidence from the 1980s. *Justice Quarterly, 4*(3), 349–407.

Geis, G. (1977). Rape-in-marriage: Law and law reform in England, the United States, and Sweden. *Adelaide Law Review, 6*, 284.

Gleason, B. (2013). Occupy wall street: Exploring informal learning about a social movement on Twitter. *American Behavioral Scientist, 57*(7), 966–982.

Greenland, C. (1972). Dangerous sexual offenders in Canada. *Canadian Journal of Criminology and Corrections, 14*(1), 44–54.

Groth, A. N., & Burgess, A. W. (1977). Rape: A sexual deviation. *American Journal of Orthopsychiatry, 47*(3), 400.

Gylys, J. A., & McNamara, J. R. (1996). A further examination of validity for the Sexual Experiences Survey. *Behavioral Sciences & the Law, 14*(2), 245–260.

Hacker, F. J., & Frym, M. (1955). The sexual psychopath act in practice: A critical. *California Law Review, 43*, 766–780.

Hanson, R. K., & Bussière, M. T. (1998). Predicting relapse: A meta-analysis of sexual offender recidivism studies. *Journal of Consulting and Clinical Psychology, 66*(2), 348–362.

Hanson, R. K., & Thornton, D. (2000). *Static-99: Improving actuarial risk assessments for sex offenders* (Vol. 2). Ottawa, Canada: Solicitor General of Canada.

Hanson, R., Morton, K. E., & Harris, A. J. R. (2003). Sexual offender recidivism risk. *Annals of the New York Academy of Sciences, 989*(1), 154–166.

Hare, R. D. (1999). *Without conscience: The disturbing world of the psychopaths among us.* New York: Guilford Press.

Hartmann, H. I., & Ross, E. (1978). Comment on "On writing the history of rape". *Signs: Journal of Women in Culture and Society, 3*(4), 931–935.

Hibey, R. A. (1973). The trial of a rape case: An advocate's analysis of corroboration, consent, and character. *American Criminal Law Review, 11*, 309–334.

Hilgartner, S., & Bosk, C. L. (1988). The rise and fall of social problems: A public arenas model. *American Journal of Sociology, 94*(1), 53–78.

Hole, J., & Levine, E. (1971). *Rebirth of feminism.* New York: Quadrangle.

Jenkins, P. (1998). *Moral panic: Changing concepts of the child molester in Modern America.* New Haven, CT: Yale University Press.

Karpman, B. (1951). The sexual psychopath. *Journal of Criminal Law, Criminology and Police Science, 42*, 184.

Karpman, B. (1952). Considerations bearing on the problems of sexual offenses. *Journal of Criminal Law, Criminology and Police Science, 43*, 13.

Karpman, B. (1954). *The sexual offender and his offenses.* Oxford: Julian Press.

Kilpatrick, D. G., Best, C. L., Saunders, B. E., & Veronen, L. J. (1988). Rape in marriage and in dating relationships: How bad is it for mental health? *Annals of the New York Academy of Sciences, 528*(1), 335–344.

Koss, M. P., Gidycz, C. A., & Wisniewski, N. (1987). The scope of rape: Incidence and prevalence of sexual aggression and victimization in a national sample of higher education students. *Journal of Consulting and Clinical Psychology, 55*(2), 162–170.

Koss, M. P., Leonard, K. E., Beezley, D. A., & Oros, C. J. (1985). Nonstranger sexual aggression: A discriminant analysis of the psychological characteristics of undetected offenders. *Sex Roles, 12*(9-10), 981–992.

Krafft-Ebing, R. (1939). *Psychopathia sexualis; A medico-forensic study.* New York, NY: Pioneer Publications.

Krisberg, B. (1991). Are you now or have you ever been a sociologist. *The Journal of Criminal Law and Criminology, 82,* 141.

La Fond, J. Q. (2005). *Preventing sexual violence: How society should cope with sex offenders.* Washington, DC: American Psychological Association.

Lalumière, M. L., & Quinsey, V. L. (1994). The discriminability of rapists from non-sex offenders using phallometric measures: A meta-analysis. *Criminal Justice and Behavior, 21*(1), 150–175.

Lalumière, M. L., Quinsey, V. L., Harris, G. T., Rice, M. E., & Trautrimas, C. (2003). Are rapists differentially aroused by coercive sex in phallometric assessments? *Annals of the New York Academy of Sciences, 989*(1), 211–224.

Launay, G. (1999). The phallometric assessment of sex offenders: An update. *Criminal Behaviour and Mental Health, 9*(3), 254–274.

Lave, T. R. (2009). Only yesterday: The rise and fall of twentieth century sexual psychopath laws. *Louisiana Law Review, 69,* 549–591.

LeGrand, C. E. (1973). Rape and rape laws: Sexism in society and law. *California Law Review, 61,* 919.

Lieb, R., Quinsey, V., & Berliner, L. (1998). Sexual predators and social policy. *Crime and Justice, 23,* 43–114.

Logan, W. A. (2000). A study in "actuarial justice": Sex offender classification practice and procedure. *Buffalo Criminal Law Review, 3*(2), 593–637.

Logan, W. A. (2003). Sex offender registration and community notification: Emerging legal and research issues. *Annals of the New York Academy of Sciences, 989*(1), 337–351.

Lussier, P. (2018). *Délinquance sexuelle: Au-delà des dérives idéologiques, populistes et cliniques.* Quebec City: Presses de l'Université Laval.

Lussier, P., & Cale, J. (2013). Beyond sexual recidivism: A review of the sexual criminal career parameters of adult sex offenders. *Aggression and Violent Behavior, 18*(5), 445–457.

Lussier, P., & Cale, J. (2016). Understanding the origins and the development of rape and sexual aggression against women: four generations of research and theorizing. *Aggression and Violent Behavior, 31,* 66–81.

Lussier, P., & Mathesius, J. (2019). Trojan horse policies: Sexual predators, SORN laws and the American experience. *Psychology, Crime & Law, 25*(2), 133–156.

Lussier, P., Tzoumakis, S., Cale, J., & Amirault, J. (2010). Criminal trajectories of adult sex offenders and the age effect: Examining the dynamic aspect of offending in adulthood. *International Criminal Justice Review, 20*(2), 147–168.

Madden, S. (2008). *The labelling of sex offenders.* Lanham, MD: University Press of America.

Magnan, V. (1890). Des exhibitionnistes. *Les Archives de l'Anthropologie Criminelle et de Sciences Pénales, 5,* 456–471.

Malamuth, N. M. (1981). Rape proclivity among males. *Journal of Social Issues, 37*(4), 138–157.

Malamuth, N. M. (1989). The attraction to sexual aggression scale: Part I. *Journal of Sex Research, 26*(1), 26–49.

Maletzky, B. M., & McGovern, K. B. (1991). *Treating the sexual offender.* Newbury Park, CA: Sage.

Marshall, W. L. (1996). Assessment, treatment, and theorizing about sex offenders: Developments during the past twenty years and future directions. *Criminal Justice and Behavior, 23*(1), 162–199.

Marshall, W. L., & Barbaree, H. E. (1978). The reduction of deviant arousal: Satiation treatment for sexual aggressors. *Correctional Psychologist, 5*(4), 294–303.

Marshall, W. L., & Fernandez, Y. M. (2000). Phallometric testing with sexual offenders: Limits to its value. *Clinical Psychology Review, 20*(7), 807–822.

Martinson, R. (1974). What works? Questions and answers about prison reform. *The Public Interest, 35*, 22–54.

McAlinden, A. M. (2012). The governance of sexual offending across Europe: Penal policies, political economies and the institutionalization of risk. *Punishment & Society, 14*(2), 166–192.

Michaud, P., & Proulx, J. (2009). Penile-response profiles of sexual aggressors during phallometric testing. *Sexual Abuse: A Journal of Research and Treatment, 21*(3), 308–334.

Murphy, L., Fedoroff, J. P., & Martineau, M. (2009). Canada's sex offender registries: Background, implementation, and social policy considerations. *The Canadian Journal of Human Sexuality, 18*(1-2), 61.

Ouimet, R. (1969). *Report of the Canadian Committee on Corrections: towards unity: Criminal justice and corrections*. Edmonton: Queen's Printer.

Peek, R. M., & Storms, L. H. (1956). Validity of the Marsh-Hilliard-Liechti MMPI sexual deviation scale in a state hospital population. *Journal of Consulting Psychology, 20*(2), 133.

Petrunik, M. (1994). Models of dangerousness: A cross jurisdictional review of dangerousness legislation and practice. Solicitor General Canada, Ministry Secretariat.

Petrunik, M. (2003). The hare and the tortoise: Dangerousness and sex offender policy in the United States and Canada. *Canadian Journal of Criminology and Criminal Justice, 45*(1), 43–72.

Petrunik, M. G. (2002). Managing unacceptable risk: Sex offenders, community response, and social policy in the United States and Canada. *International Journal of Offender Therapy and Comparative Criminology, 46*(4), 483–511.

Polk, K. (1985). Rape reform and criminal justice processing. *Crime & Delinquency, 31*(2), 191–205.

Proulx, J. (1989). Sexual preference assessment of sexual aggressors. *International Journal of Law and Psychiatry, 12*, 275–280.

Quinsey, V. L., & Earls, C. M. (1990). The modification of sexual preferences. In W. L. Marshall, D. R. Laws, & H. E. Barbaree (Eds.), *Handbook of sexual assault: Issues, theories, and treatment of the offender* (pp. 279–295). Boston, MA: Springer.

Quinsey, V. L., Harris, G. T., Rice, M. E., & Cormier, C. A. (1998). *Violent offenders: Appraising and managing risk*. Washington DC: APA.

Quinsey, V. L., Rice, M. E., & Harris, G. T. (1995). Actuarial prediction of sexual recidivism. *Journal of Interpersonal Violence, 10*(1), 85–105.

Reinhardt, J. M., & Fisher, E. C. (1948). The sexual psychopath and the law. *The Journal of Criminal Law and Criminology, 39*, 734.

Roberts, J. V., & Gebotys, R. J. (1992). Reforming rape laws: Effects of legislative change in Canada. *Law and Human Behavior, 16*(5), 555.

Robin, G. D. (1977). Forcible rape: Institutionalized sexism in the criminal justice system. *Crime & Delinquency, 23*(2), 136–153.

Robinson, M. C., Rouleau, J. L., & Madrigrano, G. (1997). Validation de la pléthysmographie pénienne comme mesure psychophysiologique des intérêts sexuels des agresseurs adolescents. *Revue Québécoise de Psychologie, 18*, 111–124.

Rose, V. M. (1977). Rape as a social problem: A byproduct of the feminist movement. *Social Problems, 25*(1), 75–89.

Roth, N. (1952). Factors in the motivation of sexual offenders. *The Journal of Criminal Law, Criminology, and Police Science, 42*(5), 631–635.

Sacco, V. F. (1995). Media constructions of crime. *The Annals of the American Academy of Political and Social Science, 539*(1), 141–154.

Sanday, P. R. (1981). The socio-cultural context of rape: A cross-cultural study. *Journal of Social Issues, 37*(4), 5–27.

Schneider, J. W. (1985). Social problems theory: The constructionist view. *Annual Review of Sociology, 11*(1), 209–229.

Schwendinger, J. R., & Schwendinger, H. (1974). Rape myths: In legal, theoretical, and everyday practice. *Crime and Social Justice, 1*, 18–26.

Seto, M. C., Lalumière, M. L., & Blanchard, R. (2000). The discriminative validity of a phallometric test for pedophilic interests among adolescent sex offenders against children. *Psychological Assessment, 12*(3), 319–327.

Shorter, E. (1978). On writing the history of rape. *Signs: Journal of Women in Culture and Society, 3*(2), 471–482.

Simon, J. (1998). Managing the monstrous: Sex offenders and the new penology. *Psychology, Public Policy, and Law, 4*(1-2), 452.

Somers, M. R., & Block, F. (2005). From poverty to perversity: Ideas, markets, and institutions over 200 years of welfare debate. *American Sociological Review, 70*(2), 260–287.

Spohn, C., & Horney, J. (1992). *Rape law reform: A grassroots revolution and its impact.* New York: Plenum Press.

Sutherland, E. (1950). The sexual psychopath laws. *The Journal of Criminal Law and Criminology, 40*, 543–554.

Szasz, T. S. (1960). The myth of mental illness. *American Psychologist, 15*(2), 113–118.

Tappan, P. W. (1951). Sentences for sex criminals. *Journal of Criminal Law, Criminology, and Police Science, 42*, 332–337.

Tappan, P. W. (1955). The young adult offender under the American Law Institute's model penal code. *Federal Probation, 19*, 20–25.

Theocharis, Y., Lowe, W., Van Deth, J. W., & García-Albacete, G. (2015). Using Twitter to mobilize protest action: online mobilization patterns and action repertoires in the Occupy Wall Street, Indignados, and Aganaktismenoi movements. *Information, Communication & Society, 18*(2), 202–220.

The (New York City) Mayor's Committee Reports on the Study of Sex Offenses. (1944). *Journal of Criminal Law and Criminology, 34*(5), 324–327.

Treas, J. (2002). How cohorts, education, and ideology shaped a new sexual revolution on American attitudes toward nonmarital sex, 1972–1998. *Sociological Perspectives, 45*(3), 267–283.

Valentich, M., & Gripton, J. (1984). Ideological perspectives on the sexual assault of women. *Social Service Review, 58*(3), 448–461.

Van Dijk, T. A. (1998). *Ideology: A multidisciplinary approach.* London: Sage.

Weisman, R. (1995). Reflections on the Oak Ridge experiment with mentally disordered offenders, 1965–1968. *International Journal of Law and Psychiatry, 18*, 265–290.

Whitting, L., Day, A., & Powell, M. (2014). The impact of community notification on the management of sex offenders in the community: An Australian perspective. *Australian and New Zealand Journal of Criminology, 47*(2), 240–258.

Wood, P. L. (1973). Victim in a forcible rape case: A feminist view. *American Criminal Law Review, 11*, 335.

Wormith, J. S., & Ruhl, M. (1986). Preventive detention in Canada. *Journal of Interpersonal Violence, 1*(4), 399–430.

Yamahiro, R. S., & Griffith, R. M. (1960). Validity of two indices of sexual deviancy. *Journal of Clinical Psychology, 16*, 21–24.

Chapter 3
Applying a Criminal Career Approach to Expose Myths, Misconceptions, and Erroneous Conclusions About Sexual Offending

Introduction

The social and legal construction of the "sex offender" has led to the idea that individuals who perpetrate a sex crime are a homogenous group characterized by a life-course persistent pattern of sexual offending. These individuals need to be stopped one way or another before they go on to offend against hundreds of victims. Politicians and government officials have been pressured into swift, unproven, and untested populist and ideologically driven sociolegal responses to address the sex offender problem. In doing so, politicians, government officials, and even policy-makers have been, consciously or not, responsible for propagating myths and misconceptions about perpetrators of sex crimes. One result is the collective idea that there are people born as sex offenders who begin committing sex offenses very early in life and do so throughout their lives more often than not and likely never stop.

As early as the 1930s, prominent public figures like J. Edgar Hoover and J. Paul De River publicly spoke about the sex fiend as a "bogeyman" who attacked women and children at random. Scientific research on perpetrators of sex crimes slowly emerged in the 1940s but it was not until the late 1970s that it became a field of research, at least in North America. From that point on, like any other field of research in the social sciences, rigorous research and scientific evidence have emerged sporadically. Researchers did not have the means of communication that are available nowadays. They did not possess the technology available today to examine systematically thousands and thousands of pieces of information about hundreds of perpetrators of sex crimes. Scientific research was not accessible in those days like it can be now. Despite this, there were some, albeit few, researchers who advocated against populist and ideological thinking around the topic. In the early 1950s, Guttmacher and Weihofen (1952) highlighted some widely held misconceptions about "sex offenders" of their era. The first was that these individuals represented a homogenous group to which they pointedly and concisely explained "the reverse is true" (p. 154). The second misconception of their era they pointed out

© Springer Nature Switzerland AG 2021
P. Lussier et al., *Understanding Sexual Offending*,
https://doi.org/10.1007/978-3-030-53301-4_3

was the perception that individuals will typically progress from minor sexual crimes, such as from exhibitionism, to serious sexual crimes like forcible rape. Again, they were unable to uncover any scientific evidence of this in their time. The third was the misconception that sex offenses were rampant in this time period. Again, they were unable to identify any trends suggesting this. Finally, the fourth was that all sex offenders tended to be recidivists. An examination of Uniform Crime Reports that were available at the time suggested the opposite. Disappointingly, almost seventy years on, we are confronted with virtually the same myths, misconceptions, and erroneous conclusions about perpetrators of sex crimes.

While sex offending research took time to establish itself as a field of scientific investigation, myths, misconceptions, and erroneous conclusions continuously proliferated. A major consequence of this is that politicians, government officials, policymakers, and the public have filled in these gaps with their own narratives about the "sex offender." They have simplified complex behavioral phenomenon such as sex offending to a single cause, be it psychiatric, psychological, social, or cultural, which has led to the propagation and accumulation of key misconceptions about the causes, but also, the nature and extent of sexual violence in society and ways to respond to it collectively. Such narratives are based on errors in reasoning such as hearsay, personal interpretation, stereotypes and personal biases, personal experiences, as well as media representation of extreme and atypical cases, and films and television series to name a few. More importantly, the accumulation of these myths and misconceptions over time has led to a substantial fragmentation of our collective understanding about the phenomenon. Our assertion is that myths and misperceptions can be corrected through scientific investigation; however, researchers have been attempting to do this, arguably with marginal success, for almost a century now.

The key point to take away from the outset is that perpetrators of sex offenses represent a heterogeneous population for which a single label (e.g., sex offender) and a single representation (e.g., life-course persistent sex offender) are not supported by research. This chapter establishes the justification for deconstructing this label and this single representation of perpetrators of sex crimes through an examination of scientific research and scientific evidence about the criminal activity of these individuals throughout their life-course. The criminal career research paradigm was used as the framework for organizing this complex scientific literature. The criminal career paradigm has been used in criminological research for several decades to study the longitudinal sequence of offending. Although some researchers have paid attention to this in the past (Gebhard, Gagnon, Pomeroy, & Christenson, 1965), it is only more recently that researchers from the field of sex offending have highlighted the benefits of this approach (Blokland & Lussier, 2015; Cale & Lussier, 2014; Lussier & Cale, 2013). This framework is useful for addressing the myths and misconceptions that thrive today. The current chapter demonstrates the utility of the criminal career framework for guiding research on key aspects of the offending patterns of perpetrators of sex crimes and that the research addressing different parameters of the criminal career has, to this point, debunked several typical misconceptions. Although empirical studies along these lines were not necessarily explicitly testing criminal career principles, they nevertheless addressed five contemporary assumptions generally held about these perpetrators. The assumptions are as follows:

1. Sex offending is highly prevalent even in the general population
2. Most "sex offenders" start their offending early in the life-course
3. Most "sex offenders" offend repeatedly against multiple victims
4. Young "sex offenders" are destined for sex offending in adulthood
5. Sex offenders are sex crime specialists (i.e., the majority of their crimes are sex offenses)

Early investigations of perpetrators of sex offenses were conducted in psychiatric hospitals and focused on the examination and description of deviant sexual behaviors (e.g., Krafft-Ebing, 1867). Sexual deviance encompasses a range of phenomena such as sexual thoughts; urges; fantasies; desires; preoccupations; drive; preferences; arousal; and behaviors. The range of these phenomena encompasses cognitive, emotional, physiological, and behavioral aspects of sexual deviance. These distinctive aspects are too often conflated and lost into what is considered and referred to as sexual deviance. This poses a significant problem from a criminal career perspective. For example, someone may experience deviant sexual fantasies without having an urge to actualize such fantasies in real life. Someone may experience sexual arousal to deviant sexual stimuli involving sexual violence without having ever actually been sexually violent or becoming sexually violent. Someone may even perpetrate a sex crime without having deviant sexual interests or preferences for such particular forms of sexual gratification. Furthermore, research suggests that deviant sexual fantasizing is more prevalent in the general population than initially thought (e.g., Joyal, 2015). When speaking of sexual deviance, clinical researchers have not always distinguished between the cognitive, emotional, physiological, and behavioral aspects of sexual deviance, therefore creating much confusion about the scope and extent of a person's sexual deviance.

The criminal career paradigm is not concerned about a person's thoughts, fantasizing, preoccupations, drive, or even urges. Criminal career research is focused on a person's behavior. From that standpoint, cognitive, emotional, and physiological aspects of sexual deviance (e.g., fantasies, preferences, arousal) are conceived as potential risk factors of sexual offending. The starting point, therefore, of a criminal career investigation is a person's sexual offending behavior. Below, before examining the empirical validity of the abovementioned assumptions, we introduce the key parameters of the criminal career that this perspective seeks to describe. Following this, we examine the empirical evidence that exists about what is actually known, and what is not, about the offending patterns among perpetrators of sex offenses.

The Criminal Career Approach

The criminal career research paradigm focuses on the longitudinal sequencing of an individual's offending pattern (e.g., Blumstein, Cohen, & Farrington, 1988; Blumstein, Cohen, Roth, & Visher, 1986; DeLisi & Piquero, 2011; LeBlanc &

Loeber, 1998; Piquero, Farrington, & Blumstein, 2003). A major focus of the criminal career framework is establishing the prevalence of offending (also referred to as participation), which refers to the proportion of offenders within a given population during a specific period. The main objective of the criminal career research paradigm is not to explain why offending is or is not prevalent but rather to more fully understand offending sequences. Criminal career researchers recognize that offending develops over time and as such to better understand this development, it is important to break down this longitudinal sequence into several parts. These parts are known as offending "parameters" and they refer to the beginning (e.g., age of onset), the unfolding (e.g., frequency, lambda), and the end (e.g., desistance) of an offender's criminal career. The criminal career paradigm does not make assumptions about the specific causes of offending. It does, however, acknowledge that different causal mechanisms are responsible for the onset, the unfolding, and the termination of offending. The criminal career paradigm also does not make assumptions that the longitudinal sequencing of offending is necessarily different across different types of offenses. Therefore, the criminal career paradigm may be an appropriate framework for understanding the beginning, the unfolding, and the end of sex offending over the life-course of an individual. We believe that one significant factor that facilitated the proliferation of myths and stereotypes about perpetrators of sex crimes, even among criminal justice professionals, is the lack of words and terms to more properly distinguish their behavior and their offending patterns. These criminal career parameters are presented and defined in Table 3.1 in order to fill this gap.

While criminal career researchers have introduced this terminology to break down the study of criminal offending into its parts, another key component of this research paradigm is its focus on the longitudinal examination of offending. Age, timing, and the passage of time are inherently important for criminal career researchers. For example, criminal offending is not assumed to be a stable and fixed trait but rather a behavior that can evolve with age. Interest in the dynamic and longitudinal aspect of offending helps to organize information about criminal career parameters. In fact, when examining criminal career parameters, a longitudinal sequence of development emerges. Researchers have described this longitudinal sequence in terms of a developmental process model of offending (LeBlanc & Fréchette, 1989; Lussier, 2017). This model is presented in Fig. 3.1. Before offending repeats itself, it needs to start. The sequence, therefore, starts at the age of onset of offending. Criminal career research has shown that the earlier offending starts, the more persistent it can be and, in the process, the more frequent and diverse it can become (e.g., Piquero et al., 2003). When offending is persistent, it can become chronic and can progress to more serious forms of offending (e.g., LeBlanc & Loeber, 1998). Research also shows that offending reaches a culmination point after which it slows down and becomes less frequent and more specific until individuals cease their offending behavior altogether.

At first, this description may suggest that all offenders are career criminals, but criminal career research has used this framework to identify much heterogeneity in longitudinal offending patterns. In fact, this framework has helped to identify a

Table 3.1 The criminal career approach

Parameters	Definition
Prevalence	The proportion of a given population committing a crime during a specific period
Age of onset	The age at first offense
Frequency (volume)	The number of offenses perpetrated
Lambda	The number of offenses perpetrated taking into account the time at risk (i.e., excluding periods during which the offender did not have the opportunity to offend (e.g., hospitalization, incarceration, death))
Continuity	The passage from juvenile offending to adult offending
Career length	The length of time between onset and termination of offending
Versatility (diversity)	The number of different offense types committed
Seriousness	The degree of gravity of offending
Specialization	The tendency to limit offending to one particular behavioral form
Desistance	Termination of offending

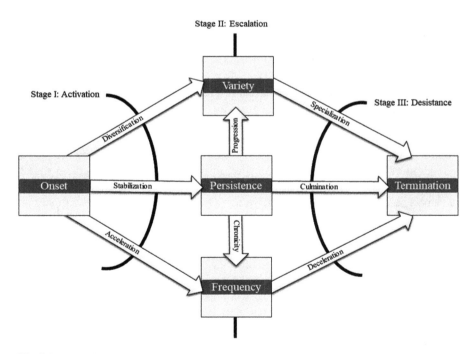

Fig. 3.1 A developmental process model of offending

diversity of longitudinal offending sequences. Some being transitory and very limited in frequency and time, while others being more sustained and frequent but limited to a certain developmental period. The same research has also shown a more concerning pattern of offending. One of these patterns is initiated early on, characterized by a high offending rate in a wide array of crime types, which persist over long time periods (Piquero, 2008). Another pattern is initiated later on, and while offending is more sporadic and intermittent, it is nonetheless diverse and persistent. While the scientific contribution of the criminal career research paradigm is undeniable and its legacy long-lasting, it was only recently that researchers extended this paradigm to the study of sexual offending (Cale & Lussier, 2012; Lussier, McCuish, Deslauriers-Varin, & Corrado, 2017). As such, it is unclear if the observation regarding general criminal careers also applies to perpetrators of sex crimes and whether the development of sexual offending mirrors that of non-sexual offending (Lussier & Blokland, 2017). While the scientific literature was first reviewed by Lussier and Cale (2013), an update of the scientific evidence characterizing the criminal careers of perpetrators of sex crimes is provided below.

The criminal career paradigm facilitates the scientific evaluation of the merits of such social constructions and policies. Some of the major criminal career parameters that have been studied, whether directly or indirectly, in the field of research on sexual offending include prevalence, age of onset, frequency, persistence/continuity, and specialization/versatility. The current chapter focuses on what research has discovered with respect to each of these parameters.

The Prevalence of Sexual Offending

Identification of the prevalence of sexual offending may seem like a simple task. After all, prevalence is simply a count of the number of instances in which the behavior occurred in a sample of individuals. However, underneath the surface of this task is the responsibility of developing a clear measure of what constitutes sex offending; only then can social scientists fulfill their role of estimating the scope and extent of the sex offender problem. When measuring sexual offending, social scientists and criminal career researchers face a series of pitfalls, challenges, and barriers. The definition of a sex crime varies across jurisdictions and over time. For example, anal penetration and selling sexual services, under Canadian law, were once criminal offenses. On the other hand, up until the 1980s rape was only considered an offense outside of marriage in many countries such as Canada and Australia; in other words, a male who committed rape against his spouse could not be charged for the crime. What's more, until the 1990s females could not be charged with the offense of rape in several countries as well, such as Canada and the Netherlands among others. Not all sex crimes are reported to the police for various reasons, such as fear, guilt, and shame, not wanting to be involved with the criminal justice system, unawareness, or being financially dependent on the perpetrator (Thompson, Sitterle, Clay, & Kingree, 2007). Moreover, not all sex crimes reported to the police lead to a criminal conviction for a multitude of reasons such as in cases where the suspect cannot be identified or located, the police lack evidence, the testimony is not reliable enough, mistakes are made with the handling of criminal evidence, and so on. There are also disparities across jurisdictions with respect to criminal justice resources available to efficiently and adequately respond to reports of a sex crime starting with the training of police, police investigators, prosecutors, and their handling of sex crimes that may affect the outcome of the criminal investigation and the court decision. In other words, there is a large gap between actual offending and official sources of information about sex crimes that are available from police, court, and correctional databases. This gap is not specific to sex crime cases, but it is true for most if not all forms of crimes. The challenge for criminal career research is to estimate this gap.

To address some of the issues with official information about crime, social scientists, criminologists, and criminal career researchers have relied on other sources of information, most commonly self-reports. Self-reported information about sexual offending is retrieved from potential and actual perpetrators through questionnaires, surveys, and structured interviews used to ask, confidentially and sometimes anonymously, sensitive questions about a person's past behavior, including sexual offending. Self-reports have been used sporadically by researchers to measure sexual offending with mixed results. Indeed, self-reports are not a panacea and these methods also have limitations that affect the measurement of sexual offending. Not everyone approached to report their offending behavior will choose to participate in such a study; those that do participate may decline to answer questions about their criminal behavior, including sex crimes, or may not be honest about them. Furthermore, the legal context can also limit the measurement of sexual offending using a self-reported approach. For example, in Canada, everyone has a legal obligation to report to the police known or suspected child (sexual) abuse which can significantly affect a person' willingness to report such behavior for research purposes. Even individuals convicted for a sex crime often persistently deny and minimize the behavior for which they were convicted (Rogers & Dickey, 1991).

Victim rights advocates, on the other hand, have argued that the most reliable source of information about sexual offending are victimization surveys. Victimization surveys have been used to provide a picture of the prevalence of sexual offending. Using these methods, not surprisingly, researchers have shown that sexual victimization is much more widespread than what can be accounted for using official data. However, while these instruments can point towards the broad scope of sexual victimization incidents in a given place during a specified period they are not as helpful from a criminal career perspective because victims are typically unable to report, for example, whether it was the offender's first offense, fifth offense, or last offense. Furthermore, victimization surveys are problematic to estimate the size of the population of sexual offenders. First, such surveys make it difficult to determine whether two different participants were victimized by the same perpetrator or separate perpetrators. When it comes to general offending, the criminal career framework has identified that a small group of perpetrators is typically responsible for a disproportionate amount of these particular crimes (e.g., Abel & Rouleau, 1990; Lussier, Van Den Berg, Bijleveld, & Hendriks, 2012). To equate each victim with a distinct offender will inflate the prevalence of sexual offending in the population. Second, long recall periods (e.g., asking participants about lifetime history of sexual victimization) typically used in these surveys simply do not allow for the estimation of the population of perpetrators in a given time period. Third, these surveys also typically will not include individuals who are not registered citizens in the respective country, such as tourists and visitors who may be sexually victimized during their stay. Victimization surveys also have issues with reaching some segments of the general population of a given country (e.g., individuals with no fixed address, no phone access, and hospitalized or incarcerated individuals), who, as a result, are not included in such large-scale surveys. This is especially problematic because such individuals may be at an elevated risk of sexual victimization. On the other hand, victimization surveys are often administered specifically to university students who may be at a heightened risk for experiencing sexual victimization given that perpetrators are in closer social proximity and the presence of shared risk factors characterizing their environment (Kania & Cale, 2018). In effect, issues with survey measures and generalizability make it difficult to make strong conclusions about the prevalence of sex offending in the general population.

More generally, there are inherent difficulties in establishing even the prevalence of sexual victimization, let alone perpetration, due to different ways sexual victimization is defined across studies. The behaviors included in some surveys are vague and/or not defined which may lead to various interpretations by those surveyed, or by researchers. For example, prior to the redesign of the large-scale American National Crime Survey (NCS) in 1993, no explicit definition of "rape" was provided to respondents; this determination was left to the interviewer based on the response to screening question regarding assaults. In other surveys (including the revised National Crime Victimization Survey), rape referred to sexual intercourse subsequent to the use of force or physical violence, but studies showed variations in the lower boundary age included in the definition (sexual victimization since age 14, 16, or 18) (e.g., Koss, Gidycz, & Wisniewski, 1987). Yet others have used the broader concept of sexual assault, which refers to being pressured or forced to have sexual contact (e.g., Sorenson, Stein, Siegel, Golding, & Burnam, 1987). Importantly, these various operational definitions lead to very different prevalence rates for sexual victimization. In the oft-cited study of Koss et al. (1987) that was based on a large sample of college women, the self-reported prevalence of sexual victimization (unwanted sexual contacts; sexual coercion, attempted rape, rape) since age 14 was 53%, however, this number dropped to 15% when considering rape alone. While this compartmentalization is desirable to address specific policy and research questions, it severely limits the possibility of estimating the size of the offender population given the abovementioned issues. This poses a serious dilemma to criminal career researchers; namely, how to best measure sexual offending given these known limitations. Researchers have advocated one measure over another while the preferred scenario, from a methodological standpoint, is to combine and compare findings across methods (e.g., see Payne & Piquero, 2017).

To be sure, the scientific literature on the prevalence of sexual offending has become more sophisticated and includes a greater emphasis on empirical data since Brownmiller (1975) claimed that rape was a "conscious process of intimidation by which all men keep all women in a state of fear" (p. 13). Numerous self-report studies have been conducted with selected groups of young men, typically undergraduate students. Malamuth (1981, 1989) surveyed a group of male undergraduate university students and asked them whether they would be likely to engage in different behaviors if they were absolutely sure that there would be no negative consequences. Three-quarters of the students surveyed (74%) said they would not commit a rape under any circumstances, thus suggesting that 26% were at least open to the idea under certain conditions. At the same time however, only about 2% of all the men surveyed by Malamuth (see also Greendlinger & Byrne, 1987) said they would "very likely" rape someone under such circumstances. While this study did not measure the percentage of men who actually raped someone, it did highlight the fact that one out of four men may contemplate the idea if given the opportunity to do so in circumstances where there would be no negative consequences. This is still a limited means of estimating prevalence because it does not reflect real-world situations where it is typically the case that there is a non-zero probability that individuals can commit such offenses without consequence.

These and similar findings drew much attention to the issue of sexual assault perpetrated by college men in the USA in the 1980s. In the study by Koss et al. (1987), one-quarter of the male college students surveyed reported having engaged in at least one form of behavior defined as sexual aggression, including unwanted sexual touching, pressuring someone into sex, sexual coercion such as the use of threats, rape, and attempted rape. However, when narrowing down the definition to acts of sexual coercion such as sexual intercourse subsequent to pressure, threats, or misuse of authority, that prevalence rate dropped to 7%. Finally, it was found that 4% of behaviors described by these male college students met the legal definition of rape. Importantly, similar findings have been reported elsewhere (e.g., Greendlinger & Byrne, 1987; Senn, Desmarais, Verberg, & Wood, 2000). Recent studies have reported lower estimates of prevalence. Kjellgren, Priebe, Svedin, and Långström (2010) estimated the prevalence of self-reported sexually coercive behavior among a Swedish sample of high school students between the ages of 17 and 20. For this study, sexually coercive behaviors were defined as someone who used pressure or forced someone to masturbate, have sex, oral sex, or anal sex. A total of 5% of the students sampled reported perpetrating coercive sexual behavior during their lifetime. There are some important points to consider surrounding these particular findings and the discrepancies of self-reported prevalence estimate of sexual offending. Namely, the extent to which these estimates are biased due to, on the one hand, underreporting of sexually coercive behaviors due to social desirability issues (e.g., Seifert, Boulas, Huss, & Scalora, 2017), and, on the other hand, misinterpretation of behaviorally specific questions out of context.

More recently, Swartout et al. (2015) examined trajectories of rape perpetrated on college campuses. Their analyses specifically targeted speculations by the media, special interest groups, and the general public that perpetrators of rape on college campuses were serial rapists. These researchers referred to such speculations as part of a campus serial rapist assumption that formed the dominant portrayal of the phenomenon despite a lack of empirical data or misinterpretation/misreporting of existing data. Two samples were used, one to identify a trajectory model ($n = 847$) and one to test the validity of such a model ($n = 795$). In this study, rape was defined as "penetration, no matter how slight, of the vagina or anus with any body part or object, or oral penetration by a sex organ of another person, without the consent of the victim" (Swartout et al., 2015, p. 1149). This study found that 72.9% of all rapes committed in college were perpetrated by individuals with no prior history of sexual offending. Unlike other community studies, this study showed that approximately 50% of individuals that perpetrated a rape in adolescence also did so during their college career. In terms of the trajectory analyses, in both the derivation and validation samples, a three-group solution was identified. This analysis found that 90% of male college students were associated with a trajectory defined by no perpetration of campus rape or perpetration that was circumscribed to a very short period of time. The second largest trajectory comprised 5% of the sample and was characterized by perpetration of rape in high school followed by a sharp decrease in frequency of perpetration over the college career. A third trajectory (2.1% of the sample) showed a pattern of campus rape that increased in frequency over the college career. There was no trajectory defined by a high-rate and persistent level of campus rape, which contradicted many of the myths and misperceptions purported by university leaders, politicians, and advocacy groups, and the media. Another important finding to note is that although the first trajectory that was defined by low or no involvement in campus-perpetrated rapes (only 7.5% of this trajectory had a lifetime history of campus-perpetrated rape), this group nevertheless accounted for 52.8% of all offenders. In other words, the majority of individuals that perpetrated rape on campus were individuals with no prior history of perpetrating such offenses, and in most if not all cases, this first offense was also their last offense.[1]

Another challenge in estimating the prevalence of sexual offending is the focus on adult victims and the neglect of self-reported sexually abusive behaviors against children. This gap in research is interesting because the rates of sexual abuse victimization among children that have been uncovered in epidemiological studies are quite substantial; a meta-analysis based on retrospective studies conducted with college students found that about 17% of men (range: 3–37%) and 28% (range: 8–71%) of women have been sexually abused as a child (Rind, Tromovitch, & Bauserman, 1998). Lower victimization rates for child sexual abuse compared to those for sexual assault against adult women are generally consistent with lower

---

[1] These findings sharply contrast with Swartout et al. (2015) review of major task forces and reports that influence federal legislation, media coverage of the phenomenon, and public discourse. Such perspectives portray campus sexual assaults as the result of an extremely small number of men perpetrating the majority of all sex offenses. Indeed, the White House Council on Women and Girls (2014) received information suggesting that 3% of college men perpetrated 90% of all rapes. Accordingly, the report concluded that the typical campus assailant is one that repeatedly engaged in such crimes. Swartout et al. (2015) findings suggested not just that such an offender was rare, but that such an offender did not exist according to their data. In sum, the problem of sex offending on high school and college campuses was an issue of prevalence rather than frequency; approximately 10% of men had a history of perpetrating rape and yet the most frequent offenders in Swartout et al. (2015) study accounted for only 13% of all individuals that perpetrated rape on a high school or college campus. Put clearly, "at least 4 of 5 men on campus who have committed rape will be missed by focusing solely on these men" (Swartout et al., 2015, p. 1153). The findings, therefore, also suggest that the prevalence of rape as reported in victimization surveys should be closer than previously believed to the perpetration rate estimated in self-reports.

sexual interest among adult males for sexual contacts with children in the broader population. For example, in Malamuth's (1989) study, 91% of men surveyed indicated that they would not engage in sexual acts with children even if they knew they would get away with it. In another study by Templeman and Stinnett (1991), approximately 5% of male respondents from a community-based sample self-reported sexual interest for children. Briere and Runtz (1989) reported similar figures where 9% of male college students that they surveyed indicated they have had sexual fantasies involving a child, and, 7% (of the whole sample) suggested they would act on them if they could get away with it. In another study of male college students, Fromuth, Burkhart, and Jones (1991) found that 3% of their sample of men reported having had a "sexual experience" with a child. Similar to the above-mentioned issues with victimization surveys, the emphasis of self-report studies on young adult male college students makes it difficult to generalize the findings to other subgroups of adult males, such as adult males in the community who do not have university education, and the prevalence of sexual aggression in that context. In addition, these self-report studies did not ask men whether they ever had been caught, arrested, or convicted for the behaviors they reported, and therefore, this does not allow researchers to estimate the actual risks of apprehension/conviction, which would add an important piece to the puzzle when it comes to estimating prevalence of sexual offending behavior.

Officially Recorded Data The prevalence of sexual offending has been directly examined using official statistics on crime. To address the issue of generalization, researchers have relied on prevalence estimates of sexual offending using birth cohort data.[2] Using data from the 1945 Philadelphia birth cohort study, Wolfgang, Sellin, and Figlio (1972) showed that 0.4% of their cohort had been arrested for rape throughout adolescence (1 out of 250 youths), whereas 1.4% had been arrested for other sex crimes. Tracy, Wolfgang, and Figlio (1990) conducted a similar birth cohort study (men born in 1958) in Philadelphia to estimate the prevalence of crime involvement during adolescence. Their study was innovative in that it allowed the examination of cohort and period effects. For youth born 13 years later than in the original study, the prevalence of being arrested for rape increased to 0.66% while the one for other sex offenses dropped to 0.43%. The rate at which individuals are arrested for rape and sex crimes can fluctuate across generations, an observation that has gone almost unnoticed in the scientific literature. Similarly, a series of birth cohort studies including individuals born in the UK in the 1950s, 1960s, and 1970s showed that the overall official prevalence of sex crimes perpetrated by adolescents ranged from about 0.3% to 0.5% (Marshall, 1997). These observations are therefore consistent with findings observed by Tracy et al. (1990) in the USA for the same period. More recently, using data from the 1984 Dutch birth cohort, Lussier and

---

[2] Birth cohort data refers to information stemming from a sample of individuals born the same year in a specific location (city, state, country). The objective of using birth cohort data is to have information representative of society as whole and not just a segment or a subgroup of the population (e.g., inmates).

Blokland (2014) estimated that the prevalence of sexual offenses committed by adolescents was 0.4%. Despite the historical, sociocultural, and legal differences across the locations where these studies were conducted, there is some consistency in official prevalence estimates of perpetration of sexual offending among adolescents. These data show that for every 1000 young people in a birth cohort, between 3 and 5 are arrested for a sexual offense. This small number shows how the phenomenon rarely comes to the attention of the police and, as a result, how difficult it is for researchers to isolate and describe possible explanations.

Furthermore, arrests for internet child pornography related offenses are even rarer; the Crimes Against Children Research Center in the USA showed that in 2006, there were an estimated 3672 arrests for these specific types of sexual crimes. That same year, there were over 92,000 reports of rape to law enforcement in the USA (U.S. Department of Justice, 2007). In a meta-analysis examining the overlap between contact sexual offending and online sex offending, Seto, Hanson, and Babchishin (2011) found that approximately 12% of men with online sex offenses had officially recorded contact sex offense histories, but that this number jumped to 55% across studies based on self-reported offending histories.

These prevalence estimates speak of the offending of individuals at some particular point in time but not about offending over their life-course. Marshall (1997) used five birth cohorts of individuals born in the UK to estimate the life-course cumulative prevalence of sex crime perpetration. The findings showed that one out of 70 men born in 1953 and followed up to age 40 had been convicted for a sexual offense involving a victim, one out of 90 men had been convicted for a serious sexual crime (i.e., hands-on behaviors against children and/or adults), and one out of 140 men had been convicted of a sexual crime against a child (Marshall, 1997). Marshall's data are difficult to interpret given the absence of similar findings from other studies. These data do show, however, that only a very small fraction of a birth cohort are convicted for a sex crime. Marshall (1997) also looked at the participation rate (not to be confused with the cumulative participation rate) and found that it steadily increased from the 20–24 age group (0.3%) to the 40 and older group (1.8%) thus suggesting that older men might be either more active in sexual offending, or more at risk of being apprehended and convicted for a sex crime. This trend is reminiscent of the one reported by Cline (1980) using arrest data on a sample of adjudicated juvenile delinquents. Using the Gluecks' longitudinal arrest data of a sample of adjudicated juvenile offenders, Cline (1980) reported that the prevalence rate for sex crimes increased from 0.3% in early adolescence to 1.6% in late adolescence, 2.4% in early young adulthood, and 2.6% in late young adulthood.

These numbers are interesting for several reasons. First, they show that only a small segment of the population is arrested for a sex crime at any point during adolescence and young adulthood. Second, these findings are also interesting from a criminal career perspective because the data is based on the same cohort of individuals as they age rather than individuals from different age groups/cohorts. These findings based on longitudinal cohort data suggest that the prevalence of sex offending perpetration steadily increased with age during that specific time frame. This is somewhat atypical given that the peak of offending, when considering all forms of crime and delinquency, usually occurs during mid-to-late adolescence. While these official prevalence estimates are surprisingly low, they are potentially inflated because they are based on a sample of youth who had problems with the law. As such, this group is not representative of the larger population of that time.

In spite of the social importance of estimating the prevalence of sex crime perpetration, there have been very few scientific innovations over the years to circumvent the methodological and conceptual limitations in doing so. The obvious key issue using any official data, be it charges or convictions, to estimate the prevalence of any crime, let alone sexual crime, is the typical problem of the "dark figure," particularly for sexual crimes which are possibly among the least reported for various reasons. In order to address this key limitation of these kind of data, Bouchard and Lussier (2015) estimated the number of perpetrators of sex offenses at risk of incarceration based on official data. Using a technique called "capture-recapture" generally used by biologists, these researchers estimated the dark figure of sex offending using official data. Their sample consisted of 387 individuals who had been convicted of a sexual offense in a Canadian province between 1995 and 1998. The findings suggested that these 387 incarcerated individuals were active among an estimated 8000 other "sex offenders" who were not incarcerated over the same time period. In other words, the results suggested that the incarcerated population of individuals who have committed sex offenses represented about just under 5% of active perpetrators of sex offenses who were not incarcerated. Furthermore, not adjusting for the age-distribution of the population, their findings suggested that there were at least three times as many older perpetrators (i.e., 36 years old and above) compared to younger ones (18–35 years old), which is broadly consistent with Marshall's (1997) estimates. Again, notwithstanding the known limitations of using official data and the degree to which they capture actual offending patterns compared to the activities of the criminal justice system, this study was the first attempt to estimate the size of the population of individuals who perpetrated sex offenses in a specific time frame and geographical context. Much more work along these lines is needed to establish the prevalence rate at different time points, also using various indicators of sex offending in the same study (e.g., self-report, official; types of sex offenses, etc.).

Any of the measures used to establish the prevalence of sex offending in a given place at a given point in time would inevitably provide an underestimate of the phenomenon. Victimization surveys will not capture all victims and do not provide accurate information about the prevalence of perpetration. There is obvious inherent social desirability bias in self-report studies of sex offense perpetration (Seifert et al., 2017), and, sex offending is characterized by a substantial dark figure. Furthermore, the attrition of sexual assault cases through the legal process means that data based on convictions for sex offenses are possibly among the most substantial underestimates (e.g., Daly & Bouhours, 2010; Langevin et al., 2004; Van Wijk, Mali & Bullens, 2007). Indeed, a report conducted by the Victorian Law Reform Commission in 2004 in Australia showed that 1 in 6 reports to police of rape, and 1 in 7 reports to police of incest or sexual assault against a child resulted in a prosecution, let alone a conviction (see also, Gregory & Lees, 1999). Again, there is a substantial literature on the multitude of reasons victims do not report sexual crimes committed against them, particularly when the perpetrator is known to them.

One key context here is intimate relationships (e.g., dating, marriage). When it comes to sexual violence in the context of intimate relationships, a major focus has been on marital rape (Bennice & Resick, 2003). As mentioned earlier, one of the reasons for this definitionally narrow focus stemmed from sociopolitical climates that up until the 1980s, at least in Western nations, saw the legal invalidation of rape in the context of marriage, (e.g., Bennice & Resick, 2003; Finkelhor & Yllo, 1985; Lussier & Cale, 2016; Russell, 1990). However, a key limitation of this approach, as discussed above and in previous chapters, is that rape reflects a set of behaviors implying that there was vaginal intercourse involved in the absence of the victim's consent and some degree of force used by the assailant (e.g., Koss, Leonard, Beezley, & Oros, 1985). Therefore, this precludes many behaviors that would fall under the category of sexual coercion or other forms of sexual aggression which we have been discussing.

To be sure, since the early studies that focused exclusively on marital rape, researchers have broadened their lens to investigate behaviors along a continuum of sexual coercion and aggression in relationships that we have been discussing (e.g., Koss et al., 1985; DeKeseredy & Kelly, 1993; Finkelhor & Yllo, 1985). In a nationally representative US sample of rape and sexual coercion in the intimate partner context, Basile (2002) found that among women who reported having unwanted sex with spouse/partner, that the most common form of sexual coercion occurred in contexts where women thought it was their duty to have sex with their spouse/partner. The next most common type of sexual coercion occurred after a romantic situation (e.g., back rub, intimate kissing), followed by sexual coercion in which a spouse/partner begged/pleaded for sex. Smith et al. (2018) estimated the lifetime prevalence rates for women experiencing *rape* (i.e., any completed or attempted unwanted vaginal, oral, or anal penetration through the use of physical force or threats to physically harm including when the victim was drunk, high, drugged, or passed out and unable to consent) in a relationship at 21.3%, *sexual coercion* (i.e., unwanted sexual penetration that occurs after a person is pressured in a nonphysical way) at 16.0%, and unwanted sexual contact (i.e., unwanted sexual experiences involving touching but not sexual penetration, such as being kissed in a sexual way, or having sexual body parts fondled, groped, or grabbed) at 37.0%. Besides these, and possibly very few other studies sexual violence in the intimate partner context has largely been overlooked in the empirical literature, undoubtedly due to the inherent difficulties in obtaining reliable data along these lines. At the same time, in many countries, official arrest data suggests that reports of sexual assaults have increased substantially in the past decade (Francis, Hargreaves, & Soothill, 2015).

In a recent study that was also based on the same five UK cohorts as the study of Marshall (1997), plus the additional cohort in 1978, Francis et al. (2015) examined the six UK birth cohorts to investigate changes in the patterning of convicted "sex offenders," and whether and to what extent these changes reflected actual changes in behavior (i.e., sex offending) or changes in how the justice system prosecuted sex

offense convictions over time. This is an important question because changing official prevalence rates over time will reflect both actual changes in behavior as well
as changes in the societal response to sex offending.

For example, Francis et al. (2015) found that over the years under observation,
cautions and convictions for "rape" increased, while other types of sex crimes, such
as indecency between males decreased eventually to the point of zero—these two
trends corresponded with legislative changes criminalizing rape in the context of
marriage and decriminalizing sex between consenting males, respectively.[3] They
also observed changes over time in the prevalence rates for sex offenses involving
male and female victims under 16 years of age; again for males this corresponded
to the timing of legal changes regarding consensual sex between males, and for
females declines were associated with less willingness to report and prosecute sexual acts between adolescents when there was evidence of consent over the years
under observation. However, their analysis also indicated that the prevalence of sex
offense convictions varied according to the proportion of younger and older males
in the population. First, the higher the proportion of younger (i.e., late adolescent/
young adults) males corresponded to a higher prevalence of sexual crimes against
adult female victims. Second, the higher the proportion of older (i.e., above 40)
males also corresponded to a higher prevalence of sexual crimes against female
victims, in addition to male victims. These trends broadly resemble a commonly
observed phenomenon regarding the prevalence of sex offending, namely, that the
age crime curve associated with sexual offenses is bimodal, with prevalence peak-
ing twice, once in adolescence/young adulthood and again in mid-adulthood some-
time in the mid-to-late 30s. The first peak includes both adult-victim and child-victim
perpetrators and resembles the general age-crime curve. The second, apparently
more prominent, peak includes predominantly child-victim perpetrators (Smallbone
& Cale, 2015).

Female Sexual Offending   As mentioned earlier, up until the 1990s in many countries it was not possible for a female to be charged with rape. Therefore, only much
more recently have studies investigated the prevalence of sex offending perpetrated
by females. In 2017, Cortoni, Babchishin, and Rat conducted a meta-analysis using
17 samples from 12 countries including data that were based on official arrests and
victimization surveys. These studies showed that there was considerable variance in
prevalence statistics when it comes to sex offending perpetrated by females. For
example, data from official records indicated that the median prevalence rate was
1.7%, with prevalence rates across the official sources they considered ranged from
0.4% to 6.8%. Data from victimization surveys (i.e., the prevalence of sexual

---

[3] It is also important to note that the impact of similar sociolegal definitional changes on prevalence
estimates of sex offending can be observed in the studies discussed earlier based on the Philadelphia
Birth Cohorts—these involved changes to laws surrounding behaviors such as sodomy, prostitution, and buggery and others that legally constituted sex crimes historically that coincided with
shifts in prevalence estimates in the 1960s and 1970s (see Zimring et al., 2009). In effect, attempts
to estimate the prevalence of sex offending over time are also plagued by the fact it is a phenomenon that has been defined differently across generations.

victimization at the hands of a female) displayed even greater variance, with prevalence rates ranging from 3.1% to 24.4% (median = 10.8%) (Cortoni, Babchishin, & Rat, 2017). Many of the challenges discussed above apply when trying to uncover the prevalence of sex offending perpetrated by females; many sex offenses go undetected by the criminal justice system, and as such are not captured by criminal justice data. In addition to some of the factors associated with underreporting sex offenses in the victimization context discussed earlier, traditional gender roles and gender stereotypes also often act as additional barriers to recognizing and reporting sexual offending committed by females (Wijkman & Sandler, 2018). For example, men may not report being sexually coerced or assaulted by a woman for fear it may detract from their masculinity. The same issues may pervade the criminal justice system given assumptions that "women don't do such things" (Wijkman, Bijleveld, & Hendriks, 2010, p. 136).

Studies are also increasingly examining the prevalence of female sex offending among young people. In the meta-analysis by Cortoni et al. (2017) the prevalence rate of female sex offenses among youth having committed a sexual offense was 2.3%—a rate that was higher than the 1.8% found for adults. Similar findings were uncovered in a US study based on a national sample of adolescents; Ybarra and Mitchell (2013) found that the prevalence rate of any sexual violence perpetration (based on self-reported items from the SES; Koss et al., 1987) in a National US sample of 1058 adolescents was approximately 10%, forced sexual contact was approximately 8%, and coercive sex was approximately 3%. Interestingly among those youth reporting the perpetration of sexual violence and coercion ($n = 108$), the prevalence of female and male perpetrators was as follows: any sexual violence 42% female versus 58% male; forced sexual contact 52% female versus 48% female; and coercive sex 25% female versus 75% male. These findings are interesting, and controversial, for a few key reasons. First, they suggest that the prevalence of female perpetrators of sex offenses may be higher among adolescent than among adult populations. Second, at the extreme end of sexual violence (i.e., forced sexual contact), the self-reported prevalence for males and females was virtually equal. Third, gender differences were evident when it came to coercive sex where it was three-quarters of males compared to one-quarter of females who self-reported ever having engaged in these behaviors. This may suggest that while males engage in a wider range of sexually coercive and aggressive behaviors, at the extreme end when it comes to sexual violence, similarly small proportions of females self-report ever having engaged in this type of behavior.

These findings are controversial because sexual violence is considered by many as a "gendered" crime; indeed, unlike non-sexual crime the gender gap when it comes to sexual violence is overwhelmingly male, yet one possibility is that like the gender gap for non-sexual crimes, the gender gap for sexual crimes may also be narrowing. It is unclear, however, if it is the case, and whether criminal justice systems have adjusted their responses to female sex offending. For example, in the Netherlands, of all female adolescents involved in sex crimes over a 15-year period, 40% were prosecuted compared to 72% of males (Wijkman, Bijleveld, & Hendriks, 2014).

The Onset of Sexual Offending

The age of onset of sex offending refers to the time of one's first sexual offense. It is an important criminal career parameter because the earlier a behavior emerges, the more frequent and persistent it is expected to be.

The age of onset in this context allows for the examination of why and under what circumstances the behavior was initiated. The age of onset has been discussed in several empirical studies on perpetrators of sex offenses, but the operationalization of this particular criminal career dimension has not always been clear. For example, in early clinical investigations, researchers primarily considered this parameter in terms of the age of onset of sexual problems experienced by adults who committed sex offenses. Using the term sexual problems encompasses noncriminal behaviors such as deviant sexual arousal, deviant sexual fantasizing, and deviant sexual behaviors as well as actual sexual offending. Using these criteria, early clinical studies suggested that the sexual deviance of incarcerated adult sex offenders typically began in adolescence (e.g., Abel et al., 1987). As discussed in Chap. 2, early clinical models also heavily emphasized the role of deviant sexual fantasies as a precursor to sexual offending (Abel & Blanchard, 1974). Subsequent clinical research, however, has shown that not only do a small proportion of adults who commit sex offenses report deviant sexual fantasies and/or paraphilia, but also that even a far smaller proportion of them report having experienced such deviant fantasies prior their sexual offending (Marshall, Barbaree, & Eccles, 1991). Furthermore, the preponderance of evidence suggests that the adolescence-onset of sexual offending is likely the exception rather than the rule among adults who have committed sex offenses which is consistent with prevalence studies as well (Lussier & Blokland, 2014; Marshall et al., 1991; Smallbone & Wortley, 2004). Studies that did identify adult sex offenders with an onset of sex offending in adolescence were sampled from a specialized court system dealing exclusively with individuals with a history of involvement in more serious and/or repeated sexual offenses and held deviant sexual fantasies/paraphilias (e.g., Abel, Osborn, & Twigg, 1993; Groth, 1977). This reinforces the importance of distinguishing deviant fantasies, deviant sexual behaviors, and sex offending and clarifying where the sample was drawn from to understand the generalizability of findings.

Criminological research suggests that the onset of crime and delinquency generally occurs between the ages of 8 and 16 (Farrington, 2003). The variation in the mean age of onset across studies is typically attributable to sample discrepancies, type of crimes considered, and data source used to estimate the age of onset (e.g., official records versus self-report). The limited research on the onset of sexual offending suggests a broader range of ages of onset. When focusing on adolescent offenders, these studies typically showed that the average age of onset of sexual offending in adolescence is around 14 years old (e.g., Cale, Smallbone, Rayment-McHugh, & Dowling, 2016; Carpentier, Leclerc, & Proulx, 2011; Miner, 2002; Vizard, Hickey, & McCrory, 2007; Waite et al., 2005). However, some researchers have also provided evidence of a departure from this trend. Researchers have shown that between 5 and 26% of adolescent offenders may have started their sexual offending prior to the age of 12 (e.g., Awad & Saunders, 1991; Carpentier et al., 2011; Ryan, Miyoshi, Metzner, Krugman, & Fryer, 1996; Vizard et al., 2007). These findings do show that for a small subgroup, by adolescence, sexual offending is already part of a pattern of continuity. For most young offenders, however, an adolescence-onset of sexual offending best characterizes their situation. For them, sexual offending starts at the peak age of general delinquency involvement during adolescence. By this age, most youth have experienced the onset of puberty, they are more anxious to be liked and appreciated by their peers. Teenagers are also becoming more independent from their parents and increasingly interested in developing friendships with both males and females as well as showing an interest in romantic relationships. That said, their first sexual offense probably occurs prior to the onset of most youth's first sexual intercourse as suggested by epidemiological studies (Zimmer-Gembeck & Helfand, 2008). Gender differences are also evident. Ybarra and Mitchell (2013) found that among adolescents surveyed in their National US sample, almost all perpetrators who reported onset at around age 15 were male (i.e., 98%), whereas onset of sexual coercion and violence was later in adolescence for females. Clearly, there is a need to examine the onset of adolescent sexual offending in the context of the development of sexuality but also antisocial behavior more broadly.

A major challenge with studying the self-reported onset of offending, especially among adults, is the challenge for perpetrators to accurately recall the age at which the behavior first occurred. Such issues can be alleviated with prospective longitudinal studies, which have shown a gap between the actual and the official age of onset depending on the type of data used to measure it (e.g., self-reports, police data) (LeBlanc & Loeber, 1998). Research with adolescents who have perpetrated a sex crime also suggests such a trend, but the difference between the actual and official age of onset remains unknown because they are typically examined in separate studies. Clearly, the existing studies highlight the need to combine official and self-reported data that can account for the onset of different types of sexual offenses. Indeed, adolescents can perpetrate a myriad of sexual offenses and the current scientific literature does not account for this variance. Some studies suggest, among other things, that young people who commit sexual offenses against significantly younger victims tend to start sexually offending younger than those whose sexual offending involves victims from the same age group (e.g., Groth, 1977; Hendriks & Bijleveld, 2004). These results suggest the importance of the physical and psychological maturity necessary to create a context conducive to a sexual offense against adolescents as opposed to children, who are much more vulnerable to such victimization, especially if the young perpetrator is in a position of authority (e.g., babysitting, older sibling, day camp counselor, sport instructor/trainer).

Other studies conducted with adult offenders have reported an older age of onset of sexual offending. Many early clinical studies conducted in psychiatric hospitals and treatment settings were conducted under the assumption that sex offending was a manifestation of a life-long underlying condition of sexual deviance that was initiated in the early years. These studies have therefore described adults who perpetrate sex offenses as grown up juvenile sex offenders.[4] Of importance, these findings suggest that the onset of sexual offending can occur across the life-course and is not limited to the period of adolescence. Not surprisingly, estimates of the age of onset based on self-report data are younger than those based on official data (e.g., Baxter, Marshall, Barbaree, Davidson, & Malcolm, 1984; Cale, 2015; Gebhard et al., 1965; Lussier, LeBlanc, & Proulx, 2005; Proulx, Lussier, Ouimet, & Boutin, 2008; Smallbone & Wortley, 2004). When looking at the official age of onset, results clearly indicate that it significantly varies across different types of adult perpetrators of sex offenses. These reports suggest that adults who commit sexual offenses against women are typically charged for a first offense in their late twenties/early thirties, while for those who commit sex offenses against children it is typically in their late thirties/early forties. There is a gap between the age of onset reported in self-report studies with adults who committed sex offenses and those found in studies based on police data. That gap, however, is relatively unknown given that self-report and official data on the age of onset are not typically analyzed in the same study, which limits conclusions that can be drawn as comparisons across samples are afflicted by differences in the population they are sampled from different jurisdictional processes, different ages/ethnicities of sample members, etc. These measures are consecutive occurrences and thus studies relying on official data such as convictions will be prone to estimating an age of onset that could more so reflect challenges with processing cases through the justice system, especially for more serious crimes with more elaborate trials (Payne & Piquero, 2017). Furthermore, the utility of other sources of information such as police reports and victim statements has not been examined in prior research.

In a series of studies, Mathesius and Lussier (2014); see also Lussier and Mathesius (2012) compared self-reported versus official data with respect to the onset of sex offending. They showed that the official age of onset, as measured with criminal justice data, provides a distorted view of the actual onset of offending, at least for some perpetrators of sex offenses. Their claim was based on the observation that official data on offending does not take into consideration the offender's

---

[4] For example, in the study by Prentky and Knight (1993), 49% of their sample of adults convicted of rape reported an onset prior to age 18, while the rest of the sample reported an onset in adulthood. These results mirrored those reported Groth et al. (1982) earlier study, which showed an average age of onset of 19 years old for a sample of males who committed sexual offenses against adult women, while in the study of Abel et al. (1993), it was 22 years old. The self-reported onset age for adults who committed sexual offenses against children appears to be different than the one reported for adults who sexually offended against women; however, these findings are not stable across studies. In the Prentky and Knight (1993) study, whereas 49% of adults who sexually offended against women committed sexual offenses in adolescence, that number increased to 62% for adults who committed sexual offenses against children. Therefore, given these results, one would expect that most adult sex offenders initiated their sex offending career during adolescence and were persisting into their adult years. This is not the case, however, and this could be attributable to sampling differences. To illustrate, in the Marshall et al. (1991) study, the self-reported age of onset was 24 years old for extrafamilial perpetrators against boys, 25 years old for extrafamilial perpetrators against girls, and 33 years old for fathers who committed acts of incest against their children. Similar numbers were reported by Smallbone and Wortley (2004).

ability to avoid and/or delay detection. In their study, official data, police data, and victim accounts were analyzed to compare and contrast the official and actual age of onset in a large sample of convicted offenders. On average, it was found that there is a gap of about seven years between the actual and official age of onset in sex offending, which may not be for the same acts. The findings showed that the gap between actual and official onset was much more important for child molesters, more specifically incestuous and pseudo-incestuous fathers. These findings may suggest that victims may take significantly longer to report the crime to the authorities (if they do), especially if the crime is committed by a parental figure. For the most part, while the actual age of onset in adulthood does not vary across sex offender types, it does for the official age of onset, suggesting differential investment in detection avoidance across offenders. Further, the findings also suggested that close to 20% of convicted offenders had already desisted or were in the process of desisting by the time they had been first convicted for a sex crime. In other words, in the time between onset and their conviction for a sex crime, there was no evidence that these individuals had been involved in other sex offenses.

There also appears to be an important overlap between child sexual abuse and the production of child pornography; part of this overlap can obviously be explained by the fact that contact child sexual abuse represents a necessary part of the production of child pornography (see Bickart, McLearen, Grady, & Stoler, 2019; Gewirtz-Meydan, Mitchell, & Rothman, 2018; Krone et al., 2017; Krone & Smith, 2017; McManus, Long, Alison, & Almond, 2015; Sheehan & Sullivan, 2010). McManus et al. (2015) found that child pornography offenders who had previously committed a sexual offense against a child were over seven times more likely to have produced child pornography than those with no previous history of contact sexual offenses. However, some producers of child pornography do so strictly online using webcams, and thus do not themselves perpetrate contact sexual abuse. Nonetheless, in a study by Gewirtz-Meydan et al. (2018), 93% of victims reported that they experienced sexual molestation as part of the child pornography production process. Bickart et al. (2019) also specifically examined the nature and extent of women's engagement in the production of child pornography. In some cases, it was restricted to activities where no direct physical contact with the victim was made, such as in the recording of child pornography images and videos, and in others it involved actions that constitute contact sex offenses, such as physically manipulating the victim into certain poses, or in fact, sexually assaulting the victim. Wolak, Finkelhor, Mitchell, and Jones (2011) descriptively analyzed 319 internet-related child pornography production arrests from the first two waves (2001/2006) of the National Juvenile Online Victimization Study (N-JOV) study. In terms of demographic characteristics, perpetrators were typically Caucasian males in early adulthood (i.e., over the age of 26 years) who were employed full-time. Using data from the second wave of the N-JOV, Clevenger, Navarro, and Jasinski (2016) found that the largest proportion of offenders who engaged in child pornography production and distribution were between the ages of 30 and 39 years old, roughly corresponding to the age of onset for intrafamilial child sexual abuse noted above. Similarly, Babchishin, Karl Hanson, and Hermann (2011) found that the average age of internet child pornography offenders was approximately 39 years old. These figures align with estimates that up to half, and possibly substantially more, of child pornography production occurs in the familial context (Bickart et al., 2019).

Most of the studies conducted thus far have been based on convenience samples of offenders in psychiatric or correctional settings. With the proliferation of longitudinal studies, more studies have highlighted a broader range of ages of onset of sexual offending and in particular the presence of an adult-onset group. Using data from the 1984 Dutch birth cohort study, Lussier and Blokland (2014) reported that only 17 of 377 (4.5%) individuals with an adult criminal record related to a sexual offense had a criminal history in adolescence in connection with a sexual offense. The lack of data from other sources makes it almost impossible to estimate the proportion of individuals with adult criminal records who have committed a sexual offense during adolescence. However, the proportion of individuals whose known sexual offenses begin in adulthood is simply overwhelming. Similarly, in a prospective longitudinal study of youth who had been incarcerated for all types of crime, Lussier et al. (2015) showed that activation of sexual offending in adulthood was more prevalent for youth who had been involved in drug trafficking and the use of firearms during adolescence, both commonly associated with gang-related criminal activities. This pattern of adult-onset sexual offending, therefore, appeared to be part of an escalating and aggravating pattern of crime and delinquency rather than a long-lasting pattern of sexual deviance (see also Cale & Lussier, 2011).

The Frequency of Sexual Offending

For criminal career researchers, the frequency of offending refers to the number of crimes perpetrated by a person. Studies conducted by the Rand Institute with inmates having been involved in all sorts of crimes showed that strict reliance on arrests and convictions can lead to a substantial underestimation of this criminal career parameter (e.g., Chaiken & Chaiken, 1982; Peterson & Braiker, 1980). The same studies have shown that a small subgroup of offenders are responsible for a disproportionate amount of all crimes perpetrated. For example, the seminal birth cohort study conducted by Wolfgang et al. (1972) showed that 6% of a birth cohort of all males born in Philadelphia the same year were responsible for more than 50% of all arrests for any crime by this cohort during adolescence. This group, dubbed "chronic offenders," were not only responsible for a large share of all crimes, but also more than 70% of all arrests for rapes by members of this birth cohort during adolescence. In other words, the Wolfgang et al. (1972) study showed that young "rapists" were, for the most part, characterized by a chronic pattern of general offending. For several years, this important finding, for some unknown reason, went unnoticed in the scientific community. These observations suggest that youth involved in sex crimes may have a lot in common in terms of risk factors with those involved in chronic offending. But what about sexual offending? Are there chronic or prolific perpetrators of sex crimes?

To many, the sex offender label is synonymous with a repetitive pattern of sexual offending. The frequency of sex offending refers to the number of sex crimes committed over the course of a criminal career, or in other words, an individual's volume of sex crimes perpetrated over their life-course. It is interesting to note that researchers, for some reason, have not spent too much time describing and explaining this aspect of sexual offending. Researchers have limited the scope of their investigation to official data sources indicating the number of convictions and reconvictions for a sex offense, which may vastly underestimate the scope of a person's sexual offending. Focusing on convictions means that offending is limited to those instances where the perpetrator was known and reported to the police, but then also charged and convicted for this criminal event. The focus on sex crime convictions also results in instances where multiple sex crime events (e.g., the repeated sexual abuse of a stepchild) are reduced to a single conviction. Like most other crime types, measuring the frequency of sex offending is not as straightforward as it may seem. In the case of sexual offending, this is due in part to the nature of the offending behavior and the various offending strategies adopted by perpetrators of sex offenses that may lead to differences with respect to opinions about "what counts" when measuring frequency of sex offenses (Lussier et al., 2012). For example, the frequency of sex offending may refer to the number of victims an individual has offended against. However, it can also refer to the number of sex crime events, or the number of times an individual has sexually offended against the same person. Some individuals may adopt an offending strategy in which they offend against different victims on a very limited number of occasions (e.g., once or twice). This victim-oriented strategy may characterize perpetrators who target strangers. Others may decide to limit the number of victims they offend against, choosing instead to maximize a single offending opportunity by reoffending on multiple occasions against the same person. This is referred to as an event-oriented strategy and characterizes incest and pseudo-incest offenders as well as intimate partner sexual violence and sex offenses perpetrated against someone whom the offender is responsible for (e.g., their step-child, a person in a nursing home, etc.). For other sex offenses, such as child pornography (e.g., production, use, distribution), the estimation of the frequency of offending becomes quite challenging.[5] Therefore, it becomes evident that it is difficult to estimate the frequency of offending based on data found in prior research because too often criminal justice indicators are used, such as the number of arrests or convictions for a sex crime.

Empirical studies conducted with clinical samples showed that youth, on average, sexually assaulted one or two victims (Cale et al., 2016; Carpentier et al., 2011; Jacobs, Kennedy, & Meyer, 1997). Using data from a clinical sample of 67 youth, Becker, Cunningham-Rathner, and Kaplan (1986) also showed that the average number of victims is limited to one, but is two for adolescents who have sexually

---

[5] For example, the Seto et al. (2011) meta-analysis showed that only 2.0% of online offenders recidivated with a contact sexual offense and 3.4% ($n = 43$) recidivated with a child pornography offense, based on studies using officially recorded information. Again, recidivism rates are not a robust measure of offending frequency as they are based on subsequent charges or convictions.

assaulted a young boy. The data on the average number of criminal events were quite similar, with the exception of those who sexually assaulted victims within the family for whom the number of events per victim was higher. Interestingly, in a comparative study, Miranda and Corcoran (2000) examined the frequency and duration of sexual abuse by youth and adults. The results showed that, on average, young abusers are involved in two incidents of child sexual abuse over an average period of about nine months. The frequency and duration of sexual abuse were lower and of a shorter duration compared to adults who had committed at least one sexual offense against a child. In short, generally, studies show that sexual offending perpetrated by youth during adolescence is not repetitive, albeit given a few exceptions.

Studies of adults who have been convicted of a sexual offense show somewhat divergent results in terms of the frequency of the acts. In particular, studies to date show some heterogeneity in the individual frequency of sexual offending over a given period. In the Lussier et al. (2012) study using a sample of convicted adult males found guilty of sexual offenses, the average number of victims was 1.8 but the number of victims varied between 1 and 13. Similarly, in an earlier study by Groth, Longo, and McFadin (1982), the number of self-reported sex crimes varied between 1 and 30. Even greater variance was uncovered in the study by Weinrott and Saylor (1991) where the range of self-reported victims varied between 1 and 200. These findings, therefore, highlight the presence of some heterogeneity in sexual offending frequency across offenders; however, the extent of such heterogeneity is unclear. For example, research suggests that individuals who have sexually assaulted children average more victims than those who assault women (e.g., Pham, Debruyne, & Kinappe, 1999). This heterogeneity becomes more evident with the use of other self-reported measures of sexual offending. In the Weinrott and Saylor (1991) study based on a clinical sample, the results showed that individuals who sexually assaulted women had, on average, two official victims, while self-reports showed, on average, nearly twelve victims (median = 6). In addition, individuals who sexually assaulted children had an average of two official victims, but self-reported an average of seven victims (Abel et al., 1987; Groth et al., 1982; Marshall et al., 1991). These results are misleading, however, as they are greatly influenced by the presence of a small subgroup of individuals whose repetitive pattern of sexual offending far exceeds those more typically observed for adult offenders.

In this regard, Lussier et al. (2012) examined the presence of a subgroup of chronic sex offenders in a sample of adult men convicted for a sex crime. With the use of multiple sources of information (self-reports, police reports, victim impact statements), individual's frequency of sexual offending was examined. The results showed much more disparity between individuals in the number of separate sex crime events that individuals were involved in compared to their respective number of victims. In fact, the individuals in the sample were involved in between 1 and 5524 sex crime events. A total of 50% of the sample had been involved in less than 6 events with only 1 victim before being arrested and convicted for their offense. A small group of individuals, however, stood out from the others in terms of their offending and their ability to avoid detection. While 50% of the sample was able to escape detection and conviction for at least 2 years, just over 11% of the individuals in the sample escaped detection and conviction for more than 16 years. Therefore, it appears that individuals differ among themselves, not so much in terms of the number of victims, but rather in the act and the ability to evade the criminal justice system. The results also revealed that these more prolific individuals, who escaped the criminal justice system longer, had a lot in common: they were older and had a rather conventional profile compared to the typical "detainee" profile; they were married or in a relationship with an adult partner; they were employed at the time of the offenses, did not have any apparent drug problems and, most importantly, they had no criminal record for a sex crime. This image stands in stark contrast with current widely publicized portrayals of the "sexual predator."

Criminal Versatility and Crime Specialization

To many, the "sex offender" label implies that individuals who commit sex offenses are different. For example, the label of "sex offender" itself typically will override any other identity characteristics (e.g., priest, business executive, teacher, etc.). In corrections, individuals who have been convicted for a sex crime who are in custody will be designated as sex offenders irrespective of the fact that have been convicted for other crime types. When someone's identity is labeled by others as a "sex offender," this also carries the implicit assumption that this label describes a long-standing and persistent behavior. Not only does this carry the assumption about the risk that the person may represent to others, but, paradoxically, also the risk that this person may be exposed to in custody given the nature of their past offending behavior and the stigma associated with such crimes.

Crime specialization is a commonly studied aspect of the criminal career of sex offenders. Various definitions of crime specialization have been proposed over the years. Criminal career researchers have generally defined specialization as the probability of repeating the same type of crime (e.g., Blumstein et al., 1986). Crime specialization is important from a crime control perspective for several reasons. If offenders specialize in a particular crime type, then the implementation of specific crime prevention strategies targeting known offenders involved in the specific crime type should be paramount. The sex offender registry, for example, reflects the assumption that sex offenders are sex crime specialists and the registry aims to prevent their sexual recidivism. Recording personal information in a database helping to track down convicted sex offenders is undoubtedly considered useful from a law enforcement standpoint. It can be used as a tool to prioritize suspects in new cases of sexual assault and abuse. According to the specialization hypothesis, if the criminal activity of a sexual offender persists, it would be primarily in sexual crime. When considering criminal careers more generally, Cohen (1986) highlighted that the level of specialization may vary across crime types as well as across offenders. Therefore, following Cohen's recommendation, one should distinguish crime specialization and crime specialists. On the one hand, specialization is understood as the tendency for some crime to involve a higher or lower level of repetition over time. In this context, researchers may be interested in comparing whether specialization in sex crime is similar or different than specialization in burglary, drug-related offenses, driving under the influence, car theft, etc. The concept of a specialist, on the other hand, refers to individuals with a higher probability of repeating the same crime over time.

Criminological studies have shown that, if offending persists over time, it tends to diversify and take different forms (Piquero et al., 2003); someone who steals a car one day may burglarize a home the next and be involved in drug-trafficking a week later. Versatility speaks of the rather opportunistic and impulsive nature of offending among persistent offenders. Longitudinal studies show that, generally, while persistent juvenile delinquency is multi-purpose (Klein, 1984), adult offending tends to be more specialized in comparison. This is possibly because individuals tend to offend at a higher rate in adolescence and then demonstrate a pattern of desistance in adulthood. In other words, versatility tends to be associated with offending frequency and specialization tends to be associated with offending desistance. Yet, public policies concerning sex offenders operate under the assumption that specialization in sex offenses implies a high frequency of sex offending. In particular, by examining data on the official delinquency of 12–26 years of a birth cohort, Piquero, Paternoster, Mazerolle, Brame, and Dean (1999) found that regardless of the age of onset of offending, persistent offending tends to be more specialized and specific after turning 18 years old. In one of the few longitudinal studies on long-term criminal specialization, Nieuwbeerta, Blokland, Piquero, and Sweeten (2011) demonstrated that the versatility of delinquency fades with age and particularly in adulthood; this versatility giving way to a certain specialization in a particular form of crime (see also, Lussier et al., 2017). In sum, versatility reflects the development of offending up until it reaches a culmination point, a development characterized by experimentation, spur of the moment and impulsive decisions, chance encounters, new and thrill-seeking opportunities that align with the period of adolescence. Crime specialization reflects the slowing down of persistent offending until its termination point. During this desistance phase, it tends to become more patterned with time, age, and experience as offenders possibly become more selective in attempting to avoid the criminal justice system one way or another; they may have more to lose at that point.

But what about sexual offending? These assertions do not seem to characterize the offending patterns of individuals having perpetrated a sex offense. Why is that so? Do individuals who have committed a sexual offense have a versatile offending pattern or, to the contrary, do they tend to specialize in sex crimes? The sex offender label used to characterize their offending suggests that crime specialization is predominant within this group (Simon, 2000). There has been little research on the crime specialization of adolescents who have committed a sexual offense. The presence of a substantial subgroup of adolescent perpetrators involved in various forms of crime and delinquency was noticed early on but did not attract much theoretical consideration. Atcheson and Williams (1954) noticed that, for adolescents who had perpetrated a sex crime, there was a certain lack of coherence as to the type of offending they were involved in. These clinical researchers were surprised by the general lack of a pattern in the offending history of these particular young people. This lack coherence was also noticed by criminologists examining offending patterns of persistent young offenders who had not necessarily engaged in sex crimes. Klein (1984), in that regard, coined the term "cafeteria-style delinquency" in order to highlight the opportunistic, if not often thoughtless and impulsive nature of persistent offending among adolescent offenders. This term suggested that young offenders were not driven by a specific motivation or reaction to a specific stressful or difficult situation. Rather, they were acting on opportunities for immediate gratification and their sex offending was in accordance with this behavioral pattern. Whether or not this cafeteria-style offending characterized all youth involved in sex crimes and the extent to which this offending pattern was involved in the perpetration of sex crimes are other issues. Clinical studies conducted with young offenders who had perpetrated a sex crime were somewhat rediscovered three decades later when research on juvenile sex offending became more prevalent. These studies highlighted that about half of young perpetrators of sex offenses had a history of non-sexual offending (e.g., Awad, Saunders, & Levene, 1984; Butler & Seto, 2002; Cale et al., 2016; Ryan et al., 1996; Seto & Lalumière, 2006).

The prevalence of a subgroup of adolescent perpetrators for whom sexual offending was part of a general offending pattern attracted more attention this second time around. Following earlier observations made by Doshay (1943), researchers distinguished adolescent perpetrators of sex offenses according to whether their offending was versatile and included non-sexual offenses as well, or was limited to sexual offending (e.g., Butler & Seto, 2002). In that regard, Blokland and van Wijk (2008) examined the arrest history pattern of a group of adolescent perpetrators of a sex crime and found the presence of three groups: (a) versatile offending, i.e., young people involved in various sexual and non-sexual delinquent activities (e.g., theft, vandalism, assault, fraud, non-compliance with supervisory conditions); (b) specialized offending, i.e., young people who were exclusively involved in sex offenses; and (c) first-time offenders, i.e., young people whose arrest for a sex crime was their first arrest. The limited research examining and comparing these groups suggests that adolescents whose offending is not limited to sex crime appear to have a distinct profile, particularly with respect to their developmental background characterized by criminogenic factors and a history of antisocial behaviors. Such classification models, however, are imperfect because they only reflect a youth's past and do not inform about the unfolding of their offending behavior over time (McCuish & Lussier, 2018). In other words, this classification reflects a snapshot of an adolescent's behavior which can subsequently take multiple routes in adolescence and in adulthood. The first-time offender can become the specialist or the versatile offender; the specialist may become more versatile with time. Hence, the offending pattern suggested by these classifications might not be one in the long-term and research should complement those with an inspection of later offending patterns during adolescence (e.g., Cale et al., 2016) and into adulthood (Lussier et al., 2012). In this regard, there is little evidence to suggest that adolescents specialize in sexual offenses in the long-term (Blokland & van der Geest, 2015).

Empirical studies of adult perpetrators of sex crimes suggest the presence of both versatility and crime specialization. The first noticeable trend that has been observed in criminal career research is the discrepancies between perpetrators of sexual offences against adult females compared to those with child victims with respect to the versatility of their offending. The simple inspection of the criminal record of convicted offenders has revealed that, more often than not, the criminal activity of perpetrators with adult female victims of women is more versatile and serious in nature (Cale, 2015; Gebhard et al., 1965; Lussier, 2005; Lussier et al., 2005). Furthermore, using transition matrices to examine the type of crimes a person has been arrested for on successive arrests, researchers have shown that crime specialization is much less important for sex offenders who offend against women compared to those who offend against children (Blumstein, Cohen, Das, & Moitra, 1988; Britt, 1996; Stander, Farrington, Hill, & Altham, 1989). This is not to say that perpetrators of adult female victims are versatile offenders and those with child victims are sex crime specialists. In fact, researchers later clarified that offenders with child victims were not all sex crime specialists (e.g., Lussier et al., 2005; Smallbone & Wortley, 2004; Soothill, Francis, Sanderson, & Ackerley, 2000). Rather, these findings appear to suggest that the extent of crime versatility is more important in offenders with adult female victims and the extent of crime specialization in sex crimes is more important for those with child victims. The most detailed analysis, however, comes from the work of Miethe, Olson, and Mitchell (2006) which has shown that the presence of criminal specialization in sexual offenses, although limited, is generally preceded by crime versatility. In other words, versatility and criminal specialization do not distinguish two groups of individuals but represent two distinct processes or phases of the development of criminal activity. These results are, to some extent, in line with the development process model that portrays diversification and specialization as two different stages of sexual delinquency development. These conclusions, however, are based on official data and further analysis using other sources of information is needed for validation purposes.

There is scarce research examining whether persistent sex offending in adolescent offenders tends to be more versatile or specialized. While there has been some research on adolescent sexual offending dating back to the 1940s (e.g., Doshay, 1943), it only emerged as a field of research in the 1990s. It remains to this day a relatively small field of scientific investigation, which explains in part the relative absence of studies. Recall also that empirical studies having examined the frequency of sexual offending among adolescents show that, more often than not, their sexual offending is not repetitive. In this context, the study of persistent sexual offending to examine patterns of versatility and sex crime specialization becomes somewhat hazardous. Such studies are difficult to conduct because of the challenges finding young persistent and repetitive offenders that are representative of this population. The little research conducted to date has examined no more than one or two dimensions of sexual offenses generally focusing on victims' characteristics. The general trend suggests that young sexual recidivists tend to commit their sexual offenses against the same victim type (Awad et al., 1984; Awad & Saunders, 1991; Fehrenbach, Smith, Monastersky, & Deisher, 1986). Other studies, however, show that young people who perpetrated their first sexual offense in childhood (i.e., early-starters) are more likely to exhibit some versatility in their sexual offending over time (Vizard et al., 2007), therefore suggesting a certain diversification process, at least for some.

Empirical examinations of the versatility and specialization in persistent sex offending with adult offenders are more conclusive. Soothill et al. (2000) came to the generally accepted conclusion within the scientific community that, while individuals who have committed a sexual offense tend to present a versatile offending pattern, their sexual offending tends to be much more specific and specialized. Similarly, Radzinowicz (1957) also found specialization in victim-choice in that only 7% of a large sample of convicted offenders had convictions for crimes against both male and female victims, a finding consistent with the early work of Gebhard et al. (1965). More recently, Cann, Friendship, and Gozna (2007) found that only about 25% of their sample of incarcerated sex offenders was versatile when considering three sexual offending dimensions (victim's age and gender, offender–victim relationship). However, when examining versatility using other sources of information about offending, versatility in sex offending increases. For example, using official data only, Weinrott and Saylor (1991) found that only 15% of their sample of offenders was versatile considering three sexual offending categories (victim's age and gender; victim–offender relationship). However, when using a self-reported computerized questionnaire with the same individuals, however, that number rose to 53%. Similarly, Abel et al. (1987) showed that 42% of their sample targeted victims in more than one age group, 20% targeted victims of both genders, and 26% committed both hands-on and hands-off crimes (Abel & Rouleau, 1990). In another study, when using a lie detector, Heil, Ahlmeyer, and Simons (2003) reported that incarcerated offenders appeared to be more versatile in their sex offending. Less dramatic numbers were reported for parolees, suggesting that difference may be explained by contextual factors and sampling differences (i.e., incarcerated offenders are more likely to be serious and repetitive offenders) and the fact that admitting a crime was a prerequisite to enter treatment. Whether this requirement influenced the reporting of valid information about the presence of additional sexual offenses remains open for debate. In all, these studies suggest that when sex offending persists, it can diversify, but the extent that of this diversity and the factors explaining it remain unclear.

To conclude that all perpetrators of sex crimes are out-of-control sex offenders are simply not supported by the scientific literature. The current state of knowledge suggests a certain specificity of sexual offending behavior (Cann et al., 2007). For example, Guay, Proulx, Cusson, and Ouimet (2001) have found some stability in sexual offending, particularly with respect to the sex of the victim, while the victim's age (i.e., child, adolescent, adult) is more likely to vary from one sexual offense to another among repeat offenders. These findings need some context, as they do not seem to reflect out-of-control sex offending. Although offenders with either adult female or child victims who sexually reoffend tend to reoffend against the same victim age group on subsequent sex offenses, the observed versatility seems to suggest that in the absence of the preferred age group, teenagers become the default option for both groups (see Cale, Leclerc, & Smallbone, 2014; Guay et al., 2001). Additional findings suggest that the out-of-control sexual offending hypothesis is not reflective of the sexual offending pattern of all perpetrators. Lussier et al. (2008) concluded that the versatility in sexual offending increased with the persistence of sexual offending over time, particularly regarding the age of the victim, the offender–victim relationship (e.g., intra-, extrafamilial), and level of sexual intrusiveness. Hence, the more repetitive sexual offending is, the more diverse it can be along specific dimensions. Other dimensions, such as the level of violence and the victim's gender remain relatively stable from one sexual offense to the next. Smallbone and Wortley (2004) showed that diversity in sexually deviant acts may be a function of general offending. Looking at different paraphilia (e.g., voyeurism, frotteurism, sexual sadism) in a sample of offenders convicted for child sexual abuse, they found that offenders involved in more types of criminal activities (e.g., theft, burglary, assault, drug trafficking) were also the ones previously involved in more types of deviant sexual activities. In sum, sexual offending appears to be a function of the interplay of a series of factors when choosing to perpetrate a sexual offense. Antisociality (e.g., impulsivity, callousness) and opportunity factors (e.g., random encounter), among other things, may facilitate the adaptation or the modification of persistent offenders' sexual offending script in order to avoid detection and apprehension.

Continuity and Persistence in Sexual Offending

It is generally assumed that perpetrators of sex crimes are life-course persistent sex offenders. It is assumed that their offending, or at least their risk of sexual offending, can span over multiple decades and across developmental periods; that their sexual offending starts in adolescence and persists into late adulthood. It is assumed that their sexual offending can defy the impact of time, age, and aging. No matter what, sexual offending will be part of a person's behavioral repertoire throughout the life-course because it is driven by a fixed and stable propensity to sexually take advantage of others and cause sexual harm. Furthermore, the perception is that this propensity can outlast the impact of criminal justice interventions, whether in the form of probation or custody. It can be resistant to change that comes with significant life events, turning points, and life transitions. Even after specialized therapy and treatment, there is always a risk that a perpetrator could revert back to sexual offending. It is under these assumptions that additional legal measures and penal dispositions are implemented to address the problem of sexual offending persistence. These measures and dispositions, such as sex offender registration and public notification, are presented as necessary and inevitable given the long-term pattern of sexual offending and the potentially devastating consequences of sexual victimization.

These sets of assumptions address another key criminal career parameter, which refers to the persistence of offending over time. Persistence differs from frequency primarily because only the former requires consideration of time. This parameter includes both a behavioral and a temporal dimension. Criminologists have struggled over the years with the estimation of this criminal career parameter given the difficult task of estimating the duration of a criminal career. First, to estimate the length and duration of individual offending, prospective longitudinal study designs are necessary. Therefore, the same cohort of individuals needs to be followed over time in each subsequent wave of data collection in a manner as to avoid, as much as possible, losing track of research participants. In that context the measurement of offending is necessary. Some prefer the use of self-reports to avoid the issue of undetected crimes while others prefer official sources of information to minimize issues of poor memory recall, personal biases, and social desirability issues. Second, research also needs to determine the duration of the study to capture the length of such criminal careers. Some criminal careers may last a week, while others may span across multiple decades. Short follow-up studies may underestimate the length of criminal careers that are more intermittent and sporadic in nature. This is sometimes referred to as right-hand censoring. Long follow-up studies that span across developmental periods are difficult to implement. There are ethical and legal barriers that prevent researchers, for example, from identifying youth who were arrested and convicted in adolescence to follow-up on their criminal career in adulthood. Retrospective studies of adults' criminal records may also be problematic because of the possibility of a record of sexual offending in youth that was sealed to prevent stigmatizing/labeling the young person as they entered adulthood. Third, researchers need to determine who they will follow and invest tremendous resources for numerous years to study the duration of offending; should it be at risk school kids, adjudicated youths, convicted offenders, or offenders in custody? These issues and challenges offer a glimpse of complex tasks involved in conducting a study on offending persistence.

Estimates of the average duration of general criminal activity vary considerably depending on the type of data used, the length of the follow-up period, and the characteristics of the sample under study (LeBlanc & Fréchette, 1989; Piquero et al., 2003). In the Cambridge Study in Delinquent Development conducted in England where a cohort of men was followed from age eight until their 60s, the findings showed that, on average, the duration of the official criminal career was about 10 years. Consistent with Wolfgang et al.'s (1972) initial research on the chronic offender, a small minority of men (9%) were associated with disproportionately longer criminal careers (Farrington, Lambert, & West, 1998). As Francis et al. (2015) demonstrated, estimates of the length of the official criminal career are highly dependent on the age at first contact with the criminal justice system. For example, they report that the average duration of criminal careers for individuals whose first contact with the criminal justice system was in connection with a violent crime perpetrated before the age of 15 is, on average, about 10 years. By comparison, individuals who first come into contact with the criminal justice system in their early twenties have significantly shorter criminal careers. Their findings show that, on average, their offending careers last about 5 years. But what about sexual offending? Do perpetrators of sex crimes have long sexual offending careers?

Much of the research conducted to date has focused on the continuity of sexual offending across the adolescence-adulthood transition. More specifically, studies along these lines have attempted to answer the following question: To what extent do adolescents who have perpetrated a sex crime perpetrate sex crimes in adulthood? In other words, are today's adolescent sex offenders tomorrow's adult sex offenders? The results of the first studies conducted in clinical settings with young offenders suggested that young sex offenders were overwhelmingly persistent sex offenders. These earlier studies used retrospective data to measure the persistence of sexual offending (e.g., Awad et al., 1984; Awad & Saunders, 1991; Becker et al., 1986; Fehrenbach et al., 1986; Groth, 1977). To determine the persistence of sexual offending, early investigators relied on offenders' past behavior and not their future behavior. In other words, in order to determine the persistence of sexual offending, rather than prospectively follow a cohort of adolescents to evaluate which ones sexually recidivate in adulthood, these studies sampled only individuals in adulthood that were convicted of a sexual offense and retrospectively examined how many of them also had a sex offense in adulthood. In effect, this approach was biased because it automatically excluded all adolescents that did not sexually offend in adulthood.

These studies contributed to the representation of adolescent offenders as persistent and sexual recidivists. This image of the young sexual recidivist emerged in the 1980s, not to mention the associated punitive policy responses, and seemed to be largely dependent on the filtering process within the youth justice system of the time, which advocated a differential judicial approach for first-time offenders compared to recidivists (e.g., see Groth, 1977). As a result, early clinical studies were more likely to have created research designs that favored including recidivists rather than one-time offenders. In short, these researchers drew inappropriate conclusions about the persistence of sexual offending among young recidivists and these findings were subsequently generalized to all youth having perpetrated a sex crime. The methodological strategies of the criminal career paradigm were developed in part to avoid this type of bias.

Strong evidence pointing to the lack of continuity in sexual offending across the adolescence-adulthood transition has been reported in prospective longitudinal studies using data from the general population (Jennings, Piquero, Zimring, & Reingle, 2015; Zimring, Jennings, Piquero, & Hays, 2009; Zimring, Piquero, & Jennings, 2007). Using police data from the 1984 Birth cohort study in the Netherlands, Lussier and Blokland (2014) examined the police records of 87,528 males between 12 and 23 years old. Of those, about 25% of the sample had a police contact during the study period for any crime. In total, only 701 individuals (0.8%) from the entire birth cohort had a police contact for a sex crime throughout the study period. Of those, only 16 individuals (0.018%) had a police contact in relation to a sex crime during both adolescence and adulthood. These findings are important for several reasons. First, these findings show that the phenomena of sexual offending continuity across the adolescence-adulthood transition are extremely rare. To further illustrate, "'persisters'" represented 4.7% of the subgroup of individuals who had a police contact during adolescence for a sex crime. Second, although not aimed to estimate the length of sex offending careers, these findings suggest that their duration are relatively short and confined to a specific developmental stage. For example, 19.7% of those who only had a police contact in adolescence for a sex crime sexually reoffended in adolescence, while 13.1% of those who only had a police contact for a sex crime in adulthood sexually reoffended in adulthood. Third, while persistence in sexual offending across the adolescence-adulthood transition increased for young sexual recidivists, it remained a relatively rare phenomenon. Indeed, 12.3% of young sexual recidivists had a police contact for a sex crime in adulthood. Finally, these findings also refute previous observations that most adult sex offenders initiated their sex offending career during adolescence. In fact, up to age 23, 95.7% of individuals who had a contact for a sex crime in adulthood had no police contact for such crimes during adolescence. It could be reasonably argued that the follow-up did not extend that long into adulthood which leads to biased findings about the continuity of sexual offending across the adolescence-adulthood transition. Yet, retrospective studies using samples of incarcerated adult offenders show that only a small proportion of these men have convictions in adolescence for sexual offenses (usually between 10% and 15%) (Cale, Lussier, & Proulx, 2009); those with child victims appear slightly more likely to have convictions for juvenile sex offenses compared to those with adult victims (Cale, 2015), which aligns with the previous literature on sex offense specialization (Miethe et al., 2006).

In short, based on the available data, while the continuity of sexual offending is greater among young repeat offenders, it remains unusual, atypical, and rare. Long sexual offending careers appear to be the exception and not the rule. This is consistent with the notion that sexual offending does not reflect a preferred mode of sexual expression or acquiring sexual encounters for most men (Cale et al., 2014). Furthermore, these empirical observations suggest that the overlap between sexual offenses perpetrated by minors and those perpetrated by adults appears to be minimal. The absence of overlap suggests, contrary to common perceptions in the general population, and also to some extent among criminal justice practitioners, that perhaps adolescent sexual offending and adult sexual offending are two relatively distinct and independent phenomena. This conclusion is drastically different from the well accepted idea that early specialized interventions with young offenders are pivotal in order to prevent the development of a life-long pattern of sexual offending. In fact, looking at the available evidence, it is unclear how such ideas are still commonly held nowadays. Instead, it could be reasonably argued from the available evidence that risk factors responsible for sexual offending may be distinct from one period to the next and specific to each developmental stage. Such a developmentally informed perspective would be a significant departure from the clinically focused orientation characterizing current prevention and intervention strategies. This hypothesis, however, has yet to gain momentum in the scientific literature despite empirical evidence pointing in such direction.

What Do We Know About Criminal Careers?

While the study of criminal careers of perpetrators of sex crime remains in its early stages, it does provide evidence-based information (Blokland & Lussier, 2015; Lussier & Cale, 2013). For the most part, the information reviewed is heavily based on official data about crime. Official information about sexual offending not only underestimates the actual instances of sexual offending, it reflects, at least in part, the work of the criminal justice system including law enforcement agencies, the courts, and correctional services. While some have argued that this information is meaningless because it underestimates the actual scope and extent of sexual offending, we found much consistency across the reviewed studies, in spite of being conducted in different jurisdictions and countries, by different researchers using various methodologies and data sources, and over the span of several decades. Therefore, while the conclusions drawn here should be interpreted cautiously, they do offer baseline information about the criminal activities of perpetrators of sex crimes. We highlight seven key conclusions below.

First, the sex offender label suggests the presence of a distinct, specific, and homogenous group of individuals. This label is deceiving not only because it is generally based on legal criteria, but also because it encompasses a group of individuals having been apprehended for a broad range of crimes. Beyond the broad range of behaviors meeting the legal definition of a sex crime, the inspection of the available scientific literature suggests the presence of much heterogeneity across perpetrators of sex crimes. This heterogeneity was observed for all criminal career parameters examined, from the age of onset to desistance of sexual offending across developmental stages, therefore suggesting the presence of multiple longitudinal sequences of sexual offending.

Second, the official prevalence of sexual offending is lower than that observed using self-reports. That being said, whether inspected on their own or when combined, these two sources of information most likely provide an incomplete picture of the actual prevalence of sexual offending in society during a given time. This is because of differences in how sex offending behaviors are defined and because changes in attitudes about the stigmatization of certain behaviors may influence how these behaviors are recorded by police and reported by victims and perpetrators. Furthermore, comparing the estimates based on the two sources of information is hazardous because self-report studies might not be exclusive to criminal behaviors. Furthermore, the range of sexual offending behavior measured might significantly vary across these studies, which can seriously influence the prevalence observed. In fact, the estimated prevalence of sexual offending is likely to vary along key dimensions such as the period being covered by the estimation, the sample's age at the time of the assessment, and the criteria used to define a sex crime. The question around the prevalence of sexual offending might be best addressed in terms of what, where, when, and who rather than drawing broad conclusions about the scope of sexual offending. More studies are needed that integrate multiple sources of information about a broad range of sexual offending behavior for the same sample of perpetrators.

Third, it has been assumed that the origins and patterns of sexual offending for most if not all perpetrators could be traced back to puberty or even earlier stages of development. There is little evidence to support such claims and the current state of knowledge suggests, instead, the presence of a continuum of ages of onset of sexual offending. This observation has implications for the study of the explanatory factors of sexual offending which have been overwhelmingly focused on the childhood period and, to a lesser extent, the period of adolescence. Such an approach is unlikely to account for the onset of sexual offending in most contexts. In fact, the continuum of ages of onset of sexual offending suggests that a fruitful approach to the explanation of sexual offending would be to focus on the examination of risk factors across developmental stages. Understanding the age of onset of sexual offending and forms of sexual offending should be a key focus of future research.

Fourth, there is a prevailing idea that perpetrators of sex crimes are out-of-control offenders that perpetrate hundreds of sex crimes and choose their victims indiscriminately. However, there is little evidence to support this claim, as the general trends appear to suggest an asymmetrical distribution of sexual offending frequency and variety for this group. While most perpetrators will offend against a very limited number of victims on a limited number of occasions, offenders who persist will be characterized by either a victim-focused offending pattern, offending on a single or limited number of occasions against several different victims or an event-focused pattern repeatedly offending against the same victim. Among persistent offenders, the former are more likely to take risks and, as a result, more likely to be apprehended for their sex crimes, while the latter might be more apt at evading detection entirely or at least delaying detection for substantial periods. We believe that given the focus and reliance on the criminal justice indicators of sexual offending, our representation of persisters might be biased toward those characterized by a victim-oriented strategy.

Fifth, a major assumption that has characterized sex offender policies from the 1990s to the present day has been the idea that adolescent sex offenders of the day are tomorrow's adult sex offenders. The idea that sexual offending starts early and persists across the adolescence-adulthood transition still resonates in the narratives of many criminal justice practitioners, psychologists, and psychiatrists working with these individuals. The evidence simply does not support such a unilateral claim for all young perpetrators of sex offenses. The resulting consequences, unfortunately, have been the overwhelming number of false positives that are not accounted for by these assumptions; that is, young persons who are falsely perceived to be on a life-long track of sexual offending with potentially dramatic and harmful consequences. Conversely, adult-onset perpetrators who are falsely presumed to be adolescent-onset offenders who do not report sexually offending during adolescence may be falsely perceived as deniers and liars. The challenge for policymakers, researchers, criminal justice professionals, therapists, and treatment program managers is to move beyond these stereotypes and to approach, first and foremost, the issue of adolescence and adult sexual offending as separate phenomena.

Sixth, the issue of versatility and specialization is incomplete without looking at the type of sex offenses perpetrated by offenders. Beyond the issue of whether these perpetrators are involved or not in non-sexual offenses is the question of whether sex crime "specialists" actually repeat the same sex crime type. Is persistent sexual offending governed by specific deviant sexual thoughts, sexual urges, and sexual preferences that lead to mirroring the same type of behavior across each sex crime event? From a researcher's perspective, measuring versatility and specialization in sex offending is a relatively complex task because sex crimes are inherently multidimensional and detailed information about these offenses are often hard to find, analyze, and validate. Indeed, sex crimes such as sexual violence and abuse can be distinguished based on victim characteristics (e.g., age, gender, offender–victim relationship), sexual aspects of the offense (e.g., contact vs. non-contact offenses, type of sexual behavior force on the victim, type of sexual behavior the victim is coerced to perform on the offender, level of sexual intrusiveness), and the level of coercion and violence used (e.g., weapon use, physical violence) (Lussier et al., 2008).

Finally, while life-course persistent sexual offending appears to be an extremely rare phenomenon, it is nonetheless one that requires specific attention given that such a long-term sexual offending pattern may become versatile, diversified, and not focused on a specific victim type. Moving beyond the idea that all perpetrators are life-course persistent sex offenders and focusing the study on the identification of sexual offending trajectories and their associated risk and protective factors will allow a platform for more evidence-based prevention strategies to emerge, prevention strategies that are tailored to the specific needs of individual adolescents and adults. Current models based on risk of sexual recidivism do not seem to be addressing this; not only do these approaches strictly focus on individuals who have been convicted for a sex crime, but the interventions happen after sexual harm has been done. This may be too limited for a global approach to prevention given that sex offending careers appear to be, for the most part, relatively brief, short-lived, and confined to a specific developmental stage.

Conclusion

There is a significant gap in the sociolegal construction of the sex offender and the scientific evidence about the offending patterns of these individuals. The criminal career research paradigm provides a bridge that can fill this gap in many ways. It provides a terminology that can be used by criminal justice professionals, policy-makers and stakeholders, clinicians and therapists, prosecutors and police investigators, policy analysts, and researchers alike. In fact, these parameters can provide a common language to define, think of, and discuss more clearly the problem of sexual offending. The absence of a common language between practitioners from various fields with various backgrounds has in part contributed to the proliferation of myths, misconceptions, and erroneous conclusions about perpetrators of sex crimes.

In this context, applying criminal career parameters forces these criminal justice professionals to think more clearly about the offending behavior of perpetrators of sex crimes while being more precise about the key objective of crime prevention policies and what criminal career parameters these policies are targeting. Prevention efforts aimed to decrease the prevalence of sexual offending should be quite different than those aimed at preventing the onset and repetition of sexual offending.

While the idea that all perpetrators of sex crimes are life-course persistent offenders remains pervasive, the criminal career research paradigm provides information that not only discredits such claims, but also highlights the presence of much heterogeneity in offending across all of the criminal career parameters that measure sexual offending. This is not to say that life-course persistent sex offenders do not exist, but rather the use of this image to characterize all perpetrators of sex crimes and to justify certain policies impacting all perpetrators of sex crimes clearly misses the point and, more importantly, leads to ineffective and potentially unfair, harmful, and even iatrogenic interventions and policies. The criminal career framework provides the foundation to unravel offending trajectories of perpetrators of sex crimes. Indeed, while the proposed parameters were examined separately in this chapter, the interrelationship between, among other things, the onset, frequency, and persistence of sexual offending can be examined in order to identify the presence, number, and shape of sexual offending trajectories more directly.

Given the examination of the existing research, a few key points about the current state of the scientific evidence and future research about the criminal careers of perpetrators of sex crimes can be highlighted. First, the description of the parameters for the development of sexual offending remains relatively preliminary and tentative rather than conclusive and definitive. The state of this scientific evidence does not allow drawing firm conclusions about gender differences across criminal career parameters of perpetrators of sex crimes. Much of the scientific literature reviewed and analyzed has been based on male adolescents and adults while neglecting the study of adolescent and adult female perpetrators of sex crimes (e.g., McCuish & Lussier, 2018; Wijkman & Sandler, 2018). Second, criminal career research conducted thus far has been almost exclusively focused on perpetrators of sexual violence and abuse. There is scarce research about the criminal career development of individuals having been involved in sexual misconduct and sexual exploitation. Given the distinctive nature of these forms of sexual offending, it is expected that their criminal career parameters will be relatively different in terms of prevalence, the age of onset, the frequency, or pattern of crime specialization. Third, several key criminal career parameters have not yet been the subject of sufficient empirical research. This is particularly the case with escalation and aggravation (e.g., Leclerc, Lussier, & DeslauriersVarin, 2015) as well as the desistance from sexual offending (e.g., Harris, 2014). The investigation of escalation and aggravation in sexual offending has been limited to the retrospective analysis of the behavior of extreme criminal careers (e.g., sexual murderers), which does not provide much information from a policy standpoint given that retrospective data provide a biased view of offending for a selected few individuals. This point is concerning given that more recent policies have been based on the idea that the offending behavior of perpetrators of sex crimes is characterized by a pathway culminating with a sexual homicide (Sample & Bray, 2003). Finally, the state of the scientific literature is overwhelmingly based on official sources of information, which limit the conclusions that can be drawn. More empirical studies relying on other sources of information are desperately needed to complement the existing literature on the criminal career parameters of sexual offending.

References

Abel, G. G., Becker, J. V., Mittleman, M. S., Cunningham-Rathner, J., Rouleau, J. L., & Murphy, W. D. (1987). Self-reported sex crimes of non-incarcerated paraphiliacs. *Journal of Interpersonal Violence, 2*(1), 3–25.

Abel, G. G., & Blanchard, E. B. (1974). The role of fantasy in the treatment of sexual deviation. *Archives of General Psychiatry, 30*(4), 467–475.

Abel, G. G., Osborn, C. A., & Twigg, D. A. (1993). Sexual assault through the life span: Adult offenders with juvenile histories. In H. E. Barbaree, W. L. Marshall, & S. M. Hudson (Eds.), *The juvenile sex offender*. New York: Guilford Press.

Abel, G. G., & Rouleau, J. L. (1990). The nature and extent of sexual assault. In *Handbook of sexual assault* (pp. 9–21). Boston, MA: Springer.

Atcheson, J. D., & Williams, D. C. (1954). A study of juvenile sex offenders. *American Journal of Psychiatry, 111*(5), 366–370.

Awad, G. A., & Saunders, E. B. (1991). Male adolescent sexual assaulters clinical observations. *Journal of Interpersonal Violence, 6*(4), 446–460.

Awad, G. A., Saunders, E. B., & Levene, J. (1984). A clinical study of male adolescent sexual offenders. *International Journal of Offender Therapy and Comparative Criminology, 28*(2), 105–116.

Babchishin, K. M., Karl Hanson, R., & Hermann, C. A. (2011). The characteristics of online sex offenders: A meta-analysis. *Sexual Abuse, 23*(1), 92–123.

Basile, K. C. (2002). Prevalence of wife rape and other intimate partner sexual coercion in a nationally representative sample of women. *Violence and Victims, 17*(5), 511–524.

Baxter, D. J., Marshall, W. L., Barbaree, H. E., Davidson, P. R., & Malcolm, P. B. (1984). Deviant sexual behavior: Differentiating sex offenders by criminal and personal history, psychometric measures, and sexual response. *Criminal Justice and Behavior, 11*(4), 477–501.

Becker, J. V., Cunningham-Rathner, J., & Kaplan, M. S. (1986). Adolescent sexual offenders: demographics, criminal and sexual histories, and recommendations for reducing future offenses. *Journal of Interpersonal Violence, 1*(4), 431–445.

Bennice, J. A., & Resick, P. A. (2003). Marital rape: History, research, and practice. *Trauma, Violence & Abuse, 4*(3), 228–246.

Bickart, W., McLearen, A. M., Grady, M. D., & Stoler, K. (2019). A descriptive study of psychosocial characteristics and offense patterns in females with online child pornography offenses. *Psychiatry, Psychology and Law, 26*(2), 295–311.

Blokland, A., & van Wijk, A. (2008). Criminal careers of Dutch adolescent sex offenders: A criminological perspective. *Child Sexual Abuse: Issues and Challenges, 2008*, 203–219.

Blokland, A. A. J., & Lussier, P. (2015). *Sex offenders: A criminal career approach*. Oxford: Wiley-Blackwell.

Blokland, A. A. J., & van der Geest, V. (2015). Lifecourse transitions and desistance in sex offenders: An event history analysis. In A. A. J. Blokland & P. Lussier (Eds.), *Sex offenders: A criminal career approach* (pp. 257–288). Chichester: John Wiley & Sons.

Blumstein, A., Cohen, J., Das, S., & Moitra, S. D. (1988). Specialization and seriousness during adult criminal careers. *Journal of Quantitative Criminology, 4*(4), 303–345.

Blumstein, A., Cohen, J., & Farrington, D. P. (1988). Criminal career research: Its value for criminology. *Criminology, 26*(1), 1–35.

Blumstein, A., Cohen, J., Roth, J. A., & Visher, C. A. (1986). *Criminal careers "career criminals".* Washington, DC: National Academy Press.

Bouchard, M., & Lussier, P. (2015). Estimating the size of the sexual aggressor population. In A. A. J. Blokland & P. Lussier (Eds.), *Sex offenders: A criminal career approach.* Chichester: John Wiley & Sons.

Briere, J., & Runtz, M. (1989). University males' sexual interest in children: Predicting potential indices of "pedophilia" in a nonforensic sample. *Child Abuse & Neglect, 13*(1), 65–75.

Britt, C. L. (1996). The measurement of specialization and escalation in the criminal career: An alternative modeling strategy. *Journal of Quantitative Criminology, 12*(2), 193–222.

Brownmiller, S. (1975). *Against our will: Men, women, rape.* New York: Simon and Schuster.

Butler, S. M., & Seto, M. C. (2002). Distinguishing two types of adolescent sex offenders. *Journal of the American Academy of Child & Adolescent Psychiatry, 41*(1), 83–90.

Cale, J. (2015). Antisocial trajectories in youth and the onset of adult criminal careers in sexual offenders of children and women. In A. A. J. Blokland & P. Lussier (Eds.), *Sex offenders: A criminal career approach* (pp. 143–170). Chichester: John Wiley & Sons.

Cale, J., Leclerc, B., & Smallbone, S. (2014). The sexual lives of sexual offenders: The link between childhood sexual victimization and non-criminal sexual lifestyles between types of offenders. *Psychology, Crime & Law, 20*(1), 37–60.

Cale, J., & Lussier, P. (2011). Toward a developmental taxonomy of adult sexual aggressors of women: Antisocial trajectories in youth, mating effort, and sexual criminal activity in adulthood. *Violence and Victims, 26*(1), 16–32.

Cale, J., & Lussier, P. (2012). Merging developmental and criminal career perspectives implications for risk assessment and risk prediction of violent/sexual recidivism in adult sexual aggressors of women. *Sexual Abuse: A Journal of Research and Treatment, 24*(2), 107–132.

Cale, J., & Lussier, P. (2014). A criminal career approach to sex offender subtypes: Is there a relationship between pathways in the offending process and the criminal career of extrafamilial sexual offenders? In *Pathways to sexual aggression* (pp. 243–272). Abington, UK: Routledge.

Cale, J., Lussier, P., & Proulx, J. (2009). Heterogeneity in antisocial trajectories in youth of adult sexual aggressors of women: An examination of initiation, persistence, escalation, and aggravation. *Sexual Abuse: A Journal of Research and Treatment, 21*(2), 223–248.

Cale, J., Smallbone, S., Rayment-McHugh, S., & Dowling, C. (2016). Offense trajectories, the unfolding of sexual and non-sexual criminal activity, and sex offense characteristics of adolescent sex offenders. *Sexual Abuse: A Journal of Research and Treatment, 28*(8), 791–812.

Cann, J., Friendship, C., & Gozna, L. (2007). Assessing crossover in a sample of sexual offenders with multiple victims. *Legal and Criminological Psychology, 12*(1), 149–163.

Carpentier, J., Leclerc, B., & Proulx, J. (2011). Juvenile sexual offenders: Correlates of onset, variety, and desistance of criminal behavior. *Criminal Justice and Behavior, 38*(8), 854–873.

Chaiken, J. M., & Chaiken, M. R. (1982). *Varieties of criminal behavior. Rand report no R-2814-NIJ.* Santa Monica, CA: Rand.

Clevenger, S. L., Navarro, J. N., & Jasinski, J. L. (2016). A matter of low self-control? Exploring differences between child pornography possessors and child pornography producers/distributers using self-control theory. *Sexual Abuse, 28*(6), 555–571.

Cline, H. F. (1980). Criminal behavior over the life span. In O. G. Brim & J. Kagan (Eds.), *Constancy and change in human development* (pp. 641–674). Cambridge: Harvard University Press.

Cohen, J. (1986). Research on criminal careers. Blumstein, A., Cohen, J, Roth, J.A., Visher, C.A. (eds.), Criminal careers and career criminals (p. 292–418). Washington D.C.: National Academy Press.

Cortoni, F., Babchishin, K. M., & Rat, C. (2017). The proportion of sexual offenders who are female is higher than thought: A meta-analysis. *Criminal Justice and Behavior, 44*(2), 145–162.

Daly, K., & Bouhours, B. (2010). Rape and attrition in the legal process: A comparative analysis of five countries. *Crime and Justice, 39*(1), 565–650.

DeKeseredy, W., & Kelly, K. (1993). The incidence and prevalence of woman abuse in Canadian university and college dating relationships. Canadian Journal of Sociology/Cahiers canadiens de sociologie, 137–159.

DeLisi, M., & Piquero, A. R. (2011). New frontiers in criminal careers research, 2000–2011: A state-of-the-art review. *Journal of Criminal Justice, 39*(4), 289–301.

Doshay, L. J. (1943). *The boy sex offender and his later career.* Oxford: Grune & Stratton.

Farrington, D. P. (2003). Developmental and life-course criminology: Key theoretical and empirical issues—The 2002 Sutherland award address. *Criminology, 41*(2), 221–225.

Farrington, D. P., Lambert, S., & West, D. J. (1998). Criminal careers of two generations of family members in the Cambridge Study in Delinquent Development. *Studies on Crime and Crime Prevention, 7,* 85–106.

Fehrenbach, P. A., Smith, W., Monastersky, C., & Deisher, R. W. (1986). Adolescent sexual offenders: Offender and offense characteristics. *American Journal of Orthopsychiatry, 56*(2), 225.

Finkelhor, D., & Yllo, K. (1985). *License to rape: Sexual abuse of wives.* New York: Holt, Rinehart, & Winston.

Francis, B., Hargreaves, C., & Soothill, K. (2015). Changing prevalence of sex offender convictions: Disentangling age, period and cohort effects over time. In A. A. J. Blokland & P. Lussier (Eds.), *Sex offenders: A criminal career approach* (pp. 199–218). Chichester: John Wiley & Sons.

Fromuth, M. E., Burkhart, B. R., & Jones, C. W. (1991). Hidden child molestation: An investigation of adolescent perpetrators in a nonclinical sample. *Journal of Interpersonal Violence, 6*(3), 376–384.

Gebhard, P. H., Gagnon, J. H., Pomeroy, W. B., & Christenson, C. V. (1965). *Sex offenders: An analysis of types.* New York: Harper and Row.

Gewirtz-Meydan, A., Mitchell, K. J., & Rothman, E. F. (2018). What do kids think about sexting? *Computers in Human Behavior, 86,* 256–265.

Greendlinger, V., & Byrne, D. (1987). Coercive sexual fantasies of college men as predictors of self-reported likelihood to rape and overt sexual aggression. *Journal of Sex Research, 23*(1), 1–11.

Gregory, S., & Lees, S. (1999). *Investigating sexual assault.* London: Sage.

Groth, A. N. (1977). The adolescent sexual offender and his prey. *International Journal of Offender Therapy and Comparative Criminology, 21*(3), 249–254.

Groth, A. N., Longo, R. E., & McFadin, J. B. (1982). Undetected recidivism among rapists and child molesters. *NPPA Journal, 28*(3), 450–458.

Guay, J. P., Proulx, J., Cusson, M., & Ouimet, M. (2001). Victim-choice polymorphia among serious sex offenders. *Archives of Sexual Behavior, 30*(5), 521–533.

Guttmacher, M., & Weihofen, H. (1952). Sex offenses. *The Journal of Criminal Law, Criminology, and Police Science, 43*(2), 153–175.

Harris, D. A. (2014). Desistance from sexual offending: Findings from 21 life history narratives. *Journal of Interpersonal Violence, 29*(9), 1554–1578.

Heil, P., Ahlmeyer, S., & Simons, D. (2003). Crossover sexual offenses. *Sexual Abuse: A Journal of Research and Treatment, 15*(4), 221–236.

Hendriks, J., & Bijleveld, C. C. J. H. (2004). Juvenile sexual delinquents: Contrasting child abusers with peer abusers. *Criminal Behaviour and Mental Health, 14*(4), 238–250.

Jacobs, W. L., Kennedy, W. A., & Meyer, J. B. (1997). Juvenile delinquents: A between-group comparison study of sexual and nonsexual offenders. *Sexual Abuse: A Journal of Research and Treatment, 9*(3), 201–217.

Jennings, W., Piquero, A., Zimring, F. E., & Reingle, J. (2015). Assessing the continuity of sex offending over the life-course: Evidence from two large birth cohort studies. In A. A. J. Blokland & P. Lussier (Eds.), *Sex offenders: A criminal career approach* (pp. 43–70). Chichester: John Wiley & Sons.

Joyal, C. C. (2015). Defining "normophilic" and "paraphilic" sexual fantasies in a population-based sample: On the importance of considering subgroups. *Sexual Medicine, 3*(4), 321–330.

Kania, R., & Cale, J. (2018). Preventing sexual violence through bystander intervention: Attitudes, behaviors, missed opportunities, and barriers to intervention among Australian university students. *Journal of Interpersonal Violence.* https://doi.org/10.1177/0886260518764395

Kjellgren, C., Priebe, G., Svedin, C. G., & Långström, N. (2010). Sexually coercive behavior in male youth: Population survey of general and specific risk factors. *Archives of Sexual Behavior, 39*(5), 1161–1169.

Klein, M. W. (1984). Offence specialisation and versatility among juveniles. *The British Journal of Criminology, 24*, 185–194.

Koss, M. P., Gidycz, C. A., & Wisniewski, N. (1987). The scope of rape: Incidence and prevalence of sexual aggression and victimization in a national sample of higher education students. *Journal of Consulting and Clinical Psychology, 55*(2), 162–170.

Koss, M. P., Leonard, K. E., Beezley, D. A., & Oros, C. J. (1985). Nonstranger sexual aggression: A discriminant analysis of the psychological characteristics of undetected offenders. *Sex Roles, 12*(9-10), 981–992.

Krafft-Ebing, R. (1867). *Psychopathia sexualis*. New York: Putnam.

Krone, T., & Smith, R. (2017). *Trajectories in online child sexual exploitation offending in Australia*. Trends & issues in crime and criminal justice (research report No. 524). Australian Government, Australian Institute of Criminology.

Krone, T., Smith, R. G., Cartwright, J., Hutchings, A., Tomison, A., & Napier, S. (2017). Online child sexual exploitation offenders: A study of Australian law enforcement data. *Criminology Research Grants, 77*, 1213.

Langevin, R., Curnoe, S., Fedoroff, P., Bennett, R., Langevin, M., Peever, C., et al. (2004). Lifetime sex offender recidivism: A 25-year follow-up study. *Canadian Journal of Criminology and Criminal Justice, 46*(5), 531–552.

LeBlanc, M., & Fréchette, M. (1989). *Male criminal activity from childhood through youth: Multi-level and developmental perspectives*. New York: Springer-Verlag.

LeBlanc, M., & Loeber, R. (1998). Developmental criminology updated. *Crime and Justice, 23*, 115–198.

Leclerc, B., Lussier, P., & DeslauriersVarin, N. (2015). Offending patterns over time: An examination of specialization, escalation and de-escalation in the commission of sexual offenses. In A. A. J. Blokland & P. Lussier (Eds.), *Sex offenders: A criminal career approach* (pp. 171–198). Chichester: John Wiley & Sons.

Lussier, P. (2005). The criminal activity of sexual offenders in adulthood: Revisiting the specialization debate. *Sexual Abuse: A Journal of Research and Treatment, 17*(3), 269–292.

Lussier, P. (2017). Juvenile sex offending through a developmental life-course criminology perspective: An agenda for policy and research. *Sexual Abuse, 29*(1), 51–80.

Lussier, P., & Blokland, A. (2014). The adolescence-adulthood transition and Robins's continuity paradox: Criminal career patterns of juvenile and adult sex offenders in a prospective longitudinal birth cohort study. *Journal of Criminal Justice, 42*(2), 153–163.

Lussier, P., & Blokland, A. (2017). A developmental life-course perspective of juvenile and adult sexual offending. In T. Sanders (Ed.), *The Oxford handbook of sex offences and sex offenders*. Oxford, UK: Oxford University Press.

Lussier, P., & Cale, J. (2013). Beyond sexual recidivism: A review of the sexual criminal career parameters of adult sex offenders. *Aggression and Violent Behavior, 18*(5), 445–457.

Lussier, P., & Cale, J. (2016). Understanding the origins and the development of rape and sexual aggression against women: Four generations of research and theorizing. *Aggression and Violent Behavior, 31*, 66–81.

Lussier, P., Corrado, R. R., & McCuish, E. (2015). A criminal career study of the continuity and discontinuity of sex offending during the adolescence-adulthood transition: a prospective longitudinal study of incarcerated youth. *Justice Quarterly, 33*(7), 1123–1153.

Lussier, P., LeBlanc, M., & Proulx, J. (2005). The generality of criminal behavior: A confirmatory factor analysis of the criminal activity of sex offenders in adulthood. *Journal of Criminal Justice, 33*(2), 177–189.

Lussier, P., Leclerc, B., Healey, J., Proulx, J., Delisi, M., & Conis, P. (2008). Generality of deviance and predation: Crime-switching and specialization patterns in persistent sexual offenders. In M. DeLisi & P. J. Conis (Eds.), *Violent offenders: Theory, research, policy, and practice* (pp. 97–118). Boston, MA: Jones and Bartlett Publishers.

Lussier, P., & Mathesius, J. (2012). Criminal achievement, criminal career initiation, and detection avoidance: The onset of successful sex offending. *Journal of Crime and Justice, 35*(3), 376–394.

Lussier, P., McCuish, E., Deslauriers-Varin, N., & Corrado, R. (2017). Crime specialization as a dynamic process?: Criminal careers, crime mix, and crime specialization in chronic, serious, and violent offenders. In A. A. J. Blokland & V. Van der Geest (Eds.), *The Routledge international handbook of life-course criminology* (pp. 112–139). Abington, UK: Routledge.

Lussier, P., Van Den Berg, C., Bijleveld, C., & Hendriks, J. (2012). A developmental taxonomy of juvenile sex offenders for theory, research, and prevention: The adolescent-limited and the high-rate slow desister. *Criminal Justice and Behavior, 39*(12), 1559–1581.

Malamuth, N. M. (1981). Rape proclivity among males. *Journal of Social Issues, 37*(4), 138–157.

Malamuth, N. M. (1989). The attraction to sexual aggression scale: Part I. *Journal of Sex Research, 26*(1), 26–49.

Marshall, P. (1997). *The prevalence of convictions for sexual offending* (Vol. 55). London: Home Office Research and Statistics Directorate.

Marshall, W. L., Barbaree, H. E., & Eccles, A. (1991). Early onset and deviant sexuality in child molesters. *Journal of Interpersonal Violence, 6*(3), 323–335.

Mathesius, J., & Lussier, P. (2014). The successful onset of sex offending: Determining the correlates of actual and official onset of sex offending. *Journal of Criminal Justice, 42*(2), 134–144.

McCuish, E. C., & Lussier, P. (2018). A developmental perspective on the stability and change of psychopathic personality traits across the adolescence–adulthood transition. *Criminal Justice and Behavior, 45*(5), 666–692.

McManus, M. A., Long, M. L., Alison, L., & Almond, L. (2015). Factors associated with contact child sexual abuse in a sample of indecent image offenders. *Journal of Sexual Aggression, 21*(3), 368–384.

Miethe, T. D., Olson, J., & Mitchell, O. (2006). Specialization and persistence in the arrest histories of sex offenders: A comparative analysis of alternative measures and offense types. *Journal of Research in Crime and Delinquency, 43*(3), 204–229.

Miner, M. H. (2002). Factors related with recidivism in juveniles: Analysis of serious juvenile sex offenders. *Journal of Research in Crime and Delinquency, 39*(4), 421–436.

Miranda, A. O., & Corcoran, C. L. (2000). Comparison of perpetration characteristics between male juvenile and adult sexual offenders: Preliminary results. *Sexual Abuse: A Journal of Research and Treatment, 12*(3), 179–188.

Nieuwbeerta, P., Blokland, A. A., Piquero, A. R., & Sweeten, G. (2011). A life-course analysis of offense specialization across age: Introducing a new method for studying individual specialization over the life-course. *Crime & Delinquency, 57*(1), 3–28.

Payne, J. L., & Piquero, A. R. (2017). The concordance of self-reported and officially recorded criminal onset: Results from a sample of Australian prisoners. *Crime & Delinquency, 64*(4), 448–471.

Peterson, M. A., & Braiker, H. B. (1980). *Doing crime: A survey of California Prison inmates. Report no R-2200-DOJ*. Santa Monica, CA: Rand.

Pham, T. H., Debruyne, I., & Kinappe, A. (1999). Évaluation statique des délits violents chez les délinquants sexuels incarcérés en Belgique francophone. *Criminologie, 32*(2), 117–125.

Piquero, A. R. (2008). Taking stock of developmental trajectories of criminal activity over the life-course. In A. M. Liberman (Ed.), *The long view of crime: A synthesis of longitudinal research* (pp. 23–78). New York: Springer.

Piquero, A. R., Farrington, D. P., & Blumstein, A. (2003). The criminal career paradigm. *Crime and Justice, 30*, 359–506.

Piquero, A. R., Paternoster, R., Mazerolle, P., Brame, R., & Dean, C. W. (1999). Onset age and offense specialization. *Journal of Research in Crime and Delinquency, 36*(3), 275–299.

Prentky, R. A., & Knight, R. A. (1993). Age of onset of sexual assault: Criminal and life history correlates. In G. C. N. Hall, R. Hirschman, J. R. Graham, & M. S. Zaragoza (Eds.), *Sexual aggression: Issues in etiology assessment, and treatment*. Washington, DC: Taylor and Francis.

Proulx, J., Lussier, P., Ouimet, M., & Boutin, S. (2008). Criminal careers of four types of sexual aggressors. In B. K. Schwartz (Ed.), *The sex offender: Offender evaluation and program strategies* (Vol. IV, pp. 1–21). Princeton: Civic Research Institute.

Radzinowicz, L. (1957). *Sexual offenses: A report of the Cambridge department of criminal justice*. London: MacMillan.

Rind, B., Tromovitch, P., & Bauserman, R. (1998). A meta-analytic examination of assumed properties of child sexual abuse using college samples. *Psychological Bulletin, 124*(1), 22.

Rogers, R., & Dickey, R. (1991). Denial and minimization among sex offenders. *Sexual Abuse: A Journal of Research and Treatment, 4*(1), 49–63.

Russell, D. E. H. (1990). *Rape in marriage*. New York: Macmillan Press.

Ryan, G., Miyoshi, T. J., Metzner, J. L., Krugman, R. D., & Fryer, G. E. (1996). Trends in a national sample of sexually abusive youths. *Journal of the American Academy of Child & Adolescent Psychiatry, 35*(1), 17–25.

Sample, L. L., & Bray, T. M. (2003). Are sex offenders dangerous? *Criminology & Public Policy, 3*(1), 59–82.

Seifert, K., Boulas, J., Huss, M. T., & Scalora, M. J. (2017). Response bias on self-report measures of sexual fantasies among sexual offenders. *International Journal of Offender Therapy and Comparative Criminology, 61*(3), 269–281.

Senn, C. Y., Desmarais, S., Verberg, N., & Wood, E. (2000). Predicting coercive sexual behavior across the lifespan in a random sample of Canadian men. *Journal of Social and Personal Relationships, 17*(1), 95–113.

Seto, M. C., Hanson, K. R., & Babchishin, K. M. (2011). Contact sexual offending by men with online sexual offenses. *Sexual Abuse, 23*(1), 124–145.

Seto, M. C., & Lalumière, M. L. (2006). Conduct problems and juvenile sexual offending. In H. Barbaree & W. Marshall (Eds.), *The juvenile sex offender* (pp. 166–188). New York: Guilford Press.

Sheehan, V., & Sullivan, J. (2010). A qualitative analysis of child sex offenders involved in the manufacture of indecent images of children. *Journal of Sexual Aggression, 16*(2), 143–167.

Simon, L. M. (2000). An examination of the assumptions of specialization, mental disorder, and dangerousness in sex offenders. *Behavioral Sciences & the Law, 18*(2-3), 275–308.

Smallbone, S., & Cale, J. (2015). An integrated life-course developmental theory of sexual offending. In A. A. J. Blokland & P. Lussier (Eds.), *Sex offenders: A criminal career approach* (pp. 43–70). Chichester: John Wiley & Sons.

Smallbone, S. W., & Wortley, R. K. (2004). Onset, persistence, and versatility of offending among adult males convicted of sexual offenses against children. *Sexual Abuse: A Journal of Research and Treatment, 16*(4), 285–298.

Smith, S. G., Zhang, X., Basile, K. C., Merrick, M. T., Wang, J., Kresnow, M., et al. (2018). *The national intimate partner and sexual violence survey (NISVS): 2015 data brief—updated release*. Atlanta, GA: National Center for Injury Prevention and Control, Centers for Disease Control and Prevention.

Soothill, K., Francis, B., Sanderson, B., & Ackerley, E. (2000). Sex offenders: Specialists, generalists—or both? A 32-year criminological study. *The British Journal of Criminology, 40*(1), 56–67.

Sorenson, S. B., Stein, J. A., Siegel, J. M., Golding, J. M., & Burnam, M. A. (1987). The prevalence of adult sexual assault the Los Angeles epidemiologic catchment area project. *American Journal of Epidemiology, 126*(6), 1154–1164.

Stander, J., Farrington, D. P., Hill, G., & Altham, P. M. (1989). Markov chain analysis and specialization in criminal careers. *British Journal of Criminology, 29*(4), 317–335.

Swartout, K. M., Koss, M. P., White, J. W., Thompson, M. P., Abbey, A., & Bellis, A. L. (2015). Trajectory analysis of the campus serial rapist assumption. *JAMA Pediatrics, 169*(12), 1148–1154.

Templeman, T. L., & Stinnett, R. D. (1991). Patterns of sexual arousal and history in a "normal" sample of young men. *Archives of Sexual Behavior, 20*(2), 137–150.

Thompson, M., Sitterle, D., Clay, G., & Kingree, J. (2007). Reasons for not reporting victimizations to the police: Do they vary for physical and sexual incidents? *Journal of American College Health, 55*, 277–282.

Tracy, P. E., Wolfgang, M. E., & Figlio, R. M. (1990). *Delinquency careers in two birth cohorts.* New York: Plenum Press.

U.S. Department of Justice. (2007). Crime in the United States, 2006. Retrieved from http://www2.fbi.gov/ucr/cius2006/index.html

Van Wijk, A. P., Mali, B. R., Bullens, R. A., & Vermeiren, R. R. (2007). Criminal profiles of violent juvenile sex and violent juvenile non–sex offenders: An explorative longitudinal study. *Journal of interpersonal violence, 22*(10), 1340–1355.

Vizard, E., Hickey, N., & McCrory, E. (2007). Developmental trajectories associated with juvenile sexually abusive behaviour and emerging severe personality disorder in childhood: 3-year study. *The British Journal of Psychiatry, 190*(S49), s27–s32.

Waite, D., Keller, A., McGarvey, E. L., Wieckowski, E., Pinkerton, R., & Brown, G. L. (2005). Juvenile sex offender re-arrest rates for sexual, violent nonsexual and property crimes: A 10-year follow-up. Sexual abuse: a journal of research and treatment, 17(3), 313–331.

Weinrott, M. R., & Saylor, M. (1991). Self-report of crimes committed by sex offenders. *Journal of Interpersonal Violence, 6*(3), 286–300.

White House Council on Women and Girls. (2014). Rape and sexual assault: A renewed call to action.

Wijkman, M., Bijleveld, C., & Hendriks, J. (2010). Women don't do such things! Characteristics of female sex offenders and offender types. *Sexual Abuse: A Journal of Research and Treatment, 22*, 135–156.

Wijkman, M., Bijleveld, C., & Hendriks, J. (2014). Juvenile female sex offenders: Offender and offence characteristics. *European Journal of Criminology, 11*, 23–38.

Wijkman, M., & Sandler, J. C. (2018). Female sexual offending. In O. Lussier & E. Beauregard (Eds.), *Sexual offending: A criminological perspective* (pp. 257–275). Abington, UK: Routledge.

Wolak, J., Finkelhor, D., Mitchell, K. J., & Jones, L. M. (2011). Arrests for child pornography production: Data at two time points from a national sample of US law enforcement agencies. *Child Maltreatment, 16*(3), 184–195.

Wolfgang, M. E., Sellin, T., & Figlio, R. M. (1972). *Delinquency in a birth cohort.* Chicago, IL: University of Chicago Press.

Ybarra, M. L., & Mitchell, K. J. (2013). Prevalence rates of male and female sexual violence perpetrators in a national sample of adolescents. *JAMA Pediatrics, 167*(12), 1125–1134.

Zimmer-Gembeck, M. J., & Helfand, M. (2008). Ten years of longitudinal research on US adolescent sexual behavior: Developmental correlates of sexual intercourse, and the importance of age, gender and ethnic background. *Developmental Review, 28*(2), 153–224.

Zimring, F., Piquero, A., & Jennings, W. G. (2007). Sexual delinquency in Racine: Does early sex offending predict later sex offending in youth and adulthood? *Criminology & Public Policy, 6*(507), 534.

Zimring, F. E., Jennings, W. G., Piquero, A. R., & Hays, S. (2009). Investigating the continuity of sex offending: Evidence from the second Philadelphia birth cohort. *Justice Quarterly, 26*(1), 58–76.

Chapter 4
Why Sexual Offending?

Introduction

There is a wide range of popular explanations as to why people perpetrate sexual offenses. For some, there is a long-held belief that the causes of sexual offending are inherently found in the people that perpetrate these acts. These people are believed to be mad or bad. Deranged or psychopaths. From this standpoint, there is something wrong with how these individuals think, feel, act or react. They are prone to commit sex offenses because of some mental defect and there is little that society can do to change such these individuals. Others claim that society is a factory of rape and sexual assault. The causes of rape and sexual assault are not found in people because everyone is capable of committing sexual harms when such behaviors are tolerated, endorsed, and even reinforced. The causes of sexual offenses are found instead in the environment, social structure, and the harmful messages that encourage such behaviors. They argue that there is a rampant rape culture endorsed by all males and that such endorsement propels them to sexually take advantage of women and children whenever there is an opportunity to do so. Others have argued that individuals who sexually take advantage of others do so because they have been abused themselves; they only mimic what they have learned to do as a result of their own sexually abusive and adverse experiences. According to this viewpoint, the main cause of sexual offending is sexual offending and its atrocious consequences on a person's sexual functioning and sexual interests. Sexual offending causes sexual offending through a vicious cycle that perpetuates sexual harm from one generation to another. These three main viewpoints have and continue to lead to profound debates. Not so much because of the theoretical importance underlying these debates, but mostly because of the resulting societal responses and policy associated with these viewpoints: locking up deranged individuals and keeping them away; enforcing profound societal changes and increasing formal and informal social control; providing help, support, and assistance to sexually abused victims hoping to break the vicious cycle of abuse. In other words, the origins of the debate have more

P. Lussier et al., *Understanding Sexual Offending*,
https://doi.org/10.1007/978-3-030-53301-4_4

to do with the preferred response to the issue at hand than with a differential analysis and interpretation of the contributing factors of sexual offending.

To date, a critical reason explaining the long-lasting debates has to do with social science's inability to clearly identify the causes of sexual offending. One of the central factors explaining such difficulties is that the nature of sexual offending is and continues to be a moving target. What is socially constructed as a sexual offense continues to change from one generation to another. It evolves faster than the scientific knowledge about the phenomenon. The medical, feminist, and actuarial periods have in turn left indelible marks on the formulation of the phenomenon of sexual offending. These formulations will inevitably have consequences for the propositions of hypotheses and explanatory models. The hypotheses evoked during these periods all contrast with one another, as do the issues raised by these perspectives and currents of thought. How is it possible for these three perspectives to be so distinct? One possibility is that these unique explanations emerged as part of social science's reaction to the types of sex offending that have received the most attention from the public, policymakers, and media. Accordingly, these explanations resemble the parable of the blind men and the elephant, in which different persons describe a phenomenon in different ways according to the small aspect of the phenomenon that they are able to touch. Here, researchers are providing an explanation for a very narrow set of behaviors that comprise a small proportion of all sexual offending. The theories and hypotheses put forward will all too often serve to support the prevailing ideology of the moment, rather than to explain the origin and development of all sexual offending. There will be exceptions, of course, but history shows that, most of the time, what is presented as a "theory" of sexual offending is merely a justification that gives credit to the dominant ideology and the practices that come from it, whether it is the treatment programs offered, the legislative changes that are required or the tools that are put in place in correctional settings.

In this field of research, history suggests that theory does not guide, it merely justifies the practices in intervention and prevention. Despite appearances, the research foundation in this field of expertise has remained shaky at best, the ideological discourse too often acting as a barrier to fruitful communication, education, exchanges and discussion between key actors (e.g., victims, perpetrators, witnesses, family members, police investigators, lawyers, prosecutors and judges, clinicians, correctional officers, and probation/parole officers) and researchers. Social scientists do not all agree about these underlying assumptions and such disagreements have been the subject of much debate and controversy for numerous years. Social scientists do not all agree about these underlying assumptions and such disagreements have been the subject of much debate and controversy for numerous years (Bryden & Grier, 2011; Lussier & Cale, 2016). Such debates are also disciplinarily framed given the complexity of the social phenomenon at hand. Sociologists tend to focus on the larger social environment in which people function and interact to find the causes of sexual offending. Psychologists tend to focus on a person's cognitive, emotional, and behavioral functioning and their interactions with the larger social environment. Others, such as social biologists, are concerned with the origins of the phenomenon from an evolutionary perspective and why such behavior exists in the first place. Such debates are useful, healthy, and necessary to establish the scientific foundation in a field of research. In this chapter, theories and explanatory models of sexual offending are reviewed.

Sexual or Pseudo-Sexual Motivation?

Why do individuals perpetrate sexual offenses? This might seem obvious to some, completely irrelevant to others. Historically, this research question has been and remains one of the most contentious and controversial theoretical elements of the understanding of the etiology of sexual offending. There are four recognizable generations of theorizing and research about the causes of sexual offending (Lussier & Cale, 2016; see Fig. 4.1).

We can trace back the study of sexual offending to the first clinical cases reported in the European literature on abnormal and deviant sexual behaviors (e.g., Gley, 1884; Krafft-Ebing, 1895; Magnan, 1885). Psychiatrists of the time were concerned about the role of brain abnormalities, brain dysfunctions, and the deterioration to the brain to explain eccentric, bizarre, atypical sexual behaviors (e.g., erotomania, compulsive masturbation). Supported by the description of single case studies, these writings somewhat laid the foundation for North American research that would gradually emerge in the early twentieth century. Indeed, the first generation of theorizing emphasized the role and importance of sexual deviance and deviant sexual motives as key components to sexual offending. For some clinical researchers who have conducted clinical assessments and therapy with individuals who have perpetrated such offenses, this motivation is not necessarily conscious on the part of the perpetrator, but such motivations take root in the developmental history of the person. This motivation is the result of profound injuries resulting from early

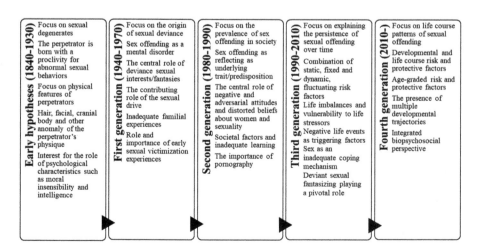

Fig. 4.1 Evolution of theorizing about sexual offending

traumas and abuse, tragic stories of neglect, abandonment and abuse that occurred very early in, and persisted throughout, the developmental trajectory of some perpetrators of sexual offenses. For others, the motivation has more to do with the goals pursued by the person committing the acts. These objectives are the results of inadequate learning experiences and social conditioning mechanisms that occurred during childhood and adolescence. Finally, for others, this motivation is purely situational and transitory and simply reflects the wants and contingencies of a particular moment in time and may have little to do with a person's early trauma or life experiences.

More fundamentally, what is the nature of this motivation that drives an individual to commit a sexual offense? Some would argue that sexual offending is simply a symptom of "abnormal" sexual development. But what is the nature of this abnormality? Are perpetrators of sexual offenses motivated by a need for immediate sexual gratification? Are they compelled to act because their sexual urges are stronger than what other people experience? Do they simply lack inhibitory mechanisms to control their relatively normal sexual urges? Is it instead that their sexual urges are relatively normal but driven by goals and objectives that are outside of what is considered socially conventional, expected, and/or tolerable? In these regards, the assumptions are numerous. Indeed, for some, sexual offending is motivated by deviant sexual drives (Abel & Blanchard, 1974). For others, sexual offenses represent a manifestation of the needs of an abnormally high sexual drive (Ellis, 1991). Some will refer to the assumption that perpetrators of sexual offenses do not have sufficiently developed or effective behavioral inhibition mechanisms to control their sexual behavior in certain circumstances (Marshall & Barbaree, 1984). All these hypotheses have been raised before and point in a very specific direction despite being formulated differently; that is, that sexual offenses are in fact sexually motivated. In effect, the key assumption here is that the etiological roots of sexual offending have something to do with a person's sexual functioning. Many others will question this hypothesis, suggesting that sexuality has little to do with sexual offenses. Indeed, for other researchers, sexual offending is not sexually motivated at all, but rather that perpetrators are motivated by other needs that are expressed through sexual violence and abuse, such as power. In this context, the key question that emerges is how to explain the expression of such needs in a sexual manner. Some of these key hypotheses are examined.

Some of the first North American assumptions underlying this key question were largely influenced by the behavioral approach. The hypothesis of deviant sexual preferences and the central role of deviant sexual fantasies in the development of a propensity for sexual offending is certainly one of the first real explanatory tracks followed by clinical researchers. These theories aimed more to explain sexual deviance (e.g., deviant sexual thoughts, needs, urges, interests and/or behavior) than sexual offending per se (that is, the acting out). Three elements are at the heart of the deviant sexual preference hypothesis.

First, these etiological models state that certain stimuli are sexually arousing and rewarding. The tenets of these models distinguish different types of sexual deviance or deviations in comparison to more conventional or normal sexual thoughts, fantasies, preferences, and behaviors. The deviation aspect, as relative as it may be, is generally approached from a statistical point of view, that is: what are the sexual thoughts, needs, urges, interests that are out of the ordinary, atypical, uncommon, unexpected? Some of these sexual deviancies represent deviations from the common sexual object, another human being (e.g., a foot, an animal, feces). There are also deviations related to the notion of consent for sexual behaviors, which include, for example, behaviors involving a child, a dead body, an intoxicated person, or an unwilling adult female. There are also deviations from typical sexual behaviors, such as inflicting physical pain. Second, these etiological models emphasize that sexually deviant stimuli are preferential for certain individuals compared to other more conventional sexual stimuli. For example, having sexual contact with a child would be preferential to having sexual contact with another adult for a pedophile. A sexual sadist would be more sexually aroused by inflicting pain to another human being than having sexual contact without some sort violence being inflicted to the sexual partner. Third, these models also suggest that individuals tend to seek out opportunities, whether actively or more passively, to act out their sexual preferences in some way or another. In all, this approach centers on the assumption that deviant sexual thoughts are the central etiological factor responsible for sexual offenses.

Different hypotheses have been proposed to explain the emergence of deviant sexual preferences by borrowing concepts from behavioral theories of human behavior and social learning theory (e.g., Laws & Barbaree, 1990). These theories emphasize early life experiences and trauma in a person's sexual development (Abel & Blanchard, 1974; McGuire, Carlisle, & Young, 1964). Similar to consensual adult sexual behaviors, proponents of this theoretical perspective agree that sexual offending reflects an amalgam of sexually deviant behaviors learned like any other sexual behavior socially considered as nondeviant or normal. These theorists hypothesized, however, that human sexual preferences are genetically predisposed (Laws & Barbaree, 1990), although these mechanisms still remain relatively unclear. Regardless of this, the assumption is that genetic predispositions, life experiences, and the consequences associated with them are pivotal to the development of deviant sexual preferences rather than other "normal" sexual preferences. As such, theorists have focused on the impact of a person's exposure to deviant sexual models on the central role of fantasies, linking orgasm and masturbation to these fantasies as catalysts for the development of deviant sexual preferences.

These theories will be particularly influenced by the observations of McGuire and his collaborators (1964) who noticed a recurrent pattern in patients seen at their clinic. Most of them reported that they had been sexually abused at a young age and that these experiences of abuse were their first sexual experiences. The same patients also reported that, at around puberty, the thoughts of their past sexual victimization served as a support for their masturbatory activities. McGuire and his colleagues (1964) hypothesized that repeated masturbatory activities to these sexual thoughts followed by orgasm, created a positive reinforcement pattern. The association of these experiences of abuse with sexual gratification, in the process, gradually shaped their sexual interests. According to McGuire and his collaborators (1964), these experiences of abuse favored the development of deviant sexual preferences, which provided a drive, or a motivation, to reproduce the same abusive acts on another person. While this model offers an explanation of the origin and development of deviant sexual preferences, the factors explaining why some individuals act upon those sexual preferences and others do not, remain somewhat elusive. The central role of deviant sexual preferences, while popular in a certain era, are no longer seen as a key concept in the explanation of sexual offending. In fact, it offers a limited explanation of sexual offenses and its importance for some form of sexual offending remains unclear or irrelevant (e.g., sexual exploitation).

For other theorists, sexual offending is not the result of deviant sexual interests or preferences, but rather a question of the intensity of a person's sexual urges in general. In short, if the hypothesis of sexual deviance emphasizes a 'deviation' from the goals pursued by the individual in relation to societal norms and expectations, this second hypothesis evokes a disturbance of the intensity of sexual urges in the pursuit of objectives that remain relatively common (Krueger & Kaplan, 2001). Some have evoked the term compulsive sexuality to describe this clinical reality, while others have alluded to sexual addiction (Carnes, 2001; Coleman, 1992). Importantly, compulsive sexuality or sexual addiction are not criminal behaviors, but they may create a context conducive to sexual offenses. These phenomena observed in clinical and psychiatric settings raise important questions related to sexual offending. Are sexual offenders sexually dependent to the point of committing a sexual offense in order to satisfy their sexual needs?

But what is a sexual addiction? Is it an addiction to sexuality or an addiction to sexual behaviors? How does this addiction manifest itself? The concept is unclear, and several researchers question the very nature of this concept (e.g., Levine, 2010). In fact, just like sexual deviance, some raise the idea that sexual addiction is a mental health problem, just like substance abuse disorders. This hypothesis has been rejected by the scientific community. Martin Kafka (1997, 2003) proposed a clearer and more operational formulation of the concept under the label of hypersexuality. Hypersexuality, as defined by Kafka, involves three specific aspects: (1) a sexual preoccupation or the extent to which the person is overwhelmed by sexual needs, fantasies, and behaviors; (2) frequent sexual behaviors of all kinds (masturbation, use of pornography, cybersex, sexting, sexual contact, sexual intercourse); and, (3) hypersexuality that has significant and negative consequences on the general and social functioning of the individual. From a psychiatric point of view, the concept of hypersexuality raises important diagnostic questions. For example, as Stein, Black, and Pienaar (2000) and Krueger and Kaplan (2001) point out, to what extent are the sexual behaviors of the individual specific symptoms of hypersexuality or rather clinical symptoms of an entirely different nature (substance abuse, manic episode, obsessive-compulsive disorder)? This question remains unanswered.

Sexual Motivation Versus Pseudo-Sexual Act: A False Debate?

While early clinical research has been conducted under the assumption that sexual offenses were sexually motivated, other researchers relied on different assumptions. Could it be that, despite the behaviors being of a sexual nature, that the underlying motives behind rape, sexual assault, and child molestation, to name a few, are not sexually motivated? Indeed, for many theorists, sexual offending represents a set of pseudo-sexual acts and behaviors to achieve nonsexual goals. Indeed, while it made sense from behaviorists to examine the root of sexual offending in the environmental sexual cues that a person has been exposed to as a leading etiological path toward sexual offending, psychologists relying on a psychodynamic and Freudian approach saw another etiological path to sexual offending, one that has less to do with sexuality (Groth & Birnbaum, 1979). Such views were also somewhat in agreement with feminists' thinking and writing on rape and sexual assault that become prominent in the 1970s.

From a feminist approach, sexual offending is generally discussed under the umbrella term of sexual violence. From this standpoint, sexual violence is considered a pseudo-sexual act where the key objectives are the social, individual, legal, and economic enslavement of women. Sexual violence, therefore, is both an expression of patriarchal values and strategy used to maintain the established patriarchal order in society. According to this position, domination, power, and control of women are the main goals of sexual offending, especially rape and sexual assault, and other acts that help to further humiliate and restrain women's assertiveness. For example, to Brownmiller (1975), drawing mainly on past wartime observations and periods of slavery in the USA, sexual offending is nothing more or less than a process of intimidation by which all men maintain women in a state of fear. In the same vein, Groth and Birnbaum (1979) stated that perceiving rape and sexual assault as sexually motivated acts had a victim blaming effect by suggesting that victims deliberately or inadvertently caused their own victimization. These interpretations and conclusions, very popular during the 1970s and 1980s, were eventually challenged by several scholars for misrepresenting the underlying causal factors of rape and sexual assault (e.g., Ellis, 1991; Felson, 2002; Lalumière, Harris, Quinsey, & Rice, 2005). In that regard, for Bryden and Grier (2011), rejecting the sexual motivation for sexual offending was not the result of scientific and empirical observations, but rather the reflection of a socially and politically engaged ideological discourse of a specific period. The main objective of this discourse was to change societal attitudes and perceptions about victims and not to explain scientific facts and observations about the phenomenon itself.

For some, however, this debate is somewhat futile and ideological because there is not a single motivation to all sexual offenses, but rather a set of motivations that characterize them all. Even simple behaviors such as eating, running, shouting, thinking, and writing can be driven by various motivations. These motivations are also shaped by the context in which these actions take place. The idea is not new and was raised by Katz (1988) who emphasized the importance of approaching criminal behavior in general and sexual offenses in particular using a phenomenological approach. This approach is concerned with the meaning and function of criminal behavior. Rather than inferring unconscious motivations that would be psychologically or socially predetermined by some uncontrollable forces, Katz (1988) and others (e.g., Felson, 2002) asked why not simply approach the complex issue from the perpetrator's point of view? This approach has the value of turning the attention to the contextual and situational contingencies that characterize the perpetrator's actions. The behaviors are diverse, and the contexts are just as numerous. For many years, psychologists and criminologists have inquired about the motives of the individual who has committed a sexual offense. Why sexually assault a young boy during a camping trip? Why expose one's private parts in front of a group of teenage girls who are waiting for the bus? Why break into a young woman's apartment to steal her underwear or to sexually assault her? Why pretend to be a professional photographer to invite a vulnerable young girl to an apartment to sexually take advantage of her? Perhaps, as these phenomenological researchers suggested, there is something to learn from their stories and that their perspective is not just lies, rationalizations, justifications, and minimization.

Despite this diversity of context and situations, over the years, researchers noticed trends and regularities in perpetrators' narratives about their motivations to commit a sexual offense (Cohen, Garofalo, Boucher, & Seghorn, 1971; Groth & Birnbaum, 1979; Knight & Prentky, 1990; Marshall, 1989; Tedeschi & Felson, 1994). Perpetrators report a wide range of motivations for sexual offending, sometimes multiple motives for the same offense. Some were seeking immediate sexual gratification. Others reported wanting to act out their sexual fantasies. Some reported not having specific motivations prior to the sexual offense but rather that they were simply taking advantage of an opportunity or that they enjoyed the thrill the situation produced. Some reported having long-lasting hostility toward women in general, others toward people in general. Some reported that their hostility was such that they were driven by anger and rage. Others by the power and control over someone else. Some have even mentioned that their behavior was driven by the need to feel masculine, vigorous, and virile. Others, quite differently, reported they were in need of intimacy with another person and that the sexual offense was, in its own distorted way, meant to achieve this goal. Some perpetrators have stressed the need to hurt someone to obtain sexual pleasure, the need to humiliate or even completely dominate another person. As these studies accumulated over the years, it became obvious that sexual offending was explained by both sexual and nonsexual motives.

Researchers not only unraveled the presence of sexual and nonsexual motives, but they also highlighted the presence of certain patterns in the narratives of perpetrators of sex crimes. In fact, clinical researchers observed the presence of distinguishable patterns that not only represented the perpetrator's motivation but also the situation and contextual element of the sexual offense, such as the victim's age, the type and level of physical violence used against the victim, the level of physical injury inflicted on the victim, whether the victim was previously known by the assailant (Proulx, St-Yves, Guay, & Ouimet, 1999). This is not to say that a perpetrator's sexual and nonsexual motives can predict the type of sexual offense perpetrated. Rather, it suggests that the type of sexual offense perpetrated may imperfectly reflect certain aspects of perpetrators' motives and other contextual factors that may have less to do with their initial motives (e.g., whether alcohol was involved, the victim's resistance, the presence and intervention of bystanders). In law enforcement jargon, this would refer to the crime scene, whereas criminologists prefer to speak of crime events. These patterns would lead researchers to propose different classification models of perpetrators of sexual offenses, especially those having been involved in sexual violence and abuse.

These classification models (also called typologies) were particularly popular from the 1970s, especially in clinical settings to guide sex offender treatment (Cohen et al., 1971; Gebhard, Gagnon, Pomeroy, & Christenson, 1965; Groth & Birnbaum, 1979; Knight & Prentky, 1990). Prior to this point there was an understanding of perpetrators of sexual offenses as a heterogeneous group. However, it was not until this typological perspective emerged that researchers began to systematically code this heterogeneity in an attempt to categorize offenders into more homogeneous groups, types or categories. A commonly held belief among proponents of this approach was that treatment should be tailored to the specific needs of these individuals and typologies provided important information about the causal factors responsible for their actions. In a way, sex offender typologies represented a certain theoretical advancement, as they brought to light key factors that distinguished individuals along sexual offending dimensions (e.g., types of sexual acts perpetrated, using some form of violence, the perpetrator–victim relationship). However, these researchers were never able to reach a general consensus about the number and nature of these types. In fact, typologies tended to differ from one researcher to another and even the types that composed these classification models differed. Too often, clinical studies relied on an inferential approach to identify "types" and their findings often were not validated through additional research using the scientific method. More sophisticated analytical methods overcame some of these limitations (see, for example, Knight & Prentky, 1990; Proulx, Beauregard, Lussier, & Leclerc, 2014). However, one fact remains: the application of the phenomenological perspective reflects the state of mind of the individual *after* the act not before, and, usually, after being arrested by the police, convicted before a court of law, and often incarcerated in a penitentiary and admitted into a sex offender treatment program. In this context, it becomes difficult to distinguish whether the words of the individual actually reflect their state of mind when acting out a sexual offense, or rather the interpretation, or even the justification, of their actions after the acts, or even the assimilation of a particular clinical discourse. The latter point refers to instances in which an offender simply parrots a narrative provided by a treatment professional for why an individual might perpetrate a sexual offense.

As a result, other researchers discounted classification models based on motivation and offenders' narratives. More recent classification models focus on factual, directly observable behavior using different sources of information (e.g., victim statement, police investigation) that are less subject to clinical interpretations that may be misleading or subject to personal and interpretation biases. For example, research has focused on the analysis of the diversity of *modus operandi* and the offending process (e.g., Deslauriers-Varin & Beauregard, 2010; Proulx et al., 2014; Polaschek, Hudson, Ward, & Siegert, 2001). These researchers examined the pre-crime, crime, and post-crime behaviors, such as the level of planning, the level of violence used, the duration of the offense, victim-offender relationship, the location of the offense, etc. These researchers dissected the sexual offense in multiple parts to better understand the diversity of offending processes that had been neglected up to that point. Others, focused their analysis on the diversity of criminal careers and offending trajectories (e.g., Blokland & Lussier, 2015; Cale, Lussier, & Proulx, 2009; Lalumière et al., 2005; Lussier, Tzoumakis, Cale, & Amirault, 2010; Lussier, Leclerc, Cale, & Proulx, 2007; McCuish, Lussier, & Corrado, 2016). These research-ers were concerned by perpetrators' entire history of offending behavior, including nonsexual offending. They exposed the heterogeneity of the longitudinal offending patterns and the dynamic aspect of offending over time. Others exposed the hetero-geneity characterizing perpetrators of sexual offenses in terms of variations of prob-abilities of sexual recidivism (notably, Hanson & Thornton, 2000; Quinsey, Harris, Rice, & Cormier, 1998). These researchers identify that not all perpetrators are characterized the same probabilities of sexual recidivism and such probabilities could also be classified along of continuum of risk (e.g., low, moderate, high). In other words, the heterogeneity characterizing this population has been documented along several dimensions such as offending process, criminal careers, and recidi-vism probabilities.

While these studies are informative about the diversity of motivations underlying a sexual offense, one question remains: Are sexual offenses the result of a unique motivation for sexual offending that is specific and distinct from the one usually associated with "normal" sexual behaviors? Typology studies have been exclusively focused on questioning perpetrators of sexual offenses, and in the process, did not question non-perpetrators of sexual offenses about their sexual motivations.

A common theme throughout this book is that a major and consistent limitation of research on sexual offending is the failure to conduct research using an appropri-ate control group. Often, what is once considered a unique aspect of sexual offend-ing eventually is revealed to also be relatively common within the general offender population. The key question might not be what drives perpetrators of sexual offenses, but rather whether their motivation is distinct from others who do not cause sexual harm. What drives an adult to engage in consensual sexual intercourse with another adult? The state of current knowledge about the underlying motiva-tions for consenting sexual behaviors is relatively limited. Until recently, scientific writings evoked three main motivations for sexual intercourse: reproduction, sexual pleasure or merely the need to release some sexual tension. More recent research, however, has shown that motivations are diverse and multiple.

Adults have consensual sexual intercourse for a multitude of reasons other than those generally mentioned in early writings on the subject. For example, a survey with young adults found a range of motivations for consenting sex, i.e., motives that are not necessarily sexual in nature (Hill & Preston, 1996). According to the study findings, researchers noted that for this group of young adults, the main motives reported can be categorized as follows: to feel important, valued or desired by their partner; to demonstrate their value and importance to their sexual partner; to express value for a partner; to enhance personal feelings of power; to free oneself from stress; to express love and affection for a partner; to experience pleasure; and, to procreate. In short, sexual intercourse between two consenting adults reflects various motives that may vary from one context to another. In other words, there are multiple sexual and nonsexual motives for sexual intercourse between consenting adults.

More recently, in a similar study by Meston and Buss (2007), the results broadened our understanding of the range of young adults' motivations for sex. These researchers identified various reasons for sex, which can be grouped according to four main motivations. The first, physical motivation, refers to a range of motives which include seeking a stress release, searching for physical pleasure, out of physical attractiveness, or simply by seeking new experiences. The second, insecurity, refers to sexual intercourse that is motivated by the desire to increase one's personal confidence, to satisfy or to please one's partner, or for fear of being rejected by that person. Affective motivations refer to sexual intercourse that is motivated by love, commitment to others, and the expression of one's emotions towards the other through sexual intercourse. Finally, sexual intercourse can be instrumentally motivated, meaning that the act is used to achieve a particular purpose, such as social status, getting money or property in return, or revenge against someone. The results of Meston and Buss's (2007) study show that the most frequently reported motives are physical attraction, seeking pleasure and sexual gratification, love and intimacy, as well as seeking out new experiences.

Moreover, the Meston and Buss (2007) study shows that for males, sexual intercourse is also motivated by the search for new experiences (having different sexual partners), out of personal revenge (so to hurt someone psychologically), in order to increase their self-esteem (in order to feel important) or merely for physical pleasure (without emotional investment). Interestingly, the key motivations for sexual offending as identified by and attributed to individuals who have committed a sexual offense are strikingly similar to the motivations for consensual sexual intercourse as reported by university students, whether it is revenge, seeking out new sensations and experience, or boosting their self-esteem. While these studies have not directly compared the motivations of perpetrators of sex offenses to those of the general population, the fact remains that the central element that seems to distinguish the two groups is not so much the motives, but the pursuit of these objectives in the absence of the victim's consent. In these circumstances, therefore, it could be reasonably argued that it is not so much the motivation that distinguishes perpetrators of sexual offenses from the general population, but the *notion of consent* and the context surrounding it.

Motivation may initiate a person's actions directed toward achieving sex but it does not explain why that person takes a particular course of action at a certain point in time, one that led to consensual activities or another that lead to a sexual assault. For example, perpetrators of a sexual offense will rely on a wide array of strategies and tactics to achieve their goals, whether sexual, pseudo-sexual, or both: taking advantage of an intoxicated or unconscious person; manipulating or persuading a young victim with gifts and privileges; lying and using a false identity to lure a young person to a secluded place; breaking and entering into the property of an adult stranger; simply acting impulsively on the spur of the moment without much thinking; taking advantage of being in a context of authority over another person; isolating, manipulating, and intoxicating a young person for the purpose of sexually exploiting him/her; using threats, a weapon or physical force to coerce a person into sexual acts (Lussier & Cale, 2016).

For some reason, these strategies have been somewhat overlooked in clinical research, which traditionally has been centered on the identification of perpetrators' motives to cause sexual harm. Yet, these strategies are inherently part of most if not all sexual offenses. What are these strategies? Why are these strategies used in a sexual context? What is the origin of these strategies? The question has not been addressed directly until very recently. Two schools of thought that are diametrically opposed to one another have indirectly attempted to address this question for some time: Are risk factors for sexual offending innate or acquired? The starting point of these two schools of thought has been relatively similar: disproportionately, sexual offenses are committed by men. Why is that so? Are men genetically predisposed to commit sexual offenses? Is sexual offending and other related tactics used by males that cause sexual harm a byproduct of human evolution? Or, is it instead that the sociocultural environment promotes sexual offending more specifically among men? Is there something about culture and social forces that promotes the use of certain tactics in sexual contexts? The purely ideological reaction to this debate has led to virulent, unhelpful exchanges, where one camp tends to caricature, simplify or misinterpret the others' views, theoretical perspectives, and hypotheses (Ward & Siegert, 2002). Yet both schools of thought are characterized by a multitude of relatively complex theoretical perspectives. These questions, far from being solved, are generally tackled by two major fields of research: on the one hand, sociobiology (as well as evolutionary psychology) and, on the other hand, sociocultural studies (as well as ethnographic studies). In order to answer these questions, sociobiology turned to the study of animal behavior, especially primates, while ethnographic studies turned to the description and analysis of the phenomenon in traditional or so-called primitive societies.

Sexual Offending: Innate or Acquired?

Innate Propensity

What is the origin of sexual offending? Is it an innate behavior that is embedded in human nature and shaped by many millions of years of evolution? Are there one or more genes that facilitate, promote or predispose some to perpetrate sexual offenses? A first series of theoretical formulations concerning the origins of sexual offending, more specifically rape and sexual assault, comes from sociobiology and evolutionary psychology (Ellis, 1991; Lalumière & Quinsey, 1996; Lalumière et al., 2005;

Thornhill & Palmer, 2000). These theoretical formulations have been focused on the phylogenetic origins of rape in the context of human evolution, taking into account the principles of natural and sexual selection. From this point of view, these researchers ask the following question: Do rape and sexual assault increase the perpetrator's evolutionary success (i.e., survival of one's genes through procreation)? Researchers have noted the presence of male coercive sexual behaviors against females in different animal species, including chimpanzees and gorillas (Goldberg & Wrangham, 1997; Lalumière et al., 2005; Smuts, 1992). As a result, rape and sexual assault are not approached as human-specific behaviors. It is from this perspective that several researchers have raised the hypothesis that these social behaviors have a genetic component that may provide certain evolutionary benefits to the perpetrator. In particular, researchers have proposed and examined two main theses about the phylogenetic origin of rape. The first stipulates that rape directly increase a male's probabilities of evolutionary success and, more specifically, gene survival. In other words, rape itself carries an evolutionary advantage. The other suggests that there are no "genes" for rape and sexual assault. That these phenotypes are the by-product of human evolution.

To date, research findings tend to support the by-product hypothesis (Lalumière et al., 2005; Thornhill & Palmer, 2000). The by-product hypothesis suggests that through the long process of evolution a particular phenotype indirectly related to rape and sexual assault may have enhanced male adaptation to their environment. These phenotypes, while increasing gene survival may also promote, facilitate or predispose someone to coerce another into sex in certain contexts. It is in that context that several researchers hypothesized that sexual offending is the result of relatively stable and fixed neurohormonal biological disturbances over time (Aromäki, Lindman, & Eriksson, 2002; Bain, Langevin, Dickey, Hucker, & Wright, 1988; Bradford & McLean, 1984; Rada, Laws, & Kellner, 1976). The central hypothesis evoked by these researchers implies a possible link between an abnormally high level of testosterone and sexual offending. To date, Ellis (1991) has proposed the most elaborate etiological model specifically to explain rape. According to Ellis (1991), rape is not only intrinsically motivated, but it is also a learned behavior. In both cases, neurohormonal factors play a determinant role in the intensity of sexual needs and sensitivity to aversive stimuli in the environment. Ellis (1991) hypothesizes that androgens, especially testosterone, influence not only the brain structure, but also its functioning. In contrast to sociocultural explanations, Ellis (1991) states that the intensity of men's sexual drive is not socially conditioned but reflects neurohormonal differences that systematically affect brain development during the intrauterine period and in the months following the birth. The intensity of the sexual drive, which is activated and accentuated at puberty, is directly proportional to the intensity of prenatal and perinatal brain exposure to testosterone—a process also described as the masculinization of the brain. This process would desensitize the brain to negative environmental stimuli, including the psychological distress of others. According to this model, individuals who are more likely to commit sexual violence would have an abnormally high sex drive while being less sensitive to the negative consequences of their own actions.

Even today, however, the testosterone-sexual offending link is not based on con-clusive empirical evidence. Indeed, laboratory studies show that the link between testosterone and aggression is stronger in animals than in humans (see Archer, 1991). In addition, the presence of a testosterone-aggression link in humans sug-gests that it is not specific to sexual offending, but rather to the use of violence in general, and in different contexts. This may explain the contradictory results observed so far regarding the link between testosterone and sexual offending (Aromäki et al., 2002; Bain et al., 1988; Berlin, 1983; Bradford & McLean, 1984). In fact, if such a link is present, it seems more conducive to the specific explanations of sexual violence. According to this hypothesis, in the animal kingdom, males can be distinguished according to their reproductive effort, also called sociosexuality. Two differential strategies are used to maximize evolutionary success and more specifically gene survival. Some males are characterized by a short-term strategy. This strategy refers to males who maximize their reproductive efforts by investing primarily in the pursuit of multiple sexual partners. As efforts are focused on pursu-ing multiple partners, these males are distinguished by their low parental investment towards their offspring (e.g., protection, security, food, housing, education). As low parental efforts are invested in their offspring, these males are more concerned with maximizing the number of offspring by maximizing the number of sexual partners. Other males are characterized by a long-term strategy, directing their reproductive efforts towards commitment to the same partner and parental investment towards their offspring. These males are focused on securing a partner and maximizing their parental investment with their offspring. The first strategy thus aims at evolutionary success through the multiplication of the number of offspring, while the second strategy tries to optimize the probabilities of survival of a more limited number of offspring.

The concept of sociosexuality therefore suggests that men who pursue a short-term strategy are more likely to encounter difficulties when their reproductive efforts are in conflict with those of women. Sociobiological research suggests that females are much more selective than males in their choice of a sexual partner and a parent given the sex differences in evolutionary costs when having offspring. From an evolutionary point of view, aside from the burden of pregnancy and birth, and early care of the infant, a female has more to lose by opting for a partner who will eventually be, as a parent, absent, not engaged or invested, with limited resources to offer to the family. This selection is therefore likely to cause conflicts, especially for males pursuing a strategy focused on maximizing the number of sex-ual partners with little concerns for parental investment. This approach, which refers to the concept of sociosexuality, should not be confused with the concept of hyper-sexuality (Kafka, 2003) in that it does not reflect an uninhibited or compulsive sexu-ality, but rather a particular behavioral strategy. Moreover, a study by Kennair, Grøntvedt, Mehmetoglu, Perilloux, and Buss (2015) on the underlying motivations for consensual sexual intercourse between adults illustrates the divergent sociosex-ual strategies of young men. Indeed, the results of this study show that those who are characterized by a long-term sociosexual strategy are more likely to be moti-vated by love and commitment towards their partner, whereas individuals with a short-term sociosexual orientation are much more likely to have sex for reasons such as looking for new experiences, revenge towards others or to assert or reaffirm a certain social status.

In this context, researchers have attempted to answer whether perpetrators of sexual offenses are characterized by a short-term sociosexual strategy. A short-term sociosexuality hypothesis of rape and sexual assault would suggest that perpetrators would have a tendency to have a greater (not fewer) number of sexual partners. This may seem somewhat surprising given the popular belief that perpetrators of sexual offenses coerced someone into sex because of their inability to find a mate through socially acceptable and more conventional means. Indeed, various reasons and factors have been offered to explain why perpetrators have difficulties and failures in finding a mate or a sexual partner: they are unpopular; clumsy and awkward; introverted and even reclusive; they have limited or very rudimentary social skills such as the capacity to express themselves, to introduce themselves to others, to hold a discussion with another person, to listen to others, to negotiate or even to express a feeling properly; their low self-esteem limits their encounters with other adults and the quality of such social interactions. In fact, when rapists were compared to the general population, the findings did show that they were more socially inept (e.g., Stermac & Quinsey, 1986). They were not different, however, from individuals involved in other crime types and sexual offenses. In other words, their social skills did not set them apart from individuals prone to perpetrate nonsexual antisocial and criminal acts, except on one dimension—their tendency to be less assertive than others. Could it be that when faced with frustrating situations, such as being turned down, ignored, rejected, or felt used, they are more prone to frustration and anger? Could it be that the underlying motivation to perpetrate a rape/sexual assault is not so much a difficulty finding a sexual partner, but episodic difficulties when faced with conflicting interests between two or more individuals?

Evolutionary psychologists argued that perpetrators of rape and sexual assault were not quite successful in finding a sexual partner and preferred sexual partner diversity. Research has shown that perpetrators of rape and sexual assault tend to have an early onset of sexual contact and sexual intercourse (Cale, Leclerc, & Smallbone, 2014; Lussier, Blokland, Mathesius, Pardini, & Loeber, 2015). They are also more likely to have more sexual partners and are more likely to have committed a sex crime (Cale et al., 2014; Lalumière & Quinsey, 1996; Lussier et al., 2015; Malamuth, 1998). This is not to say that perpetrators of sexual offenses are characterized by a short-term sociosexual strategy. Those who are, however, are more likely to have committed their first sexual offense at a younger age and to have done it more frequently over their life course (Cale & Lussier, 2011). Additional research has also shown that men who are more likely to revert to antisocial behavior and those who also show evidence of psychopathy are more likely to pursue short-term sociosexuality (Harris, Rice, Hilton, Lalumiere, & Quinsey, 2007). How can these results explain rape and sexual assault? The predominant assumption is that individuals who have a preference for multiple partners and the pursuit of "sexual conquests" are more likely to eventually use antisocial tactics to achieve their ends. For example, when faced with a refusal of a sexual advance, these individuals are more likely to resort to subterfuge, charm, and tricks (e.g., falsely claiming to have emotional feelings towards others, intentionally intoxicating the person), coercion (e.g., exerting pressure, threatening to quit or to upload compromising images) or even physical violence (e.g., grabbing, slapping, hitting) to achieve their ends.

Socially Acquired Predisposition

The sociocultural approach to the issue of sexual offending focuses on the role of the environment to explain sexual offending. According to sociocultural theories, the behaviors associated with sexual offending are not innate or a by-product of evolution, but rather socially learned through various mechanisms. The central hypothesis of these theories is that a patriarchal culture promotes, facilitates, or encourages these behaviors (Brownmiller, 1975). Most sociocultural hypotheses recognize the genetic and biological bases and foundations of human sexuality. However, according to sociocultural theories, the forms of expression of human sexuality are the reflection of sociocultural contingencies. Moreover, while sociobiology and evolutionary psychology emphasize human sexuality from a reproductive and procreation perspective, sexual behaviors fulfill many functions and needs that are socially conditioned. From a sociocultural point of view, therefore, gender inequality, the objectification of women, the early sexualization of children, the media, the Internet and pornography, as well as rape culture, are sociocultural elements at the heart of this school of thought. For Brownmiller (1975) and Clark and Lewis (1977), sexual violence, sexual misconduct, and sexual exploitation are the result of a patriarchal society characterized by unequal gender relations in which women are perceived as men's property and various social cues promote and reinforce this idea.

One of the first sociocultural perspectives on rape and sexual assault originates from the work of Sanday (1981) and it evokes two premises that are not directly addressed by sociobiological and evolutionary theses. The first refers to the prevalence of rape that varies from place to place and, more specifically, from one culture to another. The second premise of Sanday's work states that a high prevalence of rape and sexual assault is generally observed in societies with a particular sociocultural pattern. More concretely, after analyzing data collected from 156 so-called primitive societies, Sanday (1981) observed that rape and sexual assault are more common in primitive societies with certain key characteristics. She argued that the estimated prevalence of rape and sexual assault was higher in societies that are patriarchal, have unequal gender relations, and value interpersonal violence, especially when used for instrumental purposes. This was particularly true for warfare prone societies (see also Chagnon, 1988). In fact, some have reported that in times of war, women and children are particularly vulnerable to rape and sexual assault. Some even evoke the idea that these behaviors are actual war strategies (e.g., Koo, 2002). In all, Sanday (1981) concluded that when interpersonal violence was part of a society's customs, especially in patriarchal societies where gender inequalities are marked and significant, these conditions facilitated men's expression of their sexual needs.

These observations are not anecdotal and reiterate the importance of examining rape and sexual assault from a general violence perspective. Could it be that these forms of sexual offenses are just another expression of interpersonal violence? Christine Adler (1984) raised a fundamental question when she asked the scientific community whether rapists were "sex offenders" or violent offenders. The idea that perpetrators of rape and sexual assault are, first and foremost, violent offenders is shared by several researchers. For example, Quinsey (1984), and later Baron, Straus, and Jaffee (1988), hypothesized that the sociocultural mechanisms that encourage and facilitate sexual offending are not distinct from those that encourage and facilitate interpersonal violence in general. In itself, sociocultural mechanisms are not specific to sexual offending. In that regard, Baron and his collaborators (Baron et al., 1988) raised the idea that there is a ripple effect: a culture that values and reinforces interpersonal violence will undeniably have direct repercussions on interpersonal relationships between men and women. A culture that promotes violence will have consequences where someone feels prejudiced against, whether it is perceived or factual; that person may feel entitled to use whatever means necessary to repair such injustice, including physical violence (Tedeschi & Felson, 1994). The general violence hypothesis, therefore, suggests that rather than a so-called rape culture, attitudes and beliefs supportive of interpersonal violence can facilitate or encourage rape and sexual assault. According to Baron et al. (1988), this is especially true when interpersonal violence is tolerated, facilitated, and even encouraged by social institutions (e.g., corporal punishment at home or in schools, violence in the mass media, police use of violence). The more violence is widespread, systematic, and perceived to be legitimate by social institutions, the more likely individuals who endorse positive beliefs and attitudes towards violence are to use violence against men, women, and children, but also in different contexts, including sexual contexts.

For other sociocultural theorists, the general violence hypothesis is valuable but incomplete to explain rape and sexual assault. A popular hypothesis has been the role of pornography (Dworkin, 1981; Malamuth, 1989; Malamuth, Addison, & Koss, 2000). Well before the advent and proliferation of pornographic internet websites, researchers were concerned about the role of the pornography industry and the proliferation of pornographic material on rape and sexual assault. Three interrelated ideas are generally raised to explain the role of pornography in sexual offending (e.g., Baron & Straus, 1987). First, pornographic material spreads sexist attitudes that reinforce unequal gender relations. Second, pornography contributes to the perception of women and children as sexual objects. Third, the presence of sexually violent pornographic material as well as child pornography provides behavioral models that can then be reproduced. It is difficult to determine, based on empirical observations, whether the use of pornography promotes sexual offending or whether sexual offending favors the use of pornography, or both. Indeed, while the empirical and statistical association between the consumption of pornographic material and the attitudes and behavior of men towards women is complex, the results of research on this topic remain somewhat equivocal (Fisher & Grenier, 1994; Malamuth et al., 2000). The results of two meta-analyses (Allen, D'Alessio, & Brezgel, 1995; Allen, D'Alessio, & Emmers-Sommer, 1999), however, suggest a statistical association between pornography and sexual offending. Initially, the results show that exposure to stimuli (images) whose content is not violent, degrading or humiliating would not encourage men to take aggressive actions against women in the experimental laboratory context. In fact, the opposite is observed as men are less likely to exhibit aggressive behaviors when exposed to nudity alone in experimental laboratory settings. However, exposure to pornography, violent or nonviolent, appears to increase the use of aggressive behaviors in experimental laboratory setting (Allen et al., 1995). Is it possible to generalize these results outside the laboratory and the experimental setting of these studies?

The link between pornography and sexual offending remains unclear. One hypothesis is that these two variables are correlated but not causally related. The correlation exists only because: (a) some other factor is responsible for both the consumption of pornography and sexual offending; or, (b) consumption of pornography influences sexual offending only when certain other conditions are met. According to the sociocultural perspective, sexual offending does not reflect spur of the moment and impulsive acts, but reflects false beliefs about women, children, and sexuality. Repeated exposure to pornographic material can promote the development of such beliefs. More than 30 years ago, in an American study, Burt (1980) spoke of the importance of harmful stereotypes and false beliefs among the population, particularly with regard to women and victims of rape and sexual assault; women secretly want to be raped; most women lie about having been raped; women who dress provocatively want to have sex; victims deserved to be raped; a woman invites a date back to her place solely because she wants to have sex. The results of the Burt (1980) study, later confirmed by the work of Malamuth and his colleagues (1991), showed that adherence to these stereotypes are particularly important in individuals who adhere to sexist attitudes and who perceive violence as a legitimate means of resolving interpersonal problems. In other words, individuals who are prone to revert to violence tends to hold negative views about women and false beliefs about rape and sexual assault.

Clearly, these sexists and proviolence attitudes are unlikely to inhibit one's behavior in a sexual context especially if that person holds false beliefs about women's sexuality and rape. For example, the work of Polaschek and Gannon (2004) goes further by characterizing the cognitive schemas (or implicit theories) of individuals who have perpetrated a sexual offense against a woman. Their study findings revealed some relatively constant themes in these perpetrators' narratives about women and sexuality in general. More specifically, these men tended to believe that women are sexual objects, but also dangerous, harmful, and unpredictable. These men also believe that they are entitled to fulfill their own sexual needs with no regard for the needs of others, and that their sexual desires and excitement are difficult to control. These cognitive schemas are likely to significantly taint their interpretations of complex social and sexual interactions. While these observations are interesting, the research findings should be interpreted with caution: these narratives were reported after these individuals perpetrated an offense, were detected, arrested, charged, and convicted for these acts. Could it be that perpetrators' experience with the criminal justice system influenced these views about women and sexuality or that these views contributed to their offending? The origin and development of false beliefs (also called cognitive distortions) remain speculative (Beech & Ward, 2004).

Sociobiologically Driven, Socioculturally Molded

Although sociobiological and sociocultural positions are apparently diametrically opposed, these two perspectives are not irreconcilable according to Malamuth (1998) (see also Ward & Siegert, 2002). Research from sociobiology and evolutionary psychology evokes a certain predisposition for the search of impersonal sex and partner variety in certain males. However, such research does not explain the use of coercive, aggressive, and violent strategies used by these individuals who are struggling with a non-consenting partner. Sociocultural theories, without denying the biological basis of human behavior, place a decisive role on the environment, norms, values, and social representations in the expression of human behavior. Sociobiological as well as sociocultural approaches present hypotheses whose limits are obvious regarding certain manifestations associated with sexual offending. In fact, sociobiological and sociocultural theories have been limited to the description and explanation of rape and sexual assault against women, leaving out several manifestations associated with sexual offending such as sexual harassment, sexual exploitation, and other forms of sexual aggression. How, from an evolutionary point of view, does sexual contact with an eight-year-old allow the abuser to improve his or her evolutionary success? How does one explain, from the sociobiological thesis, a sexual homicide? Can the behavior of a female teacher who sexually assaults a boy be explained by a patriarchal society and societal values that reinforce the subjugation of women? These questions remain unanswered and suggest that sociobiological and sociocultural theses offer incomplete explanations to all forms of sexual offending. Clearly, these theoretical perspectives are not parsimonious and yet despite this complexity they still require additional components that are well beyond these two broad perspectives. While sociobiological and sociocultural perspectives present distinct schools of thought, more recent integrated theories of sexual offending represent, in many cases, efforts to integrate these two perspectives, while broadening the explanatory framework.

Debates between sociobiological and sociocultural theorists favored the development of a third perspective, more deeply rooted in the field of human development (e.g., Marshall, 1989; Marshall, Hudson, & Hodkinson, 1993; Smallbone, 2006; Smallbone & Cale, 2015; Ward & Siegert, 2002).

This third line of explanations was framed around the idea that sociobiological and sociocultural factors come into play in the origins and development of sexual offending. One of the most comprehensive formulations of this approach was initially proposed by Marshall and Barbaree (1984) as a theory of rape but later reformulated as a general theory of sexual offending (Marshall & Barbaree, 1990). Marshall and Barbaree's multifactorial explanatory model revolves around the key role of attachment as an etiological factor in sexual offending. According to this model, sexual offending is the result of biological and social factors that not only promote behavioral disinhibition against sexual offending but also cause significant interference in acquisition of behavior inhibitions against sexual offending. In other words, the theoretical model suggests that sexual offending does not develop overnight and involves a long developmental process with its roots in early childhood. The model suggests that, at birth, humans have two normal instincts or drives that are largely undifferentiated, namely a sexual drive and aggression. The process of socialization is really important during childhood to allow humans to dissociate these two impulses, but also to learn the skills necessary to inhibit their manifestations in certain contexts.

According to this theory, these developmental tasks can be particularly difficult for children whose parents have poor or limited parenting skills and whose family context is characterized by abuse and violence. More specifically, this theory suggests that during their childhood, perpetrators of sexual offenses are characterized by an inadequate attachment bond with their caregivers, characterized by insecurity, mistrust and lack of self-confidence. This insecure attachment is the result of difficult experiences in the family environment. This environment may include aversive childhood experiences such as parental conflicts, divorce, physical or psychological violence, parental neglect, and some form of abuse. Still according to this hypothesis, these negative childhood experiences do not allow the child to develop the necessary skills to discover and explore his social environment and establish bonds of trust and intimacy with others (see also, Cicchetti & Lynch, 1995; Marshall et al., 1993). Such difficult childhood experiences and inadequate socialization processes create a context of vulnerability in which the child cannot develop the necessary behavioral inhibitions for the regulation of aggressive and sexual behaviors. This is especially difficult during the period of adolescence, marked by puberty and an increase in testosterone for young males. According to this model, aggressive teenagers see their prosocial interactions increasingly limited, because the rejection by their peers significantly affects their confidence and their personal image. At the same time, such negative peer-to-peer interactions feed their growing hostility towards their peers. In that context, they are then more receptive to certain sociocultural messages promoting violence and negative attitudes toward others, including women, for example, through pornographic material. Continued exposure to these messages can gradually become beliefs as their negative peer-to-peer interactions continue. For Marshall and Barbaree (1990), at puberty, these negative and hostile images and false beliefs play an important role in masturbatory activities and facilitate the emergence of deviant sexual fantasies and deviant sexual interests. These individuals, struggling with hostile cognitive schemes, limited social skills, and negative and difficult interpersonal relationships, gradually become at risk of perpetrating a sexual offense, especially if situational disinhibitors are present, such as alcohol or drugs and intense negative emotions.

Ward and Siegert (2002) questioned one of the main premises of Marshall and Barbaree's (1990) multifactorial model. Indeed, Marshall and Barbaree's central premise is that, at the core of the origin of sexual offending is a disinhibition issue: perpetrators of sexual offenses have not learned the skills necessary to control innate drives that can manifest themselves in a sexual context. Without challenging this view, Ward and Siegert (2002) argue that this picture is incomplete. In other words, in their view, not all perpetrators of sexual offenses lack self-control over their aggressive and/or sexual drive. Ward and Siegert evoke other regulatory issues that can lead someone to perpetrate a sexual offense. Self-regulation refers to the psychological processes involved in setting goals and planning, monitoring, evaluating, and modifying actions to optimally achieve a goal (Barkley, 2001). Executive functions of the brain play a key role in the regulation of thoughts, emotions, and behavior. The presence and the role of executive function deficits on regulatory function of the brain have been hypothesized and shown to play a key role in the development of a persistent antisocial trajectory (Farrington, 2007; Loeber, Farrington, Stouthamer-Loeber, & White, 2008; Moffitt, 1993). The same mechanisms, therefore, could play a determining role in perpetrators' self-regulatory functions in multiple ways (e.g., Joyal, Black, & Dassylva, 2007).

In this regard, Ward and Hudson (2000) proposed a conceptual framework to study the origin and development of sexual offending by focusing on these self-regulatory mechanisms: (a) individuals who possess inadequate regulation mechanisms and may be characterized by general disinhibition of emotions and behaviors such as low self-control; (b) those who use inappropriate emotional and behavioral strategies to modulate their emotions and behavior to manage, avoid or escape intense and/or persistent negative emotions, such as anger, rage, and loneliness; and, (c) those whose self-regulation mechanisms are relatively adequate, but are distinguished by attitudes, beliefs, and values that support sexual offending, such as false or distorted beliefs about sexuality, women, children. In other words, Ward and Hudson (2000) suggested that sexual offenses could occur because someone made thoughtless and impulsive decisions, because these actions provide inadequate alternatives to cope with intense/persistent negative emotions, or out of a sense of entitlement because such actions are perceived as being justified, without serious consequences, and pleasurable. What this framework suggests is the presence of different developmental pathways leading someone to perpetrate a sexual offense.

In their integrated theory, Smallbone and Cale (2015) proposed to understand how and why particular developmental pathways can result in a specific sexual offense, at a specific time, in a specific place. At the foundational level, they argued that human evolution provides the universal potential for both prosocial and antisocial behavior. In line with the conceptual framework of Ward and Hudson and Marshall and Barbaree, they argued that positive socialization generally serves to constrain, but not eliminate, the biological potential for antisocial behavior, including sexual violence, through mechanisms like empathy, emotional regulation, and moral reasoning. At the same time, positive socialization also provides the foundation for socially responsible emotional and physical intimacy through mechanisms such as perspective-taking, self-confidence, trust and social skills. As described earlier, vulnerabilities in either of these contexts can influence an individual likelihood of perpetrating a sexual offense. The lack of exposure to prosocial models and weakening of inhibitions can come from sociocultural norms, disorganized neighborhoods, dysfunctional families, and peer influence.

The point here is that risk factors for, and protective factors against, sexual offending can be located at various levels of ecological systems over the life course in which potential perpetrators and potential victims are embedded. Furthermore, they argued that risk and protective factors more proximal to the individual exert the most direct effects; disruptions in family and peer systems that are close to the individual exert more direct effects on a person's behavior compared to neighborhood disorganization and sociocultural norms. Finally, and perhaps most critically, they argued that the development of such a propensity alone is not sufficient to robustly explain how sexual offenses occur. Various developmental risk factors for sexual offending behavior form the backdrop against which situational elements that they argue exert at least equally as strong an influence on behavior can occur (see Mischel et al., 1968). Certain situations provide opportunities for sex offense-related motivations to emerge, but they also contain dynamic properties that can serve to precipitate sexual offense-related motivations that would otherwise not occur. Taken together, their integrated theory proposes that biological and developmental factors interact to produce general individual vulnerabilities for antisocial behavior, including sexual offending, and that sex offenses occur when these vulnerabilities converge with situational factors of immediate behavioral settings that also arise from the ecological systems in which perpetrators and victims are socially embedded.

While these potential developmental pathways are informative, they remain highly speculative given the absence of empirical research testing these hypotheses. These hypothesized models, however, offer a valuable framework for the description of the propensity or propensities to perpetrate sexual offenses.

Propensity to Perpetrate Sexual Offenses

In mid 1980s, in the midst of the feminist movements and their fight against rape culture, Neil M. Malamuth, a Professor of psychology at the University of California Los Angeles surveyed a group of 367 male undergraduate students enrolled in an introductory psychology class. The survey consisted of a series of questions aiming to assess their attraction to a series of conventional and unconventional sexual activities, deviant sex and sexual aggression, which included rape (Malamuth, Check, & Briere, 1986; Malamuth, 1989). In total, 288 students returned questionnaires that provided complete data to all questions included in the survey. There are various reasons why someone did not participate in the study or did not fully complete the questionnaire. However, the researchers did not provide additional detail about why some students did not have complete data. Of particular interest, the survey included an item that asked students how likely, if at all, they would commit a rape if they could be assured that no one would know and that they could in no way be punished for engaging in such acts. Students were given a five-point scale response format, from "not at all" to "very likely." In total, 74% of these young men reported that under no circumstances would they commit a rape. Less than 2% indicated that they would very likely take the opportunity to rape someone. The remaining 24% of participants therefore were somewhat indecisive about their likelihood of perpetrating such actions. In comparison, 91% of the same men reported that under no circumstances would they engage in pedophilic acts. Men's responses were more ambiguous when asked how likely they would be to force a female to do something she did not want to. Indeed, only about 42% of this group said not at all while 5% said they were very likely to force a female if their actions went undetected and unpunished. The question was not specific to sexual activities, which might explain the ambiguity of their responses. It does suggest, however, that when looking at broad antisocial actions such as the use of force and coercion, men's responses suggest more openness to such actions than those that are social taboos such as rape or pedophilia. It also suggests that this openness to one component of complex social situations such as rape and sexual coercion might explain how and why a somewhat innocent encounter could potentially escalate to something more dramatic.

The question is hypothetical and does not inquire about having perpetrated a sexual offense but rather about a person's attitude and attractions toward such actions. The concept of attraction to sexual offenses is one of many hypotheses used by researchers to determine the presence of a propensity for sexual offending. One key element of the motive of perpetrators of a sexual offense remains: what is the nature of such propensity? Such propensity refers to relatively stable and fixed individual differences that increase someone's likelihood of perpetrating a sexual offense. As Malamuth's (1989) findings show, not all young adult men secretly desire or wish they could rape or coerce someone into sex. There are individual differences associated with the perpetration of sexual offending and such differences have been approached through the idea of individual propensity for sexual offending. As we have seen thus far, these individual differences may be genetic and biological, sociocultural and contextual, and/or developmental and psychological. Such propensity may act in a way that it disregards someone's inability to consent to sexual activities or even contribute to overcoming a victim's lack of consent. Such propensity can lead to the perpetration of sexual offenses that are sexually motivated, non-sexually motivated or a combination of both. Researchers will speak of a latent propensity for this specific reason: this propensity is not directly observable, but it can be measured and tested through the identification of its traits. Such propensity is, in many respects, somewhat elusive and difficult to circumscribe. It does not even have a name while being responsible for some of the most serious offending behaviors. Researchers have proposed various labels over the years, but they remain hypothetical. This alone speaks of the difficulties encountered by researchers whose work aims to describe and explain sexual offending.

The nature of such a propensity remains somewhat controversial and debated among researchers (Fig. 4.2.). The controversial aspect of this issue stems from the underlying assumption accepted by many that perpetrators of sexual offenses are a distinct group of individuals who share certain characteristics that compel them to

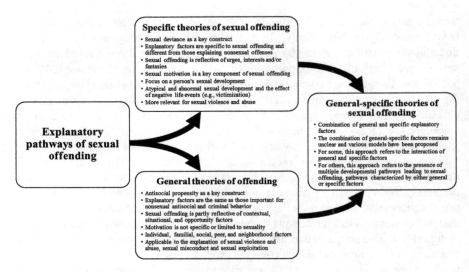

Fig. 4.2 Theoretical perspectives about sexual offending

perpetrate sexual offenses. This statement seems so obvious that even certain researchers have overlooked the issue of the specificity of perpetrators of sexual offenses. Other researchers have argued that this underlying assumption merits more scrutiny. According to Lussier, Proulx, and LeBlanc (2005), distinctive meta-theoretical perspectives have proposed propensity models of sexual offending. These meta-theoretical approaches of classifying theories of sexual offending have since been adopted by other researchers to organize the theoretical development within the field of research (e.g., Harris, Mazerolle, & Knight, 2009; Seto & Lalumière, 2010). These meta-theoretical perspectives refer to sets of theories that are based on different assumptions about the specificity of the propensity to perpetrate sexual offenses. Is sexual offending a distinct and unique form of offending? Are perpetrators of sexual offenses characterized by a unique and distinctive propensity for such actions? Does this form of offending require a distinct and unique theoretical model?

The General and Specific Propensity to Sexually Offend

The general and specific perspective on the propensity to perpetrate a sexual offense is based on the premise that the etiology of sexual offending is more or less identical to that of nonsexual antisocial and criminal behaviors (Felson, 2002; Gottfredson & Hirschi, 1990; Lussier, Proulx, & LeBlanc, 2005). Tenets of the general propensity hypothesis argue that there is little specificity to sexual offenses and that sexual offending is another manifestation of a general propensity to perpetrate antisocial and criminal acts. According to this viewpoint, there is nothing significantly different about the propensity to perpetrate a sexual offense that a general theory of antisocial and criminal behavior cannot explain. Tenets of the specificity propensity hypothesis, however, argue that perpetrators of sexual offenses have unique and distinctive characteristics that compel them to act that way. In fact, tenets of the specificity hypothesis argue that there is something specific about the propensity to perpetrate sexual offenses, but also something specific to various sex offenses. This sort of theoretical positioning has led tenets of the specificity hypothesis to elaborate theories of rape, sexual aggression of women, child sexual abuse, incest, sexual homicide, sexual aggression during wartime, sexual harassment, to name only a few. In all, the general propensity hypothesis offers a more parsimonious explanation to the perpetration of antisocial and criminal acts that can be applied to sexual offenses while specific theories of sexual offending aim to identify what is so unique and special about perpetrators of sexual offenses.

Historically, the specific propensity hypothesis has been, by and far, the most influential and advocated perspective to describe and explain sexual offending. For years, however, researchers have challenged the so-called specificity of sexual offending. More than six decades ago, Radzinowicz (1957) noted that the personal characteristics of perpetrators of sexual offenses were more or less identical to those who had perpetrated other forms of crime: burglars, con artists, bank robbers, violent intimate partners, drug dearlers, etc. Tappan (1951) criticized the untested claims of specificity characterizing perpetrators of sexual offenses. These suggestions, however, never really resonated within the clinical research community whose vision has been, and remains, focused on the assumption of specificity. These observations and the conclusions of Radzinowicz and Tappan will be rediscovered a few decades later by Adler (1984) and Simon (1997) who both questioned the sex offender label given the relatively diverse and varied criminal background of perpetrators of sexual offenses. Why such a label when these individuals have also robbed, stolen, threatened, beaten or burglarized others? Was the "sex offender" label hiding a more complex reality about these perpetrators? Could the perpetration of a sexual offense reveal more about the characteristics of a person than their involvement in other crimes? As the empirical evidence accumulated about the lack of specificity of their criminal backgrounds, researchers called into question the sex offender label, such as DeLisi (2001), Felson (2002), Lussier (2005), Smallbone and Wortley (2004) as well as Harris et al. (2009). Indeed, the measures of past criminal behavior, whether it based on police data (Adler, 1984; Bard et al., 1987; DeLisi, 2001; Gebhard et al., 1965; Lussier, Proulx, & LeBlanc, 2005; Radzinowicz, 1957; Simon, 2000) self-reported data (Weinrott & Saylor, 1991), as well as measures of post-release criminal recidivism (Broadhurst & Maller, 1992; Gibbens, Soothill, & Way, 1981; Soothill, Francis, Sanderson, & Ackerley, 2000), show that these individuals are involved in a variety of antisocial and criminal behaviors.

The general perspective recognizes, first and foremost, that sexual offending is an antisocial behavior in the same way as nonsexual antisocial behaviors (Smallbone, 2006). Proponents of the criminogenic hypothesis point to several conceptual similarities between antisocial and criminal behavior and sexual offending (see Lussier & Beauregard, 2018). Like antisocial and criminal behavior, sexual offenses involve a transgression of rules; a violation of others' rights. The conceptual similarities are such that these behaviors coexist in many ways. Perpetrators of sexual offenses will notably resort to antisocial or nonsexual criminal behaviors in order to commit a sexual offense: lying to the victim in order to gain his/her trust; using a disguise to gain the trust of a child by claiming to be a police officer; grabbing the victim's genitals without consent; not taking no for an answer and pressuring someone into sex; threatening to beat and injure the victim if he/she communicates with the police; intoxicating a victim without her/his knowledge for the purpose of sexually assaulting that person; entering the victim's residence illegally to sexually assault that person; hitting and beating a victim who resists a sexual assault; lying about his/her age to lure a child over the internet; stealing personal belongings, money and a credit card from a sexual assault victim; kidnapping a victim for the purpose of sexually assaulting that person; using or threatening to use a weapon to force a victim to comply with the perpetrator's request; killing the victim after sexually assaulting that person out of pleasure or to minimize the risk of detection and arrest, etc. In short, antisocial and nonsexual criminal actions are an integral part of most, if not all, sexual offenses. Why isolate the sexual nature of the act rather than analyze the act as a whole, including sexual and nonsexual components of the offense? If antisocial acts are an integral part of most sexual offenses, then what are such actions?

The multifaceted concept of antisocial behavior is well known to criminologists, sociologists, and psychologists. In fact, several empirical studies based on different research methodologies have confirmed the presence of an antisocial behavior syndrome (Bartusch, Lynam, Moffitt, & Silva, 1997; Dembo et al., 1992; Donovan & Jessor, 1985; LeBlanc & Bouthillier, 2003; LeBlanc & Girard, 1997; Osgood, Johnston, O'Malley, & Bachman, 1988; Zhang, Welte, & Wieczorek, 2002). These studies have shown that this syndrome which manifests itself in different ways is best characterized by various dimensions (LeBlanc & Bouthillier, 2003; LeBlanc & Girard, 1997; Osgood et al., 1988). Through empirical examination and testing, this line of research has helped to identify the presence of four distinct dimensions to this antisocial behavior syndrome: (a) authority-conflict behaviors, which refer to being oppositional, defiant, and rebellious with authority figures and rules; (b) reckless and dangerous behavior which refers to behaviors that indicates a certain disregard for someone's own safety and well-being or that of others (substance use and abuse, dangerous and reckless driving, unprotected sexual intercourse, driving while impaired, etc.); (c) covert behaviors which refer to more sneaky, illicit, and hidden behaviors such as theft, fraud, repeated lies, and; (d) overt behavior which refer to aggressive and violent behaviors such threatening, biting, hitting, assaulting, killing someone, etc.

What the antisocial syndrome suggests is that these behavioral dimensions are manifestations of an antisocial propensity: individuals prone to antisocial actions will be rebellious, reckless, and dangerous, and perpetrate covert and overt antisocial behaviors. It is also expected that these rebellious, reckless and dangerous, covert and overt antisocial behaviors can facilitate and lead to the perpetration of a sexual offense. First and foremost, sexual offending refers to a series of antisocial acts that are interpersonal transgressions. Sexual violence and abuse, sexual misconduct, and sexual exploitation are various forms of interpersonal transgression. A central component for this type of transgression is acting without the victim's consent. Sexual offending is about breaking rules of conduct, whether moral, social, interpersonal, and/or sexual. Sexual offending is also about showing a certain disregard for such rules, irrespective of what the consequences of these actions might be for others.

These transgressions include overt, covert, reckless, and authority-conflict antisocial behaviors, which can play a significant part at various stages of the perpetration of a sexual offense (i.e., before, during, after). At each stage, perpetrators may revert to the use of antisocial tactics such as intimidation, threats, dishonesty, lies and fraud, reckless and dangerous behaviors, as well as aggression and violence. Such antisocial tactics may be used to lure a potential victim, to gain the victim's trust, to access a particular location where the offense will take place, to take the victim to a specific location to perpetrate a sexual offense, or to create a context conducive to a sexual offense by grooming the victim (e.g., gifts, favors, seduction). Such antisocial behaviors, especially overt behaviors, may be also be used to force the victim to perform sexual acts, to perform sexual acts on the victim, to restraint the victim for the duration of the offense, to control a resisting victim, etc. Antisocial behaviors (e.g., threats) may also be used in such a way as to avoid detection or the reporting to the police. Considering this, it is not surprising that individuals who are repeatedly involved in antisocial and nonsexual crimes are more likely to perpetrate diverse sexual offending acts of various severity. This is not meant to say that only antisocial individuals are perpetrating sexual offenses, but rather individuals who are prone to antisocial behaviors are more likely to perpetrate a sexual offense. The important convergence of antisociality and sexual offending suggests that theories of sexual offending should start with general propensity considerations and not what is supposedly unique and different about perpetrators of sexual offenses. In all, as suggested by Wikström (2014), if we can understand why people break rules more generally, we can then begin to understand why they break the rules of consent more specifically. This simple lesson has been more or less overlooked by researchers until recently.

Antisocial Propensity to Sexually Offend

Early etiological models focused on sexual deviance discounted the role and importance of antisocial propensity to perpetrate sexual offenses (for a discussion, Lussier & Mathesius, 2018). Empirical research has shown, however, that a general antisocial propensity should be at the core of a theoretical propensity model of sexual offending (Lussier, Proulx, & LeBlanc, 2005; Lussier, LeBlanc, & Proulx, 2005).

Criminological research suggests that an antisocial propensity is composed of at least three distinctive dimensions or traits (e.g., Caspi et al., 1994; Jones, Miller, & Lynam, 2011; Lahey & Waldman, 2003, 2005; Miller & Lynam, 2001; Morizot & LeBlanc, 2003). The number and nature of these dimensions remain somewhat debatable and the subject of discussion among criminologists and psychologists (e.g., Jones et al., 2011; Morizot & LeBlanc, 2005). While early propensity theorists simply recognized the presence of stable and fixed individual differences associated with antisocial and criminal behavior, contemporary theoretical models were more specific about the nature of this antisocial propensity and its dimensions. Across these contemporary propensity models of antisocial and criminal behavior, researchers generally allude to the presence of three distinct traits or dimensions.

The most well-known and documented dimensions of this antisocial propensity refer to behavioral inhibition. This stream of criminological research has been examined primarily by control theories of antisocial and criminal behavior (e.g., DeLisi & Vaughn, 2008; Gottfredson & Hirschi, 1990; LeBlanc, 2005). This dimension is referred to when discussing perpetrators' impulsive, here-and-now orientation, as well as daring and adventurous tendencies. Individuals with limited behavioral inhibition tend to have more difficulties delaying gratification, persevering when facing difficulties, and considering consequences of their behavior prior to acting (Farrington, 2007; Gottfredson & Hirschi, 1990; Wilson & Herrnstein, 1986). Behavioral inhibitions help people adhere to the rules, moral code, and laws of a particular social environment in spite of a person's own preferences, motivations and moral code. They may be weakened, however, by situational factors such as alcohol and drugs, intense negative emotional states and moods, and peer pressure. In effect, for some, behavioral inhibitions may be low because of more innate neurocognitive or personality deficits; for others, behavioral inhibitions may be low due to situational factors. The latter may be especially important for understanding why persons may offend at one point in time but not another despite being in a similar situation or context.

The second dimension refers to the emotional component of the antisocial propensity and refers to negative emotionality. This dimension refers to a certain vulnerability when faced with frustrating, difficult, and stressful life events. This stream of research has been documented and described by more recent strain theories of antisocial and criminal behavior (e.g., Agnew, 1992, 2001; Baron, 2004; Broidy, 2001). When discussing perpetrators' individual characteristics, criminologists will refer to their tendency to overreact to difficult situations, easily lose their temper, experience anger, and even rage. Negative emotionality also refers to a person's limited coping skills when faced with difficult situations as well as their tendency to have conflictual and difficult relations with others as a result of their strong and intense negative emotional reactions. Individuals characterized by negative emotionality will be vulnerable to situations such as having difficulties reaching valued goals and objectives (e.g., being turned down by someone he/she is physically attracted to), when losing something valued (e.g., a partner who was ending an intimate relationship) or when confronted with a negative experience (e.g., being insulted by a female stranger).

The third component of the antisocial propensity is a person's moral code and consideration for others (Lahey & Waldman, 2003, 2005; Wikström, 2014). Criminologists have discussed this dimension of the antisocial propensity using many terms such as a person's tendency to be egotistic, selfish and immature, centered around their own need and well-being and disregard for other people's needs and well-being, a lack concern for others, less prone to spontaneously share, help and be kind to others. Others have also noted that perpetrators tend to be callous and unemotional, lack empathy, are emotionally detached, insensitive to other people's distress and pain, unremorseful when breaking rules, unapologetic or feeling guilty when violating the moral code and laws of a particular setting. As emphasized by Wikström (2014), crimes are moral actions that are guided by what the perpetrator believes to be the right or wrong thing to do under particular circumstances. What is right and wrong from the perpetrator's perspective may not necessarily be the same from a moral and legal standpoint in a particular social environment.

Neil Malamuth and his colleagues were among the first to empirically demonstrate the role and importance of antisociality in sexual offending (Malamuth et al., 1991; Malamuth, 1998, 2003). Their confluence propensity model of sexual offending against women integrates, on the one hand, different components of sociological and feminist theories and, on the other hand, components of sociobiological and evolutionary psychology. For Malamuth and his colleagues, the propensity for sexual offending is articulated around the following principles. This propensity is the result of the interactions between biological, cultural, and individual factors. It is deeply rooted in early family experiences and in the exposure to patterns of violence that foster the development of hostile, cynical, and conflicting cognitive patterns of male–female relationships. According to this model, children exposed to patterns of abuse and violence are more likely to associate with delinquent peers who interfere with the development of prosocial problem-solving skills, particularly with respect to frustrations and interpersonal conflicts. As a result of the continued influence of delinquent peers, according to Malamuth's thesis, these youth are more likely to develop an antisocial identity as well as a here-and-now perspective. This antisocial identity, where everything is allowed and where only the present is important, is manifested in various life functions, like school and work, but also in interpersonal relationships, including sexual activities.

In keeping with sociobiological theses, Malamuth and his colleagues hypothesized that these young people with abusive and violent cognitive schemas and under the influence of delinquent peers are more likely to be characterized by short-term mating effort or sociosexuality. In Malamuth's terms, these individuals will be prone to an impersonal sexuality characterized by a succession of one-night stands and "sexual conquests," sexual encounters without legitimate emotional investment, the use of escorts and prostitution, etc. Similar to Marshall and Barbaree's model (Marshall & Barbaree, 1990), Malamuth's model emphasized the role and importance of the sociocultural environment as contributing to the propensity to perpetrate sexual offenses against women. A sociocultural environment that promotes masculinity as a reflection of strength and power, robustness and dominance, aggression, and competitive instinct promotes the reinforcement of hostile cognitive patterns, which Malamuth and colleagues refer to as a "negative masculinity" (also called hostile masculinity). Individuals with such a negative masculinity, character-ized by an impersonal and unbridled sexuality, are more likely to use coercive and violent strategies in a sexual context. These men certainly do not fear the rejection of women, considering the negative image they have of them. For Malamuth and his colleagues, therefore, the propensity for sexual offending is articulated around two dimensions, an impersonal sexuality and a negative masculinity, both of which have distinct etiological origins. While Malamuth and colleagues' propensity model did not evoke an antisocial propensity directly, these two dimensions are certainly con-gruent with an antisocial propensity (e.g., Malamuth, 2003).

The role and importance of an antisocial propensity in the perpetration of sexual offenses subsequently became more explicit. Malamuth and colleagues' confluence propensity model did not seem to represent the clinical reality of perpetrators of sexual offenses in prison and psychiatric hospital settings. After all, the confluence model was elaborated and empirically examined by testing and interviewing college and university students. It is in this context that Knight and Sims-Knight (2003) proposed an explanation of sexual offending against women centered around fea-tures of psychopathy. This approach was not based on the already rejected concept of sexual psychopathy (e.g., Karpman, 1951), but rather on a contemporary concep-tualization of psychopathy as a personality disorder (Hare & Neumann, 2008). The empirical validation work done by Knight and Sims-Knight extended and chal-lenged Malamuth's confluence propensity model in several ways. Knight and Sims-Knight emphasized the role and importance of psychopathy and traits associated with psychopathy in individuals who have committed a sexual offense. According to this etiological model, the development of psychopathy is rooted in a family environment that is particularly abusive and violent. More specifically, according to this model, exposure to a violent family environment promotes, on the one hand, callous and unemotional features of personality, and on the other hand, the develop-ment of antisocial and aggressive behavior.

While Knight and Sims-Knight (2003) remained relatively silent about the mechanisms that explain these connections, they present a particularly distinct pic-ture of the perpetrators of sexual offenses against women. The image of Knight and Sims-Knight's perpetrator of sexual offenses was not one of a sexist and hostile individual seeking sexual conquests as espoused by Malamuth and colleagues, but of one of a tough, aggressive, rebellious, callous, and violent individual with a gen-eral insensitivity to women, men, and children alike. Knight and Sims-Knight's model presents a developmental profile that emphasizes the importance of early antisocial behavior and callousness toward others. Therefore, according to these authors, these young people have interpersonal relationships characterized by lies, manipulation, and taking advantage of others. As Malamuth (2003) pointed out, Knight and Sims-Knight's model is not entirely inconsistent with the confluence propensity model. Impersonal sexuality and negative masculinity, the two dimen-sions of Malamuth's propensity for sexual offending are conceptually related with psychopathy. Callousness and unemotional individuals, key elements of psychopa-thy, can promote adherence to hostile and sexist cognitive schemas of thinking about women. Interpersonal features of psychopathy are also conducive to negative interactions with women that involve manipulation, deceit, and interpersonal dominance.

An important departure between the two propensity models, however, is Knight and Sims-Knight's emphasis on hypersexuality. Indeed, according to these authors, perpetrators of sexual offenses are not so much characterized by a short-term mating effort, but rather by a hypersexuality which they refer to as an invasive and compulsive sexuality. The origin of hypersexuality is said to be deeply rooted in early sexual victimization experienced during childhood but the mechanisms responsible for this were not outlined by the authors. This hypersexuality, therefore, suggested a view that perpetrators of sexual offenses are characterized by intense and persistent sexual urges that manifest in various ways, including conventional and unconventional sexual activities. This propensity for sexual offending, therefore, portrays the perpetrator as an antisocial, aggressive, and callous individual, whose lack of empathy, combined with hypersexuality, favors the emergence of sexually violent thoughts, images, and fantasies that not only orient but also disinhibit their behavior in a manner that increases the risk of sexual offending.

Propensity alone does not explain the perpetration of a sexual offense as such explanations require taking into consideration situational and contextual factors (Smallbone & Cale, 2015; Gottfredson & Hirschi, 1990; LeBlanc, 2005; Wikström, 2014). Sexual offending is not simply the result of a propensity or inclination for antisocial behaviors. Circumstantial and contextual elements come into play. In this regard, Schwartz, DeKeseredy, Tait, and Alvi (2001) proposed and examined an explanatory model that draws on the assumptions of Malamuth and his collaborators, while developing the contextual dimensions of acting out. According to Schwartz and his colleagues (Schwartz et al., 2001), the routine activities of the individual play an important role in sexual offending. The authors, to support their hypothesis, rely on the phenomenon of sexual offending on American university campuses. This model is structured around the idea that the frequency and location of a crime are directly affected by the presence of three elements that meet in time and space: (a) the presence of a motivated individual to commit an offense; (b) the absence of a capable and available guardian; and (c) the presence and availability of an appropriate target.

Schwartz and his collaborators (Schwartz et al., 2001) argue that the convergence of these three criminogenic factors is conducive to sexual offending, particularly on American university campuses because of the simultaneous presence of sexually motivated young men, the presence of a pool of potential victims, in this case students, and the relative absence of guardians capable of detecting and even intervening if a potentially criminal situation unfolds. Like Malamuth and his collaborators (Malamuth et al., 1991), they argue that the university campus, especially the presence of male peer groups who subscribe to sexist attitudes and perceive violence in interpersonal relationships as legitimate, promotes acts of abuse and sexual violence against women when the opportunity arises. In addition, these individuals are reluctant to intervene when a woman is in a vulnerable position (intoxicated with alcohol), thus increasing the probability of sexual offending. Schwartz and his colleagues (Schwartz et al., 2001) conclude that students with friends who exhibit Malamuth's negative masculinity, who consume alcohol and drugs, find themselves in situations that are conducive to a sexual offense (e.g., parties, bars, initiation), are more likely to commit sexual offenses.

These situational and contextual factors are also differentially associated with different developmental pathways to sexual aggression. As described above, propensity alone cannot explain the perpetration of sexual offenses; we know the rates of sexual assault are typically higher in university settings given the convergence of potential perpetrators, potential victims, reduced guardianship, and disinhibitory situations such as parties involving alcohol, etc. Surely, however, not all university students are antisocial psychopaths. Seto and Barbaree (1997) and Lalumière et al. (2005) argued that here, the concept of "date-rape" in the adolescent and young adulthood years, can be explained by difficulties in adopting adult sexual roles in the face of social maturational barriers (e.g., lack of money, job, status, etc.). In effect, sexual aggression in this context represents a subset of risk factors that are circumstantial in nature and as individuals age and achieve positive prospects such as employment, wealth, and status, the need to employ coercion and aggression in a sexual context declines for most. In turn, this developmental pathway can be compared to one characterized by the accumulation of early risk factors (e.g., neuropsychological deficits) and the resulting consequences in adulthood such as unstable employment and lack of wealth and status, would limit the success of some men to acquire prosocial sexual encounters and maintain stable relationships. These reflect the men who are characterized by the antisocial propensity described above, who are more likely to simply opt to use coercive and aggressive tactics to acquire sexual relations. Finally, for others, they argued that sexual offending represents a third and distinct subset of causal factors. For example, rather than an inability to experience prosocial sexual encounters, some individuals purposely employ antisocial tactics such as deceit, manipulation, grandiosity, coercion, and aggression to create sexual opportunities and increase the frequency of their sexual experiences; these are the subset of men characterized by psychopathic personality characteristics described earlier whose sexual offending represents an alternative strategy to acquire multiple sexual partners, rather than a result of the inability to achieve sexual relations in a prosocial manner.

Conclusion

Sexual deviance and deviant sexual fantasies have been long considered prime candidates by researchers as key components of the propensity to perpetrate a sexual offense (e.g., Abel & Blanchard, 1974). Such views, however, cannot explain some of the basic observations about the origins and development of sexual offending. Alternatively, sociobiological, sociocultural, and psychosocial views have been provided. Sociobiological explanations' key themes are focused on the role and importance of sociosexuality and strategies used to increase the probabilities of passing on one's genes. Sociocultural explanations' key themes are centered on the gender imbalance and social processes used to maintain such imbalances. In both perspectives, sexual offenses refer to actions and means used to attain objectives that have little to do with sexual pleasure and sexual gratification. Sociobiological and sociocultural explanations of the origins of sexual offending provide an unsatisfactory and incomplete picture of the origins of sexual offending and all its manifestations. Clinical research suggests that there are multiple motives to perpetrate a sexual offense. These motives are so diverse across individuals and offenses that they can be sexual, nonsexual, and even both. Another problem is that the reasons for committing sexual offenses do not seem very unique from the reasons for why other individuals engage in consensual sexual behavior. The key underlying theme to sexual offending, however, is not perpetrators' desire to sexually harm someone, to obtain sexual gratifications, to dominate another person, to subjugate women, to feel some intimacy with another person, to act out deviant sexual fantasies or even to control and assert power over someone else. The myriad of motives only highlights the complexities of the contexts in which sexual offenses can be perpetrated.

The common underlying theme to all forms of sexual offenses is the victim's lack of consent to perpetrators' actions, irrespective of whether such action entails sexual violence and abuse, sexual misconduct or sexual exploitation. This notion of violating others by bypassing consent is not unique to sexual offending. It is associated with most all other forms of criminal behavior. At its core, sexual offending is a violation of another person and is very similar to other forms of antisocial and criminal behavior. Accordingly, some have argued that explanations of sex offending must begin with the notion of a general antisocial tendency. There are individual differences associated with sexual offending and such individual differences may be conceived as a propensity or proclivity to perpetrate sexual offenses. Contrary to popular belief, this propensity is not specific to sexual offending but it may manifest itself in a sexual context or a context conducive to sexual behaviors. Based on the current state of knowledge, an antisocial propensity appears to be a key etiological component of the origin and development of sexual offending. This is not saying all perpetrators of a sex crime meet the Diagnostic Statistical Manual-5 criteria for antisocial personality disorder. Rather, it is suggested that individuals who are more prone to perpetrate antisocial and criminal behavior are more likely to perpetrate a sex offense given the opportunity to do so.

Fundamentally, the criminogenic factors responsible for the perpetration of a sex crime are not different from those of antisocial and criminal behaviors. In fact, a common underlying theme is the perpetrator's unawareness and disregard for the victim's ability to consent to the actions or in spite of the victim's refusal and resistance to these actions. These actions are imposed through various antisocial rule-breaking means and transgressions, including coercive actions and violence, irrespective of the victim's active or passive resistance, their absence of consent, or even their inability to consent to these acts due to their mental state, age, intellectual capacity, etc. This idea is not new (Lalumière et al., 2005; Lussier, LeBlanc, & Proulx, 2005; Seto & Barbaree, 1997) but it has been broadly stated and limited to the explanation of rape and sexual assault. The conceptual link between antisocial propensity and sexual offending is such that one could think about sexual offending as *antisocial sexuality* (Cale & Lussier, 2011). Starting with the premise that sexual offending is, first and foremost, an antisocial act, may be an important way to begin theorizing about sexual offending in the twenty-first century.

References

Abel, G. G., & Blanchard, E. B. (1974). The role of fantasy in the treatment of sexual deviation. *Archives of General Psychiatry, 30*(4), 467–475.

Adler, C. (1984). The convicted rapist: A sexual or a violent offender? *Criminal Justice and Behavior, 11*(2), 157–177.

Agnew, R. (1992). Foundation for a general strain theory of crime and delinquency. *Criminology, 30*(1), 47–88.

Agnew, R. (2001). Building on the foundation of general strain theory: Specifying the types of strain most likely to lead to crime and delinquency. *Journal of Research in Crime and Delinquency, 38*(4), 319–361.

Allen, M., D'Alessio, D., & Brezgel, K. (1995). A meta–analysis summarizing the effects of pornography II aggression after exposure. *Human Communication Research, 22*(2), 258–283.

Allen, M., D'Alessio, D., & Emmers-Sommer, T. M. (1999). Reactions of criminal sexual offenders to pornography: A meta-analytic summary. *Annals of the International Communication Association, 22*(1), 139–169.

Archer, J. (1991). The influence of testosterone on human aggression. *British Journal of Psychology, 82*(1), 1–28.

Aromäki, A. S., Lindman, R. E., & Eriksson, C. P. (2002). Testosterone, sexuality and antisocial personality in rapists and child molesters: A pilot study. *Psychiatry Research, 110*(3), 239–247.

Bain, J., Langevin, R., Dickey, R., Hucker, S., & Wright, P. (1988). Hormones in sexually aggressive men: I. Baseline values for eight hormones/II. The ACTH test. *Annals of Sex Research, 1*(1), 63–78.

Bard, L. A., Carter, D. L., Cerce, D. D., Knight, R. A., Rosenberg, R., & Schneider, B. (1987). A descriptive study of rapists and child molesters: Developmental, clinical, and criminal characteristics. *Behavioral Sciences & the Law, 5*(2), 203–220.

Barkley, R. A. (2001). The executive functions and self-regulation: An evolutionary neuropsychological perspective. *Neuropsychology Review, 11*(1), 1–29.

Baron, L., & Straus, M. A. (1987). Four theories of rape: A macrosociological analysis. *Social Problems, 34*(5), 467–489.

Baron, L., Straus, M. A., & Jaffee, D. (1988). Legitimate violence, violent attitudes, and rape: A test of the cultural spillover theory. *Annals of the New York Academy of Sciences, 528*(1), 79–110.

Baron, S. W. (2004). General strain, street youth and crime: A test of Agnew's revised theory. *Criminology, 42*(2), 457–484.

Bartusch, D. R. J., Lynam, D. R., Moffitt, T. E., & Silva, P. A. (1997). Is age important? Testing a general versus a developmental theory of antisocial behavior. *Criminology, 35*(1), 13–48.

Beech, A. R., & Ward, T. (2004). The integration of etiology and risk in sexual offenders: A theoretical framework. *Aggression and Violent Behavior, 10*(1), 31–63.

Berlin, F. S. (1983). Sex offenders: A biomedical perspective and a status report on biomedical treatment. In J. G. Greer & I. R. Stuart (Eds.), *The sexual aggressor: Current perspectives on treatment* (pp. 83–123). New York: Van Nostrand Reinhold Company.

Blokland, A. A. J., & Lussier, P. (2015). *Sex offenders: A criminal career approach*. Oxford, UK: Wiley-Blackwell.

Bradford, J. M. W., & McLean, D. (1984). Sexual offenders, violence and testosterone: A clinical study. *The Canadian Journal of Psychiatry, 29*(4), 335–343.

Broadhurst, R. G., & Maller, R. A. (1992). The recidivism of sex offenders in the Western Australian prison population. *British Journal of Criminology, 32*(1), 54–80.

Broidy, L. M. (2001). A test of general strain theory. *Criminology, 39*(1), 9–36.

Brownmiller, S. (1975). *Against our will: Men, women, rape.* New York: Simon and Schuster.

Bryden, D. P., & Grier, M. M. (2011). The search for rapists' « real » motives. *The Journal of Criminal Law and Criminology, 101*(1), 171–278.

Burt, M. R. (1980). Cultural myths and supports for rape. *Journal of Personality and Social Psychology, 38*(2), 217–230.

Cale, J., & Lussier, P. (2011). Toward a developmental taxonomy of adult sexual aggressors of women: Antisocial trajectories in youth, mating effort, and sexual criminal activity in adulthood. *Violence and Victims, 26*(1), 16–32.

Cale, J., Lussier, P., & Proulx, J. (2009). Heterogeneity in antisocial trajectories in youth of adult sexual aggressors of women: An examination of initiation, persistence, escalation, and aggravation. *Sexual Abuse: A Journal of Research and Treatment, 21*(2), 223–248.

Cale, J., Leclerc, B., & Smallbone, S. (2014). The sexual lives of sexual offenders: The link between childhood sexual victimization and non-criminal sexual lifestyles between types of offenders. *Psychology, Crime & Law, 20*(1), 37–60.

Carnes, P. (2001). *Out of the shadows: Understanding sexual addiction.* Center City, MN: Hazelden Publishing.

Caspi, A., Moffitt, T. E., Silva, P. A., Stouthamer-Loeber, M., Krueger, R. F., & Schmutte, P. S. (1994). Are some people crime-prone? Replications of the personality-crime relationship across countries, genders, races, and methods. *Criminology, 32*(2), 163–196.

Chagnon, N. A. (1988). Life histories, blood revenge, and warfare in a tribal population. *Science, 239*(4843), 985–992.

Cicchetti, D., & Lynch, M. (1995). Failures in the expectable environment and their impact on individual development: The case of child maltreatment. In D. Cicchetti & D. J. Cohen (Eds.), *Wiley series on personality processes. Developmental psychopathology, volume 2. Risk, disorder, and adaptation* (pp. 32–71). Oxford, UK: John Wiley.

Clark, L. M., & Lewis, D. J. (1977). *Rape: The price of coercive sexuality.* Toronto: Women's Press.

Cohen, M. L., Garofalo, R., Boucher, R., & Seghorn, T. (1971). The psychology of rapists. *Seminars in Psychiatry, 3*, 307–327.

Coleman, E. (1992). Is your patient suffering from compulsive sexual behavior? *Psychiatric Annals, 22*(6), 320–325.

DeLisi, M. (2001). Extreme career criminals. *American Journal of Criminal Justice, 25*(2), 239–252.

DeLisi, M., & Vaughn, M. G. (2008). The Gottfredson–Hirschi critiques revisited: Reconciling self-control theory, criminal careers, and career criminals. *International Journal of Offender Therapy and Comparative Criminology, 52*(5), 520–537.

Dembo, R., Williams, L., Wothke, W., Schmeidler, J., Getreu, A., Berry, E., et al. (1992). The generality of deviance: Replication of a structural model among high-risk youths. *Journal of Research in Crime and Delinquency, 29*(2), 200–216.

Deslauriers-Varin, N., & Beauregard, E. (2010). Victims' routine activities and sex offenders' target selection scripts: A latent class analysis. *Sexual Abuse: A Journal of Research and Treatment, 22*(3), 315–342.

Donovan, J. E., & Jessor, R. (1985). Structure of problem behavior in adolescence and young adulthood. *Journal of Consulting and Clinical Psychology, 53*(6), 890–904.

Dworkin, R. (1981). Is there a right to pornography? *Oxford Journal of Legal Studies, 1*(2), 177–212.

Ellis, L. (1991). A synthesized (biosocial) theory of rape. *Journal of Consulting and Clinical Psychology, 59*(5), 631–642.

Farrington, D. P. (2007). Origins of violent behavior over the life span. In D. J. Flannery, A. T. Vazsonyi, & I. D. Waldman (Eds.), *The Cambridge handbook of violent behavior and aggression* (pp. 19–48). Cambridge, UK: Cambridge University Press.

Felson, R. B. (2002). *Violence and gender reexamined*. Washington, DC: American Psychological Association.

Fisher, W. A., & Grenier, G. (1994). Violent pornography, antiwoman thoughts, and antiwoman acts: In search of reliable effects. *Journal of Sex Research, 31*(1), 23–38.

Gebhard, P. H., Gagnon, J. H., Pomeroy, W. B., & Christenson, C. V. (1965). *Sex offenders: An analysis of types*. New York: Harper and Row.

Gibbens, T. C., Soothill, K. L., & Way, C. K. (1981). Sex offences against young girls: A long-term record study. *Psychological Medicine, 11*(02), 351–357.

Gley, E. (1884). Les aberrations de l'instinct sexuel: D'après des travaux récents. *Revue Philosophique de la France et de L'étranger, 17*, 66–92.

Goldberg, T. L., & Wrangham, R. W. (1997). Genetic correlates of social behaviour in wild chimpanzees: Evidence from mitochondrial DNA. *Animal Behaviour, 54*(3), 559–570.

Gottfredson, M., & Hirschi, T. (1990). *A general theory of crime*. Palo Alto, CA: Stanford University Press.

Groth, A. N., & Birnbaum, A. H. (1979). *Men who rape: The psychology of the offender*. New York: Plenum.

Hanson, R. K., & Thornton, D. (2000). *Static-99: Improving actuarial risk assessments for sex offenders (user report 99-02)*. Ottawa, ON: Department of the Solicitor General of Canada.

Hare, R. D., & Neumann, C. S. (2008). Psychopathy as a clinical and empirical construct. *Annual Review of Clinical Psychology, 4*, 217–246.

Harris, D. A., Mazerolle, P., & Knight, R. A. (2009). Understanding male sexual offending: A comparison of general and specialist theories. *Criminal Justice and Behavior, 36*(10), 1051–1069.

Harris, G. T., Rice, M. E., Hilton, N. Z., Lalumiere, M. L., & Quinsey, V. L. (2007). Coercive and precocious sexuality as a fundamental aspect of psychopathy. *Journal of Personality Disorders, 21*(1), 1–27.

Hill, C. A., & Preston, L. K. (1996). Individual differences in the experience of sexual motivation: Theory and measurement of dispositional sexual motives. *Journal of Sex Research, 33*(1), 27–45.

Jones, S. E., Miller, J. D., & Lynam, D. R. (2011). Personality, antisocial behavior, and aggression: A meta-analytic review. *Journal of Criminal Justice, 39*(4), 329–337.

Joyal, C. C., Black, D. N., & Dassylva, B. (2007). The neuropsychology and neurology of sexual deviance: A review and pilot study. *Sexual Abuse: A Journal of Research and Treatment, 19*(2), 155–173.

Kafka, M. P. (1997). Hypersexual desire in males: An operational definition and clinical implications for males with paraphilias and paraphilia-related disorders. *Archives of Sexual Behavior, 26*(5), 505–526.

Kafka, M. P. (2003). Sex offending and sexual appetite: The clinical and theoretical relevance of hypersexual desire. *International Journal of Offender Therapy and Comparative Criminology, 47*(4), 439–451.

Karpman, B. (1951). The sexual psychopath. *The Journal of Criminal Law, Criminology, and Police Science, 42*(2), 184–198.

Katz, J. (1988). *Seductions of crime: Moral and sensual attractions in doing evil*. New York: Basic Books.

Kennair, L. E. O., Grøntvedt, T. V., Mehmetoglu, M., Perilloux, C., & Buss, D. M. (2015). Sex and mating strategy impact the 13 basic reasons for having sex. *Evolutionary Psychological Science, 1*(4), 207–219.

Knight, R. A., & Prentky, R. A. (1990). Classifying sexual offenders: The development and corroboration of taxonomic models. In W. L. Marshall, D. R. Laws, & H. E. Barbaree (Eds.), *The handbook of sexual assault: Issues, theories and treatment of the offender* (pp. 23–52). New York: Plenum Press.

Knight, R. A., & Sims-Knight, J. E. (2003). The developmental antecedents of sexual coercion against women: Testing alternative hypotheses with structural equation modeling. *Annals of the New York Academy of Sciences, 989*(1), 72–85.

Koo, K. L. (2002). Confronting a disciplinary blindness: Women, war and rape in the international politics of security. *Australian Journal of Political Science, 37*(3), 525–536.

Krafft-Ebing, R. (1895). *Étude médico-légale: Psychopathia sexualis, avec recherches spéciales sur l'inversion sexuelle*. Paris, France: G. Carré.

Krueger, R. B., & Kaplan, M. S. (2001). The paraphilic and hypersexual disorders: An overview. *Journal of Psychiatric Practice, 7*(6), 391–403.

Lahey, B. B., & Waldman, I. D. (2003). A developmental propensity model of the origins of conduct problems during childhood and adolescence. In B. B. Lahey, T. E. Moffitt, & A. Caspi (Eds.), *Causes of conduct disorder and juvenile delinquency* (pp. 76–117). New York: Guilford Press.

Lahey, B. B., & Waldman, I. D. (2005). A developmental model of the propensity to offend during childhood and adolescence. *Advances in Criminological Theory, 13*, 15–50.

Lalumière, M. L., Harris, G. T., Quinsey, V. L., & Rice, M. E. (2005). *The causes of rape: Understanding individual differences in male propensity for sexual aggression*. Washington, DC: American Psychological Association.

Lalumière, M. L., & Quinsey, V. L. (1996). Sexual deviance, antisociality, mating effort, and the use of sexually coercive behaviors. *Personality and Individual Differences, 21*(1), 33–48.

Laws, D. R., & Barbaree, H. E. (1990). A conditioning theory of the etiology and maintenance of deviant sexual preference and behavior. In W. L. Marshall, D. R. Laws, & H. E. Barbaree (Eds.), *Handbook of sexual assault: Issues, theories, and treatment of the offender* (pp. 209–230). New York: Plenum Press.

LeBlanc, M. (2005). An integrative personal control theory of deviant behavior: Answers to contemporary empirical and theoretical developmental criminology issues. In D. P. Farrington (Ed.), *Integrated developmental and life-course theories of offending: Advances in criminological theory* (pp. 125–163). New Brunswick, NJ: Transaction Publishers.

LeBlanc, M., & Bouthillier, C. (2003). A developmental test of the general deviance syndrome with adjudicated girls and boy using hierarchical confirmatory factor analysis. *Criminal Behaviour and Mental Health, 13*(2), 81–105.

LeBlanc, M., & Girard, S. (1997). The generality of deviance: Replication over two decades with a Canadian sample of adjudicated boys. *Canadian Journal of Criminology, 39*(2), 171–183.

Levine, S. B. (2010). What is sexual addiction? *Journal of Sex & Marital Therapy, 36*(3), 261–275.

Loeber, R., Farrington, D. P., Stouthamer-Loeber, M., & White, H. R. (2008). *Violence and serious theft: Development and prediction from childhood to adulthood*. Mahwah, NJ: Lawrence Erlbaum.

Lussier, P. (2005). The criminal activity of sexual offenders in adulthood: Revisiting the specialization debate. *Sexual Abuse: A Journal of Research and Treatment, 17*(3), 269–292.

Lussier, P., & Beauregard, E. (2018). "Sex offender" theory and research in context: The relative absence of a criminological perspective. In P. Lussier & E. Beauregard (Eds.), *Sexual offending: A criminological perspective* (pp. 3–11). Abington, PA: Routledge.

Lussier, P., Blokland, A., Mathesius, J., Pardini, D., & Loeber, R. (2015). The childhood risk factors of adolescent-onset and adult-onset of sex offending: Evidence from a prospective longitudinal study. In A. A. J. Blokland & P. Lussier (Eds.), *Sex offenders: A criminal career approach*. Chichester, UK: Wiley.

Lussier, P., & Cale, J. (2016). Understanding the origins and the development of rape and sexual aggression against women: Four generations of research and theorizing. *Aggression and Violent Behavior, 31*, 66–81.

Lussier, P., LeBlanc, M., & Proulx, J. (2005). The generality of criminal behavior: A confirmatory factor analysis of the criminal activity of sex offenders in adulthood. *Journal of Criminal Justice, 33*(2), 177–189.

Lussier, P., Leclerc, B., Cale, J., & Proulx, J. (2007). Developmental pathways of deviance in sexual aggressors. *Criminal Justice and Behavior, 34*(11), 1441–1462.

Lussier, P., & Mathesius, J. (2018). Integrating general and specific theories of sex offending. In P. Lussier & E. Beauregard (Eds.), *Sexual offending: A criminological perspective* (pp. 12–43). Abington, PA: Routledge.

Lussier, P., Proulx, J., & LeBlanc, M. (2005). Criminal propensity, deviant sexual interests and criminal activity of sexual aggressors against women: A comparison of explanatory models. *Criminology, 43*(1), 249–282.

Lussier, P., Tzoumakis, S., Cale, J., & Amirault, J. (2010). Criminal trajectories of adult sex offenders and the age effect: Examining the dynamic aspect of offending in adulthood. *International Criminal Justice Review, 20*(2), 147–168.

Magnan, V. (1885). *Des anomalies, des aberrations et des perversions sexuelles*. Paris, France: Progrès médical.

Malamuth, N. M. (1989). The attraction to sexual aggression scale: Part I. *Journal of Sex Research, 26*(1), 26–49.

Malamuth, N. M. (1998). An evolutionary-based model integrating research on the characteristics of sexually coercive men. *Advances in Psychological Science, 1*, 151–184.

Malamuth, N. M. (2003). Criminal and noncriminal sexual aggressors. *Annals of the New York Academy of Sciences, 989*(1), 33–58.

Malamuth, N. M., Addison, T., & Koss, M. (2000). Pornography and sexual aggression: Are there reliable effects and can we understand them? *Annual Review of Sex Research, 11*(1), 26–91.

Malamuth, N. M., Check, J. V., & Briere, J. (1986). Sexual arousal in response to aggression: Ideological, aggressive, and sexual correlates. *Journal of Personality and Social Psychology, 50*(2), 330.

Malamuth, N. M., Sockloskie, R. J., Koss, M. P., & Tanaka, J. S. (1991). Characteristics of aggressors against women: Testing a model using a national sample of college students. *Journal of Consulting and Clinical Psychology, 59*(5), 670–681.

Marshall, W. L. (1989). Intimacy, loneliness and sexual offenders. *Behaviour Research and Therapy, 27*(5), 491–504.

Marshall, W. L., & Barbaree, H. E. (1984). A behavioral view of rape. *International Journal of Law and Psychiatry, 7*(1), 51–77.

Marshall, W. L., & Barbaree, H. E. (1990). An integrated theory of the etiology of sexual offending. In W. L. Marshall, D. R. Laws, & H. E. Barbaree (Eds.), *Handbook of sexual assault: Issues, theories, and treatment of the offender* (pp. 257–275). New York: Plenum Press.

Marshall, W. L., Hudson, S. M., & Hodkinson, S. (1993). The importance of attachment bonds in the development of juvenile sex offending. In H. E. Barbaree, W. L. Marshall, & S. M. Hudson (Eds.), *The juvenile sex offender* (pp. 164–181). New York: Guilford.

McCuish, E., Lussier, P., & Corrado, R. (2016). Criminal careers of juvenile sex and nonsex offenders: Evidence from a prospective longitudinal study. *Youth Violence and Juvenile Justice, 14*(3), 199–224.

McGuire, R. J., Carlisle, J. M., & Young, B. G. (1964). Sexual deviations as conditioned behavior: A hypothesis. *Behaviour Research and Therapy, 2*(2–4), 185–190.

Meston, C. M., & Buss, D. M. (2007). Why humans have sex. *Archives of Sexual Behavior, 36*(4), 477–507.

Mischel, W., Coates, B., & Raskoff, A. (1968). Effects of success and failure on self-gratification. *Journal of personality and social psychology, 10*(4), 381–390.

Miller, J. D., & Lynam, D. (2001). Structural models of personality and their relation to antisocial behavior: A meta-analytic review. *Criminology, 39*(4), 765–798.

Moffitt, T. E. (1993). Adolescence-limited and life-course-persistent antisocial behavior: A developmental taxonomy. *Psychological Review, 100*(4), 674–701.

Morizot, J., & LeBlanc, M. (2003). Searching for a developmental typology of personality and its relations to antisocial behaviour: A longitudinal study of an adjudicated men sample. *Criminal Behaviour and Mental Health, 13*(4), 241–277.

Morizot, J., & LeBlanc, M. (2005). Searching for a developmental typology of personality and its relations to antisocial behavior: A longitudinal study of a representative sample of men. *Journal of Personality, 73*(1), 139–182.

Osgood, D. W., Johnston, L. D., O'Malley, P. M., & Bachman, J. G. (1988). The generality of deviance in late adolescence and early adulthood. *American Sociological Review, 53*(1), 81–93.

Polaschek, D. L., & Gannon, T. A. (2004). The implicit theories of rapists: What convicted offenders tell us. *Sexual Abuse: A Journal of Research and Treatment, 16*(4), 299–314.

Polaschek, D. L., Hudson, S. M., Ward, T., & Siegert, R. J. (2001). Rapists' offense processes: A preliminary descriptive model. *Journal of Interpersonal Violence, 16*(6), 523–544.

Proulx, J., Beauregard, E., Lussier, P., & Leclerc, B. (2014). *Pathways to sexual aggression.* New York: Routledge.

Proulx, J., St-Yves, M., Guay, J. P., & Ouimet, M. (1999). Les agresseurs sexuels de femmes: scénarios délictuels et troubles de la personnalité. In D. J. Proulx, M. Cusson, & M. Ouimet (Eds.), *Les Violences criminelles* (pp. 157–185). Québec, QC: Les Presses de l'Université Laval.

Quinsey, V. L. (1984). Sexual aggression: Studies of offenders against women. In D. Weisstub (Ed.), *Law and mental health: International perspectives* (pp. 84–121). New York: Pergamon.

Quinsey, V. L., Harris, G. T., Rice, M. E., & Cormier, C. A. (1998). *Violent offenders: Appraising and managing risk.* Washington DC: APA.

Rada, R. T., Laws, D. R., & Kellner, R. (1976). Plasma testosterone levels in the rapist. *Psychosomatic Medicine, 38*(4), 257–268.

Radzinowicz, L. (1957). *Sexual offenses: A report of the Cambridge Department of Criminal Justice.* London: Macmillan.

Sanday, P. R. (1981). The socio-cultural context of rape: A cross-cultural study. *Journal of Social Issues, 37*(4), 5–27.

Schwartz, M. D., DeKeseredy, W. S., Tait, D., & Alvi, S. (2001). Male peer support and a feminist routing activities theory: Understanding sexual assault on the college campus. *Justice Quarterly, 18*(3), 623–649.

Seto, M. C., & Barbaree, H. E. (1997). Sexual aggression as antisocial behavior: A developmental model. In D. Stoff, J. Breiling, & J. D. Maser (Eds.), *Handbook of antisocial behavior* (pp. 524–533). New York: John Wiley.

Seto, M. C., & Lalumière, M. L. (2010). What is so special about male adolescent sexual offending? A review and test of explanations through meta-analysis. *Psychological Bulletin, 136*(4), 526–575.

Simon, L. M. J. (1997). Do offenders specialize in crime types? *Applied and Preventive Psychology, 6*(1), 35–53.

Simon, L. M. J. (2000). An examination of the assumptions of specialization, mental disorder, and dangerousness in sex offenders. *Behavioral Sciences & the Law, 18*(2–3), 275–308.

Smallbone, S., & Cale, J. (2015). An integrated life-course developmental theory of sexual offending. In A. A. J. Blokland & P. Lussier (Eds.), *Sex offenders: A criminal career approach* (pp. 43–70). Chichester: John Wiley & Sons.

Smallbone, S. W. (2006). Social and psychological factors in the development of delinquency and sexual deviance. In H. E. Barbaree & W. L. Marshall (Eds.), *The juvenile sex offender* (pp. 105–127). New York: Guildford Press.

Smallbone, S. W., & Wortley, R. K. (2004). Onset, persistence, and versatility of offending among adult males convicted of sexual offenses against children. *Sexual Abuse: A Journal of Research and Treatment, 16*(4), 285–298.

Smuts, B. (1992). Male aggression against women. *Human Nature, 3*(1), 1–44.

Soothill, K., Francis, B., Sanderson, B., & Ackerley, E. (2000). Sex offenders: Specialists, generalists – or both? A 32-year criminological study. *The British Journal of Criminology, 40*(1), 56–67.

Stein, D. J., Black, D. W., & Pienaar, W. (2000). Sexual disorders not otherwise specified: Compulsive, addictive, or impulsive? *CNS Spectrums, 5*(01), 60–66.

Stermac, L. E., & Quinsey, V. L. (1986). Social competence among rapists. *Behavioral Assessment, 8*, 171–185.

Tappan, P. W. (1951). Sentences for sex criminals. *Journal of Criminal Law, Criminology & Police Sciences, 42*, 332–337.

Tedeschi, J. T., & Felson, R. B. (1994). *Violence, aggression, & coercive actions.* Washington, DC: American Psychology Association.

Thornhill, R., & Palmer, C. (2000). *A natural history of rape: Biological bases of sexual coercion*. Cambridge, MA: MIT Press.

Ward, T., & Hudson, S. M. (2000). *A self-regulation model of relapse prevention. Remaking relapse prevention with sex offenders: A sourcebook* (pp. 79–101). Thousand Oaks, CA: Sage.

Ward, T., & Siegert, R. J. (2002). Toward a comprehensive theory of child sexual abuse: A theory knitting perspective. *Psychology, Crime & Law, 8*(4), 319–351.

Weinrott, M. R., & Saylor, M. (1991). Self-report of crimes committed by sex offenders. *Journal of Interpersonal Violence, 6*(3), 286–300.

Wikström, P. O. H. (2014). Why crime happens: A situational action theory. In *Analytical sociology: Actions and networks* (pp. 74–94). Chichester, UK: Wiley.

Wilson, J. Q., & Herrnstein, R. J. (1986). *Criminals born and bred: Crime and human nature*. New York: Simon & Schuster.

Zhang, L., Welte, J. W., & Wieczorek, W. F. (2002). Underlying common factors of adolescent problem behaviors. *Criminal Justice and Behavior, 29*(2), 161–182.

Chapter 5
Sex Offenders Under the Microscope: Are They Unique?

Introduction

Among all subgroups of individuals having been convicted for a criminal offense, perhaps no other group has been the focus of more curiosity, scrutiny, and empirical research than perpetrators of sex crimes. Since early writings stemming from the nineteenth century, starting with Dr. Krafft-Ebing (1886/1965) who documented the complex clinical profile of "sexual deviants" and Dr. Lombroso (1880) who reported on their abnormal physical appearance, perpetrators of sex crimes have been the unique focus of much research. One key aspect of conducting research on the causes of sexual offending is the ability to measure sexual offending. This can take many forms, as discussed in Chaps. 3 and 4, such as sexual victimization surveys, official crime rates, court data, and so on. Therefore, when one is concerned about, and interested in, perpetrators of sex crimes and what is unique about them, the measurement of sexual offending begins with the search for individuals having perpetrated a sex crime. For many obvious reasons, perpetrators of sex crimes are a difficult to reach population, creating significant challenges for researchers aiming to study the origin and development of their behavior. To gather systematic and detailed information on a large number of perpetrators of sex crimes, researchers have followed in the footsteps of Dr. Paul Gebhard and others before him by going to prisons and mental health facilities to collect systematic information about individuals who committed sex crimes. Over the years, researchers have relied on clinical interviews, checklists, questionnaires and surveys, brain scans, psychological and neuropsychological tests, phallometric assessment, and the polygraph, to name just a few methods of data collection. They have examined case histories of individuals convicted of sex crimes, looking at their upbringing during their childhood, their thoughts and attitudes, their sexual fantasies and behavior, their beliefs regarding women and sexuality, their adjustment to the period of adolescence up to their conviction for a sex crime in adulthood. Overall, these have been the methods of choice for several decades and required that individuals recollect their past, in terms

© Springer Nature Switzerland AG 2021
P. Lussier et al., *Understanding Sexual Offending*,
https://doi.org/10.1007/978-3-030-53301-4_5

of their upbringing, their sexual offending, thoughts and attitudes towards their victims, prior sexual (non-offending) behavior, and their motivation to commit such crimes. They also searched their correctional and psychiatric files, relied on self-reports, clinical assessments, police, and court data, sometimes even referring to the perpetrators' family members to acquire additional information about their upbringing, social interactions, and personality.

The search for what is unique about perpetrators of sex offenses has spanned more than eight decades. Many have raised the idea that to perpetrate a sexual offense implies that such a person must be different, not only from the general population, but even from individuals that perpetrate nonsexual offenses. Identifying characteristics more common to perpetrators of sex offenses was assumed to be the gateway to unraveling the causes of sexual offending. After all, these individuals have perpetrated crimes that are serious, morally repugnant, even inconceivable and bizarre, sometimes with physical violence, and even extreme forms of violence resulting in the death of the victim(s). Intuitively, therefore, it stands to reason that there should be something that makes them distinct as a group and that such distinctions can be identified, measured, and described through the lens of science. Thus far, this quest has primarily focused on individual-level factors. Individual-level factors are personal attributes, beliefs, skills, values, and qualities that characterize an individual. Empirical research has measured these individual-level factors by examining the biological, physiological, neuropsychological, cognitive, emotional, behavioral, sexual, and interpersonal functioning of perpetrators of sex offenses. Historically, this has been to the exclusion of the search for causes emanating from beyond the individual (e.g., situational, social, etc.).

The current chapter aims to contextualize the emergence of this research on individual-level factors and what is unique and distinct about perpetrators of sex crimes. It also aims to provide a critical analysis of this research while highlighting some tentative conclusions about what sets them apart from other offenders.

Historical Context

In the 1940s, recognizing the relative absence of an empirical study on perpetrators of sex crimes, the Legislature of the State of New York commissioned a study directed by Dr. David Abrahamsen. Abrahamsen (1950) and his team examined a group of 102 individuals incarcerated at Sing Sing Prison in the state of New York who were convicted for a serious sex crime. This prison had a notorious reputation because of its numerous executions by electrocution. These sex offenders had perpetrated felony offenses such as rape, sexual murder, child sexual abuse, indecent exposure, but also other crimes such as (sexually motivated) arson and homosexual acts. Recognizing that this group did not seem to be representative of sex offenders in general, Dr. Abrahamsen nonetheless concluded that all the men examined were suffering from serious mental or emotional disturbances. This assumption and conclusion should not be taken lightly. For example, in 1948, in the city Chicago, there had been 2001 people arrested or complained against for a sex crime. Of those, there were only 140 cases (7%) where a psychiatric evaluation had been ordered by a judge. Among those evaluated, more than 80% were found to have a psychiatric disorder of one type or another (Braude, 1950).

At first glance, these findings could be used to conclude that 80% of perpetrators of sexual offenses had a psychiatric disorder. However, another way of thinking is that for 1861 persons (93% of perpetrators), the court ruled that their case did not require a psychiatric evaluation. If nearly all evaluations positively identified a psychiatric disorder, one wonders, therefore, what the criteria were for a judge to identify a defendant in need of psychiatric evaluation? Was it the case that these individuals committed such horrific crimes, or acted so abnormally during judicial proceedings that they poorly represented the typical case of sexual offending? If so, does this call into question the generalizability of research findings that relied on samples of individuals with data pertaining to psychiatric evaluations? In effect, if psychiatric evaluations were relatively rare, what does this say about the individuals that received them? How disturbed were such individuals, or the details of the case, that led to a judge feeling that an assessment was warranted? It is possible that the research design strategies of the time were elaborated in such a way that the only conclusion one would arrive at pertaining to perpetrators of sexual offenses is that they were all serious offenders who were psychologically disturbed and typically characterized by sexual deviance.

At the same time, the inspection of psychiatric evaluations revealed to Dr. Abrahamsen the idea that the disorders that characterized perpetrators of sex crimes could not all be reduced to sexual psychopathy. Not only was the term "sexual psychopath" too vague, it also did not represent the clinical reality of these individuals. He also stressed the need to better understand the personality of these men. With his report, it was recommended "…that suitable treatment would be available for these men, making it possible to rehabilitate them" (see Glueck, 1956, p. 197). The recommendations included: (a) requiring a mental health assessment for all perpetrators before sentencing; (b) allowing a judge to impose an indeterminate sentence to be served in a mental health institution; (c) transferring the responsibility of providing psychological and psychiatric services from correctional services to the Commission of Mental Hygiene to address their specific and individual needs; and (d) establishing an institute that would promote research and training for the personnel working with this population (see also Guttmacher & Weihofen, 1952). These recommendations essentially displaced some of the legal system's responsibility for responding to sex offenses into the hands of trained professionals dealing with individuals with mental health problems. Responding to sexual offending eventually became as much a clinically based task as it was a legal one. These recommendations were accepted and eventually implemented in the State of New York.

Soon thereafter, led by Dr. Bernard Glueck, a detailed assessment protocol was developed at Sing Sing Prison by members of the Sex Delinquency Research Project. In 1957, following the work of Drs. Hammer and Glueck, members of this research group provided a detailed account of their interviews conducted with 200 perpetrators of sex crimes. They relied on the clinical tools that were available for that era, which were heavily grounded in psychodynamic personality theory and Freudian concepts. In effect, while they were conducting systematic interviews with a large number of perpetrators, the lens through which this research group was trying to understand sexual offending was focused on a relatively narrow set of individual-level characteristics. For a period of 5 years, they subjected perpetrators of sex crimes to an assessment protocol lasting between 25 and 35 h. The authors were concerned about the fact that their study had been based on individuals apprehended and incarcerated for their behavior and the pitfalls of generalizing their findings to all perpetrators of sex crimes, especially with respect to the underlying motivations characterizing this group. They were also careful to point out that because they studied perpetrators at just one point in time, they could not firmly ascertain that their findings were reflective of stable and fixed traits characterizing perpetrators of sex crimes. Their analysis and interpretation of the data collected focused on, among other things, the results of projective tests, such as Rorschach tests. Nevertheless, they argued that their methodology was sensitive enough to separate those from more context-dependent reactions (Hammer & Glueck, 1957). In other words, they recognized that for some perpetrators, there were enduring and long-lasting contributing factors responsible for their sexual offending behavior; for others, however, situational factors that had little to do with the person's upbringing and past personal experiences facilitated their sexual offending (e.g., sexual arousal, intoxication, anger, boredom, loneliness).

Their groundbreaking research of the time allowed them to identify four individual-level factors possibly contributing to sexual offending that included: (1) psychosexual disturbances (e.g., fear, forbidden sexual feelings, and feelings of sexual inadequacy); (2) what they called schizoid-schizophrenic adjustment characterizing a person who is very shy, has low self-esteem, and susceptible to psychotic ideations of not feeling appreciated by others; (3) lack of impulse control; and (4) the lack of capacity for sublimation, meaning difficulty with turning socially unacceptable thoughts and fantasies into socially acceptable behaviors. On the one hand, the latter two factors did not appear markedly different from factors hypothesized to influence the perpetration of nonsexual offenses. On the other hand, the first two factors underscored the sexual needs of these individuals that aimed to bolster their self-esteem, define themselves, or to compensate for some childhood emotional trauma (Hammer & Glueck, 1957). In short, their findings suggested that the root causes of sexual offending could be found in offenders' complex psychosexual development. Due to the cross-sectional nature of their research, what the authors were unable to conclude, for example, was whether psychosexual disturbances and schizoid-schizophrenic adjustment were driven by a lack of impulse control and capacity for sublimation.

Searching for the North Star

These and other researchers from the early postwar era set the stage for the search of what is unique and different about perpetrators of sex crimes. As clinical researchers, they were conducting their own research in psychiatric units within prisons or in psychiatric hospitals. They were well aware that their research findings should not be generalized to all perpetrators of sex crimes such as those not admitted to a psychiatric hospital, those deemed untreatable, those who had not been incarcerated for their sex crime, as well as those that had not been convicted or even apprehended for their offenses. Given the absence of victimization surveys or other sources of information about the scope of sexual offending in society (this would come much later in the 1980s), the extent of the bias in focusing on a group of perpetrators in psychiatric settings represented a major blind spot in the clinician's perspective on sexual offending. In effect, in the absence of research on other perpetrators, clinical researchers were aware of generalizability issues but could not put into perspective the scope of the generalizability issue of research findings stemming from psychiatric settings. In the absence of the use of alternative research strategies, the growing number of clinical studies became the prototypical source for information about perpetrators of sex crimes for many years to come.

Clinical research from the early postwar period, unwillingly perhaps, had established a model for conducting research on perpetrators of sex crimes, which was soon adopted by other clinical researchers across the country. This template for sexual offending research included: conducting research in psychiatric settings in close proximity to perpetrators; conducting standardized clinical assessments that would allow immediate testing of clinical hypotheses; and developing clinical tools that would allow for the collection of additional information about mental illness characterizing these individuals. The close proximity between clinical research and clinical practice further contributed to the emergence of the clinical-medical model for sexual offending. The model would lead this emerging field of research to search for the "North Star" and in the process, develop new methodologies for testing hypotheses about the causes of sexual offending. These new methodologies are described below.

At the University of California at Los Angeles, a team of researchers including Marsh, Hilliard, and Liechti (1955) proposed a sexual deviation scale that consisted of a series of items from the well-known MMPI (Hattaway & McKinley, 1989) and could assist in the clinical assessment of perpetrators of sex crimes under the Sexual Psychopathy Act. Given its adaptation from a measure of general personality functioning, the proposed sexual deviation scale had little to do with a person's sexual development and functioning such as sexual arousal, sexual thoughts and sexual fantasies, sexual urges, or sexual preferences. Rather, it consisted of a series of clinical indicators reflecting the growing consensus of the time: perpetrators of sex crimes were mentally ill and their propensity for sexual offending would be reflected in dysfunctional personality characteristics that had more to do with poor social competency and interpersonal difficulties than with attitudes about sexual behavior.

Marsh et al. (1955), therefore, identified the following clinical characteristics of their mental health that made them different: poor social relationships, being asocial and amoral, with a tendency to be suspicious of others, fearful and experiencing feelings of guilt and depression, and suffering from mental and physical complaints. In order to investigate whether these characteristics distinguished perpetrators of sex crimes from "non-sex offenders," they compared their MMPI scores to those of a group of university students. The results suggested not only that perpetrators of sex crimes had a high prevalence of personality dysfunction, but that differences in personality characteristics when compared to a group of university students would explain their sexual offending.

While the scale they developed embodied some key ideas of the time, it was met with much skepticism and the results were not replicated in subsequent research (e.g., Peek & Storms, 1956). The idea that Marsh et al. (1955) had created a scale measuring the propensity to commit a sex crime by examining the clinical profiles of individuals targeted by Sexual Psychopathy Laws raised some concerns. At the time, such laws still reflected the belief that individuals processed under such laws were nevertheless capable of benefiting from treatment. Psychiatrists became less confident that all individuals involved in sexual offenses could be rehabilitated in this way. Accordingly, there were concerns that the criteria used to identify, among all convicted perpetrators of a sex crime, those that were mentally ill and treatable created a filtering process that led to the creation of a subcategory of perpetrators that were committed to a mental health institution. A key question therefore emerged: What about those deemed to not be treatable?

Moreover, because details of Sexual Psychopathy Laws varied across jurisdictions there were concerns about generalizability even across studies using similar sampling criteria. For example, in some states, it was reported that while this type of disposition targeted perpetrators of violent sex offenses, in reality, about half of the individuals committed to a psychiatric hospital had perpetrated a nonviolent sex crime such as exhibitionism, voyeurism, and homosexuality (e.g., Burick, 1968). In other states, older offenders, those with prior convictions for a sex crime, and those with a relatively poor prognosis were more likely to be committed to a mental health institution rather than being sent to prison (Ellis, Doorbar, & Johnston III, 1954). Marsh et al.'s (1955) study, like most research of the time, focused on offenders targeted by Sexual Psychopathy Laws. Therefore, the research findings were more reflective of the legal and clinical practices of the time rather than actual risk factors for sexual offending more generally. In other words, the first series of empirical studies that aimed to discover what was unique about perpetrators of sex crimes were in fact describing which clinical profiles met the criteria for psychiatric commitment to a mental health institution. This important methodological shortcoming would characterize the clinical research for decades to come.

In that regard, Cormier and Simons (1969) were concerned that the "really dangerous sexual offenders," as they put it, were seldom found in the mental health institution, which had been specifically designed for them (p. 333). The fact that these individuals were not considered good candidates for therapy excluded them from the early clinical studies. Addressing the gap in the scientific literature that focused on committed offenders who are potentially more responsive to therapy, Cormier and Simons (1969) wanted to highlight the individual characteristics of dangerous, violent sexual offenders. They conducted a small-scale study including 8 incarcerated males who had been clinically assessed by a prison-psychiatrist. This very small group of individuals had all committed a rape. An unidentified number of them were serial rapists and two were homicide offenders. Cormier and Simons presented a profile that significantly departed from what had been presented in the scientific literature up to this point. They depicted the dangerous sex crime perpetrator as someone who acts alone, who actively searches for a potential victim, targets stranger victims, and rarely is under the influence of drugs or alcohol at the time of the offense. For Cormier and Simons (1969), what stood out was not their deviant sexual fantasies, but rather the relative lack of control these individuals had over such violent sexual fantasies. In fact, they suggested that the escalation pattern characterizing their sexual offending over time was unique and specific to dangerous sex offenders. While these results are interesting, they highlight the fact that rather than collecting data on a broader scale, these researchers narrowed their investigation to an even small subgroup of offenders, further raising issues about the generalization of their findings. This important methodological shortcoming would also characterize the clinical research for decades to come.

The interest in broadening the scope of research on sexual offending to include not just those processed under Sexual Psychopathy Laws, but those with more severe psychopathology profiles, resulted in the onset of the search for distinctive individual differences characterizing perpetrators of sex crimes. What became clear was that very contradictory findings were emerging about the profiles of perpetrators of a sex crime. To address the heterogeneity characterizing this group, it became apparent that more elaborate and diverse clinical assessment tools were needed. During that period, across the Atlantic Ocean in the country formerly known as Czechoslovakia, a researcher in the field of sexology was working on a device that would significantly alter the course of the field of sexual offending research and the work of a whole generation of scholars. Dr. Kurt Freund developed a device that allowed him, in a laboratory setting, to measure rather objectively, men's sexual arousal and sexual interests, and possibly even their sexual preferences (see, Freund, 1963). At first, the method was developed to discriminate men's arousal and attraction to adult males and females. At that time, military service was mandatory but homosexual men were excluded from the service (some men in fact faked homosexuality to avoid serving in the military). The apparatus initially consisted of, among other things, an air-proof transducer and a glass cylinder designed to measure and record penile volume changes during the presentation of various stimuli (e.g., Freund, Sedlacek, & Knob, 1965). The assessment would include the presentation of pictures of males and females of varying ages while the person being assessed would put the device on his penis. The apparatus soon also became used as a tool to measure men's sexual arousal to children, and as a possible diagnostic tool for pedophilia and sexual arousal to adolescents to diagnose hebephilia (e.g., Freund, 1963, 1967).

Up to this point in time, there were in fact several methods that had been developed to measure a man's sexual arousal (Zuckerman, 1971) but penile plethysmography provided the most objective measure (Proulx, 1989). The preliminary results observed by Dr. Freund (1967) with respect to measuring sexual interest towards children reinforced the need to investigate further the clinical utility of such a tool for the purpose of clinical assessment of the "sex offender." In the midst of political turmoil and the Soviet invasion of Czechoslovakia, Dr. Freund fled his country and moved to Canada. Not too long after, the procedure called penile plethysmography (also known as phallometric assessment) grew in popularity in North America and become a primary assessment method for clinical and research purposes.

The phallometric assessment of males' sexual arousal to deviant and nondeviant sexual stimuli and the study of sexual deviance considerably evolved over the following two decades. The procedure became somewhat less intrusive as the volumetric apparatus was replaced by a mercury-filled rubber strain gauge that measured the circumference of the penis (e.g., Laws, 1977; Rosen & Keefe, 1978). Given the legal context in which these assessments were conducted and the risk that a person could attempt to manipulate test protocols, procedures were also developed to prevent voluntary control of penile responses (e.g., Proulx, Côté, & Achille, 1993). The procedure was also expanded because the presentation of slides involving nude males and females of varying ages proved to be too limited for the assessment of complex preferences and fantasies reflected in the perpetration of sex crimes (e.g., sexual violence, rape). Indeed, images could not properly render more complex scenarios such as rape, sexual violence, and humiliation of a victim, as well as sexual sadism and the infliction of pain.

Researchers, therefore, proposed the use of audiotaped vignettes describing sexually conventional and unconventional scenarios (e.g., Earls & Proulx, 1986; Proulx, Aubut, McKibben, & Côté, 1994; Quinsey & Chaplin, 1982). Vignettes were sourced through asking perpetrators to write down a description of their sexual fantasies and sexual thoughts that could in turn be narrated and recorded. These recordings were then presented in a laboratory setting (e.g., in a systematic fashion) to other sex offense perpetrators for assessment purposes. These audiotaped recordings allowed for the measurement and assessment of pedophilia, but also sexual arousal to sexual violence, nonsexual violence, rape with physical violence, and rape with physical violence and humiliation of the victim, among others. While the promising results observed by Dr. Freund appeared justified, particularly for the assessment of pedophilia, the use of this new technology to assess deviant sexual preferences of rapists and sexual aggressors against women raised new challenges and controversies.

The study of men's sexual arousal in psychiatric settings using phallometric assessment consolidated the perceived importance of sexual deviance as a contributing factor to sexual offending (e.g., Simon & Schouten, 1991). Phallometric assessment became a pivotal device for the clinical assessment and research on perpetrators of sex offenses in psychiatric settings (e.g., Quinsey & Earls, 1990). It was used to determine sex offender treatment program objectives and whether the modification of sexual preferences should be a treatment target. It also became a treatment device that behaviorally oriented treatment providers could use in the context of aversion therapy to modify sexual preferences (Quinsey, Chaplin, & Carrigan, 1980). Later on, phallometric data also became a key indicator of risk for recidivism (e.g., Proulx et al., 1997; Quinsey, Rice, & Harris, 1995). From a research perspective, the device was used to describe the sexual interest profile of perpetrators of sex crimes (e.g., Michaud & Proulx, 2009) and to test hypotheses about the origins and development of deviant sexual preferences among perpetrators of sex crimes (Beauregard, Lussier, & Proulx, 2004; Lussier, Beauregard, Proulx, & Nicole, 2005). The relative ubiquity of phallometric assessment was such that individuals refusing to participate in the assessment were viewed with suspicion from clinical staff. This was an important issue because at the same time, there was a relative absence of professional guidelines and standards characterizing the ethical use of this technique in treatment settings.

Although deviant sexual fantasies were perceived to be central in the development of sexual offending (e.g., Abel & Blanchard, 1974), other ideas about the origin of sexual offending began to emerge from clinical research conducted in psychiatric settings. One was the notion that sexual offending was not so much the result of qualitative differences in sexual development (i.e., the clear demarcation of normative versus non-normative sexual development), but rather the result of quantitative differences in sexual development (i.e., heightened sexual drive and urges). Indeed, while the science of phallometric research was slowly evolving in North America, there had been a growing number of reports about the use of physical castration with perpetrators of sex crimes as a means to quell what would be later referred to as "hypersexuality," or certain individuals' persistent fixation on sexual activity. It was not so much deviant sexual attitudes, but normative attitudes that could not be satiated simply through opportunities for consensual sexual relations (for a review of earlier studies, Bradford, 1985; Meyer III & Cole, 1997; Prentky, 1997). Physical castration represented a drastic and controversial technique that had been tested in several European countries, especially Scandinavian countries. Castration involved the removal of the testicles, which are responsible for the production of testosterone (T), an androgen that plays a certain role in male sexual activity. Therefore, it was believed that physical castration would remove the hormonal component of a person's sexual urges.

While very low sexual recidivism rates of surgically castrated perpetrators had been reported, many questioned the procedures on ethical and empirical grounds. The use of the technique by the Nazi regime in WWII Germany against homosexual males, "sex offenders", and "disabled" people among others, according to LeMaire (1956), probably explained why it was widely met with hesitation and aversion as a treatment method in North America in the postwar period. That said, in the early twentieth century, there was growing pressure as part of a broader eugenics movement to implement a compulsory human sterilization program (e.g., vasectomy) with individuals considered to be "unfit" (e.g., habitual offenders, mentally handicapped, and sexual deviants; e.g., Millikin, 1894; Singer, 1913). The State of Indiana was the first to pass a bill allowing the use of human sterilization for crime prevention purposes and other US states and Canadian provinces (e.g., Alberta) followed their lead (for a review, Fink, 1938; Grekul, Krahn, & Odynak, 2004). Many commentators of the time argued that such techniques would not be effective given that there was no proof that crime was hereditary. Moreover, this technique did not contribute in any way to offender rehabilitation.[1]

Pressured into doing something about the sex offender problem, physicians looked for more humanistic alternatives to physical castration by finding a technique that curtailed sexual urges but was not irreversible, did not constitute cruel and unusual punishment, and did not interfere with a person's ability to procreate. At the Burden Neurological Institute in Bristol, England, known for some of the first trials of electroconvulsive therapy and the lobotomy, the neuropsychiatrist Frederick Golla was among the first to use and report on a hormonal-based procedure designed to control men's sexual urges (Golla & Hodge, 1949). Heavy doses of female sex hormones were administered daily to 13 individuals with positive outcomes (i.e., suppression of the libido) observed after about 1 month. Golla and Hodge (1949) concluded that hormonal therapy was more effective than physical castration, especially given many reports that male sexual capacity was not extinguished after physical castration. This was later confirmed by Heim (1981) who reported that close to one-third of castrated male perpetrators of sex offenses were able to engage in sexual intercourse after the surgery. Despite the reported evidence that this approach significantly impacted men's ability to control their sexual urges, the side effects of administering female hormones (e.g., nausea, enlarged breasts) led researchers to seek alternatives.

Different alternatives to these hormonal-based therapies were proposed in the 1960s and included neuroleptics and antiandrogens. Antiandrogens such as medroxyprogesterone and cyproterone were considered antilibidinal because of their capacity to block androgen receptors. Case studies were presented in terms of the dosage, short-term impact, and some side effects were noticed (e.g., Berlin & Meinecke, 1981; Money, 1970). While hormonal-based therapy highlighted the ability to control males' sexual arousal from a perceived prevention standpoint, no research up to that point had in fact shown that perpetrators of a sex crime had an abnormal sexual drive in the first place. In short, researchers at the time had put the cart before the horse; the causes of sexual offending were presumed based on strategies used to treat sexual offending. It was assumed that there was something abnormal about offenders' sexual functioning and therefore treatment strategies were developed to curtail sex drive. Physical and chemical castration had been used to control males' sexual arousal without any sound scientific evidence that these individuals had abnormal T levels in the first place, or that abnormal T levels actually played any part whatsoever in their sex crimes. In fact, this was an important revelation to emerge when considering the tenets of hormonal-based therapy. Was the behavior of perpetrators of sex crime even sexually motivated? Was their behavior the result of an abnormally high sexual drive? Was their inability to control their sexual urges a result of a specific biological anomaly? None of these questions had

[1] It was also argued that human sterilization would result in the proliferation of sexually transmitted diseases (see Fink, 1938).

been rigorously examined up to this point, yet physical and chemical castration were well underway as part of sex offender therapy. Furthermore, instead of investigating these fundamental research questions, researchers persisted to search for more precise means of measuring hormonal imbalances.

There had been sporadic scientific research reports between the 1930s and 1960s regarding the measurement of plasma T in laboratory settings. Using blood samples, methods to estimate the T level in human plasma gradually improved (e.g., Finkelstein, Forchielli, & Dorfman, 1961). The measurement and the description of T levels in humans soon followed, including observations about gender differences before and after puberty (e.g., Resko & Eik-Nes, 1966). These scientific advancements facilitated sexual offending research from a psychoendocrinological perspective, given the potential importance of T in both sexual and violent behavior. It is in that context that researchers turned their attention to psychoendocrinology and the study of biological markers for the possible discovery of what is unique about perpetrators of sex offenses (e.g., Rada, 1980).

In a study conducted at the Atascadero State Hospital in California, a team of researchers examined and compared the plasma T level between a group of rapists and child molesters and a group of men from the treatment staff (Rada, Laws, & Kellner, 1976). Like many of the early studies comparing a highly specific group of sex offenders to college students, the comparison group utilized by researchers was simply inadequate and differed from the perpetrators in many ways other than having been convicted for a sex crime, which may have confounded the findings. Rada et al. (1976) selected a group of 44 individuals among a sample of about 300–375 convicted perpetrators of sex crimes based on a number of stringent criteria (e.g., acted alone; crime was brutally violent or entirely nonviolent; victim was an adult or a child; being in good health; no history of mental illness and not on medication). Multiple blood samples were obtained in the morning and the early evening over the course of a few days. It was known at that time that a person's T level could fluctuate during the course of the day (e.g., T levels are typically higher in the morning), therefore making it difficult to draw any firm conclusions about its role in past sexual and/or violent behavior. This limitation alone represented a serious threat to the study findings and conclusions.

Nonetheless, the findings showed that the mean plasma T level of rapists was higher than that of child molesters and the comparison group; while violent and nonviolent rapists' T level did not differ, the group of violent child molesters showed the highest T level of all. These findings suggesting the role and importance of plasma T levels on human sexuality offered a potentially powerful explanation of the origins and development of sexual violence. That said, these results showed heterogeneity in T within sexual offenders that was primarily linked to involvement in violence. Later studies would also show that these results might have been confounded by age, as child molesters tend to be older, and plasma T level tends to decrease with age (e.g., Rada, Laws, Kellner, Stivastava, & Peake, 1983). Therefore, it remained unclear whether offenders matched for age would show similar T levels, which would call into question the importance of T levels to the development of sexual offending.

Like many empirical studies in the field of research of sexual offending, these early findings were met with some skepticism and caution especially given the underlying deterministic message that this line of research and therapy suggested. For one, human sexual behavior is multidetermined and not simply reflective of biological variation but also the result of environmental and learning experiences (e.g., Hucker & Bain, 1990). It was argued that such biological dysregulations could not explain most cases of sexual offending (Marshall & Barbaree, 1990). Instead, many began to suggest that the familial environment of these perpetrators had failed them in many ways. Some researchers argued that during childhood, these individuals had suffered from trauma, including being sexually abused, which also provided them with inadequate sexual learning and modeling experiences (e.g., Groth, 1979; Seghorn, Prentky, & Boucher, 1987). Others suggested that early inadequate parent–child interactions did not provide a secure attachment that allowed the development and maintenance of intimate and mutually satisfying relationships later in life (e.g., Burgess, Hartman, Ressler, Douglas, & McCormack, 1986; Marshall, 1989). These inadequate and often abusive early learning experiences did not provide the foundation necessary to express sexual urges in a socially acceptable manner. With the rise of the feminist movement and protests against the pornography industry, the role and importance of pornography and its ambiguous, stereotyped, misogynistic views of women as sexual objects were also examined as potential contributing factors with equivocal findings (e.g., Eysenck & Nias, 1978; Goldstein, Kant, Judd, Rice, & Green, 1971). These misogynistic views might become even more critical in "the heat of the moment," as Ariely and Loewenstein (2006) suggest, when sexual arousal further impacts men's decision-making.

Recognition that sexual development and negative family experiences begin early in the life course, combined with the perceived concern that adult "sexual offenders" began their deviant behaviors much earlier than adulthood, led researchers to turn their attention to the search for the cause(s) of sexual offending among adolescents. Up to this point in the 1980s, there had been little empirical research on the topic of adolescent perpetrators of sex crimes. This is somewhat surprising given that criminological research during this era was especially concerned with delinquent and criminal behavior perpetrated by adolescents (Wolfgang, Figlio, & Sellin, 1972). At that time, there was much judicial discretion in the sanctioning of juvenile offenders and criminological research highlighted that only a very small fraction of all adolescents having perpetrated a crime (i.e., any crime type) were referred to the juvenile court or to the public welfare system (e.g., Terry, 1967a, 1967b). The term "juvenile sex offender" was ambiguous given that it referred to not only adult-like sex offenses such as rape, sexual assault, voyeurism, indecent assault, and exhibitionism, but also a wide array of sexual behaviors that departed from heterosexual activities of married couples (Reiss, 1960) such as homosexual acts, sexual promiscuity, sexual intercourse, bestiality, incest (victim of), and sexual misbehaviors (e.g., Atcheson & Williams, 1954; Markey, 1950).

Possibly as a spillover effect of the child-saving movement of the early twentieth century, and *parens patriae* doctrine that guided judicial decision-making for adjudicated youth, these youths were viewed as those in need of "proper" guidance and support. Despite the fact some delinquent youth committed sexual offenses, they were often afforded far less harsh treatment than adults who perpetrated sex crimes. This was largely because of views that their sexual behavior was transitory, partly reflective of the period of adolescence (e.g., fragile self-esteem), partly reflective of their developmental stage (e.g., immaturity, puberty, developing self-control), and partly reflective personality maladjustment in reaction to a dysfunctional familial context (e.g., Atcheson & Williams, 1954; Maclay, 1960). In this context, the research conducted with youth who committed sexual offenses was characterized by much optimism at the time. Longitudinal studies, though rare at the time, suggested that most of these young persons did not sexually re-offend, and if they did commit any subsequent offenses, they were typically relatively minor infractions (e.g., Atcheson & Williams, 1954; Doshay, 1943). While several clinical researchers of the time painted a relatively positive picture of adolescent perpetrators of sex offenses with respect to their risk of sexual re-offending, they were nonetheless concerned about their underlying personality maladjustment that required some sort of professional and therapeutic intervention (e.g., Markey, 1950). Importantly, based on the perspective that personality maladjustment begins in adolescence rather than adulthood (e.g., Blonigen, 2010; Caspi, Roberts, & Shiner, 2005), researchers increasingly began to turn their attention to adolescent perpetrators of sex offenses.

After researchers investigating adult perpetrators of sex offenses observed that samples drawn from individuals processed under Sexual Psychopathy Laws poorly accounted for the most serious, violent, and persistent sex offending patterns (e.g., Cormier & Simons, 1969), a group of scholars became more and more concerned about the seemingly long-term pattern of sexual deviance characterizing individuals that initially perpetrated sex offenses in adolescence. One of the most influential researchers of the time, Groth (1977), argued that there was a reluctance from the courts and other social agencies to take the issue of juvenile sexual offending seriously. To support his claim, he examined a small sample of 26 adolescents aged between 15 and 17 years old who had been convicted for a sexual assault and referred to the Center for the Diagnosis and Treatment of Sexual Dangerous Persons located in Massachusetts. This small sample of adolescent perpetrators, therefore, only represented a small minority of all adolescents also referred to as "sex offenders" that were up to this point met with much optimism by clinical researchers regarding their prognosis. Dr. Groth also included in his sample a group of 37 adult convicted offenders assessed at the same Center who also had a history of sexual offending during adolescence. In other words, Groth identified a group of adult sexual recidivists that had come to the attention of the criminal justice system during adolescence for a sex crime. The data presented did not distinguish between those who were adolescents at the time of the study and those who were adult sexual recidivists. Instead, Groth examined them as one group of adolescent offenders.

Not only did Groth fail to examine a representative sample of young offenders, he examined a very biased sample. Indeed, for a young offender to be sent to that particular institution for an assessment, it required a very specific profile given the courts' reluctance to adjudicate adolescents, especially first-time offenders. In fact, Groth's sample was vastly overrepresented by adolescent sexual recidivists (74%) when research already showed that adolescent sexual recidivists were rarely found, and when they were, they had committed minor offenses (e.g., Doshay, 1943). In this case, sexual recidivism represented involvement in particularly serious sex crimes. These important caveats falsely depicted this small group of adolescents as life-course persistent sexual offenders. In fact, based on his analysis, Groth concluded that "the dynamics of forcible sexual assault by adolescent offenders were the same as those exhibited by adult offenders…" (p. 253). His findings, however, did not support such claims given that some of the "adolescents" in the same sample were actually adult offenders. Such conclusions were also unwarranted by the data available given that these conclusions were generalized to all adolescents having perpetrated a sexual assault.

Against the 1980s/1990s backdrop of an increasing general crime rate that was partly attributable to the changing age-structure and other societal changes occurring during that period (e.g., Steffensmeier & Harer, 1999), the perception emerged among certain circles that juvenile sexual offending was worsening, on the rise, and was an important precursor to becoming an adult "super-predator" (Campregher & Jeglic, 2016). This social context certainly fueled the need and importance of conducting scientific research to improve the understanding of juvenile sexual offending (Barbaree, Hudson, & Seto, 1993). Consequently, the number of scientific investigations significantly increased to determine what is so unique and different about adolescent perpetrators of sex crimes. Sociodemographic, developmental and familial, individual and clinical, legal and criminological factors were measured, examined, described, and compared over the next 20 years (e.g., Awad & Saunders, 1989, 1991). By the late 1980s, research on what was special or unique about juvenile sexual offending was on the rise. Parallels drawn between adult and adolescent offenders were based on research findings that were seriously flawed (e.g., Abel, Osborn, & Twigg, 1993; Groth, 1977) and a perceived increase in the prevalence of juvenile sexual offending raised concerns about the phenomenon (Barbaree et al., 1993).

The parallels drawn between adolescent and adult offenders and the portrayal of all adolescent perpetrators as potential long-term sexual predators in need of an adult-like specialized assessment and interventions blurred the line between sexual offending during adolescence and adulthood. In other words, juvenile sexual offending was treated as a distinct area of research, but the conclusions emanating from this research mimicked those from the literature on adult perpetrators. The importation of theoretical writings and scientific findings observed with adult offenders to explain juvenile sexual offending further added to this trend. Several researchers cautioned about the danger of stigmatizing minors who had caused sexual harm (e.g., Becker, 1998). The growing use of adult-like sentences and a shift away from rehabilitative toward more repressive and punitive approaches that were not in line with the philosophy of the early youth juvenile system were challenged by clinical researchers (Becker & Hicks, 2003).

In sum, from the 1940s up to the 1990s, the search for risk factors uniquely attributable to sexual offending was somewhat anecdotal, atheoretical, and at times pseudo-scientific, plagued by serious methodological limitations. Researchers agreed that of principal importance was understanding the sexual component of this behavioral manifestation, but disagreed with respect to whether this sexual component resulted from a person's personality traits, hormones, or neglectful/negative family experiences. Proponents of the biological-driven hypotheses leaned toward the idea that the causes of sexual offending could be found within the perpetrator in some way such as: (a) they had abnormal sexual urges or an abnormal sexual drive which manifested in deviant, atypical, and criminal ways; (b) they had a relatively normal sexual drive and urges but due to some mental illness they could not express their sexual needs in a prosocial and conventional way; or (c) they had deviant sexual interests and preferences and sexual offending was simply in continuity with their inner world. Tenets of environmental-driven hypotheses leaned toward the role and importance of factors external to the person which significantly impacted perpetrators' sexual development such as: (a) they were sexually victimized early in the life course and these experiences provided them with an inappropriate template for the expression of their sexual urges; (b) they came from a highly dysfunctional family environment and their experiences impacted their ability to develop and maintain adequate and respectful intimate relationships; or (c) they were exposed to inappropriate and inadequate sexual material or messages, for example, in the form of pornography, which impacted their sexual development in such a way as to motivate them to perpetrate a sex crime. Both sets of hypotheses suggested the presence of a predisposition toward the perpetration of sex crimes, whether such predisposition was biologically driven or environmentally caused. The idea that such a predisposition was a common characteristic among these adolescent perpetrators suggested to some that there was a long-lasting presence and impact of the predisposition toward the perpetration of sex crimes.

From a scientific standpoint, a number of methodological limitations stood out in most of these studies that rendered them inadequate for addressing the research questions of interest. For example, most of the studies were based on a highly selective and biased sample of individuals who had been arrested, charged, convicted, and incarcerated for a sex crime. Even the incarcerated samples were not representative of all incarcerated offenders because they relied on subsamples of individuals characterized by mental health disturbances and therefore transferred and admitted to a psychiatric institution or the psychiatric ward in a prison. As reported earlier, individuals receiving the type of psychiatric assessment that would allow for such transfers represented a tiny percentage of convicted offenders (Braude, 1950). Of importance, most of the studies conducted were retrospective, meaning that the explanatory factors assessed by researchers were measured after the perpetration of a sex crime (Lussier & Cale, 2016). This raised the question of whether the risk factors investigated were in fact a cause, consequence, or simply a correlate of sexual offending. For example, was low self-esteem influencing individuals to commit a sex crime, or was the experience of being tried, convicted, incarcerated, and admitted to a psychiatric hospital influencing an individual's perspective of themselves? Also, the relative absence of information on comparison groups of non-sex offenders raised important questions about the possibility of drawing firm conclusions from study findings. While research on perpetrators of sex crimes was plagued by methodological limitations, such limitations were not necessarily identified or considered at the time. As such, this body of research certainly helped shape many of today's assumptions about perpetrators of sex crimes.

Can 15 Meta-Analyses Be Wrong?

In the social sciences, a single study rarely if ever solves a social issue or social problem. Replication and the accumulation of scientific observations from independent studies has been and remains a fundamental pillar of science. To address the limitations of individual studies, researchers have sometimes conducted reviews of the scientific literature. There are different types of scientific reviews that can be conducted to summarize the state of research on a particular research question within a specific field of study. The most common form of scientific review found in the field of sexual offending is a narrative review in which scholars read a body of literature on a particular topic and provide their interpretation of this work. For example, this book provides a narrative review of past and current research and policy about sexual offending. Another form of review involves a more systematic inspection of all empirical studies conducted on a very specific research question. This particular approach is useful when one is interested in knowing more about how many independent studies have been conducted, how this particular type of research is done, what type of research instruments are used, what population of research participants have been targeted, and so on. A third type of review (there are more than three types) refers to what researchers call quantitative meta-analysis.

Quantitative meta-analysis offers researchers a powerful tool that can help to circumvent some of the methodological limitations of single independent studies. More specifically, quantitative meta-analysis allows researchers to combine findings from similar, yet independent empirical studies. The technique originates from the work of Smith and Glass (1977) and has since been extended and developed (e.g., Hedges & Olkin, 1985; Lipsey & Wilson, 2001). Because independent empirical studies vary on a number of factors (e.g., sample size, number of tests/trials, type of variables used) other than the statistical findings, it can be difficult to integrate findings and summarize the scientific literature as a whole. As such, quantitative meta-analyses are used to summarize and integrate the statistical findings of independent empirical studies, also known as effect sizes, on a specific topic. Therefore, a meta-analysis cannot include theoretical pieces, policy recommendations, or findings from a qualitative study or review. Also, they cannot be used to aggregate findings from empirical studies that are examining different risk factors or different explanatory variables; they cannot combine findings from studies applying different research designs. That said, given that research in the field of sexual offending is often based on small and biased samples, researchers have turned to quantitative meta-analyses to draw more reliable conclusions about risk factors of sexual offending.

The research conducted between the 1940s and the 1990s dictated the list of potential key risk factors for sexual offending, how to examine and measure these risk factors, and where to conduct such empirical research. Replication is paramount to science and researchers tested and re-tested some of the same hypotheses allowing other researchers to conduct meta-analyses to examine empirically the importance of those key risk factors. At the time that this book was being written, the scientific literature on sexual offending had produced a total of 15 unique quantitative meta-analyses that compared the prevalence or degree of a given risk factor across perpetrators of sex offenses and at least one comparison sample (e.g., nonsexual offenders). The goal of each meta-analysis was to statistically summarize what is so unique and specific about perpetrators of sex crimes. Other meta-analyses that examined risk factors that predict sexual recidivism were excluded given that these studies do not include non-sex offenders and therefore cannot be used to understand the uniqueness of perpetrators of sex crimes.

This chapter provides a systematic review of all meta-analyses conducted aiming to identify the risk factors for sexual offending. The inspection of these meta-analyses revealed some of the most common themes that researchers in the field of sexual offending have been focusing on for the past eight decades or so. In other words, in addition to elucidating differences between sexual and nonsexual offenders, the types of risk factors investigated in these meta-analyses reveal the tone of sexual offending research to date, including what have been some of the major hypotheses about the explanation of sexual offending from a research standpoint. It also exposes the extent to which some of these hypotheses have been examined through independent empirical studies. Whereas the focus of the chapter to this point has been on a narrative review of the state of sexual offending research, the inspection of these meta-analyses shows more clearly, and more objectively via statistical summaries, the most common methodological approaches used, including the research design, sampling procedures, type of measures and instruments used if any, and the analytical strategy used to address very complex questions such as the origins and the development of sexual offending. These meta-analyses are presented and summarized in Table 5.1.

The examination of these meta-analyses revealed four individual-level risk factor domains and one environmental-level risk factor domain hypothesized to distinguish the development of sexual offending: (1) biological factors (e.g., T, intelligence, neurobiological deficits); (2) physiological factors (e.g., sexual arousal); (3) psychological factors (e.g., attachment deficits, social anxiety); (4) behavioral factors (e.g., social competence skills, pornography usage); (5) environmental adversity (e.g., history of abuse). The domains identified were congruent with our observation about the heavy focus on individual-level factors as key causes of sexual offending (Fig. 5.1). This reflects the long-held idea that perpetrators of sex crimes are fundamentally different and such differences are responsible for their sexual

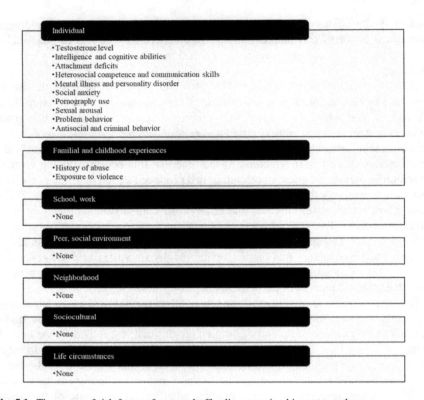

Fig. 5.1 The scope of risk factors for sexual offending examined in meta-analyses

offending. Furthermore, of these five domains examined, the level of intelligence, the presence of neuropsychological deficits, and a history of abuse have been especially prominent in research comparing "sex offenders" and a comparison group. The presence of a higher volume of research for these risk factor domains suggests that they reflect long-held hypotheses about the origins and the development of sexual offending. The inspection of findings from the 15 meta-analyses reveals a series of trends about the specificity characterizing perpetrators of sex crimes.

Researchers comparing perpetrators of sex crimes to other individuals are concerned with group differences that are both statistically significant and characterized by a large effect size. Recall that researchers do not conduct their research on all perpetrators of sexual offense in society but rather a sample of offenders said to be representing this population. In that context, statistical significance refers to the probability of rejecting the null hypothesis of no group differences between a group of sex offenders and a group of non-sex offenders given that the null hypothesis is true. More simply, statistical significance means essentially that the differences observed in a given study are not due to chance or random sampling variation but do reflect actual differences in the population. The effect size reflects the magnitude, or extent to which these differences are important between the two groups.

Table 5.1 A description of 15 quantitative meta-analyses examining potential risk factors for sexual offending

	Study identification	Factor(s) examined	Number of studies included	Samples	Measures and instruments
1	Wong and Gravel (2018)	Testosterone level	7	SO, $n = 325$ (rapists and child molesters) CG, $n = 196$ (diverse: staff, volunteers, convicts)	The testosterone level was measured using either blood sample ($k = 9$) or saliva test ($k = 2$). All studies obtained physical samples in the morning, which were measured after the perpetration of the sexual offense
2	Cantor et al. (2005)	Intelligence	75	SO, $n = 7045$ (juvenile and adult samples; sexual offenders against children sexual offenders against adults) CG, $n = 18,101$ (diverse, staff, volunteers, students, convicts)	A range of tests were used to measure cognitive capacity, including the Wechsler adult intelligence scale ($k = 36$), the Wechsler adult intelligence scale—revised ($k = 36$), the Army general classification tests ($k = 22$), the short form of any of the Wechsler intelligence tests ($k = 19$), and the Wechsler intelligence scale for children—revised ($k = 20$)
3	Joyal, Beaulieu-Plante, and de Chantérac (2014)	Neuropsychological deficits	23	SO, $n = 1063$ (rapists and child molesters) CG, $n = 693$ (non-sex offenders (violent or not) and general population)	Tests used to measure neuropsychological deficits included the following: the Stroop interference condition (time; cognitive inhibition); the trail-making B task (time; speed processing and switching); the Wisconsin card sorting task (categories, perseveration, and correct responses; reasoning and cognitive flexibility); the Halstead-Reitan category task (number of correct responses; reasoning); the Raven's standard progressive matrices (total score; reasoning and fluid intelligence); the control oral word association test (COWAT; number of correct responses; verbal fluency); the logical memory subtest (delayed recall; memory); the visual reproduction subtest (delayed recall; memory) of the Weschler memory scale

(continued)

Table 5.1 (continued)

	Study identification	Factor(s) examined	Number of studies included	Samples	Measures and instruments
4	Boommann et al. (2016)	Mental illness	8	SO, n = 2951 (juvenile sex offenders) CG, n = 18,688 (non-sex juvenile offenders)	Mental disorder measures were based on DSM or ICD classifications, assessed by use of a structured or semi-structured clinical instrument, or retrieved from file reports
5	Hall et al. (1993)	Sexual arousal	9	SO, n = 175 (prison and mental health samples) CG, n = 164 (university students, sexual offenders, staff, and non-sex offenders) Other, n = 95 (undergraduate students)	Penile response to rape audio-recorded stimuli using a penile plethysmograph
6	Lalumière and Quinsey (1994)	Sexual arousal	12	SO, n = 415 rapists (mainly correctional and mental health settings) CG, n = 192 (university students, general population, non-sex offenders)	Penile response to rape audio-recorded stimuli using a penile plethysmograph
7	Babchishin, Hanson, and Hermann (2011)	History of abuse and demographic variables	27	SO, n = 4844 online sex offenders (diverse: treatment centers, prisons, registered sexual offenders) CG, n = variable	The histories of abuse were self-reported data. For the sex offender groups, the information was generally collected through self-reported information or collected from different file documents (e.g., court, psychologist, police, etc.)
8	Jespersen et al. (2009)	History of abuse	24	SO, n = 1999 (1037 sexual offenders; 962 sexual offenders against children) CG, n = 3096 (1762 violent and nonviolent offenders; 1334 sex offenders against women)	Most of the studies included in this meta-analysis obtained abuse history information directly from the offenders (self-reported)

	Study identification	Factor(s) examined	Number of studies included	Samples	Measures and instruments
9	Ogilvie, Newman, Todd, and Peck (2014)	Attachment deficits	6	SO, $n = 268$ rapists and child molesters CG, $n = 224$ violent offenders	Standardized assessments were used to measure attachment deficits such as: relationship scales questionnaire; experiences in close relationships inventory; Cloninger's temperament and character inventory; adult attachment interview
10	Dreznick (2003)	Heterosocial competence	14	SO, $n =$ unclear (child molesters, rapists) CG, $n =$ unclear (incarcerated and non-incarcerated samples)	Tests used to measure heterosocial competence included some of the following: the affect categorization in a romantic scenario; the confederates' ratings of anxiety; the confederates' ratings of social skills; the discrepancy between predicted and actual self-efficacy in heterosocial situation; the facial affect recognition; the fear of intimacy scale; the heterosocial skills behavior checklist; the hostility discrimination index; the judges' ratings of anxiety; the judges' ratings of social skill; the relationship questionnaire, fearful attachment; the relationship scales questionnaire, fearful attachment; self-ratings of anxiety; the seduction discrimination index
11	Emmers-Sommer et al., 2004	Communication skills	11	SO, $n = 196$ (convicted sex offenders) CG, $n =$ unclear (college students, convicted offenders) Other, $n = 1568$ (university and college students)	Measures of communication skills included surveys, observational scales, and some of the following instruments: Rathus assertiveness scale; assertiveness inventory; social response inventory subscale; heterosexual skills behavior checklist

(continued)

Table 5.1 (continued)

	Study identification	Factor(s) examined	Number of studies included	Samples	Measures and instruments
12	Nunes et al. (2012)	Social anxiety	6	SO, $n = 273$ (convicted sex offenders against children) CG, $n = 397$ (inmates, sex offenders against adults, community, and university students)	Social avoidance and distress scale
13	Allen et al. (1999)	Pornography usage	13	SO, $n =$ unclear (rapists, child molesters, exhibitionists that were under arrest, convicted or in treatment) CG, $n =$ unclear (persons that had no record of criminal sexual behavior)	Measures of the use of sexual material were based on surveys which included questions/items measuring: the frequency of use (how often the person used sexually explicit material); the age at first exposure to sexual material; the use of sexual material prior to some form of sexual behavior (masturbation, consensual sex, coercive sex, or criminal sexual behavior). The measure of the physiological effects of sexual materials exposure was based on the penile plethysmograph
14	Whitaker et al. (2008)	Multiple risk factors	89	SO, $n =$ unclear (sex offenders against children, adults, and juvenile offenders) CG, $n =$ unclear (sex offenders against adult victims, non-sex offenders (prison and treatment samples), and non-offenders (university students and community))	No information was provided by the authors with respect to the instruments and measures used in the original studies as well as the scoring of those that lead to the computation of effect sizes

	Study identification	Factor(s) examined	Number of studies included	Samples	Measures and instruments
15	Seto and Lalumière (2010)	Multiple general delinquency and specific sexual offending risk factors	59	SO, $n = 3855$ (juvenile sex offenders (probation, custody, court treatment samples) CG, $n = 13,393$ (non-sex offenders)	A wide range of instruments were used to measure the following risk factors domains, which included: (a) conduct disorders (e.g., Millon adolescent personality inventory; multidimensional assessment of sex and aggression; (b) antisocial tendencies (e.g., Buss–Durkee hostility inventory; psychopathy checklist—revised); (c) Substance abuse (e.g., diagnostic interview schedule for children; young offender level of supervision inventory); (d) childhood abuse and exposure to violence (e.g., childhood trauma questionnaire; modified conflict tactics scales); (e) family problems (e.g., children's report of parental behavior inventory; family adaptability and cohesion; family attachment and changeability index); (f) interpersonal problems (e.g., adolescent temperament questionnaire; california personality inventory—revised); (g) sexuality (e.g., sexual fantasy questionnaire; sexual history form; multidimensional assessment of sex and aggression); (h) psychopathology (e.g., Beck depression inventory; minnesota multiphasic personality inventory); (i) cognitive abilities (e.g., controlled oral word association; electroencephalogram; Kaufman brief intelligence test)

Note: n sample size, *SO* sex offender sample, *CG* comparison group, *k* number of unique studies

Five key observations can be made in this regard. First, when statistically significant differences are found between perpetrators of a sex crime and the comparison group, they are relatively small. The 15 meta-analyses examined reported at least one significant difference between perpetrators of sex crimes and some comparison group. However, the differences observed were relatively small, reflected by a low effect size. The presence of a low effect size is not surprising as sexual offending is a complex, multidetermined phenomenon resulting from the effect of multiple factors. As such, meta-analyses only looking at a single risk factor at a time are bound to identify differences that are relatively small in magnitude. The identification of differences, albeit small, does not tell the whole story as the inspection of these study findings are more complex and these meta-analyses in fact show mixed findings. Indeed, the mean effect size identified often masks important variation across the studies compared with respect to nature of these deficits, type of perpetrator, and nature of the comparison group that cast doubts about the interpretation and the meaningfulness of these findings.

Second, effect sizes are more pronounced when the comparison group is composed of a sample of individuals from the general population rather than non-sex offenders. Across studies, it is noticeable that researchers were likely to find significant differences when comparing perpetrators of sex crimes to individuals from the general population. Generally speaking, samples from the general population were often university/college students, hospital staff, and other volunteers. This is particularly problematic given that this group was simply inadequate in that they differed from the perpetrators of sex crimes in so many ways other than having been convicted for a sex crime (e.g., more educated, less likely to have a mental illness, less likely to have a criminal history, etc.). In that context, it is not surprising that researchers observed individual differences between the two groups; these differences could not conclusively be interpreted as risk factors for sexual offending but could refer to differential propensity, for example, to be apprehended for a crime. In effect, such studies were not equipped to understand risk factors for sexual offending because they could not rule out important confounds such as the fact that these risk factors may be causes of other behavioral and social outcomes that were more common to sex offenders than to college students.

Third, accounting for heterogeneity *among* perpetrators of sex offenses reveals a lack of uniformity when it comes to differences with perpetrators of non-sex offenses. For example, perpetrators of sex crimes against women are very similar to non-sex offenders when compared along the dimensions included in the various meta-analyses. Indeed, while differences have been reported when compared to non-offenders (e.g., students, hospital staff members), these differences were not observed when this type of perpetrator was compared to non-sex offenders (e.g., inmates, violent offenders, individuals convicted for other crime types). One possible exception to this has been in relation to their sexual arousal pattern. Using phallometric assessment, perpetrators of sex crimes showed differential sexual arousal patterns in laboratory settings compared to controls (e.g., Allen, D'Alessio, & Emmers-Sommer, 1999; Hall, Shondrick, & Hirschman, 1993). There are two related questions that are relevant here: a) whether they are more sexually aroused by rape depictions than controls; and b) whether perpetrators of sex crimes are more sexually aroused by rape depictions than consenting sex between two adults compared to controls. Lalumière and Quinsey (1994) found supporting empirical evidence for both of these questions. This seemed to be especially true when phallometric assessment involved the use of graphic and brutal rape audiotaped stimuli (Lalumière & Quinsey, 1994).

The first question refers to a general lack of inhibition over their sexual arousal, while the second question refers to rape as a sexual preference. The latter would provide support for the earlier hypothesis that sexual offending is a result of non-normative sexual interests (i.e., deviant sexual arousal) as opposed to the result of uncontrollable sexual urges (i.e., hypersexuality). Let us recall that phallometric assessments are conducted with convicted offenders after the perpetration of their crimes. As a result, it is impossible to determine whether: (a) their sexual arousal to rape caused their sexual offending; (b) their sexual arousal to rape is a result of their sexual offending (e.g., these scenarios draw upon memories of sexually arousing experiences that occurred as part of committing sex offenses); or (c) whether the two are simply correlated because of a third factor that affects both sexual offending and sexual arousal. Potential confounds for an intervening factor in the latter scenario include: proneness to sensation-seeking behavior, preference for rough and loud situations, low self-control, callous-unemotional traits, and rape myths and false beliefs supporting rape (e.g., Hall & Hirschman, 1991; Knight & Sims-Knight, 2003; Lussier, Proulx, & LeBlanc, 2005; Malamuth, 1998).

Fourth, perpetrators of sex crimes against women tend to differ from perpetrators of sex crimes against children. Most of the meta-analyses that examined group differences along these lines reported some differences on the risk factor measures examined. Some variation was found between perpetrators of sex crimes against women (higher T level) and perpetrators with child victims (lower T level) (Wong & Gravel, 2018). However, other differences between these two groups, such as the older age of perpetrators with child victims and the higher tendency for perpetrating general violence found among perpetrators of adult women, might be responsible for these differences. Similarly, compared to aggressors against children, perpetrators of sex crimes against women showed more heterosocial competence (Dreznick, 2003), similar levels of social anxiety (Nunes, McPhail, & Babchishin, 2012), a lower likelihood of having been sexually abused, but a greater likelihood of having been physically abused (Jespersen, Lalumière, & Seto, 2009; see, however, Whitaker et al., 2008); they were somewhat more likely to show evidence of externalizing behavior, including issues of anger and hostility, but not in terms of symptoms from the internalizing spectrum (Whitaker et al., 2008). In other words, there appeared to be as much, if not more, variation within the group of perpetrators of sex offenses than between these perpetrators and perpetrators of non-sex offenses.

Fifth, once the abovementioned within-group differences were accounted for, the significant differences reported between perpetrators of sex offenses and non-sex offenses appeared to be largely attributable to perpetrators of sex crimes against children more specifically, especially when compared to individuals from the general population. More specifically, perpetrators of sex crimes against children tended to be characterized by lower intelligence, showed evidence of neuropsychological deficits, especially with respect to cognitive inhibition and control of interference and appeared to be less socially competent, more socially anxious and characterized by an anxious attachment style. Not surprisingly, they were also found to be more sexually aroused to sexual stimuli involving children than non-offenders (Allen et al., 1999). Despite these differences, these findings do not necessarily mean that all or even most perpetrators of sex crimes against children commonly present with these individual characteristics. For example, one possibility is that even after sub-dividing perpetrators of sex offenses according to victim selection (i.e., children versus adults), there is still a distinctively unique subgroup of perpetrators within the child "sex offender" subgroup that drives the observed differences compared with controls. It is important to keep in mind that the heterogeneity of these perpetrators in terms of their sexual preferences has been demonstrated in other research. For example, only a subgroup of perpetrators of sex crimes against children show evidence of pedophilic sexual interests (Barbaree & Marshall, 1989; Michaud & Proulx, 2009).

Given that these factors have been examined in different studies, it is unclear whether these differences characterize most, some, or a small proportion of perpetrators of sex crimes against children. In other words, it is not entirely clear whether these findings are indicative of a typical clinical profile or multiple profiles of adult perpetrators of sex crimes against children. These differences, however, remain difficult to interpret because they could reflect methodological limitations such as differential risk of being apprehended, charged, and convicted for a sex crime against a child or a filtering process by which the individuals presenting these characteristics are more likely to be accepted in a mental hospital and/or a sex offender treatment program. Furthermore, they could also reflect pedophilic sexual interests and/or victim-choice selection rather than sexual offending.

For adolescent perpetrators, based on a more limited number of meta-analyses (e.g.,Boonmann et al., 2016; Seto & Lalumière, 2010), a few interesting additional trends were observed. Overall, prior sexual abuse, deviant sexual interests, exposure to violence, anxiety, low self-esteem, and exposure to sex or pornography were risk factors that distinguished adolescent perpetrators of sex offenses from those of non-sex offenses. Perpetrators of sex offenses were more likely to report prior sexual abuse, atypical sexual interests, having been exposed to violence and sex growing up, as well as being somewhat more anxious and characterized by lower self-esteem. However, several major methodological issues require further consideration of the accuracy and meaningfulness of these differences. Perpetrators of sex crimes were more likely to be selected from clinical populations; such populations did not exist for perpetrators of non-sex offenses, who were more likely to be recruited from incarcerated populations (Seto & Lalumière, 2010). By being in a clinical treatment setting, it is unclear to what extent adolescent "sex offenders" may have been more open to disclosing information about pornography use, sexual interests, abuse history, etc., because they were speaking with clinicians compared to adolescent perpetrators of non-sex offenses in incarceration facilities. Similarly, it is unclear as to what extent these perpetrators of sex crimes may have been more aware of their family's sexual history because of this being a relevant factor discussed in the court process, especially for those involved in incestual sex offenses. For adolescent perpetrators of non-sex offenses, this would not necessarily be relevant information pertaining to their adjudication/sentencing and thus is less likely to be brought up/discussed in the first place. In other words, is it possible that decades of research about, for example, sexual deviance as a key factor for sexual offending has resulted in clinicians, judges, and lawyers placing great emphasis on such factors at the time of sentencing adolescents who have perpetrated a sex crime. In effect, it is possible that a long history of heightened attention to these factors has created greater awareness, rather than necessarily reflecting an actual higher prevalence, of these factors among these perpetrators compared to perpetrators of non-sex offenses.

There is little evidence that, as a group, adolescent perpetrators of a sex crime are more likely to show evidence of a mental illness compared to other adolescents (Boonmann et al., 2016; Seto & Lalumière, 2010). In fact, they are somewhat less likely to present symptoms that meet the diagnostic criteria for a mental disorder compared to youth involved in other crime types. This appears to be true for a wide range of mental health problems, especially along the internalization spectrum that are often in reaction to abuse and trauma (e.g., anxiety, depression, affective disorder, post-traumatic stress disorder). This may potentially reflect some distinction between adolescent and adult perpetrators of sex crimes. Indeed, adult perpetrators were more likely to stand out compared to their non-offender counterparts on various mental health indicators. Finally, and importantly, while Cantor, Blanchard, Robichaud, and Christensen (2005) observed a lower IQ for adult perpetrators of sex crimes against children, such a trend was not observed for adolescent offenders, further suggesting another important distinction between adolescent and adult perpetrators of sex crimes.

Differences that are more noticeable between perpetrators and non-perpetrators of sex crimes can be found along the externalizing spectrum. Perpetrators of a sex crime were less likely to meet the diagnostic criteria of an associated disorder (e.g., drug and alcohol abuse, disruptive behavior, and attention deficit hyperactivity disorder symptoms). Perpetrators of a sex crime were, overall, less frequently involved in crime and delinquency compared to perpetrators of non-sex offenses (Seto & Lalumière, 2010). However, adolescent perpetrators of a sex crime were also significantly younger at the time of their assessments. Because they were significantly younger, it is possible that such individuals simply had less exposure to opportunities for, for example, alcohol use, disruptive behavior, and juvenile delinquency. This may reflect the fact that courts are more concerned about sexual offenses than other types of offenses and are more willing to incarcerate adolescents for a first-time sex offense compared to a first-time non-sex offense. This may be especially true given Franklin Zimring's characterization of the United States' justice system fear that today's adolescent sex offender is tomorrow's adult sex offender. The higher prevalence of disorders among perpetrators of non-sex crimes could also simply reflect the fact that, the common denominator among perpetrators of sex crimes was typically a single conviction for a sex crime. On the other hand, the common denominator for youth perpetrators of non-sex crimes was typically a more extensive pattern of juvenile delinquency (e.g., chronic, serious, and violent offending) which explains why they were adjudicated and incarcerated. In other words, to be a "juvenile sex offender" in such samples typically required just a single conviction for a sex crime. To be a "juvenile non-sex offender" in such samples required perpetration of multiple non-sex crimes. These externalizing behavior differences therefore could reflect the nature of a study's research design rather than the curious finding that being less delinquent increases the risk of perpetrating a sex crime in adolescence. This is counterintuitive to findings stemming from very large and representative longitudinal birth cohort studies that are not plagued by the methodological issues characterizing studies included in these meta-analyses (e.g., Lussier & Blokland, 2014).

These findings highlight factors that have been shown to differentiate perpetrators of sex crimes from non-perpetrators of sex crimes. At face value, the findings highlight potential factors that may contribute to the perpetration of a sex crime. It is important to keep in mind that these meta-analyses were focused a priori on the study of individual-level factors that differentiate perpetrators of sex crimes from non-perpetrators of sex crime. Relatedly, researchers have specifically been looking for what is unique and different about perpetrators of sex crimes, therefore it stands to reason that what is perhaps the most important risk factor for sexual offending, antisocial propensity, was relatively absent from these meta-analyses given its obvious importance to offending more broadly. After all, there is little specificity to the concept of antisocial propensity. That said, the status of these individual-level factors remains unclear and equivocal despite the observed findings reported in these meta-analyses. The presence of individual-level differences between perpetrators of a sex crime and non-perpetrators does not prove that these characteristics are risk factors for sexual offending. Indeed, because of the methodological limitations characterizing the studies included in the meta-analyses reviewed, it remains equivocal as to whether the findings have helped to identify: (a) risk factors for sexual offending (e.g., factors increasing the odds of perpetrating a sex crime); (b) consequences of sexual offending (e.g., perpetrating a sex crimes increases the odds of experiencing these factors); (c) correlates of sexual offending (e.g., these factors and sexual offending share something in common); (d) a filtering process within the criminal justice system (e.g., individuals presenting these characteristics are more likely to be apprehended and convicted for a sex crime); or (e) a combination of these situations. In all, findings from meta-analyses raise more questions than answers and also highlight the issues and challenges that researchers are facing when trying to understand such complex phenomena.

Limitations of Existing Knowledge

In addition to the abovementioned limitations of meta-analytic work that is specific to challenges with studying sexual offending, there are also limitations of meta-analytic work more broadly that require consideration. Meta-analyses are not a panacea for concrete conclusions about complex social science questions and like any other research are characterized by conceptual and methodological limitations. Therefore, findings stemming from this type of research should be interpreted accordingly, findings of a meta-analysis are as good as the research conducted in a particular field. Taking these two important points into consideration, the findings discussed above do not provide entirely convincing evidence that risk factors for sex crime perpetration have been identified. Rather, they are showing that there are promising factors that need to be investigated further. One consistent conclusion, however, is that among perpetrators of sexual crimes, those having offended against children seem to present a relatively distinct profile from other offenders and the general population. This observation, however, seems to be true for adult offenders but not necessarily for adolescents having perpetrated similar crimes against younger children (e.g., Worling & Långström, 2003). These findings suggest that some sort of specificity characterizing perpetrators of sex offenses is not what makes them different as a group. Rather, methodological issues aside, what stands out is that specific risk factors appear to be associated with the perpetration of different sex crimes, at least for adults.

If most studies are plagued by the same specific methodological limitations, conducting a meta-analysis combining the findings of these studies will not alleviate these issues. This is quite important because many studies in the field do present very similar methodological limitations. The fact that most studies are based on retrospective rather prospective data is not corrected by the use of a meta-analysis. Likewise, meta-analysis cannot correct for the fact that several studies have relied on comparison groups (e.g., college students, treatment staff) that are inadequate because they differ from perpetrators of sex crimes found in a mental health institution on a number of ways other than being convicted for a sex crime. Meta-analyses also cannot correct for the fact that the vast majority of studies have been based on samples of perpetrators who have been arrested, convicted, and incarcerated for their crime. The use of a conviction to identify a group of perpetrators of sex offenses is certainly not a new practice in research (Ellis & Brancale, 1956), but it remains a major methodological limitation. Although this limitation is frequently acknowledged by the same research, actual attempts to address the limitation or understand how impactful this limitation is on the understanding of the uniqueness of perpetrators of sexual offenses has been relatively overlooked. In fact, it is noticeable that researchers did not report nor attempted to control for the methodological rigor of each of the empirical studies included in their meta-analysis. The methodological rigor does vary greatly across empirical studies in this field and it could explain why the effect sizes reported across studies tend to vary.

The meta-analytic approach also assumes that the "sex offender" group is homogenous, and therefore fails to account for within-group differences in this population. In other words, these findings allow one to see if the "average" perpetrator of a sex crime is statistically different from the average perpetrator of non-sex crimes. One must consider the possibility that, perhaps, there is no such thing as an "average" perpetrator of sex crimes and surprisingly this hypothesis has not been addressed rigorously. The presence of such heterogeneity within the group of perpetrators of sex offenses is highlighted by the observed findings, especially with respect to differences between perpetrators of sex crimes against adults and perpetrators of sex crimes against children. It is interesting to note that while researchers have found empirical evidence that perpetrators of sex offenses against children are different from controls, they generalize their findings to "sex offenders" more broadly. What these meta-analyses do not address is the fact even within these two groups, there is much heterogeneity that is not accounted for by these studies. There are different "types" of perpetrators of sex crimes against women and different "types" of perpetrators of sex crimes against children (e.g., Cale, 2018; Proulx, Beauregard, Lussier, & Leclerc, 2014). While several classification schemes have been proposed over the years focusing on victim characteristics, offenders' motivation, and crime-scene behaviors (e.g., Gebhard, Gagnon, Pomeroy, & Christenson, 1965; Knight & Prentky, 1990), it remains unclear how to best account for such heterogeneity from an explanatory standpoint.

The meta-analytical approach requires researchers conducting the study to aggregate findings from independent studies. The inspection of these meta-analyses reveals a deeper, more fundamental problem within the field of research on sexual offending, that is, the lack of theoretically sound research. For the most part, the research conducted thus far and included in the 15 meta-analyses is overwhelmingly inductively driven by clinical judgment and clinical hypotheses about perpetrators found in sex offender treatment programs. The relative absence of theory-driven hypotheses resonates even in the interpretation of the study findings. It is as if the research on sex offending has adopted horse blinders that require the investigation of hypotheses without any attention to research conducted outside the field of sexual offending. For example, Cantor et al. (2005) concluded that perpetrators of sex crimes tend to show a lower IQ and the evidence provided by 72 reports provided sufficient justification to move beyond further substantiating whether these offenders in fact show lower IQ, to instead understand why it is that a lower IQ was identified among perpetrators of sex crimes. However, missing from this analysis is the consideration of whether lower IQ is indeed even a meaningful risk factor for involvement in offending; identifying differences between groups does not necessarily imply that such differences represent causal risk factors. Indeed, criminological research has shown that IQ is not a pivotal contributor to crime involvement, the association of IQ with crime has been shown to be small and most likely indirect through some intervening factors (e.g., Cullen, Gendreau, Jarjoura, & Wright, 1997; Gendreau, Little, & Goggin, 1996). If IQ is not a particularly important risk factor for criminal behavior, then to what extent will understanding why sexual offenders have a lower IQ actually contribute to reducing sexual offending? Having observed the lower IQ of perpetrators of sex crimes against children, Guay, Ouimet, and Proulx (2005) hypothesized that these differences were in fact attributable to an overrepresentation of lower IQ offenders being incarcerated and admitted to sex offender treatment programs. In other words, the lower IQ observation among perpetrators of sex crimes against children was simply an artefact of the criminal justice differential response to sex offender characteristics and its differential response to what is *perceived* to be a risk factor.

The file-drawer problem is another inherent issue with respect to the interpretation of quantitative meta-analysis. The file-drawer problem refers to the reliance on published scientific work, which can be interpreted as a publication bias. This bias occurs when the probability that a study gets published is related or influenced by its statistical findings. Studies that find a lack of significant differences might be deemed less interesting or useful by journal editors and reviewers and thus will be rejected for publication; alternatively, researchers may stuff such papers in a drawer and not even bother to seek publication, hence the file-drawer problem. Put simply, new research is more likely to be published when significant findings are observed. Research that fails to identify differences between sexual and nonsexual offenders is less likely to be published and therefore less likely to be included in meta-analyses. The issue is somewhat highlighted by Emmers-Sommer et al. (2004) who decided to remove a study that *did not show* a significant difference between perpetrators of a sex crime and controls because it represented more than 50% of the whole sample. In doing so, they focused on the clinical studies that relied on small and biased samples and found statistically significant differences between perpetrators and controls. Emmers-Sommer et al.'s (2004) strategy is highly questionable but also valuable for illustrating the danger and consequence of the file-drawer effect and the absence of the "grey" literature (i.e., unpublished studies) in meta-analyses. While they removed a published study (i.e., Muehlenhard & Falcon, 1990) from their analyses, there might be other unpublished studies on the issue that were not included in meta-analyses because of the file-drawer problem. The file-drawer problem applies to all meta-analyses examined in this review.[2]

Conclusion

The nature and severity of sex crimes makes it especially difficult for the public to imagine a scenario in which one could commit such crimes. Accordingly, theorizing and research on sexual offending started with an assumption that perpetrators of sex crimes must be different, not only from people that do not offend, but also from people that commit non-sex offenses. It therefore is not surprising that the field of research on sexual offending developed almost completely independently from criminology and the study of criminal behavior (Lussier & Beauregard, 2018). It is telling that the most common criminogenic risk factors for crime and delinquency are not included in these meta-analyses (however, see Seto & Lalumière, 2010). Research on sexual offending began in response to inadequate criminal justice policies aimed at individuals having perpetrated a sex crime who were perceived to be too sexually dangerous for society. Rather than guiding policymaking, research conducted with biased samples of perpetrators in psychiatric hospitals and psychiatric

---

[2] To address this issue more directly, for example, Nunes et al. (2012) estimated the number of additional negative findings required to nullify the ones observed in their meta-analysis on social anxiety and sexual offending.

units in prison settings somewhat reinforced the idea of uniqueness of perpetrators of sex crimes, but not along the lines first imagined. Despite Sexual Psychopathy Laws, rather than finding a sexual psychopath, research found heterogeneous populations; some perpetrators were characterized by mental illness, others by low IQ and deviant sexual interests, and yet others, by none of these factors. In light of the ambiguous findings, rather than bringing theoretical and conceptual clarity, this field of research raised far more questions.

Trends in the meta-analytic findings have raised questions that are more important than the answers produced by these statistical summaries themselves. These questions can be boiled down to two main trends. The first trend requires questioning the meaningfulness of the differences identified. Effect sizes are often relatively small and perhaps not of clinical utility. It is not as if there is an all-versus-none observation when it comes to, for example, the prevalence of sexual deviance across perpetrators of sex and non-sex offenses. When stronger differences are observed, it is typically when studies compared perpetrators of sex offenses to non-offenders. By sampling from two populations that are distinct across a wide range of sociode-mographic and other important characteristics it remains unclear whether differences in risk factors reflect the origins of sexual offending or the origins of mental health issues, poverty, poor education outcomes, etc. Doing so also fails to distinguish whether the differences identified reflect risk factors specifically for sexual offending or risk factors for general offending/coming into the detection of the broader criminal justice system. When compared against individuals involved in non-sex offenses, differences are less pronounced. This is especially true when comparing perpetrators of sex crimes against women to perpetrators of non-sex offenses. In fact, differences among perpetrators of sex offenses (e.g., perpetrators against adults versus those against children) may be more prominent than when comparing differences between perpetrators of sex and non-sex offenses.

It is therefore difficult to claim that perpetrators of sex offenses are a unique, homogenous group when the degree of within-group variability is stronger than between-group differences. One approach pursued by researchers has been to subdivide perpetrators of sexual offenses into smaller and smaller groups based on their offense characteristics (e.g., sadistic sexual offenders, homosexual extrafamilial child molesters, etc.). Traditionally, this approach stems from the hypothesis that the offending behavior is a reflection of some specific individual predisposition (e.g., deviant sexual fantasies). This latter type of approach does not necessarily avoid previous concerns with research design limitations, atheoretical attention to spurious risk factors, and the tendency to focus on the offender's most recent offense rather than their entire offending pattern. In fact, such theoretical and methodological concerns may be exacerbated using this type of approach. Furthermore, this approach fails to consider the role and importance of situational and contextual factors that can shape the nature of the sexual offense (e.g., access to a potential victim, victim resistance, the absence of capable guardians, risk of detection, offender's intoxication, being a gang member). In criminology, the study of individual differences distinguishing, for example, bank robbers, burglars, car thieves, and drug dealers, has long been abandoned as it did not lead to theoretically meaningful findings and it could not be reconciled with some of the most common observations about criminal careers (e.g., Gibbons, 1975). For example, burglars can become bank robbers; drug dealers can become car thieves; and so on. Group membership can easily change with the passage of time, changing opportunity structures, human agency, and the dynamic aspects of human lives. Criminological researchers have since distinguished the study of particular crime events (e.g., bank robbery, auto theft, burglary, drug dealing) and the study of individual longitudinal patterns of offending (e.g., age of onset, frequency, diversity, seriousness, length, desistance). The former is more concerned with situational-based factors, while the latter with individual and environmental factors and their interplay over time. A similar approach to the study of specific sexual offenses and the study of sexual offending over time is needed for this field of research to move forward.

The second major trend of questions reflects a concern with whether decades of sex offending research created an acutely engrained presumption about what is and what is not important for the development of sexual offending. This not only results in a relatively engrained status quo when it comes to research designs and procedures (e.g., expectations from journal editors about what must be examined when searching for the causes of sexual offending), but also how the justice system responds to sexual offending. Because these empirical studies are overwhelmingly if not entirely based on interviews and surveys with perpetrators of sex crimes after they have been caught, tried, punished, and treated, to what extent has the sociolegal response to perpetrators of sex offenses made such offenders more aware of their attitudes towards women, sexual preferences, abuse history, etc. compared to offenders involved in non-sex offenses? Does placement in a 12-week treatment program discussing the role of sexual abuse history have no impact on a person's likelihood of disclosing their history of sexual abuse and attributing this abuse to their perpetration of a sex crime? In other words, despite several meta-analyses, research has failed to establish temporal order between risk factors and outcomes. Consequently, the legal system's hypersensitivity to the mental health and prior abuse experiences of perpetrators of sex offenses may also extend to these perpetrators' hypersensitivity to these issues. This problem reflects a similar, earlier pattern of research on sexual offending in which targeting hormones was used as a way to respond to perpetrators of sexual offenses by medical practitioners and then in turn became a central factor to be investigated by researchers, even though this factor ultimately provided little understanding of the causes of sex offending. In effect, the lack of theorizing about sexual offending, especially outside of theorizing by clinical researchers, has resulted in allowing the societal response to sexual offending to dictate the agendas of researchers in a pattern. It may be the case that history, traditions, attitudes, and responses to perpetrators of sex offenses has resulted in this group being more aware of their sexual and mental health problems compared to perpetrators of non-sex offenses. In sum, the research approach more commonly used to study perpetrators of sexual offending appears to inform more about the sociolegal response to sexual offending than about sexual offending as a phenomenon.

If much work is required to identify differences between perpetrators of sex and non-sex offenses (e.g., selecting more precise subsamples from both groups), then perhaps it is appropriate to look at what these two perpetrator groups have in common as a way to understand the origins of sexual offending. To be clear, understanding why sexual offending emerges does not necessarily require identifying factors that are only ever found for persons involved in sexual offenses. A more parsimonious "general explanation" perspective on sexual offending may be suitable. According to this perspective, individuals involved in sexual offenses have a more general antisocial propensity and their sexual offense may be in large part a reflection of the tendency to be okay with harming others as opposed to hormonal imbalances, neuropsychological deficits, IQ, self-esteem, sexual preferences, abuse experiences, etc. This is not to claim that the latter cannot be important to the development of sexual offending, but rather that sexual offending is just one manifestation of a general antisocial propensity and could occur at any point in an individual's life trajectory and criminal career (e.g., Lussier, 2005). In effect, for individuals who frequently violate the rights of others in non-discriminant ways, sexual offending may simply reflect one type of expression of a general antisocial tendency. This is not to say that all perpetrators of sex crimes are antisocial individuals or even psychopaths. Rather, we posit that individuals who are more prone to perpetrate antisocial behaviors and who are exposed to criminogenic factors (e.g., individual-level, familial-level, peer-level, neighborhood-level) are more likely to perpetrate a sex crime than those who are less prone to engage in other antisocial acts. Criminogenic factors and antisocial propensity may be the key building blocks for a host of negative outcomes, including individual-level risk factors like sexual deviance, mental illness, and abuse that have been part of the long-standing tradition of sexual offending research. The challenge for researchers is to unravel the relationship between antisocial propensity, these more traditional criminogenic risk factors, and sexual offending. The developmental and life-course criminology approach offers some insight about the nature of these building blocks that are desperately missing from this scientific literature.

References

Abel, G. G., & Blanchard, E. B. (1974). The role of fantasy in the treatment of sexual deviation. *Archives of General Psychiatry, 30*, 467–475.

Abel, G. G., Osborn, C. A., & Twigg, D. A. (1993). Sexual assault through the life span: Adult offenders with juvenile histories. In H. E. Barbaree, W. L. Marshall, & S. M. Hudson (Eds.), *The juvenile sex offender*. New York: Guilford Press.

Abrahamsen, D. (1950). Study of 102 sex offenders at Sing Sing. *Federal Probation, 14*, 26–32.

Allen, M., D'Alessio, D., & Emmers-Sommer, T. M. (1999). Reactions of criminal sexual offenders to pornography: A meta-analytic summary. *Annals of the International Communication Association, 22*(1), 139–169.

Ariely, D., & Loewenstein, G. (2006). The heat of the moment: the effect of sexual arousal on sexual decision making. *Journal of Behavioral Decision Making, 19*, 87–98.

Atcheson, J. D., & Williams, D. C. (1954). A study of juvenile sex offenders. *American Journal of Psychiatry, 111*(5), 366–370.

Awad, G. A., & Saunders, E. B. (1989). Adolescent child molesters: Clinical observations. *Child Psychiatry and Human Development, 19*(3), 195–206.

Awad, G. A., & Saunders, E. B. (1991). Male adolescent sexual assaulters clinical observations. *Journal of Interpersonal Violence, 6*(4), 446–460.

Babchishin, K. M., Karl Hanson, R., & Hermann, C. A. (2011). The characteristics of online sex offenders: A meta-analysis. *Sexual Abuse, 23*(1), 92–123.

Barbaree, H. E., Hudson, S. M., & Seto, M. C. (1993). Sexual assault in society: The role of the juvenile offender. In H. E. Barbaree, W. L. Marshall, & S. M. Hudson (Eds.), *The juvenile sex offender* (pp. 1–24). New York, NY: Guilford Press.

Barbaree, H. E., & Marshall, W. L. (1989). Erectile responses among heterosexual child-molesters, father-daughter incest offenders and matched non-offenders: Five distinct age preference profiles. *Canadian Journal of Behavioural Science, 21*, 70–82.

Beauregard, E., Lussier, P., & Proulx, J. (2004). An exploration of developmental factors related to deviant sexual preferences among adult rapists. *Sexual Abuse: A Journal of Research and Treatment, 16*(2), 151–161.

Becker, J. V. (1998). The assessment of adolescent perpetrators of childhood sexual abuse. *The Irish Journal of Psychology, 19*(1), 68–81.

Becker, J. V., & Hicks, S. J. (2003). Juvenile sexual offenders: Characteristics, interventions, and policy issues. *Annals of the New York Academy of Sciences, 989*(1), 397–410.

Berlin, F. S., & Meinecke, C. F. (1981). Treatment of sex offenders with antiandrogenic medication: Conceptualization, review of treatment modalities, and preliminary findings. *American Journal of Psychiatry, 138*, 601–646.

Blonigen, D. M. (2010). Explaining the relationship between age and crime: Contributions from the developmental literature on personality. *Clinical Psychology Review, 30*(1), 89–100.

Boonmann, C., Nelson, R. J., DiCataldo, F., Jansen, L. M., Doreleijers, T. A., Vermeiren, R. R., et al. (2016). Mental health problems in young male offenders with and without sex offences: a comparison based on the MAYSI-2. *Criminal Behaviour and Mental Health, 26*(5), 352–365.

Bradford, J. M. (1985). Organic treatments for the male sexual offender. *Behavioral Sciences & the Law, 3*(4), 355–375.

Braude, J. M. (1950). The sex offender and the court. *Federal Probation, 14*, 17.

Burgess, A. W., Hartman, C. R., Ressler, R. K., Douglas, J. E., & McCormack, A. (1986). Sexual homicide: A motivational model. *Journal of Interpersonal Violence, 1*(3), 251–272.

Burick, L. T. (1968). An analysis of the Illinois sexually dangerous persons act. *Journal of Criminal Law, Criminology, and Police Science, 59*(2), 254–266.

Cale, J. (2018). Classification of perpetrators of sexual offences: An overview of three generations of research and development. In P. Lussier & E. Beauregard (Eds.), *Sexual offending: A criminological perspective* (pp. 326–348). London, UK: Routledge.

Campregher, J., & Jeglic, E. L. (2016). Attitudes toward juvenile sex offender legislation: The influence of case-specific information. *Journal of Child Sexual Abuse, 25*(4), 466–482.

Cantor, J. M., Blanchard, R., Robichaud, L. K., & Christensen, B. K. (2005). Quantitative reanalysis of aggregate data on IQ in sexual offenders. *Psychological Bulletin, 131*(4), 555.

Caspi, A., Roberts, B. W., & Shiner, R. L. (2005). Personality development: Stability and change. *Annual Review of Psychology, 56*, 453–484.

Cormier, B. M., & Simons, S. P. (1969). The problem of the dangerous sexual offender. *Canadian Psychiatric Association Journal, 14*(4), 329–335.

Cullen, F. T., Gendreau, P., Jarjoura, G. R., & Wright, J. P. (1997). Crime and the bell curve: Lessons from intelligent criminology. *Crime & Delinquency, 43*(4), 387–411.

Doshay, L. J. (1943). *The boy sex offender and his later career*. Oxford: Grune & Stratton.

Dreznick, M. T. (2003). Heterosocial competence of rapist and child molesters: A meta-analysis. *The Journal Sex Research, 40*(2), 170–178.

Earls, C. M., & Proulx, J. (1986). The differentiation of francophone rapists and nonrapists using penile circumferential measures. *Criminal Justice and Behavior, 13*(4), 419–429.

Ellis, A., & Brancale, R. (1956). *The psychology of sex offenders*. Springfield, IL: Charles C Thomas.

Ellis, A., Doorbar, R. R., & Johnston III, R. (1954). Characteristics of convicted sex offenders. *The Journal of Social Psychology, 40*(1), 3–15.

Emmers-Sommer, T. M., Allen, M., Bourhis, J., Sahlstein, E., Laskowski, K., Falato, W. L., et al. (2004). A meta-analysis of the relationship between social skills and sexual offenders. *Communication Reports, 17*(1), 1–10.

Eysenck, H. J., & Nias, D. K. B. (1978). *Sex, violence, and the media*. New York: Saint Martin's Press.

Fink, A. (1938). *Causes of crime*. Philadelphia: University of Pennsylvania Press.

Finkelstein, M., Forchielli, E., & Dorfman, R. I. (1961). Estimation of testosterone in human plasma. *The Journal of Clinical Endocrinology & Metabolism, 21*(1), 98–101.

Freund, K. (1963). A laboratory method for diagnosing predominance of homo-or heteroerotic interest in the male. *Behaviour Research and Therapy, 1*(1), 85–93.

Freund, K. (1967). Erotic preference in pedophilia. *Behavior Research and Therapy, 5*(4), 85–93.

Freund, K., Sedlacek, F., & Knob, K. (1965). A simple transducer for mechanical plethysmography of the male genital. *Journal of the Experimental Analysis of Behavior, 8*(3), 169.

Gebhard, P. H., Gagnon, J. H., Pomeroy, W. B., & Christenson, C. V. (1965). *Sex offenders: An analysis of types*. New York: Harper and Row.

Gendreau, P., Little, T., & Goggin, C. (1996). A meta-analysis of the predictors of adult offender recidivism: What works! *Criminology, 34*(4), 575–608.

Gibbons, D. C. (1975). Offender typologies—Two decades later. *The British Journal of Criminology, 15*(2), 140–156.

Glueck, B. C. (1956). An evaluation of the homosexual offender. *Minnesota Law Review, 41*, 187.

Goldstein, M., Kant, H., Judd, L., Rice, C., & Green, R. (1971). Experience with pornography: Rapists, pedophiles, homosexuals, transsexuals, and controls. *Archives of Sexual Behavior, 1*(1), 1–15.

Golla, F. L., & Hodge, R. S. (1949). Hormone treatment of the sexual offender. *The Lancet, 253*(6563), 1006–1007.

Grekul, J., Krahn, A., & Odynak, D. (2004). Sterilizing the "feeble-minded": Eugenics in Alberta, Canada, 1929–1972. *Journal of Historical Sociology, 17*(4), 358–384.

Groth, A. N. (1977). The adolescent sexual offender and his prey. *International Journal of Offender Therapy and Comparative Criminology, 21*(3), 249–254.

Groth, A. N. (1979). Sexual trauma in the life of rapists and child molesters. *Victimology, 4*(1), 10–16.

Guay, J. P., Ouimet, M., & Proulx, J. (2005). On intelligence and crime: A comparison of incarcerated sex offenders and serious non-sexual violent criminals. *International Journal of Law and Psychiatry, 28*(4), 405–417.

Guttmacher, M., & Weihofen, H. (1952). Sex offenses. *Journal of Criminal Law, Criminology, and Police Science, 43*(2), 153–175.

Hall, G. C. N., & Hirschman, R. (1991). Toward a theory of sexual aggression: A quadripartite model. *Journal of Consulting and Clinical Psychology, 59*(5), 662.

Hall, G. C. N., Shondrick, D. D., & Hirschman, R. (1993). The role of sexual arousal in sexually aggressive behavior: A meta-analysis. *Journal of Consulting and Clinical Psychology, 61*(6), 1091.

Hammer, E. F., & Glueck, B. C. (1957). Psychodynamic patterns in sex offenders: A four-factor theory. *The Psychiatric Quarterly, 31*(1-4), 325–345.

Hattaway, S. R., & McKinley, J. C. (1989). *Minnesota multiphasic personality inventory–2*. Minneapolis: University of Minnesota Press.

Hedges, L., & Olkin, I. (1985). *Statistical methods for meta-analysis*. London: Academic Press.

Heim, N. (1981). Sexual behavior of castrated sex offenders. *Archives of Sexual Behavior, 10*(1), 11–19.

Hucker, S. J., & Bain, J. (1990). Androgenic hormones and sexual assault. In W. L. Marshall, D. R. Laws, & H. E. Barbaree (Eds.), *Handbook of sexual assault* (pp. 93–102). Boston, MA: Springer.

Jespersen, A. F., Lalumière, M. L., & Seto, M. C. (2009). Sexual abuse history among adult sex offenders and non-sex offenders: A meta-analysis. *Child Abuse & Neglect, 33*(3), 179–192.

Joyal, C. C., Beaulieu-Plante, J., & de Chantérac, A. (2014). The neuropsychology of sex offenders: A meta-analysis. *Sexual Abuse, 26*(2), 149–177.

Knight, R. A., & Prentky, R. A. (1990). Classifying sexual offenders: The development and corroboration of taxonomic models. In W. L. Marshall, D. R. Laws, & H. E. Barbaree (Eds.), *The handbook of sexual assault: Issues, theories and treatment of the offender* (pp. 23–52). New York: Plenum Press.

Knight, R. A., & Sims-Knight, J. E. (2003). The developmental antecedents of sexual coercion against women: Testing alternative hypotheses with structural equation modeling. *Annals of the New York Academy of Sciences, 989*(1), 72–85.

Krafft-Ebing, R. (1886/1965). *Psychopathia sexualis*. New York: Putnam's Sons.

Lalumière, M. L., & Quinsey, V. L. (1994). The discriminability of rapists from non-sex offenders using phallometric measures: A meta-analysis. *Criminal Justice and Behavior, 21*(1), 150–175.

Laws, D. R. (1977). A comparison of the measurement characteristics of two circumferential penile transducers. *Archives of Sexual Behavior, 6*(1), 45–51.

LeMaire, L. (1956). Danish experience regarding treatment of sex offenders. *The Journal of Criminal Law and Criminology, 473*, 274–310.

Lipsey, M. W., & Wilson, D. B. (2001). *Practical meta-analysis*. Thousand Oaks, CA: Sage.

Lombroso, C. (1880). *L'uomo delinquente*. Torino: Fratelli Bocca.

Lussier, P. (2005). The criminal activity of sexual offenders in adulthood: Revisiting the specialization debate. *Sexual Abuse: A Journal of Research and Treatment, 17*(3), 269–292.

Lussier, P., & Beauregard, E. (2018). "Sex offender" theory and research in context: The relative absence of a criminological perspective. In P. Lussier & E. Beauregard (Eds.), *Sexual offending: A criminological perspective* (pp. 3–11). Abington: Routledge.

Lussier, P., Beauregard, E., Proulx, J., & Nicole, A. (2005). Developmental factors related to deviant sexual preferences in child molesters. *Journal of Interpersonal Violence, 20*(9), 999–1017.

Lussier, P., & Blokland, A. (2014). The adolescence-adulthood transition and Robins's continuity paradox: Criminal career patterns of juvenile and adult sex offenders in a prospective longitudinal birth cohort study. *Journal of Criminal Justice, 42*(2), 153–163.

Lussier, P., & Cale, J. (2016). Understanding the origins and the development of rape and sexual aggression against women: four generations of research and theorizing. *Aggression and Violent Behavior, 31*, 66–81.

Lussier, P., Proulx, J., & LeBlanc, M. (2005). Criminal propensity, deviant sexual interests and criminal activity of sexual aggressors against women: A comparison of explanatory models. *Criminology, 43*(1), 249–282.

Maclay, D. T. (1960). Boys who commit sexual misdemeanours. *British Medical Journal, 1*(5167), 186.

Malamuth, N. M. (1998). An evolutionary-based model integrating research on the characteristics of sexually coercive men. *Advances in Psychological Science, 1*, 151–184.

Markey, O. B. (1950). A study of aggressive sex misbehavior in adolescents brought to juvenile court. *American Journal of Orthopsychiatry, 20*(4), 719.

Marsh, J. T., Hilliard, J., & Liechti, R. (1955). A sexual deviation scale for the MMPI. *Journal of Consulting Psychology, 19*(1), 55.

Marshall, W. L. (1989). Intimacy, loneliness and sexual offenders. *Behaviour Research and Therapy, 27*(5), 491–504.

Marshall, W. L., & Barbaree, H. E. (1990). An integrated theory of the etiology of sexual offending. In W. L. Marshall, D. R. Laws, & H. E. Barbaree (Eds.), *Handbook of sexual assault: Issues, theories, and treatment of the offender* (pp. 257–275). New York: Plenum Press.

Meyer III, W. J., & Cole, C. M. (1997). Physical and chemical castration of sex offenders: A review. *Journal of Offender Rehabilitation, 25*(3-4), 1–18.

Michaud, P., & Proulx, J. (2009). Penile-response profiles of sexual aggressors during phallometric testing. *Sexual Abuse: A Journal of Research and Treatment, 21*(3), 308–334.

Millikin, M. (1894). Emasculation and ovariotomy. *Journal of the American Medical Association, 23*(12), 475–475.

Money, J. (1970). Use of an androgen-depleting hormone in the treatment of male sex offenders. *Journal of Sex Research, 6,* 165–172.

Muehlenhard, C. L., & Falcon, P. L. (1990). Men's heterosocial skill and attitudes toward women as predictors of verbal sexual coercion and forceful rape. *Sex Roles, 23*(5-6), 241–259.

Nunes, K. L., McPhail, I. V., & Babchishin, K. M. (2012). Social anxiety and sexual offending against children: A cumulative meta-analysis. *Journal of Sexual Aggression, 18*(3), 284–293.

Ogilvie, C. A., Newman, E., Todd, L., & Peck, D. (2014). Attachment & violent offending: A meta-analysis. *Aggression and Violent Behavior, 19*(4), 322–339.

Peek, R. M., & Storms, L. H. (1956). Validity of the Marsh-Hilliard-Liechti MMPI sexual deviation scale in a state hospital population. *Journal of Consulting Psychology, 20*(2), 133.

Prentky, R. A. (1997). Arousal reduction in sexual offenders: A review of antiandrogen interventions. *Sexual Abuse, 9*(4), 335–347.

Proulx, J. (1989). Sexual preference assessment of sexual aggressors. *International Journal of Law and Psychiatry, 12*(4), 275–280.

Proulx, J., Aubut, J., McKibben, A., & Côté, M. (1994). Penile responses of rapists and nonrapists to rape stimuli involving physical violence or humiliation. *Archives of Sexual Behavior, 23*(3), 295–310.

Proulx, J., Beauregard, E., Lussier, P., & Leclerc, B. (2014). *Pathways to sexual aggression.* New York, NY: Routledge.

Proulx, J., Côté, G., & Achille, P. A. (1993). Prevention of voluntary control of penile response in homosexual pedophiles during phallometric testing. *Journal of Sex Research, 30*(2), 140–147.

Proulx, J., Pellerin, B., Paradis, Y., McKibben, A., Aubut, J., & Ouimet, M. (1997). Static and dynamic predictors of recidivism in sexual aggressor. *Sexual Abuse: A Journal of Research and Treatment, 9*(1), 7–27.

Quinsey, V. L., & Chaplin, T. C. (1982). Penile responses to nonsexual violence among rapists. *Criminal Justice and Behavior, 9*(3), 372–381.

Quinsey, V. L., Chaplin, T. C., & Carrigan, W. F. (1980). Biofeedback and signaled punishment in the modification of inappropriate sexual age preferences. *Behavior Therapy, 11*(4), 567–576.

Quinsey, V. L., & Earls, C. M. (1990). The modification of sexual preferences. In W. L. Marshall, D. R. Laws, & H. E. Barbaree (Eds.), *Handbook of sexual assault* (pp. 279–295). Boston, MA: Springer.

Quinsey, V. L., Rice, M. E., & Harris, G. T. (1995). Actuarial prediction of sexual recidivism. *Journal of Interpersonal Violence, 10*(1), 85–105.

Rada, R. T. (1980). Plasma androgens and the sex offender. *Journal of the American Academy of Psychiatry and the Law Online, 8*(4), 456–464.

Rada, R. T., Laws, D. R., & Kellner, R. (1976). Plasma testosterone levels in the rapist. *Psychosomatic Medicine, 38*(4), 257–268.

Rada, R. T., Laws, D. R., Kellner, R., Stivastava, L., & Peake, G. (1983). Plasma androgens in violent and nonviolent sex offenders. *The Journal of the American Academy of Psychiatry and the Law, 11*(2), 149–158.

Reiss, A. J. (1960). Sex offenses: The marginal status of the adolescent. *Law and Contemporary Problems, 25,* 309.

Resko, J. A., & Eik-Nes, K. B. (1966). Diurnal testosterone levels in peripheral plasma of human male subjects. *The Journal of Clinical Endocrinology & Metabolism, 26*(5), 573–576.

Rosen, R. C., & Keefe, F. J. (1978). The measurement of human penile tumescence. *Psychophysiology, 15*(4), 366–376.

Seghorn, T. K., Prentky, R. A., & Boucher, R. J. (1987). Childhood sexual abuse in the lives of sexually aggressive offenders. *Journal of the American Academy of Child & Adolescent Psychiatry, 26*(2), 262–267.

Seto, M. C., & Lalumière, M. L. (2010). What is so special about male adolescent sexual offending? A review and test of explanations through meta-analysis. *Psychological Bulletin, 136*(4), 526–575.

Simon, W. T., & Schouten, P. G. (1991). Plethysmography in the assessment and treatment of sexual deviance: An overview. *Archives of Sexual Behavior, 20*(1), 75–91.

Singer, H. D. (1913). The sterilization of the insane, criminal and delinquent. *The Illinois Medical Journal, 625*, 5.

Smith, M. L., & Glass, G. V. (1977). Meta-analysis of psychotherapy outcome studies. *American Psychologist, 32*(9), 752.

Steffensmeier, D., & Harer, M. D. (1999). Making sense of recent US crime trends, 1980 to 1996/1998: Age composition effects and other explanations. *Journal of Research in Crime and Delinquency, 36*(3), 235–274.

Terry, R. M. (1967a). Discrimination in the handling of juvenile offenders by social-control agencies. *Journal of Research in Crime and Delinquency, 4*(2), 218–230.

Terry, R. M. (1967b). The screening of juvenile offenders. *Journal of Criminal Law, Criminology, and Police Science, 58*(2), 173–181.

Whitaker, D. J., Le, B., Hanson, R. K., Baker, C. K., McMahon, P. M., Ryan, G., et al. (2008). Risk factors for the perpetration of child sexual abuse: A review and meta-analysis. *Child Abuse & Neglect, 32*(5), 529–548.

Wolfgang, M. E., Figlio, R. M., & Sellin, T. (1972). *Delinquency in a birth cohort*. Chicago, IL: The University of Chicago Press.

Wong, J. S., & Gravel, J. (2018). Do sex offenders have higher levels of testosterone? Results from a meta-analysis. *Sexual Abuse, 30*(2), 147–168.

Worling, J. R., & Långström, N. (2003). Assessment of criminal recidivism risk with adolescents who have offended sexually: A review. *Trauma, Violence & Abuse, 4*(4), 341–362.

Zuckerman, M. (1971). Physiological measures of sexual arousal in the human. *Psychological Bulletin, 75*(5), 297.

Chapter 6
Once a Sex Offender, Always a Sex Offender?

Introduction

Since the enactment of some of the first sex offender laws, offenders' age and aging have not been part of the equation when proposing, developing, and enacting criminal justice policies to prevent sex offenses. These laws assumed that if sexual offending emerged, it was there to stay as part of a person's criminal trajectory over the life course (see Chaps. 7, 8, and 9 for a description of how some of these policies have impacted offending). This assumption was inconsistent with criminological research of the time and especially inconsistent with the more contemporary life course criminology perspective that desistance from offending is normative for even the highest-risk offenders (Sampson & Laub, 2003). Social scientists' interests in crime and the life course emerged from a long-standing observation that offending declines with age. Sheldon and Eleanor Glueck, two pioneers of longitudinal research in criminology, spearheaded the contemporary movement to explain the relationship between aging and offending. They conducted the first longitudinal studies of adolescents and adults with histories of offending and their results reflected what Adolphe Quetelet discovered 100 years earlier: there is a clear relationship between offending and age, referred to as the age-crime curve, such that crime tends to peak in the later stages of adolescence, much sooner than most people expect, and then becomes much less common in adulthood. Whereas Quetelet was concerned with the prevalence of offending across age groups (i.e., between-group differences), the Gluecks sought to explain why a person's level of offending declined over time (i.e., within-individual change).

The Gluecks were mostly concerned with what helped explain why some offenders persisted well beyond adolescence, while others tended to follow the age-crime curve pattern described by Quetelet. To address this question, they acquired a sample of 500 delinquents from reformatory schools in Massachusetts and matched this group to 500 non-delinquents. The delinquent sample was followed up to age 32, which allowed the Gluecks to examine offending continuity and discontinuity even

P. Lussier et al., *Understanding Sexual Offending*,
https://doi.org/10.1007/978-3-030-53301-4_6

for those individuals that were involved in crime after the typical decline in offending per the age-crime curve. A major assertion from the Gluecks was that aging was just a proxy for an individual who was more mature. This process of maturation helped facilitate a person's growing up, and, growing out, of crime. The Gluecks therefore offered one of the first theoretical perspectives for what scholars would later term "desistance." However, the Gluecks' perspective was critiqued for providing a tautological explanation for within-individual declines in criminal behavior. Specifically, individuals that were mature were expected to stop offending, but individuals could be considered matured only if they stopped offending. Additionally, while the Gluecks claimed that maturation was distinct from aging, they did not attempt to disentangle what it meant to become mature (e.g., less impulsive, more forward thinking, more interested in fulfilling adult social roles). For these and other reasons (see Laub & Sampson, 1991), the Gluecks' perspective was largely ignored by researchers from their era.

Long after the Gluecks' writings, Robert Sampson and John Laub rediscovered the Gluecks' data archived in a series of boxes held at the Harvard Law School Library. They took up the task of reanalyzing and updating the Gluecks' data by examining the lives of the delinquent boys now fully grown. A subsample was followed until as old as age 72. Sampson and Laub (1997) saw the data as an opportunity to address the missing explanation for why individuals that were involved in frequent offending in adolescence experienced a change in their pattern of offending as they moved through adulthood. They felt that theories either ignored desistance in favor of explaining persistence or acknowledged desistance but did not offer hypotheses for this transformation. Breathing new life into the Gluecks' data, Laub and Sampson (2003) challenged prior theorizing about the long-term predictability of offending. Through a sociological lens, Sampson and Laub (2005) asserted that the past is not prologue, meaning that making projections about future lives based on adolescent patterns of offending will overestimate risk of offending for some and underestimate this risk for others. This was quite distinct from earlier perspectives in the 1980s and 1990s on juvenile sexual offending. They helped develop the field of life course criminology, which is primarily interested in understanding the factors responsible for desistance from crime. Life course researchers define desistance as the process by which higher-rate offenders begin slowing down in their level of offending until they reach and maintain at least a near-zero rate of offending (Bushway, Piquero, Broidy, Cauffman, & Mazerolle, 2001).

Some themes from life course criminology have been addressed in research on sexual offending. The brute fact that the risk of sexual offending recidivism for adults will steadily decline over time (e.g., Hanson, 2002; Hanson & Bussière, 1998; Lussier & Healey, 2009) is not typically accounted for by the public, some professionals working with this population, and those in charge of informing or creating policy (e.g., Sample & Kadleck, 2008). In fact, these popular assumptions suggest that convicted offenders remain at a significant risk of sexual recidivism and that this requires the implementation of various legal, penal, and therapeutic measures and interventions to prevent a sexual reoffense (e.g., English, 1998). Against the backdrop of these popular assumptions, life course criminology is optimal for, among other things, addressing why sexual offending declines with age given that it is principally concerned with explaining desistance from offending. With these themes and issues in mind, the current chapter introduces (1) the life course perspective more broadly, (2) the adaption of the life course perspective as a criminological theory of desistance, (3) the application of the life course perspective to understanding and explaining discontinuity and desistance from sexual offending, and (4) future considerations for how to think about and study the development of desistance from sexual offending.

The Life Course as Human Development

In criminology, the life course perspective emerged from the sociological work of Dr. Glen Elder. Elder's (1998) life course theory describes and explains the dynamic nature of human development, not only in the early years, but across the full life span. A key tenet of life course research is the use of longitudinal data to study human development, including continuity and change, across the life span. Longitudinal research helps avoid the "past-as-prologue" pitfall by allowing researchers to take snapshots of a single individual at multiple points in time and then weave these snapshots together to tell a story about their life. In some cases, earlier snapshots will be informative of the future, in other cases, transitions between snapshots can be observed that illustrate not just that a person changed, but also why they changed. This perspective highlights the need to study the dynamic nature of human lives, the contexts that these lives are embedded within, how these contexts change, and the macro-level structures that influence these contexts and lives. Longitudinal research on human development is used to measure a person's trajectory over the life span that demarcates a longer-term pattern of behavior across multiple life domains (e.g., work, family, interpersonal relationships, personality), whether it be behavior as an employee, friend, spouse, parent, or offender. The life course perspective emphasizes how transitions, which represent key shorter-term life events, exist along a person's life span and alter the course and shape of a person's trajectory (Elder, 1998). To make sense of the dynamic nature of human lives captured by these trajectories and turning points, life course theory describes how social roles and local life circumstances, which are tied to age, human agency, the intergenerational transition of social patterns, and historical context, influence the dynamic nature of human development, not only in the early years, but across the full life span (Elder, 1998).

Local life circumstances refer to factors such as work, marriage, military service, and parenthood that have the potential to act as positive turning points in the life course. It is not just that these events occur, it is that these events matter to the individual. For example, life events such as work impact and structure a person's circumstances in a number of ways: it structures a person's daily routine and activities; it influences the types of people he/she interacts with most of the day; it creates expectations about someone's attitude and behavior; it also potentially provides opportunities to develop new friendships and relationships and opportunities to do good and feel appreciated by others. Part of what dictates whether an individual ascribes value to these events is their age. This is what several life course researchers have termed "age-graded roles and social transitions" (Caspi, Elder, & Herbener, 1990, p. 15). What matters in childhood (e.g., attachment and parenting) may not be as important in adolescence (e.g., school and the nature of peer dynamics); what matters in adolescence may not capture what is important in emerging adulthood[1] (e.g., independence, exploration of new social environments, and identity formation); what matters in emerging adulthood may not capture what is important in adulthood (e.g., employment, marriage, housing, and other civic duties). Longitudinal research becomes critical for examining the timing of these age-graded factors and the interplay between them. Although it is not a deterministic indicator of maturation, aging speaks to maturation and maturation is informative of whether an individual will covet, value, and guard against the loss of these events and social roles that act as turning points in the life course.

Human agency is another key principle of the life course. It describes how "individuals construct their own life course through the choices and actions they take within the opportunities and constraints of history and social circumstances" (Elder, 1998, p. 4). As people age, they make their own choices when it comes to daily life activities (e.g., where they go; whom they go with; what they do; and how they behave in that situation). From a life course perspective, human agency entails that people are not passive actors compelled to attend a certain situation and behave in a specific way. Rather, they can actively contribute to the construction of their own environment. This principle pushes back against past-as-prologue notions of human development (Lewontin, 2000). Individual motivation makes prediction problematic; specifically, it introduces false positives into prediction. Individuals characterized by a specific set of risk factors associated with negative outcomes (e.g., low educational attainment as a risk factor for negative outcomes like unemployment, reliance on welfare) may not experience such outcomes because of their ability to "pull themselves up by their bootstraps" and chart a different life path. In effect, the life course perspective takes the macro-level conceptualization of the "American Dream" (Messner & Rosenfeld, 2012) and illustrates its applicability at the individual level. Childhood and adolescent factors do not preclude entry into employment; individuals are active participants in their own lives. At the same time, these lives cannot be examined in isolation; they are tied to the activities of a person's social circle.

A less commonly discussed and measured aspect of the life course perspective is the notion of linked lives. This principle speaks to the need to examine the social context that an individual is embedded within. One social context, but not the only one, is the family. The experiences and social capital of family members are transmitted to the next generation as part of a process often referred to as intergenerational

---

[1] The transition period between adolescence and adulthood is roughly between ages 18 and 25 (e.g., Arnett, 2000).

transmission. For example, parents pass along socioeconomic resources that afford individuals different life opportunities (Mustillo, Wilson, & Lynch, 2004). Parents also establish certain cultures and values that can be helpful for engaging in activities that promote positive transitions over the life course (Min, Silverstein, & Lendon, 2012). Importantly, intergenerational transmission is not solely dependent on the family's communication of values. Macro-level events help shape a family's social capital and thus also shape an individual's ties to others and their social capital. For example, historical contexts like slavery excluded specific groups from the labor market, which impacted not only the lives of individuals forced into slavery but also the lives of future generations whose parents did not have the same social capital as the parents of peers that were free to work as they pleased. Historical context is also important for understanding how social structures of the time can influence the funneling of individuals into certain roles and life events. In addition to human agency, life course theory also acknowledges that individuals can enter adult roles, not because they actively pursued them, but because macro-level social structures push individuals into these roles as they become part of specific age demographics. For example, individuals can be conscripted into military service at one time-point but not another; economic recessions can influence unemployment in one time period but booms can influence stable employment in another.

A Life Course Perspective on Desistance from Criminal Behavior

Sampson and Laub's life course theoretical perspective (Sampson & Laub, 1997, 2003) on criminal behavior was formalized over a decade of research and writings using longitudinal data originally collected by Sheldon and Eleanor Glueck in the early-to-mid-1900s. Sampson and Laub's approach utilizes the broader life course theoretical perspective developed by Elder to examine the underlying factors explaining why offenders desist from crime. Their research agenda stressed the role and importance of life transitions and turning points (e.g., entry into the labor market; the birth of a child). Similar to criminal career researchers (Chap. 3), they also relied on longitudinal research to examine questions about desistance from offending, with attention to the abovementioned principles regarding life events, human agency, linked lives, and historical context. This perspective does not altogether ignore why offending emerges and why it persists; however, part of the motivation for Laub and Sampson's (2003) life course perspective was the growing recognition of change in the lives of offenders and that this change implied less stability in criminal behavior than what was presumed by other theories of crime. Accordingly, the life course theoretical perspective presented by Sampson and Laub briefly points to the lack of social bonds as an explanation for offending onset and persistence and then turns most of its attention to examining how acquiring such bonds is important for desistance. Developing bonds with prosocial individuals may be particularly challenging for those with a criminal record characterized by limited conventional opportunities and a social network composed of individuals who also have a criminal record.

Laub and Sampson's interest in desistance evolved from concerns with the ontogenic perspective, which characterizes offenders as easily predictable organisms with a specific and well-defined life path. Laub and Sampson instead looked at offending from a sociogenic perspective, which gives greater credence to how factors like human agency and the randomness of life events make prediction messy. Humans are not just actors in a play that manipulate the stage and their environment; the "stage" (i.e., the environment) can also directly influence an individual, their life course, and their offending. There is an interaction between society and individuals (Dannefer, 1984) and in the context of life course criminology, this interaction helps explain desistance. This type of attention to social structure was especially absent from explanations of sexual offending discussed in Chap. 5. The importance of social structure and human agency meant that major turning points were expected to be a typical part of the life course for even the highest rate offenders. For most included in these longitudinal studies, their story illustrated that over the life course there was both change and stability in offending and in social circumstances, with social circumstances having implications for offending (Laub & Sampson, 2003). As people age, they are exposed to different people, social environments, expectations, opportunities, and situations, all of which can act as turning points for their offending trajectory. Desistance arises from "side bets" (Laub & Sampson, 2003) in which the new social structure that acts as a turning point was not necessarily actively pursued, or at least not actively pursued for the purpose of disengaging from crime, but nevertheless results in an offender's embeddedness within a social structure that incentivizes desistance. For example, a person may become employed, not to desist from criminal behavior, but to help with housing, affording a car, and so on. Yet, as an individual becomes embedded within the culture of their workplace (employee camaraderie, respect from a boss, pay raises), the social costs of offending and potentially losing this job and associated social environment become too great to risk.

One example of a turning point suggested by Sampson and Laub is marriage, although a cohesive and stable intimate relationship could also have potential effects on a wide range of life domains that help initiate desistance. First, a person's intimate relationship can change their attitudes toward and perceptions about the positive rewards of offending (Laub & Sampson, 2003). A person's attachment to their partner makes involvement in crime not just less appealing, but also recognized as an action that could threaten their relationship and social roles. Second, being in a stable intimate relationship creates an additional source of supervision that can help deter involvement in offending. Third, a stable intimate relationship changes a person's routine activities in ways that constrain opportunities for criminal behavior (Laub & Sampson, 2003), such as through reduced exposure to delinquent peers and negative social influences (e.g., Warr, 1998). Fourth, a stable intimate relationship can change a person's identity in ways that create a more positive sense of self and a renewed purpose in life that inspires a desire to "go straight." As an empirical illustration of the marital effect, using longitudinal data from the Gluecks' study, Laub, Nagin, and Sampson (1998) found that marital cohesiveness promoted lower levels of crime over the long-term. Such sources of informal social control also appear to be important for short-term changes in criminal behavior (Horney, Osgood, & Marshall, 1995). These four mechanisms by which an intimate relationship influences desistance are also observed in other types of informal social control such as employment (Laub & Sampson, 2003).

Importantly however, the life course perspective does not suggest that these sources of informal social control are universally valued. At the heart of life course criminology is attention to aging and age-graded informal social control. Longitudinal research is not necessary simply to establish temporal order or to utilize a follow-up period of sufficient length. Indeed, individuals of different ages, followed for an identical length of time, may nevertheless experience informal social controls differently. For a 15 year old followed for 10 years, employment 5 years later at age 20 might have minimal impact on desistance over the next 5 years. In contrast, for a 25 year old followed for 10 years, employment five years later (i.e., at age 30) might have a substantial impact on desistance over the next 5 years. Uggen (2000) provided an empirical demonstration of the age-graded nature of the effects of employment on desistance. Those employed at age 26 and younger were less likely to terminate their involvement in offending compared to those that were employed and were older than 26. Research on parenting also demonstrates similar results (Uggen & Wakefield, 2008). It is not just that the person is old enough; it is that they are more developmentally mature and more likely to value these different sources of informal social control (Nguyen & Loughran, 2018). It is not necessarily the case that an individual enters a given social role and then fully values it immediately. It takes time to acquire, value, and maintain sources of informal social control. Researchers also speak of the importance of timing to explain the variable impact of life events on the decision to persist in crime (Ouimet & Le Blanc, 1996). For example, an early entry into marital life and the associated stressful events that come with it can promote rather than deter criminal behavior.

A major debate in the life course literature concerns whether turning points are influenced by selection effects. That is, to what extent are people that are at a high risk to reoffend less likely to get married, find a job, benefit from parenthood, and so on? Developmentalists like Terrie Moffitt (1993) argued that the accumulation of disadvantage early in the life course precluded, or at least decreased the likelihood of, opportunities to experience positive turning points. She argued that individuals with certain dispositions and circumstances, such as specific personality traits and family backgrounds, tended to associate themselves with acquaintances, friends, co-workers, and intimate partners that shared similar traits (e.g., sensation-seeking, impulsivity). In that context, for the individuals most likely to offend, and thus most in need of turning points facilitating desistance, the "marital effect" may not be one promoting desistance from criminal behavior but rather facilitating, stimulating, or encouraging it. Laub and Sampson (2003) disagreed with this perspective on the basis that there is too much random variation over the life course to suggest that people limit their social environment to individuals with similar dispositions. For example, individuals move to another neighborhood, change schools/jobs, and meet new people in the process. Furthermore, if we accept that individuals are active agents seeking to improve their own personal situation, human agency dictates that their motivations can change behaviors and life outcomes regardless of personality traits or life circumstances.

The empirical evidence for selection effects is mixed. Laub and Sampson (2003) presented qualitative evidence that men with highly criminogenic backgrounds entered into quality marriages that helped promote desistance (also see quantitative analyses in Laub et al., 1998; Sampson, Laub, & Wimer, 2006). Blokland and Nieuwbeerta's (2005) long-term study of offenders from the Netherlands showed that life circumstances like marriage were associated with desistance, but that the influence of such circumstances was weaker for individuals with more active criminal histories. One factor that Laub and Sampson (2003) did consider when it comes to selection effects is the role of time spent incarcerated. Some studies suggested that incarceration may act as a barrier to marriage and employment (Hagan & Dinovitzer, 1999; Pager, 2003; Western & Beckett, 1999; Western, Lopoo, & McLanahan, 2004) and therefore incarceration may prevent or at least delay desistance through the disruption or breaking of informal social controls. Other studies showed that incarceration on its own was not necessarily a barrier to desistance. Instead, what was important was the nature of individuals' custody experiences. McCuish, Lussier, and Corrado (2018) found that when individuals experienced identity changes in custody and had good relationships with staff, they were more likely to desist from offending. However, victimization while in custody was associated with higher levels of offending upon community re-entry.

Overall, there is mixed evidence for the impact of selection effects on the ability of offenders to experience and benefit from important turning points. As outlined below, at least conceptually, involvement in sexual offending could be a type of selection effect that impacts the likelihood and quality of social roles and events in the lives of such persons.

Sexual Offending, "Sex Offenders," and Desistance

The concept of desistance from crime implies a conscious decision to stop offending. Therefore, a person's behavioral changes reflect this decision in such a way that eventually leads them to maintain a state of non-offending over the life course. Life course theory is meant to explain desistance from all offending, including sexual offending (Laub, Rowan, & Sampson, 2019). Contemporary research is now concerned whether there is anything unique about desistance for persons with a history of sexual offending. Is desistance more or less likely for such individuals compared to those committing nonsexual offenses? Are the factors related to desistance different across the different offending types? However, getting to a point at which research considered such questions was a gradual process. A decade or so ago, the idea that individuals having perpetrated a sex crime chose to stop perpetrating such acts was not given much credence because of preconceived ideas about the etiology of sexual offending. It had been assumed for so long that most if not all perpetrators of sex offenses were driven by uncontrollable sexual urges and deviant sexual interests and fantasies. In the absence of specialized sex offender therapy, the idea that life events, life transitions, and contextual factors could impact their offending behavior in a meaningful way was almost inconceivable, to a point where research addressing questions about the prevalence of desistance and what influences desistance among individuals with a history of sexual offending was uncommon, especially through the lens of a life course perspective (e.g., Farmer, McAlinden, & Maruna, 2015; Harris, 2014, 2017; Lussier, 2016). In fact, when a convicted "sex offender" encounters potentially meaningful turning points (e.g., developing an intimate relationship with a single mother, taking part in group therapy with a female counselor, finding a job that happens to be close to an elementary school, etc.), it is *assumed* that they are seeking out new opportunities to perpetrate another sex crime. This is due, in part, to a lack of interdisciplinary research, ideological thinking, and disciplinary biases but also assumptions that all convicted sex offenders are life course persistent sex offenders. These assumptions need to be reexamined in the context of life course theory and the heterogeneity characterizing this population.

The life course perspective on desistance was conceptualized by criminologists trained in sociology and sees the causes of desistance as the same for all types of offenses. It is incorrectly assumed by some that general theories of crime, including general theories of desistance from crime, may not apply to sexual offending. Others do not believe that focusing specifically on involvement in sexual offending is a necessary line of analysis because it is assumed that the same underlying factors responsible for desistance from crime must apply to desistance from sexual offending (Capaldi & Patterson, 1996; Farrington, 1989; Laub & Sampson, 2001). Perhaps some criminologists also prefer not to test their ideas and hypotheses to specific situations that could prove challenging to their theory. After all, criminologists have remained relatively silent about perpetrators of sex crimes in comparison to perpetrators of general delinquency (Chap. 1). Against the backdrop of these assumptions, numerous studies reported data on sex offender recidivism and statistical probabilities of recidivism (e.g., Hanson & Bussière, 1998). Why raise the issue of desistance from sexual offending when researchers are presenting data suggesting that there is always some risk that these offenders might perpetrate another sex crime if released from prison? Not only did the idea of examining the concept of sex offender desistance seem counter-intuitive, it seemed unnecessary given the prevailing ideas of the time.

The very unique and differential sociolegal response to individuals convicted for a sex crime is another argument for testing criminological theories of desistance. Individuals convicted for a car theft will not experience the same treatment from the criminal justice system as those convicted of, for example, child pornography offenses. The sociolegal responses to these two groups will sharply contrast in many ways. The latter group is more likely to be subject to media coverage. They will be referred to by name as a sex offender; the media may search for interviews from family members, co-workers, and intimate partners. Their experience in prison will also be different in many ways (e.g., special prison unit for sex offenders, intimidation, and threats from other inmates for being a sex offender). Their post-prison experience may also include some form of public notification. They will have to register as a sex offender to the local police. They are more likely to be the subject of intensive community supervision with a parole/probation officer monitoring the offender's behavior in the community by informing, questioning, and following up with the offender's neighbors, employers, family members, peer group, and treatment providers (e.g., therapist for an alcohol addiction). The movements of the sex offender will be held under a microscope. Why live in that neighborhood? Why that job? Why that grocery store? These differential experiences are likely to impact a person's opportunities for community reintegration. In the context of a differential criminal justice response that appears to impact key desistance factors, the study of desistance with individuals convicted for a sex crime is even more critical. After all, policymakers did not have desistance factors in mind when implementing public notification and sex offender registries, but rather the stable and high risk of sexual recidivism that they perceive such individuals to possess.

Other researchers did not see it this way. They challenged these preconceived ideas about the persistence of sexual offending over life course. Their work can be organized into three lines of research. The first topic, comprising the bulk of research on the intersection of life course criminology and sexual offending, focuses on the prevalence of desistance. Instead of addressing the origins of sexual offending or why risk factors for sexual offending are (or are not) different from risk factors for nonsexual offending, this research used longitudinal studies to address questions about the prevalence and degree of repeated sexual offending over the life course for individuals adjudicated for a sex offense. Three types of longitudinal studies were used to address this topic: (1) studies of sexual recidivism; (2) studies on the continuity of sexual offending across developmental age-stages; and (3) studies of sexual offending trajectories over the life course. The second topic steps back from the study of sexual offending and instead examines desistance from general offending among those with and without a history of sexual offending. The third research topic, covered mostly by qualitative studies using a life history calendar method, concerns the mechanisms associated with desistance. This research on desistance from sexual offending and general offending often looks at life course theory principles such as the role of informal social controls in promoting desistance.

Sexual Offending (Dis)continuity Over the Life Course

For several decades, sex offender laws and policies implied that a convicted sex offender's risk for repeated sexual offending was relatively high and stable over time. This assumption was based on the long-held belief that all perpetrators of sexual offenses were sexual recidivists or potential sexual recidivists. These beliefs emerged from early clinical descriptions of individuals in psychiatric settings (e.g., Karpman, 1951). The individuals interviewed recollected their past sexual offenses, how they encountered their victim(s), where they committed their sexual offense(s), the circumstances in which they used some form of nonsexual physical violence, the type of sexual behaviors forced on the victim, and so on. A majority of the individuals in such studies also reported that their sexual offending was frequent, began in adolescence, and persisted in adulthood (e.g., Abel, Osborn, & Twigg, 1993). Clinicians and researchers also noticed that a substantial proportion of individuals sentenced for a sex crime had been previously convicted for a sexual offense. The notion of risk, therefore, first emerged from past events—i.e., what these individuals had done prior to being arrested, convicted, and sentenced for their current sexual offense(s) that resulted in their inclusion in a particular study. Few paid attention to the scarce but slowly developing research (Frisbie, 1966) showing that the risk of sexual recidivism should be examined forward and longitudinally after discharged, rather than retrospectively. When approached from this perspective, findings showed that only a minority of individuals were ever rearrested or reconvicted for a sex crime.

In criminology, establishing the risk of future offending based on past events is of considerable importance. Equally important is the research design strategy used to establish the relationship between past events and future behavior. In the late 1970s, interested in the life course development of young males, Lee Robins showed that when using cross-sectional research designs, retrospective accounts provided by adult offenders indicated that antisocial behavior in adulthood virtually required antisocial behavior in adolescence. To some, this finding could be used to conclude that all adolescents who manifest antisocial behavior will persist acting in such a way in adulthood. Her research, however, did not show this. Instead of retrospectively asking adults about prior behavior in adolescence, Robins used a prospective longitudinal research design in which children were followed from childhood, through adolescence, and into adulthood. Her study revealed that children and adolescents that perpetrated antisocial behavior typically did not continue this behavior in adulthood. This observation, now referred to as Robins' Paradox, demonstrates that pitfalls of retrospective accounts, such as those used in early studies of adults involved in sexual offenses, in terms of overestimating the stability of offending over the life course. Since Robins' observation, even studies of high-risk offender samples showed that adolescents typically did not continue to offend into later stages of adulthood (Lussier, Corrado, & McCuish, 2016; Sampson & Laub, 2003). This paradox was mostly examined in the context of general antisocial behavior. What these studies did not address was whether Robins' Paradox was a reasonable assumption for sexual offending or whether sex offender policies were more reasonable in their assumption of the long-term stability of sex offenders' risk of sexual recidivism.

Robins' continuity paradox implies that desistance from antisocial and criminal behavior is common, even among the most active young offenders. It also suggests that amid all this discontinuity there is a much smaller subgroup of individuals whose antisocial and criminal behavior appears more stable and unaffected by society's response to such behavior. Together, these observations about the continuity and discontinuity of antisocial and criminal behavior reiterate the importance of a life course criminology approach as the past is not always prologue. What these observations did not show was whether this paradox also applied to sexual offending. More recently, three different types of studies have emerged to examine desistance from sexual offending: recidivism studies, continuity studies, and trajectory studies. A description of these three studies is shown in Fig. 6.1.

Sexual Recidivism Over the Life Course

A conceptual illustration of sexual recidivism studies is illustrated in Fig. 6.1a. Sexual recidivism studies typically involve examining whether persons with a history of sexual offending were adjudicated for a new sex crime over some length of time, typically at least a year, with most studies averaging approximately 5 years of follow-up data. Rarely do studies examine sexual recidivism beyond a 10-year period (Caldwell, 2002; McCann & Lussier, 2008), which is in part because the likelihood of sexual recidivism is dramatically lower if persons remain crime-free for at least 5 years (Thornton, Hanson, Kelley, & Mundt, 2019). According to systematic literature reviews and meta-analyses, the prevalence of sexual recidivism, typically defined as an official re-arrest or reconviction for a sexual offense, rarely reaches double digits (Caldwell, 2002; Hanson & Bussière, 1998; Sample & Bray, 2006). Even longer-term studies show that less than 10% of adolescents and adults sexually recidivated (Caldwell, 2002). These studies also showed that individuals adjudicated for sexual offenses were more likely to recidivate with non-sex offenses. For example, McCann and Lussier's (2008) meta-analysis of 18 studies showed that only 12% of adolescents sexually recidivated, yet half of these same adolescents had recidivated with a nonsexual offense.

In more recent years, researchers have used statistical techniques to determine the long-term risk of a reconviction for a sex crime. Hargreaves and Francis (2014) estimated that by the end of a 35-year follow-up period, about 13% of individuals who had been convicted for a sex crime prior to 21 years old had sexually recidivated. They also estimated that, for this group, after remaining conviction-free for 17 years, the risk of a conviction for a sex crime became equivalent to that for a comparison group that had never incurred a conviction for an offense, sexual, or otherwise (see also, Nakamura & Blumstein, 2015). Indeed, they were able to estimate how long it took for the risk level of a group of offenders to decrease to that of individuals from the general population that never had been convicted for any crime. A limitation of this research was that individuals that committed sex offenses in adolescence (defined as ages 10–17) or in young adulthood (defined as ages 18–20) were included in a single group because of a low base rate of sex offenses committed in adolescence. From a risk assessment perspective, the risk of sexual recidivism between adolescents and young adults is significantly different. Young adults have the highest probabilities of sexual recidivism. In other words, the methodological decisions taken by the researchers might have inflated risk for continued sexual offending over time, even though the 13% prevalence rate of sexual recidivism was

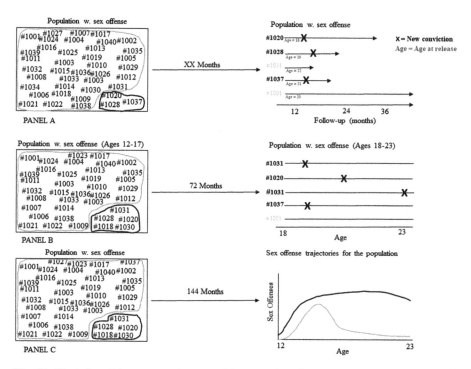

Fig. 6.1 Depiction of three approaches to studying sexual reoffending. *Notes.* Panel (**a**) depicts a recidivism study. Individuals of different ages are followed for different lengths of time. The right-hand side shows examples of recidivists and non-recidivists. Panel (**b**) depicts a continuity study. Individuals are all followed from ages 12 to 23. Ages are aggregated into adolescence (12–17) and adulthood (18–23). The right-hand side shows all individuals that engaged in a new sex offense in adulthood. Notice that #1031 did not sexually reoffend in the recidivism study but did so in the continuity study due to a longer follow-up period. Panel (**c**) shows the aggregate trajectories identified for sample members. The red trajectory depicts a higher rate and continued pattern of offending for the subsample circled in red. Note that this trajectory represents the aggregate trajectory of these individuals and may not perfectly represent the trajectory of any of these persons

still markedly lower than how such risk is portrayed in social, media, and political discourses. Despite these limitations, these researchers introduced to the field a novel statistical technique that helped to clarify developmental and life course concepts and considerations about the dynamic nature of human lives as well as the possibility that the risk of a sexual reoffense might be dynamic and subject to change, even for high-risk individuals.

In one of the longest follow-up studies using a large sample including more than 7000 individuals, Hanson, Harris, Letourneau, Helmus, and Thornton (2018) found that after 10–15 years, persons with histories of sexual offending and nonsexual offending were equally likely to sexually offend. As well, an individual's risk of sexual recidivism declined the longer they remained crime-free in the community, and this was true for even high-risk offenders. These findings showed not only that sexual recidivism risk was low, but also that sexual offending was circumscribed to a certain period. Using the same data, Hanson, Harris, Helmus, and Thornton (2014) showed that risk for sexual recidivism markedly decreased if the offender remained crime-free after the first few years of release. Even for those labeled high risk, their probability of sexual recidivism in years 6–10 of the follow-up period was five times lower than their probability of sexual recidivism in years 1–5 of the follow-up period. To illustrate, about 20% of high-risk persons sexually recidivate in years 1–5 of the follow-up period; for those high-risk individuals that did not recidivate during the first five years, only about 4% sexually recidivated in years 6–10. For low risk persons, comprising approximately 12% of the sample, sexual recidivism risk remained low (1–5%) throughout a 20-year follow-up period. In sum, these recidivism studies indicate that there is "redemption" for individuals with a history of sexual offending. Their risk of sexual recidivism is relatively low and declining with each year they remain crime-free in the community. In fact, after approximately 7–10 years crime-free, former offenders do not differ from the general public in terms of their probability of offending (e.g., Hanson et al., 2018; Kurlychek, Brame, & Bushway, 2007; Nakamura & Blumstein, 2015; Soothill & Francis, 2009). In sum, according to these studies, the mantra of "once a sex offender, always a sex offender" is simply inaccurate.

Life course criminology research is attuned to the process of age, aging, and an individual's stage in their criminal career. Recidivism studies can be somewhat limited in addressing these life course themes because rarely do they account for the fact that reoffending can occur at different stages of the criminal career. Instead, all instances of recidivism are treated the same way, even though for some individuals their recidivism represents their first reoffense and for others their recidivism represents their 10th reoffense (Lussier, Deslauriers-Varin, Collin-Santerre, & Bélanger, 2019). The age at which this recidivism is examined is also important from a life course perspective. In many recidivism studies, a person who is 20 years old and followed for 10 years is assumed to have the same risk of reoffending as a person that is 40 years old and followed for 10 years. By age 40, this person may have several prior arrests for sexual offenses compared to the person at age 20 that has just begun to sexually offend. Thus, the person who is 40 years old may even score higher on a particular risk assessment tool compared to the person at 20 years old; their prior criminal record will serve to elevate their risk status. However, based on what has been indicated by the age-crime curve, the person that is 20 years old may in fact be more likely to sexually recidivate than the person that is 40 years old. The latter is at the end of their criminal career and the former is toward the beginning of their criminal career. Nevertheless, this point will not be reflected by risk assessment tools that heavily rely on a person's prior criminal behavior without giving attention to a person's age and the stage of their criminal career. This point is illustrated in Fig. 6.1a, where the individuals that sexually recidivate are typically younger than the individuals that did not sexually recidivate. Also shown in Panel A is the fact that individuals in the same study are not necessarily followed for the same length of time. Although this can be controlled for in the analysis, one issue is that even the same length of time might have a different meaning for persons of different ages. A three-year follow-up for someone at age 20 captures more of the "at-risk" period for offending compared to the person at age 40 and another at 65. In sum, while recidivism studies have been helpful for reiterating the life course criminology notion that most offenders desist, such studies also lack some of the nuance required to investigate life course notions of the impact of age and aging. Accordingly, Lussier and Cale (2013) recommended a more nuanced approach; one option is to measure whether sexual offending is present at different age stages.

Sexual Offense Continuity Over Different Developmental Stages

Continuity studies use a dynamic classification table approach (LeBlanc & Kaspy, 1998) to examine whether a person is involved in a sexual offense during two different developmental stages. This approach seeks to bring the concepts of age and aging into the study of sexual offending by sampling from a cohort of individuals of the same age who are followed for an identical length of time. Unlike studies of sexual recidivism, continuity studies can be used to identify whether individuals with a history of sexual offending in the first age-stage under examination are more likely to sexually reoffend in the second age-stage compared to individuals *without* a history of sexually offending in the first age-stage. For example, is the person with a history of sexual offending between ages 12 and 17 more likely to sexually offend between the ages of 18 and 23 compared to an individual without a history of sexual offending between ages 12 and 17? This approach is therefore different from sexual recidivism studies in that the sample is not composed exclusively of individuals with a history of sexual offending.

Using data from a community birth cohort from Racine, Wisconsin, Zimring, Piquero, and Jennings (2007) followed approximately 6000 boys and girls until at least age 22 and found that just 8.5% of adolescents with a history of sexual offending were convicted of a sex crime in adulthood. Boys with a history of sexual offending in adolescence accounted for just four percent of all adult male sex crimes for the sample. In other words, using a person's history of sexual offending in adolescence to predict future sexual offending in adulthood would miss out on 96% of all sex crimes committed in this early stage of adulthood. This finding comports with the life course criminology perspective about the difficulty associated with making long-term projections of adult behavior based on adolescent characteristics (Laub & Sampson, 2003). What was more informative of sexual offending in adulthood was the person's frequency of general police contacts in adolescence, which once again reiterates the potential value of using a general antisocial tendency as a key building block in theorizing about the causes of sexual offending (see Chap. 5).

These findings were replicated by Zimring, Jennings, Piquero, and Hays (2009) in a longitudinal study of individuals from the Philadelphia Birth Cohort ($n =$ 27,160) who were followed from adolescence through at least age 26. Again, only approximately 10% of adolescents with a history of sexual offending were adjudicated for at least one new sex offense in adulthood. Less than eight percent of all male sex crime arrests in adulthood were accounted for by adolescents with a history of sexual offending, which resulted in false positive and false negative rates of over 90%. Like the Racine study, frequency of non-sex offending in adolescence was a better predictor of adult sexual offending. In perhaps the longest follow-up of persons with a history of adolescent sexual offending, Piquero et al. (2012) used data on males from the Cambridge Study in Delinquent Development. Participants were recruited from working class neighborhoods in London at age 8 and were followed through age 50. None of the adolescents adjudicated for a sex crime ($n = 10$) perpetrated another sex offense between ages 18 and 50. One caveat to the findings presented so far is that the data were collected during an era where certain sexual behaviors were criminalized (e.g., promiscuity, prostitution, certain sexual acts, or preferences). Accordingly, the data likely captured individuals that do not typically come to mind when most of society thinks about what it means to perpetrate a sexual offense. Thus, other studies turned toward more contemporary samples involved in more serious types of sexual offenses.

Lussier and Blokland (2014) and McCuish, Lussier, and Corrado (2016) examined data on male offenders from the Netherlands and Canada, respectively. These studies examined participants between ages 12 and 17 and then again between ages 18 and 23. Both studies found that less than 10% of adolescents adjudicated for sex crimes repeated such offenses in adulthood. Using data from the Incarcerated Serious and Violent Young Offender Study (ISVYOS), McCuish et al. (2016) found that 75% of all sex crimes in adulthood were committed by individuals with no record of sexually offending in adolescence. Lussier and Blokland (2014), like Zimring et al. (2007) found that adolescents that were frequent non-sex offenders were significantly more likely to engage in adult sex offenses. What is interesting about these studies is the fact that they are based on very different samples from different countries, with different cultures and distinct legal systems. One was based on a birth cohort of all males born in the same year in the Netherlands, while the other was based on a Canadian sample of incarcerated serious and violent youth.

In both cases, these studies showed that youth with a history of sexual offending were not the group most at-risk for committing a sex crime in adulthood. In both cases, researchers observed Robins' discontinuity paradox in full display. Young persons who had committed a sexual offense during adolescence were entering adulthood and discovering new social opportunities that come with this life transition that help terminate reinvolvement in the justice system due to the perpetration of a sexual offense. And yet, policymakers, practitioners, and police investigators remain concerned that such new life opportunities could actually increase the risk of sexual recidivism. In actuality, researchers did not find convincing empirical evidence to support such concerns, at least for most of these youth. One question that should have been raised is not why youth continue to sexually offend in adulthood, but why most of them do not.

Sexual Offense Trajectories Over the Life Course

Another way to examine the issue of continuity and discontinuity of sexual offending over time is through the examination of offending trajectories. For criminologists, offending trajectories represent patterns of onset, course, and desistance from crime (Lussier, 2017). Offenders do not start sexually offending at the same age, at the same rate, over the same period of time, and do not stop from doing so at the same rate, at the same age, and over the same period of time. There is accumulating evidence that perpetrators of sexual offenses are best represented by the presence of multiple offending trajectories (e.g., Deslauriers-Varin & Beauregard, 2014; Francis, Harris, Wallace, Knight, & Soothill, 2014; Lussier, Van Den Berg, Bijleveld, & Hendriks, 2012). Whereas earlier clinical studies characterized sex offending heterogeneity according to different personality characteristics and motivations of offenders, trajectory studies disentangle this heterogeneity through the examination of different patterns of sexual offending over the life course. Thus, trajectory studies more closely align with life course theory definitions of desistance. Trajectory studies map the interrelationship between prior offending, aging, and future offending as a dynamic process over a person's complete criminal career, at least up until the end of a study's follow-up period. This is done by looking at all offenses committed, but instead of looking at an aggregated count of the total number of offenses perpetrated over the follow-up period (e.g., how many convictions did a person incur between ages 12 and 30?), offenses are disaggregated across an age interval, typically one year, so that the number of offenses at each year of age is plotted for a given person. Age is therefore one-half of the dependent variable, making the relationship between past and future offending intrinsically connected to the process of aging. This dynamic process has been formalized through the statistical modeling of offending trajectories (see Fig. 6.1c for a conceptual example). A person's offending trajectory therefore captures different parameters of the criminal career, including age of onset, continuity, persistence, and, if applicable, desistance.

One of the first studies to look at trajectories of sexual offending focused on adult males recruited from a federal penitentiary in the province of Quebec, Canada (Lussier & Davies, 2011). Sex crime convictions were measured between ages 18 and 35 in the sample of predominantly White males. Using semi-parametric group-based modeling (SPGM), two distinct sex crime conviction trajectories were identified. Most of the samples (96%) were characterized by a very low-rate trajectory. For the second trajectory, the first sex crime conviction in adulthood tended to occur in the mid-20s, after which sex crime convictions increased in frequency through the mid-30s. In effect, nearly all individuals with a history of sexual offending showed a pattern of offending once and then never again. Thus, whereas desistance from general offending has been shown to more closely resemble a process of slowing down in frequency of offending over time (e.g., Bushway et al., 2001), desistance from sexual offending was not so much a process observable over time. Rather, in most cases, the start of a person's sexual offending criminal career also signaled its end. Instead of showing a process of slowing down in level of sexual offending, it was typically the case that individuals simply terminated their involvement in sex offenses once the first offense had been perpetrated. This observation was also made by Lussier et al. (2012) in a study of sexual offending trajectories of Dutch adolescents followed from ages 12 to 30. Approximately 90% of the sample was associated with a trajectory where sexual offending was confined to the period of adolescence. The other trajectory indicated continued sexual offending at a relatively high rate between adolescence and adulthood. Although not in line with the life course perspective on desistance as a process, these and other studies of sexual offending trajectories (e.g., Francis et al., 2014; Freiburger, Marcum, Iannacchione, & Higgins, 2012) are in line with the life course perspective that desistance is a normative part of the sexual offending criminal career, which contrasts with certain criminal justice system perspectives on the likelihood of continued sexual offending.

Looking at a more specific group of persons involved in sexual offending, Francis et al. (2014) examined trajectories of sexual offending charges of 780 adult male sexual offenders from the Massachusetts Treatment Center. This sample is unique in that it consisted of those in an institution for high-risk offenders receiving psychiatric treatment who were civilly committed between 1959 and 1984. Sex crime charges were measured between ages 9 and 58 for the sample, although offenders were followed for different lengths of time. The median age of the sample was 27 at the time sexual offending charges were measured. Of the four trajectories identified, a negative relationship between aging and sexual offending charges was observed for just one trajectory (25% of the sample). In the trajectory most typical of the sample, age had minimal impact on sexual offending charges. For the remaining two trajectories, sexual offending charges steadily increased through the 30s and 40s. One group showed a steady increase in sexual offending charges into the late 50s. Overall, the level of persistence in sexual offending found in this study was much greater compared to other sexual offending trajectory studies. There may therefore be something unique about the process of desistance from sex offending for persons that have been civilly committed. Practitioners at the MTC noted that this sample was involved in sexual offenses that required specific attention and, in some cases, longer periods of confinement (e.g., perpetrated more serious offenses). Of importance, their study did not include prospective longitudinal data after being civilly committed and instead reflects offending up until the point that they were civilly committed. This could explain the presence of offending trajectories that steadily increased, representing another example of Robins' retrospective continuity bias. These trajectories, therefore, may mainly reflect the criminal justice system filtering process and the selection of individuals deemed unlikely to desist from sex crimes.

In sum, regardless of the type of methodological approach used to study continued sexual offending over the life course (e.g., recidivism studies, continuity studies, trajectory studies), desistance from sexual offending is the norm for both adolescents and adults. Desistance may occur at different points of the life course for different people; for some, desistance may occur during adolescence; for others, it may occur in adulthood. Furthermore, rather than desistance being a process where higher-rate offenders slowly decline in their level of sexual offending over time, for most individuals, desistance from sexual offending seems to be an immediate (non) event. That is, for most persons, their first sex offense event also marked the end of their sexual offending criminal career.

There are two caveats to this conclusion. First, these studies relied on official data about sexual offending (e.g., police contacts, arrests, charges, convictions) which underestimate the actual sexual offending behavior of these individuals. Second, because studies on offending trajectories emerged from a life course criminology theoretical perspective, researchers understood that looking only at sexual offending essentially placed blinders on their ability to see broader patterns of offending over the life course for persons with a history of sexual offending. In fact, in Lussier et al.'s (2012) study, they observed that even adolescents associated with the highest rate of sexual offending committed nonsexual offenses at a much higher rate. The synchronicity between nonsexual and sexual offending warrants further examination. For instance, can information about desistance from nonsexual offending inform the underlying factors explaining desistance from sexual offending? This line of analysis sparked a movement toward looking at desistance from general offending among persons with a history of sexual offending, including whether individuals with a history of sexual offending were less likely to show a pattern of desistance or did not experience desistance until later in the life course, compared to individuals with a history of nonsexual offending only.

Pulling Back on the Microscope: General Offense Trajectories

If persons with a history of sexual offending have a low likelihood of repeating such behavior over the life course, does that mean that their first sex offense is also their last offense of any kind? From a life course theoretical perspective on desistance, involvement in a specific crime type is not believed to be informative of a person's general offending pattern (Capaldi & Patterson, 1996; Farrington, 1989; Laub & Sampson, 2001) and therefore the study of desistance among persons with a history of sexual offending should look at their broader offense patterns. Although specific examination of general desistance for persons with a history of sexual offending was not part of life course criminology's initial research interests, the possibility that adjudications for sex offenses could act as a barrier to desistance via the unique criminal justice system response and stigmatization associated with a sex offense could make it difficult for such persons to acquire and benefit from informal social controls. Initial research therefore investigated whether general desistance followed a similar process for individuals with or without a history of sexual offending.

Jennings, Zgoba, and Tewksbury (2012) compared the general offending trajectories of adults with a history of sexual offenses ($n = 247$) and nonsexual offenses ($n = 250$) following the implementation of SORN laws in New Jersey. Based on an 8-year follow-up period, they observed that persons with a history of sexual offending were associated with a trajectory defined by a lower level of involvement in criminal behavior. However, non-sex offending was certainly more common than sexual offending. Ronis and Borduin (2013) used a sample of 131 individuals with a history of engaging in sexually aggressive behavior between ages 12 and 27 and 605 individuals with a history of engaging in at least one serious nonsexual criminal offense. Sexually aggressive behavior included having sexual relations with someone against their will or using pressure or physical force. Three trajectories of antisocial behavior emerged. There were no differences in antisocial behavior trajectory patterns between individuals with a history of sexual offending versus nonsexual offending only. Looking specifically at incarcerated adolescent offenders followed until age 23, McCuish et al. (2016) compared general offending trajectory group membership between a group of adolescents with a history of sexual offending and another group with a history defined exclusively by non-sex offending. Four general offending trajectories covering adolescence and early adulthood period were identified for the sample ($n = 283$). Adolescents with a history of sexual offending were relatively equally distributed across each of the four trajectories and this distribution was mirrored by adolescents with a history of non-sex offending.

In a Canadian study (ISVYOS),[2] Reale, McCuish, and Corrado (2019) looked at whether a history of adolescent sexual offending impacted desistance from general offending in adulthood. Whereas other studies looked at general offending trajectories over the measurement period, which resulted in including the sex offense as part of the entire offense trajectory, Reale et al. looked at whether sexual offending in adolescence (ages 12–17) had implications for the nature of a person's offending trajectory between ages 18 and 25. They found that having a history of sexual offending in adolescence had no implications for the nature of an incarcerated youth's pattern of offending in adulthood. However, many aspects of an adolescent's general offending history between ages 12 and 17 were informative of desistance, including a lower frequency of general offending, less time incarcerated, and less offending versatility. Overall, since trajectory studies did not find much or any difference in the general offending patterns of those with or without a history of sexual offending, there seemed to be little validity to the hypothesis that adjudications for sex offenses were an indicator that a prolonged criminal career was to come. These studies also showed that for perpetrators of sexual offenses, their sexual offending was the rarest aspect of their criminal career; their nonsexual offending patterns were far more frequent.

In sum, youth who have been adjudicated for a sex crime present the same general offending patterns as those adjudicated for nonsexual offenses. Some are occasionally involved in criminal activities, but their level of involvement significantly decreases after turning 18. Others are repeatedly involved in criminal activity, but their offending slows down more progressively in adulthood. A rarer group shows more stability in their pattern of general offending. What research seems to repeatedly confirm is that, when prospective longitudinal studies are used, regardless of

---

[2] There are notable differences between the Canadian and American criminal justice system, including their respective responses to individuals who have been convicted for a sex crime. Some of those differences include the use of public notification and sex offender registries and are discussed in Chap. 9.

the nature of the sample, the likelihood of desistance from general offending is similar among individuals with and without a history of sexual offending. In other words, the process of desistance from sexual offending might be closely tied to that of offending in general. However, this does not preclude the possibility that there are also unique pathways to desistance for at least some persons involved in sexual offenses.

A Life Course Theoretical Perspective on Sexual Offending and Desistance

Since the enactment of the first sex offender laws (e.g., sexual psychopath laws), the therapeutic path to desistance has been a somewhat recurrent theme. This path suggests that desistance can only be achieved through the offender's participation in some form of professional and specialized therapy designed specifically for individuals having perpetrated sex crimes. Sex offender treatment can tackle the underlying causes and motivations of sexual offending in a way that promotes a person's rehabilitation. This therapeutic path has been seen by many as the only possible path to desistance from sex crimes. Others have distanced themselves from the rehabilitation goals arguing instead that "once a sex offender, always a sex offender" (see Zimring, 2004). Such views and endorsement for such assumptions have led others to reformulate sex offender treatment as a risk management strategy where treatment was initiated for the purpose of helping individuals *control* their enduring predispositions toward sexual offenses (e.g., Pithers, 1990). While the ultimate goal was to help these individuals to not sexually reoffend, constant cognitive-behavioral control over their stable and fixed predisposition toward sexual offenses was the key objective. Until recently, the therapeutic path has been assumed to be the only path to desistance advocated and such a path has been exclusively focused on the person, the offender, in a therapeutic environment. Lessons from life course criminology suggest that desistance from crime requires a broader perspective.

From a life course perspective, formal sanctions can negatively impact life events and social roles associated with desistance. Parallel to this, the literature on persons involved in sex offenses has expressed concerns that such persons have minimal community and social support following their release from custody (e.g., Bohmert, Duwe, & Hipple, 2018; Gutiérrez-Lobos et al., 2001). Therefore, although patterns of desistance do not seem to vary across persons with or without a history of sexual offending, the former individuals, because of their involvement in a sex crime, may face unique circumstances that act as barriers to desistance. In other words, the similar patterns of desistance may be in spite of the more adverse circumstances that persons with sexual offenses are exposed to as part of their processing through the justice system. Relatedly, the role of social structure in facilitating turning points is a key pillar of life course criminology and may operate in a fundamentally different way for persons with a history of sexual offending given that such persons are likely to be funneled into disadvantaged communities that provide fewer opportunities for housing, employment, and positive sources of social support (Mustaine, Tewksbury, & Stengel, 2006).

In effect, whereas life course research highlights the need for offenders to be embedded in positive social environments, criminal justice system philosophies view such environments as catalysts for the "sex offender" to commit new crimes. Relatedly, Sampson and Laub emphasize the value of human agency as a means of altering a person's life course and helping facilitate the acquisition of informal social control. Yet, many criminal justice system policies, especially those in the USA, have collateral consequences on the psychosocial functioning of perpetrators of sex offenses that may weaken human agency or inhibit action-taking. These policies often include lengthy sentences, which according to the life course criminology principle of state dependence[3] can have a negative impact on sources of informal social control and thus can increase their likelihood of continued offending (Kornhauser, 1978; Laub & Sampson, 1993). Civic reintegration is another important source of informal social control (Uggen, Manza, & Behrens, 2004) but may be more challenging given that placement on a sex offending registry may reduce opportunities to reside in a neighborhood with strong collective efficacy, which in turn makes developing prosocial ties with neighbors more difficult. The possibility of sexual offending resulting in unique challenges for experiencing desistance has been addressed by studies looking at whether informal social controls central to life course criminology were less prevalent, of a weaker quality, or had a less beneficial effect individuals with a history of sexual offending. Both qualitative and quantitative studies have approached this question by looking at various sources of informal social control and how they relate to desistance among individuals with a history of sexual offending.

Lussier and McCuish (2016) highlighted the role of peer influence as a source of informal social control influencing desistance among a sample of Canadian men with a history of sexual offending. These men, when embedded in a social environment composed of positive and noncriminal influences, were more likely to experience desistance compared to their counterparts whose social network of friends and acquaintances included criminal and negative social influences. Although prosocial peers were important for desistance, because persons with a history of sexual offending tend to be more socially isolated, they may have greater difficulty in meeting such peers. Lussier and McCuish (2016) found that positive peer relations were uncommon for the sample and speculated that sample members may be hesitant to leave antisocial peer groups for prosocial ones given that their relatively low social capital may make it difficult to transition to a positive peer group. Thus, the person would rather maintain friendships with antisocial peers than risk being completely socially isolated. Another challenge for making new friends is that individuals with a history of sexual offending may be viewed suspiciously when attempting

---

[3] State dependence can be understood as a process where the correlation between past and future criminal behavior stems from how engaging criminal behavior can profoundly impact and transform an individual's life circumstances in such a way that it alters or increases the probability of future offending (Nagin & Paternoster, 2000).

to contribute to the social life cohesiveness and collective efficacy of the community in which they reside (Lussier & McCuish, 2016). In a similar vein, ten Bensel and Sample's (2017) examination of the identities of adult males with a history of sexual offending indicated that switching to a more prosocial peer group would likely result in rejection due to the stigmatizing nature of being a known "sex offender." The use of social media was one way that persons with a history of sexual offending established informal social networks that improved loneliness and sense of empowerment, which may be particularly important given that these individuals have limited access to conventional opportunities for friendship networks (ten Bensel & Sample, 2019). Although peer networks established through social media may act as an important source of informal social control, existing criminal justice policies include explicit attempts to limit internet access to social media sites for persons on a sexual offending registry (Tewksbury & Zgoba, 2010).

Lussier and McCuish (2016) found little evidence that central life course criminology turning points like employment and marriage benefited those with histories of sexual offending in terms of helping promote desistance. Blokland and van der Geest (2015) also reported that neither marriage nor employment was associated with recidivism once controlling for other key factors (also see Kruttschnitt, Uggen, & Shelton, 2000). Kras (2019) used a mixed-methods approach to examine 72 men convicted of sex crimes in Missouri. Neither instrumental support (e.g., financial) nor expressive support (e.g., emotional) from a partner helped these men to avoid violating court orders upon release from custody. Similarly, attachments to family and intimate partners did not reduce the likelihood of reimprisonment. A recurrent theme in Farmer et al.'s (2015) review of qualitative research on desistance from sexual offending noted that employment and relationships did not appear to be important for desistance. Harris (2014) examination of the desistance narratives of 21 adults with a history of sexual offending showed not only that none of these men attributed their desistance to informal social control, they actually described their relationships in negative terms due to the stigma that stemmed from their involvement in a sex crime. Kras (2019) reported that qualitative examinations of informal social controls were especially necessary as the quality of such controls may be weaker or less effective among persons involved in sexual offenses and therefore relatively limited in promoting desistance. For example, although sexual recidivists in Kras' (2019) study received instrumental support from family members and intimate partners, Kras (2019) speculated that instrumental support in the absence of positive and prosocial emotional support may have only enabled the person to continue their behavior following release from custody.

In sum, both qualitative and quantitative studies provided evidence that an individual's history of sexual offending potentially impacted the quality of their marriage and other informal social controls. ten Bensel and Sample (2017) and Kruttschnitt et al. (2000) cautioned against strict interpretations of these findings given that binary measures of marital status were too broad for persons with a history of sexual offending. The stigmatization of being a "sex offender" may strain even strong relationships and contribute to the person internalizing a collective identity as someone on the margins of society. Simply measuring whether someone is married or unmarried misses out on this nuance. Although Laub and Sampson (2003) argued that their life course perspective on desistance was a general theory that applied to all offense-types, certain pillars of the life course perspective, especially those referring to macro-level social structures and historical contexts, may operate differently for individuals with a history of sexual offending. These structures include variability in how the criminal justice system responds to sex offending compared to non-sex offending (Cooley & Sample, 2018). As outlined in Chap. 9, a major source of strain comes directly from sex offender policies that have a stigmatizing effect and may negatively influence relationship and employment quality (Harris, Walfield, Shields, & Letourneau, 2016; Levenson & D'Amora, 2007).

Re-thinking the Process of Desistance for Persons with a History of Sexual Offending

Since Laub and Sampson's (2003) update and description of how age-graded sources of informal social control influence desistance over the life course, several scholars have taken up the goal of explaining desistance through an integration of principles from the sociologically based life course theory and principles from the psychology-based developmental criminology paradigm. One principle of the developmental perspective is the focus on person x environment interactions and their impact on a person's behavior. Exclusive focus on a person or the environment misses one of the fundamental pieces of the puzzle regarding how people change over the life course. Could it be that some experiences are necessary for individual change and maturation to occur? Could it be that some individuals ready for change seek out experiences in social/environmental contexts that will provide suitable opportunities for maturation? A notable example of this approach is Rocque's (2015) integrated theory of desistance (ITD). Half a century earlier, the Gluecks identified maturation as central to the process of desistance. Yet, aside from suggesting that maturation was not simply the result of aging, the Gluecks provided little direction in terms of what it actually meant for a person to mature. Rocque addressed this long-standing research need by defining different dimensions of maturation and examining how these dimensions are perhaps a necessary first step to being open and ready for social roles and other turning points that help with desistance. Rocque specified that maturation is a complex multidomain process that while normative can vary across individuals and within individuals. Rocque (2015) decomposed this complexity into five measurable domains that could be used to help understand the relationship between aging and desistance: psychosocial, identity, adult social role, civic, and neurocognitive. From the perspective of research on sexual offending, these maturation dimensions may be stunted by the experience of being adjudicated for a sex offense. This could explain why informal social controls have not been as useful as explanations of desistance for perpetrators of sexual offenses (Lussier &

McCuish, 2016). Rocque's perspective essentially revived the Gluecks' interest in maturation and merged it into a life course perspective on desistance.

The first maturation domain, psychosocial maturation, draws on the work of Steinberg and Cauffman (1996) and refers to improvements in perspective-taking (e.g., being future oriented), responsibility (e.g., independence), and temperance (e.g., improvements in self-control and aggression suppression). According to this view, more mature individuals are more self-reliant about how to attain their own goals, more persistent in their actions toward these goals, but also conscious about the possible long-term consequences of such actions. Psychosocial maturation improves during the transition from adolescence to adulthood and is associated with a desistance trajectory (Monahan, Steinberg, Cauffman, & Mulvey, 2009, 2013). The relationship between psychosocial maturation and desistance is robust across White, Black, and Hispanic youth (Rocque, Beckley, & Piquero, 2019). McCuish, Lussier, and Rocque (2019) showed that there was a reciprocal relationship between psychosocial maturation and offending, meaning that although psychosocial maturation promoted reduced offending, increased offending had a negative impact on psychosocial maturation. This type of relationship may be especially likely for individuals involved in sexual offenses. Sexual offending may result in disrupted bonds with family (Farkas & Miller, 2007) and limit employment (Mustaine et al., 2006), both of which are negatively associated with psychosocial maturation (DeWitt, 2016; Williams & Steinberg, 2011). In other words, sexual offending negatively impacts, in ways that perhaps no other crime type can, certain life domains that traditionally help foster psychosocial maturation. Accordingly, practitioners should be wary of the potentially negative impact of the justice system on factors that traditionally help promote desistance.

The second maturation domain, identity maturation, reflects a person's willingness to be less inflexible to allow for a cognitive transformation that facilitates a more positive perception of the self and the rejection of antisocial attitudes. Individuals become more open to positive growth, which includes improved attitudes toward society, themselves, and prosocial behavior. Several studies of identities of adolescents and adults showed that a more positive future self, defined by expectations about involvement in conventional social institutions, was associated with lower levels of offending (Abate & Venta, 2018; LeBel, Burnett, Maruna, & Bushway, 2008; Na & Jang, 2019). Even for criminally active persons, they will alter their self-identity if they forecast their future involvement in conventional social institutions. This forecasting leads such individuals to alter their behavior so that it aligns with their new self-identity and perceptions of the future (Iselin, Mulvey, Loughran, Chung, & Schubert, 2012). Another component of the identity domain is antisocial attitudes, which describe an individual's attempt to avoid internal sanctions (e.g., guilt, threat to self-worth) by rationalizing their harmful behavior to make it appear justified (Bandura, Barbaranelli, Caprara, & Pastorelli, 1996). This too is associated with desistance (Steinberg et al., 2015). Measuring identity might be especially important to understanding desistance for those with a history of sexual offending because of tendencies to experience internalizing issues following a conviction for a sex offense (Kruttschnitt et al., 2000; ten Bensel & Sample, 2017).

The constant reminder of being a convicted sex offender prior to, during, and well after the end of their sentence leaves little room for cognitive transformation and openness to become more positive toward society and themselves. This may be especially true given society's strong negative reaction and the associated stigma that results from a person's past behavior. Studies that examine within-individual change in identity prior to and following a person's adjudication for a sex offense may help to better understand how identity is influenced by sanctioning and how this in turn impacts desistance.

The third maturation dimension, adult social role maturation, represents Rocque's (2015) integration of life course theory concepts into his ITD. Social role maturation describes the acquisition of social roles like marriage/cohabitation, parenthood, and employment. These roles can serve as social controls on behavior, and the efficacy of such roles is contingent on the age at which they occur (Uggen, 2000) and their subjective value (Nguyen & Loughran, 2018). These roles and the social opportunities that come along cannot stress enough the importance of social integration. It is not enough for a person to find a job for maturation and desistance to occur. It needs to be a meaningful job, with good colleagues that can have a positive influence; who can provide advice and guidance; who can share their thoughts, their own experiences; who may partake in some social activities outside of work, which can not only foster a person's attitude toward their job, but also further disrupt time/opportunity to offend. Social integration that promotes maturation is not a status issue (e.g., being employed, married, etc.), it is more about the positive social connections and experience that favor growth.

As illustrated by Uggen (2000), the influence of employment on desistance is stronger for older individuals than younger individuals because the former may be in a better position to value their employment for reasons other than financial gain. Measuring an individual's attitudes toward work may therefore be informative of their level of maturity that in turn informs the likelihood of whether this employment will be valued and remain stable enough to facilitate desistance. The sequencing of social roles is a less examined theme, but also appears to matter for the likelihood of desistance (Kang, 2019). For example, parenthood before marriage/cohabitation or employment may less effectively promote desistance compared to the reverse sequence of events. Attitudes toward work, consideration for others, and the subjective valuation of associated roles may differ for individuals convicted of a sex offense because their ability to gain/maintain quality employment and relationships may be limited due in part to stigmatization.

The final two maturation dimensions are less often examined in the desistance literature. The fourth dimension, civic maturation, concerns an individual's orientation toward the legitimacy of social norms and values and the institutions that govern them. Civic maturation also involves a desire to volunteer or engage in the community as a means of giving back. Behaviors like voting and paying taxes also exemplify civic maturation. Schneider (1990) developed a specific measure of civic maturation via the Good Citizen Scale. Among a sample of serious and violent Canadian offenders followed from adolescence through the twenties, higher scores on this scale were associated with desistance from violent offending (McCuish,

Corrado, Hart, & DeLisi, 2015). Yet, engagement in the community may be difficult for a person with a history of sexual offending given the potential for this person to be looked upon suspiciously or perceived to have ulterior motives (Lussier & McCuish, 2016). The fifth dimension, cognitive/neurological maturation, concerns the growth and development of the brain and executive functioning, which is linked to a reduction in impulsivity and sensation-seeking behavior. This is the least commonly investigated maturation dimension, likely because of the difficulties and costs associated with measuring, for example, changes in brain development. Unlike components from other maturation dimensions, neurocognitive components likely are not as malleable, especially once individuals enter late adolescence/early adulthood, and therefore the lack of change in such components might make it a challenge to examine within-individual change in criminal behavior.

Few studies have provided a head-to-head test to compare the impact of different maturation dimensions on desistance. Rocque, Posick, and White (2015) used the Rutgers Health and Human Development study to measure all five dimensions and explore their relationship to desistance, finding that while each dimension was correlated with crime in the expected direction, in multivariate growth models, identity and psychosocial maturation were most consistently associated with desistance. In addition, an overall maturation measure, which combined all five dimensions, was related to desistance. Stone and Rydberg (2019) used data from the Pathways to Desistance Study on serious and violent male and female offenders from Phoenix and Philadelphia to examine the interaction between parenthood, different dimensions of maturation, and desistance. These authors showed that parenthood impacted maturation dimensions, that maturation dimensions were associated with desistance, but that the effect of parenthood on desistance was not mediated by maturation. This suggests the role of parenthood on desistance is not just about becoming more mature. Parenthood may change a person's routine activities in ways that constrain opportunities for criminal behavior (Laub & Sampson, 2003). Stone and Rydberg (2019) also found that the effect of parenthood on maturation was not always in the anticipated direction. For example, becoming a parent reduced males' psychosocial maturation. This provided an important illustration of the likely age-graded nature of turning points. Participants in the Pathways to Desistance Study were only followed until the early to mid-20s and may not have been at a level of maturation that prepared them for the parenthood experience. These observations align with life course theory assertions that events that take place too early in the life course may be ineffective as facilitators of desistance.

Rather than measure actual involvement in adult social roles, McCuish et al. (2019) used data from the Pathways to Desistance Study to measure expectations and attitudes toward such roles and the capacity to meet role expectations (e.g., demonstration of consideration for others). Expectations include becoming less selfish by considering others, which is consistent with moral development, allocentrism, and cognitive empathy (Martinez, Stuewig, & Tangney, 2014). In effect, McCuish et al. (2019) argued that there were specific indicators of maturation that signaled a person's preparedness for events such as employment, marriage, and parenthood. Their analyses showed that change in maturation dimensions did not occur independently of other maturation dimensions. By looking at different indicators of psychosocial, adult role, and identity dimensions, they found that indicators of maturation tended to cluster in triads composed of one indicator from each dimension. For example, participants high in responsibility (psychosocial maturation) tended to be high in self-identity (identity maturation) and work-orientation (social role maturation). Moral disengagement (identity maturation) and consideration of others (social role maturation) were the measures of different maturation dimensions most consistently related to desistance from general offending. There is currently no research that has examined the relationship between different dimensions of maturation and desistance from general or sexual offending among persons that have been adjudicated for a sexual offense. Future research examining this theme should consider whether adjudication for a sexual offense negatively impacts maturation in ways that decrease the likelihood of desistance.

In sum, the maturation-based framework for studying desistance acknowledges important interrelationships among a range of different constructs from life course (Laub & Sampson, 2003), cognitive transformation (e.g., Giordano, Cernkovich, & Rudolph, 2002; Paternoster & Bushway, 2009), and developmental (Glueck & Glueck, 1937) theories of desistance. It is not just that an individual becomes employed, it is that they have a level of psychosocial maturation and positive self-identity that makes them an attractive job candidate and allows them to benefit from employment in ways that facilitate desistance. Empirical research has not yet established the causal order of these different dimensions of maturation and adult social roles. Does employment give individuals a sense of positive identity and a rationale for suppressing aggression and impulsivity, or does a change in identity and an ability to control impulses make a person more likely to seek out, and benefit from, employment? These are unaddressed puzzles to be solved in the desistance literature, especially with respect to persons adjudicated for sexual offenses, and there are new approaches to examining desistance (e.g., Thornton et al., 2019) that might be effective for examining the efficacy of maturation and turning points.

These emerging research themes raise a potentially pivotal question for the explanation of sexual offending: could it be that life course factors thought to play a role in desistance from general offending, when absent, also operate in ways that increase the risk for sexual offending? After all, losing a job, experiencing financial problems, going through recurrent marital difficulties, persistent interpersonal conflicts with a neighbor, a colleague, or the victim, and impulsive and angry behaviors that result from these conflicts, and feelings of loneliness and intimacy needs are all common antecedents that perpetrators of a sex crime noted were present in the months, weeks, and even hours prior to their offense (e.g., Laws, 1989; Proulx, Beauregard, Lussier, & Leclerc, 2014). In fact, these situations have been previously described as significant triggers for perpetrators of sex crimes. Could these triggers reflect some of these perpetrators' difficulties coping and adjusting to age-graded life events? This assertion squares with Laub and Sampson's (2003) life course perspective that offending persistence and desistance represent two sides of the same coin. Major risk factors for continued sexual offending could simply be the opposite of turning points. The life course provides multiple age-graded transition points such as: entry to high school, college, and university, entry into the job market, becoming a colleague, starting a business or a professional career, first sexual contacts, dating, first sexual intercourse, cohabiting with a love one, marriage, and parenthood. These life transitions may represent a challenge to some who are prone to negative emotional reactions, who have a tendency to seek new experiences and sensations, who are self-centered and focused on their immediate needs. The required stability, persistence, and hardship associated with these life transition and newly acquired roles (e.g., intimate partner; parent; employer) may prove to be challenging at many levels. Could it be that these difficulties coping and adjusting to these life transitions and newly acquired roles and responsibilities escalate during the life course in such a way that it leads them to harm others psychologically, physically, and even sexually? Could it be that sexual recidivism partly reflects the persistence of these difficulties adjusting to certain age-graded roles that require a certain maturity level?

Conclusion

The life course perspective emphasizes how different sociological processes influence within-individual change in offending over time. Sampson and Laub (1997) were specifically interested in how the life course perspective explains desistance, which they viewed as something that should be studied specifically among the most high-rate and persistent offenders (Laub & Sampson, 2003). In explaining desistance, the main principles of life course theory include the role of age-graded sources of informal social control, the impact of macro-level social structures and historical contexts that facilitate (or hinder) the acquisition of informal social control, and human agency (e.g., individual motivation). Regardless of how different studies measured desistance from sexual offending, the story remains the same: sexual offending most typically represents a short-lived period of a person's life course. The behavior rarely continues between adolescence and adulthood. Studies measuring trajectories of sexual offending show that for approximately 90% of persons with a history of sexual offending the behavior is typically limited to a short period of low-rate offending. Perpetrators may experience temporary difficulties adjusting to new life events and circumstances that may trigger antisocial and criminal behaviors which can escalate to sexual offending. Desistance from sexual offending therefore is not typically something that can be examined as a process for most offenders. For most persons that come into contact with the criminal justice system, sex offending persistence and desistance, at least based on official data, happen at exactly the same time. A person becomes involved in a sex offense at one instance in time and yet this instance also marks the time that desistance starts in that it is the last time they will ever be involved in a sex offense again, at least according to official data. This is certainly not to say that this is the only pattern of desistance for persons involved in sexual offenses. However, it does appear to be the most common pattern. While researchers have been overly focused on trying to decipher the factors associated with persistence of sexual offending over the life course; perhaps another fruitful approach would be to examine why, when, and under what circumstances most perpetrators of sexual offenses cease such behavior.

Emerging research using a life course criminology perspective suggests that persons involved in sexual offending have unfinished stories; their lives following sexual offending are not simply characterized by incarcerations, releases, and reinvolvement in sex offenses. Such observations are markedly different from many policies responding to sexual offending that tend to assume that, once a "sex offender," always a "sex offender" (Zimring, 2004). However, individuals involved in sexual offending typically do not confine their offending to this one crime type. In fact, nonsexual offending is far more common for most of this group. Patterns of desistance from general offending for persons with a history of sexual offending look very similar to individuals involved only in nonsexual offending, but there is also reason to believe that future research should pay attention to the unique circumstances of persons with a history of sexual offending as the mechanisms responsible for desistance from general offending may be different for these persons. Specifically, informal social controls may be less useful for individuals with a history of sexual offending. The implication here is that life course theories of desistance from general offending may not be equally useful for explaining desistance from general offending among persons with a history of sexual offending.

References

Abate, A., & Venta, A. (2018). Perceptions of the legal system and recidivism: Investigating the mediating role of perceptions of chances for success in juvenile offenders. *Criminal Justice and Behavior, 45*(4), 541–560.

Abel, G. G., Osborn, C. A., & Twigg, D. A. (1993). Sexual assault through the life span: Adult offenders with juvenile histories. In H. E. Barbaree, W. L. Marshall, & S. M. Hudson (Eds.), *The juvenile sex offender*. New York: Guilford.

Arnett, J. J. (2000). Emerging adulthood: A theory of development from the late teens through the twenties. *American Psychologist, 55*(5), 469.

Bandura, A., Barbaranelli, C., Caprara, G. V., & Pastorelli, C. (1996). Mechanisms of moral disengagement in the exercise of moral agency. *Journal of Personality and Social Psychology, 71*(2), 364.

Blokland, A. A., & Nieuwbeerta, P. (2005). The effects of life circumstances on longitudinal trajectories of offending. *Criminology, 43*(4), 1203–1240.

Blokland, A. A. J., & van der Geest, V. (2015). Lifecourse transitions and desistance in sex offenders: an event history analysis. In A. A. J. Blokland & P. Lussier (Eds.), *Sex offenders: A criminal career approach* (pp. 257–288). Oxford: Wiley-Blackwell.

Bohmert, M. N., Duwe, G., & Hipple, N. K. (2018). Evaluating restorative justice circles of support and accountability: can social support overcome structural barriers? *International Journal of Offender Therapy and Comparative Criminology, 62*(3), 739–758.

Bushway, S. D., Piquero, A. R., Broidy, L. M., Cauffman, E., & Mazerolle, P. (2001). An empirical framework for studying desistance as a process. *Criminology, 39*(2), 491–516.

Caldwell, M. F. (2002). What we do not know about juvenile sexual offense risk. *Child Maltreatment, 7*(4), 291–302.

Capaldi, D. M., & Patterson, G. R. (1996). Can violent offenders be distinguished from frequent offenders: Prediction from childhood to adolescence. *Journal of Research in Crime and Delinquency, 33*(2), 206–231.

Caspi, A., Elder, G. H., & Herbener, E. S. (1990). Childhood personality and the prediction of life-course patterns. In *Straight and devious pathways from childhood to adulthood* (pp. 13–35). Cambridge: Cambridge University Press.

Cooley, B. N., & Sample, L. L. (2018). The difference between desistance from sexual offending and not reoffending. *Journal of Crime and Justice, 41*(5), 483–503.

Dannefer, D. (1984). Adult development and social theory: A paradigmatic reappraisal. *American Sociological Review, 49*, 100–116.

Deslauriers-Varin, N., & Beauregard, E. (2014). Consistency in crime site selection: An investigation of crime sites used by serial sex offenders across crime series. *Journal of Criminal Justice, 42*(2), 123–133.

DeWitt, S. E. (2016). Signaling desistance: using short-term signals to identify long-term desisters (Doctoral dissertation, Rutgers University-Graduate School-Newark).

Elder, G. H. (1998). The life course as developmental theory. *Child Development, 69*(1), 1–12.

English, K. (1998). The containment approach: An aggressive strategy for the community management of adult sex offenders. *Psychology, Public Policy, and Law, 4*(1-2), 218.

Farkas, M. A., & Miller, G. (2007). Reentry and reintegration: Challenges faced by the families of convicted sex offenders. *Federal Sentencing Reporter, 20*(1), 88–92.

Farmer, M., McAlinden, A. M., & Maruna, S. (2015). Understanding desistance from sexual offending: A thematic review of research findings. *Probation Journal, 62*(4), 320–335.

Farrington, D. P. (1989). Early predictors of adolescent aggression and adult violence. *Violence and victims, 4*(2), 79–100.

Francis, B., Harris, D. A., Wallace, S., Knight, R. A., & Soothill, K. (2014). Sexual and general offending trajectories of men referred for civil commitment. *Sexual Abuse, 26*(4), 311–329.

Freiburger, T. L., Marcum, C. D., Iannacchione, B. M., & Higgins, G. E. (2012). Sex offenders and criminal recidivism: an exploratory trajectory analysis using a Virginia sample. *Journal of Crime and Justice, 35*(3), 365–375.

Frisbie, L. V. (1966). Studies on sex offending in California: 1954–1966. *California Mental Health Research Digest, 4*, 135–141.

Giordano, P. C., Cernkovich, S. A., & Rudolph, J. L. (2002). Gender, crime, and desistance: Toward a theory of cognitive transformation. *American Journal of Sociology, 107*(4), 990–1064.

Glueck, S., & Glueck, E. (1937). *Later criminal careers.* New York: Commonwealth Fund.

Gutiérrez-Lobos, K., Eher, R., Grünhut, C., Bankier, B., Schmidl-Mohl, B., Frühwald, S., et al. (2001). Violent sex offenders lack male social support. *International Journal of Offender Therapy and Comparative Criminology, 45*(1), 70–82.

Hagan, J., & Dinovitzer, R. (1999). Collateral consequences of imprisonment for children, communities, and prisoners. *Crime and Justice, 26*, 121–162.

Hanson, R. K. (2002). Recidivism and age. *Journal of Interpersonal Violence, 17*, 1046–1062.

Hanson, R. K., & Bussière, M. T. (1998). Predicting relapse: a meta-analysis of sexual offender recidivism studies. *Journal of Consulting and Clinical Psychology, 66*(2), 348–362.

Hanson, R. K., Harris, A. J., Helmus, L., & Thornton, D. (2014). High-risk sex offenders may not be high risk forever. *Journal of Interpersonal Violence, 29*(15), 2792–2813.

Hanson, R. K., Harris, A. J., Letourneau, E., Helmus, L. M., & Thornton, D. (2018). Reductions in risk based on time offense-free in the community: Once a sexual offender, not always a sexual offender. *Psychology, Public Policy, and Law, 24*(1), 48.

Hargreaves, C., & Francis, B. (2014). The long term recidivism risk of young sexual offenders in England and Wales–enduring risk or redemption? *Journal of Criminal Justice, 42*(2), 164–172.

Harris, A. J., Walfield, S. M., Shields, R. T., & Letourneau, E. J. (2016). Collateral consequences of juvenile sex offender registration and notification: Results from a survey of treatment providers. *Sexual Abuse, 28*(8), 770–790.

Harris, D. A. (2014). Desistance from sexual offending: Findings from 21 life history narratives. *Journal of Interpersonal Violence, 29*(9), 1554–1578.

Harris, D. A. (2017). Desistance from sexual offending: Behavioral change without cognitive transformation. *Journal of Interpersonal Violence, 32*(20), 3049–3070.

Horney, J., Osgood, D. W., & Marshall, I. H. (1995). Criminal careers in the short-term: Intra-individual variability in crime and its relation to local life circumstances. *American Sociological Review, 60*, 655–673.

Iselin, A. M. R., Mulvey, E. P., Loughran, T. A., Chung, H. L., & Schubert, C. A. (2012). A longitudinal examination of serious adolescent offenders' perceptions of chances for success and engagement in behaviors accomplishing goals. *Journal of Abnormal Child Psychology, 40*(2), 237–249.

Jennings, W. G., Zgoba, K. M., & Tewksbury, R. (2012). A comparative longitudinal analysis of recidivism trajectories and collateral consequences for sex and non-sex offenders released since the implementation of sex offender registration and community notification. *Journal of Crime and Justice, 35*(3), 356–364.

Kang, T. (2019). The transition to adulthood of contemporary delinquent adolescents. *Journal of Developmental and Life-Course Criminology, 5*(2), 176–202.

Karpman, B. (1951). The sexual psychopath. *Journal of Criminal Law, Criminology, and Police Science, 42*, 184.

Kornhauser, R. R. (1978). *Social sources of delinquency: An appraisal of analytic models*. Chicago: University of Chicago Press.

Kras, K. R. (2019). Can social support overcome the individual and structural challenges of being a sex offender? Assessing the social support-recidivism link. *International Journal of Offender Therapy and Comparative Criminology, 63*(1), 32–54.

Kruttschnitt, C., Uggen, C., & Shelton, K. (2000). Predictors of desistance among sex offenders: The interaction of formal and informal social controls. *Justice Quarterly, 17*(1), 61–87.

Kurlychek, M. C., Brame, R., & Bushway, S. D. (2007). Enduring risk? Old criminal records and predictions of future criminal involvement. *Crime & Delinquency, 53*(1), 64–83.

Laub, J. H., Nagin, D. S., & Sampson, R. J. (1998). Trajectories of change in criminal offending: Good marriages and the desistance process. *American Sociological Review, 63*, 225–238.

Laub, J. H., Rowan, Z. R., & Sampson, R. J. (2019). The age-graded theory of informal social control. In D. P. Farrington, L. Kazemian, & A. R. Piquero (Eds.), *The Oxford handbook of developmental and life-course criminology* (pp. 295–322). New York: Oxford University Press.

Laub, J. H., & Sampson, R. J. (1991). The Sutherland-Glueck debate: On the sociology of criminological knowledge. *American Journal of Sociology, 96*(6), 1402–1440.

Laub, J. H., & Sampson, R. J. (1993). Turning points in the life course: Why change matters to the study of crime. *Criminology, 31*(3), 301–325.

Laub, J. H., & Sampson, R. J. (2001). Understanding desistance from crime. *Crime and Justice, 28*, 1–69.

Laub, J. H., & Sampson, R. J. (2003). *Shared beginnings, divergent lives: Delinquent boys to age 70*. Cambridge, MA: Harvard University Press.

Laws, D. R. (1989). *Relapse prevention with sex offenders*. New York: Guilford Press.

LeBel, T. P., Burnett, R., Maruna, S., & Bushway, S. (2008). The "chicken and egg" of subjective and social factors in desistance from crime. *European Journal of Criminology, 5*, 131–159.

LeBlanc, M., & Kaspy, N. (1998). Trajectories of delinquency and problem behavior: Comparison of social and personal control characteristics of adjudicated boys on synchronous and nonsynchronous paths. *Journal of Quantitative Criminology, 14*(2), 181–214.

Levenson, J. S., & D'Amora, D. A. (2007). Social policies designed to prevent sexual violence the emperor's new clothes? *Criminal Justice Policy Review, 18*(2), 168–199.

Lewontin, R. C. (2000). *The triple helix*. Cambridge: Harvard University Press.

Lussier, P. (2016). Desistance from crime: Toward an integrated conceptualization for intervention. In R. Laws & W. O'Donohue (Eds.), *The treatment of sex offenders* (pp. 281–322). New York, NY: Guilford.

Lussier, P. (2017). Juvenile sex offending through a developmental life course criminology perspective: An agenda for policy and research. *Sexual Abuse: A Journal of Research and Treatment, 29*(1), 51–80.

Lussier, P., & Blokland, A. (2014). The adolescence-adulthood transition and Robins's continuity paradox: Criminal career patterns of juvenile and adult sex offenders in a prospective longitudinal birth cohort study. *Journal of Criminal Justice, 42*(2), 153–163.

Lussier, P., & Cale, J. (2013). Beyond sexual recidivism: A review of the sexual criminal career parameters of adult sex offenders. *Aggression and Violent Behavior, 18*, 445–457.

Lussier, P., Corrado, R. R., & McCuish, E. (2016). A criminal career study of the continuity and discontinuity of sex offending during the adolescence-adulthood transition: A prospective longitudinal study of incarcerated youth. *Justice Quarterly, 33*(7), 1123–1153.

Lussier, P., & Davies, G. (2011). A person-oriented perspective on sexual offenders, offending trajectories, and risk of recidivism: A new challenge for policymakers, risk assessors, and actuarial prediction? *Psychology, Public Policy, and Law, 17*, 530–561.

Lussier, P., Deslauriers-Varin, N., Collin-Santerre, J., & Bélanger, R. (2019). Using decision tree algorithms to screen individuals at risk of entry into sexual recidivism. *Journal of Criminal Justice, 63*(C), 12–24.

Lussier, P., & Healey, J. (2009). Rediscovering Quetelet, again: The aging offender and the prediction of reoffending in a sample of adult sex offenders. *Justice Quarterly, 26*(4), 827–856.

Lussier, P., & McCuish, E. (2016). Desistance from crime without reintegration: A longitudinal study of the social context and life course path to desistance in a sample of adults convicted of a sex crime. *International Journal of Offender Therapy and Comparative Criminology, 60*(15), 1791–1812.

Lussier, P., Van Den Berg, C., Bijleveld, C., & Hendriks, J. (2012). A developmental taxonomy of juvenile sex offenders for theory, research, and prevention: The adolescent-limited and the high-rate slow desister. *Criminal Justice and Behavior, 39*(12), 1559–1581.

Martinez, A. G., Stuewig, J., & Tangney, J. P. (2014). Can perspective-taking reduce crime? Examining a pathway through empathic-concern and guilt-proneness. *Personality and Social Psychology Bulletin, 40*(12), 1659–1667.

McCann, K., & Lussier, P. (2008). A meta-analysis of the predictors of sexual recidivism in juvenile offenders. *Youth Violence and Juvenile Justice, 6*, 363–385.

McCuish, E., Lussier, P., & Corrado, R. (2016). Criminal careers of juvenile sex and nonsex offenders: Evidence from a prospective longitudinal study. *Youth Violence and Juvenile Justice, 14*(3), 199–224.

McCuish, E., Lussier, P., & Corrado, R. (2018). Incarceration as a turning point? The impact of custody experiences and identity change on community reentry. *Journal of Developmental and Life-Course Criminology, 4*(4), 427–448.

McCuish, E., Lussier, P., & Rocque, M. (2019). Maturation beyond age: Interrelationships among psychosocial, adult role, and identity maturation and their implications for desistance from crime. *Journal of Youth and Adolescence, 2019*, 1–15.

McCuish, E. C., Corrado, R. R., Hart, S. D., & DeLisi, M. (2015). The role of symptoms of psychopathy in persistent violence over the criminal career into full adulthood. *Journal of Criminal Justice, 43*(4), 345–356.

Messner, S. F., & Rosenfeld, R. (2012). *Crime and the American dream.* Boston: Cengage Learning.

Min, J., Silverstein, M., & Lendon, J. P. (2012). Intergenerational transmission of values over the family life course. *Advances in Life Course Research, 17*(3), 112–120.

Moffitt, T. E. (1993). Adolescence-limited and life-course-persistent antisocial behavior: a developmental taxonomy. *Psychological Review, 100*(4), 674–701.

Monahan, K. C., Steinberg, L., Cauffman, E., & Mulvey, E. P. (2009). Trajectories of antisocial behavior and psychosocial maturity from adolescence to young adulthood. *Developmental Psychology, 45*(6), 1654.

Monahan, K. C., Steinberg, L., Cauffman, E., & Mulvey, E. P. (2013). Psychosocial (im) maturity from adolescence to early adulthood: Distinguishing between adolescence-limited and persisting antisocial behavior. *Development and Psychopathology, 25*(4), 1093–1105.

Mustaine, E. E., Tewksbury, R., & Stengel, K. M. (2006). Social disorganization and residential locations of registered sex offenders: Is this a collateral consequence? *Deviant Behavior, 27*(3), 329–350.

Mustillo, S., Wilson, J., & Lynch, S. M. (2004). Legacy volunteering: A test of two theories of intergenerational transmission. *Journal of Marriage and Family, 66*(2), 530–541.

Na, C., & Jang, S. J. (2019). Positive expected selves and desistance among serious adolescent offenders. *Journal of developmental and life-course criminology, 5*(3), 310–334.

Nagin, D., & Paternoster, R. (2000). Population heterogeneity and state dependence: State of the evidence and directions for future research. *Journal of Quantitative Criminology, 16*(2), 117–144.

Nakamura, K., & Blumstein, A. (2015). Potential for redemption for sex offenders. In A. Blokland & P. Lussier (Eds.), *Sex offenders: A criminal career approach*. Oxford, UK: Wiley.

Nguyen, H., & Loughran, T. A. (2018). On the measurement and identification of turning points in criminology. *Annual Review of Criminology, 1*, 335–358.

Ouimet, M., & Le Blanc, M. (1996). The role of life experiences in the continuation of the adult criminal career. *Criminal Behavior and Mental Health, 6*, 73–97.

Pager, D. (2003). The mark of a criminal record. *American Journal of Sociology, 108*(5), 937–975.

Paternoster, R., & Bushway, S. (2009). Desistance and the feared self: Toward an identity theory of criminal desistance. *The Journal of Criminal Law and Criminology, 99*, 1103–1156.

Pithers, W. D. (1990). Relapse prevention with sexual aggressors. In W. L. Marshall, D. R. Laws, & H. E. Barbaree (Eds.), *Handbook of sexual assault: Issues, theories, and treatment of the offender* (pp. 343–361). New York: Plenum Press.

Proulx, J., Beauregard, E., Lussier, P., & Leclerc, B. (2014). *Pathways to sexual aggression*. New York, NY: Routledge.

Reale, K., McCuish, E., & Corrado, R. (2019). The impact of juvenile sex offending on the adult criminal career. *International Journal of Offender Therapy and Comparative Criminology, 61*, 3.

Rocque, M. (2015). The lost concept: The (re) emerging link between maturation and desistance from crime. *Criminology & Criminal Justice, 15*(3), 340–360.

Rocque, M., Beckley, A. L., & Piquero, A. R. (2019). Psychosocial maturation, race, and desistance from crime. *Journal of Youth and Adolescence, 48*(7), 1403–1417.

Rocque, M., Posick, C., & White, H. R. (2015). Growing up is hard to do: An empirical evaluation of maturation and desistance. *Journal of Developmental and Life-Course Criminology, 1*(4), 350–384.

Ronis, S. T., & Borduin, C. M. (2013). Antisocial behavior trajectories of adolescents and emerging adults with histories of sexual aggression. *Psychology of Violence, 3*(4), 367.

Sample, L. L., & Bray, T. M. (2006). Are sex offenders different? An examination of rearrest patterns. *Criminal Justice Policy Review, 17*(1), 83–102.

Sample, L. L., & Kadleck, C. (2008). Sex offender laws: Legislators' accounts of the need for policy. *Criminal Justice Policy Review, 19*(1), 40–62.

Sampson, R. J., & Laub, J. H. (1997). A life-course theory of cumulative disadvantage and the stability of delinquency. *Developmental Theories of Crime and Delinquency, 7*, 133–161.

Sampson, R. J., & Laub, J. H. (2003). Life-course desisters? Trajectories of crime among delinquent boys followed to age 70. *Criminology, 41*(3), 555–592.

Sampson, R. J., & Laub, J. H. (2005). A life-course view of the development of crime. *The Annals of the American Academy of Political and Social Science, 602*(1), 12–45.

Sampson, R. J., Laub, J. H., & Wimer, C. (2006). Does marriage reduce crime? A counterfactual approach to within-individual causal effects. *Criminology, 44*(3), 465–508.

Schneider, B. (1990). The climate for service: Application of the construct. In B. Schneider (Ed.), *Organizational climate and culture* (pp. 383–412). San Francisco: Jossey-Bass.

Soothill, K., & Francis, B. (2009). When do ex-offenders become like non-offenders? *The Howard Journal of Criminal Justice, 48*(4), 373–387.

Steinberg, L., & Cauffman, E. (1996). Maturity of judgment in adolescence: Psychosocial factors in adolescent decision making. *Law and Human Behavior, 20*(3), 249–272.

Steinberg, L. D., Cauffman, E., & Monahan, K. (2015). Psychosocial maturity and desistance from crime in a sample of serious juvenile offenders. Laurel, MD: US Department of Justice, Office of Justice Programs, Office of Juvenile Justice and Delinquency Prevention.

Stone, R., & Rydberg, J. (2019). Parenthood, maturation, and desistance: Examining parenthood transition effects on maturation domains and subsequent reoffending. *Journal of Developmental and Life-Course Criminology, 5*(3), 387–414.

ten Bensel, T., & Sample, L. L. (2017). The influence of sex offender registration and notification laws on fostering collective identity among offenders. *Journal of Crime and Justice, 40*(4), 497–511.

ten Bensel, T., & Sample, L. L. (2019). Social inclusion despite exclusionary sex offense laws: How registered citizens cope with loneliness. *Criminal Justice Policy Review, 30*(2), 274–292.

Tewksbury, R., & Zgoba, K. M. (2010). Perceptions and coping with punishment: How registered sex offenders respond to stress, internet restrictions, and the collateral consequences of registration. *International Journal of Offender Therapy and Comparative Criminology, 54*(4), 537–551.

Thornton, D., Hanson, R. K., Kelley, S. M., & Mundt, J. C. (2019). Estimating lifetime and residual risk for individuals who remain sexual offense free in the community: Practical applications. *Sexual Abuse, 3*, 10.

Uggen, C. (2000). Work as a turning point in the life course of criminals: A duration model of age, employment, and recidivism. *American Sociological Review, 65*, 529–546.

Uggen, C., & Wakefield, S. (2008). What have we learned from longitudinal studies of work and crime?. In The long view of crime: A synthesis of longitudinal research (pp. 191–219). Springer, New York, NY.

Uggen, C., Manza, J., & Behrens, A. (2004). Less than the average citizen: Stigma, role transition, and the civic reintegration of convicted felons: Pathways to offender reintegration. In S. Maruna & R. Immarigeon (Eds.), *After crime and punishment: Pathways to offender reintegration* (pp. 258–290). Milton Park: Willan Publishing.

Warr, M. (1998). Life-course transitions and desistance from crime. *Criminology, 36*(2), 183–216.

Western, B., & Beckett, K. (1999). How unregulated is the US labor market? The penal system as a labor market institution. *American Journal of Sociology, 104*(4), 1030–1060.

Western, B., Lopoo, L., & McLanahan, S. (2004). Incarceration and the bonds among parents in fragile families. *Imprisoning America: The Social Effects of Mass Incarceration, 2004*, 21–45.

Williams, L. R., & Steinberg, L. (2011). Reciprocal relations between parenting and adjustment in a sample of juvenile offenders. *Child Development, 82*(2), 633–645.

Zimring, F. E. (2004). *An American travesty: Legal responses to adolescent sexual offending.* Chicago: University of Chicago Press.

Zimring, F. E., Jennings, W. G., Piquero, A. R., & Hays, S. (2009). Investigating the continuity of sex offending: Evidence from the second Philadelphia birth cohort. *Justice Quarterly, 26*, 58–76.

Zimring, F. E., Piquero, A. R., & Jennings, W. G. (2007). Sexual delinquency in Racine: Does early sex offending predict later sex offending in youth and young adulthood? *Criminology & Public Policy, 6*(3), 507–534.

Part III
Understanding Sex Offender Policy

Chapter 7
Correctional *Moneyball*, Actuarial Risk, and Sexual Recidivism: Searching for the Sexual Predator

Introduction

Since the 1990s, the estimated probabilities of sexual recidivism of convicted offenders became central to the narrative of what was later dubbed the "new penology" (Feeley & Simon, 1992; Simon, 1998). The new penology marked a systemic change within the criminal justice systems in the USA and, to a lesser extent, in Canada (Petrunik, 2002, 2003). More specifically, while the postwar era was marked by a rehabilitation discourse and the 1970s by a retributive one, the new penology marked a shift toward risk management. The rehabilitation discourse, relying on a sentencing principle referred to as individualization (e.g., Coffee, 1975), was focused on the offender as a person and the need to tailor specific sentences according to the treatment needs of the individual. The retributive discourse somewhat refocused sentencing practices on the criminal act and the need to punish with attention to mitigating (e.g., remorse shown by the offender) and aggravating (e.g., the severity of the criminal event) circumstances. The new penology marked a gradual shift toward a person's level of risk of criminal recidivism. In other words, the focus shifted from what just happened to what might happen in the future. This was done as a means of addressing the criminal justice system's responsibility to maintain and monitor public safety. Ever since, psychiatrists, psychologists, and criminal justice practitioners (e.g., probation/parole officers) have been routinely called upon during various stages of a person's processing through the criminal justice system to assess the probability of sexual recidivism. Once convicted, individuals may be assessed for likelihood of recidivism to help judges identify whether they should be given a community or custody sentence. Once sentenced to custody, prison administrators can use the person's likelihood of recidivism to identify whether they should be placed in a low, medium, or high security institution. Once in this institution, decisions can be made about the intensity of intervention and treatment required to address the likelihood of recidivism. Before a person leaves the institution (e.g., parole hearing), the probability of recidivism is at least one factor used to determine

© Springer Nature Switzerland AG 2021
P. Lussier et al., *Understanding Sexual Offending*,
https://doi.org/10.1007/978-3-030-53301-4_7

the nature of a person's re-entry into the community (or if parole is even granted in the first place). In sum, the assessment of the likelihood of recidivism plays a major role in multiple phases of a person's journey through the criminal justice system.

Although the prediction of recidivism appears somewhat straightforward, that is, a person either will or will not recidivate, there are two major aspects of this question that are complex. The first relates to how recidivism probabilities are established; that is, the factors that are measured as indicators of this risk, the process by which these factors are measured, and how these factors are linked to reoffending. The second relates to how recidivism probabilities are interpreted. What constitutes a high risk for recidivism? High risk compared to what or to whom? Is recidivism the most appropriate means of measuring a person's risk to society? Broadly speaking, these two questions, especially the first one, have been the major focus of sex offender research since the 1980s. A general consensus exists about the role and importance of measuring risk of sexual recidivism in the criminal justice system; namely, that its measurement is the cornerstone to criminal justice intervention in terms of correctional planning, supervision, and intervention, as well as community re-entry and reintegration opportunities. In fact, the acceptance of sexual recidivism as a key measure and indicator of risk and needs has remained almost unquestioned and unchallenged in spite of increasingly apparent limitations. In short, sexual recidivism is a particularly complex concept, more complex than it seems at first glance. This measure, far from being perfect and unanimous within the scientific community, poses particular challenges not only for evaluators, but also for the criminal justice system. But what is the risk of sexual recidivism and is it possible to come up with a reliable and valid measure of it? The importance of sexual recidivism as a gold-standard outcome measure in the criminal justice system became such that any critiques or challenges to the concept became focus of much defensive criticism by some, and, in the most egregious cases, willful ignorance by those who adhered to the risk management principles of the new penology.

No other offender groups were impacted as greatly by this systematic shift as individuals convicted for a sex crime (Simon, 1998). In the process, terms such as sexual recidivism, predictors of sexual recidivism, actuarial risk assessment and prediction became part of the new landscape in correctional settings. Not only did sexual recidivism become the gold-standard measure of risk, it also became the gold-standard justification for the implementation and the development of new criminal justice measures; risk assessments and risk prediction scales were developed and validated using sexual recidivism as the key outcome measure. In turn, sex offender registries and public notification procedures were just some of the measures that were introduced and designed to reduce the risk of sexual recidivism. Sexual recidivism also became a gold-standard measure to determine the efficacy of the criminal justice system. Sexual recidivism was used to evaluate, for example, whether sex offender treatment programs were effective and whether intensive supervision improved community safety. In other words, sexual recidivism was not just an offending outcome being measured, it was an indicator of success, or lack thereof, of virtually all criminal justice system strategies, policies, and interventions designed to reduce future sexual offending. Indeed, risk of sexual recidivism inevitably became the gold-standard measure used to classify these individuals in the criminal justice system and to evoke to the public a certain individual's level of dangerousness once released back into the community. This systematic shift in criminal justice policy and practice marked the birth of the "low" "moderate" and "high" risk "sex offender."

In the context of this risk management movement, Dr. Soothill (2010, p. 146) observations still resonate today: "Quite simply, the public wants the issue to be 'solved.' However, as the focus on sexual offender recidivism gets more mathematically precise, is there a bigger picture that we are overlooking?" In this chapter we present the state of scientific knowledge concerning sexual recidivism as well as the factors that inform its probability. Advances in risk assessment will be highlighted. The effectiveness of risk assessment and risk prediction methods will be discussed. The validity of assessment tools will be analyzed in two ways. The first concerns the inclusion of appropriate risk and protective factors used to make decisions about risk. The second concerns whether recidivism is the most appropriate indicator of "dangerousness," which refers to the negative outcomes associated with this risk, in light of current knowledge regarding the criminal careers of perpetrators of sex offenses.

The Measurement of Sexual Recidivism

In recent decades, issues concerning the risk of sexual recidivism have been at the forefront of research and policy at the cost of looking more comprehensively at the various parameters that comprise a person's criminal career (e.g., onset). Following his review of the scientific literature, Soothill (2010) identified 168 empirical studies concerning the topic of sex offender recidivism.[1] Our own research conducted in 2020 helped to identify well over 800 empirical studies on sex offender recidivism.

For criminology scholars, recidivism is not a theoretical concept (e.g., Blumstein, Cohen, Roth, & Visher, 1986). Rather, it is an administrative indicator used by correctional services that imperfectly and indirectly assesses the criminal conduct of individuals who have completed or are about to complete any sentence following a criminal offense. Thus, criminal recidivism refers to the proportion of individuals who have committed a new crime during a given follow-up period. Recidivism does not refer to the individual's criminal history or their past, but rather to future criminal behavior that occurs during or after a supervision period (e.g., parole) or a post-release follow-up period (e.g., following the end of a sentence/sanction). It is necessary to understand at this point that the vast majority of individuals who have received a prison sentence for a sexual offense will return, one day or another, to the community. Therefore, in the field of research on sexual recidivism, it is common to

---

[1] In contrast, Lussier and Mathesius (2012) reviewed the literature on the topic of the age at first sexual offense and identified only 15 studies.

use police data (i.e., indicating if an individual is subsequently arrested and/or charged) to establish whether recidivism has occurred. In the scientific literature, recidivism does not refer to the actual presence of a new crime, but rather, to the presence of a new contact with the criminal justice system. This becomes problematic as recidivism does not measure actual criminal behavior, but rather the criminal justice response to criminal behavior.

As we know, not all sex crimes are reported to the police. In fact very few are, not all sex crimes lead to an arrest and even a fewer number lead to a conviction. Recidivism rates using administrative data, therefore, do not strictly reflect an individual's subsequent criminal behavior or more specifically the tendency to repeat sex crimes. Such rates also reflect characteristics of victims of these offenses (e.g., willingness to report to the police, officer attitudes toward the victim), sociocultural attitudes (e.g., societal view of certain behaviors as sex offenses or not), police investigation practices, legal factors (e.g., testimony in court, plea-bargaining), and other administrative and procedural factors (e.g., DNA testing and delays). While it should now be clear why this is obviously highly problematic, there are few valid alternatives to official measures of recidivism. In effect, because the measurement of sexual recidivism is based on official/administrative data, care must be taken with the legal definitions of sex crimes and how justice systems choose to investigate and respond to sex crimes, which can vary from one jurisdiction to another and from one time to another.

Methodological limitations aside, the question that continues to be asked is: what, in fact, is the sexual recidivism rate of individuals convicted for a sex crime? As Quinsey (1984) and Rice and Harris (2006) have already pointed out, it is illusory to think that there is "a" rate that provides a good description of the probability of sexual recidivism. It is illusory because recidivism can be defined in different ways (arrest, reconviction, reincarceration), jurisdictions have different practices for responding to and resolving sexual offending, and different sociohistorical contexts can further exacerbate these difficulties. It is also an illusion to believe that there is a universal measure of sexual recidivism.

It would be more relevant to conclude that there are recidivism "rates." This point is illustrated by looking at a study by Langan and Levin (2002) on the measurement of general recidivism among a sample of 272,111 individuals released from prison in 15 American states. The researchers examined the criminal records of these persons three years after their release from prison. This representative sample of the American prison population included men, women, boys, and girls. The first question concerned how to measure recidivism. The researchers considered three indicators, namely: (a) a new arrest; (b) a new conviction; and, (c) a new prison sentence. When looking at recidivism for any offense-type, after 6 months of release, 29.9% of this sample were rearrested, 10.6% were reconvicted, and 5% received a new prison sentence during the follow-up period. In short, the recidivism rate varied from 5% to 29.9% simply by changing the criteria for measuring criminal recidivism.

To complicate things further, what would happen if the follow-up period was extended? In Langan and Levin's (2002) study, the recidivism rate based on arrest statistics increased to 44.1% after 1 year of release and 67.5% after 3 years of follow-up. Therefore, if after 6 months of follow-up, approximately 3 in 10 individuals have been arrested for a new offense, this proportion increases to 2 in 3 individuals after 3 years of post-release follow-up. As a result, the longer the follow-up period, the more likely that criminal recidivism rates will increase at least to some extent. If we recapitulate the results of the study by Langan and Levin (2002), it is possible to conclude that the rate of criminal recidivism is 5.0% (if measured as a new prison sentence after only 6 months of post-release follow-up). However, it is also correct to conclude that the recidivism rate for this same group is 67.5% (if measured as a new arrest after 3 years of post-release follow-up). These results speak to some of the basic issues and challenges researchers face when examining recidivism rates. By modifying two parameters of the measurement of recidivism (i.e., duration of follow-up and criminal justice system sanction), it is possible to arrive at diametrically opposite conclusions concerning general recidivism among prisoners. The key question then is not so much "what is the sexual recidivism rate of convicted offenders?" but "what is the rate for whom, by what criteria, and over what period?".

To be sure, many researchers are familiar with the numerous limitations involving the measurement of sexual recidivism. However, as with the use of official data more generally, researchers in the field of sexual violence and abuse tend to simply acknowledge the limitations of recidivism measures as opposed to searching for new ways to measure offending or "dangerousness." As early as 1989, Weinrott, Furby, and Blackshaw noted the limits of "recidivism" as an indicator of the nature and frequency of criminal activity and concluded that due to the variability of the measurement of recidivism across studies, and the shortcomings of individual studies, it was hard to draw firm conclusions. To illustrate, because recidivism rates for different types of sex offenses are relatively low, for statistical analysis purposes, it has become common practice in the scientific community to combine all types of sex offenses under the umbrella term "sexual recidivism." In the process, crimes such as possession and distribution of child pornography, sexual interference, sexual contact with a minor, sexual assault, armed sexual assault, rape, incest, exhibitionism, and gross indecency all can represent a sex crime, and thus any of these various offenses simply become labeled as sexual recidivism. This generic measure is particularly imprecise. For example, it fails to identify critical questions about the type of sex crime committed, victim characteristics, the number of times the offender offended against the victim, the number of victims, the level of violence used, whether the modus operandi was similar across different acts or between the index offense and the offense marking recidivism, the duration of the offense, the time elapsed between offenses if the individual has acted repeatedly, etc. In sum, there is a considerable gap between "sexual recidivism" and what it means for a person to be involved in another sexual offense.

Sex Offender Recidivism Rates

One of the reasons that sexual recidivism continues to be the de facto outcome variable for studies on the risks posed by perpetrators of sexual offenses relates to, at least on the surface, the simplicity with which recidivism outcomes can be communicated to others. However, this simplicity sacrifices important nuances in offending patterns that may be critical for addressing the severity of a person's risk to harming the public. Renowned researchers reported study findings on the sexual recidivism of individuals who had been referred to a specialized sex offender clinic (Langevin et al., 2004). Taking into account different sources of information, the retrospective analysis of more than 320 files enabled them to conclude that approximately 4 out of 5 individuals were sexual recidivists. In other words, based on these findings, perpetrators of sex crimes were presented as a group of dangerous, repeat offenders who remained at risk of sexual recidivism for long periods. The simplicity of reducing someone's future to a yes/no question of sexual recidivism was also appealing to journalists. These findings would appear in newspapers across Canada in the months to come. A reporter for The *Globe and Mail*, a major Canadian newspaper, reported that researchers, judges, and the criminal justice system tend to underestimate the threat that this group represents. These findings were presented as an opportunity for the scientific community to question certain practices in terms of risk assessment and sexual recidivism (see Freeze, 2004). Not mentioned in the newspaper is the fact that a team of researchers soon challenged these findings and conclusions from the University of Ottawa and the University of Toronto. An article by Webster, Gartner, and Doob (2006) questioned not only the authors' conclusions, but also the scientific rigor of the study. According to these authors, methodological biases artificially inflated the sexual recidivism rates observed. In fact, according to the authors, the study distorted the concept of sexual recidivism because of important methodological shortcomings. Webster et al. (2006) went even further and concluded that the results of the study by Langevin et al. (2004) had little scientific value. While the scientific community attempted to reel-in exaggerated portrayals of the risk of sexual recidivism through debate in journal articles, containment of such exaggerations was far less successful in the sexual recidivism discourse that played out in the media and the living rooms of the general population. The impression established in these domains was that the most likely outcome of a person convicted of a sex offense was that they would continue this behavior (Kernsmith, Craun, & Foster, 2009).

In spite of the recognized variability in the measurement of recidivism, researchers have continued the search for an aggregate base rate of sexual recidivism for convicted offenders. Several studies have been carried out to estimate the rates of criminal recidivism of a sample of individuals who have been convicted for a sex crime (e.g., Doren, 1998; Firestone et al., 1999; Hall, 1988; Hanson, Steffy, & Gauthier, 1993; Hildebrand, De Ruiter, & De Vogel, 2004; Prentky, Knight, & Lee, 1997; Prentky, Lee, Knight, & Cerce, 1997; Proulx et al., 1997; Quinsey, Rice, & Harris, 1995; Radzinowicz, 1957; Rice & Harris, 1997; Rice, Harris, & Quinsey, 1990; Rice, Quinsey, & Harris, 1991; Soothill & Gibbens, 1978). The meta-analysis by Hanson and Bussière (1998) is one of the first to take stock of the growing scientific literature at the time on the sexual recidivism of individuals who have been convicted of a sexual offense. This study combined the findings of 61 studies of criminal recidivism and included a total of approximately 29,000 individuals, mainly adult men. The researchers noted that on average, the studies conducted by the researchers had a follow-up period of approximately 5 years during which these offenders were at risk of being arrested, charged, or convicted again. When it came to general recidivism, the findings indicated that, on average, 1 in 3 individuals recidivated during the follow-up period. Thus, with a broader definition of recidivism which includes a new arrest or conviction for any type of crime, the researchers noted that only a minority of individuals have again run into trouble with the law after their release. This was quite a different story compared to the findings from Langevin et al. (2004) that were widely cited in various media outlets. When researchers focused on sexual recidivism more specifically, the findings suggested that on average, 1 in 7 individuals, or less than 15%, have come into conflict with the law in connection with a new sex crime during the follow-up period. This is not to suggest that 15% is not a meaningful or concerning number, only that it is markedly different from how the risk of sexual recidivism has been portrayed in the media and by some researchers. If identifying sexual recidivism is going to be a fundamental goal of this research field, accurately measuring this base rate seems critical. The fact that these numbers stem from a meta-analysis combining multiple independent studies may be perceived by some as providing certainty about the risk. These results, however, do not reflect the variability of recidivism rates across this offender group and across measures of recidivism.

As mentioned earlier, one of the main reasons for variability in recidivism rates is due to differences in the length of a study's follow-up period. What is even less often considered is variability in the length of follow-up among individuals *within* the same study. For example, in a recidivism study of convicted offenders released from prison with an average follow-up period of 5 years, a given individual may have been followed for 2 months, 1 year, 8 years or maybe 15 years. In short, the period dubbed the "time at risk" during which the individual had the opportunity to commit a crime can vary considerably from one person to another. Thus, the individual who was the subject of a 2-month post-release follow-up that did not incur new arrests, charges or convictions is then considered a non-recidivist in the study context. This issue is what the literature refers to as right-censoring. What would we conclude about this person's recidivism if they were followed for a longer period of time? As such, important questions remain regarding what is the appropriate amount of time that an individual remains crime-free before they can be declared a non-recidivist. Recidivism statistics that do not take into account the length of the follow-up and the risk period are likely to produce biased results. In a subsequent study, therefore, Hanson, Morton, and Harris (2003) examined the sexual recidivism rates for individuals convicted of a sexual offense taking into consideration the length of the follow-up period. Combining the results of different studies, they estimated that the cumulative sexual recidivism rates for a 5-year follow-up period tend to vary between 10% and 15% with annual recidivism rates varying from 2% to 3%. Focusing on a subset of these studies with a longer follow-up period, the results indicated that the cumulative sexual recidivism rate would be around 20% for a 10-year follow-up with an annual recidivism rate that drops to 1% to 2% after the 5th year. Finally, an even smaller subset of empirical studies with a much longer follow-up period suggested that the cumulative rate of sexual recidivism is around

35% for a follow-up period of 20 years with an annual sexual recidivism rate of around 1% after the 10th year.

These results confirm the importance of the duration of follow-up in order to estimate recidivism rates. They also show that annual recidivism rates vary over time. Specifically, individuals are at greater risk of recidivism in the first month following their release. What is typically not investigated in such studies is whether this reflects a heightened tendency to perpetrate sex crimes in the months following release, or whether such individuals are under greater surveillance in the early period of their community re-entry and therefore are simply more likely to be detected and adjudicated for their offenses. Moreover, ensuring that individuals are followed for an identical length of time does not fully resolve issues with the research designs of recidivism studies. What about instances where researchers are interested in sexual recidivism, but an individual is reincarcerated for perpetrating a nonviolent sex offense and receives a ten-year sentence? This person is unlikely to incur new convictions for a sex crime over the study period. Is this type of non-recidivism for a sex offense the same as for a person that is free in their community for a decade and does not commit any crimes? In sum, not all recidivists are the same, nor are all non-recidivists the same. Such differences are not accounted for by using simplistic measures of offending outcomes.

Even if the concern regarding variability in the length of the follow-up for individuals in a study is addressed, other issues remain. For example, sexual recidivism rates can be misleading in some respects because they largely depend on sample characteristics. Adult men convicted and incarcerated for a sexual offense do not represent all persons who commit sex offenses; they even may even account for only a small portion of all perpetrators of such offenses. Yet, they can be a convenient population to reach. They are all located in institutions, perhaps even a single institution. Their name is on file and they may have correctional identifiers that make tracking these persons through the justice system quite straightforward. Thus, the types of studies providing the greatest amount of knowledge regarding sexual recidivism rates are also studies that do not necessarily adequately capture the heterogeneity in the population of persons involved in sex crimes.

This reality can also mask the phenomenon of recidivism among women, who are largely underrepresented within the prison population (Cortoni, Hanson, & Coache, 2010). Until recently, this issue has been overlooked and its importance may be underestimated. This oversight is all the more surprising since the specificity of women's antisocial and criminal conduct relative to that of men's is widely documented (e.g., Barker, 2009; Blanchette & Brown, 2006; Langan & Levin, 2002). In order to fill this gap, two meta-analyses were conducted to summarize the scientific literature concerning the rates of sexual recidivism for female offenders (Cortoni et al., 2010). The more recent of the two identified 10 studies including 2490 women followed over an average period of approximately 6 years. The results showed that women, on average, have relatively lower rates of sexual recidivism (between 1% and 3%) compared to what is generally observed in men. Most women in these studies were released and then had no new criminal justice system contact of any type. When such contact did occur, the odds that such contact was for a nonsexual offense was ten times higher than for a sexual offense (~20% vs ~2%, respectively). These differential rates show the importance of taking into account the specific nature of women's criminal conduct in order to not overstate the rate of sexual recidivism. These results also highlight the issues and challenges surrounding risk assessment for women convicted for a sexual offense. Indeed, over an average follow-up period of 6 years, for every 100 women convicted of a sexual offense, between 1 and 3 will have contact with the criminal justice system in connection with a new sex offense. The challenge for the criminal justice experts who must assess the dangerousness level of these women is the following: is it even possible based on current knowledge to identify such a small subgroup of women at risk of sexual recidivism? Just imagine the following situation: An expert who concludes that all women convicted of a sexual offense poses no risk of sexual recidivism would have a rate of effectiveness and accuracy of prediction of approximately 97–99%.

It is important to reiterate that these aggregate sexual recidivism rates represent general trends for groups of individuals who have been convicted for a sex crime. Fewer studies have specifically focused on looking at whether the likelihood of a convicted offender sexually recidivating over, for example, a 5-year period following release from custody is higher than the likelihood of the perpetration of a sexual offense for the first time by a former non-sex offender released from custody and followed for an identical period of time. In other words, are individuals convicted for a sex crime at a significantly higher risk of perpetrating another sex crime following their release compared to the risk that convicted non-sex offenders pose for perpetrating a sexual offense? After all, recall that sex offender policies (e.g., sex offender registries, public notification) are aimed at individuals convicted for a sex crime because of the presumption that they are more likely than anyone else to be involved in a sex offense in the future. Efforts to verify this assumption through empirical research have been rare and tended to focus on general recidivism rather than sexual offending. However, the results of such studies could be used to demystify the presumption that "sex offenders" constitute the most dangerous group of offenders.[2] As Lussier (2005) pointed out, individuals who have been convicted for a sex crime tend to have lower general recidivism rates than the general prison population. The factors explaining these differences, however, remain unclear because researchers have very rarely investigated the nonsexual offending of the population categorized as "sex offenders" (for some notable exceptions, Gebhard, Gagnon, Pomeroy, & Christenson, 1965; DeLisi, 2001; Smallbone & Wortley, 2004). These observations may also be different when separating perpetrators of sexual offenses against children from those that committed their offenses against

---

[2] For exemple, Langan et al. (2003) reported that 68% of individuals who had been previously sentenced for a non-sex crime, once released, were arrested again for a criminal offense, compared to 43% of individuals convicted for a sex crime. Using a 5-year follow-up period, Sample and Bray (2003) demonstrated that 45% of their sample of individuals convicted for a sex crime were subsequently rearrested. This percentage of criminal recidivism is lower than that observed for individuals who were arrested for armed robbery (75%), burglary (66%), assault (58%) or theft (53%).

post-pubescent victims (e.g., sexual aggressors of women). This trend also may be subject to change as a result of the implementation of legal dispositions (e.g., public sex offender registry, housing restriction laws) that limit the rights and freedoms of these individuals following their release (Chap. 9). For example, when individuals convicted for a sex crime are subjected to intensive supervision, their general recidivism rates are significantly higher, mainly because they are more likely to breach their supervisory conditions (e.g., missing a curfew, drinking alcohol, using drugs; e.g., Lussier & Davies, 2015).

Studies comparing the likelihood of sexual offending following release across individuals serving a sentence for a sexual offense compared to individuals serving a sentence for another type of crime and who have no history of sex crimes are even rarer. One of the first studies along these lines was conducted by Hanson, Scott, and Steffy (1995) with a convenience sample of inmates in a Canadian penitentiary. These researchers compared the sexual recidivism rates of a group of 191 individuals with a history of child sex offenses to the recidivism rates of a sample of 137 individuals who did not have a criminal history involving a sexual crime. The results indicated that the sexual recidivism rate of individuals convicted for a sex crime who assaulted children was 35% compared to only 1% for the non-sex offender group. The results appeared quite eloquent and seemed to give weight to the argument that there is some degree of sexual offending specificity (i.e., sexual recidivism) among individuals with a sexual offending history. However, subsequent recidivism studies found that sex offenders and non-sex offenders were quite similar in their likelihood of future involvement in sex crimes (Langan, Schmitt, & Durose, 2003; Sample & Bray, 2003).[3] More importantly, the study by Hanson et al. (1995) gives the impression that sexual offending by convicted offenders is a phenomenon almost exclusive to individuals with a history of sexual offending. However, it is important to remember that this study was based on a convenience sample, and therefore was not representative of the prison population. Indeed, when we examine study findings that are representative of the prison population more closely, it is possible to see how sexual recidivism rates can be misleading.

Langan et al. (2003) compared the rates of sexual recidivism among a large sample of prisoners followed over a three-year period in more than 15 American states. Among the group of inmates ($n = 9691$) serving a sentence for a sex offense, approximately 5% were rearrested for a sex offense during the follow-up period (3 years). Among the group of inmates ($n = 262,420$) who were incarcerated for a non-sex crime, approximately 1% were rearrested for a sex crime. Thus, these results show that individuals with a history of sex crime are more at risk of being arrested again for the same type of crime. However, in thinking about how to prevent sexual offenses, 1% of 262,420 reflects approximately 2600 new arrests for sex

---

[3] For example, Sample and Bray (2003) conducted a 5-year follow-up study on a large sample ($n = 146,918$) of American offenders arrested between 1990 and 1997. They found that 6% of individuals who were arrested for a sex crime were arrested again. When looking at other subgroups of offenders that had never before been convicted for a sexual offense, the likelihood of perpetrating such a crime during the follow-up period ranged between 0 and 3% depending on the group.

crimes, whereas 5% of 9691 reflects approximately 480 new arrests for sex crimes. While sexual recidivism rates tell one story about how to prevent sexual offenses, absolute numbers show a very different picture. Indeed, it is possible to estimate that 87% of those individuals that were arrested for a sex crime during the follow-up period *were not previously incarcerated for a sex crime*. Focusing solely on individuals convicted for a sex crime to prevent sexual offending will result in a substantial failure to prevent future sexual victimization. In other words, almost 9 out of 10 convicted offenders who were next arrested for a sex crime were not known "sex offenders." This finding is of important policy value yet continues to be overlooked because it departs from preconceived ideas about risk, the nature of risk and the social representation of individuals convicted for a sex crime as sexual recidivists. A more accurate depiction is that, based on official data, sexual offending perpetrated by a person with a criminal history involving sex crimes is a rare phenomenon. In fact, the vast majority of individuals who are convicted for a sex crime have no prior record for a sex crime (e.g., Lussier, Deslauriers-Varin, Collin-Santerre, & Bélanger, 2019). In some ways then, researchers in the field of sexual violence and abuse have been focused on preventing sexual offending by focusing on the prevention of sexual recidivism among a group that is ultimately unlikely to account for a particularly meaningful amount of all future sex crimes.

Recidivism Rates of Adolescent Perpetrators

Research on sexual recidivism has been conducted mainly with adult males but the findings have been generalized to all perpetrators of sex crimes, irrespective of their age and associated developmental issues. Are young offenders more prone to sexual recidivism because their sexual offending was initiated at a younger age? McCann and Lussier's (2008) meta-analysis combined the results of 18 studies carried out between 1986 and 2005 that included approximately 3200 minors with a history of sexual offending. The duration of the follow-up period varied between 5 and 9 years. Around 50% recidivated with a new offense of any kind. However, these general recidivism rates considerably varied within the 18 studies examined in this meta-analysis (8–79%), thus limiting the conclusions that can be drawn from them. When examining violent crimes, the researchers reported that the violent recidivism rate was significantly lower but still substantial (28.5%). Again, there was substantial variation between studies (6–54%). In terms of sexual recidivism, the researchers estimated that, on average, longitudinal studies report a sexual recidivism rate of 12% (median = 11%) with rates varying from 2% to 30% across studies.

Why do recidivism rates seem to vary so dramatically from one study to another? This is a difficult question to answer and has not been the subject of substantial attention by the scientific community. However, it is possible to hypothesize that the legal frameworks and practices influencing the sociolegal response to the delinquent and criminal behavior of young people varies considerably from place to place.

Some researchers have examined whether differences in research design have contributed to variance in recidivism rates across studies of adolescents. Like studies of adults, McCann and Lussier (2008) found that differences in the operationalization of sexual recidivism and differences in follow-up period resulted in variability in sexual recidivism rates. Another element that affects observed recidivism rates is the demographic composition of samples of young people (see Hagan, Gust-Brey, Cho, & Dow, 2001; Långström & Grann, 2000). Studies with higher rates of sexual recidivism are based on samples with a disproportionate number of young adults (under 20 years of age) compared to younger adolescents (13–14 years old). It is therefore likely that samples involving more young adults contribute to differential (i.e., higher) recidivism rates, especially since studies with adults show that individuals in their twenties have the highest rates of sexual recidivism (e.g., Lussier & Healey, 2009; Wollert, 2006). These observations clearly reiterate the fact that "recidivism" is at best an approximate measure, a construction influenced by multiple factors other than those solely associated with the perpetrators' proneness or likelihood of criminal recidivism.

In a second major analysis of the scientific literature on the sexual recidivism of minors, Caldwell (2010) combined data from 63 separate studies which included a total of 11,219 young people. Their focus questioned the social construction and preconceptions of "dangerousness" surrounding young people who commit sex offenses. The results of their study indicated that over an average follow-up of around 60 months, the prevalence of general recidivism was 43% and the prevalence of sexual recidivism was 7%. Based on these aggregate results, three conclusions stand out: (1) the majority of adolescents who have come into contact with the juvenile justice system for a sex offense do not subsequently come into contact with the law; (2) for those who do; it is typically in relation to a non-sex crime, and; (3) sexual recidivism among minors is a relatively rare event. Furthermore, by comparing the results of the Caldwell (2010) study with those of Hanson et al. (2003), it is reasonable to hypothesize at this point that, compared to adults convicted for a sex crime, adolescents represent a lower risk of sexual recidivism. This hypothesis, however, raises two more important questions. The first is whether the differential sexual recidivism rates between minors and adults is indicative of specific developmental factors at play. The second is whether the differential sexual rates recidivism rates are reflective of different approaches taken by adult criminal justice systems and juvenile justice systems when it comes to perpetrators of sex crimes. For example, does the lower sexual recidivism rate for adolescents reflect a lower tendency to commit sex crimes compared to adults; or, does it reflect the fact that adults may be more closely monitored and therefore more likely to be detected and punished for repeat involvement in a sex crime?

The results of meta-analyses examining adolescent recidivism rates suggest that sexual recidivism is a relatively unlikely event. However, considering that these results are mainly based on police data, can we and should we conclude that these rates of sexual recidivism are valid and representative of the actual offending behavior of these youth? Few empirical studies with adolescent offenders have used different sources of information to examine and compare recidivism rates. A study by Bremer (1992) on adolescent perpetrators of sex crimes is a notable exception. By using self-reported questionnaire data, she observed that approximately 11% of the young people who attended a specialized treatment program recidivated with another sexual crime.[4] Interestingly, this can be compared to a sexual recidivism rate of 6% based on conviction data from the same study. Of course, a measure of self-reported sexual recidivism also has methodological limitations, for example, it likely underestimates the true extent of recidivism among minors (e.g., some youth who committed a subsequent sex crime may not admit to doing so even in a research context for fear of being charged again). However, considering these results, the hypothesis that the low rates of sexual recidivism observed in previous studies are attributable to the use of police data that vastly underestimate the extent of sexual recidivism does not seem valid given that recidivism rates based on self-reported sex offending were also low. Of course, the study by Bremer (1992) is just one such study and included a relatively small sample of individuals attending a specialized treatment program and therefore may not be generalizable to adolescent perpetrators of sexual offenses more broadly.

From Risk to Actuarial Assessment and Prediction

It should be becoming clearer now that research based on aggregate measures of sexual recidivism have provided much empirical evidence challenging popular perceptions that all individuals convicted for a sex crime, irrespective of their gender and/or age, are sexual recidivists. At the same time, it is important to remember that these aggregate statistics provide a measure of central tendency that may not be an accurate reflection of the likelihood of sexual recidivism of all individuals convicted for a sex crime. Pooling together or aggregating, for example, all persons convicted of a sex crime in a particular prison over a particular period is beneficial for generalizability but may fail to capture nuances in the differences in sexual recidivism rates across subtypes of persons involved in sexual offenses. The results of these different meta-analyses is an important reminder that sexual recidivism rates do vary, sometimes quite substantially. Such variations should be examined, first and foremost, across different jurisdictions and settings given the reliance across studies on official measures of sexual recidivism. However, instead of considering such variations across different contexts, researchers have almost exclusively focused on variations between individuals: why is one person a sexual recidivist and not another? What do sexual recidivists have in common compared to non-recidivists? Who is more likely to sexually recidivate among a group of individuals convicted for a sex crime? Are there any specific individual characteristics informative of the

---

[4] It appears from their study that they could not verify/determine for 23 of these young persons whether they had sexually reoffended during the follow-up period (up to 8 years).

likelihood of sexual recidivism? Following the 1990s, there was a shift in research from the description of aggregate base rates of sexual recidivism among samples of prisoners to the identification of risk factors or predictors of sexual recidivism as a means of managing risk and maintaining public safety. These developments marked the emergence of actuarial risk assessment and risk prediction paradigms, particularly in correctional settings.

In the book *Moneyball: The art of winning an unfair game*, Michael Lewis (2003) tells the story of a small revolution in the world of American professional baseball. Throughout the twentieth century, professional baseball teams evaluated players based on the professional opinions of managers, coaches, and scouts. The opinions of such individuals were assumed to be valid because of their years of experience, which was often earned through having previously played professional baseball. Because these professionals tended to come from similar backgrounds, there was not a lot of diversity of opinion about which characteristics of baseball players would help teams win games. These professionals relied on their experience, judgment, and *flair* (i.e., intuition) to put together a winning team. For years, the art of professional baseball management was untested, unchallenged and not based on any advanced statistics. Rather, the belief was that the reputation, experience, and credentials of these professionals implied that their assessment of players was accurate and valuable. However, over the last 50 years the salaries associated with playing professional baseball markedly changed. The average baseball player's salary significantly increased from about $20,000 in the 1970s (which after inflation adjustment is about $130,000 in 2020) to about $4 million in the late 2010s. As such, for many baseball teams, especially those in smaller markets that had lower payrolls, the costs and consequences of poorly evaluating players became more severe. Born out of these severe consequences was a new perspective on how to evaluate players. The small revolution Lewis reports on highlights the shift from a subjective management model to a much more mechanical and objective model based on advanced statistical analyses of key indicators relevant to baseball players' performance. Lewis suggested that by using a statistical or "moneyball" approach, teams would become much more competitive even with limited financial resources. This new evaluation and management model, brought to light by Lewis, is now widespread across all professional sports.

The evolution of the management model described by Lewis in many ways mirrored changes that had occurred in the North American criminal justice system through the adoption and proliferation of actuarial risk assessment (Fig. 7.1). Dr. John Monahan played a significant role in the development of risk assessment practices that are reminiscent of the moneyball approach. Monahan (1981) made a series of observations and recommendations in the 1980s that would change the course of risk assessment practices, and what were considered best-practices in criminal justice, for years to come. He noted that individual clinicians/risk assessors tend to overestimate the risk of violent recidivism among individuals who have previously perpetrated a violent crime. Many individuals perceived by risk assessors as being too dangerous did not in fact go on to reoffend after their release. How was it that trained clinicians that assessed and treated hundreds of individuals got prediction so

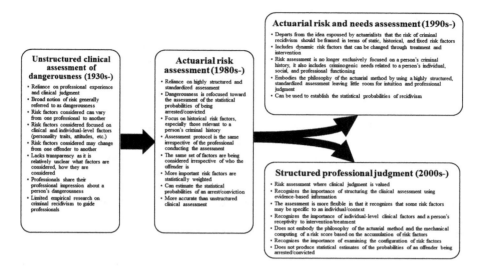

Fig. 7.1 The evolution of risk assessment practices in corrections

wrong so often? A combination of factors likely contributed to blurring the clinical judgment of risk assessors. In particular, the vague concept of dangerousness was framed almost exclusively in terms of personality characteristics for violent offenders (e.g., being impulsive, lacking self-control) and, in terms of sexual deviance for perpetrators of sex crimes. In addition, risk assessors rarely had the opportunity to verify the accuracy of their assessments or "predictions." There was a lack of systematic research evaluating (a) how decisions about risk or "dangerousness" were made and (b) whether such decisions were accurate in terms of whether the person being assessed recidivated 1 year, 5 years or even 20 years after their release. Risk assessors were unaware of aggregate or baseline recidivism rates of certain offender groups as the research on criminal, violent, and sexual recidivism was virtually non-existent at the time. Before the 1980s, there was minimal research about the sexual recidivism rates of individuals who had been convicted for a sex crime and even less research examining the predictors of sexual recidivism. This was not because decisions about risk and the identification of which factors were most likely to predict sexual recidivism did not occur, only that such themes were not investigated by researchers. It was in this context that Monahan and Steadman (1994) called for the scientific community to set in motion the implementation of longitudinal studies aimed at identifying the risk factors associated with recidivism.

The science of correctional risk assessment and risk prediction emerged from the field of forensic psychology and psychiatry. Experts from these disciplines are regularly asked by courts and parole boards to provide their assessment of a person's dangerousness. The role of these experts has become increasingly important when dealing with offenders who have committed violent and sexual crimes. Various methods and techniques have been proposed, developed, and tested to help these professionals complete accurate assessments of risk to assist and guide decisions made by the criminal justice system, especially with respect to sentencing and the granting of parole (e.g., Beech, Fisher, & Thornton, 2003). The first two generations of the assessment methods of a person's dangerousness, which dominated much of the twentieth century, contrasted unstructured clinical judgment (i.e., the first generation of risk assessment methods) with statistical prediction and mechanical methods commonly referred to as actuarial assessment (i.e., the second generation; see Meehl, 1954; Monahan & Steadman, 1996, Grove & Meehl, 1996).

Evaluations of these two approaches in terms of their ability to predict recidivism have consistently shown the relative weakness of unstructured clinical judgment and the superiority of actuarial assessment (Aegisdóttir et al., 2006; Andrews & Bonta, 2003; Hilton & Simmons, 2001). A meta-analysis performed by Aegisdóttir et al. (2006) revealed that actuarial tools are 13% points more precise than risk assessment based on unstructured clinical judgment. Such comparisons do not imply that all instances of unstructured clinical judgment are worse than all instances of actuarial assessment. Some professionals using unstructured clinical judgment may be very accurate. However, at the aggregate level, there are clear flaws in relying solely on the subjective opinions of clinicians that may vary on important variables such as level of experience, age, and skill level. Sets of scores based on standardized actuarial instruments, on the other hand, are not characterized by this kind of variance; scores on such instruments can be reproduced by different assessors quite reliably. Therefore, in light of these findings, several researchers have argued that the transition from the first generation (i.e., decisions based on unstructured clinical judgment) to actuarial tools (i.e., decisions based on statistics and probabilities derived from actuarial assessments) is one of the main progressive developments in the correctional system over the past 30 years (Bonta, Bourgon, Jesseman, & Yessine, 2005). The main advantages cited by those who favor actuarial methods reside in the elimination of biased, arbitrary, and prejudicial decisions by the justice system and its agents.

Support for the movement toward actuarial risk assessment can be largely attributed to research providing empirical evidence of its superior predictive accuracy over unstructured clinical judgment (e.g., Grove, Zald, Lebow, Snitz, & Nelson, 2000). The proliferation of actuarial instruments was also fueled by concerns surrounding standardization of assessment in the criminal justice context and greater transparency concerning the designation of "risk." Thus, in the actuarial context, the risk factors being assessed are not those determined to be most important according to clinical experience of an individual or team in a given jurisdiction and therefore necessary to include as part of risk assessment protocols. Instead, actuarial risk assessment tools are developed by using a set of hypothesized risk factors to predict recidivism within a given sample. Risk factors that were statistically associated with recidivism are included in the actuarial instrument; those not associated with recidivism are not included in the instrument. This instrument is then used across a wide range of jurisdictions and these different jurisdictions do not "add in" their own risk factors of interest. As such, the assessment of risk is the same across all jurisdictions using that particular instrument. Assessors using such an instrument, therefore, have to evaluate these factors, and only these factors, in such a way designated by the developers of the actuarial risk assessment instrument. Risk assessors could no longer add or ignore certain factors they deemed relevant or irrelevant to the prediction of risk. In fact, intuitively speaking, while more rather than less information is better when it comes to completing a clinical assessment, this is not the case from an actuarial perspective. From an actuarial standpoint, too much information becomes noise and can bias the reliability and validity of a risk assessment. In fact, actuarial instruments limit the range of factors taken into account by risk assessors, down to a series of about one or two dozen indicators. These actuarial tools also make it possible to minimize the overestimation of risk by taking into account the known statistical probabilities of sexual recidivism of a group of convicted offenders. As a result, it is possible, using these tools, to establish with relative precision the probabilities of sexual recidivism over a specific period, something that cannot be accomplished with unstructured clinical judgment. In other words, actuarial assessments were not only useful for improving the accuracy of decisions about risk for specific individuals, they also facilitated the development of research that could more accurately take stock of the probabilities of sexual recidivism.

Actuarial assessment was not universally accepted by risk assessors given that it was introduced based on the opinion, as empirically informed as it was, that risk assessors were not as accurate as they themselves believed. After all, it was their judgment and their expertise that was questioned. For some, these methods were too rigid and deterministic, based on an inexact science that dehumanizes the individual being assessed and completely replaces human expertise. Others raised concerns that these instruments simply predict and do nothing to explain a person's criminal behavior. As mentioned by Grove et al. (2000), this criticism and resistance was based on false beliefs concerning the actuarial assessment of the risk of sexual recidivism. While actuarial assessment is an imperfect science, unstructured clinical judgment deviates even further from perfection. In addition, the role of the actuarial tool is precisely to predict and not to explain the criminal sexual behavior of the individual, this explanatory task always falls to experts. Moreover, it is never recommended to use actuarial evaluation without appropriate clinical expertise. Finally, as Grove et al. (2000) suggest, the use of methods that do not consistently produce valid results, such as unstructured clinical judgment, are no more humane if they lead to the overestimation of sexual recidivism and more prediction errors.

Feeley and Simon (1992) were among the first to evoke these changes in correctional practices centered on the routine use of actuarial tools for risk management purposes at all stages of the criminal justice process (Hannah-Moffat & Maurutto, 2003), from presentence investigations to parole board decisions, including correctional risk and needs classification (e.g. Andrews, 1989; Bonta, 2002; Glaser, 1962; Gottfredson, 1987; Gottfredson & Moriarty, 2006; Hoffman, 1994; Nuffield, 1982). Risk assessment and prediction instruments became the main tool for classifying prisoners, and this was done based on their probability of recidivism.

The proliferation of risk assessment methods and tools also served to highlight a number of ethical issues that guided the developers of these instruments to take into account a relatively limited number of risk factors. Tonry (1987), for example, rightly asserted that risk assessments should not be discriminatory *vis-à-vis* visible minorities (e.g., immigrants, Indigenous people, African-Americans), because these methods could help perpetuate social and socioeconomic inequalities. In other words, he argued that irrespective of whether race, ethnic origin, and socioeconomic indicators are statistically predictive of criminal recidivism, these characteristics should not be considered in risk assessment instruments. In addition, Tonry (1987) argued that certain factors that are outside the convicted offender's control should not be taken into account for prediction and classification purposes, despite their predictive value. Furthermore, considering as part of a risk assessment a person's alleged offense(s) for which that person has never been arrested or convicted for or that are based on hearsay also raises other ethical issues. On the other hand, Gottfredson and Jarjoura (1996) argued that the omission of known risk factors from a risk assessment protocol lowers the quality of the assessment and, at the same time, creates other ethical problems from, for example, a community safety standpoint. Researchers such as Harcourt (2011), and Giguère and Lussier (2016) have stressed the importance of using risk assessment instruments with strong psychometric properties. In that regard, Harcourt (2007) mentioned that risk assessment instruments must be supported by rigorous psychometric evidence and research evaluating their predictive validity before being used by criminal justice system decision-makers. The use of inaccurate, invalid, and/or unreliable assessment instruments could have potentially dramatic consequences for individuals and their trajectory within the criminal justice system, while also adversely impacting community re-entry and reintegration possibilities. Indeed, actuarial tools did not necessarily eradicate all biases typically associated with unstructured clinical judgment.[5]

Others have raised concerns regarding actuarial tools' strict reliance on static risk factors. Static risk factors are those that cannot be modified in any way (Caudy, Durso, & Taxman, 2013; Gendreau, Little, & Goggin, 1996; Lussier & Davies, 2011; Morgan, Kroner, Mills, Serna, & McDonald, 2013). For example, a history of prior sexual offending is an example of a static risk factor; there is nothing a person can do to modify their risk score. This becomes an ethical issue because if an entire risk assessment instrument is defined by static risk factors, there is nothing a person can do, no matter how much treatment they receive and progress they make, to

---

[5] Hart (2016) argued that because actuarial tools were validated using relatively small samples of offenders, typically male and white, it is possible that such tools should not be used with individuals that are not represented by the sample used to validate the actuarial instrument. In other words, if the reliability and validity of a given actuarial instrument is based on research conducted with a sample that is not generalizable to the population that will potentially be assessed using this instrument, then questions remain about the fairness and ethics of the actuarial tool. Practitioners have an ethical and legal duty to ensure they are not contributing to the overrepresentation of minority persons in the justice system through the construction of risk assessment tools that are not as effective for such persons relative to white males (Hart, 2016).

lower their risk score. It is, however, possible for such individuals' risk score to increase. Therefore, demonstrating a desire to change and even actual change typically will not be taken into consideration by an actuarial tool designed to measure the probability of recidivism based on static risk factors. In short, static risk factors are not sensitive to individual changes over time, for example, participation in a treatment program, positive life events, life transitions and/or aging (e.g., Lussier & Healey, 2009). By definition, these static and historical factors do not change (Douglas & Skeem, 2005) and therefore are not representative of the mental state of the individual at the time of the evaluation (Côté, 2001). As a result, clinical researchers proposed the addition of dynamic risk factors that are sensitive to changes over time and informative of the changing risk of sexual recidivism. Dynamic factors tend to refer to the offender's mental state and psychological functioning that can have an impact on the likelihood of reoffending (e.g., Beech & Ward, 2004; Lussier & Cortoni, 2008). The relative importance of static versus dynamic risk factors has been and remains the subject of some debate (e.g., Beech, Friendship, Erikson, & Hanson, 2002; Dempster & Hart, 2002). At the center of this debate is the question of whether the assessment of dynamic risk factors improves the prediction of sexual recidivism and whether the successful modification of dynamic factors reduces the risk of sexual recidivism. While dynamic risk factors might help capture the changing state of a person, what if this change is not actually helpful for the prediction of sexual recidivism, especially once static factors are measured?

Canadian researchers questioned the American pessimism surrounding correctional treatment by reaffirming the importance of rehabilitation as a key guiding sentencing principle over a just deserts model. These researchers criticized the actuarial movement focused on the so-called static prediction and prediction of criminal recidivism by stressing the importance of taking into account factors that may change over time or following an intervention or a treatment aimed at modifying an offender's level of risk (Gendreau et al., 1996). The Risk-Need-Responsivity (RNR) model developed by Andrews and Bonta (1994) offered an alternative to the strictly actuarial, mechanical, and statistical version of risk assessment. The Risk principle refers to matching the level of intervention/service to the offender's specific risk of recidivism, Needs refers to targeting specific criminogenic needs in treatment, and Responsivity refers to tailoring interventions/treatment to specific offenders' abilities and strengths in order to maximize the impact of the intervention. The RNR model contrasts with actuarial assessments because of its focus on dynamic risk factors for criminal recidivism (for example, Andrews & Bonta, 2003; Douglas & Skeem, 2005; Hoge, Vincent, & Guy, 2012), which can also be targeted for intervention purposes and provides guidance for correctional interventions aimed at reducing the risk of criminal recidivism for specific individuals (Bonta & Motiuk, 1985; Gendreau et al., 1996; Raynor, Kynch, Roberts, & Merrington, 2000). Dynamic risk factors have been described as such because: (a) they have been empirically demonstrated to predict criminal recidivism; and, (b) they can theoretically change over time (e.g. Andrews, Bonta, & Wormith, 2006; Douglas & Skeem, 2005; Knight, Garner, Simpson, Morey, & Flynn, 2006). Thus, the RNR model ushered in a new way of thinking about persons as dynamic, changing, responsive to treatment, and therefore the nature of persons did not really fit with a strictly actuarial perspective of a person's risk for recidivism.

The RNR model was an important conduit for the third generation of approaches to risk assessment, which involved what is referred to as structured professional judgment (SPJ). SPJ blends together principles of actuarial assessment, the RNR model, and principles and practices of unstructured professional judgment. Like actuarial assessment, SPJ emphasizes standardization of practices and a focus on empirically validated risk factors. Whereas risk factors included in actuarial tools were the ones found to be significant in an analysis of a single sample, risk factors in SPJ instruments are those that were identified based on a systematic review of the literature on risk factors for the outcome of interest (e.g., sexual recidivism). Doing so avoids selecting risk factors that are bound to a specific sample rather than the population for which an instrument is intended to be used on. Like the RNR model, SPJ tools also include dynamic risk factors, sometimes referred to as clinical factors that are susceptible to change through treatment, intervention, time, or the person's own agency. Finally, in keeping with practices of unstructured professional judgment, SPJ allows for professional overrides, where trained users of the instrument can override a person's risk rating if important factors, unaccounted for by the instrument, clearly alter a person's level of risk. Yet, despite these advancements, in practice, actuarialists have questioned the utility of the SPJ model's inclusion of dynamic risk factors on the basis that such factors tend to be subsumed by the criminal propensity hypothesis and largely psychological view of sexual offending. In short, they are often narrowly conceptualized in the context of the psychological functioning of the individual in relation to the offense and targeted with standard interventions such as cognitive-behavioral therapy. This, of course, is to the detriment of social and contextual factors that are known to influence offending in general, and sexual offending specifically, most of which are highly prevalent in prison populations (Andrews et al., 2006).

The purpose of the current chapter is not to review all the literature concerning unstructured professional judgment, actuarial assessment, and SPJ and to determine a "winner" in terms of the best approach to predicting sexual recidivism. Rather, the point being made here is that the new risk management penology that characterizes the late twentieth century and early twenty-first century is clearly defined by the search for ways to best predict a person's likelihood of reoffending. A critical question of this new penology is whether the ability to predict sexual recidivism, regardless of the approach used, is ultimately helpful for understanding and preventing the development of sexual offending. After all, as discussed earlier, an instrument that successfully predicts 100% of all instances of sexual recidivism will still miss out on the vast majority of all future sex crimes detected by the criminal justice system given that most of these new sex crimes are perpetrated by convicted offenders without an official record of prior sexual offending.

Contemporary Risk Assessment of Sexual Recidivism

Since the 1990s, several risk assessment instruments designed for individuals convicted for a sex crime have been developed to determine their risk of sexual recidivism. These instruments were developed to assess the risk for sexual recidivism of adult offenders who have been convicted for a sex crime. These instruments were not developed to assess likelihood of perpetrating a sex crime among persons not involved in the criminal justice system. Nor were they developed for use on persons without a history of sexual offending, even those these individuals ultimately account for the majority of all sex crimes. Tools such as the Rapid Risk Assessment for Sex Offender Recidivism (RRASOR; Hanson, 1997), the Static-99 (Hanson & Thornton, 2000), the Static-2002 (Hanson, 2002), the Risk Matrix 2000-Sexual (RM2000/S; Thornton et al., 2003), the Sex Offender Risk Appraisal Guide (SORAG; Quinsey, Harris, Rice, & Cormier, 1998a), and the Minnesota Sex Offender Risk Screening Tool-Revised (MnSOST-R; Epperson, Kaul, & Hesselton, 2000) illustrate this generation of instruments designed to assess the probabilities of sexual recidivism. The risk factor items that make up these risk assessment instruments are presented in Table 7.1.

Tonry's arguments that risk factors outside an offender's control should not be included in risk assessment instruments were not echoed in the development of risk assessment instruments for sexual recidivism. While a person's criminal history and the characteristics of the sexual offense perpetrated represent some of the core aspects of these risk assessment instruments, the domains of risk factors extent beyond that. In fact, these instruments are generally composed of the following risk factor categories: (a) sociodemographic characteristics (e.g., offenders' age, marital status); (b) developmental factors (e.g., family situation growing up; behavior problems in childhood/adolescence); (c) sexual offending characteristics (e.g., number of sex crime convictions, type of sex crime convictions, juvenile sexual offending, rate of sexual offending over time); (d) victim characteristics of their sexual crime(s) (e.g., victim's gender, victim's age); (e) nonsexual criminal history (e.g., number of prior convictions, nonviolent offending; nonsexual violent offending; rule-breaking behaviors); and, (f) a history of mental health problems (e.g., drug/alcohol abuse; a diagnosis of a personality disorder). Based on the presence and number of these items that characterize different actuarial risk assessment instruments, offenders are classified as having a certain risk of sexual recidivism. Indeed, a brief survey of these instruments suggests that the typical profile of someone likely to be rearrested/reconvicted for a sex crime is as follows: a young adult with a history of both sexual and nonsexual offending who has had difficulties complying with past supervisory conditions; and whose sex offense(s) involved a non-contact crime (e.g., exhibitionism) perpetrated against a (most likely young) male victim outside the family setting (e.g., against a stranger).

These instruments are constructed in such a way that a person characterized by a high number of the abovementioned risk factors should be at a higher risk of sexual recidivism. In other words, there is no single key risk factor or "north star" among

Table 7.1 Risk predictors of sexual recidivism of different actuarial risk assessment instruments

Risk factor domain	Risk factor category	RRASOR	Static-99	RM2000/S	Static-2002	SORAG	MnSOST-R
Sociodemographic characteristics	Age	Age at release	Age at release	Age at commencement of risk	Age at release	Age at index offense	Age at release from institution
	Marital status		Ever lived with an intimate partner for at least two years	Marital status		Marital status	Employment history during the most recent 12 months in the community
Developmental factors	Family situation					Lived with both biological parents to age 16 (except when parent deceased)	
	Behavior problems					Elementary school maladjustment	Is there evidence of adolescent antisocial behavior in file
Sexual offending	Number of sex crime convictions	Number of prior arrests or convictions for a sex crime	Number of prior arrests or convictions for a sex crime (excluding index offense)	Sexual appearances	Prior sentencing occasions for sexual offenses	Number of prior sex offense convictions	Number of sex and sex-related convictions (including index conviction)
	Type of sex crime conviction		Any convictions for a non-contact sex offense	Non-contact sex offense conviction	Any sentencing occasion for a non-contact sex offense		Length of sexual offending history

Risk factor domain	Risk factor category	RRASOR	Static-99	RM2000/S	Static-2002	SORAG	MnSOST-R
	Juvenile sexual offending				Any juvenile arrest for a sexual offense and convicted as an adult for a separate sexual offense		
	Rate of sexual offending				Rate of sexual offending		
	Legal context during sexual offending						Offender was under any form of supervision when they committed any sex offense for which they were eventually charged or convicted
	Location of sexual offending that led to a sex crime conviction						Any sex offense (charged or convicted) committed in a public place
	Sex offender treatment						Sex offender treatment while incarcerated

(continued)

Table 7.1 (continued)

Risk factor domain	Risk factor category	RRASOR	Static-99	RM2000/S	Static-2002	SORAG	MnSOST-R
	Level of violence used						Force or the threat of force used to achieve compliance in any sex offense (charged or convicted)
	Number of sex crime events						Has any sex offense (charged or convicted) involved multiple acts on a single victim within any single contact event?
Victim characteristics	Victim's gender	Any male victims	Any male victims	Any male victims	Any male victims		Number of different age groups victimized across all sex/sex-related offenses (charged or convicted)
	Offender-victim relationship	Any unrelated victims	Any unrelated victims Any stranger victims	Any stranger victim	Any unrelated victims Any stranger victims		Was there a stranger victim for any sex/sex-related offense
	Victim's age				Young unrelated victims	Prior sex offense against female victims under 14 years old (exclusively)	Offended against a 13- to 15-year old victim and the perpetrator was more than 5 years older (charged or convicted)

Risk factor domain	Risk factor category	RRASOR	Static-99	RM2000/S	Static-2002	SORAG	MnSOST-R
Nonsexual criminal career	General offending		Number of prior sentencing dates (excluding index offense)	Criminal appearances	Prior involvement with the criminal justice system Number of prior sentencing occasions for any crime Years free prior to index offense (less than 36 months)		
	Nonviolent offending					Nonviolent criminal history score (Cormier-Lang system)	
	Nonsexual violent offending		Prior conviction for a nonsexual violent crime Convicted for a nonsexual violent crime (index offense)		Prior sentencing occasions for nonsexual violent crime	Violent criminal history score (Cormier-Lang system)	
	Rule-breaking behaviors				Any community supervision violation	Failure of prior conditional release	Discipline history while incarcerated

(continued)

Table 7.1 (continued)

Risk factor domain	Risk factor category	RRASOR	Static-99	RM2000/S	Static-2002	SORAG	MnSOST-R
Mental health	History of drug/alcohol problems					Any history of alcohol problems (includes parental alcoholism, teenage and adult alcoholism, etc.)	Patterns of substantial drug or alcohol abuse during the most recent 12 months in the community Chemical dependency treatment while incarcerated
	Personality disorder					Meets DSM-III criteria for any personality disorder Psychopathy checklist-revised (PCL-R) score	
						Meets DSM-III criteria for schizophrenia	
						Phallometric test results	

Note: Rapid Risk Assessment for Sex Offender Recidivism (RRASOR; Hanson, 1997); Static-99 (Hanson & Thornton, 2000) Risk Matrix 2000 Sexual (RM2000/S; Thornton et al., 2003) Static-2002 (Hanson et al., 2013) Sex Offender Risk Appraisal Guide (SORAG; Quinsey et al., 1998a, 1998b; Minnesota Sex Offender Screening Tool Revised (MnSOST-R; Epperson et al., 2000) the risk factors for sexual recidivism. To be identified as having a high risk for sexual recidivism means that the individual is associated with multiple recognized risk factors. The computation of sexual recidivism probabilities using these tools is based on what is called Burgess (1928). This method consists of summing each risk factor that is present to create an aggregate score. Sometimes different risk factors are given predetermined weights based on their strength of association with sexual recidivism. An expert thus completes the tool and adds the scores for all risk factor items in order to obtain a total score. A conversion table then makes it possible to associate the total score with the average estimated risk probabilities of sexual recidivism based on prior research. Certain instruments also make it possible to assign a qualitative "label" to this score in order to reflect a person's likelihood of risk of sexual recidivism. Generally, this categorization is quite simplistic: low risk, moderate risk, high, or very high risk. It should be noted that there is no universal standard for establishing what in fact actually constitutes a "low," "moderate," or "high" risk. In addition, the standards or thresholds used to establish specific risk levels vary from one tool to another. The simplicity of Burgess' method explains, in part, why the use of these instruments is so widespread. Moreover, very few alternative methods have been examined to date, such as hierarchical and iterative classification methods (Silver, Smith, & Banks, 2000; Steadman et al., 2000).

These instruments are not designed to explain risk and recidivism. Therefore, they are not informative, for example, as to the reason why offenders who target male victims are at a higher risk of sexual recidivism than those who do not. One way to make sense of the underlying meaning of these risk factors is to conduct certain statistical analyses (e.g., factor analyses) that allow for the identification of dimensions or factors among the items in the instruments. These types of analyses allow for the investigation of whether or not these risk factor items are possibly informative of a latent construct or antisocial propensity that is responsible for the increased likelihood of sexual recidivism. Statistical analysis of the risk factor items that make up these actuarial tools have in fact highlighted the presence of at least two significant,[6] meaningful dimensions (e.g., Allen & Pflugradt, 2013; Brouillette-Alarie, Babchishin, Hanson, & Helmus, 2016). The first dimension characterizing individuals at a higher risk of being rearrested/reconvicted for a sex crime appears to reflect an antisocial propensity. This antisocial propensity is manifested by the presence of numerous previous arrests and convictions for various crime types, including violent crimes. This antisocial propensity is also expressed by the presence of non-compliance with supervisory conditions (e.g., probation/parole) and recidivism while under some form of supervision. However, given the focus on official criminal justice indicators of offending, this could also mean that these individuals are more likely to be detected and apprehended for their actions compared to other offenders. The second dimension characterizing individuals at a higher risk of being rearrested/reconvicted for a sexual crime appears to reflect the presence of "sexual deviance." This dimension is manifested by the presence of factors such as

---

[6] Other actuarial risk dimensions have been statistically identified, but their meaning is equivocal.

a history of prior sexual crimes, which marks the persistence of sexual offending, as well as the presence of sexual deviance measured using phallometric data. Characteristics of the sex offense, such as the use of physical violence or having perpetrated a sexual offense against a child or a male victim may also be indicative of sexual interests for such acts. In other words, together, these items that comprise in the second factor suggest the presence of sexual interests for sexually deviant and coercive behaviors (e.g., sexual sadism, pedophilia).[7]

From a scientific perspective, these findings that have emerged research based on actuarial instruments suggests that the persistence of sexual offending is multidetermined. Indeed, persistence in sexual offending could be the result of two independent forces coinciding: antisocial propensity and sexual deviance. Antisocial propensity has been outlined in previous chapters. In that regard, these results are not surprising. Someone who is more inclined to break societal rules in various contexts and under various circumstances is more likely to act accordingly in a sexual context. What is more surprising is that this antisocial propensity found its way into risk assessment protocols despite the fact it has long been ignored or its importance downplayed in clinical assessment protocols of perpetrators of sex crimes (Lussier & Cortoni, 2008). In addition, rediscovering the role and importance of sexual deviance in sexual offending in actuarial risk studies is also very informative. While the findings only suggest the presence of sexual deviance as a possible explanatory construct, it appears to give credence to earlier explanations of sexual offending that focused on sexual deviance as an explanation for the persistence of sexual offending.

Therefore, yet another possibility is that among all perpetrators of sexual crimes and among all sexual recidivists, only certain individuals are more likely to be detected by the criminal justice system and identified as either potential (i.e., high risk) or actual (i.e., they have been convicted multiple times) sexual recidivists. It is well established that individuals who are known to the criminal justice system are more likely to be under scrutiny in the community and this has become increasingly the case since the enactment of sex offender registries and public notification laws. Another way of thinking about this is that actuarial risk assessment tools are designed to predict the individuals that are most susceptible to being detected for the sex offenses they perpetrate, as opposed to predicting who is more likely to perpetrate sex offenses. Therefore, could it be the case that the actuarial approach creates certain biases toward a subgroup of convicted offenders? This question has been raised before (Hart, 2016) and has even made its way into Canada's court-

---

[7] However, before concluding that there are two and only two latent constructs that explain sexual offending, it must also be considered that the identification of such dimensions is predicated on the items that are chosen to be included in the risk assessment instrument being examined. As mentioned before, such determinations are entirely atheoretical and blind to the four research agenda domains associated with criminological scholarship. As such, a major question that remains is whether the two dimensions identified would reemerge in analyses that were more inclusive of, for example, dynamic risk factors, factors reflecting openness to treatment, protective factors and informal social controls, and other factors not considered by actuarial tools.

rooms (e.g., Ewert v. Canada; R. v. Haley). There are numerous important reasons to believe that this is in fact the case. One factor that criminological research has had much to say about is a person's age and the passage of time.

Age and the Passage of Time: The Great Forgotten

Let us recall some basic, well established, criminological facts. In the early nineteenth century, Adolphe Jacques Quetelet, an illustrious Belgian mathematician and statistician, made the following observation: *"The inclination to crime, toward adulthood, grows fairly rapidly; it reaches a maximum and then decreases to the last limits of life"* (Quetelet, 1836, p. 86; translated from French by the first author). What Quetelet was alluding to is that criminal behavior and age are intimately related; criminal behavior changes across the life course. The association between a person's age and criminal behavior remains one of the most robust empirical observations in the history of criminology (e.g., Hirschi & Gottfredson, 1983; Thornberry, 1997). Although this empirical observation is well known, the interpretation of this age-crime association continues to be debated within the scientific community. Indeed, the interpretation of the age-crime relationship has been debated on theoretical grounds (e.g., Blumstein, Cohen, & Farrington, 1988; Farrington, 1986; Gottfredson & Hirschi, 1986; Greenberg, 1985; Hirschi & Gottfredson, 1983; Moffitt, 1993; Tittle, 1988). These questions reemerged in the 1980s as a group of scholars were concerned with the statistical modeling of offending trajectories over time (e.g., Blumstein et al., 1986). Simply put, researchers were concerned over the idea as to whether or not the age-crime trend observed by Quetelet was invariant.[8]

---

[8] In other words, was this trend representative of the criminal activity for everyone but to varying degrees according to their antisocial propensity? For some scholars, there is no doubt that this relationship is invariant. Criminal offending emerges at the onset of adolescence, it culminates in the middle of adolescence, and it declines thereafter (Hirschi & Gottfredson, 1983). Those with a high antisocial propensity would start earlier in their life course, they would offend at a higher rate during adolescence, and continue doing so, albeit to a lesser rate, in adulthood until the eventual termination of criminal behavior compared to those with a lower antisocial propensity (Gottfredson & Hirschi, 1990; Hirschi & Gottfredson, 1983). Others challenged the invariance assumption of the age-crime association over time, instead suggesting that it reflected at least two distinctive processes (Farrington, 1986). The first was that a substantial proportion of the population takes part in criminal activities during adolescence compared to emerging adulthood and later adulthood. The second was that the frequency at which individuals perpetrate crimes can be relatively high and stable for a small number of individuals over the life course (i.e., those who are responsible for a disproportionate volume of crime) and relatively infrequent and intermittent for others. In effect, the major debate came down to a disagreement about why crime declines between adolescence and early adulthood. From the first perspective presented, the drop in the age-crime curve is a result of all persons slowing down in their level of offending. There is an inexorable effect of aging; even the highest rate offenders cannot defy this aging process (Gottfredson & Hirschi, 1990). From the second perspective presented, the drop in the age crime curve results because the vast majority of offenders stop offending altogether, but a very small proportion of offenders continue to maintain the same rate of offending as they had in adolescence (Nagin, Farrington, & Moffitt, 1995).

Why is this relevant or important in the context of the risk assessment of individuals having been convicted for a sex crime? Let us consider the following scenario based on a real case. An adult male offender is sentenced to prison for a series of sexual assaults. Considering various aspects of the sexual assaults they perpetrated (e.g., the use of violence, presence of stranger victims, and multiple victims), the individual is sentenced to a prison term of 20 years. The parole board denied this man parole on multiple occasions because of, among other things, his high risk to sexually reoffend and his poor participation in treatment programs. After completing his sentence, actuarial risk assessment showed that this man was a high risk to sexually reoffend. Yet, 20 years had passed since the original sentencing decision and prison admission. This scenario is certainly not uncommon; a sociolegal context characterized by a focus on community protection against the threat of individuals convicted for a sex crime returning to the community means that primacy is given to the issue of this man's risk of reoffending, even though he was more than 60 years old at the end of his sentence.

This raises two important questions. The first is: should the criminal justice system put in place valuable and expensive resources for the surveillance of this individual upon his return to the community? The second is: does this person represent an actual threat to public safety based on his past behavior? The actuarial risk assessment suggested that he was in fact at a high risk to sexually reoffend. What is less clear is whether these instruments are sensitive to two major questions. First, does this person's level of risk as defined by his life 20 years ago accurately reflect their level of risk now? Keep in mind that risk factors included in actuarial assessments cannot be modified. Second, even if this individual is characterized by a wide range of risk factors, to what extent does the fact that this individual is 60 years of age mitigate this risk? When the issue of an offender's age surfaced in the field of research of sexual recidivism, two schools of thought emerged. These perspectives varied regarding how to consider an offender's age and the passage of time in the evaluation and prediction of the risk of sexual recidivism (Lussier & Healey, 2009). The divide between these two perspectives centered around the question of whether a person's probability of sexual recidivism changes over time. For example, does an individual who has been convicted of a sexual offense at the age of 25 represent the same risk for recidivism 5, 10 or even 25 years later?

The first school of thought adheres to the static perspective discussed earlier and suggests that the estimated probabilities of sexual recidivism are relatively stable over time. Therefore, the individual probabilities of recidivism should not be adjusted by risk assessors according to the offender's age at the time of the assessment. For the proponents of this perspective, the only age factor that should be considered when assessing the risk of recidivism is the person's age at the time of their first offense, which is hypothesized to be a key marker of a high antisocial or criminal propensity. In support of this perspective, Harris and Rice (2007), who were involved in the development of actuarial tools, argued that the effect of age and aging on the likelihood of recidivism is relatively small and insignificant. They hypothesized that the age at first offense provides more information on the potential for recidivism than age at the time of assessment or release. In other words, the age at which a person perpetrates a sex offense is indicative of their propensity for continued sexual offending over time; the earlier this person begins sexual offending, the higher the likelihood of continued sexual offending, regardless of their age at the time of assessment. In other words, risk for sexual offending is immutable with the passage of time.

According to this static hypothesis, young adults who present a high actuarial risk of sexual recidivism will represent the same risk of recidivism, 15, 20, or 30 years later, since the propensity to recidivate is relatively stable, fixed, and age-invariant (see also, Doren, 2004). The second school of thought proposed a maturation viewpoint. The term "maturation" is meant to invoke the process of change; risk of recidivism declines as individuals age. It also reflects that although change does occur, such change occurs in a relatively predictable fashion (Barbaree, Langton, & Blanchard, 2007; Lussier & Healey, 2009). This idea refers to the hypothesis that the age-crime relationship is invariant and therefore also applies to individuals convicted for a sex crime. The static-maturation hypothesis recognizes the presence of a relatively stable and static propensity to commit a criminal offense. However, this propensity is subject to the effect of age and aging. For example, Barbaree, Blanchard, and Langton (2003) stated that sexual drive is a key component of sexual offending but that the strength of this factor irreversibly and steadily decreases with age. In that context, it is reasonable to assume that the risk of sexual recidivism will decrease in a similar fashion.

Several studies have shown that an individual's age at the time of their release from prison is associated with differences in the likelihood of recidivism. The same finding has been observed when specifically looking at persons with a history of sexual offending. The result is always the same; older age is associated with a decreased likelihood of sexual recidivism (Barbaree et al., 2003; Barbaree & Blanchard, 2008; Hanson, 2002; Lussier & Davies, 2015; Lussier & Healey, 2009; Prentky & Lee, 2007; Thornton, 2006; Wollert, 2006; Wollert, Cramer, Waggoner, Skelton, & Vess, 2010). Young adults in their early twenties have higher rates of sexual recidivism following their release than older adults released from prison. Some actuarialists recognized the importance of age as it related to risk assessment and included the age at which a person was being assessed into their actuarial risk assessment tools (e.g., Hanson & Thornton, 2000; Quinsey, Harris, Rice, & Cormier, 1998b). However, a closer look at the actuarial instruments shows an important and critical issue: these tools differ in terms of the age limit at which the risk of sexual recidivism is considered to be higher (e.g., young adults aged under 25, 27, or 30). The clear connection between age and recidivism prompted some researchers to argue in favor of the importance of establishing base rates of sexual recidivism based on the offender's age (Wollert, 2006; Wollert et al., 2010). Wollert (2006) estimated that sexual recidivism rates for specific age groups over an average follow-up period of 8 years. These findings, reported in Table 7.2, are representative of what researchers have reported in independent studies over the years (e.g., Fazel, Sjöstedt, Långström, & Grann, 2006; Hanson, 2002; Lussier & Healey, 2009; Prentky & Lee, 2007; Thornton, 2006). It shows that the group of young adults, between 18 and 24 years old show the highest estimated probabilities of sexual recidivism. The estimated risk probabilities steadily decline for subsequent older age groups, in accordance with an age-crime curve effect. It is notable that passed age 60, the estimated probabilities of sexual recidivism are extremely low. In fact, the statistical age effect is such that even after the actuarial adjustment of the level of risk of recidivism, age statistically contributes to the "prediction" of sexual recidivism (Lussier & Healey, 2009; Thornton, 2006). In fact, the age effect on sexual recidivism is so strong that it is at least equally informative of the likelihood of sexual recidivism as a person's total risk assessment score on the Static-99 (Lussier & Healey, 2009).

Why Is the Age Effect Important?

The study of age and sexual recidivism can be used to highlight some underlying issues with the practice of risk assessment and risk prediction. While there have been some scientific advancements made since the emergence of the first actuarial-based studies of the risk of sexual recidivism, the main premises of actuarial risk assessment have remained relatively untested and unchallenged in spite of theoretical, methodological, empirical, and ethical issues. In fact, the age effect has far-reaching implications beyond making additional actuarial adjustments to the estimated probabilities of sexual recidivism (Lussier, Tzoumakis, Cale, & Amirault, 2010). Five of these implications are discussed below. First, these results show the importance of taking into account the offender's age at the time of release and of adjusting actuarial scores accordingly (Lussier & Healey, 2009; Wollert et al., 2010). Indeed, not all risk assessors take into account the offender's age in order to assess risk. In addition, it may be difficult, simply based on an unstructured clinical evaluation, to properly weigh the effect of the individual's age in order to determine their probability of sexual recidivism. This prompted the revisement of at least one instrument, the Static-99, to better account for the age effect, not only by adjusting for the higher risk of young adults, but also the declining risk of older adults (Hanson, Babchishin, Helmus, & Thornton, 2013).

Second, it is important to look back at how actuarial tools are constructed. A sample from a prison is drawn, individuals are assessed, risk factors are measured, the individuals are then followed for some length of time in the community, and sexual recidivism during this follow-up period is noted. The risk factors associated with sexual recidivism are then included in the actuarial instrument being developed. However, sexual recidivists will be disproportionately represented by younger offenders. As such, the risk factors included in actuarial risk assessment tools are going to reflect risk factors for sexual recidivism by younger adults. For example, Table 7.2 shows that individuals between ages 45 and 70+ account for approximately 20% of the sample yet only approximately 10% of sexual recidivists. Will the risk factors significantly associated with sexual recidivism more broadly also reflect the risk factors for sexual recidivism among this older group? Such questions

Table 7.2 Sexual recidivism rates of individuals convicted for a sexual offense

Age group (years)	Number of individuals (% of total)	Sexual recidivism rate	Standard error	Estimated number of sexual recidivists (% of total)
18–24	630 (13.5%)	0.271	0.018	171 (20.8%)
25–29	805 (17.3%)	0.231	0.015	186 (22.6%)
30–34	920 (19.7%)	0.197	0.013	181 (22.0%)
35–39	833 (17.9%)	0.142	0.012	118 (14.3%)
40–44	583 (12.5%)	0.139	0.014	81 (9.8%)
45–49	389 (8.3%)	0.126	0.017	49 (6.0%)
50–59	379 (8.1%)	0.087	0.014	33 (4.0%)
60–69	116 (2.5%)	0.034	0.019	4 (0.5%)
70 and over	8 (0.2%)	0.000	0.000	0 (0.0%)

Adapted from Wollert (2006). Recidivism data refer to an average follow-up of 8 years

have not been addressed appropriately. This point was made by Barbaree et al. (2007). They found that after statistically correcting actuarial risk assessment by removing the age at release effect, the predictive value of actuarial tools considerably decreased. Put more simply, the findings by Barbaree et al. (2007) suggest that actuarial scores are biased toward the risk that characterizes young adult offenders (see also, Lussier & Healey, 2009). These results raise important empirical and ethical issues about the validity of actuarial predictions, especially for older offenders.

Third, the age effect on sexual recidivism cannot and should not be confused with an *aging effect*. The age effect on sexual recidivism suggest that younger adults are more likely to be rearrested/reconvicted for a sex crime compared to older adults. The age group differential in estimated probabilities of recidivism does not directly address the issue of aging because it compares the risk of recidivism of different individuals at different points in their life course. This comparison refers to between-individual differences in age. These findings, based on the methodology used, are not informative of whether individuals experience within-individual change in risk status or the likelihood of sexual recidivism. Is the same person at age 40 irrevocably of a lesser risk of sexual recidivism than when this same person was 20 years old? The issue of aging requires looking at the same person at different points in time. The type of research design used by actuarialists cannot be used to test such a hypothesis. Only prospective longitudinal studies with a cohort of individuals of the same age followed over long periods would allow for the examination of this hypothesis.

Fourth, the age effect highlights the presence of differential estimated risk probabilities for sexual recidivism. These differential recidivism rates have been interpreted as follows: as people age, they are less impulsive, less prone to thoughtless and reckless acts and their sexual drive decreases. Despite theoretical awareness of why aging might explain declines in risk for sexual recidivism, when it comes to the actuarial risk assessment literature and development of actuarial risk assessment tools, efforts to unpack this aging effect through the measurement of a person's change in impulsivity, recklessness, and sexual drive have been lacking. Instead, age remains *the* explanation for differential recidivism rates. Some could argue, as Tonry (1987) did several decades ago, that it is frankly unethical to fail to unpack the aging effect and other characteristics that an individual cannot control. Why should a young person that has undergone significant improvements in psychosocial maturation (e.g., improvements in temperance, responsibility, resistance to peers, future-orientation) that reduce their risk of offending (McCuish, Lussier, & Rocque, 2020) be held hostage by their age? An alternative and unexplored hypothesis is that, as people age, exposure to risk and protective factors associated with sexual offending may significantly vary. Indeed, could it be that the most important factors influencing sexual recidivism can be found in emerging adulthood (e.g., between 18 and 25 years old)? Could it be that the negative impact of the criminal justice system's response (e.g., conviction, labeling, registration, notification) to individuals convicted for a sex crime is significantly more important for these young adults? These questions require important scientific scrutiny moving forward.

Fifth, actuarial studies have rarely addressed the possibility that risk factors may lose their predictive accuracy over long periods. For example, while it has been established that a criminal history including a past conviction for a sex crime is statistically associated with an increased odds of sexual recidivism, is this always true, 15, 25, 35 years after that initial conviction? This becomes especially relevant when individuals are subjected to long-term sentences and long-term disposition (e.g., sex offender registry). Criminological research has shown ways to scientifically examine this question (e.g., Bushway, Nieuwbeerta, & Blokland, 2011).[9] American researchers have questioned the increasingly common practice of background checks and its impact on job searches for individuals with a criminal record (Bushway et al., 2011; Kurlychek, Brame, & Bushway, 2006). By analyzing long-term criminal behavior, they raised the question of whether it is possible to determine how long an individual with a criminal record remains at a higher risk of

---

[9] Background checks to determine whether a person has a criminal record are relatively commonplace in the twenty-first century (Bushway et al., 2011). In the USA, more than 50% of all employers use background checks prior to hiring a potential employee. This amounts to more than 40 million background checks annually. These background checks are based on the same key principle as actuarial risk assessment instruments: past criminal behavior informs about the probability of future criminal behavior. The idea is certainly not new, but it is all the more common nowadays where police data are indexed, archived, and computerized. Furthermore, there are very few rules and guidelines that dictate such practices. In particular, there are few to no rules circumscribing the period for which to verify a person's criminal record. This begs the question: should an employer have access to the entire criminal record of a potential employee, or should this information be limited to a predetermined period, for example, only the past three years? Should the duration of time vary according to the age of the prospective employee? After all, someone age 40 that has not committed a crime in two years is less likely to reoffend than someone age 20 that has not committed a crime over the same period.

offending compared to the general population.[10] How is this area of research relevant to the discussion of "sex offenders?" Actuarial risk assessment instruments do not recognize the possibility that there is *an expiration date* to an individual's prior criminal record. In fact, these instruments are not constructed to take into account the effect of the passage of time on the meaningfulness of an individual's prior criminal record. For example, when scoring a risk assessment instrument, the information does not take into account if the person's prior convictions occurred 5, 10 or even 25 years earlier, only whether this person has a prior record of conviction or not.

In this regard, Amirault and Lussier (2011) re-examined the predictive value of a prior conviction as a risk factor for sexual recidivism in a sample of individuals convicted for a sex crime. However, rather than simply comparing the sexual recidivism rates of people with and without a previous conviction, as actuarialists traditionally have done, these researchers looked at the age of the individual at the time of each of the previous convictions. With the passage of time, a prior conviction for a sexual offense eventually loses its predictive value; that is, it eventually no longer increases the risk of general and sexual recidivism. In other words, the study findings suggest that risk assessors may overestimate or underestimate the potential for criminal and sexual recidivism by not taking into consideration how far back this person had a prior run in with the law. Nakamura and Blumstein (2015) took this one-step further by analyzing the probabilities of sexual recidivism of a group of individuals who were arrested for the first time for a sex crime in state of New York State in 1980, 1985, or 1990. Essentially, there were interested in when the value of a prior sex offense "expires" in terms of no longer being informative of future offending. They also estimated the probabilities of arrest for a sex crime for all adult citizens of state of New York State during the same time period. When these researchers compared the probabilities of arrest of individuals with a criminal record for a sex offense to that of the general population, the results show that the risk of sexual recidivism remains higher for individuals convicted for a sex crime than that of the general population for 10 years after the arrest. After this point in time, the value of knowing that a person had committed a sex offense expired in the sense that individuals were no longer at a greater risk of a new offense compared to individuals in the general population. While the statistical modeling of an expiration date for risk of sexual recidivism informs about the dynamic aspect of risk over life course, these findings should not be seen in terms of immediate policy-based implications.

---

[10] Bushway et al. (2011) estimated that individuals with a first conviction after turning 26 years old represent a significantly higher risk of reoffending than the rest of the general population for approximately 2–6 years after their release. However, those under 26 at the time of their first conviction who already had more than four convictions continue to represent for 23 years a significantly higher risk of reoffending compared to the general population. In short, they found the risk of recidivism varies depending on the age at the time in question and the number of criminal convictions. These researchers therefore raised the idea that there is an expiration date to a criminal record. Their findings also raise the question of whether it is realistic and justified to require a null probability of offending on the part of individuals with a prior criminal record when the probability of offending among the general population is in fact greater than zero?

From a policy standpoint, Nakamura and Blumstein's (2015) approach of modeling a statistical threshold for time at risk does carry important limitations and implications. Indeed, these findings may suggest a wait-and-see approach in that offenders should be socially excluded for a certain period until their risk of reoffending has reached a certain statistical threshold. Recall that these models do not take into consideration legal and systemic factors such as an offender's legal situation upon community re-entry, including type of supervisory conditions imposed, type of legal dispositions used (e.g., public notification and sex offender registration), type of service and community resources offered, programs and interventions, etc. While these statistical models can be useful from a research perspective, they do have their own limitations. The wait-and-see approach is not reflective of the process of desistance (Chap. 6) and how community reintegration works. Social capital, a pivotal aspect of desistance, takes time to develop, so does desistance, which can include lapses and relapses (e.g., missing a curfew, drinking alcohol when forbidden) without a sexual reoffense occurring. Thinking about these findings from the state dependence criminological perspective, a major concern is that wait-and-see policies restrict offenders from becoming employed, which can help to further reduce their likelihood of future offending sooner, even though such persons may no longer be at risk to offend. Not only might this further marginalize offenders, it may be needlessly costly to employers that believe that background checks are helping them to make informative decisions about a prospective employee's suitability for the position. In effect, perhaps the reason why former offenders, after a period of time, are no more likely than the general population to commit a crime is because they had an opportunity to build up social capital in ways that encouraged them to not offend. If offenders are excluded, for example, from opportunities for employment for a specific period of time, it could delay their process of desistance. In all, advancements in statistical modeling should be used as tools to think more clearly about a particular social problem. Without a clear theory of desistance, such statistical modeling remains only a tool.

Conclusion

With the rise of actuarial prediction, the concept of sexual recidivism has become *the* benchmark indicator used to assess the performance of the criminal justice system in its handling of individuals convicted of sex offenses. The importance of sexual recidivism or someone's estimated risk of sexual recidivism has been elevated to a level where it represents the key measure to: establish someone's level of risk or dangerousness; determine what sentence to impose on a convicted offender; judge what supervision an offender requires during their sentence; determine what the intensity of treatment should be that an offender is offered or mandated to participate in; judge whether an offender should be offered parole or not and under what conditions; and, determine the level of supervision and type of supervisory conditions a convicted offender should receive. In the USA, this information is even communicated to the general public so that citizens can take what they deem to be appropriate actions to protect themselves against the threat that would be sexual recidivists represent to the safety of the community. The pervasive role and importance of sexual recidivism can also be seen in terms of assessing the criminal justice system's ability to protect the community against the threat of individuals convicted for a sex crime. The sexual recidivism rates of cohorts of individuals convicted for a sex crime are reported as indicators of the criminal justice system's crime prevention and public safety performance. The impact of treatment and intervention programs are often established strictly by examining and comparing sexual recidivism rates. The performance of probation and parole are examined strictly by examining the percentage of offenders who sexually recidivate while under community supervision. In their review of the scientific literature, Furby, Weinrott, and Blackshaw (1989) noted that anyone could essentially conclude anything about sex offender recidivism because of the different methodologies used across empirical studies and the methodological shortcomings of studies that have attempted to measure sexual recidivism.

How did the criminal justice system, in a matter of a decade or so, move from the concept of sexual recidivism built on shaky grounds to a situation where it is the benchmark measure by which offenders are judged and the criminal justice system performance is established? The advancement of actuarial and other forms of risk assessment certainly played a role in the ubiquity of statistics on sexual recidivism. As mentioned earlier, risk assessors started building risk prediction models centered on the following well established empirical observation: the best predictor of future behavior is past behavior (Nagin & Paternoster, 1991, 2000). In the context of risk assessment and risk prediction of future criminal behavior this means focusing risk assessment on a person's past offending to predict future offending. In the context of the risk assessment for those convicted for sexual offenses, it means examining their criminal record to determine the risk of being arrested and convicted again. Research on the prediction of violent and sexual recidivism confirmed the assertion that past behavior is the best predictor of recidivism. The results of recidivism studies showed that individuals with a long track record of run ins with the law (e.g., high numbers of arrests, high numbers of convictions) were significantly more likely to run into trouble with the law again in the future. In other words, the more an individual recidivates, the greater their probability of future recidivism. It is important to remember that there are no certainties here, only probabilities. This also means that to more certainly identify a repeat offender, the individual must, first and foremost, have been apprehended and convicted in the past, and even have already been identified as a repeat offender. Importantly, this empirical observation was never about making scientific progress toward the understanding of a person's criminal behavior or why they are more likely to criminally recidivate, but rather, predicting it and predicting it as accurately as possible. Little attention has even gone into unpacking what "it" is; that is, what types of repeat sexual offenses are being predicted by risk assessments? Are the recidivists predicted by actuarial tools those offenders that commit the types of heinous offenses that the general public hear about in the media? Or, are risk assessment tools predicting concerning and problematic albeit certainly less serious forms of repeat sexual offending such as exhibitionism?

Although actuarialists thought they were discovering the predictors of criminal recidivism, they were in fact rediscovering empirical observations made by criminologists several decades earlier (e.g., Glueck & Glueck, 1930; West & Farrington, 1977). Criminological research on the persistence of criminal behavior had been taking place several decades prior to the risk assessment revolution in correctional and forensic psychology. This criminological literature concerning explanations of offending over time was organized around four main research agendas: (1) the sociology of crime and research on criminal achievement, the role of criminal mentorship and criminal networks, and the "career criminal" (e.g., Morselli & Tremblay, 2004); (2) the empirical study of juvenile offending, the modeling of offending trajectories, the description and prediction of the longitudinal sequence of offending, crime versatility and the study of the "chronic offender" (e.g., Blumstein et al., 1986; Piquero, Farrington, & Blumstein, 2003); (3) developmental criminology and the study of the onset and developmental course of antisocial behavior as a precursor to criminal behavior, identifying, from the earliest stages of life, risk and protective factors associated with developmental trajectories of antisocial behavior, and the study of the "early onset" offender (e.g., Loeber & LeBlanc, 1990; Moffitt, 1993); and, (4) life course research that focuses on life events, turning points and life transitions, the role of informal controls, the process by which offenders terminate their offending and the study of those who "desist" from crime (Laub & Sampson, 2003; Sampson & Laub, 1997, 2005).

Understanding the processes by which criminal activity becomes persistent has been at the center of these research agendas and criminology researchers understood that persistence in offending can occur: (a) because sometimes crime pays; (b) because sometimes crime can generate negative life circumstances that promote more criminal activity (e.g., stigmatization, labeling, weakening of social bonds); (c) because sometimes crime is the result of a series of adverse experiences and disadvantages that accumulate over the life course in such a way that limits life opportunities (e.g., peer, intimate relationship, work, income, housing), and/or (d) because it partly reflects an individuals' propensity to commit crimes. There is no reason to believe that these processes are not at play for individuals convicted for a sex crime. What this suggests is the presence of multiple pathways to sex offender recidivism that are not accounted for by actuarial research, which seriously limits intervention and prevention. Paradoxically, this research was never integrated in the development of risk assessment methods to predict criminal, violent, and sexual recidivism. Rather, actuarialists adhered to a strictly atheoretical approach driven by statistical observations to determine key risk factors and subsequently produce, from these observations, risk assessment instruments to predict recidivism. The atheoretical nature of risk assessment has rendered not just a poor understanding of the development of sexual offending, but possibly also inaccurate information about the likelihood of sexual recidivism. For example, static items in actuarial tools give the impression that a person's level of risk for sexual recidivism remains unchanged over the life course. Yet, both the process of aging as well as the length of time since last conviction are intrinsically tied to a reduced likelihood of recidivism. These within-individual processes are not attended to by the risk assessment literature, which instead has focused on between-group differences (e.g., low-, medium-, and high risk groups). Fortunately, as detailed in the next chapter, the last decade of criminological research has begun to address some of these questions.

References

Aegisdóttir, S., White, M. J., Spengler, P. M., Maugherman, A. S., Anderson, L. A., Cook, R. S., et al. (2006). The meta-analysis of clinical judgment project: Fifty-six years of accumulated research on clinical versus statistical prediction. *The Counseling Psychologist, 34*(3), 341–382.

Allen, B. P., & Pflugradt, D. M. (2013). An exploration of the latent constructs of the STATIC-99. *International Journal of Offender Therapy and Comparative Criminology, 58*, 1376–1388.

Amirault, J., & Lussier, P. (2011). Population heterogeneity, state dependence and sexual offender recidivism: The aging process and the lost predictive impact of prior criminal charges over time. *Journal of Criminal Justice, 39*(4), 344–354.

Andrews, D. A. (1989). Recidivism is predictable and can be influenced: Using risk assessments to reduce recidivism. *Forum on Corrections Research, 1*(2), 11–18.

Andrews, D. A., & Bonta, J. (1994). *The psychology of criminal conduct*. Cincinnati, OH: Anderson.

Andrews, D. A., & Bonta, J. (2003). *Prediction of criminal behavior and classification of offenders. The psychology of criminal conduct* (3rd ed.). Ohio: Cincinnati.

Andrews, D. A., Bonta, J., & Wormith, J. S. (2006). The recent past and near future of risk and/or need assessment. *Crime & Delinquency, 52*(1), 7–27.

Barbaree, H. E., & Blanchard, R. (2008). Sexual deviancy over the lifespan. In D. R. Laws & W. T. O'Donohue (Eds.), *Sexual deviance: Theory, assessment, and treatment* (pp. 37–60). New York: Guilford Press.

Barbaree, H. E., Blanchard, R., & Langton, C. M. (2003). The development of sexual aggression through the life span. *Annals of the New York Academy of Sciences, 989*(1), 59–71.

Barbaree, H. E., Langton, C. M., & Blanchard, R. (2007). Predicting recidivism in sex offenders using the VRAG and SORAG: The contribution of age-at-release. *International Journal of Forensic Mental Health, 6*(1), 29–46.

Barker, J. (2009). A typical female offender. In J. Barker (Ed.), *Women and the criminal justice system: A Canadian perspective* (pp. 63–87). Toronto, Canada: Emond Montgomery.

Beech, A., Friendship, C., Erikson, M., & Hanson, R. K. (2002). The relationship between static and dynamic risk factors and reconviction in a sample of UK child abusers. *Sexual Abuse, 14*(2), 155–167.

Beech, A. R., Fisher, D. D., & Thornton, D. (2003). Risk assessment of sex offenders. *Professional Psychology: Research and Practice, 34*(4), 339–352.

Beech, A. R., & Ward, T. (2004). The integration of etiology and risk in sexual offenders: A theoretical framework. *Aggression and Violent Behavior, 10*(1), 31–63.

Blanchette, K., & Brown, S. L. (2006). *The assessment and treatment of women offenders: An integrated perspective*. Chichester, UK: John Wiley.

Blumstein, A., Cohen, J., & Farrington, D. P. (1988). Criminal career research: Its value for criminology. *Criminology, 26*(1), 1–35.

Blumstein, A., Cohen, J., Roth, J. A., & Visher, C. A. (1986). *Criminal careers and career criminals*. Washington, DC: National Academy Press.

Bonta, J. (2002). Offender risk assessment: Guidelines for selection and use. *Criminal Justice and Behavior, 29*(4), 355–379.

Bonta, J., Bourgon, G., Jesseman, R., & Yessine, A. K. (2005). *Public safety and emergency preparedness Canada.* (Presentence Reports in Canada).

Bonta, J., & Motiuk, L. L. (1985). Utilization of an interview-based classification instrument: A study of correctional halfway houses. *Criminal Justice and Behavior, 12*(3), 333–352.

Bremer, J. F. (1992). Serious juvenile sex offenders: Treatment and long-term follow-up. *Psychiatric Annals, 22*(6), 326–332.

Brouillette-Alarie, S., Babchishin, K. M., Hanson, R. K., & Helmus, L. M. (2016). Latent constructs of the Static-99R and Static-2002R: A three-factor solution. *Assessment, 23*(1), 96–111.

Burgess, E. W. (1928). Factors determining success or failure on parole, in *The workings of the indeterminate sentence law and the parole system in Illinois* (pp. 221–234).

Bushway, S. D., Nieuwbeerta, P., & Blokland, A. (2011). The predictive value of criminal background checks: do age and criminal history affect time to redemption? *Criminology, 49*(1), 27–60.

Caldwell, M. F. (2010). Study characteristics and recidivism base rates in juvenile sex offender recidivism. *International Journal of Offender Therapy and Comparative Criminology, 54*(2), 197–212.

Caudy, M. S., Durso, J. M., & Taxman, F. S. (2013). How well do dynamic needs predict recidivism? Implications for risk assessment and risk reduction. *Journal of Criminal Justice, 41*(6), 458–466.

Coffee, J. C. (1975). The future of sentencing reform: Emerging legal issues in the individualization of justice. *Michigan Law Review, 73*(8), 1361–1462.

Cortoni, F., Hanson, R. K., & Coache, M. È. (2010). The recidivism rates of female sexual offenders are low: A meta-analysis. *Sexual Abuse, 22*(4), 387–401.

Côté, G. (2001). Les instruments d'évaluation du risque de comportements violents: mise en perspective critique. *Criminologie, 34*(1), 31–45.

DeLisi, M. (2001). Extreme career criminals. *American Journal of Criminal Justice, 25*(2), 239–252.

Dempster, R. J., & Hart, S. D. (2002). The relative utility of fixed and variable risk factors in discriminating sexual recidivists and non-recidivists. *Sexual Abuse: A Journal of Research and Treatment, 14*(2), 121–138.

Doren, D. M. (1998). Recidivism base rates, predictions of sex offender recidivism, and the sexual predator commitment laws. *Behavioral Sciences & the Law, 16*(1), 97–114.

Doren, D. M. (2004). Toward a multidimensional model for sexual recidivism risk. *Journal of Interpersonal Violence, 19*(8), 835–856.

Douglas, K. S., & Skeem, J. L. (2005). Violence risk assessment: getting specific about being dynamic. *Psychology, Public Policy, and Law, 11*(3), 347.

Epperson, D. L., Kaul, J. D., & Hesselton, D. S. (2000). Minnesota sex offender screening tool revised (MnSOST-R): Development, performance, and recommended risk level cut scores. MN Department of Corrections.

Farrington, D. P. (1986). Age and crime. *Crime and Justice, 1986*, 189–250.

Fazel, S., Sjöstedt, G., Långström, N., & Grann, M. (2006). Risk factors for criminal recidivism in older sexual offenders. *Sexual Abuse: A Journal of Research and Treatment, 18*(2), 159–167.

Feeley, M. M., & Simon, J. (1992). The new penology: Notes on the emerging strategy of corrections and its implications. *Criminology, 30*(4), 449–474.

Firestone, P., Bradford, J. M., McCoy, M., Greenberg, D. M., Larose, M. R., & Curry, S. (1999). Prediction of recidivism in incest offenders. *Journal of Interpersonal Violence, 14*(5), 511–531.

Freeze, C. (2004). Sex criminals reoffend 90 per cent of time, study finds. *Globe and Mail.* Retrieved from https://www.theglobeandmail.com/news/national/sex-criminals-reoffend-90-per-cent-of-time-study-finds/article18276236/.

Furby, L., Weinrott, M. R., & Blackshaw, L. (1989). Sex offender recidivism: A review. *Psychological Bulletin, 105*(1), 3–30.

Gebhard, P. H., Gagnon, J. H., Pomeroy, W. B., & Christenson, C. V. (1965). *Sex offenders: An analysis of types.* New York: Harper and Row.

Gendreau, P., Little, T., & Goggin, C. (1996). A meta-analysis of the predictors of adult offender recidivism: What works! *Criminology, 34*(4), 575–608.

Giguère, G., & Lussier, P. (2016). Debunking the psychometric properties of the LS\CMI: An application of item response theory with a risk assessment instrument. *Journal of Criminal Justice, 46*, 207–218.

Glaser, D. (1962). Prediction tables as accounting devices for judges and parole boards. *NPPA Journal, 8*(3), 239–258.

Glueck, S., & Glueck, E. T. (1930). 500 criminal careers. AA Knopf.

Gottfredson, D. M. (1987). Prediction and classification in criminal justice decision making. *Crime and Justice, 9*, 1–20.

Gottfredson, M., & Hirschi, T. (1986). The true value of lambda would appear to be zero: An essay on career criminals, criminal careers, selective incapacitation, cohort studies, and related topics. *Criminology, 24*(2), 213–234.

Gottfredson, M., & Hirschi, T. (1990). *A general theory of crime*. Palo Alto: Stanford University Press.

Gottfredson, S. D., & Jarjoura, G. R. (1996). Race, gender, and guidelines-based decision making. *Journal of Research in Crime and Delinquency, 33*(1), 49–69.

Gottfredson, S. D., & Moriarty, L. J. (2006). Statistical risk assessment: Old problems and new applications. *Crime & Delinquency, 52*(1), 178–200.

Greenberg, D. F. (1985). Age, crime, and social explanation. *The American Journal of Sociology, 1985*, 1–21.

Grove, W. M., & Meehl, P. E. (1996). Comparative efficiency of informal (subjective, impressionistic) and formal (mechanical, algorithmic) prediction procedures: The clinical- statistical controversy. *Psychology, Public Policy, and Law, 2*, 293–323.

Grove, W. M., Zald, D. H., Lebow, B. S., Snitz, B. E., & Nelson, C. (2000). Clinical versus mechanical prediction: A meta-analysis. *Psychological Assessment, 12*(1), 19.

Hagan, M. P., Gust-Brey, K. L., Cho, M. E., & Dow, E. (2001). Eight-year comparative analyses of adolescent rapists, adolescent child molesters, other adolescent delinquents, and the general population. *International Journal of Offender Therapy and Comparative Criminology, 45*(3), 314–324.

Hall, G. C. N. (1988). Criminal behavior as a function of clinical and actuarial variables in a sexual offender population. *Journal of Consulting and Clinical Psychology, 56*(5), 773.

Hannah-Moffat, K., & Maurutto, P. (2003). *Youth risk-need assessment: An overview of issues and practices*. Ottawa: Department of Justice Canada.

Hanson, R., Morton, K. E., & Harris, A. J. R. (2003). Sexual offender recidivism risk. *Annals of the New York Academy of Sciences, 989*(1), 154–166.

Hanson, R. K. (1997). The development of a brief actuarial risk scale for sexual offense recidivism (no 1997). Solicitor General Canada.

Hanson, R. K. (2002). Recidivism and age. *Journal of Interpersonal Violence, 17*, 1046–1062.

Hanson, R. K., Babchishin, K. M., Helmus, L., & Thornton, D. (2013). Quantifying the relative risk of sex offenders: Risk ratios for Static-99R. *Sexual Abuse: A Journal of Research and Treatment, 25*(5), 482–515.

Hanson, R. K., & Bussière, M. T. (1998). Predicting relapse: A meta-analysis of sexual offender recidivism studies. *Journal of Consulting and Clinical Psychology, 66*(2), 348–362.

Hanson, R. K., Scott, H., & Steffy, R. A. (1995). A comparison of child molesters and nonsexual criminals: Risk predictors and long-term recidivism. *Journal of Research in Crime and Delinquency, 32*(3), 325–337.

Hanson, R. K., Steffy, R. A., & Gauthier, R. (1993). Long-term recidivism of child molesters. *Journal of Consulting and Clinical Psychology, 61*(4), 646.

Hanson, R. K., & Thornton, D. (2000). *Static-99: Improving actuarial risk assessments for sex offenders* (Vol. 2). Ottawa, Canada: Solicitor General of Canada.

Harcourt, B. (2007). *Against prediction: Profiling, policing, and punishing in an actuarial age*. Chicago, IL: University of Chicago Press.

Harcourt, B. E. (2011). Surveiller et punir à l'âge actuariel. *Déviance et société, 35*(2), 163–194.

Harris, G. T., & Rice, M. E. (2007). Adjusting actuarial violence risk assessments based on aging or the passage of time. *Criminal Justice and Behavior, 34*(3), 297–313.

Hart, S. D. (2016). Culture and violence risk assessment: The case of Ewert v. Canada. *Journal of Threat Assessment and Management, 3*(2), 76–96.

Hildebrand, M., De Ruiter, C., & De Vogel, V. (2004). Psychopathy and sexual deviance in treated rapists: Association with sexual and nonsexual recidivism. *Sexual Abuse: A Journal of Research and Treatment, 16*(1), 1–24.

Hilton, N. Z., & Simmons, J. L. (2001). The influence of actuarial risk assessment in clinical judgments and tribunal decisions about mentally disordered offenders in maximum security. *Law and Human Behavior, 25*(4), 393.

Hirschi, T., & Gottfredson, M. (1983). Age and the explanation of crime. *American Journal of Sociology, 1983*, 552–584.

Hoffman, P. B. (1994). Twenty years of operational use of a risk prediction instrument: The United States Parole Commission's Salient Factor Score. *Journal of Criminal Justice, 22*(6), 477–494.

Hoge, R. D., Vincent, G. M., & Guy, L. S. (2012). Prediction and risk/needs assessments. In *From juvenile delinquency to adult crime: Criminal careers, justice policy, and prevention* (pp. 150–183).

Kernsmith, P. D., Craun, S. W., & Foster, J. (2009). Public attitudes toward sexual offenders and sex offender registration. *Journal of Child Sexual Abuse, 18*(3), 290–301.

Knight, K., Garner, B. R., Simpson, D. D., Morey, J. T., & Flynn, P. M. (2006). An assessment for criminal thinking. *Crime & Delinquency, 52*(1), 159–177.

Kurlychek, M. C., Brame, R., & Bushway, S. D. (2006). Scarlet letters and recidivism: does an old criminal record predict future offending? *Criminology & Public Policy, 5*(3), 483–504.

Langan, P. A., & Levin, D. J. (2002). Recidivism of prisoners released in 1994. *Federal Sentencing Reporter, 15*(1), 58–65.

Langan, P. A., Schmitt, E. L., & Durose, M. R. (2003). *Recidivism of sex offenders released from prison in 1994*. Washington, DC: Bureau of Justice Statistics.

Langevin, R., Curnoe, S., Fedoroff, P., Bennett, R., Langevin, M., Peever, C., et al. (2004). Lifetime sex offender recidivism: A 25-year follow-up study. *Canadian Journal of Criminology and Criminal Justice, 46*(5), 531–552.

Långström, N., & Grann, M. (2000). Risk for criminal recidivism among young sex offenders. *Journal of Interpersonal Violence, 15*(8), 855–871.

Laub, J. H., & Sampson, R. J. (2003). *Shared beginnings, divergent lives: Delinquent boys to age 70*. Cambridge, MA: Harvard University Press.

Lewis, M. (2003). *Moneyball: The art of winning an unfair game*. New York: WW Norton & Company.

Loeber, R., & LeBlanc, M. (1990). Toward a developmental criminology. *Crime and Justice: A Review of Research, 12*, 375–473.

Lussier, P. (2005). The criminal activity of sexual offenders in adulthood: Revisiting the specialization debate. *Sexual Abuse: A Journal of Research and Treatment, 17*(3), 269–292.

Lussier, P., & Cortoni, F. (2008). The development of antisocial behavior and sexual aggression: Theoretical, empirical and clinical implications. In B. K. Schwartz (Ed.), *The sex offender: Offender evaluation and program strategies* (Vol. IV). Princeton: Civic Research Institute.

Lussier, P., & Davies, G. (2011). A person-oriented perspective on sexual offenders, offending trajectories, and risk of recidivism: A new challenge for policymakers, risk assessors, and actuarial prediction? *Psychology, Public Policy, and Law, 17*, 530–561.

Lussier, P., & Davies, G. (2015). Offending trajectory and residual offending of adult sex offenders. In A. A. J. Blokland & P. Lussier (Eds.), *Sex offenders: A criminal career approach* (pp. 289–320). Oxford, UK: Wiley.

Lussier, P., Deslauriers-Varin, N., Collin-Santerre, J., & Bélanger, R. (2019). Using decision tree algorithms to screen individuals at risk of entry into sexual recidivism. *Journal of Criminal Justice, 63*, 12–24.

Lussier, P., & Healey, J. (2009). Rediscovering Quetelet, again: The aging offender and the prediction of reoffending in a sample of adult sex offenders. *Justice Quarterly, 26*(4), 827–856.

Lussier, P., & Mathesius, J. (2012). Criminal achievement, criminal career initiation, and detection avoidance: The onset of successful sex offending. *Journal of Crime and Justice, 35*(3), 376–394.

Lussier, P., Tzoumakis, S., Cale, J., & Amirault, J. (2010). Criminal trajectories of adult sex offenders and the age effect: Examining the dynamic aspect of offending in adulthood. *International Criminal Justice Review, 20*(2), 147–168.

McCann, K., & Lussier, P. (2008). A meta-analysis of the predictors of sexual recidivism in juvenile offenders. *Youth Violence and Juvenile Justice, 6*, 363–385.

McCuish, E., Lussier, P., & Rocque, M. (2020). Maturation beyond Age: Interrelationships among Psychosocial, Adult Role, and Identity Maturation and their Implications for Desistance from Crime. *Journal of Youth and Adolescence, 49*(2), 479–493.

Meehl, P. (1954). *Clinical versus statistical prediction: A theoretical analysis and a review of the evidence.* Minneapolis: University of Minnesota Press.

Moffitt, T. E. (1993). Adolescence-limited and life-course-persistent antisocial behavior: A developmental taxonomy. *Psychological Review, 100*(4), 674–701.

Monahan, J. (1981). *Predicting violent behavior: An assessment of clinical techniques.* Beverly Hills, CA: Sage Publications.

Monahan, J., & Steadman, H. J. (1994). Toward a rejuvenation of risk assessment research. In *Violence and mental disorder: Developments in risk assessment* (pp. 1–17).

Monahan, J., & Steadman, H. J. (1996). Toward a rejuvenation of risk assessment research. In J. Monahan & H. J. Steadman (Eds.), *Violence and mental disorder: Developments in risk assessment* (pp. 1–17). Chicago: University of Chicago Press.

Morgan, R. D., Kroner, D. G., Mills, J. F., Serna, C., & McDonald, B. (2013). Dynamic risk assessment: A validation study. *Journal of Criminal Justice, 41*(2), 115–124.

Morselli, C., & Tremblay, P. (2004). Criminal achievement, offender networks and the benefits of low self-control. *Criminology, 42*(3), 773–804.

Nagin, D., & Paternoster, R. (2000). Population heterogeneity and state dependence: State of the evidence and directions for future research. *Journal of Quantitative Criminology, 16*(2), 117–144.

Nagin, D. S., & Paternoster, R. (1991). On the relationship of past to future participation in delinquency. *Criminology, 29*(2), 163–189.

Nagin, D. S., Farrington, D. P., & Moffitt, T. E. (1995). Life-course trajectories of different types of offenders. *Criminology, 33*(1), 111–139.

Nakamura, K., & Blumstein, A. (2015). Potential for redemption for sex offenders. In A. A. J. Blokland & P. Lussier (Eds.), *Sex offenders: A criminal career approach.* Oxford, UK: Wiley.

Nuffield, J. (1982). *Parole decision-making in Canada: Research towards decision guidelines.* Ottawa, Canada: Communication Division, Solicitor General of Canada.

Petrunik, M. (2003). The hare and the tortoise: Dangerousness and sex offender policy in the United States and Canada. *Canadian Journal of Criminology and Criminal Justice, 45*(1), 43–72.

Petrunik, M. G. (2002). Managing unacceptable risk: Sex offenders, community response, and social policy in the United States and Canada. *International Journal of Offender Therapy and Comparative Criminology, 46*(4), 483–511.

Piquero, A. R., Farrington, D. P., & Blumstein, A. (2003). The criminal career paradigm. *Crime and Justice, 30*, 359–506.

Prentky, R. A., Knight, R. A., & Lee, A. F. (1997). Risk factors associated with recidivism among extrafamilial child molesters. *Journal of Consulting and Clinical Psychology, 65*(1), 141–149.

Prentky, R. A., & Lee, A. F. (2007). Effect of age-at-release on long term sexual re-offense rates in civilly committed sexual offenders. *Sexual Abuse: A Journal of Research and Treatment, 19*(1), 43–59.

Prentky, R. A., Lee, A. F., Knight, R. A., & Cerce, D. (1997). Recidivism rates among child molesters and rapists: A methodological analysis. *Law and Human Behavior, 21*(6), 635–659.

Proulx, J., Pellerin, B., Paradis, Y., McKibben, A., Aubut, J., & Ouimet, M. (1997). Static and dynamic predictors of recidivism in sexual aggressor. *Sexual Abuse: A Journal of Research and Treatment, 9*(1), 7–27.

Quetelet, A. J. (1836). *Sur l'homme et le développement des facultés*. Brussels: Hauman.

Quinsey, V. L. (1984). Sexual aggression: Studies of offenders against women. In D. Weisstub (Ed.), *Law and mental health: International perspectives* (pp. 84–121). New York: Pergamon.

Quinsey, V. L., Harris, G. T., Rice, M. E., & Cormier, C. A. (1998a). *Violent offenders: Appraising and managing risk*. Washington DC: APA.

Quinsey, V. L., Harris, G. T., Rice, M. E., & Cormier, C. A. (1998b). Actuarial prediction of violence. In *Violent offenders: Appraising and managing risk* (pp. 141–169). Washington, DC: American Psychological Association.

Quinsey, V. L., Rice, M. E., & Harris, G. T. (1995). Actuarial prediction of sexual recidivism. *Journal of Interpersonal Violence, 10*(1), 85–105.

Radzinowicz, L. (1957). *Sexual offenses: A report of the Cambridge Department of Criminal Justice*. London: MacMillan.

Raynor, P., Kynch, J., Roberts, C., & Merrington, S. (2000). *Risk and need assessment in probation services: An evaluation*. London: Home Office.

Rice, M., & Harris, G. (2006). What population and what question? *Canadian Journal of Criminology and Criminal Justice, 48*(1), 95–101.

Rice, M. E., & Harris, G. T. (1997). Cross-validation and extension of the violence risk appraisal guide for child molesters and rapists. *Law and Human Behavior, 21*(2), 231–241.

Rice, M. E., Harris, G. T., & Quinsey, V. L. (1990). A follow-up of rapists assessed in a maximum-security psychiatric facility. *Journal of Interpersonal Violence, 5*(4), 435–448.

Rice, M. E., Quinsey, V. L., & Harris, G. T. (1991). Sexual recidivism among child molesters released from a maximum-security psychiatric institution. *Journal of Consulting and Clinical Psychology, 59*(3), 381.

Sample, L. L., & Bray, T. M. (2003). Are sex offenders dangerous? *Criminology & Public Policy, 3*(1), 59–82.

Sampson, R. J., & Laub, J. H. (1997). A life-course theory of cumulative disadvantage and the stability of delinquency. *Developmental Theories of Crime and Delinquency, 7*, 133–161.

Sampson, R. J., & Laub, J. H. (2005). A life-course view of the development of crime. *The Annals of the American Academy of Political and Social Science, 602*(1), 12–45.

Silver, E., Smith, W. R., & Banks, S. (2000). Constructing actuarial devices for predicting recidivism: A comparison of methods. *Criminal Justice and Behavior, 27*(6), 733–764.

Simon, J. (1998). Managing the monstrous: Sex offenders and the new penology. *Psychology, Public Policy, and Law, 4*(1-2), 452.

Smallbone, S. W., & Wortley, R. K. (2004). Onset, persistence, and versatility of offending among adult males convicted of sexual offenses against children. *Sexual Abuse: A Journal of Research and Treatment, 16*(4), 285–298.

Soothill, K. (2010). Sex offender recidivism. *Crime and Justice, 39*(1), 145–211.

Soothill, K. L., & Gibbens, T. C. (1978). Recidivism of sexual offenders: A re-appraisal. *British Journal of Criminology, 18*(3), 267–276.

Steadman, H. J., Silver, E., Monahan, J., Appelbaum, P. S., Clark Robbins, P., Mulvey, E. P., et al. (2000). A classification tree approach to the development of actuarial violence risk assessment tools. *Law and Human Behavior, 24*(1), 83.

Thornberry, T. P. (1997). *Developmental theories of crime and delinquency*. New Brunswick, NJ: Transaction Publishers.

Thornton, D. (2006). Age and sexual recidivism: A variable connection. *Sexual Abuse: A Journal of Research and Treatment, 18*(2), 123–135.

Thornton, D., Mann, R., Webster, S., Blud, L., Travers, R., Friendship, C., et al. (2003). Distinguishing and combining risks for sexual and violent recidivism. *Annals of the New York Academy of Sciences, 989*, 225–235.

Tittle, C. R. (1988). Two empirical regularities (maybe) in search of an explanation: Commentary on the age/crime debate. *Criminology, 26*(1), 75–85.

Tonry, M. (1987). Prediction and classification: Legal and ethical issues. *Crime and Justice, 9*, 367–413.

Webster, C., Gartner, R., & Doob, A. (2006). Results by design: The artefactual construction of high recidivism rates for sex offenders. *Canadian Journal of Criminology and Criminal Justice, 48*(1), 79–93.

West, D. J., & Farrington, D. P. (1977). *The delinquent way of life: Third report of the Cambridge study in delinquent development.* Portsmouth: Heinemann Educational Books.

Wollert, R. (2006). Low base rates limit expert certainty when current actuarials are used to identify sexually violent predators: An application of Bayes's theorem. *Psychology, Public Policy, and Law, 12*(1), 56–85.

Wollert, R., Cramer, E., Waggoner, J., Skelton, A., & Vess, J. (2010). Recent research (N = 9,305) underscores the importance of using age-stratified actuarial tables in sex offender risk assessments. *Sexual Abuse: A Journal of Research and Treatment, 22*(4), 471–490.

Chapter 8
The Lapse and Relapse of Correctional-Based Sex Offender Treatment and Intervention

Introduction

Unlike labels such as "depression," "schizophrenia," and "substance abuse," the legal label "sex offender" for those convicted of a sex crime carries very little clinical significance (e.g., Saleh, Grudzinskas, & Malin, 2015) in terms of a clear intervention or treatment strategy connected to the origins of the sex crime. Yet, from a criminal justice perspective, it is somewhat agreed upon that during the course of their sentence most if not all individuals who have been convicted for a sex crime need to undergo some form of "sex offender" therapy. In Canada, this has been formalized through the adoption of Sex Offender Treatment Program (SOTP) policies and interventions. Such a paradox has and continues to characterize the policy landscape surrounding treatment for individuals who commit sex offenses. The psychological-based treatment of individuals who have been convicted for a sex crime has long been part of the criminal justice system's response to the problem of sex offending, or more specifically, sexual reoffending. Sex offender laws as early as the postwar period espoused the role and importance of psychological intervention with individuals who had committed a sex crime. Early on it was suggested, but not scientifically demonstrated, that individuals convicted for a sex crime did not respond well to traditional criminal justice measures, most notably incarceration. The rationale for this assumption was that because of their underlying mental illness responsible for their offending behavior, sentencing principles such as deterrence and just deserts did not apply to this category of mentally ill offenders. The more fundamental issue, however, is that incarceration has no rehabilitation impact, irrespective of the type of crime a person has been convicted for (e.g., Gendreau, Cullen, & Goggin, 1999). Therefore, psychological-based interventions were seen as preferable and more likely to successfully rehabilitate these individuals in ways that incarceration could not. Psychological profile analysis and the specific aspects of the sexual criminal behavior of these individuals lead to the emergence of specialized therapeutic models. The nature, principles, and objectives of specialized

© Springer Nature Switzerland AG 2021
P. Lussier et al., *Understanding Sexual Offending*,
https://doi.org/10.1007/978-3-030-53301-4_8

therapeutic models, or "sex offender" therapy, have changed considerably since their inception.

Contrary to what many believe or want to believe, the evolution of specialized therapeutic models to treat sexual offending has not been propelled by scientific advancements with respect to the understanding of the origins and the development of sexual offending. In fact, the evolution of sex offender-based therapy, guiding principles, objectives, and methods have by far outpaced the development of scientific knowledge on the causes of sex offending. We posit that the evolution of psychological-based interventions for sex offenders has been in large part influenced by a combination of factors, including evolving sociopolitical and legal contexts, the rise of predominant social movements, the rise and fall of popular yet not necessarily evidence-based psychological approaches to understanding human behavior, and to a dramatically lesser extent, scientific observations about perpetrators of sexual offenses. The clinical-medical model, the legal-feminist model, the community risk protection model, and more recently, the emerging social justice model, all provide different guiding principles that have been proposed and implemented in sex offender treatment settings over the years. Despite these changes over time, research has continued to raise fundamental questions about the efficacy of sex offender treatment, questions that to this day are either minimized, overlooked, or simply ignored. In effect, the dominant treatment and intervention strategies in a given era often mimicked the social movement of the time. As such, up to a certain point, treatment strategies have been targeting the conception of sex offenders in the minds of the general public, politicians, policymakers, practitioners, and even some researchers. This has led to wide swings in approaches to treatment. How could the focus of therapy move, within a matter of decades, from a focus on mental health to a focus on deviant sexual preferences, to another focus where individuals lack control over their sexual urges. We assert that varied treatment strategies and the changing focus of sex offender treatment have been fleeting because of the lack of rigorous scientific evidence regarding the cause(s) of sexual offending. The trial and error approach to sex offender treatment is not based on solid theoretical and empirical grounds.

To set the background for this chapter, we suggest that since its inception, sex offender treatment was defective in practice, required major transformations from the start, and subsequently experienced substantial changes over the years. However, these changes did little to alter fundamental problems with treatment strategies. It evolved in a tumultuous context characterized by much uncertainty by some, unbridled confidence by others, and vehement debate about the root causes of the behavior, where therapy was offered to individuals who varied greatly in terms of their motivation to change, and in a prison context where offenders may feel pressured and obligated to take part in a SOTP. As such, many fundamental unanswered questions surround the practice of sex offender therapy to this day. Perhaps the most basic question that remains largely unanswered is whether all convicted sex offenders are in fact even in need of treatment. For example, is sex offender treatment a necessary path to ensure that sexual reoffending does not occur? Is it possible for a single program to address the treatment needs of such a heterogeneous population?

In the relative absence of evidence-based information about the origin and the development of sexual offending, how can effective guiding treatment principles and objectives be developed and implemented? Below we begin by providing a brief overview of the evolution of sex offender treatment from early behavioral approaches to contemporary approaches.

The chapter focuses on the North American experience with relapse prevention principles and its implication for risk management of individuals convicted for a sex crime. More specifically, the chapter examines the complex issue of the impact of contemporary sex offender treatment, the underlying ideological battles characterizing this issue, and the challenges associated with understanding and measuring the impact of therapy on offenders. To highlight these issues and the evolution from therapeutic to risk-based approaches, this chapter also discusses a Canadian community-based risk management initiative for high-risk sex offenders returning to the community after their sentence. The findings from a quasi-experimental evaluative study of this community risk management initiative highlight the issues and challenges for convicted offenders and criminal justice practitioners assigned to their supervision. This chapter also traces the origins and philosophic principles of sex offending treatment through to the more contemporary, cognitive-based approach. The complex issue of whether psychological-based sex offender therapy is effective remains open for debate.

Since the 1990s, sex offender therapy has been predominantly characterized by a cognitive-behavioral approach or cognitive-behavioral therapy (CBT). A survey of more than 1700 sex offender treatment programs in North America conducted in the early 1990s showed that more than 88% of these programs included a modality focusing on relapse prevention principles that typify CBT (Freeman-Longo, Bird, Stevenson, & Fiske, 1995). The same survey showed that only 22% of these programs included an aversive modality aimed at modifying deviant sexual interests. How can we explain this widespread adoption of relapse prevention principles to prevent sexual reoffending? This approach marked a significant turning point in sex offender therapy because of the focus of the intervention on risk and the prevention of sexual recidivism. Sex offender therapy in this context was framed around the importance of the assessment and intervention on the offender's thoughts, emotions, attitudes, beliefs, and behaviors around the time of the sex offense. Understanding the immediate context of the offender in the months, weeks, days, and even hours leading up to the sex offense became paramount to this form of therapeutic intervention. This approach focused on specific sexual crimes and the risk factors for perpetrating them. The main idea behind this approach was that these perpetrators have thought patterns that encourage, facilitate, justify, and/or predispose them to commit a sexual crime. Therefore, the modification of these thought and behavioral patterns became a central aspect of sex offender therapy. Furthermore, this approach also recognized that certain environmental factors and cues can function to disrupt these individuals' cognitive-behavioral schemas in such a way as to increase the risk of sexual offending. Knowledge of these "risky situations" and appropriate actions to prevent them became guiding principles for this form of therapeutic intervention (i.e., relapse prevention).

The cognitive-behavioral approach is not concerned with the origin and the development of sex offending over the course of someone's life, but rather, on making sure that a person does not sexually reoffend. In some ways, this approach mirrored the nature of risk assessment; individuals always have some probability of sexual recidivism and therefore the focus is on ensuring that this probability does not manifest. In this chapter we trace the journey of rehabilitation in criminal justice for individuals who have committed sex offenses to understand how we have arrived at the contemporary context described above.

Sex Offender Treatment

A Prelude to Community Risk Management

The history of the development of sex offender treatment programs is characterized by a series of unpredictable events, significant bifurcations, turning points, and cul-de-sacs. The first sexual psychopathy laws emerged in the context of what legal and criminology scholars have described as the rise of the rehabilitation ideal (e.g., Allen, 1959; Sutherland, 1950). This movement can be traced back to, among others, the writings of the eighteenth Century English philosopher Jeremy Bentham and his critical views of the criminal justice system of his time. The concept of rehabilitation is based on the notion that offenders eventually will not reoffend because they do not want or need to, not because of an underlying fear of being punished again (i.e., deterrence). The prominence of rehabilitation ideals in the criminal justice system in the 1930s and 1940s favored the emergence of some of the first psychological-based interventions in correctional settings for individuals convicted for a sex crime. These individuals included those who had engaged in homosexual acts, exposed their genitals to strangers, or had sexual contact with a child. In other words, this group included a variety of individuals responsible for different deviant sexual acts. Thus, at the time the perceived proper response to individuals having perpetrated deviant sexual acts, or "paraphiliacs," as Karpman (1951) stated, did not involve simply confinement and deterrence, but rather psychotherapy. These "paraphiliacs" were described as mentally abnormal because of the rare and atypical crimes they committed, and case studies were briefly outlined in the scientific literature by practitioners (e.g., Pascoe, 1961). The development of treatment strategies at this time was somewhat tautological: the evidence for the unique treatment needs of perpetrators of sex offenses was drawn from the assumption that perpetrating a sex crime made someone unique.

These case studies firmly established the heterogeneity of this legally defined population in terms of not only their deviant sexual acts, but also their motivations, character, background, and criminal history. Karpman (1951, 1954), which were influenced by the writings of Sigmund Freud, helped spawn the emergence of a psychotherapeutic approach to the treatment of sexual offending. Therefore, these treatment programs were focused on emotional processes and a person's character underlying them (e.g., Kopp, 1962). Sexual offending was perceived as the expression of very specific needs that conventional sexual activities could not satisfy (Cormier & Simons, 1969; Karpman, 1951). Early psychologically based treatment programs were largely framed around group psychotherapy consisting of multiple sessions with groups of 6–10 individuals. These sessions offered individuals, namely men, an opportunity to express their feelings, and often repressed feelings (e.g., fears, anger, anxiety, insecurity, humiliation), into words in a permissive, engaging, and supportive environment in a way that was conducive for other individuals in the group to do the same (e.g., Roth, 1952; Turner, 1961). These programs were clearly focused on rehabilitation, which involved the assessment and identification of the root cause of a person's deviant sexual behavior, often assumed to be buried in childhood trauma.

In this context, the focus therefore was not on the deviant sexual acts themselves, but rather on the underlying psychopathology responsible for them. Turner (1961) described the objective of their sex offender group psychotherapy in an outpatient psychiatric clinic as follows: "In the 4 years that the group has been operating, ten patients have been discharged as relieved of their symptoms and as having sufficient modification of their underlying psychopathology as to be regarded as cured" (emphasis by the author; p. 486). This sort of language has more or less completely vanished nowadays under the concept of risk and the probabilities of sexual recidivism because, even after treatment, offenders are believed to remain "at risk" of sexual recidivism irrespective of the treatment outcome. However, the clash between this medical approach and the legal response to sexual offending emerged almost immediately alongside the introduction of these early psychologically oriented treatment programs. Concerns over the ability to develop an effective therapeutic environment promoting and favoring rehabilitative goals in a prison-based setting constituted a serious limitation raised by many (e.g., Pacht, Halleck, & Ehrmann, 1962). Furthermore, while legal criteria defined the sex offender as a lawbreaker, clinical issues and considerations limited the possibility of treatment for some of these legally defined offenders. For example, concerns were quickly raised over the fact that not all offenders seemed to be amenable to therapy, not to mention that their behavior in therapy could threaten the efficacy of therapy for others in the group. It was apparent that some benefited from group psychotherapy more than others. Exclusion criteria, therefore, were quickly established so that certain offenders did not access sex offender treatment. Criteria such as being older, of lower intelligence, homosexuality, a repeat offender, or being diagnosed as having a psychopathic personality would eventually exclude offenders from being able to take part in a sex offender treatment program (e.g., Cabeen & Coleman, 1962).

The practice of psychiatry, sexual psychopathy laws, and hospital-based sex offender therapy quickly came under much scrutiny due in part to a lack of scientific rigor (e.g., Sutherland, 1950; Tappan, 1955). As such, sex offender treatment programs gradually experienced a shift to behavioral-oriented interventions focused on the modification of deviant sexual preferences. While psychotherapy offered a semi-directive, supportive, engaging, and permissive environment, behavioral-oriented treatment program environments could not offer a more contrasting setting. These sex offender treatment programs were highly standardized, individually focused, accompanied by a laboratory apparatus, manuals with strict procedures and instructions, and multiple assessment periods with specific and measurable objectives and procedures to examine the impact of therapy. Influenced by the work of Burrhus Frederic (also known as B.F.) Skinner, behavioral-oriented therapy offered a more objective approach to offender treatment that psychiatrists and psychotherapy could not offer to their critics. Sexual arousal, sexual attractiveness, sexual fantasies, and sexual behavior became key components of sex offender therapy in this context. For example, it was believed that heterosexual fear and anxiety were key contributors to homosexuality and homosexual behaviors. In a laboratory setting, therefore, aversion therapy (e.g., electric shock during the presentation of homosexual pictures) and desensitization procedures (e.g., simultaneously exposing a patient to relaxing music and heterosexual pictures) were some of the methods developed to modify this "deviant sexual preference." The goal of such procedures was to reduce heterosexual anxiety while behavioral training could help to learn adequate heterosexual skills (e.g., Barlow, 1973). Similar procedures were used to address the treatment needs of individuals characterized by other deviant sexual behaviors such as pedophilia, exhibitionism, child molesting behaviors, etc.

McGuire, Carlisle, and Young (1964) were among the first to propose an aversion therapy to modify deviant sexual preferences for individuals with deviant sexual behaviors. Building from such ideas, Maletzky (1980) used a covert sensitization technique which involved simultaneously exposing offenders to an aversive odor (e.g., decaying tissue) with aversive images involving deviant sexual behaviors (e.g., a pedophilic man laying next to a young boy, and next to him was a pile of dog feces; see also, Alford, Webster, & Sanders, 1980; Earls & Castonguay, 1989). These types of procedures evolved over the years and the goal was to reduce attractiveness to deviant sexual fantasies while increasing attractiveness to appropriate sexual fantasies of the time. Other procedures involving multiple sessions, such as orgasmic reconditioning, required offenders to masturbate to ejaculation using sexual fantasies involving adult partners (as instructed) after which they were required to verbalize their deviant sexual fantasies for several minutes after ejaculation (e.g., Johnston, Hudson, & Marshall, 1992). The latter part of the procedure was intended to associate boredom and exhaustion with the targeted deviant sexual fantasies. Many highlighted the complex and often paradoxical impact of behavioral-based methods on deviant sexual arousal patterns in the laboratory setting (e.g., Bancroft, 1971). Furthermore, while evaluative studies showing a positive treatment impact emerged, they were often based only on a single case study (e.g., Laws, 1980; Mees, 1966) or very small samples (Marshall, 1973). In fact, while the laboratory procedures were aimed at modifying a specific deviant sexual behavior, treatment providers were exposed to the fact that some offenders presented with more than one type of deviant sexual behavior (e.g., obscene phone calling and pedophilia) and the treatment of one deviant sexual interest did not always impact another.

The advent of the measurement of sexual arousal using phallometric assessment in laboratory settings provided behavioral therapists with an objective measure of the impact of behavioral therapy. While phallometric assessment was initially used for assessment purposes, it soon became an integral part of behavioral therapy. Related treatment procedures involved repeatedly associating an unpleasant/noxious stimulus with deviant sexual stimuli, with the goal of modifying sexual arousal patterns. An example of this is referred to as an external biofeedback procedure that was implemented in a laboratory setting to modify deviant sexual arousal. The biofeedback procedure occurred in a laboratory setting and was designed to increase the offender's awareness of their physiological response (e.g., erection) to certain stimuli (e.g., a young boy). Over the course of multiple sessions, a person was exposed to deviant and nondeviant images and was informed of their deviant sexual arousal using a light (connected to the plethysmograph), which was signaled back to the offender to make them aware of their sexual arousal and the possibility of punishment (e.g., electric shock). The offender was allowed the opportunity to modify his arousal over a brief period (e.g., 30 s), otherwise an electric shock would be administered to a leg or arm (e.g., Quinsey, Chaplin, & Carrigan, 1980). The uncertainty of punishment was introduced as an additional aversive component of therapy designed to modify offenders' sexual behavior. Others developed a procedure by which offenders were instructed to develop, through conscious effort, their own self-control strategy over their deviant sexual arousal (e.g., Laws, 1980). A series of indicators and measures were also used to examine goal attainment and offenders' behavioral change (e.g., sexual arousal using phallometric assessment, self-reports of deviant sexual fantasies and sexual urges, ratings of sexual attractiveness, collateral information, and observation from a significant other). Although the prevention of sexual recidivism was an inherent part of the ultimate goal of this form of sex offender treatment, it was certainly not the immediate objective of this type of therapy.

In a sociopolitical context characterized by rape law reforms, and the court system shifting from rehabilitation to just desert sentencing principles, the 1970s set the stage for important changes to sex offender treatment programs. Martinson's (1974) famous claim that correctional treatment programs do not work still echoes in 2020. At the same time, feminist scholars stressed the importance of changing how society perceives certain situations and contexts, and most importantly, rape victims (e.g., Brownmiller, 1975). Sexist attitudes, rape myths, and acceptance of interpersonal violence became important ideas about the root causes of rape and sexual assault (e.g., Malamuth, 1988). Researchers in the field of sexual offending eventually conceded that most convicted sex offenders did not have a paraphilia or deviant sexual preferences and those who did were different from a majority of individuals convicted for sexual crimes on many other individual factors (e.g., Malamuth & Check, 1983). Therefore, researchers acknowledged the importance of cognitive factors in deviant sexual arousal (Hall & Hirschman, 1992) but also shifted their attention toward the lack of empathy for victims that characterized many of these offenders, as well as their cognitive distortions or false beliefs with respect to sexuality, women, and children. The influential work of Aaron T. Beck on the cognitive basis of anxiety, depression, and personality disorder significantly contributed to a gradual shift away from behavioral-oriented approaches to treatment and toward cognitive-based assessment and intervention. Beck's work was influential in showing that mentally ill individuals were often characterized by rigid, negative, and distorted thought patterns that formed the basis of their core belief system. In addition, certain distorted thinking patterns were specific to certain types of mental illness. For example, the core beliefs of a person characterized by an antisocial personality disorder (e.g., "life is much like a jungle, only the strongest survive") were strikingly different than those characterized by an avoidant personality disorder (e.g., "if people get to know the true me, they will reject me"). In this context, it became reasonable to ask the following question: could it be that the root cause of sexual offending was found in sex offenders' thinking patterns?

Cognitive therapy became more and more prominent with clinical observations of distorted thinking patterns among individuals who committed sexual crimes. Clinical researchers conducted interviews to document, code, classify, describe, and analyze such distorted beliefs (e.g., Abel et al., 1989; Abel & Rouleau, 1990; Mann & Beech, 2003; Murphy, 1990). Much like their predecessors, cognitivists ran into an important issue: did distorted thinking patterns cause the person to perpetrate a sexual crime or were such thinking patterns and distorted beliefs simply rationalizations and justifications used by offenders confronted about their motivation for committing a sex crime? For example, individuals who have committed sexual offenses against children have been documented reporting thinking some of the following: "many children who are sexually abused do not experience problems as a result of the abuse"; "some children are eager to have sexual experiences with adults"; "sexual experiences with adults help to educate children about their own sexuality." In other words, the challenge is to understand whether such cognitive patterns are a cause or consequence of sexual offending. Further to this, a more practical question also emerges—will focusing cognitive interventions on these distorted thoughts and beliefs result in a significant improvement to sex offender treatment programs? Unfortunately, this issue was never resolved because clinical researchers were mainly conducting their research after, rather than before, the perpetration of a sexual offense. Furthermore, in the absence of clear guidance about the value of one approach compared to another (i.e., cognitive versus behavioral approaches), sex offender treatment programs gradually took the shape of multimodal interventions that included both behavioral and cognitive treatment modalities. The simple rationale was that *potentially* effective treatments should be combined in hopes that one or both of these modalities would have a significant impact. While behavioral-based programs focused on offenders' sexual behavior, the introduction of cognitive-based therapy set the stage for the combination of the two; the emergence of CBT dramatically changed the nature of SOTPs in North America.

Around the early 1990s, there was a certain consensus regarding what therapy or treatment for sex offenders should look like. A large-scale survey of the field conducted by Freeman-Longo et al. (1995) highlighted that the vast majority of SOTPs in North America were characterized by a multimodal cognitive-behavioral approach. According to Marshall, Anderson, and Fernandez (1999), North American treatment programs generally pursued two main objectives. The first objective was centered around intervention aimed to prevent high-risk situations. Although the conceptualization and definitions of "high-risk" situations varied considerably, they were generally understood to be environmental, situational contexts conducive to the perpetration of a sex crime (e.g., Laws, 1989). From one program to another, different methods and techniques were used to help offenders recognize their own high-risk situations. For proponents of this approach, sex offending was thought to be relatively predictable and that offenders could develop the ability to recognize the early warning signs of a high-risk situation. These sex offender treatment programs, therefore, aimed to help offenders not only recognize these warning signs but also develop skills to manage these situations in such a way as to avoid perpetrating a sexual crime. Thus, depending on the offender's deficits and treatment needs, various psychoeducational workshops or modules were offered where offenders could develop these skills. The modules were adapted to the specific needs of the offender that were also considered to be important in the emergence of a "high-risk" situation, such as social competence and life skills, stress and mood management skills, anger management techniques, sexual education, and addressing substance use and abuse. CBT elements of this treatment approach involved rewriting offender scripts; for example, how to change an offender's reaction to an opportunity to perpetrate a sexual offense. There was a general consensus that specific lifestyle changes needed to be made in order for offenders to avoid high-risk situations conducive to a sex crime.

If the first therapeutic objective was aimed at offenders' deficits and difficulties indirectly related to sex offending, the second series of therapeutic objectives and methods were more directly aimed at the specific sexual offending behavior. Typically taking the form of group therapy sessions, these modules aimed to address empathy toward the victim; issues of denial and minimization of a sex offending problem; distorted beliefs and negative attitudes about sex offending, sexuality, women and/or children; deviant sexual interests and preferences; and, relapse prevention. In effect, these modalities involved intervening on the cognitive, emotional, and behavioral aspects of sex offending. While the specific content, duration, tasks, objectives, and expectations varied across SOTPs, there again was a general consensus as to what such a program should look like. It is important to reiterate that these programs were not reflective of scientific advancements at the time regarding the etiology, causes, and the developmental course of sex offending. Rather, consensus surrounding such an approach was rooted in the growing optimism generated by a new intervention philosophy and approach: the relapse prevention model. For proponents of this approach, individuals having perpetrated a sex crime share some features with people fighting addiction. Hence, the underlying assumption "once a sex offender, always a sex offender" was taken to heart; but for dramatic intervention strategies, there would be nothing in the way of a person's inevitable perpetration of a new sexual offense. Thus, this new treatment modality did nothing to dissuade the perception that individuals convicted for a sex crime, without specialized treatment, were on an unalterable path to sexual recidivism. A longer-term consequence of this perception was that the path of sex offender treatment gradually changed from a focus on rehabilitation to risk management. In effect, much like the perspective of addiction, the thinking became: if we cannot cure them, we need to manage the risk they pose and sex offender therapy could become an outlet for risk management.

Once a Sex Offender, Always a Sex Offender: From Rehabilitation to Risk Management

The rehabilitation ideal is based on the premise that specific treatment and interventions will cause individual changes in such a way as to significantly impact a person's *motivation* to perpetrate a sex crime. However, in the 1990s, treatment providers and managers gradually shifted their attention toward risk and risk prevention. The gradual shift was facilitated by the writings of Dr. Alan Marlatt.

Dr. Marlatt developed an innovative therapeutic model, the relapse prevention model (RPM), for individuals fighting addiction (e.g., nicotine, alcohol, drugs, gambling). The model and its guiding principles were later adapted for use with convicted sex offenders by a group of clinical researchers (i.e., Pithers, 1990; Pithers, Marques, Gibat, & Marlatt, 1983). The guiding principles of the RPM are based on the idea that individuals who have been convicted for a sex crime present a clinical picture similar to that of individuals fighting addiction. But one critical question to this day remains unanswered; namely, what in fact is the addiction being dealt with in the sexual offending context? An addiction to sex? An addiction to deviant sex? An addiction to sexual fantasizing? An addiction to sexual offending? Although the fundamental basis for RPM in the substance use context was the notion that drugs were addictive, clinicians responsible for extending the RPM to sexual offending did not seem concerned with first clarifying the presence or nature of a presumed addiction among persons involved in a sex offense. The idea that individuals convicted for a sex crime were battling a sexual addiction was not considered an important hypothesis in the scientific literature up to this point and the scientific evidence supporting such a view was simply lacking. Clinicians did not buy into the idea of convicted sex offenders as being addicted to sex, but they did buy into the RPM approach as a way to help prevent sexual recidivism. Theoretical propositions were then formulated, clarified, and further adapted by Laws and his colleagues (Laws, 1989; Laws, Hudson, & Ward, 2000) into a comprehensive therapeutic approach with descriptive data supporting some of the key components of the model. The therapeutic model offered several comprehensive key components that made it not only attractive to treatment managers and providers, but also therapists and criminal justice practitioners. In fact, the popularity of this therapeutic model was such that, within about 10 years after having been presented to the scientific community, several researchers designated it as representing state-of-the-art treatment for sex offenders (Freeman-Longo & Knopp, 1992; Laws, 1999).

The RPM offered a cognitive-behavioral approach that was based on the premise that individuals convicted for a sex crime are inevitably on a path toward sexual recidivism. This was not necessarily because offenders are addicted to sexual offending per se, but rather because of a series of factors such as lifestyle imbalances, a lack of self-control and self-efficacy, the use of deviant sexual behavior as a coping mechanism, distorted beliefs about sex offending or the victims targeted by this behavior, a lack of guilt and remorseful feelings, as well as the intense gratification and rewards that sexual offending can provide the offender. In other words, the path to sexual recidivism is a highly complex one that bears little resemblance to the popular notion of the sexual predator who is actively on the lookout for their next prey. In fact, the RPM provided many reasonable answers to the puzzling and complex question of "why" people sexually reoffend. The RPM depicted convicted sex offenders as individuals who wanted to avoid causing sexual harm, but because of a confluence of certain factors, felt incapable of doing so without help, assistance, and therapy. This image can be contrasted with another of the time that viewed the sex offender as an out-of-control individual who offered little hope for rehabilitation. This latter perspective was based mainly on clinical observations that certain individuals do not necessarily seek to avoid sexual reoffending or feel remorseful after their sexual offending (Ward & Hudson, 1998). Indeed, certain individuals do seek out sexual offending opportunities and do not feel distressed or guilty in any way about causing sexual harm. As a result of these two contrasting views, the RPM was subjected to various revisions and modifications over the next decade, but the underlying principles and assumptions remained relatively unchallenged. This gradually marked a shift in sex offender treatment from pursuing rehabilitation goals to one characterized by risk management objectives.

The shift away from rehabilitation to risk management of sex offenders in the criminal justice context was facilitated by two key intervention components of the RPM (Laws, 1989, 1999; Pithers et al., 1983; Pithers, Martin, & Cumming, 1989). The first component concerns the therapeutic approach and it provides a three step description of the process leading up to a sexual reoffense. This component is adapted as necessary to the reality of the individual. The three steps are as follows. First, sexual recidivism begins with a high-risk situation, that is, one that threatens the individual's sense of control over their own behavior. This results in interpersonal conflict, negative mood, and situations that generate negative emotions and threaten feelings of control. Individuals who fail to properly cope with a high-risk situation then progress to the second step of the sexual recidivism component. This second step, also called a lapse, suggests that these individuals become overwhelmed by deviant sexual fantasies. This step is based on an important assumption of the RPM; namely that offenders use sexual behavior in order to inappropriately cope with negative feelings and moods. Therefore, this suggests that the lapse leads the individual to experience a sense of failure as well as feelings of remorse and guilt. Third, faced with unbearable feelings of failure after having experienced deviant sexual fantasies, the individual accepts the fact that he/she may not be cured and then refocuses on the positive and gratifying aspects of sex offending (e.g., sexual pleasure, a release of tension), and commits a subsequent sex offense. This third step has been disputed, however, because some offenders who present deviant sexual preferences do not experience such personal distress as a result of their sexual deviance (e.g., Laws et al., 2000). In the subsequent stages of the model, cognitive distortions impact offenders in such a way that they actually begin to plan future sex offenses.

To a certain extent, the RPM is practical and flexible because it requires adapting to the reality of each individual. What are different individuals' triggers? What situations lead different people to experience strong negative emotions such as anger and humiliation? How does an individual typically react and cope with those situations? Do they seek help and talk to someone about it, do they isolate themselves and fantasize, or perhaps they become mean and hostile toward others? Consequently, a key therapeutic challenge becomes, on the one hand, to help individuals in understanding their own "cycle of sexual offending" and, on the other hand, to help them establish and develop skills specifically in order to break this cycle. Clearly, this type of therapy helped offenders to understand some of the connections between daily life events, their behavior and reactions to those events, and how sex offending somehow was connected to these events. At this stage, it is important to point out that studies had yet to empirically demonstrate a connection between experiencing negative life events, having trouble dealing and responding appropriately to these events and perpetrating a sex crime. Descriptive studies in clinical settings had shown that sex offending did not typically occur unexpectedly in the absence of any adversity or triggering experience (e.g., McKibben, Proulx, & Lussier, 2001; Proulx, McKibben, & Lusignan, 1996); there were certainly some correlations between negative life events and sex offending. That said individuals typically do not sexually offend every time they experience anger, hostile thoughts, or sexual arousal. They may also experience various emotional states, even conflicting emotional states, during a period considered a high-risk period. Yet, as we mentioned earlier, upon closer examination of the RPM, a key assumption was that sexual recidivism was somehow inevitable for those being treated as they were trapped in a cycle of sex offending characterized by a series of predictable thoughts, emotions, and behaviors (Lussier, Proulx, & McKibben, 2001; McKibben et al., 2001; Proulx et al., 1996). As shown in Chap. 7, sexual recidivism rates certainly did not support such a view, but this did not stop treatment providers from embracing the components of the RPM. In fact, the RPM was developed even further, based on concerns about the individual's ability to detect and recognize their own progression toward a sexual reoffense upon their return to the community, and their ability to use strategies and skills learned during the course of treatment. These concerns led to the development of the second major component of the RPM.

The second component of the RPM relates to the supervision of convicted offenders in the community (e.g., Cumming & McGrath, 2000; Pithers et al., 1989). This component is based on the notion that sex offender treatment in prison must continue in the community following an offender's release. In other words, the idea that therapy and treatment in prison must be supplemented by subsequent external supervision and monitoring became an extension of the ideology behind the RPM. Ideally, this external supervision includes four key elements. First, the RPM allows certain guidelines to be established for probation and parole officers in order to personalize and adapt supervision and monitoring in the community according to specific "risk factors" that are relevant to each individual. These risk factors, however, do not refer to risk factors established in scientific research on the topic, but rather to those factors that were present at the time of their previous sex offense(s), such as experiencing an interpersonal conflict with a woman, loneliness and feelings of emptiness, financial and professional difficulties causing anger and despair. Indeed, another key assumption that was commonly made by therapists and practitioners was that the process of sexual recidivism will essentially reflect previous sexual offending. Without therapy, therefore, offenders will "relapse" into a sexual reoffense if certain contextual and circumstantial factors reoccurred. The model, therefore, assumes continuity in sexual offending and the process of sex offending over time. The RPM also emphasizes the role and importance of probation and parole officers in identifying community resources that can help stabilize the risk factors specific to different offenders, such as deviant sexual preferences, alcohol and substance use, anger and hostility, and impulsivity. Under this approach, the RPM encourages collaboration and close ties between various stakeholders, criminal justice professionals, and community resources, which includes sharing and exchanging information concerning the individual in question.

The RPM was particularly attractive to treatment providers because it offered a comprehensive intervention model that implemented risk management strategies from prison to community re-entry. The 1990s saw the rapid rise of risk assessment and risk prediction characterized by the emergence of actuarial risk assessment instruments for sexual recidivism. Against the backdrop of systematic changes that occurred in corrections during that time (see Feeley & Simon, 1992), where risk management became a *raison d'être* of correctional assessment and intervention, also known as the new penology, the RPM provided a therapeutic approach that was consistent with such changes in correctional practices and philosophy. The RPM left little room for actual rehabilitation, emphasizing instead supervision and monitoring of risk factors, high-risk situations conducive to a sexual reoffense, and the ongoing work of stabilizing risk factors to prevent sexual recidivism. In some ways, there was more of a focus on monitoring whether an offender attended treatment sessions and reported to their probation officer than there was on measuring rehabilitation. Even the terminology employed by the RPM (i.e., risk factors, sexual recidivism, risk management, and supervision) was consistent with the direction that corrections were heading with the advent of actuarial risk assessment, the identification of high-risk offenders, and risk management of dangerous offenders. Like the assumption that persons with a substance addiction remain at a lifelong risk of relapsing, the RPM model also espoused the idea that persons with a history of sexual offending were, and would continue to be, at risk of sexual reoffending over the life course.

The RPM reinforced the idea to offenders that they should always be on the lookout for high-risk situations to prevent a sexual reoffense. They were taught to never forget that they were, and remain, sex offenders. It seems hard to reconcile such practices with the notion of any kind of rehabilitation. While the ideology of RPM rapidly gained popularity during the 1990s, the empirical evaluation of sex offender programs based on this approach was slow to emerge. Indeed, program evaluation requires time, multiple collaborations and partnerships, data access, and formal and ethical approvals. It also requires the mobilization of substantial personal, professional, financial, and political resources. Therefore, while this approach was gaining popularity across North America, the lack of scientific evidence demonstrating a positive impact on the prevention of sexual recidivism remained concerning. But in the absence of comprehensive and sound alternatives, the RPM persisted as the *sine qua non* of treatment modalities.

The Effectiveness of Sex Offender Treatment Programs

In North America, following the enactment of sexual psychopath laws, the first reports of the impact of sex offender treatment outcomes slowly emerged (e.g., Morrow & Peterson, 1966). The evaluation of these treatment programs generally involved a follow-up period focusing on a cohort of offenders having gone through a program and subsequently were discharged from a prison-hospital or psychiatric hospital. Researchers then measured occurrence of rearrests, reconvictions, and/or reincarcerations following their discharge. These early program evaluation studies did not show differential sexual recidivism rates between individuals who had completed their sex offender treatment program and those who had not participated in such programs (e.g., Davidson, 1984; Dix, 1976; Frisbie, 1969; Meyer & Romero, 1980; Peters & Roether, 1971; Sturgeon & Taylor, 1980). These evaluative studies focused on the sex offender treatment programs of the time, which then were based on psychotherapeutic methods and psychodynamic ideas and concepts. To some, the first set of findings emerging from the evaluative studies of sex offender treatment programs were somewhat reminiscent of Martinson's (1974) now famous conclusions that correctional treatment programs with rehabilitation objectives simply did not work. Therefore, these programs eventually evolved or were replaced by sex offender treatment programs based on cognitive-behavioral concepts, methods, and ideas (Laws & Marshall, 2003; Marshall, 1996; Marshall et al., 1999).

Optimistic Versus Pessimistic Stances

For various reasons, including ideological ones, the impact of sex offender treatment programs became the subject of heated debate within the scientific community. In the context of such heated debates, the wisdom of Marques (1999) was remarkable. She correctly pointed out that, while the scientific evaluation of the impact of sex offender treatment programs remained an unresolved empirical question, most people seemed to have a firm opinion about it. As a result, as Marques further noted, researchers report empirical evidence and draw conclusions based on scientific evidence that is not always welcome by some practitioners and therapists, treatment program managers and providers, as well as some policymakers. Indeed, decisions about how to most effectively respond to sexual offending are not made in a vacuum where science, empirical observations, and knowledge of evidence-based practices are all that factor into such decisions. The public, politicians, policymakers, and special interest groups have a vested interest in how perpetrators are responded to, and too often researchers in the field have been the bearers of unexpected, disappointing, and perhaps unpleasant news. As such, scientific findings have often been simply ignored, even ridiculed by some, and/or minimized in favor of ideological thinking and the status quo. In the early 1990s, two radically opposite positions regarding the impact of sex offender treatment programs would characterize the field of sex offending research. In addition, these two positions are still very much alive to this day.

The first school of thought is optimistic regarding the effect of sex offender treatment programs. This school of thought can be attributed, at least in part, to the influential writings of Dr. Marshall, Jones, Ward, Johnston, and Barbaree (1991). According to them, it was too early to draw firm conclusions regarding the impact of sex offender treatment programs. The science of correctional treatment and intervention with perpetrators of sex crimes was still in its infancy and therefore it was too early to draw any firm conclusions about the absence of a significant treatment impact on sexual recidivism rates. Marshall and his collaborators also highlighted positive findings stemming from the first evaluative studies regarding CBT combined with pharmacological therapy. These programs were therefore seen as promising. Indeed, the early evaluative research on sex offender treatment programs based on a cognitive-behavioral approach presented encouraging findings, particularly with regard to individuals who had perpetrated a sex crime against a child and those who were involved in exhibitionism (Marshall & Barbaree, 1990; Marshall & Pithers, 1994). Their optimism would certainly contribute to the development and proliferation of CBT in North America in spite of the modest findings of these initial evaluative studies.

Marshall and colleagues represented a minority of the scientific community. Several researchers, especially Dr. Vernon Quinsey and colleagues, doubted the conclusions drawn from early evaluative studies suggesting that CBT had a positive impact of sexual recidivism. Their key argument was that, because of the significant and important methodological shortcomings of these program evaluation studies, firm conclusions could not be drawn (e.g., Furby, Weinrott, & Blackshaw, 1989; McConaghy, 1999; Quinsey, Harris, Rice, & Lalumière, 1993). These researchers, who advocated a more pessimistic stance, noted the somewhat complacent tone of the conclusions reached by their colleagues. They also raised the issue that treatment programs were offered on a voluntary basis. As a result, individuals who participated in these treatment programs might have been those who were less likely to sexually reoffend in the first place, regardless of their participation in a cognitive-behavioral sex offender treatment program (e.g., Quinsey et al., 1993). The simple fact that individuals were motivated to attend treatment may have indicated their likelihood of correcting their behavior. Indeed, this type of identity change is a critical aspect of desistance from general offending (Giordano, Cernkovich, & Rudolph, 2002). In addition, Quinsey and others noted that evaluative studies only reported the recidivism rates of individuals who successfully completed therapy, thereby excluding those who had abandoned or had been expelled from the program for various reasons (e.g., inappropriate behavior, poorly motivated to change). This selection bias is certainly far from trivial. Later empirical studies on sexual recidivism showed that individuals who do not complete their sex offender treatment have significantly higher rates of sexual recidivism (Hanson et al., 2002). This then begs the question: How can we speak of an effective treatment program in a context where those most in need either are excluded, choose not to attend, drop out, or are simply expelled from such a program? Finally, researchers pessimistic about the efficacy of existing treatment strategies highlighted that these evaluative studies had been carried out on small samples of individuals, which made it difficult to generalize the possible effect of these sex offender treatment programs for all individuals convicted for a sex crime.

Two possible options were raised to address the complex question of the impact of sex offender treatment programs. The first option was to perform a quantitative meta-analysis (e.g., Wilson & Lipsey, 2001), that is, to combine the empirical results of separate evaluative studies and to analyze them as a whole. Rather than examining the findings of evaluative studies independently, which was a common practice at the time, quantitative meta-analysis combined and analyzed findings across studies in a much more systematic matter. In other words, rather than rely on possible personal biases in the interpretation of the scientific literature on the impact of sex offender treatment programs on sexual recidivism, meta-analysis offered a more objective method. This method is interesting for several reasons. First, it overcomes an inherent problem in several of the evaluative studies of the time, namely the presence of small samples of individuals who took part in a treatment program being assessed. Second, this method is much less subjective in that meta-analysis allows researchers to "quantify" the statistical effect of sex offender treatment programs on rates of sexual recidivism. Third, it also helps to address and to statistically control for some of the methodological shortcomings or variations in treatment programs across studies (e.g., one program lasted 6 months, another 2 years; one program was an outpatient treatment program, another an in-patient, prison-based program; one study looked at post-release recidivism over a 1-year period, but another examined sexual recidivism over a 5-year period). The reality of sex offender treatment programs in practice is that beyond very broad programmatic underpinnings (e.g., the program aims to "treat" sex offenders; it uses a cognitive-behavioral approach in general; and relapse prevention techniques specifically), there are substantial variations in the treatment programs being assessed and who conducts the evaluation. The absence of standardization cannot be emphasized enough. Quantitative meta-analysis addresses this issue at least to some extent. Finally, the meta-analysis makes it possible to statistically determine whether a specific aspect of a treatment program is associated with higher or lower rates of sexual recidivism. In sum, considering the state of knowledge at the time and the heated debates within the scientific community and policy circles, this avenue seemed promising in order to clarify the impact of sex offender treatment.

Following these recommendations, several quantitative meta-analyses were performed (e.g., Alexander, 1999; Hanson et al., 2002; Lösel & Schmucker, 2005; Schmucker & Lösel, 2015). In one of the first quantitative meta-analyses to examine the impact of sex offender treatment, Hall (1995) had two main conclusions. First, not all specialized sex offender treatment programs significantly impacted sexual recidivism. The treatment impact varied according to the therapeutic approach used. Second, individuals who completed a cognitive-behavioral treatment with a relapse prevention component had slightly lower sexual recidivism rates. These results seemed, at first glance, to reiterate the optimistic position of some regarding the value of CBT and the RPM. After all, the meta-analysis was based on the findings of 12 evaluative studies, which included a total 1313 individuals and thus helped address more pessimistic concerns about small sample sizes. While Hall's (1995) observations and conclusions could have been seen as somewhat premature given only 12 studies were included, later studies supported these early findings. Indeed, similar findings were reported in the meta-analysis conducted by Hanson et al. (2002) which was based on observations stemming from 43 evaluative studies, which included more than 9400 individuals. A subsequent meta-analysis by Lösel and Schmucker (2005) that included 69 independent studies and more than 22,181 individuals also reiterated some of Hall's initial conclusions. Results of this newer and larger study showed that sex offender treatment programs were associated with reductions of sexual recidivism rates of 6 percentage points (or a 37% reduction), with cognitive-behavioral treatment programs showing the most substantial impact on sexual recidivism rates.

Despite these encouraging results, researchers remained relatively skeptical. For example, Hanson et al. (2002) were concerned with the weakness of research designs of evaluative studies. The absence of evaluative studies based on rigorous experimental designs limited the conclusions that can be drawn about sex offender treatment, regardless of whether conclusions were positive or negative. The field required experimental study designs that used random assignment to a treatment condition or non-treatment control group to clarify whether findings can be interpreted as a real treatment effect or due to differences between persons that did or did not participate in treatment. In other words, under an experimental study design, participation in a treatment program would not be based on offenders' individual characteristics such as psychopathology/degree of risk for repeat sexual offending, their recognition of being in need of treatment, or wanting to change.

It should be evident that the implementation of such an experimental research design in a correctional setting represents an ethical problem. Namely, can we, for the sake of science, withhold treatment from a convicted offender (i.e., by assigning them to the non-treatment group for research purposes) who wants to take part in a sex offender treatment program? Can we, for the sake of science, offer treatment to someone with little or no inclination to change, instead of another person who appears motivated to change? What about the ramifications to potential future victims by withholding treatment from a person at an extremely high risk of future sex offending? For some who share the view that there is no empirical evidence on the effectiveness of sex offender treatment programs, there is no ethical problem evident. Few, however, agree with this opinion, especially because the findings of meta-analyses appear to suggest at least some sort of a positive treatment effect. Legislative changes in the state of California in the 1980s, however, opened the door for such an experimental study that addressed the ethical issues discussed above, thus allowing researchers to conduct perhaps one of the most important evaluative studies on the effectiveness of a sex offender treatment program.

SOTEP

The California Sex Offender Treatment and Evaluation Project (SOTEP) remains one of the most ambitious evaluative studies concerning the impact of a sex offender treatment program on sexual recidivism (Marques, 1999; Marques, Day, Nelson, Miner, & West, 1991; Marques, Day, Nelson, & West, 1994; Marques, Wiederanders, Day, Nelson, & Van Ommeren, 2005). In the 1980s, legislative changes in the State of California made it mandatory for convicted sex offenders to participate in a sex offender treatment program. As resources available at the time did not allow the state government to meet such a demand, researchers saw an opportunity to set up an experimental research design with random assignment to sex offender treatment. After obtaining the approval of the courts, researchers launched an experimental study in 1985. The random assignment procedure was such that convicted offenders were assigned to a sex offender treatment program at the Atascadero State Hospital or assigned to serve their custodial sentence in one of the state penitentiaries without taking part in this program. This context is not trivial given that members of the treatment program team were directly associated with the development of the relapse prevention model, originally proposed by Dr. Marlatt. In other words, the program in place, based on a cognitive-behavioral approach espousing RPM principles, was reflecting what was becoming, according to many optimistic circles of the time, the state-of-the-art approach to sex offender treatment. The 2-year program was also combined with a 1-year community re-entry program, a key feature of the relapse prevention approach. The SOTEP had all the necessary ingredients to succeed, at least from the understanding of treatment providers of the time.

The first report from the SOTEP gave the scientific community, the therapeutic community, and various policy circles every reason to be optimistic about the impact of this treatment. In 1994, researchers showed that 8% of individuals who had completed the sex offender treatment program had sexually recidivated compared to 20% for those who had abandoned the program and 13% for those who had not participated in the program. These numbers could not be influenced by external factors given that participation in the program was based on random assignment. While these findings were still preliminary, many outsiders were quick to jump to certain conclusions. Despite the cautious conclusions of the researchers, some therapists, treatment managers, and treatment providers saw sufficient scientific evidence to conclude that cognitive-behavioral therapy using relapse prevention principles was effective in preventing sexual recidivism. Finally, it seemed that "science" got it right this time.

Results that followed, however, justified the relatively cautious initial conclusions of the researchers of the SOTEP. Beginning in 1999, researchers presented updates regarding the impact of the sex offender treatment program on sexual recidivism. Some were looking to confirm their beliefs that CBT with relapse prevention principles was in fact state-of-the-art practice. What possibly could have happened between 1994 and 1999? For one, more offenders took part in the treatment program. Furthermore, those who participated in the program in the early days had now been back in the community for longer periods of time. In fact, some of them were no longer even under any form of community supervision. Thus, in the second report presented in 1999, Dr. Marques' team showed that individuals who had completed the program had a sexual recidivism rate of 13%. The problem, however, was that the same sexual recidivism rate was observed for individuals who did not take part in the treatment program. The researchers noted, however, an unforeseen event, as is often the case in research: despite the randomization procedure, individuals randomly assigned to the treatment and non-treatment subgroups were no longer equivalent on certain individual characteristics that may have been important to the perpetration of sexual offenses. In effect, one of the fundamental strengths of an experimental research study was diminished, which somewhat blurred the interpretation of the study findings. The presence of differences between the two groups was unexpected given the randomness with which individuals were assigned to either treatment or control groups. In the 2005 final report, after more than 500 individuals had taken part in the study, researchers on the SOTEP concluded that the treatment program did not have the expected outcome: offenders who had completed the program did not show lower rates of sexual recidivism than those who did not take part in the program. More specifically, 22% of the treated group had sexually recidivated compared to 20% of the untreated group. Marques et al. (2005) questioned the utility of providing treatment to all individuals convicted of sex offenses. Was it possible that for some individuals convicted of sex offenses, treatment is not in fact necessary to prevent them from sexually reoffending? Was it possible that some individuals did not benefit from treatment, at least in terms of the modalities used by the SOTEP?

The SOTEP study findings presented a unique opportunity to inspect, with methodological rigor never before seen in this field, the impact of a "state-of-the-art" treatment program. As such, the societal response to these lackluster and unexpected findings are as important, if not more important, to the understanding of the sex offending problem than the research findings themselves. In fact, the implications of the SOTEP findings are an opportunity to understand what is at stake and what ideological forces often come into play with respect to societal responses to sexual offending and the "sex offender" problem. As one example, the observation that some participants that received treatment, once in the community for substantial periods of time and no longer receiving treatment or supervision, went on to sexually recidivate, could be used as evidence that more intensive interventions were required. This perspective reiterated the lifelong risk posed by this offender group. Based on our experience and our interpretation of policy documents, legislative changes, and scientific research that followed, we highlight the presence of the main reactions to the SOTEP findings.

Reaffirmation of the Rehabilitation Ideology

One of the general reactions to the SOTEP findings was to reaffirm the importance of treatment for sex offenders despite the empirical results that were observed. Some treatment managers and treatment providers were not concerned with the results of a single study, regardless of the methodological rigor behind it. Many minimized the results of this single evaluative study, preferring to refer to the more optimistic conclusions of meta-analyses. This was perhaps a hypocritical stance given the methodological limitations of the SOTEP were not as severe as those of studies included in prior meta-analyses. Nevertheless, many distanced themselves from the RPM and the SOTEP by reaffirming the uniqueness of their own sex offender treatment programs. After all, it was not their own treatment program that was evaluated. Other researchers would even go so far as to question the importance of experimental studies with random assignment in this context (e.g., Marshall & Marshall, 2007), a position that is not common in the scientific community (Seto et al., 2008). Some programs shifted their practices by espousing the principles of correctional intervention brought forward by Andrews, Bonta, and Wormith (2006) and the risk-need-responsivity approach that stressed the need to assess, identify, and intervene on known risk factors for criminal recidivism. Following these ideas, researchers would seek to identify dynamic risk factors for sexual recidivism that could be targeted and changed through sex offender treatment (e.g., Beech & Ward, 2004; Hanson & Harris, 2000, 2001). Finally, others, such as Laws (2003), who had himself significantly facilitated the formalization of the RPM for preventing sexual recidivism a decade earlier, even went so far as to essentially sign the epitaph of the RPM.[1] In this turbulent context, two questions desperately needed attention. First, was there anything to learn from the SOTEP study from a policy standpoint? Second, what were the lessons learned from the cognitive-behavioral approach and the RPM guiding principles?

---

[1] In that regard, Laws (2003, p. 28) observed: "I have been a part of this movement from the beginning when, in 1978, a postgraduate student named Janice Marques gave me a photocopied manuscript by Alan Marlatt which described a treatment called relapse prevention. She suggested that this model just might work with sex offenders. I became infatuated with it as did so many of my colleagues. It seemed an uncommon breakthrough, and perhaps it was. It has served us well but the time has come to move forward."

The Black Box Stance

When a plane crashes, investigators' first task involves locating, recovering, and inspecting the flight recorder, more popularly known as the "black box" (nowadays, these boxes are not black but of a bright orange color). The flight recorder preserves detailed flight information, including conversations of the pilots as well as performance and condition of the aircraft. Virtually all commercial aircraft carry these flight recorders, some even have two, by international civil aviation standards. The purpose of these recording devices is to assist with the investigation of aircraft accidents, crashes, and other incidents. The "black box" is used here as a metaphor to characterize another typical reaction from social scientists following the unexpected discovery of negative/null findings. In such a context, social scientists will ask for the treatment program's "black box" and stress the importance of examining its contents. In terms of sex offender treatment programs, however, often the "black box" does not exist, and when it does, the information recorded is often too limited to provide satisfactory information about the observed findings. Indeed, in a context where a plane safely and successfully lands at its destination, pilots can recount in-person, and in their own words, their flight experience. In this context, there is no need for a black box, nor is there as much interest in non-events and expected findings.

The "black box" metaphor, therefore, is typically raised in science when unexpected findings are observed and reported. In that regard, the "black box" metaphor is a call to conduct additional research to better understand how, why, and under what circumstances a treatment program works or not. However, the call is much more often made in the latter scenario compared to the former. This explains, at least in part, the rapid acceptance of certain therapeutic principles. The search for the "black box" reflects a second series of reactions to the results of the SOTEP study, which can also be described as a realistic perspective or scientific realism (e.g., Pawson & Tilley, 1997). From a realist perspective, researchers will recall that the science of sex offender treatment is still very young and that the empirical findings of a single study does not solve the bigger issue of offender rehabilitation and the impact of sex offender treatment. Indeed, this is a very complex issue that cannot be solved with broad generalizations. Realists emphasize the importance of better understanding what contexts and circumstances certain intervention methods can be effective for rehabilitation purposes (Marques et al., 2005). In particular, researchers will call on others to mobilize forces and investigate the complex issue of opening the sex offender treatment program's "black box" in order to better understand the effect of the various components of the program. In short, how can the specialized treatment program be better adapted to the specific needs of each individual? From this perspective, the aim is not to question the premises of the therapeutic intervention; the focus is instead on the adequacy of the program in addressing specific needs of the individual, taking into account the offender's receptivity for such intervention.

Increased Public Safety and Risk Management

Perhaps the single most important aspect of the fallout from the SOTEP evaluation findings was the reaffirmation of the importance of public safety and community protection. As discussed earlier, the 1990s marked a significant shift in correctional practices toward the identification of the high-risk offender and the reliance on actuarial risk assessment instruments (e.g., Feeley & Simon, 1992). It witnessed the rise of sex offender registries and public notification laws (e.g., Lussier & Mathesius, 2018). The findings from the 1999 and 2005 evaluations of SOTEP stood little chance against the momentum of this movement toward reaffirming the importance of public safety and community protection against the threat of sex offenders returning to the community. In effect, while some researchers sought to take the time to peer into the black box of this project, for others, it was necessary to move on as soon as possible and search for entirely new ways of protecting the public. The results of the SOTEP evaluation fuelled the pessimistic interpretation of the meaning of these findings, resulting in a push toward even more aggressive community risk management. This was true even though the SOTEP evaluation showed that the overall risk of sexual recidivism was low for all individuals from that jurisdiction with a history of prior adjudications for sexual offenses.

It is in this context that English (1998) carried out a survey of various American correctional services. The point of the survey was to get a better idea of the measures and dispositions that were commonly used with individuals convicted for a sex crime after their return to the community. Importantly, this study identified the emergence of new measures aimed to empower the community by providing aggressive means to monitor and supervise these individuals upon release from prison. The results of the survey painted a picture of the emergence of a community risk management model focused on community protection where safety and the needs of victims of sexual abuse and violence were paramount. This "containment model," as suggested by English, revolves around restricting the privacy of individuals who have been convicted of a sex crime and limiting their access to potential victims. The containment model in some ways adopted similar principles as the RPM in that it presumed that individuals incarcerated for committing a sex crime will return to communities despite their constant threat of perpetrating a new sex crime. Also like the RPM, it sought to ensure offenders were not exposed to certain triggers. However, rather than a therapeutic approach to doing so, this approach involved, for example, making the viewing of pornography a violation of a person's conditions for release into the community (English, 1998). Unlike the rehabilitative principles of RPM, this containment strategy emphasized multiagency efforts to monitor virtually all aspects of the lives of these individuals. Part of the basis for this model was an assumption that "many offenders have multiple paraphilias" (English, 1998, p. 223), which was not necessarily an accurate reflection of the literature to this point. Nevertheless, clinical researchers and practitioners in the field of sexual violence and abuse had adopted the RPM with relatively little consideration for how underlying principles of the RPM fit with what was known about the prevalence and nature of sexual recidivism. One of the main RPM principles was that those with a substance addiction remained at a lifelong risk of relapsing. This opened the door for justifying the adoption of this principle within the literature, treatment circles, and public discourse on sexual offending, regardless of whether this principle comported with existing scientific evidence on sexual recidivism.

The absence of a positive impact of sex offender treatment on sexual recidivism meant that participation in such a program was not grounds for perceiving an individual as having a lower risk for sexual recidivism. However, even if this was definitively true, it is perhaps because base rates of sexual recidivism are so low to begin with that it is difficult for treatment strategies to have a meaningful impact on lowering these rates. Despite this fact, the idea of high-risk persistent sex offenders remained strong. As English (1998) pointed out, this view of the high risk and lifelong persistent sex offender is widely accepted among American criminal justice professionals, which explained, at least in part, their support for the implementation of a containment model allowing for long-term community supervision. The containment model is also based on the additional premise that these offenders routinely manipulate situations in such a way as to prepare for their next sex offense. In other words, from this standpoint, individuals convicted for a sex crime are constantly overwhelmed by deviant sexual fantasies that are routinely actualized through the perpetration of a sex crime. All of their actions, therefore, are essentially motivated by the desire to create situations or contexts conducive to acting out their deviant sexual fantasies. While a former non-sex offender may be praised for finding a home and paying rent, the "sex offender" may be looked at with more scrutiny. Why this home, in this neighborhood, next to that park? Obtaining employment is not viewed as evidence of "going straight" but as a cause for concern that individuals convicted of sex crimes may manipulate their employment opportunity into opportunities to identify new victims. English did not elaborate on the origins of these widespread and broad generalizations about convicted sex offenders, but they might take their roots, at least in part, in the RPM and the writings of Pithers (1990). After all, the RPM model suggested that individuals who perpetrate a sex crime shared commonalities with individuals fighting an addiction. While Pithers' (1990) therapeutic model had rehabilitative objectives, its legacy in the historical context of societal changes and correctional policy evolution was one characterized by repression, increased social controls, and risk management.

A Canadian Example of Community Risk Management

The Canadian Legal Context

In Canada in the 1990s, a specific legal disposition was implemented allowing the court to impose supervisory conditions on individuals representing a risk[2] of perpetrating a sex crime. Using a disposition that had long been part of the Criminal Code

---

[2] It remains unclear what constitute a risk.

of Canada (CCC), the government made important amendments by making specific reference to the prevention of sex crimes. In 1995, the federal government introduced Bill C-42, which amended section 810 of the CCC to include sections 810.1 and 810.2. Section 810.1 directly focused on individuals at risk of committing a sex crime against a person 16 years of age and under, while section 810.2 indirectly targeted individuals at risk of committing a sex crime through its focus on individuals who are at risk of committing an offense causing serious personal harm. Section 810.2 has been applied to people at risk of sexual assault, particularly against women. Section 810 of the CCC is not framed as a punitive sanction imposed on someone who has been convicted for a sex crime, but rather as a preventive measure limiting the freedom of individuals considered to be at risk of perpetrating a sex crime. Any individuals exiting prison may be subjected to these orders if there are reasonable grounds to believe that this person could commit a sex crime in the future. Importantly, any citizen can inform the police and initiate proceedings to request that the court impose such a recognizance order on an individual perceived as representing a risk of committing a particular type of crime (e.g., a sexual or violent crime). If a section 810 order is imposed by a judge, it takes effect for a period of 12 months, after which it can be renewed upon a request made before the court. In this context, a judge may impose conditions ordering the person to keep the peace and be of good behavior, but also other conditions such as participating in a treatment program, wearing an electronic monitoring device, keeping away from certain people and/or locations, abstaining from drugs or alcohol, abiding by a curfew, and meeting a probation officer on a regular basis. In the context of sexual crimes concerned by the order, the judge may issue much more specific conditions such as: keeping away from playgrounds and parks, not to come into contact with a specific victim, not to be alone in the presence of a child, not to use the Internet, etc. Failure to comply with the conditions specified in the order is considered a criminal offense punishable under section 811 of the CCC.

How is this provision relevant in the context of sex offender treatment and the rehabilitation of perpetrators of sex crimes? After amendments were made to section 810 of the CCC, this disposition was increasingly used with individuals who had been convicted for a sex crime and were returning to the community at the end of their custodial sentence. It illustrates the growing concerns of the time that additional measures were needed against convicted sex offenders. It reflects the growing perception that custodial sentences would not deter these individuals from sexually reoffending and that these individuals represented a threat to public safety long after completing their sentence. This should not be surprising. The previous dominant paradigm came from RPM principles. The public, practitioners, and government officials were told that sex offenders were at a lifelong risk for relapse similar to those addicted to drugs and alcohol. Very importantly, this same paradigm, under the influence of RPM principles, then failed to establish that treatment programs like those from SOTEP were useful for reducing the likelihood of "relapse." The failure of RPM to establish one of its central premises, that is, that individuals could be successfully treated, effectively left outside viewers with the impression that perpetrators of sex offenses were likely to relapse and that rehabilitation strategies were not going to prevent this reality. In effect, the imposition of a custodial sentence and correctional programming clearly were not perceived to be effective or sufficient in their rehabilitation objectives, at least in some cases. Section 810 of the CCC therefore represented an additional safeguard against potentially dangerous offenders. In short, since 1995, these amendments to the CCC virtually created a new "legal" category of individuals who were at risk of committing a sex offense. This practice, like many other Canadian legal dispositions aimed at individuals who had been convicted for a sex crime, was not the subject of any substantial scientific scrutiny after its enactment. Therefore, many unanswered questions were evident. In particular, who exactly were the people targeted by this legal provision and in what context were these individuals being targeted using this disposition? In addition, the CCC remained particularly vague as to what represented "reasonable" grounds to suspect that an individual would perpetrate a subsequent sexual offense. It was not until over a decade after these amendments were made to the CCC that the first scientific study partially looked into the black box of this new legally defined population at risk for subsequent sexual offending.

In the province of British Columbia in Canada, with the enactment of sections 810.1 and 810.2 of the CCC, the criminal justice system gradually established a process by which "good" candidates for a recognizance order were identified before the expiry of the sentence they were serving (Lussier, Deslauriers-Varin, & Râtel, 2010). Generally speaking, the main candidates targeted were individuals convicted for a sex crime who were about to complete their custodial sentence in a federal penitentiary. In Canada, federal penitentiaries are reserved for those individuals that received a custody sentence of at least 2 years. While there has been very little scientific research on this, some Canadian researchers have shown that adults serving federal custodial sentences for sex offenses are more likely to have been convicted of a serious sex crime (e.g., sexual assault, sexual assault using a weapon or causing bodily harm), crimes involving a greater number of victims, and/or have a significantly more extensive criminal history than those individuals serving provincial sentences where the maximum sentence length is less than 2 years (e.g., Guay, Ouimet, & Proulx, 2004). Therefore, it was among this pool of convicted offenders who were about to complete their custodial sentence that additional criteria were introduced to identify potential candidates for a section 810 order. Part of these additional criteria included: evidence of a risk for sexual recidivism per an actuarial risk assessment tool; evidence of refusal to participate in treatment during the custodial sentence; and, failure to be granted parole or failure to respect their parole conditions. The files of these potential candidates were then forwarded to an advisory committee assembled by the British Columbia Correctional Services department that was tasked with the responsibility of deciding on whether to initiate legal proceedings in connection with section 810 of the CCC.

In British Columbia, probation officers were responsible for following up with individuals who received a section 810 order[3]. In many ways, this population represented a serious challenge for probation services. This group was characterized by multiple criminogenic needs and returned to the community after long periods of incarceration. A qualitative study carried out with criminal justice professionals working with this group highlighted some of the issues and challenges surrounding their community re-entry. Lussier, Dahabieh, Deslauriers-Varin, and Thomson (2010) highlighted that the main concerns and needs of these individuals have in fact little to do with sexual deviance or sexual offending. Rather, probation officers were primarily concerned with these individuals' history of substance use and abuse, the poor quality of their social network, as well as their history of antisocial and criminal behavior. They were also concerned by their many needs in terms of housing, employment and income, therapy and care (mainly addiction and mental health). Probation officers were also concerned by the lack of community-based resources to address these needs and stressed that the legal dispositions of this group created various obstacles for these individuals to even attempt to address their multiple needs.[4] While these examples reflect some of the competing interests of different stakeholders in the community risk management context, ultimately, conflicting decisions are reconciled along the lines of community protection principles in the short term. For example, restricting an individual's movements may provide some community protection from a crime occurring in the short term, but in the end, many of these principles will negatively impact successful community reintegration and rehabilitation prospects—both of which are central to community protection in the long term. To investigate some of these issues, particularly with this new legally defined population characterized by multiple needs, the British Columbia Correctional Services Branch set up a pilot project known as the Coordinated High-Risk Offender Management team (CHROME).

---

[3] Lussier, Dahabieh, et al. (2010) carried out the first empirical study describing this population in British Columbia. Over a period of approximately 2 years, they identified 59 individuals who had been the subject of a section 810 recognizance order in connection with a sex crime. These individuals were all men, poorly educated and mainly single. In adulthood, more than 60% of them were convicted on four or more occasions for a criminal offense. These individuals, for the most part, had serious and extensive criminal careers. They were also particularly old for a group of convicted offenders considered to be at risk of sexual recidivism (in their forties on average). Second, the sample was characterized by an overrepresentation of Indigenous people (Kelly-Scott & Arriagada, 2016; Rugge, 2006) and there is good reason to question the broader effect of these legal practices on the Indigenous people of Canada who are marked by historical and structural inequalities and, more specifically, the consequences of these newly implemented risk management practices on social reintegration opportunities.

[4] For example, an individual who received an 810 order wanted to take part in a drug addiction program, the only one in his region, but could not do so because the program was housed in a building adjacent to a park. Part of this offender's conditions in the community included remaining a certain distance from all parks. Another individual was unable to have his mental health needs addressed because his therapy was scheduled with a female therapist. Participation in this therapy would violate part of his section 810 conditions stipulating that he could not be alone with a woman.

The CHROME Pilot Project and Intensive Community Supervision

In 2006, in order to provide improved services and supervision to individuals subject to section 810 orders, the CHROME program was implemented by British Columbia Correctional Services. The rationale for this program aligns with some of the main principles of the RPM (Laws, 1989; Pithers et al., 1983), especially the second component of RPM that emphasizes community supervision (Cumming & McGrath, 2000). Although the external supervision component of the RPM constituted an interesting framework, in the eyes of policymakers and corrections, one of the drawbacks of the RPM model was that it lacked a comprehensive strategy to mobilize various community resources in a coordinated manner. In addition, contrary to the main principles of the RPM, a dual mandate was necessary. While the RPM placed great emphasis on the supervision and the monitoring of convicted offenders returning to the community, the RPM model did not sufficiently consider transient and contextual factors that could potentially destabilize the individual during community re-entry. Thus, not only was community supervision necessary, but so too was some form of assistance and support during the re-entry period. Therefore, this dual mandate, with somewhat conflicting objectives (e.g., monitoring the offender and identifying violations of court orders while also supporting the person in the community), became part of the CHROME global and collaborative strategy of bringing together professionals from within and outside of the criminal justice system. The CHROME project was, in many ways, another community-based risk management initiative for convicted offenders; one that espoused a multidisciplinary and interagency approach (see also Craissati, 2004; Galloway & Seupersad, 2008; Kemshall, 2008; Wood & Kemshall, 2010). More specifically, the CHROME team included a psychologist, police investigators, probation officers with specialized training in sex offending supervision, social/community workers, and a program coordinator.

CHROME emerged as a pilot project designed to examine ways to improve the community supervision of convicted offenders representing a high risk of sexual recidivism. Through a collaborative and interagency approach, the supervisory team were assigned individuals who had been imposed an 810 order. In accordance with the RPM and certain aspects of the containment approach, the CHROME program aimed to prevent an individual's progression to sexual recidivism by first facilitating the exchange of information between members of the CHROME team about the individual's personal situation. The CHROME team also aimed to help assist these individuals while monitoring their behavior in the community. While these two objectives are not necessarily incompatible (Clear & Latessa, 1993), Canadian studies show that probation officers tend to spend too much time reviewing and ensuring that conditions are met at the expense of other tasks and responsibilities, such as counseling and providing support (Bonta et al., 2010; Bonta, Rugge, Scott, Bourgon, & Yessine, 2008). Social workers were included as part of the CHROME team specifically to fill this gap. In order to neutralize potential risk factors, these social workers were given the mandate to offer their services and support in facilitating community re-entry. This included support in finding a job, securing a stable source of income, helping to open a bank account, finding suitable accommodation, and facilitating transportation to treatment programs and meetings with probation officers. The probation officer was responsible for monitoring risk factors that could precipitate criminal recidivism, including sexual recidivism (e.g., negative emotional states, negative mood, interpersonal conflict, stressful life events, sexual fantasies, access to victims). Although there were a number of similar community-based interagency risk management initiatives operating at the time in other jurisdictions such as the USA (English, 1998; Kemshall, 2008), none of these initiatives had been subjected to a rigorous longitudinal empirical evaluation.

A Quasi-Experimental Evaluative Study

A prospective longitudinal study was set up in British Columbia to assess the impact of the CHROME team as a community protection measure (Lussier & Gress, 2014; Lussier, Gress, Deslauriers-Varin, & Amirault, 2014). To do this, all individuals who had received a section 810 order between January 2003 and February 2009 in the province of British Columbia were selected for this longitudinal study ($n = 269$). This represents on average just over forty new cases annually for the entire province. Generally, the 810 order came into effect upon a person's prison release and offenders were at that point subjected to the conditions of their order. According to these conditions, all individuals were to report and to meet regularly with a British Columbia probation officer for at least a 1-year period. Face-to-face meetings took place on a weekly basis, along with telephone follow-ups and random home checks. In addition, individuals had to remain in the province for the duration of the order. They were required to inform the police and their probation officer if their residential address changed and were required to request permission for trips outside the province. Other conditions could be imposed by the court and these varied from one individual to another (e.g., restricted access to certain locations, restrictions on the use of alcohol, surrendering their passport to authorities, prohibited from possessing firearms and ammunition, random checks on computers and hard drives, etc.).

For ethical reasons, the implementation of an experimental design in the criminal justice system is virtually impossible in Canada. The quasi-experimental approach becomes the most desirable alternative for program evaluation research. This approach includes both a treatment and control group, but group assignment is not random. A quasi-experimental design is considered ethical when there are no obvious reasons to expect differences between the experimental group and the control group before taking part in the program (Hanson et al., 2002; Marshall & Marshall, 2007). It is in this context that the evaluative study of the CHROME project was carried out. In the absence of financial resources to implement the program throughout the province, the program was implemented in two regions. Individuals residing in one of the two recruitment zones were supervised by the CHROME team for the duration of their 810 order, while those whose residence was outside these zones were subjected to ordinary supervision by a probation officer. In total, 46 individuals were monitored by the CHROME team and 223 individuals, also subjected to an 810 order, were included in the control group.

Lessons from the CHROME Pilot Project

The CHROME pilot project and the quasi-experimental study provided a unique opportunity to examine the impact of intensive community supervision on individuals considered to be high-risk offenders. It provided an opportunity to examine the fallout and the consequences of this systematic shift of correctional interventions from rehabilitation toward objectives that were more and more tailored toward a containment model defined by risk assessment, risk prediction, and risk management.

First, the results of the CHROME project outlined the risk of recidivism of the individuals who were the subject of 810 orders specifically to do with sexual crimes. Individuals who are the subject of this peace bond do not constitute a representative group of all individuals who have been convicted for a sex offense. These individuals, on the contrary, present "reasonable grounds" to believe, at least in the eyes of the court, that they were at risk of committing another sex crime. The results of the CHROME project, however, show that in the short term the majority of these individuals followed the conditions of their orders without committing another offense of any type. Moreover, of the 269 individuals followed in the study by Lussier et al. (2014), only 8 (2.97%) were convicted of a new sex offense. A greater percent of the sample (16.3%) were convicted for a nonviolent, nonsexual crime (e.g., theft, drug trafficking). More importantly, the most likely scenario for those who were convicted again was violating the conditions of their 810 order. Such conditions typically included noncriminal behaviors such as drinking alcohol, being in a bar, being in a park, not respecting a curfew, associating with a person who has a criminal record, not requesting permission from a probation officer to travel, etc.

Second, the evaluative study showed mixed results regarding the influence of the CHROME team on criminal recidivism rates. Contrary to what one may expect, the intensive supervision program offered by the CHROME team did not appear to have an effect on criminal and sexual recidivism. Individuals supervised by the CHROME team showed general recidivism rates equivalent to those who were simply supervised as usual by a probation officer. However, researchers reported that individuals who were subjected to intensive supervision by the CHROME team were more likely to breach the conditions of their supervisory order (Lussier & Gress, 2014). One explanation for this is that being under more intensive supervision facilitated the identification of situations where individuals did not respect their conditions; in other words, detection was easier because these people were under more scrutiny than those who were not being supervised by the CHROME team. Indeed, individuals supervised by the CHROME team were regularly in contact with social workers, probation officers, sometimes psychologists, and even police officers, all of whom were routinely checking in on these persons. From a criminal justice system stand-point, however, these violations were perceived as steps toward more serious prob-lems, such as a sexual or violent crime; these violations were the early signs of someone progressing toward sexually reoffending. As others have pointed out, from a risk management and community protection perspective, these results could in fact be interpreted as a positive impact of the CHROME team in preventing progres-sion to a sex crime (see Wood & Kemshall, 2008).[5]

From the criminal justice practitioner's standpoint, there is a constant struggle between, on the one hand, the role of supervising and monitoring the offender and, on the other hand, providing counseling, assistance, and support to that person. When confronted by the non-complying behavior of individuals considered at risk of sexual offending, when other professionals are also part of the supervision of this person labeled a danger to reoffend, and when society could react strongly if there is indeed progression toward sexual recidivism, community protection and public safety likely will be preferred over rehabilitation. The reality is that scientists have failed to provide criminal justice practitioners useful information to guide their pro-fessional judgment in such specific contexts. Is there justification for electing to not punish a person for violating conditions of their release if doing so is in the best interests of longer-term rehabilitation and prevention of sexual offending?

Third, the study findings of the CHROME project also show that certain indi-vidual characteristics are associated with the likelihood of criminal recidivism. More specifically, among this small, new legally defined group of individuals, an even smaller subset of individuals stood out as being obstinate to criminal justice interventions. Indeed, the results show that regardless of the type of supervision (i.e., intensive supervision, regular supervision by a probation officer), those who were young adults with a higher actuarial risk of sexual recidivism, who were less educated, and who were at risk of perpetrating a sexually violent crime, were more likely to be convicted again for any crime while under their supervisory order (Lussier, Deslauriers-Varin, & Râtel, 2010; Lussier & Gress, 2014). These factors indicated the presence of a subgroup of younger adults who were more antisocial and impulsive and less likely to be deterred from committing a crime despite being

---

[5] It is worth noting here that, in similar evaluative studies with other at-risk criminal populations (e.g., drug traffickers), research had shown that intensive supervision is associated with higher rates of non-compliance (e.g., Harris, Gingerich, & Whittaker, 2004; Petersilia & Turner, 1993). In short, the results observed during the CHROME project were not unique nor specific to individuals at risk for a sex crime or even to the CHROME team but seem more directly related to the impact of intensive supervision. Indeed, there is reason to wonder, in this context, whether the intensive supervision did not further ostracize and marginalize these individuals. Even after completing their custody sentence, these individuals were imposed a preventive order with strict conditions under the supervision of various professionals who were in contact with them on a regular basis. These individuals were consistently reminded that they were convicted sex offenders and were at risk to perpetrate another sex crime. To what extent does breaching conditions of these orders reflect actual signs that a person was progressing toward sexual reoffending? Could it also reflect an inability for a person that is somewhat impulsive, poorly educated, and suffering from substance use and mental health problems to consistently follow a swath of rules regulating their behavior, including noncriminal behavior?

subjected to legal dispositions and community supervision. In other words, the intensive supervision combined with the assistance and support offered by the CHROME program did not seem to have had an impact for these individuals.

Fourth, contextual and transient factors helped to understand the community risk management of these individuals. The results of the CHROME study showed that the two contextual factors most strongly associated with criminal recidivism were the presence of a negative social environment as well as the difficulties engaging with the supervision process (Lussier & Gress, 2014). Thus, individuals that recidivated during the supervision process were more likely to present a criminogenic social environment that encourages, promotes, or facilitates antisocial and criminal behavior (Lussier & McCuish, 2016). The presence of this criminogenic social environment could partly explain their lack of engagement with the supervision process. Such individuals were not only often in the presence of antisocial individuals; they were also rarely in the presence of prosocial ones. Accordingly, there was little reason to abstain from criminal behavior to avoid letting down prosocial peers. In fact, code of the street mentalities may have resulted in such offenders being actively encouraged by others to violate conditions. That is to say, for these offenders, violating conditions may have also helped to earn status among peers; at the very least, deciding to abide by conditions may have resulted in ostracization by an antisocial peer group. This implies that supervisory conditions in the absence of a positive social support system may do little to deter young, antisocial, and impulsive men from violating conditions of their supervision.

Despite the recommendations of their probation officer, these individuals may have preferred to reconnect with their peers upon their return to the community. For these individuals, social interactions with their peers are preferable to social isolation in a context where prosocial interactions are very limited. Who wants to go for a coffee with a convicted sex offender? Who wants to hire a convicted sex offender? Who wants to rent a room or an apartment to an individual who is just out of prison in connection with a sex crime conviction? Who wants to associate with a person supervised by a probation officer and regularly checked by police officers? Who wants to give a car ride to a convicted sex offender who has an appointment with their probation officer? Further, who wants to do such things and have others in the community aware of such actions? The desire to help others may be offset by how members of the community may interpret this help. These potentially negative social interactions take on their full meaning in a context of community re-entry following a prison sentence and the issues and challenges of the re-entry and reintegration process (e.g., finding a place to sleep, securing a source of income, etc.). In the absence of familial support (Walker, Kazemian, Lussier, & Na, 2017), these individuals might have turned to individuals who themselves had similar problems with the criminal justice system. It is therefore possible, in this context, that probation officers tightened the supervision of these individuals in particular and, by the same token, detected their noncompliant and criminal behavior. Moreover, a person is more likely to be detected for violating conditions when in the presence of other offenders known to the criminal justice system and also under close supervision and monitoring.

In all, against the backdrop of a risk management philosophy, these studies helped to shed light on the issues and challenges associated with community re-entry and community reintegration. While the CHROME project was about the implementation of a coordinated and multiagency community risk management endeavor, the study findings highlighted the inherent issues that treatment providers have been dealing with since the 1930s. Who should be the target population for this program? What criteria should be used to identify this population? What is the ultimate goal and the associated objectives of this program? How might these goals and objectives interfere with what is known about factors that help promote desistance? Is this program based on evidence-based information about sexual offending, individual change, and crime prevention? Following their release, in what legal, residential, social, work/professional, and familial context are these individuals returning to? Do these contexts represent risky situations and sources of strain or opportunities to help facilitate desistance? Difficulties articulating legal and clinical aspects into a meaningful, scientific-based prevention program has been and continues to be a critical issue for the prevention of sexual offending. The reality is that we do not know much about individuals who have perpetrated sexual offense in terms of their social, familial, and work environment prior to their sexual offending, during their offending, and post release. We do not know much about their routine activities, their human agency, their life choices, their values and beliefs, and their life goals and expectations. The microscope has been so focused on the offender and finding individual-level deficits specific to their sexual functioning that along the way, practitioners and researchers have largely neglected various key components involved in community re-entry and reintegration. Actuarialists have been so focused on establishing accurate recidivism rates, that the context of recidivism and non-recidivism has been vastly overlooked. Before we can speak of risk management and community reintegration, perhaps we should know whether these individuals were integrated in the community in the first place?

Conclusion

Sex offender treatment has gone through major changes in the past 80 years. The unbalanced development and evolution of sex offender treatment reflects the influence of various underlying forces, most of which have little to do with scientific developments surrounding knowledge of the risk and protective factors of sexual offending.

Initially, supported by a rehabilitation movement, psychotherapy-based interventions offered offenders help in understanding the origin of their sex offending. However, scientific evidence had not yet evolved to a point where researchers themselves were certain about the origins of sex offending. Accordingly, this practice may have been overly optimistic. Not only was the scientific understanding of sexual offending rudimentary at this stage, but also, the prison-hospital was a less than ideal therapeutic environment for promoting positive individual change. The evaluative studies that followed did not find much support to further pursue this treatment context. This approach was gradually replaced by behavioral-oriented approaches aimed at changing offenders' sexual preferences and providing them with the social skills necessary to express their sexuality in a prosocial and more conventional manner. Sex offender treatment moved from group therapy sessions to individualized sessions in a laboratory setting. However, all of the associated protocol, standardization, transparency of methods, and clearer objectives did not result in differential sexual recidivism rates for those completing these types of behaviorally oriented treatment programs. The lack of differential sexual recidivism rates for those completing treatment compared to those not taking part were misconstrued as evidence that all sex offenders were untreatable. Already at that time, studies were highlighting that sexual recidivism was relatively rare to begin with. However, the failure of treatment programs to establish a "treatment effect" resulted in misconstruing sexual recidivism as something that could not be avoided as opposed to something that was rare to begin with and thus difficult to reduce even further.

The misconception of the untreatable sex offender led to rapid acceptable of a new approach focused on the prevention of sexual recidivism. This approach, the RPM, was attractive for several reasons. It gave practitioners a shared language and a rationale. It was not reinventing the wheel; it was based on a model established by colleagues in other research areas and adapted for a different type of clientele. It was simple enough for offenders to also understand. It gave treatment providers a model and a pseudo-theory of sexual recidivism. It gave the correctional service system a comprehensive model to structure intervention and risk management from prison admission to the end of a sentence. In the 1990s there was a major shift in North American correctional practices. Gradually, the discourse and measures focusing on treatment and rehabilitation gave way to the primacy of public safety and risk management. New measures and legal dispositions were put in place that had nothing to do with rehabilitating or "transforming" the person, but rather, with controlling them. This approach had public appeal as new policies could be sold as an approach that was getting tough on crime and protecting the public. Some of the guiding principles of RPM fit nicely with this policy shift. While the RPM was presented as a treatment program, some of the core aspects of the model were very much in line with a risk management approach. Therapy and social control became fused under a risk management strategy. The RPM offered a static vision of sex offending as a permanent problem that all offenders must learn to manage on a daily basis for the rest of their lives. No scientific observations supported this viewpoint, but still, the idea was widely embraced. The presence of methodological shortcomings of evaluative studies aimed at determining the impact of sex offender treatment raised doubts about the effectiveness of these state-of-the-art treatment programs despite some promising findings. While the pessimistic stance endorsed increased reliance on a risk management and actuarial approach to risk, the more optimistic stance endorsed a treatment program philosophy that ultimately also led to a risk management strategy.

The narrative for increased public safety and additional community risk management strategies created a context where offenders, irrespective of their risk, were doomed to fail by design. This failure did not, for the most part, involve sex crimes, but rather crimes related to the administration of justice such as breaching conditions of parole or probation orders. Science could not keep up with the speed at which these policy changes occurred. In some ways, even if science showed that this approach was not effective in protecting the public, it would be like shutting the barn door after the horse had already escaped. While researchers were making significant discoveries with respect to risk factors of sexual recidivism, the dynamic aspect of risk of sexual recidivism over time, and the offending trajectories of these individuals over long time periods, these scientific advancements were not readily available at the time these policy changes were made, or were simply at odds with the popular perception of individuals convicted for a sex crime as life course persistent sex offenders. In fact, the clash between science and policy could not be greater than what was introduced by the emergence of research on desistance from crime.

Criminology and criminal justice researchers were more knowledgeable about the dynamic aspect of risk and offending over the life course. These researchers were increasingly concerned about the underlying factors explaining why offenders stop offending at some point during their life course, some earlier than others. These researchers even claimed that the termination of offending at some point during the life course was almost inevitable (e.g., Sampson & Laub, 2003). It was the norm. This image of the desisting offender could not be more at odds with the social construction of the sex offender as a life course persistent offender. Could criminology and criminal justice research on the mechanisms responsible for desistance from crime be theoretically and policy-relevant in the context of sexual offending? Could it be that the risk management approach endorsed and pursued by the criminal justice system unwittingly created structural and social barriers that negatively impacted some of the key factors responsible for desistance for individuals convicted for a sex crime?

References

Abel, G. G., Gore, D. K., Holland, C. L., Camps, N., Becker, J. V., & Rathner, J. (1989). The measurment of the cognitive distortions of child molesters. *Annals of Sex Research, 2*(2), 135–152.

Abel, G. G., & Rouleau, J. L. (1990). The nature and extent of sexual assault. In *Handbook of sexual assault* (pp. 9–21). Boston, MA: Springer.

Alexander, M. A. (1999). Sexual offender treatment efficacy revisited. *Sexual Abuse, 11*(2), 101–116.

Alford, G. S., Webster, J. S., & Sanders, S. H. (1980). Covert aversion of two interrelated deviant sexual practices: Obscence phone calling and exhibitionism. A single case analysis. *Behavior Therapy, 11*(1), 15–25.

Allen, F. A. (1959). Criminal justice, legal values and the rehabilitative ideal. *The Journal of Criminal Law and Criminology, 50*, 226.

Andrews, D. A., Bonta, J., & Wormith, J. S. (2006). The recent past and near future of risk and/or need assessment. *Crime & Delinquency, 52*(1), 7–27.

Bancroft, J. (1971). The application of psychophysiological measures to the assessment and modification of sexual behaviour. *Behaviour Research and Therapy, 9*(2), 119–130.

Barlow, D. H. (1973). Increasing heterosexual responsiveness in the treatment of sexual deviation: A review of the clinical and experimental evidence. *Behavior Therapy, 4*(5), 655–671.

Beech, A. R., & Ward, T. (2004). The integration of etiology and risk in sexual offenders: A theoretical framework. *Aggression and Violent Behavior, 10*(1), 31–63.

Bonta, J., Bourgon, G., Rugge, T., Scott, T. L., Yessine, A. K., Gutierrez, L. K., et al. (2010). *The strategic training initiative in community supervision: Risk-need-responsivity in the real world 2010–01.* Ottawa: Public Safety Canada.

Bonta, J., Rugge, T., Scott, T. L., Bourgon, G., & Yessine, A. K. (2008). Exploring the black box of community supervision. *Journal of Offender Rehabilitation, 47*(3), 248–270.

Brownmiller, S. (1975). *Against our will: Men, women, rape.* New York: Simon and Schuster.

Cabeen, C. W., & Coleman, J. C. (1962). The selection of sex-offender patients for group psychotherapy. *International Journal of Group Psychotherapy, 12*(3), 326–334.

Clear, T. R., & Latessa, E. J. (1993). Probation officers' roles in intensive supervision: Surveillance versus treatment. *Justice Quarterly, 10*(3), 441–462.

Cormier, B. M., & Simons, S. P. (1969). The problem of the dangerous sexual offender. *Canadian Psychiatric Association Journal, 14*(4), 329–335.

Craissati, J. (2004). *Managing high risk sex offenders in the community: A psychological approach.* London: Routledge.

Cumming, G. F., & McGrath, R. J. (2000). External supervision. In D. R. Laws, S. M. Hudson, & T. Ward (Eds.), *Remaking relapse prevention with sex offenders: A sourcebook* (pp. 236–253). New York: Sage Publications.

Davidson, P. R. (1984). Behavioral treatment for incarcerated sex offenders: Post-release outcome. *Sexual Abuse: A Journal of Research and Treatment, 11*, 101–116.

Dix, G. E. (1976). Differential processing of abnormal sex offenders. *Journal of Criminal Law, Criminology, and Police Science, 67*, 233–243.

Earls, C. M., & Castonguay, L. G. (1989). The evaluation of olfactory aversion for a bisexual pedophile with a single-case multiple baseline design. *Behavior Therapy, 20*(1), 137–146.

English, K. (1998). The containment approach : An aggressive strategy for the community management of adult sex offenders. *Psychology, Public Policy, and Law, 4*(1-2), 218.

Feeley, M. M., & Simon, J. (1992). The new penology: notes on the emerging strategy of corrections and its implications. *Criminology, 30*(4), 449–474.

Freeman-Longo, R. E., Bird, S., Stevenson, W. F., & Fiske, J. (1995). *1994 nationwide survey of treatment programs and models: Serving abuse-reactive children and adolescent and adult sex offenders.* Brandon. VT: Safer Society Press.

Freeman-Longo, R. E., & Knopp, F. H. (1992). State-of-the-art sex offender treatment: Outcome and issues. *Annals of Sex Research, 5*(3), 141–160.

Frisbie, L. V. (1969). *Another look at sex offenders in California. Mental Health Research Monograph (No. 12).* Sacramento: CA: State of California, Department of Mental Hygiene.

Furby, L., Weinrott, M. R., & Blackshaw, L. (1989). Sex offender recidivism: A review. *Psychological Bulletin, 105*(1), 3.

Galloway, S., & Seupersad, A. (2008). Multi-agency or multidisciplinary working with sexual offenders. *Forensic Focus, 28*, 212.

Gendreau, P., Cullen, F. T., & Goggin, C. (1999). *The effects of prison sentences on recidivism.* Ottawa, Canada: Solicitor General Canada.

Giordano, P. C., Cernkovich, S. A., & Rudolph, J. L. (2002). Gender, crime, and desistance: Toward a theory of cognitive transformation. *American Journal of Sociology, 107*(4), 990–1064.

Guay, J. P., Ouimet, M., & Proulx, J. (2004). Criminal justice institutional referrals and selections: A comparative portrait of sexual aggressions and aggressors. *International Journal of Offender Therapy and Comparative Criminology, 48*(3), 330–346.

Hall, G. C. N. (1995). Sexual offender recidivism revisited: A meta-analysis of recent treatment studies. *Journal of Consulting and Clinical Psychology, 63*(5), 802.

Hall, G. C. N., & Hirschman, R. (1992). Sexual aggression against children: A conceptual perspective of etiology. *Criminal Justice and Behavior, 19*(1), 8–23.

Hanson, R. K., Gordon, A., Harris, A. J. R., Marques, J. K., Murphy, W., Quinsey, V. L., et al. (2002). The first report of the collaborative outcome data project on the effectiveness of psychological treatment for sexual offenders. *Sexual Abuse: A Journal of Research and Treatment, 14*, 169–194.

Hanson, R. K., & Harris, A. J. (2000). Where should we intervene? Dynamic predictors of sexual offense recidivism. *Criminal Justice and Behavior, 27*(1), 6–35.

Hanson, R. K., & Harris, A. J. (2001). A structured approach to evaluating change among sexual offenders. *Sexual Abuse: A Journal of Research and Treatment, 13*(2), 105–122.

Harris, P. M., Gingerich, R., & Whittaker, T. A. (2004). The "effectiveness" of differential supervision. *Crime & Delinquency, 50*(2), 235–271.

Johnston, P., Hudson, S. M., & Marshall, W. L. (1992). The effects of masturbatory reconditioning with nonfamilial child molesters. *Behaviour Research and Therapy, 30*(5), 559–561.

Karpman, B. (1951). The sexual psychopath. *Journal of Criminal Law, Criminology, and Police Science, 42*, 184.

Karpman, B. (1954). *The sexual offender and his offenses.* Oxford: Julian Press.

Kelly-Scott, K., & Arriagada, P. (2016). *Aboriginal peoples: Fact sheet for British Columbia.* Statistics Canada.

Kemshall, H. (2008). *Understanding the community management of high risk offenders.* Maidenhead: Open University Press.

Kopp, S. B. (1962). The character structure of sex offenders. *American Journal of Psychotherapy, 16*(1), 64–70.

Laws, D. R. (1980). Treatment of bisexual pedophilia by a biofeedback-assisted self-control procedure. *Behaviour Research and Therapy, 18*(3), 207–211.

Laws, D. R. (1989). *Relapse prevention with sex offenders.* New York: Guilford.

Laws, D. R. (1999). Relapse prevention: The state of the art. *Journal of Interpersonal Violence, 14*(3), 285–302.

Laws, D. R. (2003). The rise and fall of relapse prevention. *Australian Psychologist, 38*, 22–30.

Laws, D. R., Hudson, S. M., & Ward, T. (2000). The original model of relapse prevention with sex offenders: Promises unfulfilled. In D. R. Laws, S. M. Hudson, & T. Ward (Eds.), *Remaking relapse prevention with sex offenders: A sourcebook* (pp. 3–24). New York: Sage Publications.

Laws, D. R., & Marshall, W. L. (2003). A brief history of behavioral and cognitive behavioral approaches to sexual offenders: Part 1. Early developments. *Sexual Abuse: A Journal of Research and Treatment, 15*(2), 75–92.

Lösel, F., & Schmucker, M. (2005). The effectiveness of treatment for sexual offenders: A comprehensive meta-analysis. *Journal of Experimental Criminology, 1*(1), 117–146.

Lussier, P., Dahabieh, M., Deslauriers-Varin, N., & Thomson, C. (2010). Issues and challenges for community risk management. In L. Gideon & H. E. Sung (Eds.), *Rethinking corrections: Rehabilitation, reentry, and reintegration* (pp. 219–252). Thousand Oaks, CA: Sage Publications.

Lussier, P., Deslauriers-Varin, N., & Râtel, T. (2010). A descriptive profile of high-risk sex offenders under intensive supervision in the province of British Columbia, Canada. *International Journal of Offender Therapy and Comparative Criminology, 54*(1), 71–91.

Lussier, P., Gress, C., Deslauriers-Varin, N., & Amirault, J. (2014). Community risk management of high-risk sex offenders in Canada: Findings from a quasi-experimental study. *Justice Quarterly, 31*(2), 287–314.

Lussier, P., & Gress, C. L. (2014). Community re-entry and the path toward desistance: A quasi-experimental longitudinal study of dynamic factors and community risk management of adult sex offenders. *Journal of Criminal Justice, 42*(2), 111–122.

Lussier, P., & Mathesius, J. (2018). Integrating general and specific theories of sex offending. In P. Lussier & E. Beauregard (Eds.), *Sexual offending: A criminological perspective* (pp. 12–43). Abington: Routledge.

Lussier, P., & McCuish, E. (2016). Desistance from crime without reintegration: A longitudinal study of the social context and life course path to desistance in a sample of adults convicted of a sex crime. *International Journal of Offender Therapy and Comparative Criminology, 60*(15), 1791–1812.

Lussier, P., Proulx, J., & McKibben, A. (2001). Personality characteristics and adaptive strategies to cope with negative emotional states and deviant sexual fantasies in sexual aggressors. *International Journal of Offender Therapy and Comparative Criminology, 45*(2), 159–170.

Malamuth, N. M. (1988). Predicting laboratory aggression against women and men targets: Implications for sexual aggression. *Journal of Research in Personality, 22*, 474–495.

Malamuth, N. M., & Check, J. V. (1983). Sexual arousal to rape depictions: Individual differences. *Journal of Abnormal Psychology, 92*(1), 55.

Maletzky, B. M. (1980). Self-referred versus court-referred sexually deviant patients: Success with assisted covert sensitization. *Behavior Therapy, 11*(3), 306–314.

Mann, R. E., & Beech, A. R. (2003). Cognitive distortions, schemas, and implicit theories. In T. Ward & D. R. Laws (Eds.), *Sexual deviance: Issues and controversies* (pp. 135–153). Thousand Oaks: Sage Publications.

Marques, J. K. (1999). How to answer the Question: "does sex offender treatment work?". *Journal of Interpersonal Violence, 14*(4), 437–451.

Marques, J. K., Day, D. M., Nelson, C., Miner, M. H., & West, M. A. (1991). *The sex offender treatment and evaluation project: Fourth report to the Legislature in response to PC 1365*. Sacramento: California Department of Mental Health.

Marques, J. K., Day, D. M., Nelson, C., & West, M. A. (1994). Effects of cognitive/behavioral treatment on sex offenders' recidivism: Preliminary results of a longitudinal study. *Criminal Justice and Behavior, 21*, 28–54.

Marques, J. K., Wiederanders, M., Day, D. M., Nelson, C., & Van Ommeren, A. (2005). Effects of a relapse prevention program on sexual recidivism: Final results from California's sex offender treatment and evaluation project (SOTEP). *Sexual Abuse: A Journal of Research and Treatment, 17*(1), 79–107.

Marshall, W. L. (1973). The modification of sexual fantasies: A combined treatment approach to the reduction of deviant sexual behavior. *Behaviour Research and Therapy, 11*(4), 557–564.

Marshall, W. L. (1996). Assessment, treatment, and theorizing about sex offenders: Developments during the past twenty years and future directions. *Criminal Justice and Behavior, 23*(1), 162–199.

Marshall, W. L., Anderson, D., & Fernandez, Y. (1999). *Cognitive behavioural treatment of sexual offenders*. New York: John Wiley.

Marshall, W. L., & Barbaree, H. E. (1990). An integrated theory of the etiology of sexual offending. In W. L. Marshall, D. R. Laws, & H. E. Barbaree (Eds.), *Handbook of sexual assault: Issues, theories, and treatment of the offender* (pp. 257–275). New York: Plenum Press.

Marshall, W. L., Jones, R., Ward, T., Johnston, P., & Barbaree, H. E. (1991). Treatment outcome with sex offenders. *Clinical Psychology Review, 11*(4), 465–485.

Marshall, W. L., & Marshall, L. E. (2007). The utility of the random controlled trial for evaluating sexual offender treatment: The gold standard or an inappropriate strategy? *Sexual Abuse: A Journal of Research and Treatment, 19*, 175–191.

Marshall, W. L., & Pithers, W. D. (1994). A reconsideration of treatment outcome with sex offenders. *Criminal Justice and Behavior, 21*(1), 10–27.

Martinson, R. (1974). What works? Questions and answers about prison reform. *The Public Interest, 35*, 22–54.

McConaghy, N. (1999). Methodological issues concerning the evaluation of treatment for sexual offenders: Randomization, treatment dropouts, untreated controls, and within-treatment studies. *Sexual Abuse: A Journal of Research and Treatment, 11*, 183–193.

McGuire, R. J., Carlisle, J. M., & Young, B. G. (1964). Sexual deviations as conditioned behavior: A hypothesis. *Behaviour Research and Therapy, 2*(2-4), 185–190.

McKibben, A., Proulx, J., & Lussier, P. (2001). Sexual aggressors' perceptions of effectiveness of strategies to cope with negative emotions and deviant sexual fantasies. *Sexual Abuse: A Journal of Research and Treatment, 13*(4), 257–273.

Mees, H. L. (1966). Sadistic fantasies modified by aversive conditioning and substitution: A case study. *Behaviour Research and Therapy, 4*(4), 317–320.

Meyer, L. C., & Romero, J. (1980). *A ten-year follow-up of sex offender recidivism*. Philadephia, PA: JJ Peters Institute.

Morrow, W. R., & Peterson, D. B. (1966). Follow-up of discharged psychiatric offenders: Not guilty by reason of insanity and criminal sexual psychopaths. *The Journal of Criminal Law, Criminology, and Police Science, 57*, 31–34.

Murphy, W. D. (1990). Assessment and modification of cognitive distortions in sex offenders. In W. L. Marshall, D. R. Laws, & H. E. Barbaree (Eds.), *Handbook of sexual assault* (pp. 331–342). Boston, MA: Springer.

Pacht, A. R., Halleck, S. L., & Ehrmann, J. C. (1962). Diagnosis and treatment of the sexual offender: A nine-year study. *American Journal of Psychiatry, 118*(9), 802–808.

Pascoe, H. (1961). Deviant sexual behaviour and the sex criminal. *Canadian Medical Association Journal, 84*(4), 206.

Pawson, R., & Tilley, N. (1997). An introduction to scientific realist evaluation. In E. Chelimsky & W. R. Shadish (Eds.), *Evaluation for the 21st century: A handbook* (pp. 405–418). London: Sage Publications.

Peters, J. J., & Roether, H. A. (1971). *Success and failure of sex offenders*. Philadelphia: AAAS.

Petersilia, J., & Turner, S. (1993). Intensive probation and parole. *Crime and Justice, 17*, 281–335.

Pithers, W. D. (1990). Relapse prevention with sexual aggressors. In W. L. Marshall, D. R. Laws, & H. E. Barbaree (Eds.), *Handbook of sexual assault* (pp. 343–361). Boston, MA: Springer.

Pithers, W. D., Marques, J. K., Gibat, C. C., & Marlatt, G. A. (1983). Relapse prevention with sexual aggressives: A self-control model of treatment and maintenance of change. In J. G. Greer & I. R. Stuart (Eds.), *The sexual aggressor: Current perspectives on treatment* (pp. 214–239). New York: Van Nostrand Reinhold.

Pithers, W. D., Martin, G. R., & Cumming, G. F. (1989). Vermont treatment program for sexual aggressors. In D. R. Laws (Ed.), *Relapse prevention with sex offenders* (pp. 292–310). New York: The Guilford Press.

Proulx, J., McKibben, A., & Lusignan, R. (1996). Relationships between affective components and sexual behaviors in sexual aggressors. *Sexual Abuse: A Journal of Research and Treatment, 8*(4), 279–289.

Quinsey, V. L., Chaplin, T. C., & Carrigan, W. F. (1980). Biofeedback and signaled punishment in the modification of inappropriate sexual age preferences. *Behavior Therapy, 11*(4), 567–576.

Quinsey, V. L., Harris, G. T., Rice, M. E., & Lalumière, M. L. (1993). Assessing treatment efficacy in outcome studies of sex offenders. *Journal of Interpersonal Violence, 8*(4), 512–523.

Roth, N. (1952). Factors in the motivation of sexual offenders. *The Journal of Criminal Law, Criminology, and Police Science, 42*(5), 631–635.

Rugge, T. (2006). *Risk assessment of male Aboriginal offenders: a 2006 Perspective*. Ottawa: Public Safety and Emergency Preparedness Canada.

Saleh, F. M., Grudzinskas, A. J., & Malin, H. M. (2015). Treatment of incarcerated sex offenders. In R. L. Trestman, K. L. Appelbaum, & J. L. Metzner (Eds.), *Oxford textbook of correctional psychiatry* (pp. 336–340). New York: Oxford University Press.

Sampson, R.J., & Laub, J.H. (2003). Life-course desisters? Trajectories of crime among delinquent boys followed to ge 70. *Criminology, 41*, 319–339.

Schmucker, M., & Lösel, F. (2015). The effects of sexual offender treatment on recidivism: An international meta-analysis of sound quality evaluations. *Journal of Experimental Criminology, 11*(4), 597–630.

Seto, M. C., Marques, J. K., Harris, G. T., Chaffin, M., Lalumière, M. L., Miner, M. H., et al. (2008). Good science and progress in sex offender treatment are intertwined: A response to Marshall and Marshall (2007). *Sexual Abuse, 20*(3), 247–255.

Sturgeon, V. H., & Taylor, J. (1980). Report of a five-year follow-up study of mentally disordered sex offenders released from Atascadero State Hospital in 1973. *Criminal Justice Journal, 4*, 31–63.

Sutherland, E. (1950). The sexual psychopath laws. *The Journal of Criminal Law and Criminology, 40*, 543–554.

Tappan, P. W. (1955). The young adult offender under the American Law Institute's Model Penal Code. *Federal Probation, 19*, 20–25.

Turner, R. E. (1961). The group treatment of sexual deviations. *Canadian Journal of Corrections, 3*(4), 485–491.

Walker, A., Kazemian, L., Lussier, P., & Na, C. (2017). The role of family support in the explanation of patterns of desistance among individuals convicted of a sexual offense. *Journal of Interpersonal Violence, 73*, 1–23.

Ward, T., & Hudson, S. M. (1998). A model of the relapse process in sexual offenders. *Journal of Interpersonal Violence, 13*(6), 700–725.

Wilson, D. B., & Lipsey, M. W. (2001). The role of method in treatment effectiveness research: Evidence from meta-analysis. *Psychological Methods, 6*, 413–429.

Wood, J., & Kemshall, H. (2010). Effective multi-agency public protection: Learning from the research. In K. Harrison (Ed.), *Managing high-risk sex offenders in the com- munity: Risk management, treatment, social responsibility* (pp. 39–60). Portland, OR: Willan.

Chapter 9
A Scarlet Letter in the Digital Age: Sex Offender Registration and Public Notification

Introduction

Free and democratic societies require a balance between community safety and the right to avoid being unnecessarily or unjustly incarcerated. Achieving both objectives can be challenging, especially when an extremely rare but severe and dramatic event occurs. About 20 years ago, in the Province of Quebec, Canada, a 13-year-old boy was taken to an isolated area where he was brutally murdered. He had taken the bus to go out of town for his first day working on a farm picking vegetables. On his way back home, he was seen getting out of the bus about 3 miles away from home. He later called his mother to tell her that he would not be home for dinner as he was going to a friend's house. About 5 days later, his partially buried body was found by workers in a quarry about half a mile from where he was last seen. As the details came in through the local media, multiple conflicting reports emerged: he had been stabbed, or possibly asphyxiated; he had possibly been sexually assaulted; he had been kidnapped or lured away; he was fully clothed or partially clothed when he was found; his hands might have been tied behind his back, and so on. As more and more information made the headlines of local news outlets, the case received more and more attention from the public. A few days later, a man was interrogated by police investigators. He was quickly identified as a suspect because he had been seen getting off the bus at the same stop as the victim. He was therefore believed to be the last person to have seen the boy alive. It was later revealed that the two had met earlier that day while the boy was working and he had invited the boy to his house. He was interrogated by the police a second time and later charged after he had reached out to a television news broadcast to proclaim his innocence. After the interview was broadcasted, he was recognized by criminal justice professionals who were familiar with his past. At the time of the offense, the suspect was serving a sentence in a provincial prison, and although he was not yet eligible for parole, was granted a temporary absence from prison on the day of the boy's disappearance. In Quebec, incarceration sentences of less than 2 years are served in provincial prisons.

© Springer Nature Switzerland AG 2021
P. Lussier et al., *Understanding Sexual Offending*,
https://doi.org/10.1007/978-3-030-53301-4_9

At the time, there were very limited intervention programs offered in these prisons because the population was typically serving short sentences and therefore often were better served by attending programs in the community.

The suspect was not a convicted sex offender but had been convicted on multiple occasions, mainly for thefts and breaking and entering. In fact, there was no evidence that he had ever committed a sex crime in adulthood. What would be discovered later is that, while serving a previous prison sentence in a federal penitentiary, he had mentioned to a psychologist that he had pedophilic thoughts and, as a result, he was given the opportunity to participate in a sex offender treatment program. This disclosure warrants some additional attention. While disclosure of pedophilic interests by someone incarcerated for perpetrating a sexual offense against a child might be unsurprising, for someone with no such history, the motivation for doing so may be different. His pedophilic thoughts were unrelated to his conviction at the time that he disclosed them. Acknowledging such thoughts was not going to reduce his sentence or demonstrate to a probation officer that he was appropriately progressing through his treatment program. One factor that possibly motivated his disclosure to the prison therapist was his desire to receive help for his sexual interest in children, especially because such help was not available in the community. Indeed, in this case, aside from the desire to receive treatment for his pedophilic thoughts, there was not much for this person to personally gain from their disclosure. Typically, sex offender treatment programs, particularly in prisons, are for individuals who have been convicted for sex crimes and not for individuals struggling with deviant sexual fantasies. However, the suspect may have perceived that being in prison was a safer place to divulge his struggles with pedophilic thoughts. Then again, individuals labeled "pedophiles" are generally not welcomed by other inmates and are often the target of prison violence. Years later, but still prior to the offense against the young boy, he was reconvicted for a minor crime and sentenced to a provincial prison. Of importance, the federal and provincial prison systems in Canada did not have a centralized data sharing system. His federal correctional files, therefore, were not accessed by the provincial prison staff. As a result, the prison staff was not aware of his pedophilic thoughts and thus did not prevent him from being granted a temporary absence, or at least from establishing conditions of this absence (e.g., not to be in the presence of a young person). Individuals convicted for a nonsexual offense typically are not clinically assessed to determine whether they have deviant sexual interests. Furthermore, as mentioned above, he did not have a criminal record involving sex crimes of any kind. For the prison staff at the provincial facility, he was just another inmate, one of many with a criminal record including a series of convictions for relatively minor, nonviolent crimes.

After he was found guilty of homicide, the judge criticized the correctional service for granting this man a temporary absence. The case became an exemplar of correctional mishaps in the Province of Quebec and the failure of the criminal justice system to ensure public safety against dangerous sexual predators. Some critics and representatives of other political parties blamed the government for their irresponsible handling of the situation. Books and editorials were written about the inefficiencies and problems of the criminal justice system. Budget cuts, an overcrowded prison system, and governmental orders to use temporary absences to address overcrowding and a lack of treatment options were pinpointed as instrumental in the decision by prison staff to grant an extended temporary absence. After learning about the offender's criminal and psychological history, and the handling of his case by the prison staff, the victim's family sued the government. The tragedy had severe long-term consequences for the victim's parents, which was well-documented by the media over the years, culminating with the father's death, following his struggles with health and financial problems. The victim's mother's feelings of injustice were still very palpable a decade after the tragedy. A public enquiry ensued, and numerous recommendations were made, some urging the government to improve public safety by enhancing risk assessment and risk management procedures.

The story of the perpetrator, like many other offenders, was not told. We do not know much about him.[1] When a horrific crime, such as the murder of a child, is brought into the public's eye, it is not surprising that the public has little interest in understanding the perspective of the offender. Attempts at doing so may be perceived as an interest in protecting the offender, finding excuses for their behavior, and displacing accountability by describing negative events associated with the offender's life. As such, it becomes risky for researchers to look more closely at the circumstances and experiences of the offender given the potential for the public, policymakers, and criminal justice system professionals to view this inquiry as being "on the side of the offender." There are very important reasons for seeking to understand the person behind the offense. Doing so is not meant to rationalize or excuse their behavior. Understanding this background context is necessary to make sense of why the crime occurred, what precipitated the crime, whether the behavior is likely to continue, and what can be done to prevent similar events. Ultimately, the answers to these questions can be used to help improve public safety. Thus, it is extremely important to communicate to the public that looking more closely at the story of the offender is not simply about finding factors that mitigate a person's responsibility for their behavior or forgiving the harm done; rather, doing so can help better understand the types of policies that should be in place to ensure that such crimes do not happen again. Accordingly, we look closer at the background of the perpetrator and what was known about their offense to evaluate whether policies that emerged in response to the case appear as a clear, scientific, evidence-based response to a horrific offense.

---

[1] This man, who was in his late 20s when he committed the homicide, was intellectually impaired with a very difficult upbringing. At a very young age, he was put in a foster home. It was alleged by someone close to the situation that his birth was the product of incestuous sexual abuse. At his court hearing, he was met with an angry mob of people who were waiting for him outside the courthouse. This might have played a factor in his decision, about a week later while awaiting his trial, to call a journalist to discuss his case. Despite pleading not guilty in court, during the phone call he referred to himself as a monster who had done a terrible thing. The state of mind he was in when making what seemed to be a confession and his motives remained unclear.

Overall, the implications of this case for policymaking did not play out at the desks of journal editors and across the rooms of academic conferences. The discussions were held in public and were, understandably, laden with emotion. The discussion also did not involve looking closely at the case and attempting to understand why this offense occurred. For example, it was swiftly presumed that the young boy was killed as part of sexual deviancy and homicidal fantasy. Other explanations were not given similar consideration, such as whether the offense was instead committed because the perpetrator panicked, or feared detection and the potential serious consequences of being recognized as a pedophile and as a child molester. Developing policies based on a single case and then generalizing these policies to all perpetrators of sexual offenses is already a potentially flawed approach. To add in the fact that this single case was not scrutinized more carefully and with greater consideration of a wider possible range of motives and contexts makes the development of policies based on a single case even more concerning. Struggling with pedophilic thoughts is not a criminal act punishable by the law, but it could be evidence of a mental disorder requiring some form of treatment. Furthermore, there are, to this day, no risk assessment tools designed to determine the risk of sexual offending for individuals with no criminal history of sex crimes. As discussed in prior chapters, the risk is simply too low to be reliably detected in the general population or even a general prison population. The truth, which was never brought up despite the heavy media coverage and the numerous commentators that reflected on the situation, is that temporary absence or not, within the next year or so the perpetrator would have been released back into the community.

This case was certainly not met with indifference, socially and politically. To this day, about 20 years later, the boy's name still resonates across the province. This tragic and complex case led to significant policy changes in the Province of Quebec. From the public's perspective, a take-home message from this case was that the criminal justice system is too lenient with dangerous sexual predators. These arguments raised again and again have little to do with the facts of the case. The case drove intense discussion regarding the need for the assessment of risk for sexual recidivism and how to manage this risk, even though in this particular case, the perpetrator would not be part of the pool of individuals assessed for risk of sexual recidivism given that they had no prior conviction for sexual offenses. However, in the minds of many politicians, members of the public, and criminal justice system practitioners, it was a perfect storm for the enactment of new sex offender laws. However, rather than follow America's lead with the establishment of sex offender registries that emerged via Megan's Law, the Quebec government reaffirmed the importance of prisons in supporting rehabilitation and the community reintegration of offenders. This road included the implementation of broad-based risk assessment tools to examine the risk of general and sexual recidivism. About a decade after the victim's death, these policy changes culminated with the opening of a prison-based facility whose purpose was to offer sex offender treatment to convicted offenders serving provincial sentences. Despite this measured approach, a tragic case in the adjacent Province of Ontario would eventually lead to the enactment of the first Canadian non-public sex offender registry. This pressured other Canadian provinces to follow suit, which ultimately paved the way for Canada's federally run non-public sex offender registry.

Time and time again, supporters of sex offender registration in Canada refer to this case to justify a publicly accessible registry. The demand for such registries is based on the public's presumption that this would significantly improve how the criminal justice system responds to sexual predators while increasing public safety, especially the safety of children (Lussier & Mathesius, 2019b). This chapter addresses whether the scientific evidence supports such presumptions by reviewing what has been learned from the American experience with public notification and public sex offender registries.

Sex offender laws such as sex offender registries and notification (SORN) did not emerge from a noted rise in the rate of sexual offending within a given jurisdiction. They were not in response to research that revealed offenders were likely to be deterred from committing a future sex crime if SORN laws were enacted. Instead, to understand the development of SORN it is necessary to understand perhaps the most heinous crime imaginable: sexual homicide; more precisely, the sexual homicide of a child. While this event is extremely atypical, poorly understood, and rarely examined from a scientific perspective, it is very often the catalyst for changes in laws that are then extended to a much broader group of individuals (i.e., beyond the individuals that have perpetrated a sexual homicide offense). Why are laws enacted against a much broader group of persons (e.g., all sex offenders) based on the behavior of a smaller subset of this population? One possibility, investigated below, is that sexual homicide offenses are virtually always examined retrospectively with the benefit of hindsight. Such hindsight reveals the impression that sexual homicides were the result of a clear, predictable pattern of previous sexual offending that culminated in an escalation in behavior to the point of a homicide. From this lens, these rare events have a clearly defined pattern that starts with earlier involvement in a sex crime. Accordingly, policies that go to great lengths to prevent future sexual offending can eliminate child sexual homicide offenses. Before we discuss the efficacy of such an approach, we look more closely at why these rare crimes result in such dramatic shifts in policy.

Sexual Homicide: The *Black Swan* of Sexual Offenses

As discussed throughout the book, since the 1990s, the predominant response to sexual offending has been via community protection model in which actuarial risk assessment, prediction, and risk management have become imperative (Feeley & Simon, 1992). This philosophy brought especially profound changes with respect to how the criminal justice system responds to individuals who have been convicted for a sex crime. In that regard, Simon (1998) observed: "A new generation of sex offender laws is being produced that reflects a profound change in contemporary penality. This change is taking place on a number of different levels, including the targets of penal efforts, the forms of expertise that provide them with authority, and the image of state power they communicate. Behind the superficially consistent object of sex offender, a distinctly new and far more pessimistic vision has emerged. Sex offenders are the embodiment not of psychopathology, with the potential for diagnostic and treatment knowledge to provide better controls over such offenders, but of the monstrous and the limits of science to know or change people."

As researchers have pointed out (La Fond, 2005; Simon, 1998), this actuarial-based approach has marked the emergence of a new generation of sex offender laws, especially in the USA, but also, in Canada, Australia, and the UK (McAlinden, 2012; Petrunik, 2003). Despite the growth of risk assessment instruments used to predict sexual recidivism, the reality is that the vast majority of persons incarcerated for a sex crime will return to the community. This is not something that the risk assessment and prediction model is especially well equipped to handle. Risk assessment can be used to help justify delaying a person's return to the community or the imposition of conditions associated with a person's release, but ultimately, especially from the perspective of the public, another system was needed to fill a gap that the risk assessment model could not address; that is, how to monitor individuals once they are released from prison. While public concern about offenders' release from prison is certainly not new, from the 1990s on, this situation would be socially constructed as a significant public safety problem in need of concrete governmental action. Given the progression toward a risk-based philosophy, especially in the USA, two major changes in the sociolegal response to the problem of sexual offending and sex offenders emerged: sex offender registration (SOR) and sex offender notification (SON), commonly collectively referred to as SORN (Sex Offender Registry and Notification) laws.

The enactment of SORN laws is reminiscent of the "Black Swan" metaphor popularized by Nassim Nicholas Taleb's book of the same name (Taleb, 2007). The Black Swan metaphor describes the impact of highly improbable and unpredictable events that have an extreme impact and whose occurrences are explained *after* the fact, making them appear as if they are in fact very much predictable. A "Black Swan" is an exception, an outlier, a phenomenon that falls outside the realm of what seems possible and probable even to most experts. A sexual homicide meets these characteristics, even more so when the victim is a child. No qualified expert in human behavior, or expert in the field of risk assessment and risk prediction of sexual recidivism can predict that a specific individual, with no such prior behavior, is likely to perpetrate a sexual homicide. It is simply too rare. In fact, there are no risk assessment instruments even capable of determining accurately the probabilities of such an event occurring in the future. Even when it comes to general homicide offending, the phenomenon is difficult to accurately predict. Over 90% of the time that an individual is characterized by factors hypothesized to increase the risk of homicide (e.g., substance abuse, gang involvement, history of physical and sexual abuse), the homicide actually does not occur (Farrington, Loeber, & Berg, 2012). This false positive problem epitomizes the Black Swan metaphor in which factors that seem obvious or specific to one type of event or person are actually common to other events or persons as well.

That said, the sexual homicide of a child is of extreme social significance. If and when it does happen, society comes to a halt, followed by the mobilization of heavy and continued media coverage, which immediately captures public attention, transcends the jurisdiction where it occurs, it even transcends group and identity divisions. Such mobilization always includes a demand for some form of governmental intervention. The gravity of such a situation demands a swift response; some intervention and/or some form of action to reassure the community that they are safe, and that justice will be served. From a societal perspective, forcing a child to engage in sexual behavior is completely irrational, as is the act of killing a child. When both of these inexplicable and irrational events coincide, society reacts with anger, fear, and incomprehension. The search to identify the culpable person and obtain justice for the victim, the victim's parents and relatives, and the community more broadly, becomes paramount.

Society tends to respond to "Black Swan" events of any kind (e.g., consider many policy responses to terrorism) by applying the narrative fallacy. Taleb (2007) describes this as our collective inability to look back at an extraordinary event without constructing an easily recognizable and logical sequence of events explaining what happened and how it can be prevented in the future. Victim's rights advocates, lawyers, and criminal justice critics all will look back at these cases and highlight the flaws of the system that led to the sexual homicide. With certitude, some will conclude that the killing of the young victim was in fact predictable and preventable. We raise this issue, not because we are arguing that these offenses are never preventable or that the criminal justice system is perfect, quite to the contrary. Our assertion is that it is extremely common that a false and misconstrued narrative will be presented after the fact as part of the discourse surrounding these rare events. These characteristics of "Black Swan" events can be used to understand the enactment of SORN laws. Public outcry in response to tragic and brutal cases, usually involving the murder of a child, and a sexual dimension to the crime, has been a common denominator in the enactment of these sex offender laws in the USA and other Western countries (e.g., Dugan, 2001; Lussier, 2018; Petrunik, 2003; Whitting, Day, & Powell, 2014). The enactment of these laws in turn affected thousands and thousands of individuals that have never perpetrated a sexual homicide, never perpetrated a sex crime against a child, nor acted violently against one.

This is not to suggest that the individuals impacted by these laws were not guilty of having previously committed potentially serious crimes. What we will suggest, however, is that such individuals represented an extremely low probability of perpetrating the types of sexual homicide offenses described above and placing such an individual on a sex offender registry was unlikely to do anything to reduce this probability any further. As noted by Fitch (2006), the implementation of sex offender registry laws is not an evidence-based policy, but rather a reaction to a series of particularly sordid and wretched sex crimes against children. Reminiscent of the enactment of sexual psychopath laws decades earlier, the emergence of sex offender registration and public notification laws are inadequate policies produced by a Black Swan dynamic. In this regard, Logan (2003) appropriately qualified the implementation of American SORN laws as an article of faith given the lack of empirical evidence demonstrating their effectiveness in preventing sex crimes. For others such as Simon (1998), the emergence of these laws indicated a dangerous shift toward populist-fuelled punishment.

The Rise of a New Class of Sex Offender Laws

The American Model

Although the first laws requiring SOR were enacted in the 1940s, it was in the 1990s that all American states passed specific sex offender laws. Laws relating to SOR require that when released, those convicted of a sex offense must regularly provide personal information to law enforcement officials. Registered individuals must communicate with the police at least once a year, for a minimum of 10 years, to verify and update their personal information. These SOR laws were enacted following recommendations from the report on the Jacob Wetterling Crimes against Children and Sexually Violent Registration Program (more recently referred to as the Jacob Wetterling Law). This law, which became effective in 1994, mandates the establishment of a sex offender registry in all US states, without exception. The content of the SOR is at the discretion of each state, but it generally includes: the name and aliases of the registered individual, the sex and ethnicity of the person, a recent photograph and the person's physical characteristics (tattoos, scars, etc.), the place of residence and information concerning the sexual offense history, especially if the victim(s) were minors (Brewster, DeLong, & Moloney, 2012). The information less commonly recorded in these registries includes the person's education level, profession and workplace address, their vehicle's serial number and license plate, the offense/arrest date and location, the utilization of physical violence (or a weapon) when committing the sexual offense(s), and the registered individual's relationship to the victim (Brewster et al., 2012).

SON laws make information contained in SOR publicly available by various means, including online databases operated by state correctional services. Proposed by the State of New Jersey following the death of 7-year-old Megan Kanka, Megan's Law established SON as federal law in 1996. Together, SOR and SON laws, commonly called "SORN laws," currently exist in all the American states. However, there is significant discretion regarding what is included in these laws (Letourneau, Bandyopadhyay, Armstrong, & Sinha, 2010) and the result has been wide variation in the nature and extent of information provided in SORs from state to state (Brewster et al., 2012; Lees & Tewksbury, 2006). More specifically, Megan's Law has not provided specific instructions or directives on how to display information about registrants (Anderson, Evans, & Sample, 2009). For example, there have been differing views as to whether the application of SOR and SON laws should be retroactive or not. While this discretion is not without controversy (Agan, 2011), it favored the emergence of different models of SORN.[2]

The Adam Walsh Child Protection and Notification Act, also known as the Adam Walsh Act (AWA), was introduced in 2006 to broaden the scope of SORN laws and to standardize public notification practices in order to reduce disparities across states (Anderson et al., 2009; Wright, 2008). The AWA introduced key changes to SORN laws, most notably: (a) broadening the range of recognized offenses leading to the individual's registration (for example, possession of child pornography); (b) extending the nature of the information contained in registries (e.g., the DNA of registered offenders); and (c) implementing a classification system based on the level of risk of sexual recidivism. In addition, key changes to the SORN laws following the AWA also allowed the scope of the registry and the public notification to be extended to include all minors at least 14 years of age who have committed certain types of sex crimes.

The main rationale for *public* SORN laws was based on the assumption that using the information contained therein, the community in general, and parents specifically, can make more informed decisions about their own safety and the safety of their children. In fact, informing citizens about sex offenders living in their neighborhoods is what Winick (1998) described as *informational control*, which aims to improve the perception of being more in control of one's environment. In this regard, a study by Anderson and Sample (2008) conducted in the state of Nebraska provided some support for this notion. Their study found that the general public have a positive view of SORN laws and that the vast majority of those interviewed felt more secure as a result of the implementation of such laws. There is also some evidence that these laws are perceived positively by some law enforcement officials insofar as they feel that these laws assist them with community protection (Connor & Tewksbury, 2017; Masters & Kebbell, 2019; Powell, Day, Benson, Vess, & Graffam, 2014. In a way, Winick (1998) argues that SORN laws help to diffuse responsibility for the application of the law in terms of community protection through prevention and deterrence. However, other research has demonstrated that SORN implementation can have a negative net psychological effect on members of

---

[2] In this regard, there are four "models" for informing the public about the arrival of a sex offender in the community (Cohen & Jeglic, 2007; Finn, 1997; La Fond, 2005): (a) an agency identified in the legislation or by the State (e.g., law enforcement, parole and probation, prosecutor) determines the level of risk an offender poses and then implements a notification plan that reflects the level of risk. Frequently, the plan provides for three "tiers" depending on offender risk: the first tier may involve notification only to selected local organizations (e.g., schools), the second tier adds community residents, and the third includes the media; (b) state statutes that stipulate which types of offenders are to be subject to notification and what notification methods to use; a designated agency carries out the notification but plays no role in determining which offenders will be subject to notification or how notification will be implemented; (c) offenders themselves are required to do the actual notification, although they may be supervised closely by a criminal justice agency (e.g., to verify that the offender has appropriately notified the community within which they reside); (d) community groups and individuals must take the initiative to request information about whether a sex offender is living in their community and to ask for information about the person (e.g., Alaska, California, Colorado, New York).

the community when they are made aware of the presence of sex offenders in their neighborhood. For example, Zevitz (2004) and Beck and Travis (2004) reported that public notification procedures increase feelings of insecurity and the fear of being sexually assaulted. These seemingly contradictory findings underscore the mixed feelings and perceptions that exist about the public release of information about sex offenders.

SOR and SON laws are not exclusive to the USA. They have been implemented elsewhere, in the form of pilot projects or new laws, particularly in Canada and Australia (e.g., Lussier & Mathesius, 2018; Murphy, Fedoroff, & Martineau, 2009; Whitting et al., 2014), and are characterized by significant differences in scope, rules, and procedures across different jurisdictions. Below we briefly examine Canadian and Australian initiatives along these lines, which although modelled to some extent off US SORN laws, are different in many ways (see Table 9.1).

The Canadian Model

Over the past two to three decades, the Canadian criminal justice system has undergone various changes to better respond to sex crimes; changes that to some extent are reminiscent of those that were witnessed over time in the USA. As emphasized by Ruby, Hasan, and Enenajor (2017), protecting the Canadian public "from 'dangerous' individuals who constitute a grave future risk to public safety has become an increasingly important factor in sentencing" (661). This trend toward risk management of dangerous individuals can be traced back to the mid-1990s with the enactment of various laws and legal dispositions aimed at individuals convicted for a sex crime. The major change that these dispositions embodied was that sentences became less based on the nature of the crime a person committed and more on their perceived risk of future offending. These provisions specifically targeted individuals at risk of committing a sexual offense and include what are known as *Dangerous Offender* and *Long-Term Offender* orders. The former allows the court to impose an indeterminate prison sentence on individuals convicted for a crime who are at-risk of violence. The latter allows the court to impose long-term supervisory orders on individuals convicted for a crime who are at-risk of perpetrating a sex crime. The Canadian government also amended the Criminal Code of Canada to add peace bond orders for individuals at-risk of perpetrating a sex crime. Peace bonds are not used as a sentence following a conviction but rather as a preventive measure applied to individuals who may not even have a criminal record (Lussier & Gress, 2014; Lussier, Gress, Deslauriers-Varin, & Amirault, 2014).

Although similar concerns have been raised in Canada and the USA regarding policy responses to sexual offending and sex offenders, the Canadian government has been far more reluctant to implement public SOR. According to Petrunik (2003), this reluctance is due, at least in part, to constraints imposed by the Canadian Charter of Rights and Freedoms which limits the implementation of policies similar to those currently in effect in the USA. American SORN laws would violate the rights,

Table 9.1 Characteristics of the American, Canadian, and Australian sex offender registries

	American model	Canadian model	Australian model
Registry type	Public registry	Non-public registry	Non-public registry
Registered individuals	State-to-state variations. Generally, any individual convicted of a sexual crime or accused of a sexual crime, but subsequently found not criminally responsible on account of mental disorder (rape, sexual assault with violence against a child under 14 years of age, violent sexual assault against a person having intellectual disability, violent rape of a child under 16, rape and abuse of a child under 16, having non-consensual sex with an intoxicated person)	Anyone convicted for a series of designated offenses or charged for such offenses but renders a verdict of not criminally responsible on account of mental disorder for such offense (e.g., sexual assault, sexual interference, invitation to sexual touching, sexual exploitation, parent/ guardian procuring sexual activity, incest, luring a child, child pornography, bestiality, indecent acts, voyeurism)	Convictions for serious and violent crimes involving children, and/ or that have a sexual aspect to the offense. These vary slightly across the states but include such crimes as murder, sexual assault, sex crimes against children, acts of indecency, human trafficking, child pornography possession/production offenses
Registry access	State-to-state variations. Generally, all residents of the state have online access. Some states offer an "alert" service, that is, an email sent to the citizen who requests it when someone is added to the registry	Royal Canadian Mounted Police	Law enforcement agencies or other specific individuals authorized by the state Police Commissioner
Registry's objectives	General and specific deterrence (crime prevention)	Support for police investigations	Improve accuracy of intelligence on offenders who are registered. Facilitation of information sharing between different law enforcement agencies across the country. Act as a deterrent for reoffending. Increase sense of public safety
Registry mode	State-to-state variations. A separate registry for each state and even for the county	A centralized Canadian registry	Offender registration legislation differs slightly between the states and territories. There is no national register as of 2020 although some politicians have routinely called for one

(continued)

Table 9.1 (continued)

	American model	Canadian model	Australian model
Length of registration	For most American states, the required registration time is 10 years. For some, however, registration is required until the individual dies. Since 2006, a system with three risk levels has been in effect – Duration of 15 years for level I individuals (low risk of sexual recidivism); – Duration of 25 years for level II individuals (moderate risk of sexual recidivism); – Lifetime for level III individuals (high risk of sexual recidivism)	The duration of registration varies between 10 years and perpetuity, according to certain criteria – Duration of 10 years if the maximum sentence for the index crime is 2–5 years – Duration of 20 years if the maximum sentence for the index crime is 10–14 years. – Perpetuity if the maximum sentence for the index crime is lifetime or if the individual has committed a targeted offense	Types of convictions subject to the registry are classified as Class 1 up to Class 4 (in some states; most states have Class 1 and 2 type convictions); the higher the class of conviction typically reflects the level of severity of the offense. Across the states the least serious convictions are accompanied by an 8-year registration period The more serious classified convictions are accompanied by a 15-year registration period and multiple convictions can result in a life-long registration period
Information contained in the registry	Many variations from state to state. Most American registries include the individual's name, current residential address, ZIP code, city, and region, at least one updated photograph, date of birth, gender, ethnicity, height and weight, hair and eye color, offense committed, date of conviction	The registrant's name, date of birth, current residential address, workplace address, education or voluntary work, telephone number, height, weight and description of distinctive physical marks, license plate, driver's license and passport number, recent photograph, and sex crime for which the person was convicted	Offender's name, aliases, date of birth, any government issued identification, current addresses, details of employment, motor vehicle information, tattoos or distinguishing features, whether the offender has been charged in other jurisdictions, previous registrations, details of mobile and internet services registered, as well as social media information (e.g., accounts, emails, instant messaging names, names of any children regularly associated in some way to the offender)

(continued)

Table 9.1 (continued)

	American model	Canadian model	Australian model
Consequences relating to non-compliance with registration requirements	A person subject to the law who does not register correctly can face a 10 year prison term. In addition, if the person does not comply with the requirements of the law and commits a violent crime, the individual may face a prison sentence of 30 years	Upon summary conviction, imprisonment for up to 6 months or a fine of up to $10,000, or both. Upon conviction by indictment, imprisonment for up to 2 years or a fine not exceeding $10,000, or both	Monetary fines ranging from approximately $ 6000 up to $55,000: Varies across the states, and/or; 6 months up to 5 years imprisonment: Varies across the states

freedom, and security of individuals who have been convicted of a sex crime as defined under the Canadian Criminal Code. In addition, the role and importance of victim's rights advocacy groups has been pivotal in the emergence of SORN laws in the USA (Petrunik, 2003). Among others, Christian right wing and conservative ideological groups have fostered the emergence of a populist movement embodied by a retributive approach toward individuals convicted for a sex crime. Although such groups also exist in Canada, Petrunik (2003) argued that they were not as directly involved in the process leading to the legislative changes around sexual offending made in the 1990s. Another factor that may have played a role in the differences between the US and Canadian experiences is related to broader differences in correctional policies (Lussier, Dahabieh, Deslauriers-Varin, & Thomson, 2010; Petrunik, 2003). In the USA, the implications of Martinson's (1974) conclusions that prison rehabilitation programs do not work still resonates to this day. In contrast, in Canada, rehabilitation ideology remains a key objective of sentencing that is carried out as part of correctional services' intervention strategies, embodied by the well-known Risk-Needs-Responsivity model (Bonta & Andrews, 2007). In other words, in Canada, some of the key principles of the Canadian criminal justice system and the Canadian Charter of Rights and Freedoms (see Lussier & Mathesius, 2019a).

Canadian SOR laws are very distinct from those in the USA in terms of scope, rules and procedures, and objectives. At the federal level, the National Sex Offender Registry (NSOR) was announced in 2002 and implemented in 2004 (Murphy et al., 2009). Proposed under Bill C-16, the Sex Offender Information Registration Act (SOIRA) stipulates that anyone convicted of a designated sex crime must comply with the rules and procedures of the NSOR. The NSOR rules and procedures also apply to minors who have been sentenced as adults, a particularly rare situation in Canada. The information contained in the NSOR is only accessible by police agencies and such access is only provided for the purpose of a police investigation. The Royal Canadian Mounted Police (RCMP), Canada's national police service, is responsible for operating and managing the NSOR. Following Bill S-2, which came into force in 2011, important changes were made to the registry including: automatic inclusion in the registry for all eligible individuals including those convicted of a sexual offense abroad; the obligation to provide a DNA sample; the power to inform police forces in different jurisdictions when a registered individual moves; the offender's obligation to inform the police when travelling for more than seven straight days; and the obligation of the registered individual to inform the authorities of their work (and volunteering) address. The period of registration may last indefinitely and non-compliance with the rules and procedures is considered a criminal offense that can result in up to 2 years of imprisonment, a fine of up to $10,000, or both.

The NSOR is not the first sex offender registry initiative in Canada. At the provincial level, Ontario created such a registry in a similar context to the one that led to Megan's Law in the USA (Welchans, 2005) and Sarah's Law in the UK (Kemshall & Weaver, 2012). The Ontario (non-public) Sex Offender Registry (OSOR) was introduced as Bill 31 (also known as Christopher's Law;[3] Petrunik, 2003) 3 years before the implementation of the NSOR. The OSOR is operated by the Ontario Provincial Police service. As Murphy et al. (2009) have pointed out, there are several key differences between the OSOR and NSOR including: the duration of registration; the personal information contained in the registry; and the legal consequences for non-complying registered sex offenders.

There have been several independent provincial initiatives across Canada surrounding issuing public notifications about offenders who are deemed to be at a high risk of reoffending that are released back into the community. However, such initiatives are not always specific to individuals convicted for a sex crime or registered sex offenders; they often include individuals who may have committed certain types of nonsexual violent crimes as well. These practices vary considerably from province to province. For example, in 2002, the Province of Alberta created an online website that includes an individual's name, recent photo, and the individual's city of residence. In addition, this information is usually followed by a press release to inform the public that a violent or sex offender has moved into, or been released to, a specific area. The website can be accessed from anywhere in the world. The Province of Saskatchewan allows for applications to a database that provides information on individuals released into the community who are considered to be at a high-risk of reoffending. In this province, there is a committee made up of various stakeholders (e.g., clergy representatives, police investigators, psychologists, lawyers, victims' rights representatives) who assess the relevance of public notification requests. In Ontario, four strategies are generally considered if an individual is deemed to be at a high risk of reoffending and returns to the community, including: peace bonds; internal notification and follow-up (within law enforcement agencies); targeted public notices (in the individual's surrounding neighborhood); and general public notifications. A government website in the Province of Manitoba posts information on certain individuals who have been convicted of a sexual offense when the

---

[3] In reference to Christopher Stephenson, an 11-year-old boy whose perpetrator was, at the time of the offense, on parole. Contrary to the case presented at the beginning of the chapter, the offender in this case was a known (convicted) offender with a criminal history involving multiple convictions, including convictions for sex crimes.

information has already been made public by the police. This provincial website has a section that includes recent notices (e.g., press releases issued by the police in the past 12 months) as well as previous notices. There are no such initiatives in the Province of Quebec. That said, in recent years there has also been a growth in Canadian non-government sanctioned public initiatives to mimic the American public SORN laws.

Much of Canadian research to date has been almost exclusively focused on the development and evaluation of risk assessment and prediction tools for individuals convicted of a sexual offense. There have been no formal nor independent assessments of the implementation of non-public sex offender registries in Canada (NSOR, OSOR) and the implementation of public notification initiatives regarding "high-risk offenders" in some provinces. Some researchers have suggested that if the Canadian NSOR becomes public, the compliance rate of registered individuals would decrease significantly across the country (Murphy et al., 2009). However, there have yet to be any formal assessments of compliance rates in the first place. A Canadian study examined the perceptions of individuals registered to the Canadian NSOR and their feelings about the possibility that the registry and the personal information it contains become public (Murphy & Fedoroff, 2013). The results showed that 64% of individuals consulted expressed fears regarding this possibility, particularly with regard to their risk of sexual recidivism; some respondents indicated they would be motivated by anger, or become non-compliant with their conditions as a result of their personal information and history becoming public. While this may indicate negative implications of moving to a public SOR, a rival explanation is that such offenders were simply suggesting to the researchers that they would engage in negative behavior to help deter the creation of a public SOR. Unfortunately, SOR data have not been made available in order to, for example, compare the likelihood of sexual recidivism for those that were/were not placed on a public SOR.

The Australian Model

The establishment of SOR in different states in Australia followed templates established in the UK and the USA, and therefore, like Canada, SOR only began to appear in Australia in the 2000s. To some extent, this allowed for the policies to be adapted and tailored to the Australian context. For example, unlike the USA, SOR are not public, although in 2012 the state of Western Australia introduced community notification protocols through a website. Anyone can apply to access certain information about sex offenders in the community, similar to the example above regarding the Canadian Province of Saskatchewan. Furthermore, there is no national public SOR, although as recently as 2019 there have been calls from the conservative federal government to introduce one. A substantial consultation process was put in place by the Australian federal government which called for submissions from various stakeholders (e.g., community groups, research institutes, victim's rights groups, etc.) as to whether they supported the implementation of a national public registry. Many submissions were made, but some notable ones were from the Institute of Child Protection Studies, the Law council of Australia, and an organization known as Bravehearts, a victim advocacy group. Interestingly, among these specific submissions, there was a consensus that they did not support the establishment of SOR because, in their view, it would not enhance safety nor would it protect children from sexual abuse.

Similar to Canada, the implementation of SORN-type laws in Australia reflects a much more measured approach when compared to the USA. Nonetheless, momentum for a public SOR has gained, and continues to gain, traction. Some states in Australia, like in Canada, also have introduced legal provisions for preventative and/or indefinite detention of sex offenders; Queensland and South Australia have specific legal provisions for the indefinite detention of sex offenders, and four states as well as the Northern Territory have post-sentence preventative detention and supervision schemes for individuals convicted of sex offenses (Keyzer & McSherry, 2015).

In Australia, registries are typically referred to as "child protection" registries, as opposed to "sex offender" registries. The state of New South Wales was the first to implement legislation (i.e., the *Child Protection (Offender's registration) Act*) in 2000 with all the other states eventually adopting similar legislation by 2007 (Napier, Dowling, Morgan, & Talbot, 2018). In fact, the introduction of "child protection" registration legislation emerged from The Wood Royal Commission into corruption in the NSW police force in 1997 that, among many other things, detailed apparent inadequacies in policing pedophilia and protecting victims from sexual abuse. Part of the Wood Commission's task was to investigate existing laws and penalties, monitoring and screening of victims, and the adequacy of the police investigatory process in cases of child sexual abuse (Taylor, 2017). At the time, the Wood Commission received numerous submissions in support of SOR; this also came off the heels of American legislation such as Megan's Law, but part of the policy rationale for its introduction was also to implement a more controlled system of access to information among police.

Today, for the most part, offender registries are quite similar across the Australian states; some of the key differences include offenses eligible for registration (i.e., some states focus exclusively on offenses against children but others include offenses against adults or violent nonsexual offenses; Vess, Langskaill, Day, Powell, & Graffam, 2011). While there is no national public SOR, the registers in each state are more-or-less linked through the Australian Child Protection Reporting Scheme. This is, in effect, a national registry, but one in which only law enforcement agencies have access to for the purpose of recording, case managing, and sharing information, similar in scope of access to Canada's national registry. In fact, the Australian Bureau of Criminal Intelligence, which is a national common police service designed to facilitate the exchange of criminal intelligence between state and federal law enforcement agencies that was established in 1981, began doing so in relation to sex offenses against children in 1989. Far before the advent of registries, this practice was only publicly acknowledged in 1995 (Victorian Law Reform Commission, 2014).

Why a Public Sex Offender Registry?

Legal scholars have challenged and criticized laws such as the Jacob Wetterling Act and Megan's Law on ideological, ethical, moral, and legal grounds (e.g., La Fond, 2005; Logan, 2003; Socia & Stamatel, 2010; Simon, 1998). Nonetheless, SORN laws have generally received favorable public support in the USA, even though public notification procedures can increase feelings of insecurity and fear of being sexually assaulted (Beck & Travis, 2004; Zevitz, 2004). This support seems to arise directly from fear of convicted offenders and the social construction of all persons eligible for placement on a SOR as a sexual predator likely to perpetrate another crime. Again, this does not comport with empirical literature demonstrating the generally low likelihood of sexual recidivism. To be sure, this feeling of fear is understandable and very real, particularly among individuals who have children. This support is largely based on myths and false beliefs about these individuals and their risk of sexual offending (Levenson, Brannon, Fortney, & Baker, 2007). Indeed, the rationale for SORN laws seems to stem directly from the numerous misconceptions and stereotypes concerning these individuals. An increasing body of empirical research on the criminal activity and recidivism of these individuals has helped to begin disrupting these myths and misconceptions (Chap. 3) (e.g., Caldwell, 2002; Letourneau & Miner, 2005; Lussier, 2005; Lussier & Blokland, 2014; Sample & Bray, 2003; Simon, 1998, 2000; Zimring, 2004).

The fundamental basis on which SORN laws have been developed stands in stark contrast with the available evidence on their efficacy. In fact, SORN laws are based on a sensationalist perspective of sexual offending and the individuals perpetrating sex offenses, which generally revolves around very unusual, if not exceptional, cases that have been widely publicized. Most commonly, sexual homicides of children have driven the development of SORN laws. Although the key aim is to prevent the sexual homicide of children, American SORN laws do not specifically apply to individuals who have committed a sexual homicide, but rather any individuals convicted for any sexual offense. The underlying rationale is that perpetrators of sex offenses will continue to escalate in the severity of their sexual offenses; without intervention, their sexual offending trajectory will eventually culminate in the perpetration a sexual homicide. This again resembles Taleb's (2007) description of the narrative fallacy, a key ingredient of Black Swan events; looking back at events after they happened and attributing causal power and causal mechanisms to some situations, contexts, and events. A story is told, repeatedly, and it gains momentum, it makes sense; people accept it at face value, and it becomes the leading explanation as to why such a tragic event happened. Citizens, journalists, lawyers, judges, and policymakers who look at these events *after* the fact falsely assume that criminal justice practitioners and others tasked with preventing sexual offending and ensuring safety of the public were able to view the unfolding of the event from the same perspective as those looking at the event in hindsight and that these groups failed to take appropriate action.

Public Safety, Public Awareness, and Vigilance

Public outcry from unusual, atypical, and widely publicized cases has fueled a desire for increased protection and security to prevent sexual crimes (Logan, 2003; Prescott & Rockoff, 2011). Therefore, one critical question in this context is: what is the rationale for SORN laws? Supporters of notification laws claim that such measures can help prevent sex crimes by promoting awareness, while encouraging increased vigilance by community members; this will limit opportunities for sexual offenses and thus reduce sexual recidivism (La Fond, 2005). Another hypothesis is that public notification can also help prevent sex crimes by facilitating collaboration and partnership between multiple agencies within the criminal justice system (courts, law enforcement, corrections; e.g., Finn, 1997). This high level of support for SORN laws is not surprising given the role played by the public in the development of these laws in the USA. However, this perspective is not necessarily shared by all stakeholders. For example, many public health professionals have questioned the relevance and effectiveness of these measures (Malesky & Keim, 2001). Welchans (2005) pointed out that the implementation of SORN laws represents a burden for the criminal justice system as a whole. Likewise, these laws imply that there is no other adequate solution to address and prevent sex crimes.

For SORN laws to be effective, one vital prerequisite is arguably that the public registry needs to be accessible and that residents consult it on a relatively regular basis. Indeed, if citizens do not have access or do not use the information contained in public SOR, the main objective of such laws would be seriously compromised. Surprisingly, there has not been much research on the access and use of SOR information (Beck & Travis, 2004). Limited research to date suggests that while citizens are aware of and supportive of these laws, most tend not to consult SOR websites and information contained in the registries (e.g., Anderson & Sample, 2008; Kernsmith, Comartin, Craun, & Kernsmith, 2009). Those who tend to access these websites are generally women, young adults, people living in urban areas, and individuals with children. It could be argued that the enactment of these laws has reinforced a sense of insecurity for specific segments of the general population living in certain areas. In addition, empirical research suggests that citizens are not well aware of the presence of individuals with past convictions for a sex crime in their neighborhood.[4] This is possibly because registered sex offenders, after release from prison, tend to move to communities characterized by greater social disorganization, implying that these communities are less equipped to monitor and prevent sex crimes (Hughes & Kadleck, 2008; Mustaine, Tewksbury, & Stengel, 2006). Furthermore, among those who consult the registry's website, only a minority take

---

[4] For example, in a passive notification area (where residents are responsible for self-information), it has been reported that less than one-third of residents who lived near a registered sex offender were even aware of their presence in the neighborhood (Craun, 2010; Kernsmith et al., 2009). When active public notification is used, not surprisingly, public awareness tends to be higher (Beck & Travis, 2006).

preventive action (Anderson & Sample, 2008). Therefore, SORN laws do not seem to have a substantial impact on citizens' behavior, and if they do, it currently is unclear whether this actually contributes to the prevention of sex crimes.

Supporting Police Investigations, Deterrence, and Symbolic Value

One of the principles that led to the development of SORN laws is the concept of deterrence (Drake & Aos, 2009; La Fond, 2005). The theoretical foundation for a deterrence approach to sexual offending is rational choice theory (RCT; e.g., Cornish & Clarke, 2014). RCT states that individuals perform a rational calculus that weighs the benefits (gains) and costs associated with perpetrating an offense (e.g., Beauregard & Leclerc, 2007; Beauregard, Rossmo, & Proulx, 2007). From the logic of SORN laws, the occurrence of a sex crime is significantly decreased if the negative consequences of perpetrating such acts are real, immediate, and proportional to the act itself. Registries and public notification are therefore added to the legal consequences that result from a conviction for a sex crime. Hence, it is believed that the being publicly registered as a sex offender and subjected to public notification would significantly increase the costs of offending in such a way as to deter individuals from perpetrating a sex crime. This can happen in two ways. First, this idea suggests that individuals who are publicly registered as a sex offender, and who are thus the subject of some form of public notification, will re-evaluate the costs of sexual offending in such a way that will stop them from perpetrating a subsequent sex crime. This refers to a hypothesized specific deterrence effect of SORN laws. For example, proponents of SORN laws argued that the registry has a deterrent effect because it increases the likelihood of detection (Prescott, 2012). If a sex crime is committed, police can quickly identify individuals who have a criminal record for a sex crime in the area (Finn, 1997), trace where they live, and link their place of residence to this new offense (La Fond, 2005). This was one of the main rationales provided for the implementation of SOR laws in Canada and in Australia. Second, there is also a rationale for a general deterrent effect in which citizens that may consider perpetrating such acts and those who are struggling with deviant sexual fantasies witness the negative consequences that convicted offenders are subjected to and, as a result, re-assess the cost-benefit ratio in such a way that the perceived costs of perpetrating a sex crime outweigh the perceived benefits.

For deterrence to be effective in preventing any crime, some very basic and well-established conditions need to be met. Certainty and celerity (i.e., speed) are two of these conditions; they are among the key principles of criminal sentencing that are inherently related to the potential deterrent effect of any sanction imposed following a conviction for a sex crime. Therefore, before evaluating whether SORN laws have the potential to carry a deterrent effect, the entire criminal justice system first needs to be scrutinized. What is the certainty of being detected, caught, apprehended, charged, and convicted for a sex crime? For the relatively few individuals who end up being convicted for a sex crime (e.g., relative to even those who are arrested; see Daly & Bouhours, 2010), what then was the speed at which the criminal justice system detected, apprehend, charged, and convicted these individuals? From the RCT standpoint, individuals considering committing a sex crime would consider: (a) the difficulties targeting and offending against a victim; (b) the perceived likelihood of being arrested, convicted, and sanctioned for their crime; (c) the certainty and celerity, nature and type, of sanction; and (d) the negative consequences of engaging in different types of sexual crimes (Lussier, Bouchard, & Beauregard, 2011; Prescott, 2012). From a RCT perspective, for crime prevention efforts to be effective, the perceived costs of engaging in any given criminal behavior must outweigh the anticipated or perceived gains, rewards, or benefits resulting from the criminal behavior. Taking all these previous points into consideration, researchers have questioned whether there is even any potential general or specific deterrence effect of SORN laws. It remains unclear whether individuals contemplating the idea of perpetrating a sex crime actually consider SORN-type laws prior to taking action (e.g., Drake & Aos, 2009). The reality is that we do not know much, scientifically speaking, about the thought process involved in sexual offending, let alone the specific forms of sex crimes that resulted in calls for SORN in the first place.

Ultimately, from a general population standpoint, whether SORN laws produce a deterrent effect or not might not matter. From this perspective, what matters more is the message that SORN laws send to convicted offenders and individuals contemplating such crimes. In fact, a survey from the state of Alabama showed that respondents supported SORN laws *regardless* of their effectiveness in preventing sex crimes (Koon-Magnin, 2015). These research findings suggest that sex offender registries and public notification carry far more symbolic rather than instrumental value to the public.

The Effect of Public Sex Offender Registries

American research on SORN laws has not been focused on the underlying assumptions and principles of these laws as a crime prevention strategy. Rather, the focus of evaluation research has been limited to the examination of the impact of these policies on sexual offending. Welchans (2005) conducted one of the first syntheses of evaluation studies on the deterrent and preventative impact of public SOR laws. She reviewed 12 evaluation studies; most were focused on perceptions regarding the impact of these policies. Of these studies, Welchans (2005) found only two examining the actual impact of public registries on sex crimes, one of which was based on retrospective data, thus preventing any firm conclusions regarding the deterrent impact of public registries. Welchans (2005) considered other studies on the effect of SORN laws on crime and recidivism rates, particularly in terms of their preventative influence on different forms of violent and sexual crimes. Overall, Welchans offered a cautiously optimistic evaluation of the effect of SORN laws as a crime prevention strategy, while acknowledging that evaluation studies were far too scarce to draw any firm conclusions. Levenson and D'Amora (2007) offered a second opinion on the deterrent effect of public SOR. Their assessment of five independent studies led them to conclude that there was little empirical evidence that these measures had a deterrent effect. Levenson and D'Amora presented three issues associated with the implementation of public registries. First, they expressed concern about the accuracy of the information in public registries. If information is inaccurate, it cannot help police detect potential suspects nor can it help the public make informed decisions about how to remain safe. Second, they observed that the establishment of the public registry, particularly public notifications, had a negative effect on the community (e.g., fear and anxiety) as well as on correctional professionals (e.g., increased workload). Third, Levenson and D'Amora warned about the fact of analyzing the deterrent effect of public registries without also considering the collateral effects on registered individuals. This latter point refers to how SORN may lead to difficulties becoming employed, maintaining positive relationships with a spouse, intimate partner, and family members, and securing housing. Not all agree with this perspective. Some have argued that formal social control would facilitate informal social control (Cooley, Moore, & Sample, 2017; Meloy, 2005; ten Bensel & Sample, 2017).

The first systematic review on the deterrent effect of public registries was conducted by Drake and Aos (2009). They identified eighteen relevant studies; nine were excluded from their evaluation because they did not meet certain strict methodological criteria. It should be noted that four of the five studies cited by Levenson and D'Amora (2007) that led to the conclusion that there was no deterrent effect of public registries were excluded from the analysis by Drake and Aos due to methodological issues. Seven of the nine studies included in the evaluation examined specific deterrence, five of which focused on adults, and two of which focused on juveniles. Using a quantitative meta-analytical approach, Drake and Aos (2009) did not find a statistically significant deterrent effect on rates of sexual recidivism.[5] To that effect, Socia Jr and Stamatel (2010) argued that it is impossible to confirm whether SOR influences a reduction in sexual crimes. They mentioned that evaluation studies share an obvious methodological limitation, namely the inability to control for other external factors that may have influenced the sex crime rates following the implementation of SOR. Socia Jr & Stamatel, 2010also raised concerns that, in general, sex crime rates had started to drop *before* the implementation of SOR (see also, Zgoba, Witt, Dalessandro, & Veysey, 2008). Therefore, external factors other than public SOR could well have explained why certain evaluation studies found a general deterrent effect. Finally, Socia Jr and Stamatel (2010) warned of the

---

[5] Drake and Aos (2009) selected two evaluation studies that looked at the general deterrent effect, or in other words, the effect of public registries on recorded rates of sexual offending in the community. The two studies examining general deterrence lead these authors to conclude that there was some evidence supporting the view that public registries were associated with lower sex crime rates. They were also cautious about these results given the small number of studies on which these conclusions were based.

dangers of generalizing the results of a study considering that the provisions and the rules regarding public registries vary from one state to another.

Prescott (2012) presented contrasting conclusions by highlighting that public registries have a much more complex effect than what is generally reported in the scientific literature. First, he argued that public SOR can have a specific deterrent effect. The registry, he adds, can help reduce the sexual recidivism of registered individuals to the extent that it improves supervision and increases vigilance about their behavior. On the other hand, he maintains that public notification does not necessarily have the same effect on recidivism of convicted offenders. He hypothesized that while public notification may have a deterrent effect on sexual recidivism, it may, however, have the opposite effect on nonsexual recidivism because the collateral effects of SORN laws on social reintegration diminish the ability or the desire of registered offenders to live crime-free. Third, Prescott argues that these SORN laws are more likely to be effective when they apply to a small number of individuals rather than to all individuals who have been convicted of a sex crime. Consequently, public notifications should be limited to dangerous individuals at high risk of sexual recidivism. Referring to this group as the "worst cases," however, Prescott is unclear as to the criteria by which they can be identified among all individuals convicted for a sex crime, or even the period during which this group should be submitted to the public registry.

More recently, Lussier and Mathesius (2018) raised the hypothesis that the quest for a specific deterrent effect for all individuals on public registries is perhaps illusory and masks the possibility that public registries may have differential effects on individuals subject to such laws (see also, Caldwell, Ziemke, & Vitacco, 2008; Freeman, 2012; Schram & Milloy, 1995; Zevitz, 2006). The difficulty interpreting the findings of evaluation studies is due to numerous methodological shortcomings. Of importance, none of these studies are based on an experimental research design and the findings may be explained by external factors other than the SORN laws. As a result, there are numerous contradictory findings. For example, Freeman (2012) reported that registered individuals who were the subject of a much larger and more intensive public notification had higher rates of sexual recidivism. According to Freeman (2012), the high sexual recidivism rates in this study could be a function of the negative social consequences of such laws. Public notification may facilitate a labeling and marginalization effect among registered individuals subjected to more intense and widespread public notification. Is this marginalization effect generalized or specific to a subgroup of registered individuals? Firm conclusions are difficult to draw because the study does not contain information about sexual recidivism rates prior to the implementation of public registries. In sum, depending on the study one reads, they could conclude virtually anything about the impact of SORN. In some ways then, the literature on SORN has not provided useful information on the topic, which also reflects research that has attempted to understand the deterrent effect of capital punishment (Nagin, 2013).

An alternative to the evaluation of the deterrent impact of SORN laws is to implement a pre/post event research design. This approach involves the identification of a group of high-risk offenders prior to the enactment of SORN laws who have not been subjected to registration and public notification, and to match them with a comparable group of offenders who were convicted after the enactment of these laws. Duwe and Donnay (2008) have provided empirical evidence suggesting that, in Minnesota, the establishment of a public registry had a deterrent effect on individuals at a high-risk of sexual recidivism. These results tend to highlight the importance of a differential approach in modulating the scope of public notifications according to the individual's recidivism risk. These results, however, are difficult to reconcile with Freeman's (2012) observations and conclusions of a marginalization effect that increased the likelihood of sexual recidivism. Tewksbury and Jennings (2010) compared patterns of sexual offending among individuals from Iowa; some of whom were examined pre-SORN laws and some whom were examined post-SORN laws. These authors found similar patterns across both groups, implying such laws had neither a deterrent nor a marginalization effect. One outstanding issue involved in the non-experimental design of the Duwe and Donnay (2008) and Tewksbury and Jennings (2010) studies is the need to account for the numerous social, cultural, political, legal, and correctional changes that also occurred during the pre/post study periods, which may also explain the differential recidivism rates. Indeed, it is reasonable to assume that supervision practices, incarceration experiences, and treatment and intervention programs also may have changed since the implementation of SORN laws and that such changes, and not SORN, were responsible for any differences observed; alternatively, such changes could also have counteracted any changes that would have occurred following the implementation of SORN. The task of examining the impact of these laws is a complex one comprised of many pitfalls, issues, and challenges.

In all, the research conducted to date has neither produced convincing evidence demonstrating a crime prevention effect nor has it demonstrated the mechanism by which SORN laws could have a crime prevention effect. In that regard, in a recent qualitative analysis based on interviews conducted with a small sample of registered offenders, researchers were able to highlight offenders' perceptions of what might have deterred them from having sexually reoffended (Cooley et al., 2017). The study findings suggested that if there is a deterrent effect operating on the behavior of these registered offenders, it is the threat of legal sanctions associated with breaching registration conditions, rather than public notification, that acts as a deterrent. While there is a gap between offenders' perception and their actual behavior, these findings reiterate the lack of scientific knowledge about the role of deterrence and deterrence mechanisms in sexual offending.

External Factors that Minimize or Negate Public Registries' Deterrent Effect

The integrity of public SOR is conditional on the quality, accuracy, and validity of the information it contains. However, researchers have raised important issues regarding the reliability of the information contained in the registries over the years

(Lees & Tewksbury, 2006). For example, Tewksbury's (2002) study verified some of the information in Kentucky's public SOR. Less than 75% of the residential addresses of registered individuals were correct. Another study conducted in the state of Massachusetts suggested that the actual location of nearly half of registered sex offenders was unknown (Mullvihill, Wisniewski, Meyers, & Wells, 2003). More recently, another study found that up to 100,000 individuals listed in various public registries across the USA were missing or had vanished (see Harris, Levenson, & Ackerman, 2014). The reasons for all of these scenarios remain unclear: some individuals may be missing as a result of early mortality, hospitalization, or incarceration in another state; some may be homeless or transient; others may be on the run and trying to escape justice and the negative consequences of registration; and in other circumstances there may simply be errors in maintaining such a high volume of up-to-date records. No matter the reason, the bottom line is that if data maintained in registries are incorrect, imprecise, or invalid, it is unlikely that such registries will meet the objective of enhancing public safety and preventing sex crimes.

In addition, the quality, accuracy, and validity of the information contained in public registries has implications on resources within the criminal justice system. Indeed, the collection, verification and updating of the data contained in public registries mobilizes a lot of financial and human resources. As the number of registered individuals increases, more resources are mobilized, especially as individuals on US public registries are increasingly registered for very long periods. An increase in the number of registrations may also affect any potential deterrence impact of the measure. In the USA, more than one million people are currently listed on a public SOR. As the number of people entered in the register increases, more people are subjected to surveillance by citizens, who in turn communicate various sorts of information to law enforcement that is not always relevant. This accumulation of information can quickly become a burden on law enforcement, particularly when it is not accurate or valid (e.g., Zevitz & Farkas, 2000). In addition, the sizes of registries and the growing number of registrants yearly could have a negative impact on the quality of police investigations into sexual crimes. As Agan (2011) points out, having a registry can have the effect of quickly prioritizing registered individuals and neglecting the investigation of suspects who have no history of sex crimes and who, therefore, are not included in the sex offender registries. As shown earlier in the book, the majority of sex crimes detected by the criminal justice system are perpetrated by individuals without a history of sexual offending. From an investigative standpoint, if a SOR fails to distinguish low-risk versus high-risk persons, then police may be tasked with following up with hundreds of persons on a registry when in fact the offense was perpetrated by someone not included in the registry.

Researchers have also hypothesized that public notifications may nullify any potential deterrent effect of public registries in several ways (Dugan, 2001). First, the time spent monitoring compliance with the rules and procedures related to the registry represents time that is not devoted to the usual activities of law enforcement and probation officers (e.g., surveillance, monitoring, and counselling). Many tasks are required to maintain the efficacy of a SOR. Has the individual recently released from prison reported to the police department in their neighborhood? Is the information disclosed accurate and precise? Has the individual moved? Does the individual live alone? Does a child live in the same residence? Are the residents of the building and building manager aware of the individual's prior sex crimes? Not only are there many pieces of information to verify, but this information often changes over time, and such circumstances can change quite quickly. Second, the public registry could foster *crime displacement effect* through a process by which individuals who commit sex crimes could in fact be less likely to be detected given that they are more careful in the way they perpetrate their offenses in order to avoid being registered (e.g., Agan, 2011). One way this could occur is if perpetrators select victims who are more vulnerable and less likely to report the offense, or by committing sex crimes far from their place of residence. On this subject, Logan (2003) raised the idea that public notifications concerning the presence of a sex offender in the neighborhood are unlikely to help prevent sex crimes committed by an individual far from his residence outside the notification area (see also Petrosino & Petrosino, 1999). Third, being registered in and of itself could possibly neutralize any deterrent effect since the individual already suffers the negative consequences related to the registration (Agan, 2011); what is left to lose when an individual is already on a registry and is already the subject of public notification? Fourth, public registries may create a false sense of security among the general population (Dugan, 2001). In particular, some may falsely conclude that all sex offenders are known and listed. In this regard, public registries can draw the attention of parents on registered individuals who are the subject of a public notification in their region, to the detriment of individuals motivated to commit a sexual offense, but who are not registered (no criminal record), or even of registered individuals, but outside the notification area of the parents' place of residence.

Taken together, according to Lussier and Mathesius (2018), these study findings do not provide convincing empirical evidence to conclude that SORN laws are good crime prevention policies (see also, Bouffard & Askew, 2019). Indeed, the examination of SORN laws cannot be limited to the impact of differential sex crime rates and sexual recidivism rates; several other factors need to be considered as part of any policy analysis along these lines.

Public Sex Offender Registries and Collateral Effects

A number of studies have examined the collateral effects of public SOR on registered individuals, their families, and the community at large. Indeed, the presence of public registries raised questions regarding the safety of individuals publicly recognized as sex offenders and labeled as sexual predators. Do these public registries and public notification encourage citizens to take the law into their own hands? Are the registered individuals subject to public notifications the object of some form of retaliation or vigilantism? Are registered offenders subject to discrimination and prejudices that may disrupt their ability to reintegrate into society? Is the reach of SORN laws such that it makes it impossible for these individuals to participate in any civic duties that are traditionally associated with desistance from general offending? In other words, what is the impact of SORN laws beyond public safety and the prevention of sex crimes? Could it be that these SORN laws carry negative consequences that were not considered, foreseen, or envisioned by those that contributed to their development, implementation, and enactment? That said, in criminology, there is a long tradition of research on labeling theory and most importantly how official labels can place individuals in difficult circumstances that may promote deviant and criminal behaviors (e.g., Becker, 1963). For example, in agreement with a labeling effect, research has shown that after a conviction, self-reported offending tended to increase (e.g., Farrington, 1977), notably by affecting subsequent involvement in deviant social groups (e.g., Bernburg, Krohn, & Rivera, 2006). Individuals convicted for a sex crime are purposely labeled as sex offenders in unprecedented ways to inform the public of their legal status. Some may feel that such circumstances are the just desserts for a person that has committed a harmful offense. However, such consequences may destabilize the individual in a way that jeopardizes public safety by increasing their likelihood of committing new crimes.

Life Circumstances and Psychosocial Effects

Several studies examined the collateral effects of SORN laws on registrants. Lasher and McGrath's (2012) meta-analysis combined the results of eight American studies involving 1503 registered individuals. All studies were conducted using surveys and questionnaires that included relatively similar questions from one study to the next, making the results directly comparable. Approximately 45% of registrants reported having been threatened by a neighbor, 30% lost their jobs, 20% were forced to leave their homes, and 14% had their property damaged (Lasher & McGrath, 2012). In other words, the prevalence of negative life events associated with being placed on a sex offender register is far from nominal. Levenson, D'Amora, and Hern (2007) showed that young adults were especially likely to experience these collateral consequences. This is concerning because younger individuals are also the ones most at risk of sexual recidivism (Lussier & Healey, 2009). In other words, collateral consequences are most likely to be felt by the individuals that are most in need of positive events that can prevent their sexual reoffending. Instead, these negative events may amplify their already high risk to sexually reoffend. Similar consequences are also experienced by the families of persons on registries (Bailey & Sample, 2017; Tewksbury & Levenson, 2009). However, it is also important to note that these studies suffer from the same methodological shortcomings as evaluation studies mentioned earlier that focused on the impact of SORN laws on sex crime rates and sexual recidivism rates. For example, are the reported adverse life circumstances in fact the result of SORN laws specifically? Or is it also possible that they are the result of pre-existing social conditions or individual characteristics? It may also be possible that they reflect the broader impact of the criminal justice system and the criminogenic effect of incarceration. In short, disentangling the impact of SORN laws from other sociocultural, legal, correctional, social, situational, and individual factors is exceptionally challenging.

Despite these challenges, differences in collateral consequences have been observed depending on the risk classification of individuals surveyed. In the USA, individuals classified as being at high risk of sexual recidivism are generally subject to a wider and more intensive dissemination of public notification compared to registered individuals classified as representing a low or moderate risk of recidivism. Consequently, it is reasonable to hypothesize that the broader the public dissemination, the more the registrants are exposed to the collateral effects of SORN laws. When looking at the results of two studies that included the largest number of individuals assessed at a high-risk of recidivism, 54% lost a job, 24% had to move out of their residence when the owner discovered they were a sex offender, 83% were forced to leave their home, 34% had a family member or partner who was harassed or assaulted, 62% were threatened by a neighbor, and 30% had their property damaged (Mercado, Alvarez, & Levenson, 2008; Zevitz & Farkas, 2000). Taken together, the results of these studies therefore suggest that the life circumstances of those subject to wider and more intensive dissemination of public notification, and specifically, those assessed as high-risk offenders, are likely to be destabilized by these negative events during their community re-entry.

In terms of potential psychosocial consequences, Lasher and McGrath's meta-analytic results showed that 60% of registrants believed that SORN laws interfered with their community reintegration due to increased stress, 57% reported feelings of shame that prevented them from participating in social activities, 52% said they were pessimistic about their future, 51% said they had lost friends, 49% felt isolated, and 40% said they feared for their own safety. The mental health well-being of these individuals during the stressful period of community re-entry after spending a substantial amount of time incarcerated should be concerning for several reasons, but perhaps most especially the fact that these collateral consequences are also known risk factors for offending. In other words, while some may have little sympathy for isolation felt by perpetrators of sexual offenses, such isolation should still be concerning because it increases the risk of reoffending and therefore bringing further harm to potential victims. That this distress occurs early in the community re-entry process is also concerning because sexual recidivism is most likely to take place during the first few months/years of release. Another reason for concern is that SORN may negatively impact the mental health of individuals close to them.[6] Therefore, the negative consequences of SORN laws can extend to family members

---

[6]Levenson and Tewksbury (2009) observed that, among the family members of registrants, 86% felt stressed, 77% said they were isolated, 50% lost friends, 66% were ashamed, and 49% were concerned about their safety. In addition, they suggested that SORN laws may also adversely impact children of registered offenders. Following public notification, these children are likely to experience anger (80%), symptoms of depression (77%), anxiety (73%) and fear (63%), or even to entertain suicidal thoughts (13%). Socially, these children are likely to feel excluded from their peer group (65%), to be ridiculed (59%) or harassed (47%) by other children, or even to be physically assaulted (22%).

and those close to the individual, all of whom are critical in providing social support that can facilitate successful reintegration and work to prevent the likelihood of the individual reoffending, sexually or otherwise.[7]

Finally, although it is evident based on research that the majority of registered offenders have difficult life circumstances, citizens' perception of these individuals' circumstances appears to be quite different. For example, Schiavone and Jeglic (2009) examined the opinion and perceptions of citizens ($n = 115$) about the experience of registrants subjected to SORN laws. These researchers found that, in general, 60% of those surveyed believed that registered offenders do not in fact feel isolated, 50% believed that they have not been ostracized, 55% believed that registered offenders do not voluntarily exclude themselves from social activities because of shame, and about 50% believed that they do not fear for their safety. In short, it appears that only about half of citizens seem to be aware of the negative consequences of SORN laws on registered individuals. At the same time, some citizens seem to believe that the threats, harassment, and experiencing physical assault, etc. may be common experiences among registered individuals in the community. The results of Schiavone and Jeglic's study therefore indicate that citizens tend to support SORN laws, but this is perhaps at least in part because they are not aware of the extent of the negative consequences of these laws on the social reintegration of registered sexual offenders, nor are they aware of how such consequences could increase the risk of offending and harm to the public.

Crime, Deviance, and Marginalization

The policy intention of public registries and notifications is to increase public safety by decreasing the risk of sexual offending. However, considering the evidence surrounding the psychosocial consequences to registered individuals and their families, an important question is whether these policies actually encourage criminal and

---

[7] The complexity of the psychosocial impact of SOR should not be underestimated. On the one hand, results from some studies with offenders highlight several negative psychosocial consequences of registration, but other results suggest that certain registered individuals perceive some benefit in registration and public notification. Lasher and McGrath's study showed that 62% of offenders thought that the people informed of their situation believed in their rehabilitation potential and 74% were motivated not to sexually reoffend in order to demonstrate to those around them that they were not a "bad person." Is it possible to conclude based on these results that the presence of public SOR may in fact promote abstention from offending? On the one hand, 74% of registered offenders surveyed indicated that they were motivated not to reoffend (Lasher & McGrath, 2012). On the other hand, only 27% of these individuals believed that SORN laws played a role in their motivation to reoffend. Thus, their motivation to not sexually reoffend did not stem from SORN laws. In fact, one possibility is that the motivation to not sexually reoffend is attributable, at least in part, to the nature and quality of the social support and assistance around them upon release in spite of their legal status and the consequences of SORN laws. Whether this motivation is any sort of guarantee on the individual's behavior in the medium or long term is another important question.

deviant behavior through the marginalization of these individuals. Indeed, SORN laws purposely label convicted individuals as sex offenders and as dangerous sexual predators. As Winick (1998) points out, this labeling effect demonizes, depersonalizes, and demoralizes registered individuals. Burchfield and Mingus' (2008) qualitative interviews with persons on a SOR provided evidence that this labeling was felt by offenders, who perceived their registration as an attempt to mobilize against offenders seeking to obtain jobs, housing, and families. In recent years, some US states (e.g., Michigan, Illinois, Ohio, Wisconsin), faced with the financial burden that registration creates on the criminal justice system, have gone so far as to impose annual registration fees on registered offenders. Again, this is important to consider because such labeling and marginalization may increase the likelihood of further harm to potential victims. SORN policies do not necessarily share this concern; in fact, offenders that are not marginalized and instead are more tightly embedded within society are viewed as offenders that possibly have more opportunity for sexual offenses and therefore intervention is required to disrupt these ties (see McAlinden, 2012). This perspective contrasts with prior assertions that those who are most disadvantaged are at the greatest likelihood of having formal sanctions negatively impact their structural embeddedness, social capital, and likelihood of benefiting from informal social control (Hagan, 1991). At least three key questions need to be considered surrounding the potential for SORN laws to facilitate, promote, or encourage crime, deviance, and marginalization among registered individuals.

The first is whether SORN laws, by demonizing and depersonalizing a subgroup of registered citizens, essentially make these individuals targets for crime due to their status as a registered sex offender (i.e., vigilantism)? A significant proportion of these individuals are harassed, and even physically assaulted by other citizens (Younglove & Vitello, 2003). The prevalence and severity of these acts, however, has been debated by researchers (Zevitz & Farkas, 2000). In Lasher and McGrath's (2012) meta-analysis, approximately 20% report having been threatened or harassed by someone other than a neighbor and about 8% were physically assaulted (Lasher & McGrath, 2012). Importantly, an increasing number of adolescents are subjected to SORN laws. One of the reasons this is concerning is based on longstanding criminological theories suggesting that the effects of labeling on adolescents have a particularly detrimental effect on the perpetration of future crimes (e.g., Tannenbaum, 1938). The current state of scientific knowledge also suggests that registries and public notification laws do not have a specific deterrent effect on adolescents who have committed a sexual offense (e.g., Caldwell & Dickinson, 2009; Letourneau, Bandyopadhyay, Sinha, & Armstrong, 2009). Recent studies have also shown that SORN laws have significant negative consequences on youth, particularly with respect to their mental health, but also to the greater risks of sexual and nonsexual victimization (Letourneau et al., 2018). Adolescent offenders subjected to SORN laws are more likely to suffer from mental health problems, harassment, and school problems (Harris, Walfield, Shields, & Letourneau, 2016). The impact of SORN laws on adolescents may therefore jeopardize their mental health but also their safety, defeating the initial purpose of these laws.

The second question concerns whether SORN laws help to foster crime, deviance, and marginalization of registered individuals. While SORN laws may facilitate the supervision of certain offenders in the community, public notification, and the associated negative consequences may lead them to fail to comply with SORN rules and procedures (e.g., failing to report to their neighborhood police station, failing to inform police of their moves, etc.; Dugan, 2001).[8] The impact of labeling does not only flow through perceptions from the public. SORN policies transcend the practices of probation and parole officers such that these practitioners may view their "sex offender" clients as a collective identity; this identity being one of riskiness, dangerousness, and an individual that should be feared (see Bailey & Sample, 2017). Relatedly, few studies have examined the effect of SORN laws on the nonsexual criminal conduct of registered individuals. A recent longitudinal study by Jennings, Zgoba, Donner, Henderson, and Tewksbury (2014) found that the implementation of SORN laws had a significant effect on the general criminal recidivism of registrants. More specifically, by comparing offenders' criminal recidivism trajectories before and after the implementation of SORN laws, they demonstrated that registered individuals were much more likely to have had problems with the criminal justice system in connection with drug-related offenses (e.g., possession, trafficking) post-SORN laws. These results provide some evidence of the marginalization hypothesis; could it be that by being under more formal and informal scrutiny, these individuals were more likely to be arrested for minor crimes that would otherwise have gone unnoticed? Could it be that because of their difficult life circumstances, they turn to alcohol and drug use as a coping mechanism? Or, could it be that they turned to drug trafficking because of their difficulty finding and maintaining a job due to their status as a registered sex offender?

The third question is whether or not SORN laws are especially likely to contribute to the marginalization of certain groups. Could it be that SORN laws are another manifestation of institutionalized racism that maintains historical and structural socioeconomic disparities and disadvantages across social and racial groups? For example, Ackerman and Sacks (2018) examined the sociodemographic characteristics of a very large sample of registered offenders across various US states (see also, Hoppe, 2016). Their study revealed that Blacks were overrepresented in sex offender registries. Ticknor and Warner (2020) further reported that in the state of Ohio, Blacks were overrepresented as high-risk offenders. In the absence of a known crime prevention effect combined with the possible adverse psychosocial consequences of SORN laws, the disproportionate application of SORN laws to certain social groups is a cause of great concern and potentially a source of social injustice and inequality.

---

[8] Others have raised concerns about the inappropriate use of these individuals' personal information available on the Internet, which may encourage deviant or criminal activity. For example, some have speculated that individuals could use the public registry to contact sex offenders and facilitate the development of pedophile networks as well as the distribution of child pornography (e.g., Zevitz & Farkas, 2000). These claims, however, have not been validated from empirical data and remain, at this stage, hypotheses.

The Unintended Growth of a Misguided Initiative

An additional collateral problem of the enactment of misguided registration and notification policies has been the unintended growth of initiatives indirectly associated with SORN laws (Lussier & Mathesius, 2018). These additional measures were introduced as a result of the implementation issues and challenges that were being experienced across US states. For example, the AWA was passed in 2006 with the goal of reducing disparities between states while expanding the scope of SORN laws (Anderson et al., 2009; Wright, 2008). These issues and challenges were perceived as opportunities to question the underlying assumptions and objectives of SORN laws. However, these issues and challenges were instead interpreted as barriers to achieving the original objectives and purposes of SORN laws. Therefore, to remedy the situation, additional measures were enacted to address these barriers, including the enactment of residential restriction laws.

For individuals convicted of sex offenses, the widespread publication of personal information, such as their residential address, allowed citizens, especially victim's rights advocacy groups, to eventually discover that registered offenders often lived near locations considered to be "risky places" that are likely to be targeted by sexual predators. These "risky places" were not based on scientific evidence but rather on public perception of a "sexual predator's" preferred modus operandi. Not surprisingly therefore, these locations included places where children go to have fun, go to school, wait for the school bus, play with friends, etc. Although these locations are relatively typical in most cities and suburbs, especially in densely populated areas, the presence of the registered offenders near public parks, daycares, elementary schools, high schools, and bus stops were socially constructed as potentially risky situations. Pressure was exerted on government representatives in various US states to quickly remedy the situation. More and more states therefore began to propose, develop, and implement residential restriction laws. These laws aim to create "safe zones" where people who have already been convicted of a sex crime cannot establish a place of residence. Unsurprisingly, these new measures have received the approval of a significant proportion of Americans with young children (Mancini, Shields, Mears, & Beaver, 2010). Yet, the "safe zones" were based on social perceptions of areas that constituted a high risk for sexual offending. In reality, the areas identified contrasted with environmental criminology research on what are considered most likely sites for criminal behavior.

At the time of this book, about 35 states have residential restriction laws for sex offenders. Although these laws differ from state to state, safe zones generally ban offenders from coming within a radius anywhere from about 900 to 2000 feet (i.e., 300–600 m) from specific and predetermined geographic locations, such as public parks, daycares, and schools. It is unclear how and why these specific distances were established, as well as the rationale underlying the creation for these safe zones and the identification of criteria to determine what constitutes a safe zone. The few empirical studies that have examined the geographical and environmental aspects of sexual offending show that sex crimes are not committed in or near the places specifically covered by these laws (e.g., Barnes, Dukes, Tewksbury, & De Troye, 2008; Calkins, Colombino, Matsuura, & Jeglic, 2015). In fact, there are several studies that demonstrate that the variety of locations where these crimes generally take place are typically sites that are not considered by residential restriction laws. Indeed, Canadian studies have identified places that are more conducive to the commission of sex crimes, including shopping malls, bars, and victims' residences (Beauregard, Proulx, Rossmo, Leclerc, & Allaire, 2007; Deslauriers-Varin & Beauregard, 2010, 2014a, 2014b). It is also important to reiterate the fact that in a majority of sex offenses, the victim knows the offender prior to the abuse and the specific location may not matter that much from a prevention standpoint. More recently, Savage and Windsor (2018) added weight to criticism of the expansion of US laws limiting access to certain geographic areas to people convicted of a sex crime. They showed that the safe zones created by residential restriction laws were not sites normally considered to be at risk for sex crimes. These findings do not seem to be the result of perpetrators adapting the locations that they typically offend due to restrictions on entering these safe zones given that observations regarding the locations where offenders typically offend were made outside the USA, where such safe zone laws are not in force (e.g., Deslauriers-Varin & Beauregard, 2010).

Although the stated purpose of these residential restriction laws was to create safe zones, these laws appear to have contributed to the increased marginalization of some entire neighborhoods. Following the enactment of SORN laws, registered offenders were faced with difficulties finding a place to live, which was exacerbated by the enactment of residential restriction laws. Indeed, these laws represent additional obstacles that can hinder their re-entry and reintegration processes by separating offenders from their spouse and their children; forcing offenders to move away; having to move further away from their friends and family members; having to establish residence away from employment opportunities; having to move into criminogenic environments and/or neighborhoods, and being surrounded by negative social influences. Critically, they can also force individuals to move away from certain community resources and outpatient treatment programs. These pitfalls can also destabilize these individuals in unpredictable ways and increase the potential for sexual and nonsexual reoffending. Some research suggests that following their release from prison, registered offenders tend to establish their residence in disadvantaged neighborhoods characterized by greater social disorganization, including individuals more vulnerable to various forms of victimization (e.g., Hughes & Kadleck, 2008; Mustaine et al., 2006). The effect of SORN laws and SORN related laws may therefore create a displacement effect that leads to the emergence of what some criminologists have coined as crime "hot spots."

Assessment of the Effect of SORN Laws: Problems, Difficulties, and Challenges

Revisiting the Black Box Problem

Evaluation studies to date have focused on the general and specific deterrence effect of SORN laws irrespective of their variations across states. These laws have led to the enactment of complex procedures that require the coordination of various inter-related components; these logistical factors of the policy operation are rarely considered in evaluation studies. Consequently, SORN laws remain "black boxes" as the details of each of these components and how they interact together are very difficult to measure. Pawson (2002b) proposed a realist approach which is based on the understanding that SORN laws are multifaceted crime prevention strategies that are comprised of several interrelated components (Pawson & Tilley, 1994, 1997) such as: who is the targeted population; what are the administrative components of these measures; what are the legal and ethical considerations that dictate the practical operation of these measures; what are the implementation procedures; are any risk assessment and risk management procedures used; what are citizens' and offenders' reactions to these measures; and what is the cost/benefit of these measures. In short, rather than combining the results and analyzing them as a whole in order to determine which program works best (the "what works" approach), the realist approach builds on the diversity of prevention programs in order to better grasp the possible results. Indeed, before one draws conclusions about the effectiveness of a crime prevention policy, it is necessary to understand why and under what set of circumstances a policy or program works. Therefore, from a realist point of view, it is not so much a question of finding out what always works, but what works, for whom, how it works, why it works, and under what circumstances it is successful. Studies to date rarely address such questions. Not surprisingly therefore, researchers like Pawson (2002a) and others (e.g., La Fond, 2005) have argued that the current state of knowledge does not allow valid conclusions to be drawn regarding SORN laws.

An Illusory Utility?

To date, despite several studies, researchers have not been able to empirically demonstrate the efficacy or usefulness of SORN laws as a crime prevention tool. For example, while registries have been touted as a tool for police and investigators to quickly locate suspects in sex crime investigations, to date, no data have been produced indicating they actually contribute to police investigations of sex crimes and solving such cases (La Fond, 2005; Logan, 2003). Rather, key questions that need to be answered include whether and to what extent police investigators actually access and utilize data contained in registries, whether registries do in fact play a role in the identification and prioritization of suspects, and to what extent SOR has contributed to the arrests and convictions of individuals in connection with specific sex crimes? Currently, we simply do not have answers to these questions. These answers are necessary before drawing firm conclusions about the effectiveness of registries in terms of their utility to aid law enforcement. Another question that also deserves attention is that if the registry does in fact help prioritize suspects, to what extent has the establishment of SORN laws led to miscarriages of justice in matters of sex crimes? Could arrests made by police relying on SOR data be less likely to result in conviction because officers limited the scope of their investigation and therefore may have excluded relevant suspects not found in the registry?

The Overlooked Issue of Official Measures of Sexual Offending

To date, evaluation studies on the effectiveness of SORN laws have been based exclusively on official indicators of sexual offending (e.g., number of police complaints, number of arrests, and number of convictions). It is well known that there is a significant gap between the actual rates of sexual offending and the official data on sexual offenses (e.g., Lussier & Cale, 2013). Following the enactment of SORN laws, researchers have attempted to minimize the problem of official data by using incidents reported to the police rather than arrests or convictions (Prescott & Rockoff, 2011). Despite this, only a minority of sexual offenses are even reported to the police. This issue is compounded by concerns that those who are subjected to registration or that fear being registered will be especially careful in the way they perpetrate offenses (e.g., Agan, 2011). Strict reliance on official indicators of sexual offending, be it reports to police, arrests, or convictions, inevitably leads to a complex interpretation of crime preventive policies. For example, evaluation studies reporting that sex crime rates decreased following the implementation of SORN laws can be interpreted in many ways that researchers have not sufficiently emphasized. For example, the most straightforward interpretation is that there are fewer sex crimes perpetrated because of the implementation of SORN laws. However, another possibility is that perpetrators of sex crimes are more aware of the risk and take extra precautions when committing a sex crime so as to avoid detection (Agan, 2011). Could it be that registered offenders are more likely to perpetrate sex crimes out of the state or out of the country?[9] It could be that following the enactment of SORN laws, valuable criminal justice resources are diverted to the supervision and monitoring of a small group of individuals and non-registered offenders more easily get away with sex crimes.

---

[9] In Canada, for example, although only anecdotally discussed in the media, there have been concerns about Canadians traveling to countries such as Thailand for the purposes of "sex tourism" in which such individuals take advantage of lax laws or marginalized individuals, including children, to perpetrate sexual offenses with less risk of detection. In other words, what might appear as a deterrent effect could well be a displacement effect.

Another possibility for a post-SORN decline in the rate of sex crimes is that the criminal justice system is more reluctant to prosecute less serious forms of sexual offending because of the severely negative consequences that would be experienced by the perpetrator, especially if they are an adolescent. Other sources of information, such as victimization surveys and capture-recapture techniques (Bouchard & Lussier, 2015), could provide valuable information about the impact of SORN laws.

Alternatives to the Criminal Justice System?

The American experience with SORN laws also highlights the problems of focusing almost exclusively on the criminal justice system to prevent sex crimes by reacting to individuals that have already perpetrated one. Several researchers have questioned the strict reliance on the criminal justice system and the need to redefine the problem as a public health issue (e.g., Basile, 2003; Becker & Reilly, 1999; McMahon, 2000). The public health approach highlights the importance of proactive prevention, meaning that prevention efforts should not be limited to intervention targeted at those who have perpetrated sex crimes. Prevention initiatives should start before the occurrence of the behavior in the form of educational programs. These may include prevention efforts targeting the general population (e.g., campaigns against sexual violence; sexual harassment), also known as primary prevention. They may also include interventions targeting individuals considered at-risk of perpetrating a sex crime, also known as secondary prevention. One group that may be the focus of such secondary prevention are those struggling with deviant sexual fantasies.

Perhaps the most notable primary prevention initiative along these lines that exists today is located in Germany. This initiative is designed to intervene with individuals struggling with pedophilic sexual thoughts and fantasies, but who have not necessarily acted on those thoughts or fantasies. Prevention Project Dunkelfeld[10] was launched in 2005 and is aimed toward providing treatment for individuals who self-identified as having a sexual interest in children. This prevention program essentially aims to offer specialized counseling and treatment services to individuals without a legal status (i.e., those who have not committed sexual offenses), but who consider themselves at risk of perpetrating a sex crime against a child (e.g., Beier et al., 2009; Schaefer et al., 2010). This project was accompanied by a large-scale media campaign to encourage potential participants who were experiencing distress because of their sexual interests to seek treatment, while ensuring their anonymity and confidentiality to avoid labeling or societal stigma. While the program focuses on preventing the onset of child sexual abuse (CSA), and therefore includes many individuals who have never committed an act of CSA, it is possible that some participants may have in the past committed an act of CSA. The project provides treatment broadly based on cognitive-behavioral therapy to prevent these

---

[10] Which means "dark field" or "dark figure."

individuals from acting on their impulses and committing acts of CSA. The program provides therapy and teaches skills and techniques including, but not limited to: self-efficacy; self-monitoring of sexual fantasies and interests, positive coping strategies, and self-regulation techniques (see also, Cale, Burton, & Leclerc, 2017).

In the first 18 months after the launch of the advertising campaign, 476 people had contacted the clinic. Of the 476 individuals, 241 completed an in-person assessment at the clinic's office. It should be noted that even though the advertising campaign was carried out in Berlin, individuals from all over Germany, but also from Austria, Switzerland, and England, contacted the clinic to get help. Of all those who contacted the clinic, 58% had never had contact with the criminal justice system, despite the fact that 53% reported having ever had sexual contact with a minor. The typical clientele of the clinic are, firstly, individuals who have pedophilic thoughts but who avoid or minimize contact with children and, secondly, individuals struggling with pedophilic sexual thoughts who feel that they are gradually losing control over their behavior. The former individuals are those who experience some form of psychological distress because of their deviant sexual thoughts, while the latter group are those who experience distress to the extent that they feel they are increasingly losing control over their sexual fantasies. Although the Dunkelfeld project is not a panacea to the problem of child sexual abuse, it offers a humanistic and preventative approach to the issue of sexual offending. In 2015, a study by Beier and colleagues that was published in the Journal of Sexual Medicine provided an initial evaluation study of Prevention Project Dunkelfeld. The findings from their research suggested evidence that their treatment group experienced decreases in emotional deficits and cognitions supportive of CSA as well as increases in sexual self-regulation. They concluded that the program had an effect on reducing certain risk factors associated with the perpetration of CSA.

Conclusion

SORN laws did not emerge from a noted rise in the rate of sexual offending within a given jurisdiction. Nor were they a response to research that revealed offenders were likely to be deterred from committing a future sex crime if SORN laws were enacted. Instead, to understand the development of SORN laws, it is necessary to understand perhaps the most heinous crime imaginable: sexual homicide, more precisely, the sexual homicide of a child. While this event is extremely atypical, poorly understood, and rarely examined from a scientific perspective, it is very often the catalyst for change in laws that are then extended to a much broader group of individuals (i.e., beyond the individuals that have perpetrated a sexual homicide offense). Why are laws enacted against a much broader group of persons (e.g., all sex offenders) based on the behavior of a smaller subset of this population? One possibility is that sexual homicide offenses are virtually always examined retrospectively with the benefit of hindsight. It is potentially problematic to think that using hindsight to identify the "causes" of extremely rare events like sexual homicide of a child can be effective for preventing similar events in the future. Such hindsight reveals the impression that sexual homicides were the result of a clear, predictable pattern of previous sexual offending that culminated in an escalation in behavior to the point of a homicide. From this lens, these rare events have a clearly defined pattern that starts with earlier involvement in a sex crime. This is because in most cases the presence of these so-called causes is rarely associated with the outcome of interest (e.g., sexual homicide). Put differently, while it may be the case that a substantial proportion of individuals that perpetrate a sexual homicide offense against a child have a sexual attraction to children or have perpetrated a sexual offense in the past, the vast majority of individuals with a sexual attraction to children or whom have perpetrated a sexual offense in the past do not commit a sexual homicide offense.

The presence and diffusion of SORN laws signals the decline of the role and importance of experts' opinion on crime prevention. For most American researchers, the preventive effect of SORN laws on sex crimes is virtually null. Indeed, experts' opinions on the matter suggest that SORN laws, registries, and public notification have only symbolic value for the general public; they have no real or significant effect on preventing or reducing sexual crimes (Ackerman, Sacks, & Greenberg, 2012; Levenson & Cotter, 2005; Logan, 2008; Sample, 2011). Analysis of the scientific literature appears to confirm these conclusions by offering certain nuances. However, the presence of important methodological problems and shortcomings limits the conclusions that can be drawn from policy evaluation studies. As a result, there is no solid empirical evidence showing that SORN laws are effective as a measure to prevent sexual offending. In addition, the reliability and validity of the information contained in publicly available sex offender registries seems to be questionable; in some cases, key information about individuals is missing, raising questions about the integrity of data contained in public registries. Furthermore, researchers have conducted studies suggesting that the implementation of such laws have significant adverse collateral consequences for registered offenders and even their family members or other close social support networks. The widespread and aggressive public notification of individuals considered to be a high-risk for sexual recidivism is associated with even greater collateral effects. These collateral effects (e.g., residential eviction, job loss, harassment, ostracism, and victimization) represent significant barriers to successful community re-entry and community reintegration that are supposed to be helpful in promoting desistance from offending. Ultimately, SORN laws were based on false assumptions and the American experience with these laws suggests that they do not achieve their public safety and deterrent objectives; they may in fact be counterproductive to public safety and contribute to the ostracization and marginalization of citizens and as a result increase the likelihood of reoffending.

SORN laws explicitly symbolize the populist sociolegal construction of sexual offending that characterized the start of the twenty-first century. Despite the findings of much empirical research that at the very least calls into question the efficacy and utility of SORN laws, and possibly even provides evidence pointing toward the potential iatrogenic impact of these policies, it is unlikely that sex offender registries and public notification will disappear anytime soon. Almost 10 years ago,

Logan (2008) stated the hope that science would lead to better informed political decisions in this context; clearly, this has not happened despite a continuously growing body of empirical research. In light of almost 20 years of research, SORN laws continue to expand. The continued expansion of SORN laws has led Carpenter and Beverlin (2012) to describe the current state of policy making in this area as an unpredictable spiral. It seems that the elimination of these measures, which originated from a populist movement, now seems a hopeless task. In fact, given this context, it is not surprising to increasingly see requests for public registries for different categories of offenders, such as intimate partner violence offenders and drug traffickers. Sample (2011) even argues that it is unlikely that additional scientific research will modify or help redefine public perception of these laws and, more broadly, perceptions of the problem of sexual offending. SORN laws are unlikely to disappear in the absence of the general public calling for them to be repealed. Ackerman et al. (2012) offer an even darker vision into the future; given that SORN laws are so expensive, perhaps when US states are faced with significant financial deficits, the government will need to take a more critical look at the appropriateness of such measures. This type of scenario has played out with the enactment of three strikes laws that were later ignored due to costs associated with their implementation (e.g., Zimring, 1996; Zimring, Hawkins, & Kamin, 2001). At the same time, the reluctance of other countries to follow in the footsteps of American SORN laws highlights the importance of sociocultural and sociopolitical factors in the development and enactment of such policies.

Non-evidence based and ineffective criminal justice policies divert important resources away from social policies that can have a positive impact on human lives, and in turn, make society a safer place. In the current context, the continued reliance on misguided "one-size fits all" criminal justice policies that aim to demonstrate a near immediate impact on sexual offending are ever increasingly costly and possibly iatrogenic. In other words, vast amounts of taxpayer money are being diverted into criminal justice policies that not only likely do not achieve what they set out to do, but possibly make the problem even worse. Rather than proposing criminal justice policies that can promote, facilitate, or trigger deviant and criminal behaviors, the focus should be redirected toward the development of evidence-based policies aiming to prevent sexual offending. Starting early in the life course, such policies should be aimed toward the prevention of key risk factors for sexual offending while promoting protective factors across the life course. Tackling the issue in a proactive manner requires a developmental life course perspective. It requires an understanding of the origin and the development of sexual offending.

References

Ackerman, A. R., & Sacks, M. (2018). Disproportionate minority presence on US sex offender registries. *Justice Policy Journal, 16*, 1–20.

Ackerman, A. R., Sacks, M., & Greenberg, D. F. (2012). Legislation targeting sex offenders: Are recent policies effective in reducing rape? *Justice Quarterly, 29*(6), 858–887.

Agan, A. Y. (2011). Sex offender registries: Fear without function? *The Journal of Law and Economics, 54*(1), 207–239.

Anderson, A. L., Evans, M. K., & Sample, L. L. (2009). Who accesses the sex offender registries? A look at legislative intent and citizen action in Nebraska. *Criminal Justice Studies, 22*(3), 313–329.

Anderson, A. L., & Sample, L. L. (2008). Public awareness and action resulting from sex offender community notification laws. *Criminal Justice Policy Review, 19*(4), 371–396.

Bailey, D. J., & Sample, L. L. (2017). An examination of a cycle of coping with strain among registered citizens' families. *Criminal Justice Studies, 30*(2), 158–180.

Barnes, J. C., Dukes, T., Tewksbury, R., & De Troye, T. M. (2008). Analyzing the impact of a statewide residence restriction law on South Carolina sex offenders. *Criminal Justice Policy Review, 20*(1), 21–43.

Basile, K. C. (2003). Implications of public health for policy on sexual violence. *Annals of the New York Academy of Sciences, 989*(1), 446–463.

Beauregard, E., & Leclerc, B. (2007). An application of the rational choice approach to the offending process of sex offenders: A closer look at the decision-making. *Sexual Abuse: A Journal of Research and Treatment, 19*(2), 115–133.

Beauregard, E., Proulx, J., Rossmo, K., Leclerc, B., & Allaire, J.-F. (2007). Script analysis of hunting process in serial sex offenders. *Criminal Justice and Behavior, 34*(8), 1069–1084.

Beauregard, E., Rossmo, D. K., & Proulx, J. (2007). A descriptive model of the hunting process of serial sex offenders: A rational choice perspective. *Journal of Family Violence, 22*(6), 449–463.

Beck, V. S., & Travis, L. F. (2004). Sex offender notification and fear of victimization. *Journal of Criminal Justice, 32*(5), 455–463.

Beck, V. S., & Travis, L. F. (2006). Sex offender notification: An exploratory assessment of state variation in notification processes. *Journal of Criminal Justice, 34*(1), 51–55.

Becker, H. S. (1963). *Outsiders*. New York: Free Press.

Becker, J. V., & Reilly, D. W. (1999). Preventing sexual abuse and assault. *Sexual Abuse: A Journal of Research and Treatment, 11*(4), 267–278.

Beier, K. M., Ahlers, C. J., Goecker, D., Neutze, J., Mundt, I. A., Hupp, E., et al. (2009). Can pedophiles be reached for primary prevention of child sexual abuse? First results of the Berlin Prevention Project Dunkelfeld (PPD). *The Journal of Forensic Psychiatry & Psychology, 20*(6), 851–867.

Bernburg, J. G., Krohn, M. D., & Rivera, C. J. (2006). Official labeling, criminal embeddedness, and subsequent delinquency: A longitudinal test of labeling theory. *Journal of Research in Crime and Delinquency, 43*(1), 67–88.

Bonta, J. L., & Andrews, D. A. (2007). *Modèle d'évaluation et de réadaptation des délinquants fondé sur les principes du risque, des besoins et de la réceptivité*. Ottawa: Sécurité publique Canada.

Bouchard, M., & Lussier, P. (2015). Estimating the size of the sexual aggressor population. In A. A. J. Blokland & P. Lussier (Eds.), *Sex offenders: A criminal career approach*. Chichester: John Wiley & Sons.

Bouffard, J. A., & Askew, L. N. (2019). Time-series analyses of the impact of sex offender registration and notification law implementation and subsequent modifications on rates of sexual offenses. *Crime & Delinquency, 65*(11), 1483–1512.

Brewster, M. P., DeLong, P. A., & Moloney, J. T. (2012). Sex offender registries: A content analysis. *Criminal Justice Policy Review, 24*(6), 695–715.

Burchfield, K. B., & Mingus, W. (2008). Not in my neighborhood: Assessing registered sex offenders' experiences with local social capital and social control. *Criminal Justice and Behavior, 35*(3), 356–374.

Caldwell, M. F. (2002). What we do not know about juvenile sexual offense risk. *Child Maltreatment, 7*(4), 291–302.

Caldwell, M. F., & Dickinson, C. (2009). Sex offender registration and recidivism risk in juvenile sexual offenders. *Behavioral Sciences & the Law, 27*(6), 941–956.

Caldwell, M. F., Ziemke, M. H., & Vitacco, M. J. (2008). An examination of the sex offender registration act as applied to juveniles: Evaluating the ability to predict sexual recidivism. *Psychology, Public Policy, and Law, 14*, 89–114.

Cale, J., Burton, M., & Leclerc, B. (2017). Primary prevention of child sexual abuse: Applications, effectiveness, and international innovations. In *Crime prevention international* (pp. 147–170). Milton Park: Taylor and Francis.

Calkins, C., Colombino, N., Matsuura, T., & Jeglic, E. (2015). Where do sex crimes occur? How an examination of sex offense location can inform policy and prevention. *International Journal of Comparative and Applied Criminal Justice, 39*(2), 99–112.

Carpenter, C. L., & Beverlin, A. E. (2012). The evolution of unconstitutionality in sex offender registration laws. *Hastings Law Journal, 63*, 1071–1645.

Cohen, M., & Jeglic, E. L. (2007). Sex offender legislation in the United States: What do we know? *International Journal of Offender Therapy and Comparative Criminology, 51*(4), 369–383.

Connor, D. P., & Tewksbury, R. (2017). Public and professional views of sex offender registration and notification. *Criminology, Criminal Justice, Law & Society, 18*, 1–27.

Cooley, B. N., Moore, S. E., & Sample, L. L. (2017). The role of formal social control mechanisms in deterring sex offending as part of the desistance process. *Criminal Justice Studies, 30*(2), 136–157.

Cornish, D. B., & Clarke, R. V. (2014). *The reasoning criminal: Rational choice perspectives on offending*. Piscataway: Transaction Publishers.

Craun, S. W. (2010). Evaluating awareness of registered sex offenders in the neighborhood. *Crime & Delinquency, 56*(3), 414–435.

Daly, K., & Bouhours, B. (2010). Rape and attrition in the legal process: A comparative analysis of five countries. *Crime and Justice, 39*(1), 565–650.

Deslauriers-Varin, N., & Beauregard, E. (2010). Victims' routine activities and sex offenders' target selection scripts: A latent class analysis. *Sexual Abuse: A Journal of Research and Treatment, 22*(3), 315–342.

Deslauriers-Varin, N., & Beauregard, E. (2014a). Consistency in crime site selection: An investigation of crime sites used by serial sex offenders across crime series. *Journal of Criminal Justice, 42*(2), 123–133.

Deslauriers-Varin, N., & Beauregard, E. (2014b). Unravelling crime series patterns amongst serial sex offenders: Duration, frequency, and environmental consistency. *Journal of Investigative Psychology and Offender Profiling, 11*(3), 253–275.

Drake, E., & Aos, S. (2009). *Does sex offender registration and notification reduce crime? A systematic review of the research literature*. Washington, DC: Washington State Institute for Public Policy.

Dugan, M. J. (2001). Megan's law or Sarah's law-a comparative analysis of public notification statutes in the United States and England. *Loyola of Los Angeles International and Comparative Law Review, 23*, 617–644.

Duwe, G., & Donnay, W. (2008). The impact of Megan's law on sex offender recidivism: The Minnesota experience. *Criminology, 46*(2), 411–446.

Farrington, D. P. (1977). The effects of public labelling. *British Journal of Criminology, 17*, 112–125.

Farrington, D. P., Loeber, R., & Berg, M. T. (2012). Young men who kill: A prospective longitudinal examination from childhood. *Homicide Studies, 16*(2), 99–128.

Feeley, M. M., & Simon, J. (1992). The new penology: Notes on the emerging strategy of corrections and its implications. *Criminology, 30*(4), 449–474.

Finn, P. (1997). Sex offender community notification. *Alternatives to Incarceration, 3*(6), 26.

Fitch, K. (2006). *Megan's law: Does it protect children*. London: NSPCC.

Freeman, N. J. (2012). The public safety impact of community notification laws: Rearrest of convicted sex offenders. *Crime & Delinquency, 58*(4), 539–564.

Hagan, J. (1991). Destiny and drift: Subcultural preferences, status attainments, and the risks and rewards of youths. *American Sociological Review, 56*, 567–582.

Harris, A. J., Levenson, J. S., & Ackerman, A. R. (2014). Registered sex offenders in the United States: Behind the numbers. *Crime and Delinquency, 60*(1), 3–33.

Harris, A. J., Walfield, S. M., Shields, R. T., & Letourneau, E. J. (2016). Collateral consequences of juvenile sex offender registration and notification: Results from a survey of treatment providers. *Sexual Abuse, 28*(8), 770–790.

Hoppe, T. (2016). Punishing sex: Sex offenders and the missing punitive turn in sexuality studies. *Law & Social Inquiry, 41*(3), 573–594.

Hughes, L. A., & Kadleck, C. (2008). Sex offender community notification and community stratification. *Justice Quarterly, 25*(3), 469–495.

Jennings, W. G., Zgoba, K. M., Donner, C. M., Henderson, B. B., & Tewksbury, R. (2014). Considering specialization/versatility as an unintended collateral consequence of SORN. *Journal of Criminal Justice, 42*(2), 184–192.

Kemshall, H., & Weaver, B. (2012). The sex offender public disclosure pilots in England and Scotland: Lessons for "marketing strategies" and risk communication with the public. *Criminology and Criminal Justice, 12*(5), 549–565.

Kernsmith, P. D., Comartin, E., Craun, S. W., & Kernsmith, R. M. (2009). The relationship between sex offender registry utilization and awareness. *Sexual Abuse: A Journal of Research and Treatment, 21*(2), 181–193.

Keyzer, P., & McSherry, B. M. (2015). The preventive detention of sex offenders: Law and practice. *University of New South Wales Law Journal, 38*, 792–822.

Koon-Magnin, S. (2015). Perceptions of and support for sex offender policies: Testing Levenson, Brannon, Fortney, and Baker's findings. *Journal of Criminal Justice, 43*(1), 80–88.

La Fond, J. Q. (2005). *Preventing sexual violence: How society should cope with sex offenders.* Washington, DC: American Psychological Association.

Lasher, M. P., & McGrath, R. J. (2012). The impact of community notification on sex offender reintegration: A quantitative review of the research literature. *International Journal of Offender Therapy and Comparative Criminology, 56*(1), 6–28.

Lees, M., & Tewksbury, R. (2006). Understanding policy and programmatic issues regarding sex offender registries. *Corrections Today, 68*(1), 54–55.

Letourneau, E. J., Bandyopadhyay, D., Armstrong, K. S., & Sinha, D. (2010). Do sex offender registration and notification requirements deter juvenile sex crimes? *Criminal Justice and Behavior, 37*(5), 553–569.

Letourneau, E. J., Bandyopadhyay, D., Sinha, D., & Armstrong, K. S. (2009). The influence of sex offender registration on juvenile sexual recidivism. *Criminal Justice Policy Review, 20*(2), 136–153.

Letourneau, E. J., Harris, A. J., Shields, R. T., Walfield, S. M., Ruzicka, A. E., Buckman, C., et al. (2018). Effects of juvenile sex offender registration on adolescent well-being: An empirical examination. *Psychology, Public Policy, and Law, 24*(1), 105.

Letourneau, E. J., & Miner, M. H. (2005). Juvenile sex offenders: A case against the legal and clinical status quo. *Sexual Abuse: A Journal of Research and Treatment, 17*(3), 293–312.

Levenson, J., & Tewksbury, R. (2009). Collateral damage: Family members of registered sex offenders. *American Journal of Criminal Justice, 34*(1-2), 54–68.

Levenson, J. S., Brannon, Y. N., Fortney, T., & Baker, J. (2007). Public perceptions about sex offenders and community protection policies. *Analyses of Social Issues and Public Policy, 7*(1), 137–161.

Levenson, J. S., & Cotter, L. P. (2005). The effect of Megan's law on sex offender reintegration. *Journal of Contemporary Criminal Justice, 21*(1), 49–66.

Levenson, J. S., & D'Amora, D. A. (2007). Social policies designed to prevent sexual violence the emperor's new clothes? *Criminal Justice Policy Review, 18*(2), 168–199.

Levenson, J. S., D'Amora, D. A., & Hern, A. L. (2007). Megan's law and its impact on community re-entry for sex offenders. *Behavioral Sciences & the Law, 25*(4), 587–602.

Logan, W. A. (2003). Sex offender registration and community notification: Emerging legal and research issues. *Annals of the New York Academy of Sciences, 989*(1), 337–351.

Logan, W. A. (2008). Sex offender registration and community notification: Past, present, and future. *New England Journal on Criminal and Civil Confinement, 34*, 3–16.

Lussier, P. (2005). The criminal activity of sexual offenders in adulthood: Revisiting the specialization debate. *Sexual Abuse: A Journal of Research and Treatment, 17*(3), 269–292.

Lussier, P. (2018). *Délinquance sexuelle: Au-delà des dérives idéologiques, populistes et cliniques*. Québec: Presses de l'Université Laval.

Lussier, P., & Blokland, A. (2014). The adolescence-adulthood transition and Robins's continuity paradox: Criminal career patterns of juvenile and adult sex offenders in a prospective longitudinal birth cohort study. *Journal of Criminal Justice, 42*(2), 153–163.

Lussier, P., Bouchard, M., & Beauregard, E. (2011). Patterns of criminal achievement in sexual offending: Unravelling the "successful" sex offender. *Journal of Criminal Justice, 39*(5), 433–444.

Lussier, P., & Cale, J. (2013). Beyond sexual recidivism: A review of the sexual criminal career parameters of adult sex offenders. *Aggression and Violent Behavior, 18*(5), 445–457.

Lussier, P., Dahabieh, M., Deslauriers-Varin, N., & Thomson, C. (2010). Issues and challenges for community risk management. In L. Gideon & H. E. Sung (Eds.), *Rethinking corrections: Rehabilitation, re-entry, and reintegration* (pp. 219–252). Thousand Oaks, CA: Sage Publications.

Lussier, P., Gress, C., Deslauriers-Varin, N., & Amirault, J. (2014). Community risk management of high-risk sex offenders in Canada: Findings from a quasi-experimental study. *Justice Quarterly, 31*(2), 287–314.

Lussier, P., & Gress, C. L. (2014). Community re-entry and the path toward desistance: A quasi-experimental longitudinal study of dynamic factors and community risk management of adult sex offenders. *Journal of Criminal Justice, 42*(2), 111–122.

Lussier, P., & Healey, J. (2009). Rediscovering Quetelet, again: The "aging" offender and the prediction of reoffending in a sample of adult sex offenders. *Justice Quarterly, 26*(4), 827–856.

Lussier, P., & Mathesius, J. (2018). Integrating general and specific theories of sex offending. In P. Lussier & E. Beauregard (Eds.), *Sexual offending: A criminological perspective* (pp. 12–43). Abington: Routledge.

Lussier, P., & Mathesius, J. (2019a). Not in my backyard: public sex offender registries and public notification laws. *Canadian Journal of Criminology and Criminal Justice, 61*(1), 105–116.

Lussier, P., & Mathesius, J. (2019b). Trojan horse policies: sexual predators, SORN laws and the American experience. *Psychology, Crime & Law, 25*(2), 133–156.

Malesky, A., & Keim, J. (2001). Mental health professionals' perspectives on sex offender registry Web sites. *Sexual Abuse: A Journal of Research and Treatment, 13*(1), 53–63.

Mancini, C., Shields, R. T., Mears, D. P., & Beaver, K. M. (2010). Sex offender residence restriction laws: Parental perceptions and public policy. *Journal of Criminal Justice, 38*(5), 1022–1030.

Martinson, R. (1974). What works? Questions and answers about prison reform. *The Public Interest, 35*, 22–54.

Masters, K. B., & Kebbell, M. R. (2019). Police officers' perceptions of a sex offender registration scheme: Identifying and responding to risk. *Psychiatry, Psychology and Law, 26*(3), 396–413.

McAlinden, A. M. (2012). The governance of sexual offending across Europe: Penal policies, political economies and the institutionalization of risk. *Punishment & Society, 14*(2), 166–192.

McMahon, P. M. (2000). The public health approach to the prevention of sexual violence. *Sexual Abuse: A Journal of Research and Treatment, 12*(1), 27–36.

Meloy, M. L. (2005). The sex offender next door: An analysis of recidivism, risk factors, and deterrence of sex offenders on probation. *Criminal Justice Policy Review, 16*(2), 211–236.

Mercado, C. C., Alvarez, S., & Levenson, J. (2008). The impact of specialized sex offender legislation on community re-entry. *Sexual Abuse: A Journal of Research and Treatment, 20*(2), 188–205.

Mullvihill, M., Wisniewski, K., Meyers, J., & Wells, J. (2003). Monster next door: State losing track of sex offenders. *Boston Herald, 2003*, 1.

Murphy, L., & Fedoroff, J. P. (2013). Sexual offenders' views of Canadian sex offender registries: A survey of a clinical sample. *Canadian Journal of Behavioural Science/Revue Canadienne des Sciences du Comportement, 45*(3), 238.

Murphy, L., Fedoroff, J. P., & Martineau, M. (2009). Canada's sex offender registries: Background, implementation, and social policy considerations. *The Canadian Journal of Human Sexuality, 18*(1-2), 61.

Mustaine, E. E., Tewksbury, R., & Stengel, K. M. (2006). Social disorganization and residential locations of registered sex offenders: Is this a collateral consequence? *Deviant Behavior, 27*(3), 329–350.

Nagin, D. S. (2013). Deterrence: A review of the evidence by a criminologist for economists. *Annual Review of Economics, 5*(1), 83–105.

Napier, S., Dowling, C., Morgan, A., & Talbot, D. (2018). What impact do public sex offender registries have on community safety? *Trends and Issues in Crime and Criminal Justice, 550*, 1–20.

Pawson, R. (2002a). *Does Megan's law work? A theory-driven systematic review.* London, UK: ESRC UK Centre for Evidence Based Policy and Practice.

Pawson, R. (2002b). Evidence-based policy: The promise of realist synthesis. *Evaluation, 8*(3), 340–358.

Pawson, R., & Tilley, N. (1994). What works in evaluation research? *British Journal of Criminology, 34*(3), 291–306.

Pawson, R., & Tilley, N. (1997). An introduction to scientific realist evaluation. In E. Chelimsky & W. R. Shadish (Eds.), *Evaluation for the 21st century: A handbook* (pp. 405–418). London: Sage Publications.

Petrosino, A. J., & Petrosino, C. (1999). The public safety potential of Megan's law in Massachusetts: An assessment from a sample of criminal sexual psychopaths. *Crime & Delinquency, 45*(1), 140–158.

Petrunik, M. (2003). The hare and the tortoise: Dangerousness and sex offender policy in the United States and Canada. *Canadian Journal of Criminology and Criminal Justice, 45*(1), 43–72.

Powell, M., Day, A., Benson, M., Vess, J., & Graffam, J. (2014). Australian police officers' perceptions of sex offender registries. *Policing and Society, 24*(1), 120–133.

Prescott, J. J. (2012). Do sex offender registries make us less safe? *Regulation, 35*(2), 48–55.

Prescott, J. J., & Rockoff, J. E. (2011). Do sex offender registration and notification laws affect criminal behavior? *The Journal of Law and Economics, 54*(1), 161–206.

Ruby, C., Hasan, N. R., & Enenajor, A. (2017). *Sentencing.* Toronto, Canada: LexisNexis.

Sample, L. L. (2011). The need to debate the fate of sex offender community notification laws. *Criminology & Public Policy, 10*(2), 265–274.

Sample, L. L., & Bray, T. M. (2003). Are sex offenders dangerous? *Criminology & Public Policy, 3*(1), 59–82.

Savage, J., & Windsor, C. (2018). Sex offender residence restrictions and sex crimes against children: A comprehensive review. *Aggression and Violent Behavior, 43*, 13–25.

Schaefer, G. A., Mundt, I. A., Feelgood, S., Hupp, E., Neutze, J., Ahlers, C. J., et al. (2010). Potential and Dunkelfeld offenders: Two neglected target groups for prevention of child sexual abuse. *International Journal of Law and Psychiatry, 33*(3), 154–163.

Schiavone, S. K., & Jeglic, E. L. (2009). Public perception of sex offender social policies and the impact on sex offenders. *International Journal of Offender Therapy and Comparative Criminology, 53*(6), 679–695.

Schram, D. D., & Milloy, C. D. (1995). *Community notification: A study of offender characteristics and recidivism.* Washington, DC: Washington State Institute for Public Policy.

Simon, J. (1998). Managing the monstrous: Sex offenders and the new penology. *Psychology, Public Policy, and Law, 4*(1-2), 452.

Simon, L. M. (2000). An examination of the assumptions of specialization, mental disorder, and dangerousness in sex offenders. *Behavioral Sciences & the Law, 18*(2-3), 275–308.

Socia Jr., K. M., & Stamatel, J. P. (2010). Assumptions and evidence behind sex offender laws: Registration, community notification, and residence restrictions. *Sociology Compass, 4*(1), 1–20.

Taleb, N. N. (2007). *The black swan: The impact of the highly improbable*. New York: Random House.

Tannenbaum, F. (1938). *Crime and the community*. New York: Columbia University Press.

Taylor, S. C. (2017). Community perceptions of a public sex offender registry introduced in Western Australia. *Police Practice and Research, 18*(3), 275–290.

ten Bensel, T., & Sample, L. L. (2017). The influence of sex offender registration and notification laws on fostering collective identity among offenders. *Journal of Crime and Justice, 40*(4), 497–511.

Tewksbury, R. (2002). Validity and utility of the Kentucky sex offender registry. *Federal Probation, 66*, 21–26.

Tewksbury, R., & Jennings, W. G. (2010). Assessing the impact of sex offender registration and community notification on sex-offending trajectories. *Criminal Justice and Behavior, 37*(5), 570–582.

Tewksbury, R., & Levenson, J. (2009). Stress experiences of family members of registered sex offenders. *Behavioral Sciences & the Law, 27*(4), 611–626.

Ticknor, B., & Warner, J. J. (2020). Evaluating the accuracy of SORNA: Testing for classification errors and racial bias. *Criminal Justice Policy Review, 31*(1), 3–21.

Vess, J., Langskaill, B., Day, A., Powell, M., & Graffam, J. (2011). A comparative analysis of Australian sex offender legislation for sex offender registries. *Australian & New Zealand Journal of Criminology, 44*(3), 404–424.

Victorian Law Reform Commission. (2014). *Sex offenders registration: Final report*. Melbourne: Victorian Law Reform Commission.

Welchans, S. (2005). Megan's law: Evaluations of sexual offender registries. *Criminal Justice Policy Review, 16*(2), 123–140.

Whitting, L., Day, A., & Powell, M. (2014). The impact of community notification on the management of sex offenders in the community: An Australian perspective. *Australian and New Zealand Journal of Criminology, 47*(2), 240–258.

Winick, B. J. (1998). Sex offender law in the 1990s: A therapeutic jurisprudence analysis. *Psychology, Public Policy, and Law, 4*(1-2), 505.

Wright, R. G. (2008). Sex offender post-incarceration sanctions: Are there any limits. *New England Journal on Criminal and Civil Confinement, 34*, 17–50.

Younglove, J. A., & Vitello, C. J. (2003). Community notification provisions of "Megan's law" from a therapeutic jurisprudence perspective: A case study. *American Journal of Forensic Psychology, 21*(1), 25–38.

Zevitz, R. G. (2004). Sex offender placement and neighborhood social integration: The making of a scarlet letter community. *Criminal Justice Studies, 17*(2), 203–222.

Zevitz, R. G. (2006). Sex offender community notification: Its role in recidivism and offender reintegration. *Criminal Justice Studies, 19*(2), 193–208.

Zevitz, R. G., & Farkas, M. A. (2000). Sex offender community notification: Examining the importance of neighborhood meetings. *Behavioral Sciences & the Law, 18*(2-3), 393–408.

Zgoba, K., Witt, P., Dalessandro, M., & Veysey, B. (2008). *Megan's law: Assessing the practical and monetary efficacy*. Rockville: National Criminal Justice Reference Service.

Zimring, F. E. (1996). Populism, democratic government, and the decline of expert authority: Some reflections on "three strikes" in California. *McGeorge Law Review, 28*(1), 243–256.

Zimring, F. E. (2004). *An American travesty: Legal responses to adolescent sexual offending*. Chicago: University of Chicago Press.

Zimring, F. E., Hawkins, G., & Kamin, S. (2001). *Punishment and democracy: Three strikes and you're out in California*. Oxford: Oxford University Press.

Part IV
Conclusion

Chapter 10
The Great Policy Gap: Toward More Proactive Sex Offending Research

Introduction

The rise of the #metoo movement marks another turning point in the history of sex offender policy. Various new claims about sexual offending and perpetrators of sexual offenses have been made. The image of the sex offender is once again challenged and deconstructed. This time we see a transition from the perception of the sex offender as a male with a long history of prior sexual offending that preys on stranger victims as a result of features of psychopathy, deviant sexual fantasies, and an inability to benefit from treatment provided by the justice system, to the sex offender as a middle-aged, upper-class male in a position of power over others that for too long has avoided sanctions from the justice system in part because of their status. Atypical cases usually involving offenders in high-profile positions are used by this movement to typify the types of injustices experienced by victims in vulnerable positions; such cases establish the purpose for the movement and its call for change. Socially, culturally, and politically, however, it is difficult to pinpoint a single theme that the movement is intended to address. Sexual offending? Gender inequality? Social injustice? A new wave of feminism? This becomes problematic because it creates a lack of clarity regarding what the path forward is to developing new policies to address this emerging problem. The actions of perpetrators are clear, as are the negative consequences of these actions, but what needs to change, and how this change can be brought about is unclear. To be sure, the behavior of perpetrators is what needs to change, but larger questions of how to effect this change remains less clear. Many may have opinions on what needs to change and how to create this change, but the research to support such opinions is lacking. Once again, researchers are not in front of the problem; they are responding to it. Various social groups, victims' rights movements, and other activists are requesting immediate actions and measures. The government is being pressured into tackling this problem by implementing new policies and laws. Other institutions are ushering in new rules, norms, and measures. Yet, researchers still do not understand the scope and

© Springer Nature Switzerland AG 2021
P. Lussier et al., *Understanding Sexual Offending*,
https://doi.org/10.1007/978-3-030-53301-4_10

nature of the problem. As presented throughout this book, there is already a long history of policy, often developed with good intentions, that ultimately is also extremely flawed because it relies on myths and misconceptions about the problem at hand. It will become important for policies that respond to sexual harassment and other forms of sexual offending highlighted by the #metoo movement to avoid the traps fallen into by prior policies. Calls for justice and desire for action are understandable, but it is the role of researchers and policymakers to identify how the response should take shape. Developing a response in the absence of an understanding of the phenomenon has a long history of failure. It is also the responsibility of researchers to not just identify appropriate responses to the types of sexual offenses characterized by the #metoo movement, but to develop proactive strategies that help prevent such behaviors from happening in the first place.

This is not the first time that the public, advocates, and key stakeholders have called governments to action to respond to the problem of sex offending (e.g., see Lieb, Quinsey, & Berliner, 1998; Spohn & Horney, 2013). However, these past history lessons have shown that rushed governmental responses to poorly understood behavior are unlikely to produce the desired effect. Pseudo-scientific analysis, ideological discourse, and populist approaches are also unlikely to shed light on the phenomenon and how to best respond to it. It is easy to have an opinion on what the government should and should not be doing. Polarizing discussions about the nature, scope, causes, and best way to tackle this new social problem are becoming too familiar. This movement highlights, among other things, the dynamic aspect of sexual offending and sex offender policy. While the context, actors, and type of sexual offending under scrutiny have changed, the patterns of public response and call to action are all too familiar. In fact, another set of reactive research is already taking place. Yet, again, sexual offending researchers are all too unprepared and research too limited to address such social movements and the dynamic aspect of sexual offending over time. Is the nature of sexual offending changing? Are norms, values, and beliefs evolving? Are certain forms and manifestations of sexual offending on the rise or are they just becoming unveiled and were in fact always there? Is the sudden focus on sexual misconduct in the workplace a sign that more violent forms of sexual offending have become less concerning from a societal standpoint? The inability to approach the phenomenon from a proactive standpoint remains a critical and pivotal shortcoming of this entire field of research. This begs the question of whether this movement represents an opportunity to tackle the sexual offending problem from a public health perspective (e.g., O'Neil, Sojo, Fileborn, Scovelle, & Milner, 2018).

A number of integrative and overarching topics were addressed in the preceding chapters about the understanding of sexual offending. These topics are rarely addressed in a single book as they tend to be viewed as separate issues. We believe that by examining them together, a more comprehensive understanding of the issues and their interrelatedness emerges. The book is based on the premise that, from a societal perspective, the prevention of sexual offending tends to be reactive. We believe there is overwhelming evidence for the need for proactive prevention. More often than not, this social response has been based on populist, ideological, and pseudo-scientific ideas about sexual offending and perpetrators of sexual offenses. A common theme throughout the book is the fact that this reactive approach was sometimes introduced, not just in the absence of scientific evidence supporting it, but even in the presence of scientific evidence presenting a different, more complex, picture of the phenomenon. In the 1960s, Dr. Paul Gebhard and his team accumulated an impressive number of observations highlighting the heterogeneity among individuals convicted for a sex crime (Gebhard, Gagnon, Pomeroy, & Christenson, 1965). More than five decades later, unilateral and one-size-fits-all sex offender policies are alive and well in the policy landscape.

The emergence of ideologically driven policies has been fuelled by personal biases, human error, misconceptions, and erroneous conclusions. The number of false claims about perpetrators of sex crimes, made not just by the general population but also by policymakers, is staggering. A few of these notable myths and misconceptions include: individuals convicted for a sex crime are all sexual recidivists; adolescents having perpetrated a sex crime will accumulate hundreds of victims over their life course; offenders that exhibit their genitals to an unknown child are on an unstoppable path toward sexual homicide; all perpetrators of a sex crime are mentally ill; criminal justice interventions have little to no impact on convicted offenders; convicted offenders who return to the community are an immediate threat to the population; all sex offenders prey on strangers. In fact, these myths and misconceptions are, more often than not, calls to do something about an event already transpired in order to remedy the situation out of a sense of fear, doubt, injustice, and/or anger. In that regard, a survey study on public attitudes toward individuals convicted for a sex crime showed that hostility and punitiveness tend to be higher among citizens who endorse stereotypes suggesting that these offenders are unreformable and driven to crime by immorality (Pickett, Mancini, & Mears, 2013). In other words, populist ideas about how governments should respond to perpetrators of sexual offenses tend to be fueled by a misunderstanding of such individuals, their treatment and intervention needs, and their risk for future offending.

In some ways, this book is also about researchers' failure to shape public opinion about sexual offending and perpetrators of sexual offenses. While an explicit theme of the book is that sex offender policies have been reactive, research also has been reactive in that it has followed, rather than guided, the development of policies. This reactive approach has painted a somewhat confusing picture. Like police investigators arriving at a crime scene, researchers have examined sexual offenses, contributing factors, and sex offender policies only after the fact. The first wave of observations about perpetrators of sexual offenses stemmed from clinical psychologists and psychiatrists conducting assessments to determine the rehabilitation potential of these offenders. Offenders were met by researchers and completed questionnaires, psychological tests, and phallometric assessments after perpetrating their sexual offense. The second wave of observations stemmed from research conducted mainly with victims of sexual offenses. Researchers met with victims after their sexual victimization to gain insight about the context of the victimization, the type of abuse, who was responsible, and the nature of the consequences of their victimization. The third wave of observations stemmed from researchers examining the profile of sexual recidivists and serial offenders. The characteristics of these individuals were collected, examined, and described after their string of sexual offenses. These three waves of research were conducted in such a way that while a large body of research emerged, findings were based on observing perpetrators of sexual offenses after the fact (see Lussier & Cale, 2016). From an exploratory standpoint, when a new phenomenon emerges, this approach is necessary and understandable. The truth is that, after nearly 80 years of studying sexual offending, research on this issue is still in an exploratory mode rather than an explanatory one. The consequence of this is the development of misguided policies.

Research on sex offender treatment followed the implementation of such programs in psychiatric wards and hospitals; not the other way around. Research on risk management of sex offenders followed the implementation of new policies and practices in corrections; not the other way around. Research on public notification and sex offender registries followed their implementation; not the other way around. The *"we will figure out the science later"* approach is a common theme in sex offender policy, and as Dr. Janice Marques once wrote, it has become the customary role of the social sciences to deliver the bad news later on. This book is a call to researchers to deliver to policymakers their ideas for what should be done to prevent sexual offending, rather than to deliver to policymakers the conclusion that their policies are not useful. Breaking this mold is difficult because it requires researchers to develop new ideas for how to study sexual offending. In the past, public, government, and policy responses to sexual offending provided researchers with the impetus to examine whether these responses were appropriate. The time has come for researchers to develop their own agendas for the prevention of sexual offending and to present these agendas to those responsible for implementing policy and protecting the public. This chapter lays out a few directions for future research on the proactive prevention of sexual offending.

This is not to say that all research on sexual offending is misguided, but rather, that significant human, professional, financial, logistical, and technological resources have been invested for the scientific testing of misguided sex offender policies that are based on false premises, myths, and misconceptions about sexual offending and perpetrators of sex crimes. It is not as if these misguided policies are a one-time occurrence. For nearly 80 years it has been the trend for science to follow such sex offending policies rather than the other way around. It is disconcerting that, while several social scientists, clinical researchers, and graduate students around the world are busy conducting research on the impact of misguided policies and programs to prevent sex crimes, this field of research still cannot clearly identify the risk and protective factors associated with why a person first commits a sexual offense. This field of research cannot answer basic questions like where a particular variable or characteristic is a risk factor for sexual offending, a consequence of sexual offending, or an artifact of the criminal justice system's response to the "sex offender." The understanding of the risk and protective factors identified through research should guide policies rather than having policies guide what the risk and protective factors ought to be. New, horrific, and well-publicized cases of sex offending emerge that tend to shift the goal-posts of what the root causes of sex offending are in the minds of the public and policymakers. As a result researchers subsequently shift their focus to answering whether these perspectives are accurate. There are sufficient theories, research methods, and analytic strategies that now allow graduate students, and academics to move away from whack-a-mole sex offending research.

This chapter is not simply a summary of the preceding chapters. Rather, it aims to draw on lessons from past experiences and to provide some much needed direction for future research. Various lenses and approaches, many of which were detailed in the book, have been proposed over the years to describe, explain, and prevent sexual offenses: the medical-psychopathological approach; the feminist and socio-legal perspective; the social psychology approach; the humanist and social work approach; the biosocial and evolutionary perspective, as well as sociological and criminological approaches. These various perspectives all have provided valuable insight into the possible biological, psychological, familial, peer, social, and inter-personal, as well as cultural and media-related risk factors. However, when con-fronted with the simple fact that these risk factors were virtually all identified using retrospective rather than longitudinal research, it is clear that they have limited value as explanatory factors for sexual offending. For example, if experiencing sex-ual victimization during childhood is a key explanatory factor for juvenile sexual offending, why is that the vast majority of sexually abused children do not cause any harm to others, let alone sexual harm (Widom & Massey, 2015)? Moreover, among those who have been sexually abused and have abused others themselves, why do the vast majority of young people who commit sexual offenses not sexually offend beyond adolescence? If such a traumatic experience has such an impact on a young person's cognitive, emotional, and behavioral development as to lead them to cause sexual harm to others, then why is this impact limited to the period of adolescence? Despite these facts, sexual abuse remains one of the most commonly studied risk factors for sex offending and several major theoretical perspectives are centered around this risk factor (see Seto & Lalumiere, 2010). The gaps in the scientific lit-erature in this field are far too vast to currently understand the process by which sexual offending develops over time. The gaps are too vast to develop evidence-based prevention and intervention programs before sexual offending occurs.

Understanding Sexual Offending

This book addressed three main overarching themes and questions about sexual offending. First, to many, a pivotal aspect of sexual offending research involves defining the scope of behaviors that constitute sexual offenses. For example, what constitutes a sexual offense from a non-offending sexual behavior or an offending behavior that is not sexual? Second, for others, the focus of sexual offending research is on identifying the underlying risk and protective factors of sexual offend-ing. Third, for other individuals, the understanding of sexual offending refers to the ability to prevent these acts. For example, what is required for a sex offender treatment program to be effective? We are claiming that, to a certain extent, these three themes have been tackled in silos. The silo mentality refers to the idea that, despite the interrelated nature of these themes, they mostly have been addressed in isolation from one another. The consequence has been the pursuit of distinct goals and objectives rather than working toward a common one: how can we proactively prevent sexual offending?

The first set of themes and questions involves questions of "what?" and more specifically key conceptual and operational issues characterizing sexual offending. What is sexual offending? What are its dimensions and manifestations? What is the scope of these manifestations and its developmental course over time? What is the social science perspective of sexual offending as opposed to the medical-psychiatric perspective? What is the sociolegal approach of sexual offending? This set of questions led us to examine the phenomenon of sexual offending from a medical, legal, and social science standpoint (Chap. 1). It also led us to the examination of, from one generation to another, the construction of certain manifestations of sexual offending as more important and more urgent of a social problem (Chap. 2). This examination highlighted that perceptions of sex offending are dynamic and the construction of some of its manifestations as a social problem evolves in such a way that outpaces the development of scientific knowledge on the matter. This evolution is perpetuated by myths, misconceptions, and erroneous conclusions about sexual offending and perpetrators of sexual offending (Chap. 3). In spite of research highlighting the presence of much heterogeneity in sexual offending patterns, the pattern of sex offending portrayed by popular beliefs is one characterized by early involvement in sexual behaviors that escalate over time due to the ineffectiveness of criminal justice policies and ultimately concludes with horrific forms of abuse such as sexual homicide. In virtually all empirical research that exists on the topic, this type of pattern is clearly atypical.

Sexual offending is not limited to rape and sexual assault. Sexual offending is a complex, multidimensional phenomenon and its manifestations can be categorized as sexual violence and abuse, sexual misconduct, and sexual exploitation. It is also a phenomenon that evolves with societal change. Some sexual offenses in the 1930s are considered normative behaviors in the twenty-first century. In the twenty-first century, new types of sexual offenses such as revenge pornography and the dissemination of child pornography over the internet have emerged. While there are notable exceptions to this dynamic trend (i.e., there typically has been consensus over time surrounding the most severe (and least common) forms of sexual violence and abuse against non-consenting victims), research has largely neglected the study of other manifestations of sexual offending, or at least prioritized severe sexual violence and sexual offenses involving child victims. Sexual offending can occur in a myriad of contexts and can involve a wide range of perpetrators and victims (e.g., Proulx, Beauregard, Lussier, & Leclerc, 2014). From one generation to another, however, certain types of sexual behaviors have been defined as more important social problems than others. Importantly, it is not the social sciences and scientific knowledge that labeled these behaviors as criminal offenses deserving of punishment. Rather, sociocultural and political factors over time dictated that certain manifestations of the phenomenon were important social problems that needed to be addressed, while others were not (e.g., marital rape until the 1980s). Whether this has been the result of sociocultural changes with respect to norms, values, and beliefs of what is acceptable or not, or the result of the emergence of new sexual offending manifestations from sociocultural changes, cannot be ascertained without a clear conceptualization of what sexual offending is. This is further complicated by the fact that scientific research has yet to map out human sexual development over the life course (e.g., Elkovitch, Latzman, Hansen, & Flood, 2009; Friedrich et al., 2001; Lussier, McCuish, Mathesius, Corrado, & Nadeau, 2018). Societal norms, values, and beliefs influence which behaviors are defined as illegal and criminal. They play an important part defining, to a certain extent, what is normative, expected, and accepted. One of the key outstanding research issues is understanding which sexual behavioral manifestations are considered normative, which are considered concerning, and which are considered nonnormative. Such an approach should be complemented by the examination of the harmfulness (i.e., in relation to the consequences for the victim) and the wrongfulness (i.e., moral blameworthiness of those actions) of those manifestations.

From sexual deviants to sexual recidivists and sexual predators, the portrayal of the sex offender has evolved considerably over time. The social construction of the sex offender problem is partly dependent on social reactions to high-profile, emotionally charged, and atypical cases, often involving brutal sexual violence (Chap. 2). The social construction based on such atypical and rare cases contributed to the proliferation of the image of the sex offender as a life course persistent perpetrator of sex crimes. This is not suggesting that public opinion on perpetrators of sex offenses is uniform (e.g., see King & Roberts, 2017), but rather that such a unilateral portrayal has been used in the context of policy change. Research has shown much heterogeneity in sexual offending patterns. A late-onset, short-lived pattern is the most common one, but certainly not the only one (e.g., Lussier & Healey, 2009). For the most part, researchers, while recognizing the importance of myths and misconceptions about sexual offending and perpetrators of sexual offenses, have neglected the process by which certain sexual offending phenomenon becomes social problems, while others are overlooked and neglected; they have also neglected the study of the behavioral development of sexual offending over time. Consistent with the general tradition of sex offending research, research on the development of sex offending over time focused on public and policymaker concern about escalation in sex crimes. Does an individual progress from deviant sexual behaviors to violent sex crimes because of, for example, a lack of a consensual outlet for their deviant fantasies? Once again, such research has been retrospective in that patterns in escalation of sexual offending behavior have been examined only once individuals have been detected by the criminal justice system. It is important to question whether and to what extent such patterns, when observed, reflected dominating perceptions and preconceived notions on sexual offending of the time versus what was actually the reality of specific longitudinal behavioral patterns. In short, missing from the literature is a prospective longitudinal examination of the emergence, course, and desistance from sexual behaviors of all kinds, beginning in childhood (e.g., Lussier et al., 2018) and extending through adulthood.

The second theme involves questions of "why?", that is, the investigation of key explanatory factors related to sexual offending. Why do individuals perpetrate these acts? Why is this part of their behavioral repertoire? Why did one person perpetrate a sex crime but not another? Why did certain hypothesized risk factors contribute to sex offending behaviors? Why is sex offending limited to a certain life stage for some and yet persists over the life course for others? These themes and questions allowed us to examine the current state of knowledge and the numerous and necessary debates about the origins of sexual offending (Chap. 4). While it has long been assumed that perpetrators of sexual offenses are driven by deviant sexual thoughts, research suggests instead a multiplicity of motives, sexual and nonsexual, many of which are not necessarily "deviant." Acting without a victim's consent is universal to all sexual offenses. Therefore, behavioral inhibition issues as well as difficulties dealing with negative emotions appear to be a key aspect of committing a sexual offense; these features are also not specific to the perpetration of sexual offenses, which explains the tendency of perpetrators of such offenses to be involved in a myriad of antisocial and nonsexual criminal offenses. Indeed, while researchers have been heavily focused on finding what is special and unique about sexual offending, they have vastly overlooked what is common and shared with individuals involved in antisocial and nonsexual criminal behavior (Chap. 5). The best predictor of sexual offending may in fact be a general tendency to engage in broader antisocial behavior. This explanation may be unsatisfying to some because it leaves the impression that sex offending is not in fact any different from non-sex offending. To the public, it may be the case that explanations of sex offending must involve some supremely atypical personality trait, mental disorder, or sexual deviancy to help understand how someone could perpetrate such acts.

The message of this book is that research on sexual offending should depart from responding to what the public feels is the cause of sex offending. Researchers should instead help to construct the public's viewpoint of sexual offending. To some, explaining sexual offending as a manifestation of a general antisocial tendency may feel threatening or perceived as calling into question the existence of professional bodies, groups, expertise, and training centered around the presumption that sexual offending is definitively unique. However, emphasizing that sexual offending may manifest as a result of a general antisocial tendency and focusing on developing intervention and prevention strategies unique to this group can coexist. The tendency to approach the risk factors for sexual offending strictly in terms of a fixed and stable individual propensity to perpetrate sex crimes limits researchers in their ability to explain fundamental empirical observations about sexual offending, such as the continuity and discontinuity of offending over the life course (Chap. 6). In sum, a propensity implies a stable disposition or tendency toward a specific behavior and therefore is not likely useful for resolving the explanation of the most typical pattern of sexual offending, which is a pattern defined by limited involvement in the behavior over a brief period of the life course. Therefore, more fully explaining sexual offending, especially the typical pattern of sexual offending, requires much more attention to dynamic, transitory risk factors that may be present during just a short period of a person's life.

The theoretical development of the explanation of sex offending has been slow and irregular, focused on the origins and development of the motivation and propensity to perpetrate sex crimes. In some ways, misconceptions propagated by earlier sex offending themes have subsequently fed into others. In this case, the first theme regarding "what is" sex offending largely assumed that this behavior was repeated over the life course, often with behaviors escalating in severity from one to the next. Accordingly, theoretical explanations addressing "why" have not been addressing sex offending more broadly, but sex offending as a series of behaviors that escalate over the life course. Accordingly, theories have been centered around explaining an aspect of sexual offending that does not appear to describe the criminal careers of most perpetrators. Theoretical formulations of the explanation of sexual offending have not been supported by adequate empirical verification and, for the most part, remain as unproven and untested hypotheses. The tendency to propose theoretical models and hypotheses as the guiding light for explanations of sex offending and associated treatment and intervention programming, without putting such models to the test of scientific observation, is certainly a limitation of this field of research (e.g., Ward & Beech, 2006). When models are put to the test, their empirical findings do not provide much information about the development of sexual offending over time because of the retrospective nature of the research. The research effectively tests the question of "why did this person possibly commit this offense in the past?" instead of "did these risk factors influence the future perpetration of a sexual offense?". In fact, various aspects of the developmental course of sexual offending remain relatively unknown and unexplained, such as the onset, continuity/persistence, and desistance from sexual offending, which are key components of a developmental-oriented prevention program. Because of significant methodological and conceptual limitations, research conducted on the characteristics of perpetrators of sex offenses informs little about what the risk and protective factors of sexual offending in fact are. In effect, what has been shown to be promising factors might in fact characterize only a very small subset of all perpetrators of sexual offenses or may characterize what perpetrators feel and experience as a consequence of their sexual offending. In investigating risk factors for sexual offending, researchers have found many similarities with perpetrators of non-sex crimes. This empirical regularity continues to be ignored, minimized, or simply overlooked in policy development, therapeutic models, and even in community re-entry programs.

Understanding sexual offending starts with the understanding of antisocial and criminal behavior and the recognition of the importance of criminogenic factors (e.g., Cale & Lussier, 2011; Lalumière & Quinsey, 1996; Lussier & Cale, 2016; Lussier, Proulx, & LeBlanc, 2005). Just like other nonsexual antisocial behaviors, sexual offending is a significant social transgression. A central component for this type of transgression is acting without the victim's consent. Sexual offending is about breaking rules of conduct, whether moral, social, interpersonal, and/or sexual. Sexual offending is also about showing a certain disregard for such rules, irrespective of what the consequences of these actions might be for others. In the process, sexual offending involves the perpetration of antisocial behaviors, such as intimidation, threats, dishonesty, lies, and fraud, reckless and dangerous behaviors, as well as aggression and violence. Considering this, it is not surprising that individuals who are repeatedly involved in antisocial and nonsexual crimes are more likely to perpetrate diverse sexual offending acts of various severity. This is not meant to say that only antisocial individuals are perpetrating sexual offenses. To be sure, this is not meant to suggest that all individuals involved in crime are chronic and serious offenders with an antisocial personality disorder. Rather, this is meant to say that criminogenic factors that are pivotal for the understanding of antisocial and criminal behavior are also pivotal for sexual offending but have been overlooked in this field of research, likely at least in part because of assumptions that the causes of sexual offending must differ from other forms of offending.

The third set of themes involves questions of "how"?; specifically, how to best respond to sexual offending. This involves a series of questions that policymakers, practitioners, and researchers have attempted to address over several decades (e.g., Laws, 2016; Prentky, Janus, & Seto, 2003). How best to deal with convicted offenders? How to prevent them from sexually reoffending? How to rehabilitate them? How to determine if a convicted offender is at risk of reoffending? How to best monitor their behavior in the community to prevent high-risk situations? This set of questions led us to examine the scientific literature on sex offender recidivism and the correctional practices used to prevent sexual recidivism (Chap. 7). The findings from this literature seriously challenged the idea that all convicted offenders are sexual recidivists. The gaps in the scientific literature, however, are sufficient enough to maintain myths and misconceptions about the probabilities of sexual recidivism. The development of atheoretical instruments designed to identify individuals at risk of sexual reoffending exemplifies the important policy shift that occurred in the 1990s, where rehabilitation became an afterthought in favor of risk management strategies. The challenge of developing effective therapeutic programs in the absence of key evidence-based information about the development of sexual offending and associated risk and protective factors certainly represented a significant policy issue (Chap. 8). The absence of compelling information clearly demonstrating the positive impact of sex offender treatment programs on sexual recidivism suggested to some the need to invest in risk management strategies. Such investment took the form of public notification, sex offender registries, and residential restriction laws (Chap. 9). In the process, valuable resources increasingly shifted toward the management of individuals convicted for a sex crime even if they were responsible for a small proportion of all sexual offenses perpetrated in society. The presence of well-intended but misguided and ineffective policies reflects the misalignment of the "what," the "why," and the "how" of sexual offending. A more global, integrated, evidence-based approach is necessary to remedy the situation.

The study of sex offender recidivism has indeed provided valuable insight about risk, risk factors, and sexual recidivism. This research has demonstrated that sexual recidivism is not as frequent and repetitive, irrational, and impulsive, as previously imagined. This research has shown that the probabilities of being convicted again for a sex crime can be established through proper structured assessment guidelines (e.g., Hanson & Thornton, 2000; Quinsey, Rice, & Harris, 1995). To a certain extent, offenders' past and current situation provides valuable information about the likelihood of recidivism. This research has shown that key information about the extent of past sexual and nonsexual offending also provides valuable information about the likelihood of recidivism. The empiricism of risk management strategies used in corrections cannot compensate, however, for a lack of theoretical understanding of risk, offending behavior over time, and sexual offending more specifically. Of importance, while sex offender recidivism is often portrayed as relatively static, fixed, and predictable, research continues to unmask, through prospective longitudinal designs, the dynamic aspect of risk and offending over time (e.g., Lussier, Tzoumakis, Cale, & Amirault, 2010). Despite this, we know very little about the mechanisms behind the dynamic aspects of sex offending. When looking at sex offending from a prevention standpoint, the main question is often centered on how policies can prevent sexual offending from continuing. Longitudinal studies showing that sex offending is unlikely to continue in the first place have not been reciprocated with equivalent attention as to why sex offending occurred in the first place and why it tends to stop rather abruptly for most offenders who come into contact with the criminal justice system.

This dynamic aspect of sexual offending has not been properly captured by tenets of the rehabilitation approach either. In fact, in the absence of a solid and rigorous scientific foundation, the history of sex offender treatment is one characterized by trial and error. This is not meant to take away from the fact that much has been learned about perpetrators, risk, and possible risk factors for sexual recidivism, but rather that along the way, less has been learned about the process of change and rehabilitation. The relative failure of tackling fundamental issues about the origin and the development of risk and sexual offending through the lens of social science has contributed to the proliferation of populist-based movements that influenced flawed and ineffective sex offender policies such as sex offender registries and public notification (e.g., Schiavone & Jeglic, 2009). Public sex offender registration and public notification are not effective or efficient sex offending policy. It cannot be more clear; there is a glaring lack of a demonstrated crime prevention effect of such policies. What is more, this is also combined with the negative individual, familial, and social impact these measures can have on registrants, their families, and the broader social environment that in turn can influence offending of all forms. Furthermore, in response to many of the fundamental issues and problems with such policies, additional misguided policies have been implemented, further widening the criminal justice net while reinforcing the symbolic nature of the public registration and public notification (e.g., Tewksbury, 2007). In the end, much effort and resources are being invested in ineffective and potentially detrimental policies.

The overreliance on the criminal justice system and its actors to address a multifaceted social problem and a complex public health phenomenon remains at the heart of the issue. Flawed and misguided criminal justice policies that are developed in response to dramatic, high-profile, and atypical cases cannot compensate for the lack of an evidence-based, well-coordinated, multi-ministerial, multidisciplinary, and multifaceted approach to the prevention of sexual offending that extends well beyond the purview of the criminal justice system. Research has not followed through with recommendations for what a broader approach to sexual offending prevention should look like. In order to achieve this, a dramatically different approach to the study of sexual offending needs to be undertaken. One that is more proactive. One that really informs the prevention of sexual offending.

A More Proactive Approach to Sexual Offending Research

Despite the fact we offer a critical view on the development of scientific knowledge in the field of sexual offending research, it is without doubt that to date the contributions of scientific research to advancing the understanding of sexual offending are undeniable. A number of methodological advancements have been highlighted throughout the book. Scientific findings have been contrasted with myths, misconceptions, and erroneous conclusions about sexual offending and perpetrators of sexual offenses. These efforts however have been predominantly reactive in that they challenged myths and misconceptions rather than proactively educated in a way that could possibly have prevented the proliferation of these misconceptions and erroneous ideas in the first place. This is not a problem specific to this field of research. Nonetheless, research has failed in finding ideas to replace the common mindset of the general public that sex offenders will continue to sexually offend until placed behind bars. Instead, researchers were called upon to examine already enacted laws and policies based on "common sense" notions, ideological thinking, and pseudo-scientific observations. Researchers tested the impact of misguided policies already proposed by policymakers and enacted by the government rather than proposing guidelines for best practices in the prevention of sexual offending. Researchers looked at the impact of sex offender treatment programs that remained "black boxes" even after years of implementation in hospital and correctional settings. They proposed risk assessment tools after several decades of clinical practices where practitioners relied on their subjective professional experience and judgment to determine an offender's dangerousness.

Research has been relied upon to put to the test existing policies and practices, to improve and adjust them, and to determine their impact on sexual offending. Resistance to what is perceived as challenging research findings has been another barrier to the emergence of evidence-based policies. In other words, researchers have been working within a system whose foundation is flawed and misguided. In turn, they have been working to improve policies that are rooted in this foundation; improvements and adjustments to policies that were originally based on false, inadequate, or incomplete premises. As a result, scientific advances pertaining to sexual offending and perpetrators of sexual offenses look quite underwhelming. Research findings have often challenged these policies and practices and, rather than changing those or making necessary adjustments, a call for additional research or simply overlooking these findings have been the main response of officials and policymakers. In short, unless systemic changes are made, research will continue to be underwhelming, incomplete, and disappointing. This change begins with respect to the culture of conducting research and research practices in this field.

Overcoming Common Methodological Shortcomings

The culture of conducting research in this field should be scrutinized and reassessed. There are some clear norms and expectations about how to conduct research within this field. Such expectations are framed within the mold of reactive research. Reactive research has been unraveling for several decades now and research is expected to be produced in a certain way. Much could be gained by broadening the research and methodological perspectives within this field of research. The clinical approach to the understanding of sexual offending remains the predominant approach in the field. While it is impossible to conduct research on a complex social phenomenon such as sexual offending without some form of methodological limitations, the clinical research way of conducting scientific investigations is relatively similar. As a result, a large proportion of studies conducted in this field share the same methodological shortcomings that seriously compromise the ability to draw firm conclusions about the phenomenon. Greater confidence in research findings is obtained when similar conclusions are reached by researchers having conducted independent studies that do not share the same methodological limitations. Research designs that share the same methodological limitations raise validity, reliability, and generalization issues. Can findings apply to all perpetrators of sex crimes, or just those who have been convicted, incarcerated, and admitted to a sex offender treatment program? The challenge for researchers is to understand all forms of sexual offending and all perpetrators of sexual offenses, not just a few who are known to the criminal justice system. The challenge is formidable but necessary for the development and implementation of an effective evidence-based prevention program. So, the key question then becomes what are the methodological limitations and shortcomings that researchers need to overcome to improve the understanding of sexual offending?

From a research perspective, perpetrators of sexual offenses represent a difficult to reach population. The societal perception of perpetrators of sex crimes as monsters, perverts, deviants, and pariahs makes it even more difficult for researchers to identify these individuals and to convince them to take part in a research study. Indeed, the stigma behind having committed a sex offense implies that people may be less willing to advertise to anyone, including researchers promising confidentiality, that they have perpetrated this type of crime. To do research from a clinical perspective requires the identification of individuals who have perpetrated such behaviors. To accomplish this, research is not conducted on individuals who have perpetrated a sex crime, but rather, individuals who have been convicted for a sex crime. Therefore, clinical research traditionally has been done with individuals who have been caught, apprehended, and convicted for a sex crime. This leaves out a sizeable portion of individuals who have been arrested but not convicted and even more that have escaped adjudication altogether. Given that only a minority of victims report their crime to the police and the well-known attrition problem within the criminal justice system, it is unclear whether and to what extent convicted offenders accurately represent the broader population of perpetrators of sex crimes.

The identification of the convicted offender for research purposes in this context is generally based on legal criteria. Furthermore, these studies are often based on small convenience samples that have been filtered through the criminal justice system and are the easiest to access. Rarely do studies conducted on convicted offenders include all individuals convicted for a sex crime in a given jurisdiction in a given time period. How were individuals in these samples selected for the study? Were there specific criteria used to identify the participants? How many declined to participate? What type of sex crimes have they perpetrated in the past? When were they approached to take part in the study? Did the offenders consent to taking part in the study? Indeed, research is typically conducted in either hospital or correctional settings, often in a sex offender treatment program. Importantly, not all convicted offenders can take part in such programs as admissibility and admission criteria vary from program to program. Motivation to change and acknowledging their guilt are examples of such criteria. Together, these issues raise important but often unaddressed questions about the group that "sex offenders" found in studies actually represent.

Another important pillar of research in the field is the ability to collect sensitive information that is complete and detailed, accurate and truthful, relevant, precise, and informative about sexual offending and perpetrators of sexual offenses. This is certainly a challenging task given that the information needed to accomplish it is not only sensitive, but can be painful, shameful, stressful, and traumatic for participants to disclose to a stranger for the purpose of research. Collecting valuable information about individuals' past and childhood experiences can be challenging. Such information includes whether they have been abused; whether they have deviant sexual fantasies and whether they masturbate to such fantasies; whether they still experience deviant sexual thoughts and whether they would reoffend. Some of this information may also be illegal and divulging it could have legal implications for the participants interviewed. In fact, in some jurisdictions, it can also be the responsibility of researchers to inform relevant authorities if a person has made a direct threat to hurt someone else or who has a history of committing crimes against children. Recall the context in which research participants take part in studies along these lines, generally following a lengthy judicial process (e.g., police investigation; court proceedings; remand and detention; sentence hearings; media portrayal of the perpetrator). Critically, the effect of the judicial process on the data collected is rarely if at all taken into consideration. The same questions arise with respect to custody and the experience of incarceration and how it affects participation in a study and the data collected. It has been argued that because of the extraordinary nature of the crimes they have perpetrated, such sensitive questions are necessary to understand the origin and the development of sexual offending. The hallmark of good research is the presence of a control or comparison group. In that context, it requires recruiting individuals with no evidence of having perpetrated sexual offenses and asking them the same sensitive questions about their experiences and behaviors. Not surprisingly, only a limited subset of empirical research includes such a comparison/control group. When there is such a group, too often this group is simply inadequate in that it poorly reflects the general population of offenders (e.g., they are often more criminally involved than perpetrators of sex crimes; comparisons often involve perpetrators of violent nonsexual crimes).

The nature of the data collected is also pivotal with respect to the type of conclusions researchers can draw about their study findings. Traditionally, researchers have preferred clinical-based information about perpetrators that includes details about their mental health and personality characteristics, their sexual development, their beliefs and attitudes toward women, children, and sexuality, their mood, their cognitive and emotional state at the time of their sexual offense, and so on. Because of the reactive nature of the research, researchers only meet with participants after they perpetrated a crime. In fact, only after they have been convicted for their crime, which can be months and sometimes even years after the offense. The data collected by researchers, for the most part, was retrospective and cross-sectional. In other words, researchers gather information about offenders' past which can be biased by a number of factors other than those previously mentioned (e.g., poor memory recall; intoxicated at the time of the offense; psychotic at the time of the offense; too distant to recall accurately). Not only does this create a formidable problem for researchers to establish the quality of the information collected, but it also raises issues about the accurate ordering of events as they unfolded and why they unfolded over months, years, and sometimes decades. This situation is even more problematic because of the context and the nature of the data gathered. Indeed, researchers in the field are consistently faced with triangulation questions. Triangulation of the data refers to the use of multiple methods (e.g., questionnaires; police reports; face-to-face interviews) and multiple sources (e.g., offender, victim, witness, family member) to verify the information and to assess the quality of the information gathered (e.g., whether it is consistent). Unfortunately, it is quite rare that researchers have the luxury of working with multiple methods and multiple sources which raises questions about the quality of the data.

Taken together, these limitations and shortcomings highlight the daunting tasks faced by researchers aiming to understand the origin and the development of sexual offending; they work in less than ideal conditions and circumstances. It is like trying to solve a jigsaw puzzle, not knowing what the image is, not knowing whether or not some pieces are missing, and trying to solve the puzzle in a situation where some of the pieces found in the mix might not even belong to that particular puzzle.

Focusing on Sexual Offending Rather than Sex Offenders

Clinical researchers have focused on perpetrators designated as sex offenders as a result of their conviction for a sex crime. The "sex offender" label is also a reflection of researchers' focus on perpetrators and their behavior as an extension of who they are, their state of mind, motives, deficits, and dangerousness. In the process, by focusing almost exclusively on individual-level factors making this group of individuals distinct and unique, researchers somewhat neglected the very behavior that they try to explain, predict, and prevent. This is evident by the lack of work on the conceptualization and operationalization of sexual offending. In comparison, the concept of antisocial behavior and its key dimensions (e.g., recklessness, authority-conflict, overt and covert aggressive behaviors) are well known and have been the subject of several empirical tests (e.g., Le Blanc & Bouthillier, 2003). It has been suggested that there are three dimensions of sexual offending: sexual violence and abuse, sexual misconduct, and sexual exploitation. This dimensional model, however, has not been empirically tested. In fact, there is no instrument capable of measuring a person's involvement in what is believed to be the three dimensions of sexual offending. The absence of a valid and reliable multifaceted measure of sexual offending remains a critical outstanding issue. This three-dimensional model should be seen as a starting point for an evidence-based multidimensional model of sexual offending. Understandably, research has been heavily focused on sexual violence and abuse (e.g., sexual homicide, rape and sexual assault, sexual aggression). Research on these serious and extreme forms of sexual offending is and will continue to be important, but the lack of empirical research on other dimensions and behavioral manifestations limits our understanding of other forms and dimensions of sexual offending, such as sexual misconduct and sexual exploitation. The lack of empirical and scientific information about various forms of sexual offenses, even those that are not currently sociopolitically defined as such contributes to the emergence of myths, misconceptions, and erroneous conclusions.

While research has been and continues to be focused on who sex offenders are, more can be gained from studying the situations and life circumstances leading to a sexual offense. For example, we know very little about the situations conducive to a sexual offense where a sexual offense *did not* take place. In everyday life, there are numerous situations that are prone to the perpetration of a sexual offense. For example, situations where there is a vulnerable victim (e.g., an intoxicated adult; an unsupervised child) in a context where there are no suitable guardians (e.g., individual that can and will intervene and prevent a crime from happening), in the presence of a potential offender. From a scientific standpoint, knowledge about situations that did not escalate to a sexual offense as opposed to those that did can provide valuable policy information from a prevention standpoint. This is not just about comparing the context and life circumstances of offenders and non-offenders. Even individuals that have perpetrated sexual offenses do not act on every opportunity that they have to sexually offend. Why does a sexual offense occur in one of these opportunities but not another? Research is in fact rather clear on this: sexual offenses, for the most part, are perpetrated under exceptional circumstances. Thus, instead of looking for factors that are typical of perpetrators of sexual offenses, perhaps it would be valuable to look at circumstances within a person's life that were atypical for them. Circumstances that they were not typically exposed to or not well equipped to deal with. Knowing more about life circumstances and the thought process that stopped someone from committing a sexual offense, or influenced their perpetration of one, can provide additional insight to the offending process. As it stands, from a scientific standpoint, we know very little about these non-offending situations and their accompanied circumstances.

Criminal career research is another concrete step toward a more proactive approach to sexual offending research (e.g., Blokland & Lussier, 2015). Criminal career researchers study the longitudinal sequence of sexual offending along with associated criminal career parameters. Some of these key parameters include sexual offending age of onset, frequency, diversity, persistence and duration, as well as the age of offset. There have been some improvements and significant advancements in the description of the longitudinal sequence of sexual offending (e.g., Lussier & Cale, 2013). We know, for example, that not all perpetrators of sex crime start young and persist into the later stage of adulthood. There is a continuum of ages of onset of sexual offending. We also know that while there are prolific offenders, both in terms of the number of sex crime events and number of victims, sexual offending consists of a limited number of occurrences for most offenders. We also know that perpetrators are not, for the most part, out-of-control offenders who commit various types of sexual offenses against a myriad of victim types. One area where persistent offenders might diversify their sexual offending to a certain extent relates to the victim's age where adolescents may become surrogate victims for those who have offended against adults and those who have offended against children. To this day, however, little is known about the behavioral progression of persistent offenders and whether the development of sexual offending follows a specific path or different paths. The scientific advancements have been modest because of the lack of specificity of research combined with the absence of a valid and reliable measure of sexual offending. As a result, criminal career research has typically aggregated all forms of sexual offending into a single "sexual offending" category that is not specific enough about the different dimensions and manifestations that this behavior can take on. This is especially true for sexual misconduct and sexual exploitation. More can be gained by the examination, description, and measurement of specific forms of sexual offending and their development over time. This can be hard to do because some forms of sexual offending are rare. Moreover, many of the sexual offenses of interest may be too minor in a legal context to warrant being sentenced to a custody facility.

To observe, measure, and track the perpetration of a wide range of different sexual offending behaviors requires extremely large and representative samples. There is a long tradition of population-based research on antisocial and criminal behavior. For example, prospective longitudinal birth cohort studies have contributed to the understanding of the development course of antisocial behavior (e.g., Wolfgang, Figlio, & Sellin, 1972). Some of those birth cohort studies, in the process, allowed the prospective examination of some of the earliest developmental risk factors and their unfolding throughout childhood, adolescence, and adulthood (e.g., Moffitt, Caspi, Harrington, & Milne, 2002). Prospective longitudinal cohort studies based on samples of school-aged children and adolescents have also contributed to the understanding of antisocial and criminal behavior during adolescence, the continuity and discontinuity of antisocial and criminal behavior into adulthood, as well as

desistance from crime (e.g., Farrington et al., 2006). Similarly, prospective longitudinal cohort studies of at-risk children have also expanded our understanding of the
development course of antisocial behavior, including some of the most severe forms
of criminal behaviors (e.g., Loeber et al., 2005). It is unfortunate that these prospective criminological studies did not look at sexual offending or, at best, used crude
and limited indicators to measure sexual offending (e.g., rape) not allowing for the
examination of the full spectrum of sexual offending behaviors. This approach used
to study the developmental course of antisocial and criminal behavior should be
mirrored for the investigation of sexual offending behaviors, keeping in mind that
behavioral manifestations causing sexual harm can occur throughout the life course.
This could mean, for example, reaching to various institutions to survey the prevalence, nature, frequency, and seriousness of various sexual offending behaviors
(e.g., school system, college and university campuses). Although relatively rare, this
type of investigation has been conducted as early as the preschool period by conducting survey research with daycare workers about the sexual behavior of preschoolers (e.g., Lindblad, Gustafsson, Larsson, & Lundin, 1995). Others examined
a large sample of at-risk children to study the developmental course of inappropriate
and sexually harmful behaviors (e.g., Lussier, Chouinard-Thivierge, McCuish,
Nadeau, & Lacerte, 2019). Being specific about criminal career parameters, such as
the age of onset for specific behavioral manifestations, can help the development
and implementation of concrete prevention programs targeting specific aspects of
sexual offending.

    A proactive approach to research on sexual offending also involves examining
the behavioral progression before the onset of sexual offending. Criminology has
gained much insight into the developmental origins of juvenile delinquency and
adult criminality by examining their behavioral precursors during childhood (e.g.,
Loeber, Farrington, Stouthamer-Loeber, & White, 2008; Piquero, Farrington, &
Blumstein, 2007). The examination of conceptually related behaviors of crime and
delinquency, that is, childhood antisocial behavior (also referred as externalizing
behavior problems, oppositional defiant disorder behaviors, and conduct disorder
behaviors), has contributed to the identification of a pattern of life course persistent
crime and delinquency, but also the recognition that not all adolescents involved in
crime and delinquency continue this behavior in adulthood. In the field of sexual
offending research, these underlying processes are relatively unknown. While
there has been some research into the examination of the early antisocial behavior
of youth and adults involved in sexual offenses, not much is known about early
sexual behavioral development and whether it provides insightful information
about the unfolding of sexual offending behavior over time. Prospective research
addressing such questions is especially lacking. Of importance, researchers examining childhood behavioral problems have neglected the study of sexual behavioral
problems prior to the teenage years. Misconceptions about the onset and development course of human sexual behavior might have contributed to this situation. As
a result, there is a significant lack of knowledge as to what constitutes a typical as
opposed to an atypical and a concerning sexual behavioral development (e.g.,
DeLamater & Friedrich, 2002; Friedrich, Grambsch, Broughton, Kuiper, & Beilke,

1991). Childhood sexual behavioral problems can take different forms across at least three different dimensions: (1) coercive and harmful sexual behaviors (e.g., forced sexual touching of another child's genitals); (2) repetitive and compulsive sexual behaviors (e.g., repetitively asking another child to engage in sex play; frequently talking about sex); and (3) inappropriate sexual behavior given the developmental stage of the child (e.g., oral sex). While the occurrence of childhood sexual development problems is unlikely to be the starting point for most individuals involved in sexual offending over the life course, it could be informative from a preventive standpoint for some developmental patterns of sexual offending. Unfortunately, to this day, the proportion of adolescents and adults who experienced childhood sexual development problems and the developmental context characterizing their emergence remains unclear.

Community-Based Research

A more proactive approach to the study of sexual offending also requires a significant shift in research design practices. This includes where researchers conduct their studies, with whom, and in what context. Traditionally, research on sexual offending and perpetrators of sex crimes took place in psychiatric wards, prisons, and sex offender treatment programs. It is engrained in the culture of this field of research that those are the optimal settings to conduct such research to improve our understanding of sexual offending and perpetrators of sexual offenses. After all, this is a difficult to reach population and these settings provide access to some of these perpetrators. Research continues to be heavily focused on small samples of individuals that are known to the criminal justice system who were assessed and took part in a sex offender treatment program. We know little about individuals who have perpetrated sexual offenses but have not been convicted for their crimes. We also know little about those individuals prior to their conviction for a sex crime and more importantly, prior to their onset of sexual offending. This is not to suggest that this type of clinical research in psychiatric and prison settings should be abandoned. Rather, this field of research needs to be significantly broadened to better understand the scope of sexual offending, the full range of individuals involved in such offenses, and the various forms of sexual offenses. For example, individuals who have perpetrated acts of sexual misconduct (e.g., sexual harassment) and those who have sexually exploited others are not typically found in prison-based sex offender treatment programs. Such settings are overrepresented with individuals having perpetrated acts of sexual violence and abuse. In order to move beyond the description of the clinical profiles of convicted offenders and toward more explanatory-oriented research for all forms of sexual offending, other forms of scientific investigation need to be undertaken, expanded, and enhanced. While broad-based community research is unlikely to be very useful for the scientific investigation of more serious forms of sexual offenses (e.g., sexual aggression with physical violence, aggravated sexual assault, sexual homicide) it can provide much needed information for proactive actions.

A small revolution took place in the 1980s when some researchers took their research agenda to university campuses to study rape and sexual assault and associated risk factors (e.g., Greendlinger & Byrne, 1987; Koss & Gidycz, 1985; Malamuth, 1981; Rapaport & Burkhart, 1984). To be sure, at the time it seemed to be an odd place to study such extreme forms of criminal behaviors.

This line of research broke the mold of what research on sexual offending was supposed to be. It significantly helped, from a scientific standpoint, in breaking the image of the perpetrator of a sexual offense as someone with mental health problems committing a sex crime against a stranger. Rather than focusing on offenders, this line of research focused on sexual offending. The research was focused on locations where sexual offenses could occur due to the confluence of shared risk factors for both perpetrators and victims (e.g., age group, attitudes, peer influence, alcohol use, reckless behavior). The measurement of sexual offending was pivotal to these researchers' agenda. It relied on individual experiences of sexual offending and introduced the idea of using self-reported information about the perpetration of sexual offending and self-reported information about sexual victimization. Using self-reported data, ensuring confidentiality and anonymity, and in many cases introducing social desirability measures to statistically control for the possibility some individuals likely respond in socially desirable ways given the contents of such surveys, studies investigated whether and to what extent individuals self-reported engaging in a range of sexually coercive and aggressive behaviors. Some of these studies also investigated hypothetical scenarios, such as asking respondents whether they would ever engage in a range of sexually coercive and aggressive behaviors under specific sets of conditions (e.g., if they could be sure nobody would ever know they did it or ever find out). Acknowledging that self-report data are not without important limitations, this line of research nonetheless provided new and important insights about the behavior to a point that challenged commonly held ideas at the time about the risk factors for sexual offending. Three to four decades later, the research findings stemming from this line of investigation remain extremely valuable today.

More recently, important observations were made with respect to the course of sexual offending across a person's college trajectory. Individuals that committed rape on college campuses, with rape defined as "penetration, no matter how slight, of the vagina or anus with any body part or object, or oral penetration by a sex organ of another person, without the consent of the victim" (Swartout et al., 2015, p. 1149), showed that most rapes on campuses were perpetrated by individuals that did not have a prior history of committing rape in adolescence. Unlike traditional studies, these findings were based on the self-reports of male college students. Such perspectives portray campus sexual assaults as the result of an extremely small number of men perpetrating the majority of all sex offenses. Indeed, the White House Council on Women and Girls (2014) received information suggesting that 3% of college men perpetrated 90% of all rapes. Accordingly, the report concluded that the typical campus assailant is one that repeatedly engaged in such crimes. Swartout et al. (2015) findings suggested not just that such an offender was rare, but that such an offender did not exist according to their data. The most frequent offenders in their sample accounted for less than 20% of all instances of rape perpetrated by males on campus. In sum, this prior work demonstrates that important, policy-relevant findings can be captured by research not conforming to the norm of focusing on offender samples. While community-based research on sexual victimization is quite common, it remains a rarity for the study of the perpetration of sexual offenses, and this situation is causing significant policy gaps.

Disentangling the Risk Factors and Correlates of Sexual Offending

There is a prevailing and widespread misconception that the risk and protective factors for sexual offending are well known. Part of the reason why this is a misconception is because studies that do repeatedly identify the same risk factors for the perpetration of sexual offenses are characterized by the same research design flaws: retrospective research, narrow samples of serious offenders, reliance on official data that excludes persons that committed their crimes undetected. As such, at best, there are risk factors that are associated with sexual recidivism among men typically in their thirties that have come into contact with the justice system for sexual offending at least once in the past and have once again come into contact with the justice system for an additional sex crime. The reality is that there is no generally accepted theory of sexual offending. In fact, knowledge about the risk and protective factors is largely based on beliefs, inferences, and hypotheses (e.g., see Nunes et al., 2019).

Knowledge about the clinical profile of individuals convicted for a sex crime is certainly a step toward the understanding of sexual offending. But it is not a scientifically rigorous demonstration of what the risk factors for sexual offending are. Most of the clinical research conducted in psychiatric wards and hospitals as well as those conducted in prisons are in fact inductive. The single case studies, the examination of the characteristics of a small sample of individuals enrolled in a treatment program, the clinical profiles of individuals who have been assessed by a clinical team to identify treatment needs, and the risk of reoffending provide little empirical verification about the broader risk factors for sexual offending. This accumulation of information, irrespective of how methodologically rigorous the information was collected, has served clinical researchers in the construction of theory after the fact. There are various examples of such inductive work with very little empirical verification testing the hypotheses put forth. The construction of a theory after the fact without proper scientific assessment is problematic and leads to numerous inferences, especially in the absence of a control/comparison group. Yet, these explanatory models are generally accepted at face value because authors of these models base them on clinical observations and practitioners working with this population value these observations. The practicality of these models, however, speaks little about their scientific value. Intuitively, this is certainly a start, but the field of research has been unable to move passed this sort of inductive work. One clear implication of using such research designs and data is the inability of researchers to disentangle risk factors and correlates of sexual offending.

From a proactive research standpoint, disentangling the risk factors and correlates of sexual offending should be a priority. Statistical significance does not prove that a certain characteristic is a risk factor for sexual offending. A risk factor is a measurable characteristic of each subject in a specified population that precedes the outcome of interest (Kraemer et al., 1997). The presence/absence of a risk factor should allow researchers to distinguish a high-risk from a low-risk group. A risk factor is one that is associated with significantly different probabilities of occurrence of the measured outcome. The magnitude of this difference must also be measured. The association is reflected by the differential probabilities of the occurrence of sexual offending between a low and high-risk group. Furthermore, the modification of a risk factor should lead to the observation that these changes are associated with subsequent changes in the probability of the outcome occurring. Therefore, any changes in the presence/absence or intensity of the risk factor should be associated with changing probabilities of sexual offending. Because of the reactive research approach relying on retrospective and cross-sectional data, a correlate of sexual offending can easily be confused with a risk factor for sexual offending. A correlate of sexual offending is a factor that does not precede the outcome, but is associated with sexual offending. They can also be concomitant, that is, some factors can actually occur during the perpetration of a sexual offense (e.g., deviant sexual arousal, being angry, using physical force to overcome the victim's resistance). Correlates can also be factors that result from the perpetration of sexual offending (e.g., the development of cognitive distortions supportive of rape and sexual assault, deviant sexual interests, etc.).

A more proactive approach involves a program of research where the possible risk and protective factors for sexual offending are measured prior to the onset of sexual offending. Research, and especially clinical research, has outlined several possible candidates and promising factors that likely play a role in the origins and development of sexual offending. To test for the relevance of these factors, community-based longitudinal studies are needed. Longitudinal studies have been a major contributor to the understanding of the origins and the development of antisocial and criminal behavior more broadly. They have helped to broaden the understanding of the development of antisocial and criminal behavior with important policy implications. More specifically they have helped considerably to move from a static-fixed propensity perspective on the risk factors for antisocial and criminal behavior toward a more complex perspective recognizing the dynamic aspect of human development over the life course. To be clear, longitudinal studies involve taking repeated measurements of a single cohort of individuals ideally over very long periods of time. They allow for the collection of information about the risk and protective factors of phenomenon that have yet to occur. When properly designed, implemented, and executed, not only can longitudinal data provide key information about the development of sex offending, but also about the development of key risk and protective factors. From a preventive standpoint, these longitudinal and prospective studies can inform about how exactly certain individuals could be more likely to perpetrate a sex crime compared to others; they also would provide crucial information about the development of an individual prior to, during, and following the perpetration of a sex crime. In other words, with prospective longitudinal data, an individual becomes his or her own "control." The longitudinal design helps to address complex but necessary questions that are the foundation of evidence-based and effective prevention programs.

To date, the implementation of longitudinal studies has been heavily focused on the study of sexual recidivism among individuals convicted for a sex crime. While this line of research is not without its shortcomings, it has completely changed our perception of risk and the way risk assessment is conducted; it had a dramatic impact on the nature and type of factors considered to be important versus those not considered to be important. The implementation of longitudinal study designs has had a dramatic impact on our understanding of sexual recidivism. Critically, the same dramatic changes can be expected from longitudinal studies examining the onset of sexual offending.

Sexual Offending, Age and the Life Course

There has been an important consequence of conducting research on sexual offending primarily from a reactive, after the fact approach; this approach has contributed to an important oversight in this field of research. More specifically, this oversight is that researchers have largely neglected to examine the process by which sexual offending develops over time: its onset, course, and termination. Relatedly, the issue of age, time, and development has been grossly overlooked in the field. Age, time, and development matter in sexual offending much more than research has suggested.

To this day, there is scarce longitudinal research designed specifically to explore factors that contribute to the onset of sexual offending. Understanding, for example, the early signs of sexual offending has not been a critical research question for most researchers in the field. While there are a plethora of descriptive studies on convicted offenders' cognitions, fantasies, thoughts, emotions, sexual preferences, behavior before and after they committed their offense, we have little reliable information about who they were before perpetrating sexual offenses. Researchers have attempted to address this issue by questioning these individuals about their childhood and adolescence, but this is almost always after the fact. In this context, what these research findings are suggesting is how these individuals recollect their childhood and adolescence; what these individuals want to remember or recollect about their upbringing; what these individuals want us to know about their past experiences; their own perception of what probably happened and what might have happened. Such a retrospective and subjective narrative is usually constructed in the most unpleasant context (e.g., prison), which can impact the quality, reliability, and validity of the information collected. Convicted offenders have few incentives and little to gain by providing accurate information about their past. Research is conducted under less than ideal conditions and the study limitations are too important to draw firm conclusions about the developmental antecedents of these individuals before their offending started.

While biological age is certainly important for understanding developmental issues, the recognition of the impact of age on sexual offending is paramount. Age needs to be examined in terms of the different developmental stages and contexts in which sexual offending can emerge. The biopsychosocial developmental contexts for an 8 year old, a 14 year old, a 21 year old, a 40 year old, and a 65 year old are all quite different. This developmental context should guide the analysis of the context in which sexual offending occurs (e.g., where, with whom, under what life circumstances). Studies with preschoolers have shown that certain intrusive behaviors (e.g., running naked in front of a stranger) occur spontaneously as part of the child's development at home, at daycares, or even in public. After school entry, these spontaneous behaviors are less frequent and more covert. Some school-aged children, however, manifest overt and harmful sexual behaviors. We are learning that these children have been exposed to very difficult family environments, characterized by various forms of child maltreatment, including very early and persistent parental negligence, physical abuse, and parental abandonment. This line of research has also shown the importance of behavior problems of these children, including physical aggression. While sexual victimization can be part of the developmental context of the childhood onset of harmful sexual behaviors, it is not a pivotal one. Polyvictimization on the other hand appears to be (Lussier et al., 2019). Studies conducted with adolescents highlight that it is not so much victimization experiences but rather antisocial and criminogenic factors that are commonly referred to as risk factors for juvenile delinquency. Living in a bad neighborhood, low self-control, early involvement in crime and delinquency, and early onset of sexual intercourse are part of the developmental context conducive to sexual offending at this particular development stage. Studies conducted with young adults and college/university students have shown the importance of cognitive-based factors, such as attitudes toward women, sexuality, and interpersonal violence as well as attitudes and beliefs about sexual offending and perpetrators of sexual offenses. The profile also shows that these individuals' sexuality is far from limited to acts of sexual offenses. Rather, studies with this age group suggest that individuals who are more prone to using harmful and coercive tactics are characterized by an impersonal sexual lifestyle involving multiple sexual partners.

Put together, research findings observed among samples of individuals from various age groups do not appear to suggest that there is a single pathway to sexual offending, but rather, signs of age-graded risk factors for sexual offending. In other words, not all roads to sexual offending begin in infancy with parental negligence, attachment issues, and so on. The focus on a single developmental period to tackle the sexual offending phenomenon is unlikely to yield significant results. For a small subgroup of individuals, sexual offending is probably a reflection of the accumulation of risk factors starting as early as birth and infancy. For most individuals, however, age-graded and context-dependent life circumstances and factors are more likely operating. If this indeed is the case, an age-graded approach to understanding sexual offending manifestations should be prioritized along with age-graded interventions. Researchers need to turn their attention to the continuum reflecting the age of onset of sexual offending and the respective risk and protective factors at different age stages.

Researchers have not only neglected offenders' past but also their futures. While researchers have collected information about sexual recidivism following convicted offenders' returns to the community, little is known about these individuals following the criminal justice system's response to their behavior (e.g., McCuish & Lussier, 2017). While we know, for example, that young children with harmful and coercive sexual behaviors are very unlikely to commit a sexual offense during adolescence, we do not really know why. Such uncertainties and gaps in the scientific literature allow for the emergence and perpetuation of misconceptions and erroneous beliefs. Similarly, while we know a great deal about sexual recidivism, we do not in fact know much outside of offenders' probabilities of being convicted again during some follow-up period after their prison release. In fact, we know little about the nature, context, frequency, seriousness, or persistence of their offending until termination. How many more victims do they offend against? Under what circumstances? What was the level of planning? Was offending more sophisticated or more impulsive? For those who sexually reoffend, is there an escalation or a de-escalation over time? Is there a change in the type of victim, offending location, and duration of sex crime events? In sum, aside from the impact of criminal justice interventions on subsequent convictions, we know little of what goes on after offenders complete their sentences. Besides their subsequent offending, researchers neglected the study of their psychological, familial, social, and professional functioning following release from prison. Where do they live? Whom do they affiliate with? How do they cope with community re-entry? What kind of shape is their health and mental health in after spending years in prison? What is the impact of media coverage on their subsequent psychological, familial, and social functioning? Are they being marginalized, stigmatized, and isolated as a result of their conviction for a sex crime? Were these processes already in place prior to their conviction and even perhaps before their sexual offending occurred? It is only after the enactment of preventive measures such as public notification and sex offender registries that researchers started examining the life circumstances of convicted offenders after their return to the community.

The age-graded approach to understanding perpetrators' future involvement in sexual offenses will also likely provide extremely useful information. Although this is not reflected in sex offender policies, researchers have acknowledged the need and importance of distinguishing adolescent from adult perpetrators. The differential general and sexual recidivism rates of these two groups support this approach. Researchers have proposed, developed, and tested risk assessment tools to be used specifically with adolescent perpetrators of sex offenses. There are significant developmental differences between a 12 year old and a 17 year old. One key question is: Are those developmental differences accounted for in the development of risk assessment protocols? Should risk assessment protocols distinguish young and older adolescents and their associated risk and protective factors? Currently, this is very unlikely given that research investigating such questions is relatively non-existent. In fact, the same can be said about adult perpetrators of sex offenses. Researchers have shown that not recognizing offenders' age at the time of the assessment leads to overestimation of risk for older offenders. These revelations have led to adjustments of existing actuarial risk assessment instruments, but not a reconsideration of risk assessment practices more generally. Are the risk factors for a 21 year old convicted offender the same as for a 65 year old offender? These sorts of questions have not been adequately addressed in scientific research. The same reasoning can be applied to intervention and treatment, community re-entry and community reintegration, risk management, and community supervision. Following a sentence for a sexual offense, the contexts for a teenager going back to school, a young adult looking for employment, or an older adult with children are very different. To date, research has provided very little guidance and insight about these realities. Appropriately contextualizing the life circumstances of perpetrators of sexual offenses should become an important policy and theory-focused research agenda.

In short, the lack of theoretical and empirical research examining links between offenders' past, present, and future seriously limits the development and implementation of rigorous and evidence-based policies and prevention programs focused on perpetrators of sex crimes.

Disaggregating Profiles and Patterns

The legal characterization of individuals convicted for a sex crime as "sex offenders" perhaps has been *the* hallmark of research in the field. At first, it made sense to distinguish individuals having perpetrated what were considered to be odd, irrational, and atypical crimes. After close to 100 years of clinical research using this term, it might be time to consider turning the page. Conceptually, this term creates more confusion than it provides clarity because of the wide range of behaviors it reflects. Theoretically and clinically, the similarities far exceed the differences compared with other offenders who have perpetrated nonsexual crimes. Empirically, the sex offender label does not reflect the fact that many if not most perpetrators are involved in various crime types and among those whose offending persists, it more likely involves nonsexual offenses. Ethically, this term unnecessarily labels individuals and this label might carry long-term stigmatizing and marginalizing effects, all of which can in fact contribute to an increase in the likelihood of future offending.

There now exists a consensus among researchers that there is much heterogeneity characterizing this group of offenders. Researchers, however, have long struggled with the operationalization of this heterogeneity. How do you best characterize differences and within-group variance for individuals having perpetrated a sexual offense? Many paths have been taken and several propositions have been tested. Researchers initially categorized offenders based on the underlying motivation to perpetrate a sexual offense. This approach evolved into the categorization of offenders using certain clinical constructs (e.g., denial, empathy, intimacy, psychopathy). Researchers have also categorized offenders based on the nature and type of sexual offense perpetrated, taking into consideration information such as a victim's age, offender–victim relationship, the level of violence and injuries inflicted to the victim, etc. This eventually evolved to the categorization of offenders using crime scene indicators. More recently, researchers have categorized offenders based on their aggregate level of risk of sexual recidivism (e.g., low-risk, moderate-risk, high-risk) or whether they are sexual recidivists or not. The focus of any of these categorizations again has been reactive in nature; whatever the categorization proposed, it generally aimed to address some practical needs such as: determining offenders' treatment needs, assisting and guiding police investigations, orientating risk management practices, etc. A more proactive approach on the other hand can be pursued to better inform intervention and prevention programs for preventive purposes.

One aspect of categorization that has been somewhat left to the wayside is the characterization of homogeneity among perpetrators of sexual offenses in terms of underlying developmental processes. What are the routes and pathways leading to sexual offending? How does sexual offending develop over time? Research suggests that there are multiple pathways leading to sexual offending. Furthermore, there are multiple developmental patterns characterizing the evolution of sexual offending over time. Knowledge of these pathways and developmental patterns should be a priority for research and prevention. To that effect, there have been methodological innovations that contribute to disaggregating information to better understand the underlying processes involved in the origin and development of sexual offending. For example, analytical strategies such as group-based modeling have been used to identify the evolution of offending over time in a more dynamic fashion.

Broadening the Scope of the Risk and Protective Factors

The study of risk factors for sexual offending has been guided almost purely by research traditions in forensic psychology. What must be kept in mind is that historically, clinicians working in hospitals, psychiatric wards, and incarceration facilities were exposed to a very narrow subgroup of persons involved in sexual offenses. Researchers have long acknowledged their awareness of the fact that prison-based samples are not generalizable to community-based populations. Yet, little has been done to address this limitation by collecting longitudinal data on cohort(s) of children in the community and studying their involvement in sexual and other offending behaviors through adulthood. Such samples and associated research designs are needed, and when such studies are conducted it will be important to avoid focusing narrowly only on risk factors specified by traditional, forensics-based approaches to sexual offending and risk factors specified in sex offending risk assessment tools.

Sex offending research has been overwhelmingly focused on finding what is unique and different about the perpetrator of sexual offenses. As a result, research has been focused on the examination of individual-level factors associated with sexual offending behaviors. Of importance, the focus has been and continues to be on sexuality and sexual development of these individuals (e.g., deviant sexual thoughts, abnormal sexual preferences, deviant sexual urges, cognitive distortions, sex as coping). This research is and continues to be important, but it is also severely limited on many levels. In contrast, the study of risk and protective factors for anti-social and criminal behavior has been much broader. There is well over 100 years of criminological research on the risk and protective factors for antisocial and criminal behavior. The wide array of risk and protective factors for antisocial and criminal behavior has been reviewed extensively elsewhere (e.g., Loeber & Farrington, 2012; Morizot & Kazemian, 2014) and the key domains are presented in Fig. 10.1. We can distinguish three domains of risk and protective factors: (a) individual-level, (b) environmental-level, and (c) developmental processes representing an individual x environment interplay. In terms of sex offending specifically, of the biopsychosocial factors that have been examined in criminology, mainly personality, attitudes and beliefs, and mental health factors and to some extent antisocial and criminal behavior have been examined in clinical research. Of the environmental-level factors, child maltreatment, culture and media-related exposure, and, to some extent, the familial context have been more extensively investigated in sexual offending research. Finally, of the process variables, bonding (mainly limited to early parental attachment) and social learning (in the context of victimization) have been the subject of more rigorous clinical research with perpetrators of sex offenses.

Criminological research on the identification of risk and protective factors for antisocial and criminal behavior has shown that not only is the variety of risk and protective factors important, but the accumulation and the persistence of the risk factors over time. Criminological research has also shown that some risk factors

Risk and protective factor domains for sexual offending

Individual	Environmental	Key processes and individual x environment interplay
• **Genetic, hereditary, and biological factors** (e.g., sex, MAO-A, in utero exposure to teratogens, low resting heart rate)	• **Child maltreatment and parental neglect** (e.g., sexual abuse, physical abuse)	• **Bonding** (e.g., to social institutions such as family, school, work, etc.)
• **Neuropsychological functioning** (e.g., executive functions, attention, impulsivity, planning)	• **Familial context, parental skills, norms, values and attitudes** (e.g., supervision, investment, commitment, exposure to family violence, attitudes toward crime and law enforcement)	• **Learning** (e.g., the acquisition of norms, values, beliefs, code of conduct, etc.)
• **Temperament, personality and coping skills** (e.g., daring, low self-control, negative emotionality, emotional detachment, problem solving skills)	• **Peer relationships and victimization** (e.g., bullying, peer pressure, social capital)	• **Constraining** (e.g., development of social and personal control mechanisms)
• **Attitudes, beliefs and information-processing** (e.g., attitudes and beliefs regarding antisocial and criminal behavior, personal biases and cognitive distortions supportive of antisocial and criminal behavior)	• **Gang-related factors** (e.g., membership, peer delinquency, access to weapons)	• **Labeling** (e.g., labels, stigma, justifications for deviant actions)
• **Self-identity** (e.g., self image, self-efficacy, masculinity and gender identity)	• **School, education** (e.g., learning difficulties, motivation, conflict with authority-figures, school dropout)	• **Coping and adapting** (e.g., life transitions and life events, school, moving out, work, intimate relationship, parenthood)
• **Antisocial and criminal behavior** (e.g., lying frequently, breaking rules, arrests, conviction)	• **Work and income** (e.g., motivation to work, ability to maintain a job, securing a regular and legal source of income)	• **Maturation and growth** (e.g., brain maturation, individual growth, developing a long-term view, taking others into consideration, moral development, etc.)
• **Mental health and substance use** (e.g., drug abuse, alcohol abuse)	• **Neighborhood related factors** (e.g., crime-prone neighborhood, social disorganization)	
• **Resilience** (e.g., overcoming stressful and difficult life circumstances and psychosocial adversities)	• **Life circumstances and adversities** (e.g., marital conflicts, financial difficulties)	
• **Human agency and rational-choice** (e.g., preferences, decision-making)	• **Ethnicity and immigration** (e.g., social and structural inequalities, socioeconomic disparities, racism)	
	• **Culture and media-related exposure** (e.g., exposure to media violence, acceptance of violence across cultures and social groups)	
	• **Political and sociocultural factors** (e.g., tough on crime policies, attitudes toward rehabilitation, fear of crime, norms, beliefs)	

Fig. 10.1 Risk and protective factor domains relevant to proactive research on sexual offending

occur very early (e.g., exposure to teratogens in utero), while others appear at later stages in development (e.g., gang membership). We posit that not only do these risk and protective factor domains have implications for antisocial and criminal behavior more generally, they also have implications for human behavior in the context of sexual offending: whether it is forcing someone into sex, sexually harassing someone at work, or sexually exploiting someone for profit. These factors can potentially impede a person's ability to assess and interpret the appropriateness of a situation and/or to set inappropriate personal goals and objectives that may lead to a sexual offense. These factors may also impede a person's ability to seek, validate, and re-evaluate, to recognize and understand, to value and to respect another person's consent or lack thereof within a particular context. Some individuals may not understand, take the time to assess, or may fail to recognize that a situation is inappropriate and even perhaps criminal to begin with. Some individuals may not even seek another person's consent. Some individuals may seek the other person's consent but make their own interpretation about the person's desire and needs or even what the person is consenting to. Some individuals may simply knowingly disregard the other person's lack of consent. Individual and environmental factors and their interplay speak about the origin and the development of this propensity to disregard or to transgress another person' interest and well-being. Individual, environmental factors and their interplay can also create a context conducive to sexual offending. For sexual offending research to move forward, integrating individual and environment factors, including how they interact, in explanatory models is pivotal, especially in the context of consent. Currently, the research on the issue of consent in the context of sexual offending is almost exclusively focused on the victim's perceptions and perspective.

One way to broaden the scope of risk and protective factors for sex offending involves viewing sexual offending from a public health perspective. Prior research identified general antisocial behavior as a critical risk factor for sexual offending. Early childhood behavior of all sorts should be measured repeatedly over the life course. This behavior should not be limited to classic authority-conflict, covert, overt, and reckless antisocial dimensions identified in prior criminological literature. The behavior should be extended to much more nuanced social interactions that demonstrate social competency (e.g., willingness to share, acceptance of others, respectfulness of boundaries). Online behaviors should also be monitored, including the use of harassment and shaming via social media. Measurement should be attuned to the fact that some behaviors may be more normative in some developmental stages than others. Sexual education within schools can be used as an opportunity for proactive methods of prevention of sexual offending behaviors and also an opportunity to evaluate children and teens' understanding of consensual sexual behavior, what constitutes harassment or sexual misconduct, and what the qualities of a healthy relationship look like. While it may seem extreme to examine such behaviors among individuals at an early age, such data are being collected already. Teen dating violence has similarly become an important public health concern that is now being addressed within schools through, for example, the British Columbia Adolescent Health Survey (BC AHS; Shaffer, Adjei, Viljoen, Douglas, & Saewyc, 2018). Most importantly, results from these surveys administered by public health nurses illustrated that students ranging from ages 12 to 19 did not show signs of discomfort when responding to highly personal questions about behavior, health, sexuality, and other sensitive topics. In fact, some students reported that questions about abuse made them feel like they were not alone and that persons were taking what happened to them seriously. Accordingly, it will become necessary for research ethics boards and other agencies to become more open to permitting the collection of sensitive data necessary for understanding methods of preventing sexual offending. For example, the BC AHS collected data on refusal skills; that is, the ability of teens to be able to say "no" if they were asked to engage in sexual activity that they did not want to participate in. This survey demonstrated that younger adolescents felt more skilled than older adolescents. This discrepancy was possibly related to the increased interpersonal sophistication of older teens. As individuals age, their ability to be more manipulative in pressuring others to engage in sexual activity increased, which in turn may have decreased the confidence of other teens in saying "no." As well, older teens may feel that sexual behaviors are more normative and therefore feel less confident in saying "no" to these perceived normative behaviors.

The BC AHS findings highlight opportunities from a public health standpoint to equip teens with the skills to be able to refuse to engage in sexual activity while maintaining social stature. From a risk factor perspective, the findings of this survey also contrast with forensic psychology theories that suggest sexual offending is the result of low social competence. This is usually because samples from such studies focus on, for example, individuals that sexually offended against children or who have long histories of sexual offending that stem from general antisocial behavior and social dysfunction. This survey of high school students showed that teens with interpersonal sophistication may be more adept at coercing someone to be involved in sexual activity. This is the type of behavior that perhaps is also most likely to go undetected/unreported because victims fear potential repercussions from peers for reporting on another peer. Indeed, bullying research indicated that bullies are actually often popular among their peers (Koh & Wong, 2017). Accordingly, factors such as interpersonal dominance and popularity should be measured, and researchers should examine whether attitudes toward sexual behavior interact with such personal qualities in ways that amplify risk for perpetrating sexual offenses.

Lessons from public health research related to sexual behaviors might not be found in journals traditionally associated with research on sexual offending. It is necessary for sexual offending research to broaden the scope of their literature searches and what journals they traditionally read. Important trends in sexual behavior are often reported in sexuality journals (e.g., Journal of Adolescent Health; The Canadian Journal of Human Sexuality). Lessons from this body of research should be absorbed by researchers of sexual offending. Often missing from the public health literature however is the focus on within-individual change over time. This literature tends to instead focus on population-level trends (e.g., is condom use becoming more/less prevalent?). What should be endeavored to understand from a sexual offending research perspective is whether within-individual changes in health, sexual behaviors, and other antisocial behaviors are informative of within-individual change in sexual offending. Adolescent health research has also identified protective factors against certain sexual behavior. The BC AHS, for example, demonstrated that connectivity to family or school lowered the odds of risky sexual behavior (Saewyc et al., 2008). While this study defined sexual behavior as risky primarily with respect to exposure to sexually transmitted infections, using similar methods to study the social circumstances of sexual behavior, beginning in childhood/adolescents and continuing through adulthood, would provide useful opportunities for understanding risk and protective factors.

Experimental-Based Research

Experimental research in the field of sexual offending is extremely difficult because of ethical concerns. Randomly assigning individuals to a control group that does not receive treatment could endanger the lives of others. However, experimental research can be used in other ways to begin to understand the circumstances in which sexual offenses emerge. Virtual reality experiments are one new avenue that may provide insight into decisions to sexually offend or not sexually offend (Van Gelder, Hershfield, & Nordrgen, 2013). Virtual environments can be adapted, and persons can be assigned at random to control versus experimental environments in ways that might provide insight into how a person's decision to sexually offend or not sexually offend could vary according to different environmental circumstances. After all, sexual offending is circumscribed for most individuals. It represents an unusual circumstance/event in their life. A more precise understanding of what this circumstance may look like could be useful for understanding the development of sexual offending. This type of research has been conducted to understand bystander effects (Slater et al., 2013) and may be useful for replacing the sexual offending research tradition of using vignettes describing sexual offending scenarios (Whatley, 1996). Persons are typically in a neutral state when exposed to vignettes asking them to report on how they would act when in a state of intense emotion (e.g., Loewenstein, 1996). Virtual reality experiments can help to correct some of these past limitations. Such research has been used to study how burglars make decisions to offend or not offend (e.g., Nee et al., 2019). Studies on domestic violence and virtual reality found that although offenders had poorer facial recognition skills compared to controls, when their body movements were mimicked by a female victim, the ability to detect fearful facial expressions improved (Seinfeld et al., 2018). Extending this research to sexual offending and varying conditions in which sexual offending might occur is one way to gain better insight into the decision-making process of sexual offending.

From a sexual offending prevention perspective, virtual reality can be used to help persons meet their "future self" (see van Gelder et al., 2013). Individuals that were exposed to their "future self" were less likely to engage in cheating behavior during an experiment. This might be helpful for showing that the reward of immediate sexual gratification can provide long-term negative consequences. Exposure to a person's "future self" might help individuals understand the longer-term consequences of their behavior and in turn be useful for deterring involvement in sexual offending. The use of virtual reality in sex offending research is already under way (for a review, Fromberger, Jordan, & Müller, 2018). However, this research has remained within the domain of traditional forensic psychology research and as such has focused almost exclusively on sexually deviant preferences of small samples of individuals involved in child molestation that were detected and adjudicated by the criminal justice system (e.g., Fromberger et al., 2018). Rarely are there appropriate control groups. On a positive note, the virtual reality literature has echoed concerns from others about risk assessment in that associated tools are uninformative of how offenders acted in concrete situations (Logan, 2016). Virtual reality can assist in addressing this gap, but we recommend that it be used within a specific theoretical and methodological framework. Namely, developmental life course criminology principles should be used to study how behavior emerges, why it persists, and why it desists. This can be done through an experimental virtual reality process by modifying situations to evaluate whether individuals change their behavior.

On another positive note, broadening the scope of virtual reality research in the domain of sexology, Binter et al. (2016) examined the efficacy of virtual reality for understanding courtship behaviors. Such behaviors can be examined in childhood, adolescence, and adulthood to unravel, for example, when the onset of courtship begins, how or whether courtship behaviors change across age, and whether there are inhibitory mechanisms at different age stages that alter the types of verbal and nonverbal courtship behaviors that an individual uses in different scenarios, circumstances, and situations (Binter et al., 2016). Similarly, Hubal et al. (2008) used VR technology to help at-risk adolescents practice social skills. Those assigned to treatment that included virtual vignettes demonstrated more positive interaction skills. Overall, this relatively new technology may be useful for randomizing offenders to different experimental conditions that help improve coping skills in response to opportunities for sexual offending and can be done so without exposing others to risk (Dellazizzo et al., 2019). However, there are still major ethical implications of this new technology. For example, to what extent does exposure to virtual children induce sexual arousal that could influence individuals to seek opportunities to satiate this arousal after the virtual experience is over (Cornet & van Gelder, 2020)?

Conclusion

It is time to move sexual offending theorizing and research into the twenty-first century and this book more generally and this chapter more specifically offer various avenues for researchers to do this. A scientific approach to the description, understanding, and prevention of sexual offending should not be one of the various equally valid options available to policymakers. Knowledge, science, and progress should be the very foundation of the description, understanding, and prevention of sexual offending. Thinking, debating, measuring, testing, and re-testing using the scientific method should be the cornerstone of this foundation. To this day, research on the topic of sexual offending has been uneven and reactive, plagued by serious conceptual and methodological limitations. In a constant search to provide near immediate policy-based information, more fundamental issues about sexual offending have been simplified, set aside, or simply overlooked. The relative absence of theoretical and conceptual research on the origin and the development of sexual offending remains one of the ongoing issues. The inability to support this research on the origin and the development of sexually using conceptually sound and methodologically rigorous research remains a challenge. The implementation of prospective longitudinal community-based research to identify the key age-graded risk and protective factors of sexual offending across the life course is a pivotal step to improve the understanding of sexual offending. Reactionary research will always be necessary to begin to explore a complex and dynamic phenomenon such as sexual offending. However, to address emerging myths and misconceptions, we posit that a proactive research approach is necessary for the development of effective policies. While the social sciences cannot predict what sexual offending manifestations will be defined as the main social problem 20 years from now, an understanding of the key underlying processes of the origins and development of sexual offending will allow more appropriate actions to be taken in the future. Moving toward more proactive research on sexual offending will help address the myths, misconceptions, and erroneous conclusions, not only about sexual offending and perpetrators of sexual offenses, but also about what the commensurate social policies should be. Rather than testing misguided policies and policies based on false assumptions and public opinion, research should be at the forefront of policy development and implementation, policy evaluation and monitoring, as well as policy adjustments and amendments. A more proactive research approach to the phenomenon will help but it will certainly not solve the ongoing role of ideologically based, populist, and pseudo-scientific thinking. Researchers will have to engage in proactive research but also adopt a more proactive and leadership role to avoid the development and implementation of ineffective and misguided policies. In this day and age characterized by fake news, cyber propaganda, misinformation, and social media, without proactive research and a more proactive role in the community, research might continue to be an afterthought to policymaking.

References

Binter, J., Klapilová, K., Zikánová, T., Nilsson, T., Bártová, K., Krejčová, L., et al. (2016). Exploring the pathways of adaptation: Avatar 3D animation procedures and virtual reality arenas in research of human courtship behaviour and sexual reactivity in psychological research. In *Virtual worlds: The virtual reality and augmented reality intersections* (pp. 35–44). Leiden: Brill.

Blokland, A. A., & Lussier, P. (2015). *Sex offenders: A criminal career approach*. New York: John Wiley & Sons.

Cale, J., & Lussier, P. (2011). Toward a developmental taxonomy of adult sexual aggressors of women: Antisocial trajectories in youth, mating effort, and sexual criminal activity in adulthood. *Violence and Victims, 26*(1), 16–32.

Cornet, L. J., & Van Gelder, J. L. (2020). Virtual reality: a use case for criminal justice practice. *Psychology, Crime & Law, 2020*, 1–17.

DeLamater, J., & Friedrich, W. N. (2002). Human sexual development. *Journal of Sex Research, 39*(1), 10–14.

Dellazizzo, L., Potvin, S., Bahig, S., & Dumais, A. (2019). Comprehensive review on virtual reality for the treatment of violence: implications for youth with schizophrenia. NPJ Schizophrenia, 5(1), 1–12.

Elkovitch, N., Latzman, R. D., Hansen, D. J., & Flood, M. F. (2009). Understanding child sexual behavior problems: A developmental psychopathology framework. *Clinical Psychology Review, 29*(7), 586–598.

Farrington, D. P., Coid, J. W., Harnett, L., Jolliffe, D., Soteriou, N., Turner, R., et al. (2006). *Criminal careers up to age 50 and life success up to age 48: New findings from the Cambridge Study in Delinquent Development.* London, UK: Home Office Research, Development and Statistics Directorate.

Friedrich, W. N., Fisher, J. L., Dittner, C. A., Acton, R., Berliner, L., Butler, J., et al. (2001). Child sexual behavior inventory: Normative, psychiatric, and sexual abuse comparisons. *Child Maltreatment, 6*(1), 37–49.

Friedrich, W. N., Grambsch, P., Broughton, D., Kuiper, J., & Beilke, R. L. (1991). Normative sexual behavior in children. *Pediatrics, 88*(3), 456–464.

Fromberger, P., Jordan, K., & Müller, J. L. (2018). Virtual reality applications for diagnosis, risk assessment and therapy of child abusers. *Behavioral Sciences & the Law, 36*(2), 235–244.

Gebhard, P. H., Gagnon, J. H., Pomeroy, W. B., & Christenson, C. V. (1965). *Sex offenders: An analysis of types.* New York: Harper & Row.

Greendlinger, V., & Byrne, D. (1987). Coercive sexual fantasies of college men as predictors of self-reported likelihood to rape and overt sexual aggression. *Journal of Sex Research, 23*(1), 1–11.

Hanson, R. K., & Thornton, D. (2000). Improving risk assessments for sex offenders: A comparison of three actuarial scales. *Law and Human Behavior, 24*(1), 119–136.

Hubal, R. C., Fishbein, D. H., Sheppard, M. S., Paschall, M. J., Eldreth, D. L., & Hyde, C. T. (2008). How do varied populations interact with embodied conversational agents? Findings from inner-city adolescents and prisoners. *Computers in Human Behavior, 24*, 1104–1138.

King, L. L., & Roberts, J. J. (2017). The complexity of public attitudes toward sex crimes. *Victims & Offenders, 12*(1), 71–89.

Koh, J. B., & Wong, J. S. (2017). Survival of the fittest and the sexiest: Evolutionary origins of adolescent bullying. *Journal of Interpersonal Violence, 32*(17), 2668–2690.

Koss, M. P., & Gidycz, C. A. (1985). Sexual experiences survey: Reliability and validity. *Journal of Consulting and Clinical Psychology, 53*(3), 422.

Kraemer, H. C., Kazdin, A. E., Offord, D. R., Kessler, R. C., Jensen, P. S., & Kupfer, D. J. (1997). Coming to terms with the terms of risk. *Archives of General Psychiatry, 54*(4), 337–343.

Lalumière, M. L., & Quinsey, V. L. (1996). Sexual deviance, antisociality, mating effort, and the use of sexually coercive behaviors. *Personality and Individual Differences, 21*(1), 33–48.

Laws, D. R. (2016). *Social control of sex offenders.* London: Palgrave Macmillan.

Le Blanc, M. L., & Bouthillier, C. (2003). A developmental test of the general deviance syndrome with adjudicated girls and boys using hierarchical confirmatory factor analysis. *Criminal Behaviour and Mental Health, 13*(2), 81–105.

Lieb, R., Quinsey, V., & Berliner, L. (1998). Sexual predators and social policy. *Crime and Justice, 23*, 43–114.

Lindblad, F., Gustafsson, P. A., Larsson, I., & Lundin, B. (1995). Preschoolers' sexual behavior at daycare centers: An epidemiological study. *Child Abuse & Neglect, 19*(5), 569–577.

Loeber, R., & Farrington, D. P. (2012). *From juvenile delinquency to adult crime: Criminal careers, justice policy, and prevention.* Oxford, UK: Oxford University Press.

Loeber, R., Pardini, D., Homish, D. L., Wei, E. H., Crawford, A. M., Farrington, D. P., et al. (2005). The prediction of violence and homicide in young men. *Journal of Consulting and Clinical Psychology, 73*(6), 1074.

Loeber, R. E., Farrington, D. P., Stouthamer-Loeber, M. E., & White, H. R. E. (2008). *Violence and serious theft: Development and prediction from childhood to adulthood.* Abingdon: Routledge/Taylor & Francis Group.

Loewenstein, G. (1996). Out of control: Visceral influences on behavior. *Organizational Behavior and Human Decision Processes, 65,* 272–292.

Logan, C. (2016). Structured professional judgment: Applications to sexual offender risk assessment and management. In A. Phenix & H. M. Hoberman (Eds.), *Sexual offending: Predisposing antecedents, assessments and management* (p. 571–588). Springer.

Lussier, P., & Cale, J. (2013). Beyond sexual recidivism: A review of the sexual criminal career parameters of adult sex offenders. *Aggression and Violent Behavior, 18*(5), 445–457.

Lussier, P., & Cale, J. (2016). Understanding the origins and the development of rape and sexual aggression against women: Four generations of research and theorizing. *Aggression and Violent Behavior, 31,* 66–81.

Lussier, P., Chouinard-Thivierge, S., McCuish, E., Nadeau, D., & Lacerte, D. (2019). Early life adversities and polyvictimization in young persons with sexual behavior problems: A longitudinal study of child protective service referrals. *Child Abuse & Neglect, 88,* 37–50.

Lussier, P., & Healey, J. (2009). Rediscovering Quetelet, again: The "aging" offender and the prediction of reoffending in a sample of adult sex offenders. *Justice Quarterly, 26*(4), 827–856.

Lussier, P., McCuish, E., Mathesius, J., Corrado, R., & Nadeau, D. (2018). Developmental trajectories of child sexual behaviors on the path of sexual behavioral problems: Evidence from a prospective longitudinal study. *Sexual Abuse: A Journal of Research and Treatment, 30*(6), 622–658.

Lussier, P., Proulx, J., & LeBlanc, M. (2005). Criminal propensity, deviant sexual interests and criminal activity of sexual aggressors against women: A comparison of explanatory models. *Criminology, 43*(1), 249–282.

Lussier, P., Tzoumakis, S., Cale, J., & Amirault, J. (2010). Criminal trajectories of adult sex offenders and the age effect: Examining the dynamic aspect of offending in adulthood. *International Criminal Justice Review, 20*(2), 147–168.

Malamuth, N. M. (1981). Rape proclivity among males. *Journal of Social Issues, 37*(4), 138–157.

McCuish, E. C., & Lussier, P. (2017). Unfinished stories: From juvenile sex offenders to juvenile sex offending through a developmental life course perspective. *Aggression and Violent Behavior, 37,* 71–82.

Moffitt, T. E., Caspi, A., Harrington, H., & Milne, B. J. (2002). Males on the life-course-persistent and adolescence-limited antisocial pathways: Follow-up at age 26 years. *Development and Psychopathology, 14*(1), 179–207.

Morizot, J., & Kazemian, L. (2014). *The development of criminal and antisocial behavior.* Cham: Springer.

Nee, C., White, M., Woolford, K., Pascu, T., Barker, L., & Wainwright, L. (2019). Expertise in residential burglars: An empirical test. *Psychology, Crime & Law, 21*(5), 507–513.

Nunes, K. L., Pedneault, C. I., Filleter, W. E., Maimone, S., Blank, C., & Atlas, M. (2019). I know correlation doesn't prove causation, but...: Are we jumping to unfounded conclusions about the causes of sexual offending? *Sexual Abuse: A Journal of Research and Treatment, 31*(2), 220–236.

O'Neil, A., Sojo, V., Fileborn, B., Scovelle, A. J., & Milner, A. (2018). The #MeToo movement: An opportunity in public health? *The Lancet, 391*(10140), 2587–2589.

Pickett, J. T., Mancini, C., & Mears, D. P. (2013). Vulnerable victims, monstrous offenders, and unmanageable risk: Explaining public opinion on the social control of sex crime. *Criminology, 51,* 729–759.

Piquero, A. R., Farrington, D. P., & Blumstein, A. (2007). *Key issues in criminal career research: New analyses of the Cambridge Study in delinquent development*. Cambridge: Cambridge University Press.

Prentky, R. A., Janus, E. S., & Seto, M. C. (2003). *Sexually coercive behavior: Understanding and management* (Vol. 989). New York: New York Academy of Sciences.

Proulx, J., Beauregard, E., Lussier, P., & Leclerc, B. (Eds.). (2014). *Pathways to sexual aggression*. Abingdon: Routledge.

Quinsey, V. L., Rice, M. E., & Harris, G. T. (1995). Actuarial prediction of sexual recidivism. *Journal of Interpersonal Violence, 10*(1), 85–105.

Rapaport, K., & Burkhart, B. R. (1984). Personality and attitudinal characteristics of sexually coercive college males. *Journal of Abnormal Psychology, 93*(2), 216.

Saewyc, E. M., Poon, C. S., Homma, Y., & Skay, C. (2008). Stigma management? The links between enacted stigma and teen pregnancy trends among gay, lesbian, and bisexual students in British Columbia. *Canadian Journal of Human Sexuality, 17*, 123–139.

Schiavone, S. K., & Jeglic, E. L. (2009). Public perception of sex offender social policies and the impact on sex offenders. *International Journal of Offender Therapy and Comparative Criminology, 53*(6), 679–695.

Seinfeld, S., Arroyo-Palacios, J., Iruretagoyena, G. et al. (2018). Offenders become the victim in virtual reality: Impact of changing perspective in domestic violence. Scientific Reports, 8, 2692. https://doi.org/10.1038/s41598-018-19987-7

Seto, M. C., & Lalumiere, M. L. (2010). What is so special about male adolescent sexual offending? A review and test of explanations through meta-analysis. *Psychological Bulletin, 136*(4), 526.

Shaffer, C. S., Adjei, J., Viljoen, J. L., Douglas, K. S., & Saewyc, E. M. (2018). Ten-year trends in physical dating violence victimization among adolescent boys and girls in British Columbia, Canada. *Journal of Interpersonal Violence, 1*, 88367.

Slater, M., Rovira, A., Southern, R., Swapp, D., Zhang, J. J., Campbell, C., et al. (2013). Bystander responses to a violent incident in an immersive virtual environment. *PLoS One, 8*(1), e52766.

Spohn, C., & Horney, J. (2013). *Rape law reform: A grassroots revolution and its impact*. Cham: Springer.

Swartout, K. M., Koss, M. P., White, J. W., Thompson, M. P., Abbey, A., & Bellis, A. L. (2015). Trajectory analysis of the campus serial rapist assumption. *JAMA Pediatrics, 169*(12), 1148–1154.

Tewksbury, R. (2007). Exile at home: The unintended collateral consequences of sex offender residency restrictions. *Harvard Civil Rights Civil Liberties Review, 42*, 531–540.

Van Gelder, J. L., Hershfield, H., & Nordrgen, L. (2013). Vividness of the future self reduces delinquency. *Psychological Science, 24*, 974–980. https://doi.org/10.1177/0956797612465197

Ward, T., & Beech, A. (2006). An integrated theory of sexual offending. *Aggression and Violent Behavior, 11*(1), 44–63.

Whatley, M. A. (1996). Victim characteristics influencing attributions of responsibility to rape victims: A meta-analysis. *Aggression and Violent Behavior, 1*, 81–95.

White House Council on Women and Girls. (2014). *Rape and sexual assault: A renewed call to action*. Retrieved January 21, 2014, from https://www.whitehouse.gov/sites/default/files/docs/sexual_assault_report_1-21-14.pdf

Widom, C. S., & Massey, C. (2015). A prospective examination of whether childhood sexual abuse predicts subsequent sexual offending. *JAMA Pediatrics, 169*(1), e143357–e143357.

Wolfgang, M. E., Figlio, R. M., & Sellin, T. (1972). *Delinquency in a birth cohort*. Chicago: University of Chicago Press.

Index

© Springer Nature Switzerland AG 2021
P. Lussier et al., *Understanding Sexual Offending*,
https://doi.org/10.1007/978-3-030-53301-4

Printed in the USA
CPSIA information can be obtained
at www.ICGtesting.com
LVHW010614211123
764513LV00003B/73

9 783030 533038